CW00340547

Newton

Revised History of Ancient Kingdoms

❖———————————————❖

A Complete Chronology
Sir Isaac Newton

Edited by Larry and Marion Pierce

First printing: January 2009

Master Books®, P.O. Box 726, Green Forest, AR 72638.

ISBN-13: 978-0-89051-556-3
ISBN-10: 0-89051-556-5
Library of Congress Number: 2008940813

Cover by Diana Bogardus

Printed in the United States of America

Please visit our website for other great titles:
www.masterbooks.net

For information regarding author interviews,
please contact the publicity department at (870) 438-5288.

*The
Chronology
of
Ancient Kingdoms
Amended.
Prefixed by
A Short Chronicle from the Earliest
History of Europe, to the Conquest
of Persia by Alexander the Great.*
By Sir Isaac Newton.
London:

Printed for J. Tonson in the Strand, and J. Osborn
and T. Longman in Pater-noster Row.
MDCCXXVIII.

Revised Edition by Larry and Marion Pierce, 2008.

Master
Books®
A Division of New Leaf Publishing Group
www.masterbooks.net

TABLE OF CONTENTS

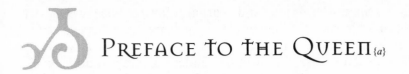
Madam,

As I could never hope to write anything myself, worthy to be laid before your majesty. {A3} I think it is a very great happiness that it should be my lot to usher into the world, under your sacred name, the last work of as great a genius as any age ever produced. It is an offering of such value in itself, as to be in no danger of suffering from the lowliness of the hand that presents it.

The impartial and universal encouragement which your majesty has always given to arts and sciences, entitles you to the best returns the learned world is able to make. The many extraordinary honours your majesty has given to the author of the following pages, gives you a just right to his productions. {A4} These, above the rest, lay the most particular claim to your royal protection; for the chronology would never have appeared in its present form without your majesty's influence. The short chronicle, which precedes it, is entirely owing to the commands with which you were pleased to honour him. It was the result of your singular care for the education of the royal offspring, earnest desire to form their minds early and lead them into the knowledge of truth.

The author has himself acquainted the public that the following treatise was the fruit of his idle hours, {A5} and the relief he sometimes had recourse to, when tired from his other studies. What an idea does it raise of his abilities, to find that a work of such labour and learning, as would have been a sufficient employment and glory for the whole life of another, was to him a diversion only, and amusement! The subject is in its nature incapable of that demonstration upon which his other writings are founded, but his usual accuracy and judiciousness are here no less observable. At the same time that he supports his suggestions, with all the authorities and proofs that the whole compass of science can furnish, he offers them with the greatest caution. {A7} By a modesty that was natural to him and always accompanies such superior talents, he sets a becoming example to others not to be too presumptuous in matters so remote and dark. Though the subject be only chronology, yet, because the mind of the author abounds with the most extensive variety of knowledge, he frequently intersperses observations of a different kind. He occasionally instills principles of virtue and humanity, which seem to have been always uppermost in his heart, and, as they were the constant rule of his actions, appear remarkably in all his writings. {A8}

Here your majesty will see astronomy, and a just observation on the course of nature, assisting other parts of learning to illustrate antiquity. A penetration and sagacity peculiar to the great author, dispels that mist, with which fable and error had darkened it. This work will with pleasure contemplate the first dawnings of your favourite arts and sciences, the noblest and most beneficial of which he alone carried further in a few years, than all the most learned who went before him, had been able to do in many ages. Here too, madam, you will observe that an abhorrence of idolatry and persecution {A9} (the very essence and foundation of that religion, which makes so bright a part of your majesty's character) was one of the earliest laws of the divine legislator. It was the morality of the first ages, and the primitive religion of both Jews and Christians. The author adds that it ought to be the standing religion of all nations, being for the honour of God, and good of mankind. Nor will your majesty be displeased to find his sentiments so agreeable to yours, while he condemns all oppression and every kind of cruelty, even to brute beasts. He does this with so much warmth, inculcating mercy, charity, and the indispensable duty of doing good, and promoting the general welfare of mankind. {A10} Those are the great ends, for which government was first instituted, and to which alone it is administered in this happy nation, under a king, who distinguished himself early in opposition to the tyranny which threatened Europe, and chooses to reign in the hearts of his subjects. He, by his innate benevolence, and paternal affection to his people, establishes and confirms all their liberties. By his valour and magnanimity, he guards and defends them.

That sincerity and openness of mind, which is the darling quality of this nation, has become more conspicuous, by being placed upon the throne. {A11} We see, with pride, our sovereign the most eminent for a virtue by which our country is so desirous to be distinguished. A prince, whose views and heart are above all the lowly arts of disguise, is far out of the reach of any temptation to introduce blindness and ignorance. Since his majesty is, by his incessant personal cares, dispensing happiness at home, and peace abroad, you, madam, lead us on by your great example to the most noble use of that quiet and ease. This we enjoy under his administration, while all your hours of leisure are employed in cultivation in yourself that learning which you so warmly patronise in others. {A12} Your majesty does not think the instructive pursuit, an entertainment below your exalted station; and are yourself a proof that the more abstract parts of it are not beyond the reach of your sex. Nor does this study end in barren speculation. It reveals itself in a steady attachment to true religion, in liberality, beneficence, and all those amiable virtues, which increase and heighten the felicities of a throne, at the same time that they bless all around it. Thus, madam, to enjoy, together with the highest state of public splendour and dignity, all the retired pleasures and domestic blessings of private life, is the perfection of human wisdom, as well as happiness.

The good effects of this love of knowledge, will not stop with the present age. It will diffuse its influence with advantage to later posterity. What may we not anticipate in our minds for the generations to come under a royal progeny, so descended, so educated, and formed by such patterns! {A13}

The glorious prospect gives us abundant reason to hope that liberty and learning will be perpetuated together; and that the bright examples of virtue and wisdom, set in this reign by the royal patrons of both, will be transmitted with the sceptre to their posterity, {A14} until this and the other works of Sir Isaac Newton will be forgotten, and time itself be no more, which is the most sincere and ardent wish of madam, may it please your majesty.

Your majesty's most obedient and most dutiful subject and servant,

John Conduitt.

{a} The reigning monarch in 1728 when this book was published was George II. He became king on June 11, 1727, and was the husband of Caroline of Ansbach. It was to his queen that this book was dedicated. John Conduitt was husband of Newton's half-niece, Catherine, and was responsible for publishing Newton's unpublished works when he died intestate on March 20, 1727.

Notice to the Reader

Although *The Chronology of Ancient Kingdoms Amended*, was written by the author many years ago, he had recently revised it, and was actually preparing it for the press at the time of his death. The short chronicle was never intended to be made public, and therefore had not been recently corrected by him. The reader must consider this fact when he finds any places where the short chronicle does not accurately agree with the dates assigned in this larger work. The sixth chapter was not copied out with the other five, which makes it doubtful whether he intended to print it. However, it was found among his papers, and evidently appeared to be a continuation of the same work. Since an abridged version of the chapter appeared in the short chronicle, it was thought proper to add the chapter to this work.

If the great author himself had lived to publish this work, there would have been no occasion for this notice. As it is, please excuse any imperfections that are always found in posthumous publications.

Notice by the Editor

Newton noted that his dates were accurate to about five years. Page numbers to the original work are noted in footnotes within the text at the end of the sentence and may not be on an exact page boundary. When you see {E55} it means *page 55* in the original 1728 AD publication. We have not rearranged the text but have added considerable material to it to make his work more understandable. We have added titles and subtitles to make his arguments easier to follow. Otherwise the original work was a monolith with huge paragraphs and sentences to match. We have broken these into smaller units to aid comprehension and added titles to aid in following his logical arguments. We translated all quotations from the Latin and Greek. Where the translations were from published works, we did not include the original Greek and Latin. Where you see Greek text followed by an English translation, the translation was done by Dr. Maurice Robinson. For the Latin with the accompanying English translation, the editor is to blame. My wife Marion typed in the original book, helped me reword it, and proofed it with me at least five times. A special thanks to Dr. Floyd Jones, Dr. Elizabeth Mitchell, and Dr. John North, who proofed the final copy before we sent it to the publishers. Dr. Jason Lisle used his knowledge of astronomy to help unravel astronomical portions of this book for me.

We made the following amendments to Newton's work:

1) Newton thought that Saul reigned for only ten years, whereas he reigned for forty. {Ac 13:21} A few dates before Saul's reign were changed accordingly and noted.

2) We assumed Ussher's biblical chronology was correct. Newton thought that it was exactly three hundred and ninety years from the time Solomon died until Nebuchadnezzar attacked Jerusalem. Had he worked out a detailed chronology for the biblical period like Ussher had, he would have seen his error. This makes most dates before Solomon's death four years too old, as well as some of the dates after his death for next the fifty years. We judiciously corrected this.

3) Newton did not take into account the fact that Artaxerxes was made viceroy in 474 BC by his father Xerxes. Ussher was the first to make that discovery, which was confirmed by archaeology two hundred and fifty years later. This makes his dates for Ezra and Nehemiah too late, which we corrected.

4) Newton assumed the old empires used non-accession dating, which is not the case. (See Appendix B.) This makes many of his dates for these periods off by one. We corrected these.

5) We corrected the spellings to reflect modern usage.

6) We documented all date changes made to the *Shorter Chronology*.

7) We corrected all obvious arithmetic errors. Newton the mathematician was not as careful with his arithmetic as Ussher the cleric was!

8) We tried to reconcile all differences between the *Shorter Chronology* and the main work.

9) We added as many BC dates as possible into the body of the work so the modern reader can easily relate this work to other works of history. We replaced any date using the *Era of Nabonassar* with the appropriate BC date, which is more easily comprehended by the modern reader.

10) We added some appendices to help the reader understand better what Newton took for granted. We also created an exhaustive index of every proper noun in his work. In so doing, we gained a much better appreciation for the depth of knowledge Newton had of this subject, which to him was just an idle diversion. The index contains a wealth of information in itself. We were careful to include the relationships for each individual (e.g. his father, mother, sisters, brothers, etc.), where the body of the text contained such information. In reading the index, you find a small bibliography for each individual. The index is almost as large as the book and ties together pieces of information you could easily overlook if you just read the book alone.

We also created an *Alias Index*. In doing the work we noted that historians (ancient and modern), had called individuals and places by many different names. This index indicates just how big a muddle they have made of ancient names and gives new meaning to the skit by Abbott and Costello, "Who's on First."

Another useful appendix contains the list of the kings for various empires which Newton and others documented.

Fortunately, most of these changes are minor and do not affect Newton's conclusions.

The more we worked on this book, the more we realised how brilliant Newton was. The conclusions he reached over three hundred years ago rest on a solid foundation of classical research and are devastating to modern archaeological conjectures. Archaeologists usually have an abysmal knowledge of the ancient classical writers, not to mention biblical history! Most of secular history before 700 BC needs a drastic revision in the light of this remarkable work. Modern Egyptology receives a full broadside from Newton and is left in a complete shambles. His conclusions are so obvious, it is a wonder how they have been overlooked for so long! After bringing order to the physical universe with his three laws of motion, Newton used his great intellect to boldly go where no historian had dared go before—into fable land. With the same success he had in the physical realm, he unravelled the Gordian Knot of the early history for the secular nations, bringing order out of chaos. He convincingly proves that most of the gods and goddesses of the ancient kingdoms were in fact real people who lived in real time and performed great exploits. Only over time did they turn into the myths we have today. What Ussher is to biblical history, Newton is to the early history of the secular nations which Ussher dared not touch.

Newton assumed the biblical history to be correct. When you throw a rock into a pond, you get ripples. Newton looks for the ripples in other nations that were triggered by events in biblical history. The Canaanites did not sit idle waiting to be slaughtered by Joshua, but many fled to other countries. Their flight into other nations was noted by various secular writers. When David defeated the Edomites, their mass exodus into Egypt, Greece, and Philistia had a major impact on these countries and was well documented. Their sophisticated knowledge of science and technology radically transformed the countries they fled to. Solomon's excellent relationships with Egypt and Hiram of Tyre were not accidents. The worldwide conquests of Sesostris had a definite impact on Judah and Rehoboam in particular. The defeat of Zerah and his huge army by Asa, destabilised Egypt and Ethiopia for many years. And the list goes on and on.

It is fascinating to see modern scholarship worship Manetho's dynasties of kings as if it were the *Gold Standard*. They know it contradicts other portions of history, but nonetheless, they cling to it like a drowning man to a piece of flotsam. Newton demonstrates that Manetho's dynasties are almost a complete work of fiction, and bad fiction at that! They were so bad the priests who created them, forgot to pass their lies on to the next generation of priests, and in a short time the dynasties were soon forgotten by the Egyptian priests. By the time Diodorus Siculus wrote about two hundred years later, these dynasties were completely forgotten and not a word of them was mentioned to Diodorus. Likewise, the Egyptian priests with whom Herodotus talked two hundred years earlier, knew absolutely nothing of these dynasties. If they had known of them, why did they withhold this information from Herodotus? It is these fictitious dynasties that are used to date the Great Pyramid at around 2800 BC instead of around 800 BC and the same dynasties are the basis for the greatly exaggerated early Egyptian history. From the time of Herodotus to the time of Manetho, the list of kings covered from Herodotus had grown from slightly more than twenty to over one hundred and thirty and the time period had magically expanded from about five hundred years to well over twenty-seven hundred years. There are better rotten reeds to lean on, when trying to recreate Egyptian history than the mess recorded by Manetho. Newton shows us a better way.

The supposed antiquity of the Assyrian Empire has really fooled modern archaeologists. The fictional history of this empire by the sixth century BC historian Ctesias pales compared to modern-day fairy tales about it. The supposed battle of Quaqar in 853 BC, in which Ahab was allegedly attacked by the Assyrians, is a good case in point. Dr. Jones, in his work, *The Chronology of the Old Testament,* shows the impossibility of this interpretation. Further, it is not a difficult exercise to show that Ahab was dead for over thirty years before this supposed battle happened in which he fought! Newton shows conclusively that there was no Assyrian Empire before Pul in 790 BC. Biblical scholars have never asked the right question of these Assyrian *scholars, What Assyrian Empire?* Dr. Thiele was duped by his lack of critical thinking on this matter, as was his successor, Dr. Leslie McFall. Worse, just about every biblical work published since Thiele, has been corrupted by his unbiblical analysis of the Hebrew chronology. Newton has done a masterful job exposing the fraudulent history of Assyria and winnows the wheat from all the chaff.

Newton also solved a little mystery concerning Homer and Hesiod. It has long perplexed historians how these two men could write such a detailed account of the fall of Troy and the Argonaut Expedition that happened almost three hundred years before they lived. After Newton redated the Argonaut Expedition to within two generations of these men and the fall of Troy to within one generation, the mystery disappears. There were still many people alive who had first-hand knowledge of both of these events with whom these two men could converse.

Newton establishes certain key dates upon which to build a better history:

1) Lycurgus the legislator, around 708 BC,

2) The return of the Heraclides, around 825 BC,

3) The fall of Troy, around 904 BC,

4) The Argonaut Expedition, around 933 BC.

All these dates, in addition to many others, he relates to the death of Solomon in 975 BC. Upon these foundation stones he erects a more credible history that is more in accord with the normal course of nature and common sense.

Newton, like a first rate prosecuting attorney, cross-examines the ancient writers, using their own words against them and exposing their logical inconsistencies. He then develops a more sound chronology using the scientific method based on logic, observations, astronomy, and just plain common sense. He is not satisfied with just showing one way of determining a historical date but overwhelms the reader with many independent ways of using the classical data to establish the approximate date for many important secular historical events.

If you search the Internet for Sir Isaac Newton, you will find all sorts of wild claims for what people think he believed or did not believe. Take these with a *large* grain of salt! A friend of mine said, "Light attracts bugs!" When you are as famous as Newton, you attract lots of bugs! Not one of the articles we have examined has footnotes to the material Newton actually wrote to prove their claims. What vague allusions there are to Newton's writings show that the writer has either not read it for himself, or read it with an agenda, or did not understand what he read at all! Much appears to rest on hearsay evidence, which everyone knows is inadmis-

inadmissible in any just court of law. They are trying to either discredit him as a Christian or claim him as one of their own to bolster their own pet unbiblical theories. Their illogic usually runs like this:

1) I believe X.

2) Newton was very clever.

3) Newton believed X (or so I think).

Therefore, X must be true.

The fact that they cannot prove Newton believed X, does not seem to bother them. Even if they could, it still does not prove the X is true. Never let facts interfere with the development of a ridiculous theory! Their arguments ought to find less obvious logical fallacies to rest on.

Keep an open mind as you read this book. Your view of ancient history will never be the same again!

— Larry Pierce

The Ancient Calendar of Israel

Scholars differ on the type of calendar Israel used before the Babylonian captivity. Newton thinks they used lunar months and intercalated extra months to keep the festivals in synchronisation with the seasons. Ussher thinks they used a tropical or solar year of three hundred and sixty-five and a quarter days similar to the Julian year introduced by Julius Caesar. This type of year would also keep the festivals in their proper seasons. It appears the antediluvians did not use a lunar year. Noah used thirty day months which are too long for a lunar month. Some have conjectured that the length of the year increased during the time of the flood. However they are unable to find any mechanism that would cause this to happen which does not create more problems than it solves. It is quite possible that the antediluvians knew the true length of the year and intercalated extra days at the end of the twelfth month to keep it in synchronisation with the tropical year. This is what Ussher thought. If they were smart enough to build a wooden ship so large that it was not until the mid 1800s we were able to build a larger ship, then Ussher's assumption that they knew the true length of the year is not unreasonable. Most of the families who migrated away from the Tower of Babel likely lost this knowledge about the length of the year. However, it may have survived in a few families of the descendants of Shem of whom Abraham was one. We did not alter the section where Newton deals with the type of calendar Israel used. The calendar question is not as simple as it first appears and we may never know the answer to it.

Osymandias

By Percy Bysshe Shelley, 1817

I met a traveller from an antique land
Who said:—Two vast and trunkless legs of stone
Stand in the desert. Near them on the sand,
Half sunk, a shatter'd visage lies, whose frown
And wrinkled lip and sneer of cold command
Tell that its sculptor well those passions read
Which yet survive, stamp'd on these lifeless things,
The hand that mock'd them and the heart that fed.
And on the pedestal these words appear:
'My name is Osymandias, king of kings:
Look on my works, ye mighty, and despair!'
Nothing beside remains: round the decay
Of that colossal wreck, boundless and bare,
The lone and level sands stretch far away.

From: Francis T. Palgrave, ed. (1824–1897).

The Golden Treasury. 1875. http://www.bartleby.com/106/246.html

1. The history of the antiquities of the Greeks is full of poetic fiction, because the Greeks wrote nothing in prose before the conquest of Asia by Cyrus the Persian. After that time, Pherecydes Scyrius and Cadmus Milesius introduced writing in prose. Pherecydes Atheniensis, about the end of the reign of Darius Hystaspes around 490 BC, wrote his history, and organised his work by genealogies, and was considered one of the best genealogists. {*E2*} Epimenides the historian proceeded also using genealogies as the basis for his history. Hellanicus, who was twelve years older than Herodotus, organised his history by the generations of the priestesses of Juno Argiva. Others organised their history by the kings of the Lacedemonians, or the archons of Athens. Hippias the Elean, around 360 BC (about thirty years before the fall of the Persian Empire), published a breviary or list of the Olympic victors. About ten years before the fall of the Persian Empire, Ephorus, the student of Isocrates, formed a chronological history of Greece, beginning with the return of the Heraclides into Peloponnesus in 825 BC, and ending with the siege of Perinthus in 340 BC, in the twentieth year of Philip, the father of Alexander the Great. He organised things by generations, since the reckoning by Olympiads was not yet in use, nor does it appear that the reigns of kings were yet set down by numbers of years. The Arundelian Marbles were written around 265 BC, (sixty years after the death of Alexander the Great), and do not mention the Olympiads. However, in the next Olympiad Timaeus

Siculus published a history in several books down to his own times, according to the Olympiads, comparing the ephori, the kings of Sparta, the archons of Athens, and the priestesses of Juno Argiva, {*E3*} with the Olympic victors. He tried to make the Olympiads, the genealogies, the successions of kings, the archons, the priestesses and poetic histories agree with one another, according to the best of his judgment. Where his history ended, Polybius began and carried on the history.

2. Shortly after the death of Alexander the Great around 300 BC, they began to record the generations, reigns and successions, in numbers of years. They made reigns and successions equivalent to generations. By assuming three generations to a hundred or a hundred and twenty years (as appears by their chronology) they have made the history of Greece three or four hundred years older than the truth. This was the origin of the detailed chronology of the Greeks. Eratosthenes wrote around 220 BC, about a hundred years after the death of Alexander the Great. He was followed by Apollodorus, and these two have been followed ever since by chronologers.

3. How uncertain their chronology is, and how doubtful it was reputed by the Greeks of those times, may be understood by this passage from Plutarch: {*E4*}

> Some say that he (Lycurgus) lived at the same time with Iphitus, and in concert with him established the Olympic truce in 776 BC. Among these is Aristotle the philosopher, and he alleges as proof the discus at the Olympia on which the inscription preserves the name of Lycurgus. But, those who compute the time by the succession of kings at Sparta, like Eratosthenes and Apollodorus, prove that Lycurgus lived many years earlier than the first Olympiad. {*Plutarch, Lives-Lycurgus, l. 1. c. 1. s. 1. 1:205*}

4. First Aristotle and later others made Lycurgus over a hundred years older than the Olympiads. In another place Plutarch states:

> As for the interview with Croesus [by Solon], some think to prove by chronology that it is fictitious. However, when a story is so famous and well attested, and, what is more to the point, when it comports so well with the character of Solon, and is so worthy of his magnanimity

and wisdom, I do not purpose to reject it out of deference to any chronological canons, so called, which thousands are to this day revising, without being able to bring their contradictions into any general agreement. {*Plutarch, Lives-Solon, l. 1. c. 27. s. 1,2. 1:479}

5. It seems the chronologers had made the legislature of Solon too old to be consistent with that interview with Croesus.

6. To reconcile such contradictions, chronologers have sometimes doubled the number of men. So when the poets had changed Io, the daughter of Inachus, into the Egyptian Isis, chronologers made her husband Osiris or Bacchus and his wife Ariadne as old as Io. Hence, they feigned that there were two Ariadnes, one the wife of Bacchus, and the other the wife of Theseus, and two Minoses their fathers, and a younger Io, the daughter of Jasius, writing Jasius corruptly for Inachus. {E5} So they have created two Pandions, and two Erechtheuses, giving the name of Erechthonius to the first; Homer calls the first, Erechtheus. By such corruptions they have exceedingly confused ancient history.

7. The chronology of the Latins is still more uncertain. Plutarch notes the great uncertainties in the original records of Rome and so does Servius. Sixty-seven years before the death of Alexander the Great in 323 BC, the old records of the Latins were burned by the Gauls in 390 BC. Quintus Fabius Pictor, the oldest historian of the Latins, lived around 220 BC, about a hundred years later than Alexander.

8. In biblical history the Assyrian Empire began with Pul and Tiglathpileser, and lasted about one hundred and seventy years. Accordingly, Herodotus has made Semiramis only five generations, or about one hundred and sixty-six years older than Nitocris, who was the mother of the last king of Babylon. {*Herodotus, l. 1. c. 184. 1:229} However, Ctesias has made Semiramis fifteen hundred years older than Nitocris, and feigned a long series of kings of Assyria, whose names are not Assyrian, nor have any affinity with the Assyrian names in the scriptures. {*Diod. Sic., l. 2. c. 21,22. 1:421,423} {E6}

9. The priests of Egypt told Herodotus that Menes built Memphis and the sumptuous temple of Vulcan, in that city, and that Rhampsinitus, Moeris, Asychis and Psammitichus added magnificent porticos to that temple. It is not likely that Memphis could be famous before Homer, who does not mention it, or that a temple could be more than two or three hundred years in construction. The sole reign of Psammitichus began about 655 BC and I place the founding of this temple by Menes about two hundred and fifty-seven years earlier, in 912 BC. However, the priests of Egypt had so exaggerated their history before the days of Herodotus, as to tell him that from Menes to Moeris (who reigned two hundred years before Psammitichus), there were three hundred and thirty kings, whose reigns took up as many ages or generations, that is, eleven thousand years. They had filled up that interval with imaginary kings, who had done nothing! Before the days of Diodorus, they had inflated their history so much as to place six, eight, or ten new reigns of kings between those kings, whom they had told Herodotus had succeeded one another immediately.

10. In the kingdom of Sicyon, chronologers have split Apis Epaphus or Epopeus into two kings, whom they call Apis and Epopeus, and between them have inserted eleven or twelve imaginary names of kings who did nothing! {E7} Thereby, they have made its founder Aegialeus three hundred years older than his brother Phoroneus! Some have made the kings of Germany as old as the flood, and yet before the use of writing, the names and actions of men could scarcely be remembered over eighty or a hundred years after their deaths. Therefore, I accept no chronology of things done in Europe, older than eighty years before Cadmus introduced writing into Europe and none of the things done in Germany, before the rise of the Roman Empire.

11. Eratosthenes and Apollodorus organised their history using the reigns of the kings of Sparta, and (as appears by their chronology still followed), they have made the seventeen reigns of these kings in both families, (between the return of the Heraclides into Peloponnesus and the battle of Thermopylae), to last six hundred and twenty-two years. This is about thirty-six and a half years to a reign, and yet a dynasty of seventeen kings of that length is nowhere to be found in real history. Kings at a moderate reckoning reign only eighteen or twenty years each. I have calculated the time of the return of the Heraclides around 820 BC by the last way of reckoning, placing it about three hundred and forty years before the battle of Thermopylae in 480 BC. According to Thucydides, I made the taking of Troy eighty years older than that return, {E8} and the Argonaut Expedition a generation older than the Trojan War, and the wars of Sesostris in Thrace and the death of Ino, the daughter of Cadmus a generation older than the Argonaut Expedition.

12. I have drawn up the following chronological table, so as to make the chronology suit with the course of nature, with astronomy, with biblical history, and with itself, without the many contradictions which Plutarch complained about. I do not pretend to be exact to the year. There may be errors of five or ten years, and perhaps twenty, but not much more.

13. 1445 BC. The Canaanites, who fled from Joshua, retreated in great numbers into Egypt, and there conquered Timaeus, Thamus or Thammuz, the king of Lower Egypt. They reigned there under their kings Salatis, Boeon, Apachnas, Apophis, Janias, Assis, etc., until the days of Eli and Samuel. They ate meat and sacrificed men after the custom of the Phoenicians. They were called Shepherds by the Egyptians, who only lived off the fruits of the earth and hated meat eaters. Upper Egypt was in those days under many kings, reigning at Coptos, Thebes (Egyptian), This, Elephantis, and other places. {E10} By conquering one another, they slowly formed one kingdom, over which Misphragmuthosis reigned in the days of Eli. (Newton left this event undated. Editor.)

14. 1121 BC. Mephres reigned over Upper Egypt from Syene to Heliopolis. His successor Misphragmuthosis made a lasting war upon the Shepherds soon after that, and caused many of them to flee into Palestine, Idumaea, Syria, and Libya. Under Lelex, Aezeus, Inachus, Pelasgus, Aeolus, Cecrops I and other captains, they fled into Greece. Before those days Greece and all Europe was inhabited by wandering Cimmerians and Scythians from the far side of the Black Sea. They lived a rambling wild sort of life, like the Tartars in the northern parts of Asia. Ogyges was the same nationality as they were and lived at the time these Egyptian strangers came into Greece. The rest of the Shepherds were confined by Misphragmuthosis, in a part of Lower Egypt called Abaris or Pelusium. (Newton's date was 1125 BC. Editor.)

15. 1117 BC. The Philistines, strengthened by the influx of the Shepherds, conquered Israel and captured the ark. Samuel judged Israel. (Newton's date was 1100 BC. Editor.)

16. 1096 BC. By the influx of the Shepherds, the Philistines became very numerous. (Newton's date was 1070 BC. Editor.)

17. 1095 BC. Saul was appointed king of Israel. (Newton's date was 1069 BC. Editor.)

18. 1094 BC The Philistines brought into the field against Saul thirty thousand chariots, six thousand horsemen, and people as the sand on the seashore for multitude. By the hand of Jonathan, Saul got a great victory over the Philistines. (Newton's date was 1069 BC. Editor.)

19. 1081 BC. Haemon, the son of Pelasgus, reigned in Thessaly. (Newton's date was 1085 BC. Editor.)

20. 1076 BC. Lycaon, the son of Pelasgus, built Lycosura. Phoroneus, the son of Inachus, built Phoronicum, which was later called Argos. {E11} Aegialeus, the brother of Phoroneus and the son of Inachus, built Aegialea, which was later called Sicyon. These were the oldest towns in Peloponnesus. Until then they built only single houses scattered up and down in the fields. About the same time Cecrops I built Cecropia in Attica, which was later called Athens. Eleusinus, the son of Ogyges, built Eleusis in Attica. These towns were the beginning of the kingdoms of the Arcadians, Argives, Sicyonians, Athenians, Eleusinians, etc. Deucalion also lived at that time. (Newton's date was 1080 BC. Editor.)

21. 1066 BC. Amosis I or Tethmosis, the successor of Misphragmuthosis, abolished the custom of the Phoenicians in Heliopolis of sacrificing men, and drove the Shepherds from Abaris. Abas, the father of Acrisius and Praetus, came from Egypt to Rhodes. (Newton's date was 1070 BC. Editor.)

22. 1065 BC. Eurotas, the son of Lelex, and Lacedemon, who married Sparta, the daughter of Eurotas, reigned in Laconia and built Sparta. (Newton's date was 1069 BC. Editor.)

23. 1060 BC. Samuel died.

24. 1055 BC. David was appointed king. (Newton's date was 1059 BC. Editor.) {E12}

25. 1044 BC. The Edomites were conquered and dispersed by David. Some of them fled into Egypt with their young King Hadad and others fled to the Persian Gulf under the command of Oannes. {1Ki 11:17} Others fled from the Red Sea to the coast of the Mediterranean Sea and fortified Azoth against David, and captured Sidon. The Sidonians who fled from them built Tyre and Aradus, and made Abibalus the king of Tyre. These Edomites carried into all places their knowledge of navigation, astronomy, and writings, for in Idumaea they had determined the constellations and had a written language before the days of Job, who mentioned them in his book. It was there Moses learned to write also. These Edomites who fled to the Mediterranean Sea, translated the word *Erythraea* into that of *Phoenicia*, giving the name of Phoenicians to themselves, and that of Phoenicia to all the seacoasts of Palestine from Azoth to Sidon. From this came the tradition of the Persians and of the Phoenicians themselves, mentioned by Herodotus, that the Phoenicians came originally from the Red Sea and soon undertook long voyages on the Mediterranean. (Newton's date was 1048 BC. Editor.)

26. 1043 BC. Acrisius married Eurydice, the daughter of Lacedemon and Sparta. The Phoenician mariners, who fled from the Red Sea and who were used to long voyages for the sake of trade, began similar kinds of voyages on the Mediterranean Sea from Sidon. {E13} After sailing as far as Greece, they carried away Io, the daughter of Inachus, who along with other women, came to their ships to buy their merchandise. Pirates began to infest the seas of Greece. (Newton's date was 1047 BC. Editor.)

27. 1042 BC. David conquered the Syrians from Zobah and Damascus. Nyctimus, the son of Lycaon, reigned in Arcadia during the lifetime of Deucalion. (Newton's date was 1046 BC. Editor.)

28. 1041 BC. Many of the Phoenicians and Syrians fled from Sidon and from David. They were led by Cadmus, Cilix, Phoenix, Membliarius, Nycteus, Thasus, Atymnus and other captains into Asia Minor, Crete, Greece and Libya. At that time they introduced writing, music, poetry, the Octaeteris, the fabrication of metals, and other arts, sciences and customs of the Phoenicians. At this time Cranaus, the successor of Cecrops I, reigned in Attica. The Greeks placed the flood of Deucalion in the reign of Cranaus and the beginning of the reign of Nyctimus. This flood was succeeded by four ages or generations of men. In the first generation Chiron, the son of Saturn (Cretan) and Philyra, was born and the last generation, according to Hesiod ended with the Trojan War. {*Hesiod, Theogony, l. 1. v. 999-1002. 1:83} {*Hesiod, Works and Days, l. 1. v. 160-165. 1:101} This places the destruction of Troy four generations or about one hundred and forty years later than that flood and the coming of Cadmus into Europe. This was computed by the ancients using three generations to a hundred years. {E14} With these Phoenicians came a mysterious religious sect bringing arts and sciences of Phoenicia, who settled in various places under the names of Curetes, Corybantes, Telchines, and Idean Dactyli. (Newton's date was 1045 BC. Editor.)

29. 1039 BC. Hellen, the son of Deucalion, and the father of Aeolus, Xuthus and Dorus, lived. (Newton's date was 1043 BC. Editor.)

30. 1031 BC. Erechtheus reigned in Attica. Aethlius, the grandson of Deucalion and the father of Endymion, built Elis. The Idean Dactyli discovered iron in Mount Ida in Crete, and smelted it into armour and iron tools. This was the origin of the trade of metallurgy and weaponry in Europe. While wearing their armour, they used to sing, keeping time by striking upon one another's armour with their swords. They introduced music and poetry to the country. At the same time, they found the Cretan Jupiter in a cave of the same mountain and danced around him in their armour. (Newton's date was 1035 BC. Editor.)

31. 1030 BC. Ammon reigned in Egypt. He conquered Libya, and elevated that people from a wandering savage life to a civil one, and taught them to store the fruits of the earth. Libya, and the desert above were named after him and was anciently called Ammonia. He was the first to build long and tall ships with sails, and had a fleet of such ships on the Red Sea, and another fleet on the Mediterranean Sea at Irasa in Libya. {E15} Until then they used small round cargo vessels invented on the Red Sea, and always sailed within sight of the shore. To enable them to cross the seas without seeing the shore, the Egyptians began in his days to study the stars. It was from this time that astronomy and sailing began. Up until now, the luni-solar year was used. This year varied in length and hence was unsuitable for astronomy. During his lifetime, and of his sons and grandsons, they determined the length of the solar year by observing the heliacal rising and settings of the stars. They made this year five days longer than the twelve calendar months of the old luni-solar year. Creusa, the daughter of Erechtheus, married Xuthus the son of Hellen. Erechtheus initiated the Panathenaea Festival and won the chariot race. Aegina, the daughter of Asopus, and the mother of Aeacus, was born. (Newton's date was 1034 BC. Editor.)

32. 1026 BC. When Ceres, a woman from Sicily who was looking for her kidnapped daughter Proserpina, came to Attica, she taught the Greeks to sow grain. For this benefaction she was deified after her death. The first person she taught to cultivate grain was Triptolemus, the young son of Celeus, the king of Eleusis. (Newton's date was 1030 BC. Editor.)

33. 1024 BC. Oenotrus, the youngest son of Lycaon who was the Roman god Janus of the Latins, led the first colony from Greece into Italy, and there taught them to build houses. {E16} Perseus was born. (Newton's date was 1028 BC. Editor.)

34. 1016 BC. Arcas, the son of Callisto and the grandson of Lycaon, and Eumelus, the first king of Achaia, received grain for making bread from Triptolemus and learned agriculture from him. (Newton's date was 1020 BC. Editor.)

35. 1015 BC. Solomon reigned and married the daughter of Ammon. Because of this marriage, he was supplied with horses from Egypt. His merchants also brought horses from there for all the kings of the Hittites and Syrians, because horses originally came from Libya. At that time Neptune was called *Equestris*. Tantalus, king of Phrygia had kidnapped Ganymede, who was the son of Tros, the king of Troy. (Newton's date was 1019 BC. Editor.)

36. 1013 BC. Solomon, assisted by the Tyrians and Aradians who had mariners among them familiar with the Red Sea, sent out a fleet of ships on that sea. Those assistants founded colonies on the Persian Gulf islands called Tyre and Aradus. (Newton's date was 1017 BC. Editor.)

37. 1012 BC. Solomon laid the foundation for the temple. Minos reigned in Crete, expelling his father Asterius, who fled into Italy and became the Saturn (Cretan) of the Latins. Ammon took Gezer from the Canaanites and gave it to his daughter, Solomon's wife. (Newton's date was 1015 BC. Editor.)

38. 1010 BC. Ammon appointed Cepheus king of Joppa. (Newton's date was 1014 BC. Editor.)

39. 1006 BC. Sesostris, during the reign of his father Ammon, invaded Arabia Faelix, and set up pillars at the mouth of the Red Sea. Apis Epaphus or Epopeus who was the son of Phroroneus, and Nycteus who was king of Boeotia, were killed. {E17} Lycus inherited the kingdom of his brother Nycteus. Aetolus, the son of Endymion, fled into the country of the Curetes in Achaia, and called it Aetolia. From Pronoe, the daughter of Phorbas, Aetolus fathered Pleuron and Clydon, who built cities in Aetolia, calling them after their own names. Antiope, the daughter of Nycteus was sent home to Lycus by Lamedon, who was the successor of Apis Epaphus. On the way back, she gave birth to twins, Amphion and Zethus. (Newton's date was 1010 BC. Editor.)

40. 1004 BC. Sesostris, during his father Ammon's reign, invaded North Africa and Spain, and set up pillars in all his conquests, particularly at the entrance to the Mediterranean Sea. He returned home by the coast of Gaul and Italy. (Newton's date was 1008 BC. Editor.)

41. 1003 BC. After Ceres had died, Eumolpus instituted her mysteries in Eleusis. The mysteries of Rhea (Cretan) were instituted in the city of Cybele in Phrygia. About this time they began building temples in Greece. Hyagnis the Phrygian invented the pipe. Using the common council of the five rulers of the Philistines as their example, the Greeks set up the Amphictyonic Council, first at Thermopylae, under the leadership of Amphictyon, the son of Deucalion. A few years later, another council was set up at Delphi, under the leadership of Acrisius. Among the cites whose representatives met at Thermopylae, I could not find Athens, and therefore I doubt that Amphictyon was king of that city. {E18} If he was the son of Deucalion and the brother of Hellen, he and Cranaus may have reigned together in various parts of Attica. However, I discovered a man named Amphictyon at a later date who entertained the great Bacchus. This council worshipped Ceres and therefore was instituted after her death. (Newton's date was 1007 BC. Editor.)

42. 1002 BC. Minos built a fleet and cleared the Greek seas of pirates, and sent colonies to the Greek islands. Some of these islands were not inhabited before. Cecrops II reigned in Attica. Caucon taught the mysteries of Ceres in Messene. (Newton's date was 1006 BC. Editor.)

43. 1001 BC. Perseus took Andromeda away from Joppa. Pandion, the brother of Cecrops II, reigned in Attica. Car, the son of Phoroneus, built a temple to Ceres. (Newton's date was 1005 BC. Editor.)

44. 998 BC. Sesostris reigned in Egypt and embellished Thebes (Egyptian), dedicating it to his father Ammon. He named it No-Ammon or Ammon-No, which means the people or city of Ammon. This is why the Greeks called it Diospolis, meaning The *City of Jupiter Ammon*. Sesostris also erected temples and oracles to his father in Thebes (Egyptian), Ammonia and Ethiopia, causing his father to be worshipped as a god in those countries and I think also in Arabia Faelix. This was the origin of the worship of Jupiter Ammon, and the first mention of oracles that I have seen in secular history. {E19} Pandion warred with Labdacus, the grandson of Cadmus. (Newton's date was 1002 BC. Editor.)

45. 990 BC. Aegeus reigned in Attica. (Newton's date was 994 BC. Editor.)

46. 989 BC. Pelops, the son of Tantalus, came into Peloponnesus and married Hippodamia, who was the granddaughter of Acrisius. He then captured the country of Aetolia from Aetolus, who was the son of Endymion. He became powerful using money he had stolen from Aetolus. (Newton's date was 993 BC. Editor.)

47. 986 BC. Amphion and Zethus murdered Lycus, forcing Laius, the son of Labdacus, to flee for his life. He reigned in Thebes (Greek) and fortified the city with high walls. (Newton's date was 990 BC. Editor.)

48. 985 BC. Daedalus and his nephew Talus invented the saw, turning lathe, auger (wimble), chip axe, and other carpentry tools, originating the trade of carpentry in Europe. Daedalus also created the first statues with

their feet apart to appear as though they were walking. (Newton's date was 989 BC. Editor.)

49. 984 BC. Minos made war against the Athenians for killing his son Androgeus. Aeacus lived at this time. (Newton's date was 988 BC. Editor.)

50. 983 BC. Daedalus murdered his nephew Talus and fled to Minos. A priestess of Jupiter Ammon was brought by Phoenician merchants into Greece and set up the oracle of Jupiter at Dodona. This was the start of oracles in Greece and the beginning of the universal worship of the dead. (Newton's date was 987 BC. Editor.) {E20}

51. 979 BC. Sisyphus, the son of Aeolus and the grandson of Hellen, reigned in Corinth, and some assume that he built that city. (Newton's date was 983 BC. Editor.)

52. 976 BC. Laius recovered the kingdom of Thebes (Greek). Athamas, the brother of Sisyphus and the father of Phrixus and Helle, married Ino, the daughter of Cadmus. (Newton's date was 980 BC. Editor.)

53. 975 BC. Rehoboam reigned. Thoas was sent from Crete to Lemnos and reigned there in the city of Hephaestia. He worked in copper and iron. (Newton's date was 979 BC. Editor.) Jeroboam I set up the worship of Egyptian gods in Israel. (Newton's date was 974 BC. Editor.)

54. 974 BC. Electryo, who was the son of Perseus and Andromeda, and his wife Lysidice, the daughter of Pelops, had a daughter, Alcmena. (Newton's date was 978 BC. Editor.)

55. 971 BC. Sesostris plundered the temple at Jerusalem, invaded Syria and Persia, and set up pillars in many places. Sesostris conquered Rehoboam. (Newton's date was 974 BC. Editor.)

56. 968 BC. Sesostris invaded India and returned in triumph the next year. This is the origin of the triennial festival called *Trieterica Bacchi*. He set up pillars on two mountains at the mouth of the Ganges River. (Newton's date was 971 BC. Editor.)

57. 965 BC. After overcoming the minotaur, Theseus reigned and soon united twelve cities of Attica under one government. (Newton's date was 968 BC. Editor.) {E21}

58. 964 BC. Sesostris crossed the Hellespont and conquered Thrace, killing Lycurges, their king. He gave the kingdom of Lycurgus and one of his Muses or singing women named Calliope to Oeagrus, the father of Orpheus. Sesostris had Ethiopians in his army who were commanded by Pan, and Libyan women commanded by Myrina or Minerva. It was customary for the Ethiopians to dance when they were entering into a battle. They also painted their bodies with goat's feet to look like skipping satyrs. (Newton's date was 967 BC. Editor.)

59. 963 BC. After Sesostris appointed Thoas king of Cyprus, Thoas went there with his wife, Calycopis. They left their daughter Hypsipyle at Lemnos. (Newton's date was 966 BC. Editor.)

60. 962 BC. The Greeks and Scythians defeated Sesostris. He lost many of his women with their Queen Minerva in this battle. He was received by Amphictyon at a feast. He buried his wife Ariadne, and went back through Asia Minor and Syria into Egypt with many captives, among whom was Tithonus, the son of Laomedon, who was the king of Troy. He left his Libyan Amazons at the Thermodon River under Marthesia and Lampeto, who were the successors of Minerva. He left the geographic tables of his conquests in Colchis. It was from this time that geography had its beginning. His singing women were celebrated in Thrace by the name of the Muses. The daughters of Pierus, who was a Thracian, imitated these singing women and were celebrated with the same name. (Newton's date was 965 BC. Editor.) {E22} Sesostris left his nephew Prometheus on Mount Caucasus and Aeetes at Colchis. (Newton's date was 968 BC. Editor.)

61. 961 BC. While at war with Cocalus, the king of Sicily, Minos was killed by him. Minos was famous for his kingdom, laws and justice. Pythagoras went to visit his sepulchre on which was written the inscription, ΤΟΥ ΔΙΟΣ, the sepulchre of Jupiter. Danaus and his daughters fled to Greece from his brother, Egyptus, also called Sesostris. Upon the advice of Thoth, who was his secretary, Sesostris divided Egypt into thirty-six nomes or administrative districts. In each nome he erected a temple and appointed various gods, festivals, and ceremonies. In these temples were the sepulchres of his great men who were worshipped after their death. Sesostris and his queen were each given the names of Osiris and Isis, and at their death were worshipped throughout all of Egypt. These were the same temples Lucian saw and described eleven hundred years later. This was the origin of the various nomes, gods, festivals and ceremonies of Egypt. Sesostris also divided and measured the land of Egypt among his soldiers from which geometry had its origin. Hercules (Idean) and Eurystheus were also born in this year. (Newton's date was 964 BC. Editor.)

62. 959 BC. Amphictyon brought the twelve gods of Egypt into Greece. These were the *Dii magni maiorum gentium* or the *Great Gods of the Greater Nations* to whom the earth, planets, and elements were dedicated. (Newton's date was 963 BC. Editor.) {E23}

63. 958 BC. Phrixus and Helle fled from their stepmother Ino, who was the daughter of Cadmus. However, Helle drowned in the strait of the Hellespont,

which was named after her, but Phrixus arrived safely in Colchis. (Newton's date was 962 BC. Editor.)

64. 956 BC. There was war between the Lapithae and the people of Thessaly, who were called Centaurs. (Newton's date was 960 BC. Editor.)

65. 954 BC. Oedipus killed his father Laius. Sthenelus, the son of Perseus, reigned in Mycene. (Newton's date was 958 BC. Editor.)

66. 951 BC. Japetus murdered his brother Sesostris. After Japetus died, he was deified in North Africa, and given the name of Neptune, but the Egyptians named him Typhon. Orus reigned and routed the Libyans, who were led by Japetus and his son Antaeus or Atlas, and had invaded Egypt. Sesostris had made the Nile River useful by cutting channels from it to all the cities of Egypt. These channels were called Sihor or Siris, Nilus and Egyptus. When the Greeks heard the Egyptian's lament saying, *Oh Siris* and *Bou Siris,* they called him Osiris and Busiris. However, the Arabians called him Bacchus the Great because of his great acts. The Phrygians named him Ma-sors or Mavors the Valiant, and shortened his name to Mars. Since Sesostris had set up pillars in all his conquests and during his father Ammon's reign, he fought against the Africans with clubs and he was painted with pillars and a club. {E24} According to Cicero, this was the same Hercules who was born on the Nile. {*Cicero, De Natura Deorum, l. 3. c. 16. (42) 19:325} {*Cicero, De Natura Deorum, l. 3. c. 22. (55) 19:339} Eudoxus claims Hercules was killed by Typhon and Diodorus states Hercules was an Egyptian who went over a great part of the world and set up pillars in North Africa. He seems also to be called Belus (Egyptian), whom Diodorus claims led a colony of Egyptians to Babylon and while there instituted priests called Chaldeans. These priests were free from paying taxes, and observed the stars, just as they did in Egypt. Up until this time, Israel was oppressed by the Egyptians, but after this king, Asa of Judah had peace from them for ten years. (Newton's date was 956 BC. Editor.)

67. 942 BC. The Ethiopians invaded Egypt and drowned Orus in the Nile. As a result of this, Bubaste, the sister of Orus, killed herself by jumping from a housetop and their mother Isis, who was also called Astraea, went mad, thus ending the reign of the gods of Egypt. (Newton's date was 947 BC. Editor.)

68. 941 BC. Asa defeated the Ethiopians under Zerah. The people of Lower Egypt then appointed Osarsiphus their king who called in two hundred thousand Jews and Phoenicians against the Ethiopians. Menes, who was also called Amenophis, the young son of Zerah and Cissia then reigned in Upper Egypt that year as well. (Newton's date was 946 BC. Editor.)

69. 940 BC. The Ethiopians, who were under Amenophis' rule, retreated from Lower Egypt and fortified Memphis against Osarsiphus. These wars and the Argonaut Expedition, destroyed the great empire of Egypt. {E25} Eurystheus, the son of Sthenelus reigned in Mycene. (Newton's date was 944 BC. Editor.)

70. 939 BC. Evander and his mother Carmenta introduced writing into Italy. (Newton's date was 943 BC. Editor.)

71. 938 BC. Orpheus deified the son of Semele by naming him Bacchus and created ceremonies to honour him. (Newton's date was 942 BC. Editor.)

72. 936 BC. The great men of Greece decided to send an embassy to the countries subject to Egypt, because the Greeks had heard of the civil wars and disorders taking place there. Hence, they commissioned that a ship named *Argo* should be built to sail on the Black and Mediterranean seas. (Newton's date was 940 BC. Editor.)

73. 935 BC. The ship *Argo* was built patterned after the long ship which Danaus sailed to Greece. This was the first long ship the Greeks had ever built. Chiron was born during the Golden Age. He charted the constellations for the Argonaut Expedition. He placed the points of the solstice and equinox in the fifteenth degree, which was in the middle of the constellations of Aries, Cancer, Chelae (Scorpio), and Capricorn. However, in 432 BC, Meton observed the summer solstice in the eighth degree of Cancer, which accounted for the solstice having gone back seven degrees. It goes back one degree in every seventy-two years, and about seven degrees every five hundred and four years. {E26} If one reckons back from 432 BC, it should place the Argonaut Expedition around 935 BC. Gingris, the son of Thoas, was killed and then deified by his father under the name of Adonis. (Newton's date was 939 BC. Editor.)

74. 934 BC. Theseus, who was fifty years old, kidnapped the seven-year-old Helen. Pirithous, who was the son of Ixion, tried to kidnap Persephone, who was the daughter of King Orcus of the Molossians, but he was killed by the dog of Orcus. His companion Theseus was taken prisoner. Helen was then set free by her own brothers. (Newton's date was 938 BC. Editor.)

75. 933 BC. The Argonaut Expedition took place. Prometheus left Mount Caucasus after being freed by Hercules (Idean). Laomedon, the king of Troy was killed by Hercules (Idean), hence, Priam succeeded him. Talus, the son of Minos, was a man from the Bronze Age who was killed by the Argonauts. Aesculapius and Hercules (Idean) were both Argonauts. Hippocrates was the eighteenth generation from Aesculapius on the father's side, and the nineteenth from Hercules

(Idean) on the mother's side. Since these generations have been noted in history, they were most probably the chief of the family, or at least the oldest sons. By this we may allow about twenty-eight to thirty years to a generation and thereby for the seventeen generations on the father's side and the eighteen by the mother's equal about five hundred years. {E27} If one reckons backwards from the beginning of the Peloponnesian War in 431 BC when Hippocrates was living, it should place them at the time of the Argonaut Expedition. (Newton's date was 937 BC. Editor.)

76. 932 BC. Theseus freed by Hercules (Idean). (Newton's date was 936 BC. Editor.)

77. 931 BC. In the hunt, Meleager kills the Calydonian boar. (Newton's date was 934 BC. Editor.)

78. 930 BC. Calycopis died and was deified by Thoas with temples at Paphos and Amathus in Cyprus, and at Byblus in Syria, and with priests and sacred rites. She was the Venus of the ancients and the *Dea Cypria*, the goddess of Cyprus, and *Dea Syria*, the goddess of Syria. From these and other places where temples were erected to her, she was also called Paphia, Amathusia, Byblia, Cytherea, Salaminia, Cnidia, Erycina, Idalia, etc. Her three female attendants became the three Graces.

79. 928 BC. The war of the seven captains against Thebes in Greece occurred.

80. 927 BC. Hercules (Idean) and Aesculapius were deified. Eurystheus drove the Heraclides from Peloponnesus and was killed by Hyllus, the son of Hercules (Idean). Atreus, the son of Pelops, succeeded him in the kingdom of Mycene. {E28} Menestheus, the great-grandson of Erechtheus, reigned at Athens.

81. 926 BC. Amenophis, with an army from Ethiopia and Thebes (Egyptian), invaded Lower Egypt, conquered Osarsiphus, and drove out the Jews and Canaanites. This was considered the second expulsion of the Shepherds. (Newton's date was 930 BC. Editor.)

82. 925 BC. Theseus was thrown down from a rock and killed.

83. 924 BC. Atreus died. Agamemnon reigned in Mycene. In the absence of Menelaus, who went to look after what his adoptive father Atreus had left to him, Paris kidnapped Helen, the wife of Menelaus. (Newton's date was 919 BC. Editor.) When Hyllus invaded Peloponnesus, he was killed by Echemus.

84. 918 BC. The second war against Thebes in Greece happened.

85. 912 BC. Thoas, the king of Cyprus and part of Phoenicia, died. He was deified for making armour for the kings of Egypt with a sumptuous temple at Memphis under the name of Baal Canaan or Vulcan. This temple was said to be built by Menes, the first king of Egypt who reigned next after the gods. That is, by Menoph or Amenophis who reigned next after the death of Osiris, Isis, Orus, Bubaste and Thoth. The city of Memphis was also said to be built by Menes. He began to build it when he fortified it against Osarsiphus. It was named after Menes and was called Menoph, Moph, Noph, etc. To this day it is called Menus by the Arabians. Therefore Menes, who built the city and temple, was Menoph or Amenophis. {E29} The priests of Egypt over time made this temple more than a thousand years older than Amenophis. Some of them made it five or ten thousand years older! However, it could not be more than two or three hundred years older than the reign of Psammitichus, who finished it and died in 614 BC. When Menoph or Menes built the city, he built a bridge there over the Nile River, which was a work too great to be older than the kingdom of Egypt.

86. 909 BC. Amenophis, called Memnon by the Greeks, built the city of Memnonia at Susa, while Egypt was under the government of Proteus, his viceroy.

87. 904 BC. Troy was taken. While Amenophis was still at Susa, the Greeks imagined that he came from there to the Trojan War.

88. 903 BC. Demophoon, the son of Theseus by Phaedra the daughter of Minos, reigned at Athens.

89. 901 BC. Amenophis built small pyramids in Cochome.

90. 897 BC. Teucer built Salamis in Cyprus. (Newton's date was 895 BC. Editor.)

91. 896 BC. Ulysses found Calypso on the island of Ogygia (perhaps Cadis or Cales in the Atlantic Ocean). She was the daughter of Atlas, according to Homer. The ancients at length imagined that this island, (which they called Atlantis after the name of Atlas) had been as large as all Europe, Africa and Asia, and sank into the sea.

92. 895 BC. Hadad or Benhadad II, the king of Syria, died and was deified at Damascus with a temple and ceremonies. {E30}

93. 887 BC. Amenophis died and was succeeded by his son Ramesses or Rhampsinitus, who built the western portico of the temple of Vulcan. The Egyptians dedicated the five days added to the year to Osiris, Isis, Orus Senior, Typhon and Nephthe, the sister and the wife of Typhon. These days were added to the twelve calendar months of the old luni-solar year. The Egyptians said that these days were added when these five

princes were born. Therefore, they were added in the reign of Ammon, the father of these five princes.

94. This year was scarcely brought into common use before the reign of Amenophis, for in his temple or sepulchre at Abydus, they placed a circle of three hundred and sixty-five cubits in circumference, which was covered on the upper side with a plate of gold. It was divided into three hundred and sixty-five equal parts, to represent all the days of the year. Each part recorded the heliacal risings and settings of the stars for that day. This circle remained there until Cambyses plundered the temples of Egypt in 523 BC. From this monument, I deduced that it was Amenophis who established this year, fixing its beginning to one of the four cardinal points of the heavens marking the beginnings of each season. Until these points had been fixed, the heliacal rising and settings of the stars could not have been noted for its days. {E31} Therefore, the priests of Egypt in the reign of Amenophis continued to observe the heliacal risings and settings of the stars for every day. Using the sun's meridional altitudes, they had determined the solstices and equinoxes according to the sun's mean motion. The equation of the sun's motion was not yet known. They started the beginning of this year at the vernal equinox and in its memory erected this monument.

95. When this year was introduced into Chaldea, the Chaldeans began their year of Nabonassar on the same month of Thoth as the Egyptians, and made their year the same length. The month of Thoth of the first year of Nabonassar happened on the 26th day of February in 747 BC. This was thirty-three days and five hours before the vernal equinox, according to the sun's mean motion. The month of Thoth of this year moved backwards thirty-three days and five hours in one hundred and thirty-seven years. Therefore, this month started on the vernal equinox one hundred and thirty-seven years before the start of the era of Nabonassar in 884 BC. If the month of Thoth began on the day following the vernal equinox, it might begin three or four years earlier and there we may place the death of this king around 888 BC. The Greeks imagined that Amenophis was the son of Tithonus. Therefore, he was born after the return of Sesostris into Egypt, with Tithonus and other captives, and so might be about seventy to seventy-five years old when he died. {E32}

96. 883 BC. Dido built Carthage and the Phoenicians soon began to sail as far as to the Strait of Gibraltar and beyond. Aeneas was still alive according to Virgil.

{*Virgil, Aeneid, l. 1. v. 297-305. 1:263}

97. 870 BC. Hesiod was in his prime. He said that he lived in the next age or generation after the wars of Thebes (Greek) and Troy and that this age would end, when the men then living had all died. Therefore, the generation was of a normal length of time. Herodotus states that Hesiod and Homer lived about four hundred years before him. Hence, it follows that the destruction of Troy was not earlier than we have determined.

98. 860 BC. Moeris reigned in Egypt. He embellished Memphis and moved the capital of his empire there from Thebes (Egyptian). At Memphis, he built the famous labyrinth, and the northern portico of the temple of Vulcan, and dug the great lake called the Lake of Moeris. On its bottom, he built two large brick pyramids. These things were not mentioned by Homer or Hesiod and were unknown to them. Therefore, these works must have been done after they died. Moeris also wrote a book of geometry.

99. 852 BC. Hazael, the successor of Hadad at Damascus, died and was deified, as was Hadad before him. These gods, together with Arathes, the wife of Hadad, were worshipped in their sepulchres or temples, until the days of Josephus. {E33} He stated that the Syrians boasted of their antiquity, not knowing that they were of recent origin.

100. 844 BC. The Aeolic migration occurred. Boeotia, formerly called Cadmeis, was captured by the Boeotians.

101. 838 BC. Cheops reigned in Egypt. He built the largest pyramid for his sepulchre, and forbade the worship of the former kings, intending to be worshipped himself.

102. 825 BC. The Heraclides, after three generations, or a hundred years, reckoned from their former expedition, returned to Peloponnesus. From this time to the end of the first Messenian War in 633 BC, ten kings of Sparta reigned from one family and nine from another. Ten kings reigned in Messene and nine in Arcadia. If one calculates (according to the normal course of nature) about twenty years to a reign, one reign following another, about one hundred and ninety years elapsed. From the end of the first Messenian War to the battle at Thermopylae in 480 BC, there were seven reigns in one of the families of the kings of Sparta, and eight in the other family. This would take up about one hundred and fifty more years and place the return of the Heraclides at about 820 BC.

103. 824 BC. Chephron reigned in Egypt and built the second large pyramid.

104. 808 BC. Mycerinus reigned in Egypt and began the third large pyramid. He enclosed the body of his daughter in a hollow ox and caused her to be worshipped daily with perfumes. {E34}

105. 804 BC. There was a war between the Athenians and Spartans, in which Codrus, the king of the Athenians, was killed.

106. 802 BC. Nitocris, the sister of Mycerinus, succeeded him, and finished the third large pyramid.

107. 794 BC. The Ionic migration occurred under the leadership of the sons of Codrus.

108. 790 BC. Pul founded the Assyrian Empire.

109. 788 BC. Asychis reigned in Egypt and built the eastern portico of the temple of Vulcan very elaborately. He also built a large brick pyramid made from the mud dug from the Lake of Moeris. Egypt broke up into several kingdoms. Gnephactus and Bocchoris reigned successively in Upper Egypt; Stephanathis, Necepsos and Nechus reigned at Sais; Anysis or Amosis II reigned at Anysis or Hanes; and Tacellotis reigned at Bubaste.

110. 776 BC. Iphitus restored the Olympic Games from which the era of the Olympiads began. Gnephactus reigned at Memphis.

111. 772 BC. Necepsos and Pelosiris invented astrology in Egypt.

112. 760 BC. Semiramis was in her prime. Sanchoniatho started to write his *Theology of the Phoenicians.*

113. 751 BC. Sabacon, the Ethiopian, invaded Egypt, which was now divided into various kingdoms. They burned Bocchoris alive, killed Nechus, and forced Anysis to flee. {E35}

114. 747 BC. Pul, the king of Assyria, died and was succeeded at Nineveh by Tiglathpileser and at Babylon by Nabonassar. The Egyptians, who fled from Sabacon, introduced their astrology and astronomy to Babylon, and founded the era of Nabonassar based on the Egyptian year.

115. 740 BC. Tiglathpileser, the king of Assyria, captured Damascus and enslaved the Syrians.

116. 728 BC. Tiglathpileser, the king of Assyria, was succeeded by Salmanasser.

117. 721 BC. Salmanasser, the king of Assyria, transplanted the ten tribes of Israel into captivity.

118. 719 BC. Sennacherib reigned over Assyria. Archias, the son of Evagetus, of the family of Hercules (Idean), led a colony from Corinth into Sicily, and built Syracuse.

119. 717 BC. Tirhakah reigned in Ethiopia.

120. 712 BC. The Ethiopians and Egyptians defeated Sennacherib. (Newton's date was 714 BC. Editor.) The Medes revolted from the Assyrian Empire. (Newton's date was 711 BC. Editor.)

121. 710 BC. Sennacherib was murdered by his two sons and Esarhaddon succeeded him. This was that Esarhaddon-Pul, or Sardanapalus, the son of Anacyndaraxis, or Sennacherib, who built Tarsus and Anchiale in one day. (Newton's date was 711 BC. Editor.) Lycurgus brought the poems of Homer from Asia into Greece. {E36}

122. 708 BC. Lycurgus, became tutor to Charillus or Charilaus, the young king of Sparta. Aristotle made Lycurgus as old as Iphitus because his name was on the Olympic discus. However, the discus was for one of the five games called the Quinquertium, and the Quinquertium game was first instituted in the 18th Olympiad. Socrates and Thucydides wrote that the institutions of Lycurgus happened about three hundred years before the end of the Peloponnesian War in 404 BC.

123. 701 BC. Sabacon, after a reign of fifty years, turned Egypt over to his son Sevechus, or Sethon, who became a priest in the temple of Vulcan and neglected military affairs.

124. 698 BC. Manasseh reigned in Judah.

125. 697 BC. The Corinthians were the first to build ships with three banks of oars, called triremes. Before this the Greeks had used long vessels of fifty oars.

126. 687 BC. Tirhakah reigned in Egypt.

127. 681 BC. Esarhaddon invaded Babylon.

128. 677 BC. The Jews were conquered by Esarhaddon, and Manasseh was taken captive to Babylon. (Newton's date was 673 BC. Editor.) He was released shortly thereafter. (Newton's date was 668 BC. Editor.)

129. 670 BC. Esarhaddon invaded Egypt. The government of Egypt was committed to twelve princes. (Newton's date was 671 BC. Editor.)

130. 668 BC. The western countries of Syria, Phoenicia and Egypt revolted from the Assyrian Empire. Esarhaddon died and was succeeded by Saosduchinus. {E37}

131. 658 BC. The Prytanes reigned in Corinth after expelling their kings.

132. 657 BC. The Corinthians defeated the Corcyreans at sea, which was the oldest recorded naval battle in history. <Phraortes reigned in Media.> (Newton's date was 658 BC for text in <>. Editor.)

133. 655 BC. Psammitichus became king of all Egypt by conquering the other eleven kings with whom he had already reigned for fifteen years. He reigned about thirty-nine more years. After this, the Ionians had access to Egypt and introduced their philosophy, astronomy and geometry there.

134. 652 BC. The first Messenian War began and lasted for twenty years.

135. 647 BC. Charops was the first decennial archon of the Athenians. Some of these archons might have died before the end of their ten years and the remainder of the ten years been completed by a new archon. Hence, the seven decennial archons might have ruled for no more than forty or fifty years. Saosduchinus, the king of Assyria died and was succeeded by Chyniladon.

136. 641 BC. Josiah reigned in Judah. (Newton's date was 640 BC. Editor.)

137. 635 BC. Phraortes, the king of the Medes, was killed in a war against the Assyrians. (Newton's date was 636 BC. Editor.) Astyages succeeded him.

138. 634 BC. The Scythians invaded the Medes and Assyrians. {E38} (Newton's date was 635 BC. Editor.)

139. 633 BC. Battus built Cyrene on the site of the city of Irasa in Libya, where Antaeus had reigned.

140. 627 BC. Rome was built.

141. 625 BC. Nabopolassar revolted from the Assyrian Empire and reigned over Babylon. Phalantus led the Parthenians into Italy and built Tarentum.

142. 617 BC. Psammitichus died, and his son Nechaoh ruled Egypt.

143. 610 BC. Josiah was killed. Cyaxeres and Nebuchadnezzar overthrew Nineveh, divided up the Assyrian Empire between them, and became great. (Newton's date was 609 BC. Editor.)

144. 607 BC. Creon was the first annual archon of the Athenians. The second Messenian War began. <The princes of the Scythians were killed in a feast by Cyaxeres.> (Newton's date was 610 BC for the text in <>. Editor.) Cyaxeres made the Scythians retreat beyond Colchis and Iberia, and seized the Assyrian provinces of Armenia, Pontus and Cappadocia. <Nebuchadnezzar invaded Syria and Judah.> (Newton's date was 606 BC for the text in <>. Editor.)

145. 605 BC. Nabopolassar died and was succeeded by his son Nebuchadnezzar, who had already reigned for two years with his father. (Newton's date was 604 BC. Editor.)

146. 600 BC. Cyaxeres reigned over the Medes. (Newton's date was 611 BC. Editor.) Darius the Mede, the son of Cyaxeres, was born.

147. 599 BC. Cyrus was born of Mandane, who was the sister of Cyaxeres and the daughter of Astyages. {E39}

148. 594 BC. Susiana and Elam were conquered by Nebuchadnezzar. Caranus and Perdiccas were banished and forced to flee from Phidon and co-founded the kingdom of Macedon. Phidon introduced weights and measures, and the coining of silver money. (Newton's date was 596 BC. Editor.)

149. 590 BC. Cyaxeres made war on Alyattes, the king of Lydia.

150. 588 BC. The temple of Solomon was burned by Nebuchadnezzar. When the Messenians were defeated, they fled to Sicily and built Messana.

151. 585 BC. In the sixth year of the Lydian war, a total eclipse of the sun on May 28th occurred as predicted by Thales, ending a battle between the Medes and Lydians. Thereupon, they made peace and ratified it by a marriage between Darius the Mede, the son of Cyaxeres, and Ariene, the daughter of Alyattes.

152. 584 BC. In the 49th Olympiad, Phidon presided over the Olympic Games.

153. 580 BC. Phidon was overthrown. Two men were chosen by lot from the city Elis to preside over the Olympic Games.

154. 572 BC. Draco was archon of the Athenians and made laws for them.

155. 571 BC. Nebuchadnezzar conquered Egypt.

156. 568 BC. The Amphictyonic Council declared war on the Cirrheans, by the advice of Solon, and captured Cirrha after a ten-year war. Clisthenes, Alcmaeon and Eurolicus commanded the forces of the Amphictyons, and were contemporary with Phidon. {E40} For Leocides, the son of Phidon, and Megacles, the son of Alcmaeon, simultaneously courted Agarista, the daughter of Clisthenes.

157. 562 BC. When Solon was archon of Athens, he made laws for them.

158. 560 BC. Darius the Mede reigned. (Newton's date was 569 BC. Editor.)

159. 557 BC. Periander died, and Corinth was freed from tyrants.

160. 555 BC. Nabonadius reigned at Babylon. His mother Nitocris embellished and fortified that city.

161. 550 BC. Pisistratus became tyrant at Athens. Solon met Croesus.

162. 549 BC. Solon died, when Hegestratus was archon of Athens.

163. 544 BC. Sardis captured by Cyrus. Darius the Mede recoined the Lydian gold and silver coins into *Darics*.

164. 538 BC. Cyrus captured Babylon.

165. 537 BC. Cyrus defeated Darius the Mede and the empire became Persian.

166. 536 BC. The Jews returned from captivity and started to build the second temple.

167. 530 BC. Cyrus died after the month of Thoth, and Cambyses reigned. His first regal year was 529 BC.

168. 521 BC. Darius the son of Hystaspes reigned. The Magi were killed. The religions of the various nations of Persia, which consisted in the worship of their ancient kings, was abolished. Under the influence of Hystaspes and Zoroaster, the worship of one god at altars without temples, was set up in all Persia. {E41}

169. 520 BC. The second temple was being built at Jerusalem by the command of Darius Hystaspes.

170. 515 BC. The second temple was finished and dedicated.

171. 513 BC. Harmodius and Aristagiton murdered Hipparchus, the son of Pisastratus, the tyrant of Athens.

172. 508 BC. The Romans expelled their kings and replaced them with consuls.

173. 490 BC. The first battle of Marathon was fought. (Newton's date 491 BC. Editor.)

174. 485 BC. Xerxes I reigned.

175. 480 BC. Xerxes I crossed over the Hellespont into Greece. The Persians fought and won the battle of Thermopylae and lost the naval battle of Salamis.

176. 474 BC. Artaxerxes Longimanus became viceroy with his father Xerxes I. (Newton had no entry for this date. Editor.)

177. 467 BC. Ezra returned into Judah. Johanan the father of Jaddua had now grown up, having a room in the temple. (Newton's date was 457 BC. Editor.)

178. 465 BC. Artaxerxes Longimanus reigned as sole king. (Newton's date was 464 BC. Editor.)

179. 454 BC. Nehemiah returned to Judah. (Newton's date was 444 BC. Editor.)

180. 444 BC. Herodotus started to write his histories.

181. 438 BC. Nehemiah expelled Manasseh, the brother of Jaddua, because he had married Nicaso, the daughter of Sanballat. (Newton's date was 428 BC. Editor.)

182. 432 BC. Sanballat built a temple in Mount Gerizim and appointed his son-in-law Manasseh as its first high priest. (Newton's date was 422 BC. Editor.)

183. 431 BC. The Peloponnesian War began.

184. 424 BC. Darius Nothus reigned. {E42}

185. 422 BC. Before this time the priests and Levites were numbered and written in the chronicles of the Jews, before the death of Nehemiah, when either Johanan or Jaddua was the high priest. This ends the biblical history of the Jews. (Newton's date was 412 BC. Editor.)

186. 404 BC. Artaxerxes Mnemon reigned. The Peloponnesian War ended. (Newton's date was 405 BC. Editor.)

187. 359 BC. Artaxerxes Ochus reigned.

188. 338 BC. Arogus reigned.

189. 336 BC. Darius Codomannus reigned.

190. 331 BC. The Persian Empire was conquered by Alexander the Great near Gaugamela. (Newton's date was 332 BC. Editor.)

191. 330 BC. Darius Codomannus, the last king of Persia, was murdered. {E43} (Newton's date was 331 BC. Editor.)

CHAPTER I Early Greek History

Part 1 — Establishing the Times of the Key Events in Greek History

192. This chapter has two main parts. In the first part we lay the foundation for building the chronology of the ancient times. In the second part of this chapter, we show how the rest of the Greek history fits within this framework.

1. The Uncertainty in Early Histories

1.1 The Exaggeration of Early Histories

193. All nations, before they began to keep exact records of time, have been prone to exaggerate their antiquity, and this fiction has been promoted by the contentions between nations about their origins. Herodotus says that the priests of Egypt reckoned that from the reign of Menes around 900 BC to that of Sethon around 700 BC that there were three hundred and forty-one generations of men, with as many priests of Vulcan, and as many kings of Egypt. {*E44*} They equate three hundred generations to ten thousand years. Herodotus states that three generations of men equates to a hundred years. The remaining forty-one generations make thirteen hundred and forty years: and so the whole time from the reign of Menes to that of Sethon was eleven thousand three hundred and forty years! {*Herodotus, l. 2. c. 142. 1:449*} By this way of reckoning, and allotting longer reigns to the gods of Egypt than to the kings who followed them, Herodotus relates from the priests of Egypt that from Pan around 15570 BC to Amasis in 570 BC were fifteen thousand years and from Hercules (Egyptian) around 17570 BC to Amasis were seventeen thousand years. {*Herodotus, l. 2. c. 145. 1:453*} {*Herodotus, l. 2. c. 43. 1:329*}

194. Likewise the Chaldeans boasted of their antiquity, for Callisthenes, the student of Aristotle, sent astronomical observations from Babylon to Greece. Babylon is said to have been founded nineteen hundred and three years before the time of Alexander the Great. (2234 BC) {*Simplicius, De Caelo, l. 2.*} The Chaldeans boasted further, that they had observed the stars for seven hundred and thirty thousand years, around 730300 BC, and there were others who made the kingdoms of Assyria, Media and Damascus, much older than the truth. {*Pliny, l. 7. c. 56. (193) 2:637*}

195. Some of the Greeks called the times before the reign of Ogyges unknown, because they had no history of them. The times between his flood and the beginning of the Olympiads was composed of fables because their history was much mixed with poetic fiction. The time after the beginning of the Olympiads was called historical because their history was free from such fables. {*E45*} The fabulous ages lacked a good chronology and so did the historical for the first sixty to seventy Olympiads, from 776 BC to about 500 BC.

1.2 The Inaccuracies of the History before the Persian Empire

196. The Europeans had no chronology before the times of the Persian Empire and whatever chronology they now have of older times has been composed since by deduction and conjecture. When the Persian Empire began, Acusilaus made Phoroneus as old as Ogyges and his flood, and that flood one thousand and twenty years older than the first Olympiad in 1796 BC, which is more than seven hundred and twenty years older than the truth! To justify his history his followers have increased the reigns of kings in length and number. Plutarch says that the philosophers of old delivered their teachings in verse, as Orpheus, Hesiod, Parmenides, Xenophanes, Empedocles and Thales. However, later ones used prose. Aristarchus, Timocharis, Aristillus and Hipparchus did not make astronomy less notable by describing it in prose after the time of Eudoxus, Hesiod and Thales, who had written in verse. {*Plutarch, Moralia-The Oracles at Delphi, l. 1. c. 18. (402F) 5:305*} Solon wrote in verse and all the seven wise men of Greece preferred to write in verse; however, Anaximenes of Lampsacus wrote in prose. {*Diogenes Laertius, Anaximenes, l. 1. c. 2. (2) 1:133*} {*Plutarch, Lives-Pubicola, l. 1. c. 9. s. 7. 1:527*} Anaximenes affirms that in his time men usually wrote in verse. {*Diogenes Laertius, Solon, l. 1. (61) 1:63*} Until those days, the Greeks wrote only in verse, and while they did so there could be no chronology, nor any other history than such as was mixed with poetic fantasies. {*E46*}

1.3 The Early Greek Historians

197. Pliny, in discussing various inventors, says that Pherecydes the Syrian taught men to write in prose in the reign of Cyrus (537-530 BC), and Cadmus Milesius to write history. {*Pliny, l. 7. c. 56. (205) 2:645} In another place, he says that Cadmus Milesius was the first one who wrote in prose. {*Pliny, l. 5. c. 31. (112,113) 2:305} Josephus states that Cadmus Milesius and Acusilaus lived shortly before the Persian invasion of Greece in 480 BC. {*Josephus, Against Apion, l. 1. c. 3. (13) 1:169} Suidas calls Acusilaus a most ancient historian, and says that he wrote genealogies based on tables of bronze, which his father is reported to have found in a corner of his house. It is not known who hid them there, for the Greeks had no public tables or inscriptions older than the laws of Draco. {*Josephus, Against Apion, l. 1. c. 4. (21) 1:171} Note the various methods in recording history.

1) Pherecydes of Athens, in the reign of Darius Hystaspes or soon after around 490 BC, wrote of the antiquities and ancient genealogies of the Athenians in ten books. He was one of the first European historians and one of the best from whence he had the name of *Genealogus;* and Dionysius of Halicarnassus said that he was not inferior to any other historian. {*Dionysius, l. 1. c. 13. s. 1. 1:41}

2) Epimenides, (not the philosopher but the historian), wrote also of ancient history in the late seventh century BC. Hellanicus, who was twelve years older than Herodotus and lived from around 480 BC to 395 BC, organised his history by the ages or successions of the priestesses of Juno Argiva. {E47} Others organised theirs by the archons of Athens or the kings of Sparta.

3) Hippias of Elis published a breviary of the victors of the Olympic Games but had no authoritative basis for his work. {*Plutarch, Lives-Numa, l. 1. c. 2. s. 4. 1:309} He lived in the one hundred and fifth Olympiad around 360 BC and was derided by Plato for his ignorance. This breviary seems to have contained nothing more than a short account of the victors in each Olympiad.

4) Ephorus was the student of Isocrates and lived from around 405 BC to 330 BC. He wrote a chronological history of Greece, beginning with the return of the Heraclides into Peloponnesus in 825 BC, and ending with the siege of Perinthus, in the nineteenth year of Philip, the father of Alexander the Great, that is, ten years before the fall of the Persian Empire in 340 BC. {*Diod. Sic., l. 16. c. 76. s. 5. 8:51,53} Ephorus organised his history

by generations. The reckoning by the Olympiads or by any other era was not yet in use among the Greeks. {*Polybius, l. 9. c. 1. (1-4) 4:3}

5) The Arundelian Marbles were composed sixty years after the death of Alexander the Great in the 4th year of the 128th Olympiad in 265 BC. They contain no mention of the Olympiads, nor any other standing era, but record the times relative to the date of their writing.

6) Chronology was now simplified to a reckoning by years. In the next Olympiad, Timaeus Siculus, who lived from around 350 to 260 BC, improved it. He wrote a history in several books, down to his own times, according to the Olympiads. {E48} He compared the ephori, the kings of Sparta, the archons of Athens, and the priestesses of Juno Argiva with the Olympic victors, so as to make the Olympiads, and the genealogies and successions of kings and priestesses, and the poetic histories agree with one another according to the best of his judgment. Where he left off Polybius, who lived around 200 to 118 BC, began and carried on the history. Eratosthenes wrote around 220 BC, about a hundred years after the death of Alexander the Great. He was followed by Apollodorus, and these two have been followed ever since by chronologers.

1.4 The Uncertainty of Early Greek History

198. How uncertain their chronology is, and how doubtful it was reputed by the Greeks of those times, may be understood by this passage from Plutarch.

> Some say that he (Lycurgus) flourished at the same time with Iphitus, and in concert with him established the Olympic truce. Among these is Aristotle, the philosopher, and he alleges as proof the discus at Olympia on which an inscription preserves the name of Lycurgus. But those who compute the time by the succession of kings at Sparta, like Eratosthenes and Apollodorus, prove that Lycurgus was many years earlier than the first Olympiad. {*Plutarch, Lives-Lycurgus, l. 1. c. 1. s. 1. 1:205}

199. Lycurgus was in his prime in the 17th or 18th Olympiad around 708 BC, and at length Aristotle made him as old as the first Olympiad in 776 BC and so did Epaminondas, as he is cited by Aelian and Plutarch. Then Eratosthenes, Apollodorus and their followers made him more than a hundred years older, living about 876 BC. {E49}

200. In another place Plutarch says:

As for his (Solon's) interview with Croesus, some think to prove by chronology that it is fictitious. But when a story is so famous and so well attested, and, what is more to the point, when it comports so well with the character of Solon, and is so worthy of his magnanimity and wisdom, I do not propose to reject it out of deference to any chronological canons, so called, which thousands are to this day revising, without being able to bring their contradictions into a general agreement. {*Plutarch, Lives-Solon, l. 1. c. 27. s. 1. 1:479}

1.5 The Uncertainty of Early Roman History

201. The chronology of the Romans is even more uncertain. Plutarch documents great uncertainties in the origin of Rome, and so does Servius. {*Plutarch, Lives-Romulus, l. 1. c. 1-2. 1:91-97} {*Plutarch, Lives-Numa, l. 1. c. 1. s. 1. 1:307} {*Virgil, Aeneid, l. 7. v. 678. 2:49,51} The old records of the Romans were burned by the Gauls in 390 BC, one hundred and eighteen years after their last king in 508 BC and sixty-seven years before the death of Alexander the Great in 323 BC. {*Diod. Sic., l. 14. c. 116. (8) 6:315} Quintus Fabius Pictor, the oldest historian of the Romans, lived around 225 BC, about a hundred years later than Alexander, and copied most of his work from Diocles of Peparethius, a Greek. {*Plutarch, Lives-Romulus, l. 1. c. 3. s. 1. 1:97}

1.6 The Uncertainty in the Early History of Other Countries

202. The chronologers of Gaul, Spain, Germany, Scythia, Sweden, Britain and Ireland wrote much later. Scythia beyond the Danube River had no written language until Ulphilas, their bishop, created it around 280 AD. This was about six hundred years after the death of Alexander the Great. {E50} Germany had none until they received it from the western empire of the Romans around 380 AD, more than seven hundred years after the death of Alexander. The Huns had none in the days of Procopius around 530 AD, who lived about eight hundred and fifty years after the death of Alexander. Sweden and Norway received a written language still later. Things said to have happened more than one or two hundred years before the use of writing, are of little credit.

2. The Time of the Return of the Heraclides into Peloponnesus

2.1 The Time of the Return According to Ancient Historians

203. Diodorus in the beginning of his history states that he did not write any history preceding the Trojan War,
because he had no accurate records to rely on. {*Diod. Sic., l. 1. c. 5. s. 1. 1:21} From the Trojan War in 1184 BC (according to the reckoning of Apollodorus whom Diodorus followed), there were eighty years to the return of the Heraclides into Peloponnesus in 1104 BC. From that period to the first Olympiad in 776 BC, there were three hundred and twenty-eight years computing the times based on the reigns of the kings of Sparta. Apollodorus followed Eratosthenes, and both of them followed Thucydides, in reckoning eighty years from the Trojan War to the return of the Heraclides. {*Thucydides, l. 1. c. 12. s. 3. 1:23} In reckoning three hundred and twenty-eight years from that return to the first Olympiad, Diodorus says that the times were computed from reigns of the kings of Sparta. Plutarch relates that Apollodorus, Eratosthenes and others followed that method of reckoning. {*Plutarch, Lives-Lycurgus, l. 1. c. 1. s. 2. 1:205} {E51} Since this method is still accepted by chronologers and was deduced by computing the times from the kings at Sparta, that is, from their number, let us re-examine that computation.

2.2 Method 1 — Dating the Return by the Average Length of a King's Reign

2.2.1 The Length of a King's Reign According to Ancient Historians

204. The Egyptians, Greeks and Romans have calculated the reigns of kings equal to generations of men with three generations to a hundred years. Accordingly, they have made their kings reign an average of thirty-three or more years each. This results in the following:

1) The seven kings of Rome who preceded the consuls have reigned two hundred and forty-four years, which averages to thirty-five years each.

2) The first twelve kings of Sicyon: Aegialeus, Europs, etc., are said to have reigned five hundred and twenty-nine years, which averages to forty-four years each.

3) The first eight kings of Argos: Inachus, Phoroneus, etc., are said to have reigned three hundred and seventy-one years, which averages to more than forty-six years each.

4) Between the return of the Heraclides into Peloponnesus, and the end of the first Messenian War, the ten kings of Sparta in one family: Eurysthenes, Agis, Echestratus, Labotas, Doryagus, Agesilaus, Archelaus, Teleclus, Alcamenes, and Polydorus; the nine in the other family: Procles, Sous, Eurypon, Prytanis, Eunomus, Polydectes,

Charillus, Nicander, Theopompus; the ten kings of Messene: Cresphontes, Epytus, Glaucus, Isthmius, Dotadas, Sibotas, Phintas, Antiochus, Euphaes, Aristodemus; {E52} and the nine of Arcadia: Cypselus, Olaeas, Buchalion, Phialus, Simus, Pompus, Aegineta, Polymnestor, Aechmis, according to chronologers, took up three hundred and seventy-nine years. This averages to thirty-eight years for each of the ten kings, and to forty-two each for the nine kings.

5) The five kings of the family of Eurysthenes, between the end of the first Messenian War, and the beginning of the reign of Darius Hystaspes: Eurycrates I, Anaxander, Eurycrates II, Leon, Anaxandrides, reigned two hundred and two years, which averages to forty years each.

2.2.2 The Average Length of a King's Reign According to Observed History

205. Thus the Greek chronologers, who follow Timaeus and Eratosthenes, have made the kings of their various cities, who lived before the times of the Persian Empire, to reign about thirty-five to forty years each, which is a time so much beyond the normal course of nature it is incredible! For by the ordinary course of nature some kings reign five or six years longer while others reign much shorter times. Eighteen or twenty years is an average length of a reign. Consider the following twelve examples taken from history that we know to be accurate:

1) The eighteen kings of Judah who succeeded Solomon reigned three hundred and eighty-eight years, 975-588 BC, which averages twenty-one and a half years each.

2) The fifteen kings of Israel after Solomon reigned two hundred and fifty-five years, 975-721 BC, which averages seventeen years each.

3) The eighteen kings of Babylon: Nabonassar, etc., reigned two hundred and nine years, which averages eleven years and eight months each. {E53}

4) The ten kings of Persia: Cyrus, Cambyses, etc., reigned two hundred and eight years, which is almost twenty-one years each.

5) The sixteen successors of Alexander the Great in Syria: Seleucus, Antiochus Soter, etc., reigned two hundred and forty-four years, which averages fifteen years and three months each.

6) The eleven kings of Egypt: Ptolemy Lagus, etc., reigned two hundred and seventy-seven years, which averages twenty-five years each.

7) The eight kings in Macedon: Cassander, etc., reigned one hundred and thirty-eight years, which averages seventeen years and three months each.

8) The thirty kings of England: William the Conqueror, William Rufus, etc., reigned six hundred and forty-eight years, which averages twenty-one and a half years each.

9) The first twenty-four kings of France: Pharamundus, etc., reigned four hundred and fifty-eight years, which averages nineteen years each.

10) The next twenty-four kings of France: Ludovicus Balbus, etc., reigned four hundred and fifty-one years, which averages eighteen years and nine months each.

11) The next fifteen kings of France: Philip Valesius, etc., reigned three hundred and fifteen years, which averages twenty-one years each.

12) All the sixty-three kings of France reigned one thousand two hundred and twenty-four years, which averages nineteen and a half years each.

2.2.3 The Average Length of a Generation Compared to a King

206. Generations from father to son may be reckoned one with another at about thirty-three or thirty-four years each, or about three generations to a hundred years. However, if you calculate by the oldest sons, they are shorter, so that three of them may be reckoned at about seventy-five or eighty years. {E54} The reigns of kings are still shorter because kings are succeeded not only by their oldest sons, but sometimes by their brothers, and sometimes they are killed or deposed and succeeded by others of an equal or greater age, especially in turbulent kingdoms.

2.2.4 Dating the Heraclides' Return by the Average Length of a King's Reign

207. In more recent times, when chronology has been more exact, there is no example to be found anywhere of ten kings reigning in continual succession for more than two hundred and sixty years. However, Timaeus and his followers, (and I think some of his predecessors), follow the example of the Egyptians. They have taken the reigns of kings for generations and have calculated three generations to a hundred years and sometimes to one hundred and twenty years and founded the chronology of the Greeks upon this way of reckoning. Let the reckoning be reduced to the normal course of nature, by setting the reigns of a king to about eighteen or twenty years each. Then the time between the return of the Heraclides into

Peloponnesus and the end of the first Messenian War around 633 BC, during which:

1) ten kings of Messene reigned,

2) ten kings of Sparta by one family reigned,

3) nine by another family of Spartan kings reigned,

4) nine kings of Arcadia reigned (previously mentioned),

will scarcely take more time than one hundred and eighty or ninety years. This places the return of the Heraclides around 830 to 840 BC. However, according to chronologers, the return was in 1104 BC which amounts to more than four hundred and seventy years. This would have these kings reigning for an average of forty-five to fifty years each! {E55}

2.3 Method 2 — Dating the Return by the Average Generation Length

2.3.1 The Average Generation Length

208. For confirming this reckoning, I may add another argument. Euryleon, the son of Aegeus, commanded the main body of the Messenians in the fifth year of the first Messenian War around 648 BC. {*Pausanias, Messenia, l. 4. c. 13. 2:241-247*} {*Pausanias, Messenia, l. 4. c. 7. 2:205-211*} {*Pausanias, Laconia, l. 3. c. 15. 2:89-97*} He was in the fifth generation from Oiolicus, who was the son of Theras. Theras was the brother-in-law of Aristodemus and the tutor to his twin sons Eurysthenes and Procles. {*Pausanias, Messenia, l. 4. c. 7. 2:205-211*} Hence, from the return of the Heraclides, which was in the days of Theras, to the battle, which was in the fifth year of this war, there were six generations, which I think were reckoned by the oldest son. Therefore, there would scarcely exceed thirty years to a generation, and so the elapsed time would be one hundred and seventy or eighty years. That war lasted nineteen or twenty years; add the last fifteen years, and there will be about one hundred and ninety years to the end of that war. However, the followers of Timaeus reckon the time to be more than four hundred and seventy years, which is almost eighty years to a generation!

2.3.2 Calculations by the Average Reign of Kings

209. By this reasoning, chronologers have increased the period between the return of the Heraclides into Peloponnesus and the first Messenian War by about one hundred and ninety years and thereby they have also increased the period between that war and the rise of the Persian Empire. For in the family of the Spartan kings who descended from Eurysthenes,

after Polydorus, these kings reigned: Eurycrates I, Anaxander, Eurycratidas or Eurycrates II, Leon, Anaxandrides, Cleomenes, Leonidas, etc. {*Herodotus, l. 7. c. 204. 3:521*} {E56} In another family descended from Procles after Theopompus, these kings reigned: Anaxandrides, Archidamus I, Anaxilas, Leutychides I, Hippocratides, Agasicles, Ariston, Demaratus, Leutychides II. {*Herodotus, l. 8. c. 131. 4:135*} These kings reigned until the sixth year of Xerxes I in 480 BC, in which Leonidas was killed by the Persians at Thermopylae. Leutychides II soon after this fled from Sparta to Tegea and died there. The seven reigns of the kings of Sparta, which succeeded Polydorus, when added to the ten reigns previously mentioned, which began with Eurysthenes, make up seventeen reigns of kings between the return of the Heraclides into Peloponnesus and the sixth year of Xerxes I in 480 BC. The eight reigns succeeding Theopompus, when added to the nine reigns previously mentioned, which began with that of Procles, also make up seventeen reigns. Taking these seventeen reigns at an average of twenty years each, amounts to three hundred and forty years. Count these three hundred and forty years back from the sixth year of Xerxes I to 819 BC. Add one or two years more for the war of the Heraclides and the reign of Aristodemus, the father of Eurysthenes and Procles. Then this places the return of the Heraclides into Peloponnesus in 821 BC, about one hundred fifty-four years after the death of Solomon and forty-five years before the first Olympiad, in which Coraebus was victor. {E57} However, the followers of Timaeus have placed this return two hundred and eighty-three years earlier in 1104 BC.

2.3.3 The Results of an Inaccurate Chronology

210. This is the foundation, according to Plutarch and Diodorus, upon which Greek history is based. For the times before Cyrus died, the history must be shorted in the proportion of almost two to one. The history after the death of Cyrus is accurate.

2.4 Method 3 — The Dating of the Return by the Time of Lycurgus

2.4.1 The Time of Lycurgus According to More Recent Ancient Historians

211. This unrealistic chronology has resulted in chronologers making Lycurgus, the legislator, as old as Iphitus, who restored the Olympiads, and Iphitus a hundred and twelve years older than the first Olympiad! To justify this chronology they have created twenty-eight Olympiads older than the first Olympiad in 776 BC, when Coraebus was the victor.

2.4.2 The Time of Lycurgus According to Thycydides and Plato

212. These things were feigned after the days of Thucydides and Plato, for Socrates died in 399 BC, five years after the end of the Peloponnesian War. Plato introduces him, saying that the institutions of Lycurgus were not much more than three hundred years old. {*Plato, Minos, l. 1. (318C) 12:411} {E58} Thucydides, in the reading followed by Stephanus, says that the Lacedemonians had good laws at an earlier time than any other land and had been free from tyranny. That time period, during which they had been enjoying the same constitution, covers about three hundred years (or a little more) down to the end of the Peloponnesian War. {*Thucydides, l. 1. c. 18. s. 1. 1:31,33} (The Loeb version says *four hundred years*, Editor.) Count back three hundred years from the end of the Peloponnesian War, and that places the legislature of Lycurgus in the 19th Olympiad in 704 BC, and according to Socrates, it might be in the 22nd or 23rd, which is 692 or 688 BC.

2.4.3 The Time of Lycurgus According to Athenaeus

213. Athenaeus relates from the ancient authors (Hellanicus, Sosibius and Hieronymus) that Lycurgus the legislator was contemporary with Terpander the musician, and that Terpander was the first man who won the music awards instituted in those festivals at Carnea in the 26th Olympiad in 676 BC. {*Athenaeus, l. 14. (635ef) 6:431} He won four times in those Pythic Games, and therefore lived at least until the 29th Olympiad in 664 BC, and he began to be popular in the days of Lycurgus. It is not likely that Lycurgus lived much before the 18th Olympiad in 708 BC.

2.4.4 How the Incorrect Time Dating Happened

214. Since the name of Lycurgus is on the Olympic discus, Aristotle assumed that Lycurgus was the companion of Iphitus in restoring the Olympic Games. This argument might be the basis of the opinion of chronologers that Lycurgus and Iphitus were contemporary.

2.4.5 The Correct Time for Lycurgus

215. However, Iphitus did not restore all the Olympic Games. He restored indeed the racing in the first Olympiad in 776 BC, when Coraebus was the victor. {E59} In the 14th Olympiad in 724 BC, the double foot race was added and Hypenus was the victor. This race was two stadia or about a quarter mile long. In the 18th Olympiad in 708 BC, the pentathlon and wrestling events were added, and Lampis and Eurybatus, both from Sparta, were the victors of these. {*Pausanias, Elis I, l. 5. c. 8. s. 5. 2:421,423} The discus was for one of the games of the pentathlon. Pausanias says that there were three discs kept in the Olympic treasury at Altis. {*Pausanias, Elis II, l. 6. c. 19. s. 1,4. 3:111} Since these have the name of Lycurgus upon them, it shows that they were given by him at the institution of the pentathlon in the 18th Olympiad in 708 BC.

216. Polydectes, the king of Sparta, was killed before the birth of his son Charillus or Charilaus and left the kingdom to Lycurgus, his brother. Lycurgus initially became the guardian to the child when he was born. After about eight months, he travelled into Crete and Asia until the child was fully grown. Lycurgus brought back with him the poems of Homer and soon after published his laws, likely in the 22nd or 23rd Olympiad in 692 or 688 BC, for by then he was growing old.

217. Terpander was a lyrical poet and began to become famous about this time, for he imitated Orpheus and Homer. He sang Homer's verses and his own and wrote the laws of Lycurgus in verse, and was the victor in the Pythic Games in the 26th Olympiad in 676 BC, as noted before. {*Plutarch, Moralia-On Music, l. 1. c. 5. (1132F) 14:363} {*Clement, Stromata, l. 1. c. 21. ANF2:330} He was the first who distinguished the modes of lyrical music by several names. {E60} Ardalus and Clomas soon after did the same for wind music. From henceforth, by the encouragement of the institution of the Pythic Games, several eminent musicians and poets became popular in Greece: as Archilochus, Eumelus Corinthius, Polymnestus, Thaletas, Xenodemus, Xenocritus, Sacadas, Tyrtaeus, Tlesilla, Rhianus, Alcman, Arion, Stesichorus, Mimnermnus, Alcaeus, Sappho, Theognis, Anacreon, Abycus, Simonides, Pindar, by whom the music and poetry of the Greeks was perfected.

2.4.6 Dating the Heraclides' Return by Lycurgus and Agesilaus

218. Lycurgus published his laws in the reign of Agesilaus, who was the son and successor of Doryagus, in the family of the kings of Sparta who descended from Eurysthenes. There were six kings from the return of the Heraclides into Peloponnesus to the end of the reign of Agesilaus. Also from the return of the Heraclides to the reign of Polydectes, there were six kings in the family of the Spartan kings who descended from Procles. At about twenty years each these reigns total one hundred and twenty years. This excludes the short reign of a year or two of Aristodemus, the father of Eurysthenes and Procles, for Aristodemus came to the throne as Herodotus and the Lacedemonians themselves affirmed. {*Herodotus, l. 6. c. 52. 3:197,199} {E61} It is not known when Agesilaus and Polydectes died, but it may be presumed that Lycurgus did not modify the Olympic Games before he became king.

Therefore, Polydectes died in the beginning of the 18th Olympiad in 708 BC or shortly before. It is likely that in the 20th Olympiad in 700 BC or very near to the middle of the Olympiad between the deaths of the two kings, Polydectes and Agesilaus, that Lycurgus made these changes. Then one hundred and twenty-one years before that time (allowing one year for the reign of Aristodemus) places the return of the Heraclides in 820 BC, about forty-five years before the first Olympiad in 776 BC.

219. Based on the information from these five methods of dating the return of the Heraclides, we selected a date of 825 BC as a good approximation and used that date in the *Short Chronology*.

2.5 Method 4 — Dating the Return by the Time of Iphitus

220. Iphitus restored the Olympic Games. {*Pausanias, Elis I, l. 5. c. 4. s. 5. 2:399*} He was a descendant of Oxylus, who was the son of Haemon the grandson of Thoas and the great-grandson of Andraemon. Hercules (Idean) and Andraemon married two sisters. Thoas fought at Troy. Oxylus returned into Peloponnesus with the Heraclides and commanded the body of the Aetolians, and recovered Elis. {*Pausanias, Elis I, l. 5. c. 1. s. 8. 2:385*} {*Pausanias, Elis I, l. 5. c. 2. s. 3,4. 2:403*} {*Pausanias, Elis I, l. 5. c. 8. s. 5. 2:421*} {*Strabo, l. 8. c. 3. s. 33. (357) 4:103*} Oxylus' ancestor Aetolus (the son of Endymion and the grandson of Aethlius) had been driven from Elis by Salmoneus, the grandson of Hellen. By the friendship of the Heraclides, Oxylus had the care of the Olympic temple entrusted to him. For his services to them, the Heraclides promised him that the country of the Eleans would be free from war and be defended by them. {*E62*} When the Eleans were thus protected, Oxylus restored the Olympic Games. After his reign, they were discontinued and later restored by Iphitus their king. {*Pausanias, Elis I, l. 5. c. 4. s. 5. 2:399*} {*Pausanias, Elis I, l. 5. c. 8. s. 5. 2:421*} He made the games quadrennial. Iphitus is considered by some to be the son of Haemon and by others the son of Praxonidas, who was the son of Haemon. Since Haemon was the father of Oxylus, I think Iphitus was the son of Praxonidas, the grandson of Oxylus, the great-grandson of Haemon. Hence, the return of the Heraclides into Peloponnesus is two generations calculated by the oldest sons, or about fifty years before the Olympiads around 825 BC.

2.6 Method 5 — Dating the Return by the Time of Melas

221. Pausanias states that Melas is the son of Antissus of the descendants of Gonussa, who was the daughter of Sicyon, and was not more than six generations older than Cypselus, the king of Corinth. {*Pausanias, Elis I, l. 5. c. 18. s. 7. 2:489*} Melas was a contemporary of Aletes, who returned with the Heraclides into Peloponnesus. According to chronologers, the reign of Cypselus began in year two of Olymiad 31 in 654 BC. If you allow thirty years for each of the six generations, then this amounts to one hundred and eighty years. This places the return of the Heraclides in 833 BC, which is fifty-eight years before the first Olympiad in 776 BC. {*E63*} However, it might not be so early if the reign of Cypselus began three or four Olympiads later, since he reigned before the Persian Empire began.

3. Dating the Argonaut Expedition

3.1 Method 1 — Dating the Argonaut Expedition by Aristodemus the Heraclide

222. Hercules (Idean) was the father of Hyllus, the grandfather of Cleodius, the great-grandfather of Aristomachus, the great-great-grandfather of Temenus, Cresphontes and Aristodemus. Aristodemus led the Heraclides into Peloponnesus. Eurystheus, who lived in the time of Hercules (Idean), was killed in the first attempt of the Heraclides to return. Hyllus was killed in the second attempt, Cleodius in the third attempt, and Aristomachus in the fourth attempt. Aristodemus died as soon as they had returned and left the kingdom of Sparta to his sons Eurysthenes and Procles. Hence, their return was four generations later than the Argonaut Expedition. These generations were short ones being reckoned by the fathers of the family and agree with the reckoning of Thucydides and the ancients that the taking of Troy was about seventy-five or eighty years before the return of the Heraclides into Peloponnesus. The Argonaut Expedition was one generation earlier than the taking of Troy. Therefore, if you count eighty years back from the return of the Heraclides into Peloponnesus to the Trojan War, the taking of Troy will be about seventy-one years after the death of Solomon in 904 BC. Since the Argonaut Expedition was one generation earlier, it would be about forty-two years after the death of Solomon in 933 BC. {*E64*} From the taking of Troy to the return of the Heraclides could scarcely be more than eighty years, because Orestes, the son of Agamemnon, was a youth at the taking of Troy, and his sons Penthilus and Tisamenus lived until the return of the Heraclides.

3.2 Method 2 — Dating the Argonaut Expedition by Aesculapius and Hippocrates

223. Aesculapius and Hercules (Idean) were Argonauts, and Hippocrates was the eighteenth generation inclusively on his father's side from Aesculapius, and the nineteenth generation from Hercules (Idean) on his mother's side. Most writers likely note these generations by the head of the family, and so for the most part by the oldest sons. Therefore, we may reckon about twenty-eight or at most about thirty years to a generation. And thus the seventeen generations on his father's side, and eighteen on his mother's sum to about five hundred and two years. Counting back from the beginning of the Peloponnesian War, at which time Hippocrates began to be popular, brings you to forty-two years after the death of Solomon, placing the time of the Argonaut Expedition in 933 BC.

3.3 Method 3 — Dating the Argonaut Expedition by the Time of the Trojan War

3.3.1 Method 3.1 — Dating the Trojan War by the Carthaginian Archives

224. When the Romans conquered Carthage, the archives of Carthage came into their hands. Hence, Appian says that from the time of the founding of Carthage until the end of the first Punic War in 241 BC was approximately seven hundred years. {*Appian, Punic Wars, l. 1. c. 2. 1:405*} Solinus adds about thirty-seven years to the number.

> *Adrymento atque Carthagini auctor est a Tyro populus. Urbem istam, ut Cato in Oratione Senatoria autumat, cum rex Hiarbas rerum in Libya potiretur, Elissa mulier extruxit, domo Phoenix, & Carthadam dixit, quod Phoenicum ore exprimit civitatem novam; mox sermone verso Carthago dicta est, quae post annos septingentos triginta septem exciditur quam fuerat extructa.* {*Solinus, Polyhistor, c. 30.*}

Adrymentum and Carthage were founded by the city state of Tyre. When King Hiarbas became master of affairs in Libya, as Cato affirms in a senatorial speech, Elissa (Dido) his wife founded the city of Carthage itself from the home city of the Phoenicans and called it Carthadas, which she called the new city state in the Phoenican language. Soon it was changed by speech to Carthage, which after seven hundred and thirty years was destroyed after its founding.

225. Elissa was Dido. Carthage was destroyed in the consulship of Lentulus and Mummius in 146 BC. Count back seven hundred and thirty-seven years to the *Encaenia* or dedication of the city in 882 BC, which is the sixteenth year of Pygmalion, the brother of Dido and the king of Tyre. She fled in the seventh year of Pygmalion, but the era of the city began with its dedication. Virgil, and his commentator Servius, who might have had access to the archives of Tyre and Cyprus, as well as from those of Carthage, relate the following. Teucer came from the war of Troy to Cyprus in the days of Dido, a little before the reign of her brother Pygmalion. Together with her father, she seized Cyprus and ejected Cinyras. The Arundelian Marbles say that Teucer came to Cyprus seven years after the destruction of Troy and built Salamis. Apollodorus states that Cinyras married Metharme, the daughter of Pygmalion, and built Paphos. {*E66*} Hence, the arrival of Teucer at Cyprus is in the reign of the predecessor of Pygmalion, and by consequence the destruction of Troy is about seventy-one years after the death of Solomon in 904 BC.

3.3.2 Method 3.2 — Dating the Trojan War by the Latin Kings

226. Dionysius of Halicarnassus says that in the time of the Trojan War, Latinus was king of the natives in Italy, and that in the sixteenth generation after that war, Romulus built Rome. {*Dionysius, l. 1. c. 9. (3) 1:31*} After Latinus he names sixteen kings of the Latins, the last of whom was Numitor, in whose days Romulus built Rome. Romulus was contemporary to Numitor, and after him Dionysius and others reckon six more kings over Rome to the beginning of the consuls. These twenty-two reigns, at about eighteen years to a reign (for many of these kings were murdered), took up three hundred and ninety-six years. Counting back from the first consuls, Junius Brutus and Valerius Publicola, in 508 BC places the end of the Trojan War about seventy-one years after the death of Solomon in 904 BC. {*E67*} The Argonaut Expedition occurred about a generation before this, and if you allow three generations per one hundred years, this would place that expedition about 937 BC.

3.4 Method 4 — Dating the Argonaut Expedition by the Expedition of Sesostris

227. The expedition of Sesostris was one generation earlier than the Argonaut Expedition, for on his return to Egypt in 962 BC, he left Aeetes in Colchis, who reigned there until the Argonaut Expedition. Sesostris left Prometheus with a body of men at Mount Caucasus to guard that pass. He was there for thirty years before he was released by Hercules (Idean). The Argonauts Phlias and Eurymedon were the sons of the great Bacchus (whom the poets called Sesostris) and of Ariadne, the daughter of Minos.

228. On the return of Sesostris into Egypt, his brother Danaus fled from him into Greece with his fifty daughters in a long ship patterned after the *Argo.*

30

Argus, the son of Danaus, built the ship *Argo*. Nauplius the Argonaut was the son of Amymone, one of the daughters of Danaus, and of Neptune, who was the brother and admiral of Sesostris. The two other daughters of Danaus married Archander and Archilites, the sons of Achaeus and the grandsons of Creusa, who was the daughter of Erechtheus, the king of Athens. Therefore, the daughters of Danaus were three generations younger than Erechtheus and as a result, contemporary with Theseus, the son of Aegeus who was the adopted son of Pandion who was the son of Erechtheus. Theseus, at the time of the Argonaut Expedition, was about fifty years old, and so he was born about the thirty-third year of Solomon in 983 BC, for he kidnapped Helen just before that expedition. {*Apollonius, Argonautica, l. 1. v. 101. 1:9} At that time she was only seven, or as some have said, ten. {E68}

229. Pirithous the son of Ixion helped Theseus to kidnap Helen. {*Plutarch, Lives-Theseus, l. 1. 1:41} Theseus went with Pirithous to kidnap Persephone, the daughter of Orcus or Aidoneus, the king of the Molossians. The king killed Pirithous and captured Theseus. While he was imprisoned, Castor and Pollux returned from the Argonaut Expedition. They released their sister Helen and captured Aethra, the mother of Theseus. Since the daughters of Danaus are contemporary with Theseus and some of their sons were Argonauts, then Danaus with his daughters fled from his brother Sesostris into Greece about one generation before the Argonaut Expedition. Therefore, Sesostris returned into Egypt in the reign of Rehoboam. He came from Egypt in the fifth year of Rehoboam in 971 BC, and spent nine years in that expedition against the eastern nations and Greece. {*Diod. Sic., l. 1. c. 55. 1:191-195} {1Ki 14:25,26 2Ch 12:2-4} Therefore, he returned back into Egypt in the fourteenth year of Rehoboam in 962 BC. Hence, Shishak and Sesostris were kings of all Egypt at the same time. They agree not only in the time but also in their actions and conquests. God gave Shishak ממלבות הארצות *the kingdoms of the lands.* {BHM 2Ch 12:8}

230. Where Herodotus describes the expedition of Sesostris, Josephus says that Herodotus described the expedition of Shishak and attributed his actions to Sesostris, thus erring only in the name of the king. {*Herodotus, l. 2. c. 102,103. 1:389,391} {*Josephus, Antiquities, l. 8. c. 10. s. 2. (253) 5:709} Corruptions of names are frequent in history. {E69} Sesostris was otherwise called Sesochris, Sesochis, Sesoosis, Sethosis, Sesonchis and Sesonchosis. Take away the Greek ending and the names become Sesost, Sesoch, Sesoos, Sethon, Sesonch, Sesac, which differ very little from Sesach. Sesonchis and Shishak differ no more than Memphis and Moph, two names for the same city. Also, Josephus relates from Manetho that Sesostris was the brother of Armais, and that these brothers were otherwise called Aegyptus and Danaus. On the return of Sesostris or Aegyptus from his great conquests to Egypt, Armais or Danaus fled from him into Greece. {*Josephus, Against Apion, l. 1. c. 15. (97-102) 1:201-205}

231. Egypt was at first divided into many small kingdoms and like other countries grew into one kingdom by degrees. Ammon, the father of Solomon's queen, was the first king of Egypt and came into Phoenicia with an army. He only took Gezer and gave it to his daughter. Sesostris, the next king, came from Egypt with an army of Libyans, Troglodytes and Ethiopians, and therefore was then king over all those countries. {2Ch 12:3} We do not read in the scriptures that any former king of Egypt, who reigned over all those countries, came from Egypt with a great army to conquer other countries. The biblical history of the Israelites, from the days of Abraham to the days of Solomon, mentions no such conqueror. {E70} Sesostris reigned over all the same nations of the Libyans, Troglodytes and Ethiopians, and came from Egypt with a great army to conquer other kingdoms. The Shepherds reigned for a long time in Lower Egypt, and according to Manetho were expelled from there around the time of the building of Jerusalem. While they reigned in Lower Egypt, Upper Egypt was under other kings. While Egypt was divided into several kingdoms, there was no place for any such king over all Egypt as Sesostris. No historian makes him later than Shishak, and therefore he was one and the same king of Egypt with Shishak.

232. This is not a new opinion. Josephus discovered it when he affirmed that Herodotus erred only in ascribing the actions of Shishak to Sesostris. This is as much as to say that the true name of him who did those things described by Herodotus was Shishak and that Herodotus erred only in calling him Sesostris or that he was called Sesostris by a corruption of his name. Our great chronologer, Sir John Marsham, was also of the opinion that Sesostris was Shishak. If this is granted, it is then most certain that

1) Sesostris came from Egypt in the fifth year of Rehoboam in 971 BC to invade the nations and returned to Egypt in the fourteenth year of that king in 962 BC. {E71}

2) Danaus then fled from his brother and came into Greece within a year or two later, about 961 BC.

3) The Argonaut Expedition was one generation later than that invasion by Sesostris and the coming of Danaus into Greece. Hence, the expedition

was certainly about forty-two years after the death of Solomon, about 933 BC.

4) Prometheus stayed on Mount Caucasus thirty years and then was released by Hercules (Idean) about 933 BC. {*Hyginus, Fabulae, l. 1. c. 144. 1:147}

233. Therefore, the Argonaut Expedition was about thirty years after Sesostris left Prometheus on Mount Caucasus, that is, about forty-two years after the death of Solomon in about 933 BC.

3.5 Method 5 — Dating the Argonaut Expedition by Astronomical Observations

234. Before we can discuss this method we must discuss the length of the year and how it was determined by ancient nations.

3.5.1 Determining the Length of the Year

3.5.1.1 The Length of the Year of the Greeks

235. Before the correct length of the solar year was known, all countries calculated months by the moon and calculated years by the return of winter and summer, spring and autumn. {Ge 1:14 8:22.} {*Censorinus, De Die Natali, c. 19,20. 1:44-48} {*Cicero, Against Verres II, l. 2. c. 52. (129) 7:431} {*Geminus, l. 1. c. 6. s. 5. 1:162} When making calendars for their festivals, they calculated thirty days to a lunar month, and twelve lunar months to a year, rounding up to the nearest month. Hence came the division of the ecliptic into three hundred and sixty degrees. So in the time of Noah's flood, when the moon could not be seen, Noah calculated thirty days to a month. If the moon appeared a day or two before the end of the month, they began the next month with the first day of its appearing. {*Cicero, Against Verres II, l. 2. c. 52. (129) 7:431} This was done generally, until the Egyptians of Thebes determined the length of the solar year. {E72} So Diodorus says that the Egyptians of Thebes use no intercalary months, nor deduct any days from the month as is done by most of the Greeks. {*Diod. Sic., l. 1. c. 50. s. 2. 1:177}

236. Cicero states:

It is the custom of the Sicilians, as of all the Greeks, as they like to secure the agreement of the days of the month with the motions of the sun and moon, to correct an occasional discrepancy by shortening a month by some one, or two days at the most, which they term *eliminated*; also they sometimes lengthen a month [legally thirty days long] by a day, or by two days. {*Cicero, Against Verres II, l. 2. c. 52. (129) 7:431} {E73}

237. Geminus states:

6. Since neither the month nor the solar year is composed of [a] whole [number of] days, a time [interval] was therefore sought by the astronomers that will contain [a] whole [number of] days, whole months, and whole years. The goal for the ancients was to reckon the months by the Moon and the years by the Sun. 7 For the command, by the laws as well as the oracles, to sacrifice in the manner of the fathers, was taken by all the Greeks to mean reckoning years in accordance with the Sun and the days and months by the Moon. 8 Reckoning years by the Sun means for the same sacrifices to the gods to be performed in the same seasons of the year, the spring sacrifice always to be performed in the spring, and the summer in the summer, and, in the same way, for the same feasts to fall at the remaining proper times of the year; 9 for this they took to be suitable and pleasing to the gods. And this could not come about in any other way if the solstices and the equinoxes were not in the same months. 10 Reckoning the days by the Moon means for the names of the days to be in conformity with the phases of the Moon, 11 for the names of the days were names for the phases of the Moon. Thus, on the day the Moon appears new, it [the day] was named, by contraction, *noumenia* or *new moon*; on the day it makes its second appearance they called it *second;* and they called the phase of the Moon occurring at the middle of the month *dichomonia* or *dividing the month* from this circumstance. 12 And in general they named all the days for the phases of the Moon; thus they also called the thirtieth day of the month, which is last, *triakas* or *thirty*, from this very circumstance. {*Geminus, l. 1. c. 8. s. 6-12. 1:176,177}

238. The ancient calendar year of the Greeks consisted of twelve lunar months, with each month having thirty days. From time to time, they corrected these years and months by the courses of the sun and moon. They omitted a day or two in the month as often as they found the month too long for the course of the moon, and added a month to the year as often as they found the twelve lunar months too short for the return of the four seasons. {E75} Cleobulus, one of the seven wise men of Greece, alluded to this year of the Greeks in his riddle:

One father there is, he has twelve sons, and each of these has twice thirty daughters different in feature; some of the daughters are white, the others are black; they are immortal, and yet they all die. {*Diogenes Laertius, Cleobulus, l. 1. c. 6. (90) 1:93}

239. Thales called the last day of the month τριακαδα, *the thirtieth*. {*Diogenes Laertius, Thales, l. 1. c. 1. (24) 1:25} After the twentieth day of the month, Solon did not count the days by adding them to the twentieth, but by subtracting them from the thirtieth, on a descending scale, like the waning of the moon. He called the thirtieth day of the month ενην και νεαν, the *Old and New*, or the last day of the old month and the first day of the new. He introduced months of twenty-nine or thirty days alternately, making the thirtieth day of every other month to be the first day of the next month. {*Plutarch, Lives-Solon, l. 1. c. 25. s. 3. 1:475}

240. To the twelve lunar months the ancient Greeks added a thirteenth every other year, which made their *Dieteris*. {*Censorinus, De Die Natali, c. 18. s. 2. 1:40} {*Herodotus, l. 2. c. 4. 1:279} Since this year was too long by a month in eight years, they omitted an intercalary month once in eight years, which made their *Octaeteris*, one half of which was their *Tetraeteris*. These periods seem to have been almost as old as the religions of Greece, being used in their various sacred festivals. The *Octaeteris* was the *Great Year* of Cadmus and Minos, and seems to have been brought into Greece and Crete by the Phoenicians. {*Apollodorus, Library, l. 3. c. 4. s. 2. 1:317} {*Strabo, l. 10. c. 4. s. 8. (476) 5:131} {*Homer, Odyssey, l. 19. v. 177-183. 2:247,249} These came there with Cadmus and Europa and continued until after the days of Herodotus. {E76} In determining the length of seventy years, he calculates thirty days to a lunar month, and twelve such months or three hundred and sixty days to the ordinary year without the intercalary months, and twenty-five such months to the *Dieteris*: and according to the number of days in the calendar year of the Greeks. {*Herodotus, l. 1. c. 32. 1:37,39} Athenians built three hundred and sixty statues to Demetrius Phalereus. The Greeks—Cleostratus, Harpalus, and others—to make their months agree better with the course of the moon, in the times of the Persian Empire varied the manner of intercalating the three months in the *Octaeteris*. When Meton determined the lunar cycle, they intercalated seven months in nineteen years.

3.5.1.2 The Length of the Year of the Romans

241. The ancient year of the Romans was also lunisolar, for the year of Numa consisted of twelve lunar months, with intercalary months to make up what the twelve lunar months lacked of the solar year. {*Plutarch, Lives-Numa, l. 1. c. 18. s. 2. 1:376} The ancient year of the Egyptians was also luni-solar, and continued to be so until the days of Hyperion, or Osiris, a king of Egypt, the father of Helius and Selene, or Orus and Bubaste. The Israelites brought this year out of Egypt, and Diodorus states that Uranus the father of

Hyperion used this year. {*Diod. Sic., l. 3. c. 56. s. 4. 2:265} In the temple of Osiris the priests filled three hundred and sixty bowls with milk each day. {*Diod. Sic., l. 1. c. 22. s. 4. 1:71} {E77} I think he means one bowl each day and three hundred and sixty in all to count the number of days in the calendar year. By this they would determine the difference between the lunar year and the true solar year, and they added five days to it to make a solar year of three hundred and sixty-five days.

3.5.1.3 The Length of the Year of the Israelites

242. The Israelites also appear to have used the lunisolar year. Their months began with their new moons. Their first month was called Abib from the earing of grain in that month. Their passover was kept upon the fourteenth day of the first month, when the moon was full. If the grain was not then ripe enough for offering the first fruits, the festival was put off by adding an intercalary month to the end of the year, and the harvest was brought in before the Pentecost. and the other fruits gathered before the feast of the seventh month.

3.5.1.4 The Length of the Year of the Various Asian Countries

243. Simplicius, in his commentary on the first of Aristotle's *Physical Acroasis*, says that some begin the year on the summer solstice, as the people of Attica, or upon the autumnal equinox, as the people of Asia, or in winter, as the Romans, or about the vernal equinox, as the Arabians and the people of Damascus. The month began either on the new moon or the full moon. {*Theodorus of Gaza 1400-1475 AD, Concerning the Months*} {E78} The years of all these nations were therefore luni-solar, thus keeping the four seasons. The old year of the Romans began at first in the spring, as I seem to gather from the names of their months, Quintilis, Sextilis, September, October, November, December, which correspond to the months numbered five, six, seven, eight, nine and ten. Julius Caesar later moved the start of their year to the beginning of winter. The ancient civil year of the Assyrians and Babylonians was also luni-solar. This year was also used by the Samaritans, who came from various parts of the Assyrian Empire, and the Jews, who came from Babylon and called the months of their luni-solar year after the names of the months of the Babylonian year. Berosus in his *Babylonian History* states that the Babylonians celebrated the festival called *Sacaea* on the sixteenth day of the month Loos. {*Athenaeus, l. 14. (639c) 6:451} This was the lunar month of the Macedonians and occurred in the same season each year. The Arabians who live in the area of Babylon use lunar months to this day. Suidas states that the *Sarus* of the Chaldeans

contains two hundred and twenty-two lunar months. This is eighteen years, each consisting of twelve lunar months besides six intercalary months. {*Suidas, in Σαροι.} When Cyrus cut the Gindus River into three hundred and sixty channels, he seems to have alluded to the number of days in the calendar year of the Medes and Persians. {*Herodotus, l. 1. c. 190. 1:237}

3.5.1.5 The Length of the Year of the Egyptians

244. The emperor Julian writes:

> For when all other people, that I may say it in one word, adjust their months to the course of the moon, we alone with the Egyptians measure the days of the year by the course of the sun.
> {*Julian, Orations, l. 4. (156AB) 1:427,429} {E79}

245. The Egyptians, for the sake of navigation, studied the stars. By noting their heliacal risings and settings, they determined the true length of the solar year to be five days longer than the calendar year and added five days to the twelve calendar months. This made the solar year to consist of twelve months and five days. Strabo and Diodorus ascribe this innovation to the Egyptians of Thebes. {*Diod. Sic., l. 1. c. 50. s. 2. 1:177} {*Strabo, l. 17. c. 1. s. 46. (816) 8:125} Diodorus said the priests of Thebes (Egyptian) excelled more than others in astronomy and philosophy. They invented the reckoning of days not by the course of the moon, but by the course of the sun. They add yearly five days to twelve months each of thirty days. {*Diod. Sic., l. 1. c. 50. s. 1,2. 1:175,177} In memory of this amendment to the year they dedicated the five additional days to Osiris, Isis, Orus Senior, Typhon and Nephthe, the sister and the wife of Typhon. They imagined that those days were added to the year when these five gods were born, that is, in the reign of Uranus, or Ammon, the father of Sesostris. {*Plutarch, Moralia-Isis and Osiris, l. 1. c. 12. (355) 5:33,35} {*Diod. Sic., l. 1. c. 13. s. 4. 1:47}

246. From Hecataeus we learn that in the sepulchre of Amenophis or Osymandias, who reigned soon after Sesostris, the priests placed a golden circle of three hundred and sixty-five cubits in circumference and divided it into three hundred and sixty-five equal parts. On each part the days in the year are noted, and the heliacal risings and settings of the stars are noted for each day. This circle remained until the invasion of Egypt around 525 BC by Cambyses, the king of Persia. {*Diod. Sic., l. 1. c. 49. s. 5. 1:175} {E80} Until the reign of Uranus, the father of Hyperion, and the grandfather of Helius and Selene, the Egyptians used the old luni-solar year. In his reign, that is, in the reign of Ammon, the father of Osiris or Sesostris, and the grandfather of Orus and Bubaste, the Thebans began

to study navigation and astronomy. Using the heliacal risings and settings of the stars, they determined the correct length of the solar year. They added five days to the old calendar year and dedicated them to his five children previously to commemorate their birthdays. After further observations in the reign of Amenophis, they accurately determined the time of the solstices and they began to start their New Year on the vernal equinox in the beginning of spring.

3.5.1.6 The Length of the Year of the Chaldeans

247. This year was used in Chaldea and was the basis for the year of Nabonassar since the years of Nabonassar and those of Egypt began on the same day and in the same month called Thoth. They were equal and in all respects the same. The first year of Nabonassar began on February 26, 747 BC. {E81} It was thirty-three days and five hours before the vernal equinox, according to the sun's mean motion, for it is not likely that the equation of the sun's motion would be known when astronomy was just getting started. This year of three hundred and sixty-five days is short by five hours, forty-eight minutes and forty-six seconds of the tropical year. The start of this year will move backwards thirty-three days and five hours in a hundred and thirty-seven years. By consequence, when this year was instituted in Egypt, it started on the vernal equinox. Therefore, according to the sun's mean motion, this was one-hundred and thirty-seven years before the era of Nabonassar began, in 883 BC. If it began on the day after the vernal equinox, it might have begun four years earlier or 887 BC, eighty-eight years after the death of Solomon. About that time Amenophis died, for he did not come from Susa to the Trojan War but died later in Egypt. This year was received by the Persian Empire from the Babylonians, and the Greeks also used it in the era of Philip, which started with the death of Alexander the Great. Julius Caesar corrected it by adding an extra day every four years and made it the standard year of the Romans.

248. George Syncellus says that the five days were added to the old year by the last king of the Shepherds. {*Syncellus, l. 1. (143) 1:178} {E82} The time between the reign of this king and Ammon is small, for the reign of the Shepherds ended only one generation or two before Ammon began to add those days. The Shepherds were not skilled in the arts and sciences.

3.5.2 Determining the Solstices and Equinoxes

249. In the rest of section 3.5, Newton is using coordinates relative to the ecliptic, not right ascension and declination that astronomers normally use. By

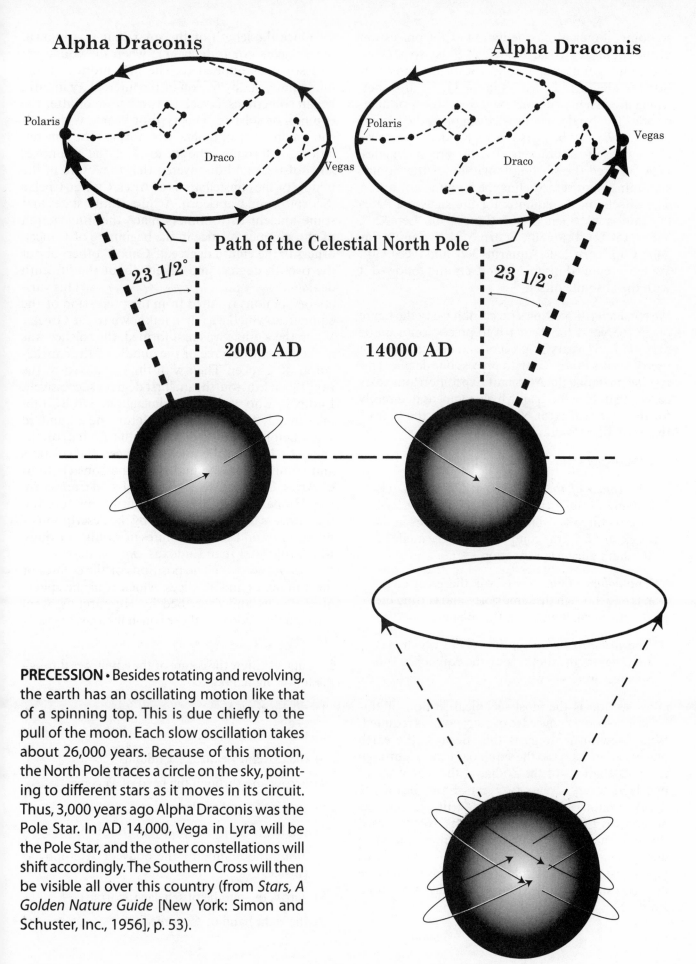

Alpha Draconis

Alpha Draconis

Polaris

Draco

Vegas

Polaris

Draco

Vegas

Path of the Celestial North Pole

23 1/2°

23 1/2°

2000 AD

14000 AD

PRECESSION • Besides rotating and revolving, the earth has an oscillating motion like that of a spinning top. This is due chiefly to the pull of the moon. Each slow oscillation takes about 26,000 years. Because of this motion, the North Pole traces a circle on the sky, pointing to different stars as it moves in its circuit. Thus, 3,000 years ago Alpha Draconis was the Pole Star. In AD 14,000, Vega in Lyra will be the Pole Star, and the other constellations will shift accordingly. The Southern Cross will then be visible all over this country (from *Stars, A Golden Nature Guide* [New York: Simon and Schuster, Inc., 1956], p. 53).

35

so doing, it makes the calculation of the precession of the equinoxes trivial. Read 2° 5' 7" as two degrees, five minutes and seven seconds. Stars in a constellation are identified by letters in the Greek alphabet, which are assigned according to brightness or magnitude. The brightest star is *Alpha* or α, the second brightest *Beta* or β, and so forth. Modern constellation names are in brackets after the original names. Newton used the starting longitude of the Zodiac signs plus an offset to define the longitude of a star. The offsets on the equinox for the signs are Aries 0°, Taurus 30°, Gemini 60°, Cancer 90°, Leo 120°, Virgo 150°, Libra 180°, Scorpio 210°, Sagittarius 240°, Capricorn 270°, Aquarius 300° and Pices 330°. We have retained his relative offsets and followed it with the absolute offset.

We recalculated Newton's precession using the figure of 25,765 years for the earth to precess once on its axis, or 71.57 years to precess one degree. Newton used 72 years for the earth to precess one degree. This resulted in dating the Argonaut Expedition four years earlier than Newton had, which compensated nicely for the four-year error Newton made in the year of the death of Solomon.

The following terms are used in this section:

> The *colure of the equinoxes* is the great circle passing through the poles of the equator, and intersecting the ecliptic in the equinoxes in an angle of 66.5°, the complement of the angle of the sun's greatest declination.

> The *colure of the solstices* is the great circle passing through the same poles, and cutting the ecliptic at right angles in the solstices.

> The *primitive sphere* is the sphere which was used before the motions of the equinoxes and solstices were known.

(This section is the most technical section of this book, and some knowledge of astronomy is required. What Newton is doing is this. Because the earth precesses on its axis, the equinoxes move through the constellations of the Zodiac at the rate of about one degree every seventy-two years. From the time of the Argonaut Expedition until 146 BC, the Greeks noted a drift of about eleven degrees. Newton used this information to redate the expedition and in so doing deleted almost three hundred years of fictitious Greek history. This calculation confirms the date he derived using other methods to date the expedition. Editor.)

250. Once the length of the solar year was known, the ancients could determine when the equinoxes and solstices happened. The first month of the luni-solar year, by reason of the intercalary month, began sometimes a week or two before or after the equinox or solstice. This type of year was the reason the first astronomers, who formed the constellations, determined the location of the equinoxes and solstices and discovered that they were in the middle of the constellations of Aries, Cancer, Chelae (Scorpio), and Capricorn. Achilles Tatius states that some ancient astronomers place the intersection of the summer solstice in the beginning of Cancer, others in the eighth degree of Cancer, others about the twelfth degree, and others about the fifteenth degree. {*Porphyry, Isagoge, s. 23, from Petavius' edition*} This variety of opinions resulted from the precession of the equinoxes, which was then unknown to the Greeks. When the Zodiac was first formed, the solstice was in the fifteenth degree or the middle of the constellation of Cancer. Then with time it moved to the twelfth, eighth, fourth, and first degrees successively. Eudoxus, who was in his prime about 370 BC (approximately sixty years after Meton and a hundred years before Aratus), described the Zodiac of the ancients. He said the ancients placed the solstices and equinoxes in the middle of the constellations of Aries, Cancer, Chelae (Scorpio), and Capricorn. {*E83*} Hipparchus of Bithynia confirms this, too, and this appears to be the case also by the description of the equinox and solstice colures in Aratus' writings, who wrote later than Eudoxus. {*Hipparchus, ad Phaenom., l. 2. s. 3. from Petavius edition*} The positions of the colures of the equinoxes and solstices, which is in the sphere of Eudoxus and described by Hipparchus, went through the middle of those constellations. {*Hipparchus, ad Phaenom., l. 1. s. 2.*}

251. Eudoxus drew the colure of the equinoxes through the following ten points:

1) the back of Aries,

2) the head of Cetus,

3) the extreme flexure of Eridanus,

4) across and through the head of Perseus,

5) the right hand of Perseus,

6) the left hand of Arctophylax (Bootes),

7) along the middle of the body of Arctophylax (Bootes),

8) across the middle of Chelae (Scorpio),

9) the right hand of Centaur

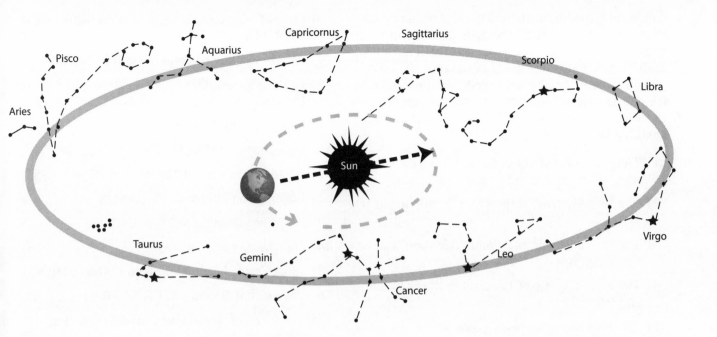

THE ZODIAC is a belt of 12 constellations: Aries, Taurus, Gemini, Cancer, Leo, Virgo, Libra, Scorpius, Sagittarius, Capricornus, Aquarius, and Pisces. These star groups circle the sky close to the ecliptic, which is the great circle of the earth's orbit around the sun. The sun, moon, and planets look as though they move against the background of these constellations and seem to be "in" them. Easiest to observe is the moon's path. The journeys of the planets take longer, depending on their distance from the sun.

The sun itself seems to move through the Zodiac constellations each year. The change of constellations seen just before sunrise or after sunset confirms this movement. Note, in the diagram, the earth circling the sun. From the earth, the sun seems to be in the constellation Libra. As the earth revolves, the sun will seem to move through Scorpius and Sagittarius, till finally it is back in Libra again.

Babylonians and other ancient astronomers recognized this apparent motion of the sun, moon, and planets. This knowledge helped them predict the seasons. Nowadays, the Zodiac is often linked to astrology, which claims to interpret the influence of stars on people and worldly events. Astronomers are convinced that astrology has no scientific foundation (from *Stars, A Golden Nature Guide* [New York: Simon and Schuster, Inc., 1956], p. 100–101).

10) the foreknee of Centaur.

252. He drew the colure of the solstices through the following ten points:

1) the middle of Cancer the crab,

2) the neck of Hydra,

3) the star between the poop deck (now called Puppis) and the sail (now called Vela) of Argo,

4) the middle of Sagitta the arrow,

5) the middle of Capricorn,

6) the tail of the southern fish (Piscis Austrinus),

7) the middle of the Great Bear (Ursa Major),

8) the neck of Cygnus the swan,

9) the right wing of Cygnus the swan,

10) the left hand of Cepheus.

3.5.3 Chiron's Sphere, the Constellations and the Argonaut Expedition

253. Chiron, who was the ancient author of *The Battle of the Titans*, listed the constellations of his time. Both he and his daughter Hippo were good astronomers. {E84} {*Clement, Stromata, l. 1. c. 15. ANF2:317} Musaeus, the son of Eumolpus and the teacher of Orpheus, was on the

Argonaut Expedition. He was the first of the Greeks to record a genealogy of the gods and to construct a sphere. {*Diogenes Laertius, Prologue, l. 1. (3) 1:5} The sphere itself shows that it was made in the time of the Argonaut Expedition, for that expedition is recorded in the constellations, together with several others from the more ancient history of the Greeks and not from anything later.

1) The golden ram (Aries), the ensign of the ship in which Phrixus fled to Colchis.

2) The bull (Taurus) with brazen hoofs tamed by Jason.

3) The twins, Castor and Pollux (Gemini), two of the Argonauts.

4) The swan (Cygnus) of Leda, the mother of Castor and Pollux.

5) The ship *Argo*. (now three constellations, Carina, the keel of the ship, Puppis, the poop deck, Vela, the sails and Pyxis, the compass. Editor.)

6) The watchful dragon (Hydra) with Medea's cup (Crater) and the raven (Corvus) on its carcass, the symbol of death.

7) Chiron (Sagittarius) the teacher of Jason with his altar and sacrifice.

8) The Argonaut Hercules (Idean) with his arrow (Sagitta) and the vulture falling down.

9) The dragon (Draco), crab (Cancer) and lion (Leo), whom Hercules (Idean) killed.

10) The harp (Lyra) of the Argonaut Orpheus.

254. All these constellations relate to the men of the Argonaut Expedition. (The name of the constellations are in capitals. Editor.)

1) ORION, the son of Neptune, or as some say, the grandson of Minos, with his dogs (CANIS MAJOR and CANIS MINOR), and hare (LEPUS), and river (ERIDANUS), and scorpion (SCORPIO). {E85}

2) Perseus in the constellations of PERSEUS, ANDROMEDA, CEPHUS, CASSIOPIA and CETUS.

3) Callisto and her son Arcas, in URSA MAJOR and ARCTOPHYLAX (BOOTES).

4) Icareus and his daughter Erigone in BOOTES, PLAUSTRUM (BIG DIPPER) and VIRGO.

5) One of the nurses of Jupiter to URSA MINOR.

6) One of the charioteers of Erechthonius to AURIGA.

7) Phorbas killing the snake OPHIUCHUS.

8) CHIRON (SAGGITTARIUS) related to Crolus, the son of the nurse of the Muses.

9) Pan to CAPRICORN.

10) Ganymede to AQUARIUS.

11) Ariadne's crown to CORONA BORNEALIS.

12) Bellerophon's horse to PEGASUS.

13) Neptune's dolphin to DOLPHINUS.

14) Ganymede's eagle to AQUILA.

15) Jupiter's goat with her kids to CAPRICORN.

16) The asses of Bacchus to CANCER THE CRAB.

17) The fishes of Venus and Cupid to PISCES.

18) Their parents the southern fish to PISCES AUSTRINUS.

255. These with Aries or Delton are the old constellations mentioned by Aratus. They all relate to the Argonauts and their contemporaries or to persons one or two generations older and nothing later than that expedition. The constellations of Antinous (created about 110 AD) and Coma Bernices (created about 240 BC) were added much later than the Argonaut Expedition.

256. Therefore, the sphere seems to have been formed by Chiron and Musaeus for use in the Argonaut Expedition, for the ship *Argo* was the first long ship built by the Greeks. {E86} Before this, they used small round cargo vessels and kept within sight of the shore. Now they ventured on an embassy to several rulers on the coasts of the Black and Mediterranean seas. By the command of the oracle and consent of the rulers of Greece, the flower of Greece set sail on an expedition through the deep in a long ship with sails and guided by the stars. {*Apollodorus, Library, l. 1. c. 9. s. 16. 1:93,95} The people of the island of Corcyra attributed the invention of the sphere to Nausica, the daughter of Alcinous, the king of the Pheaces in that island. {Suidas, in Αναγαλλις} It is most probable that she had received it from the Argonauts, who on their return voyage home stopped at that island and stayed with her father for a long time. {*Apollodorus, Library, l. 1. c. 9. s. 25. 1:115} So then, at the time of the Argonaut Expedition, the cardinal points of the equinoxes and solstices were in the middle of the constellations of Aries, Cancer, Chelae (Scorpio), and Capricorn.

3.5.4 An Analysis of the Colures of Eudoxus

257. At the end of 1689 AD the star called α Aries was at the starting longitude of Aries plus 28° 51' 0" or 28° 51' 0" with a north latitude above the ecliptic of 7° 8' 58". The star called *ultima caudae* τ at the end of the tail in Aries was at the starting longitude of Taurus plus 19° 3' 42" or 49° 3' 42" with a north latitude of 2° 34' 5". The colure of the equinox passed through the midpoint between those two stars, cutting the ecliptic at the longitude of Taurus longitude 6° 44' or 36° 44'. Hence, in 1689 AD the equinox has gone back 36° 44' since the Argonaut Expedition. {E87} This assumes that this colure passed through the middle of the constellation of Aries. The equinox goes back fifty seconds in one year, and about one degree in seventy-two years and 36° 44' in two thousand six hundred and thirty-five years. This places the time of the expedition about thirty-five years after the death of Solomon in about 940 BC. However, it is not necessary that the middle of the constellation of Aries should be the exact midpoint between the two stars called α Aries and τ.

258. It may be better to fix the cardinal points by the stars through which the colures passed in the primitive sphere according to Eudoxus. {E88}

3.5.4.1 Determining the Ancient Colure of the Equinoxes

259. Using the first five stars in the list of Eudoxus, which the colure of the equinoxes pass through, we can determine the intersection of that colure with the ecliptic.

1) In the back of the constellation of Aries is a star of the sixth magnitude marked ν by Bayer. At the end of 1689, its longitude was the starting longitude of Taurus plus 9° 38' 45" or 39° 38' 45" and its north latitude was 6° 7' 56". The colure of the equinox was drawn through it according to Eudoxus and intersects the ecliptic at the starting longitude of Taurus plus 6° 58' 57" or 36° 58' 57".

2) In the head of the constellation of Cetus are two stars of the fourth magnitude, called ν and ξ by Bayer. At the end of 1689 AD they were located as follows. The longitude of the first was at the starting longitude of Taurus plus 4° 3' 9" or 34° 3' 9" and its south latitude was 9° 12' 26". The longitude of the other was at the starting longitude of Taurus plus 3° 7' 37" or 33° 7' 37" and its south latitude was 5° 53' 7". The colure of the equinox passed midway between them, intersecting the ecliptic at the starting longitude of Taurus plus 6° 58' 51" or 36° 58' 51".

3) In the extreme flexure of the constellation of Eridanus is a star of the fourth magnitude, recently referred to as the breast of Cetus and called ρ by Bayer. It is the only star in Eridanus that this colure can pass through. At the end of 1689 AD, its longitude was at the starting longitude of Aries plus 25° 22' 10" or 25° 22' 10" and its south latitude was 25° 15' 50". The colure of the equinox passed through it, intersecting the ecliptic at the starting longitude of Taurus longitude 7° 12' 40" or 37° 12' 40".

4) In the head of the constellation of Perseus is a star of the fourth magnitude, called τ by Bayer. At the end of 1689 AD, its longitude was at the starting longitude of Taurus plus 23° 25' 30" or 53° 25' 30" and its north latitude was 34° 20' 12". The colure of the equinox passed through it, intersecting the ecliptic at the starting longitude of Taurus plus 6° 18' 57" or 36° 18' 57".

5) In the right hand of the constellation of Perseus, is a star of the fourth magnitude, called η by Bayer. At the end of 1689 AD, its longitude was at the starting longitude of Taurus plus 24° 25' 27" and its north latitude was 37° 26' 50". The colure of the equinox passed through it intersecting the ecliptic at the starting longitude of Taurus plus 4° 56' 40" or 34° 56' 40".

260. The average of these five places where the ecliptic is intersected is at the starting longitude of Taurus plus 6° 29' 15" or 36° 29' 15". Therefore, the great circle, which in the primitive sphere, according to Eudoxus and at the time of the Argonaut Expedition, was the colure of the equinox, passed through the stars just described. At the end of 1689 AD, it intersects the ecliptic at the starting longitude of Taurus plus the longitude 6° 29' 15" or 36° 29' 15". This is the best that we could determine from the rough observations of the ancients.

3.5.4.2 Determining the Ancient Colure of the Solstices

261. Using the first five stars in the list of Eudoxus, which the colure of the solstices passes through, we can determine the intersection of that colure with the ecliptic.

1) In the middle of Cancer is the South Asellus, a star of the fourth magnitude, called by Bayer δ. At the end of 1689 AD, its longitude was at the starting longitude of Leo plus 4° 23' 40" or 124° 23' 40".

2) In the neck of the constellation of Hydra is a star of the fourth magnitude, called by Bayer δ. At the end of 1689 AD, its longitude was at the

starting longitude of Leo plus 5° 59' 3" or 125° 59' 3". {E90}

3) Between the poop and mast of the constellation of the ship *Argo* is a star of the third magnitude, called ι by Bayer. At the end of 1689 AD, its longitude was at the starting longitude of Leo plus 7° 5' 31" or 127° 5' 31".

4) In the constellation Sagitta is a star of the sixth magnitude, called θ by Bayer. At the end of 1689 AD, its longitude was at the starting longitude of Aquarius plus 6° 29' 53" or 306° 29' 53".

5) In the middle of the constellation of Capricorn is a star of the fifth magnitude, called η by Bayer. At the end of 1689 AD, its longitude was at the starting longitude of Aquarius plus 8° 25' 55" or 308° 25' 55".

262. The fifth part of the sum of the three first longitudes and of the complements of the two last to 180 degrees is the starting longitude of Leo plus 6° 28' 46" or 126° 28' 46". This is the new longitude of the old colure of the solstices passing through these stars. The same colure passes between the mid-point of the stars η and χ, of the fourth and fifth magnitudes, in the neck of the Cygnus the swan, about 1° from each star. It also passes the star χ of the fourth magnitude, in the right wing of Cygnus and by the star o, of the fifth magnitude in the left hand of Cepheus and by the stars in the tail of Pisces Austrinus. It is at right angles to the colure of the equinox, which we determined previously, and so has the characteristics of the colure of the solstices. {E91}

3.5.5 Dating the Argonauts Using Precession Based on Recent Observations

263. Therefore, the two colures, which in the time of the Argonaut Expedition intersected the ecliptic at the cardinal points of 0°, 90°, 180° and 270°, have drifted by the end of 1689 AD to intersect the ecliptic at 36° 29', 126° 29', 206° 29' and 306° 29'. This is at the distance of 36° 29' from the cardinal points set by Chiron as nearly as we have been able to determine from the rough observations of the ancients. Therefore, the cardinal points from the time of that expedition to the end of 1689 AD have gone back from those colures by 36° 29'. At the rate of about 72 years to a degree, this amounts to two thousand six hundred and eleven years. This places the Argonaut expedition about fifty-three years after the death of Solomon in approximately 922 BC.

264. By the same method, the place of any star in the primitive sphere may readily be found by subtracting one sign (30°) plus 6° 29' or 36° 29' from the longitude

that it had at the end of 1689 AD. The longitude of α in Aries in the end of 1689 AD was at the starting longitude of Aries plus 28° 51' or 28° 51'. Adjust by one sign (30°) plus 6° 29' from the equinox in the middle of the constellation of Aries, then in the time of the Argonaut Expedition its longitude is at the longitude of Pisces plus 22° 22' or 352° 22'. Using the same reasoning, at the time of the expedition the longitude of the brightest star in Pleiades was at the starting longitude of Aries plus 19° 26' 8" or 19° 26' 8", and the longitude of Arcturus was at the starting longitude of Virgo plus 13° 24' 52" or 163° 24' 52", and so for any other star.

3.5.6 Dating the Argonaut Expedition Using Precession Based on Ancient Observations

265. After the Argonaut Expedition, we hear no more of astronomy until the days of Thales. He revived the study of astronomy, wrote a book of the solstices and equinoxes, and predicted eclipses. {*Diogenes Laertius, Thales, l. 1. c. 1. s. 23. 1:25} {*Pliny, l. 2. c. 9. (53) 1:203} Pliny says that he determined the morning setting of the Pleiades to be on the twenty-fifth day after the autumnal equinox. {*Pliny, l. 18. c. 57. (213,214) 5:325} Using this information, Dionysius Petavius computed the longitude of Pleiades at the starting longitude of Aries plus 23° 53' or 23° 53'. {Petavius (1583-1652 AD), Var. Dist., l. 1. c. 5.} By consequence, since the Argonaut Expedition, the brightest star in Pleiades has moved along the equinox by 4° 26' 52". At the rate of about seventy-two years to a degree this amounts to three hundred and eighteen years. From the time Thales started astronomical studies in the 41st Olympiad in 616 BC, this places the time of the Argonaut Expedition about forty-two years after the death of Solomon around 933 BC. In the days of Thales, the solstices and equinoxes were in the eleventh degree of the signs. {E93} However, Thales might conservatively place the solaces and the equinoxes in the twelfth degree of the signs to agree with earlier astronomers.

3.5.6.1 Ancient Observations of Precession

266. To compute the lunar cycle of nineteen years, Meton and Euctemon started their observations beginning at the time of the summer solstice in 432 BC, the year before the Peloponnesian War began. {Petavius (1583-1652 AD), Doct. Temp., l. 4. c. 26.} They placed it in the eighth degree of Cancer, which is at least seven degrees back farther than at first. {*Columella, l. 9. c. 14. s. 1. 2:485} {*Pliny, l. 18. c. 59. (221) 5:329} The equinox, at the rate of about one degree in seventy-two years, goes back seven degrees in five hundred and one years. Counting back from this time, from 432 BC, places the Argonaut Expedition approximately in the forty-two years after the death of Solomon, around 933 BC. This verifies the writing of Achilles Tatius, who wrote that some of the ancients placed the summer solstice in the eighth degree of Cancer, others about the twelfth degree, and others about its fifteenth degree.

267. Hipparchus, the great astronomer, comparing his own observations with those of former astronomers, was the first man who determined that the equinoxes move backward with respect to the fixed stars. {E94} He thought they went back one degree in about a hundred years. He observed the equinoxes between 162 BC and 130 BC. The midpoint 146 BC is two hundred and eighty-six years after the observations of Meton and Euctemon in 432 BC. During this time, the equinoxes went back four degrees and were in the fourth degree of Aries in the days of Hipparchus. Also, they have then gone back eleven degrees since the Argonaut Expedition. This is one thousand ninety years according to the chronology of the ancient Greeks and amounts to about one degree per hundred years according to Hipparchus, thus placing the Argonaut Expedition around 1230 BC. However, it really went back a degree in about seventy-two years, resulting in an eleven-degree shift in seven hundred and eight-seven years. This places the time of the expedition about forty-two years after the death of Solomon around 933 BC. Therefore, the Greeks have made the Argonaut Expedition about three hundred years too old, and this is the basis for the opinion of Hipparchus that the equinox went back at the rate of one degree in every hundred years. {E95}

268. Hesiod relates that sixty days after the winter solstice the star Arcturus rose just at sunset. {*Hesiod, Works and Days, l. 1. v. 564-567. 1:133} Therefore, Hesiod lived around 880 BC, about ninety-five years after the death of Solomon, or in the generation after the Trojan War, as Hesiod himself states. {*Hesiod, Works and Days, l. 1. v. 174-176. 1:101,103}

3.5.7. The Date of the Argonaut Expedition Based on Astronomy

269. From all these facts, based on the approximate observations of the ancient astronomers, we are certain that the Argonaut Expedition did not happen before the reign of Solomon. If these astronomical arguments are considered with the conclusions reached by the average length of the reigns of kings, then we may confidently conclude that the Argonaut Expedition was after the death of Solomon, and most likely that it was about forty-two years after his death around 933 BC.

4. The Time of the Trojan War

270. We have dated the Argonaut Expedition using at least five different methods. Using that information, we shall now date the time of the Trojan War. The Trojan War was one generation later than that expedition. If you allow three generations per one hundred years, then the war occurred around 900 BC. Several captains of the Greeks in that war were sons of the Argonauts. The ancient Greeks said Memnon or Amenophis, the king of Egypt, reigned in the times of that war. They thought that he was the son of Tithonus, the older brother of Priam, and at the end of that war, to have come from Susa to the assistance of Priam. {E96} Therefore, Amenophis was as old as the older children of Priam, who were with his army at Susa in the last year of that war. After he had finished building Memnonia in Susa, he returned to Egypt and beautified it with buildings, obelisks and statues, and died about eighty-five to ninety years after the death of Solomon around 887 BC. He had determined the length of the year to be three hundred and sixty-five days and commenced the Egyptian year on the vernal equinox. This was noted on a monument to him.

5. The Time of David's Expulsion of the Edomites

271. Rehoboam was born in the last year of King David and was forty-one years old at the death of Solomon {1Ki 14:21}, and therefore his father Solomon was probably born on or before the eighteenth year of King David's reign around 1038 BC. Two or three years before his birth, David besieged Rabbah, the capital of the Ammonites, and committed adultery with Bathsheba. The year before this siege began, David defeated the Ammonites and their confederates the Syrians of Zobah, Rehob, Ishtob, Maacah and Damascus. {2Sa 10:8} He extended his dominion over all these countries as far as to the entering in of Hamath and the Euphrates River around 1042 BC. Before this war began, he defeated Moab, Ammon, and Edom, and made the Edomites flee around 1044 BC. Some fled to Egypt with Hadad their king, who was then a little child. {E97} Others fled to the Philistines and fortified Azoth against David. I think others fled to the Persian Gulf and any other place where they could escape. Before this, he had various battles with the Philistines, which took place after the eighth year of his reign, when he came from Hebron to Jerusalem in 1048 BC

272. Therefore, we cannot be off by more than two or three years, if we place this victory over Edom in the eleventh or twelfth year of his reign around 1044 BC and his victory over Ammon and the Syrians in the

fourteenth in 1042 BC. After the flight of Edom, the king of Edom grew up and married Tahaphenes or Dathnis, the sister of the queen of Pharaoh. Before the death of David, she gave birth to a son for him called Genubah, and this son grew up among the children of Pharaoh. Among these children, the oldest of her mother's children was married by Solomon in the beginning of his reign. It was her little sister who at that time had no breasts and her brother who then nursed on the breasts of his mother. {So 6:9 8:1,8}

6. Sesostris, Bacchus and Osiris — The Same Person

273. Sesostris, who was about the same age as these children, became king of Egypt in the reign of Solomon. {1Ki 11:40} Before he began to reign, he warred under his father and, while he was very young, conquered Arabia Faelix, Troglodytica and Libya. {E98} He then invaded Ethiopia, and after succeeding his father, he reigned until the fifth year of Asa in 951 BC. Therefore, he was about the same age as the children of Ammon mentioned previously. He might be one of them and have been born near the end of David's reign around 1016 BC. Then he would be about forty-six years old when he came out of Egypt with a large army to invade the east in 971 BC. For his great conquests, he was celebrated in several nations by various names. The Chaldeans called him Belus (Egyptian), which in their language means *The Lord*. The Arabians called him Bacchus, which in their language means *The Great*. The Phrygians and Thracians called him Ma-sors, Mavors and Mars, which means *The Valiant*. For this reason, the Amazons, whom he transplanted from Thrace and left at the Thermodon River, called themselves the *Daughters of Mars*. The Egyptians before his reign called him their *Hero* or *Hercules*. After his death, because of his great works done to the Nile River, they dedicated that river to him and deified him by its names Sihor, Nilus and Aegyptus. When the Greeks heard them lament *Oh Sihor, Bou Sihor,* they called him Osiris and Busiris. The Arabians worshipped only two gods, Caelus and Bacchus or Dionysus, and they only worshipped the latter for his invasion of India. {*Arrian, l. 7. c. 20. (1) 2:271} {E99}

274. The *Dionysus* of the Arabians was Bacchus, and all agree that Bacchus was the same king of Egypt as Osiris. The *Caelus* or *Uranus* or *Jupiter Uranus* of the Arabians I take to be the same king of Egypt as his father Ammon, according to the poet:

Quamvis Aethiopum populis, Arabumque beatis
Gentibus, atque Indis unus sit Iupiter Ammon.

Although Ethiopia is populous and Arabia blessed,
The nations and also India are one under Jupiter Ammon.

7. Egypt after Sesostris

275. I place the end of the reign of Sesostris in the fifth year of Asa in 951 BC, because in that year Asa became free from the dominion of Egypt. He was able to fortify Judah and raise that large army with which he met Zerah and routed him. Therefore, Osiris was murdered in the fifth year of Asa by his brother Japetus. The Egyptians called Japetus by the names of Typhon, Python and Neptune. The Libyans, under Japetus and his son Atlas, invaded Egypt and started that famous war between the gods and the Titans, from whence the Nile River had the name of Eridanus. However, Orus, the son of Osiris, with the assistance of the Ethiopians, prevailed and reigned until the fifteenth year of Asa. Then the Ethiopians under Zerah invaded Egypt, drowned Orus in the Nile River, and were routed by Asa in 941 BC, so that Zerah was irreparably defeated. {E100} Zerah was succeeded by Amenophis, a youth of the royal family of the Ethiopians and, I think, the son of Zerah. However, the people of Lower Egypt revolted from him and made Osarsiphus their king. They summoned to help them a large body of men from Phoenicia and I think a part of the army of Asa. Thereupon, Amenophis, with the remnants of his father's army of the Ethiopians, retired from Lower Egypt to Memphis. They directed the Nile River into a new channel under a new bridge that he built between two large hills. At the same time he built and fortified that city against Osarsiphus, calling it after his name, Amenoph or Memphis. Then he retired into Ethiopia and remained there thirteen years. After that, he came back with a large army and conquered Lower Egypt, expelling the people that had been called in from Phoenicia around 926 BC. This I take to be the second expulsion of the Shepherds. Dr. Castel says that in the Coptic language, this city is called Manphtha, whence by contraction come its names Moph or Noph. {Castel, Moph}

276. While Amenophis stayed in Ethiopia, Egypt was in great civil disorder. I think that when the Greeks heard this, they conceived the Argonaut Expedition. Then they sent the best Greek young men in the ship *Argo* to persuade the coastal countries of the Black Sea and Mediterranean Sea to revolt from Egypt. {E101} They could then set up independent kingdoms as the Libyans, Ethiopians and Jews had done before. This is another argument for placing that expedition in 933 BC, about forty-two years after the death of

Solomon, for in this period Egypt was in civil disorder. Amenophis might return from Ethiopia and conquer Lower Egypt in about eight years. When he had established his government over it, to stop the revolt of the eastern countries, he might lead his army into Persia and leave Proteus at Memphis to govern Egypt in his absence. He would stay some time at Susa and build Memnonia, fortifying that city as the capital of his dominion in those regions.

8. The Time of Theseus and Ariadne

277. When the young Androgeus, the son of Minos, was victorious in the Athenaea, or quadrennial games at Athens, he was insidiously murdered. Thereupon, Minos made war upon the Athenians and compelled them to send to Crete every eight years seven beardless youths and as many young virgins. These were to be given as a reward to the victor in the similar games instituted in Crete in honour of Androgeus. These games seem to have been celebrated in the beginning of the Octaeteris (every eight years) and the Athenaea in the beginning of the Tetraeteris (every four years). {*E102*} These children were brought into Crete from Greece by the Phoenicians. On the third payment of the tribute of children, that is, about seventeen years after the end of the war with Athens, and about nineteen or twenty years after the death of Androgeus, Theseus became victor and returned from Crete with Ariadne, the daughter of Minos, and arrived at the island of Naxos or Dia. {*Athenaeus, l. 7. (296abc) 3:327,329*} Ariadne was abandoned there by Theseus and she took up with Glaucus, an Egyptian naval commander. She became the wife of the great Bacchus who at that time returned from India in triumph. She had two sons by him, Phlias and Eurymedon, who were Argonauts. {*Hyginus, Fabulae, l. 1. c. 14. s. 10. 1:101*} {*Hyginus, Fabulae, l. 1. c. 14. s. 19. 1:103*}

278. According to Homer, in Phrygia Bacchus was caught in bed with Venus, the mother of Aeneas, just before he came over the Hellespont and invaded Thrace. {*Homer, Odyssey, l. 8. v. 292-294. 1:293*} He married Ariadne, the daughter of Minos, according to Hesiod. {*Hesiod, Theogony, l. 1. v. 947,948. 1:79*} Therefore, by the testimony of both Homer and Hesiod, who wrote before the Greeks and Egyptians corrupted their antiquities, Bacchus was one generation older than the Argonaut Expedition and so was the king of Egypt at the same time as Sesostris. Therefore, they must be one and the same king, for they both did similar exploits. {*E103*} Bacchus invaded India and Greece. After he was routed by the army of Perseus and the war was settled, the Greeks honoured him and built a temple to him at Argos, calling it the temple of the Cretan

Bacchus because he buried Ariadne there. {*Pausanias, Corinth, l. 2. c. 23. s. 7,8. 1:373*} Therefore, Ariadne died in the last year of the war, just before Sesostris returned to Egypt, that is, in the fourteenth year of Rehoboam in 962 BC. She was taken from Naxos when Bacchus returned from India, and then became the wife of Bacchus and accompanied him on his victories. Therefore, the expedition of Theseus to Sicily and the death of his father Aegeus was about the ninth or tenth year of the reign of Rehoboam around 966 BC. At that time Theseus was a beardless young man, supposedly about nineteen or twenty years old, and Androgeus was murdered about twenty years earlier, when he was twenty or twenty-two years old, around 985 BC. His father Minos might have been about fifty years old and so have been born about the middle of David's reign around 1035 BC. He would then have been about seventy years old when Theseus came to Daedalus in Crete around 1065 BC. Europa and her brother Cadmus might have come into Europe about five years before the birth of Minos around 1040 BC.

9. The Founding of Tyre, Aradus and Other Colonies

279. Justin says:

Many years after, their city (Sidon) being stormed by the king of the Ascalonians, they sailed away to the place where Tyre stands, and there they built that city the year before the fall of Troy. {*Justin, Trogus, l. 18. c. 3. s. 5. 1:154*}

280. Strabo states that Aradus was built by the men who fled from Sidon. {*Strabo, l. 16. c. 2. s. 13. (754) 7:257*} {*E104*} Hence, Isaiah calls Tyre, the *Daughter of Sidon*, the inhabitants of the isle whom the merchants of Sidon have repopulated. {*Isa 23:2,12*} In the beginning of his reign, Solomon calls the people of Tyre Sidonians, for in a message to Hiram, the king of Tyre, he says:

Now therefore command thou that they hew me cedar trees out of Lebanon; and my servants shall be with thy servants: and unto thee will I give hire for thy servants according to all that thou shalt appoint: for thou knowest that *there is* not among us any that can skill to hew timber like unto the Sidonians. {*1Ki 5:6*}

281. The new inhabitants of Tyre had not yet lost the name of Sidonians, nor had the old inhabitants, if there were any number of them, gained the reputation for carpentry as the new inhabitants had. They would have had this reputation had they been expert sailers for a long time before this. The craftsmen who came from Sidon were not dead, and the flight of the

43

Sidonians was in the reign of David. Therefore, this flight was in the beginning of the reign of Abibalus, the father of Hiram, who was the first king of Tyre mentioned in history. As noted previously, David in the twelfth year of his reign in 1044 BC conquered Edom. He forced some of the Edomites, mainly the merchants and seamen, to flee from the Red Sea to the Philistines on the Mediterranean Sea, where they fortified Azoth. Stephanus says:

Ταυτηω εκλτισεν εις των επανελθοντων απ Ερυθρας θαλασσης φευγαδων {*Stephanus, Azoth} {E105}

They created this fortification with the help of the Edomites fleeing to Philistia from the Red Sea.

282. One of the fugitives from the Red Sea, a prince of Edom who fled from David around 1044 BC, fortified Azoth for the Philistines against David. The Philistines were now becoming very strong by the influx of the Shepherds from Egypt and the Edomites. With their help, they invaded and conquered Sidon. It had a good harbour for the merchants who fled from the Red Sea. After this the Sidonians fled by sea to Tyre and Aradus and to other safe havens in Asia Minor, Greece and Libya with whom they had previously traded. The great wars and victories of David their enemy prompted them to flee by sea. They went in large numbers, not to find Europa as was pretended, but to seek new homes and hence flee from their enemies. {Conon, Narrat. 37.} While some fled under Cadmus and his brothers to Cilicia, Asia Minor and Greece, others fled under different leaders to seek new homes in Libya. There Nonnus says they built many walled towns. {*Nonnus, Dionysiaca, l. 13. (333-335) 1:453,455} Their leader was also called Cadmus, which means *an eastern man*, and his wife was called Sithonis, a Sidonian. Many from those cities joined the great Bacchus in his armies. {E106}

283. The following events,

1) the taking of Sidon,

2) the flight of the Sidonians under Abibalus, Cadmus, Cilix, Thasus, Membliarius, Atymnus and other leaders to Tyre, Aradus, Cilicia, Rhodes, Caria, Bithynia, Phrygia, Calliste, Thasos, Samothrace, Crete, Greece and Libya,

3) the building of Tyre and Thebes (Egyptian),

helped to establish the following events. The beginning of Tyre and Thebes (Egyptian) and the start of the reigns of Abibalus and Cadmus over those cities happened approximately in the fifteenth or sixteenth year of David's reign around 1041 BC. By means of these colonies of Phoenicians, the people of Caria learned nautical skills in the small oar-powered vessels, which were then in use. They frequented the Greek seas and started to colonise some of its islands before the reign of Minos. When Cadmus came to Greece, he arrived first at Rhodes, an island on the borders of Caria, and left a colony of Phoenicians there who sacrificed men to Saturn (Cretan). When Phoroneus drove out the Telchines, they retired from Argos to Rhodes with Phorbas, who purged the island of snakes. Triopas, the son of Phorbas, conducted a colony from Rhodes to Caria and there settled in a promontory, which was called Triopium. This and similar colonies introduced nautical skills and skilled seamen to Caria, which was also called Phoenicia. {*Athenaeus, l. 4. (174f) 2:293} Strabo and Herodotus state that the Carians were subject to Minos and were called *Leleges*. They first lived on the islands of the Greek seas and migrated into Caria, a country inhabited previously by the Leleges and Pelasgians. {*Strabo, l. 14. c. 2. s. 27. (661) 6:301} {*Herodotus, l. 1. c. 171. 1:213,215} {E107} Hence, it is probable that when Lelex and Pelasgus first came into Greece to find new homes, they left some of their colonies in Caria and the neighbouring islands.

284. The Sidonians still actively traded on the Mediterranean Sea, as far west as Greece and Libya along with the very rich trade route of the Red Sea. The Tyrians traded on the Red Sea in conjunction with Solomon and the kings of Judah until after the Trojan War. Likewise so did the merchants of Aradus, Arvad or Arpad. In the Persian Gulf there were two islands called Tyre and Aradus, which had temples similar to Phoenician temples. {*Strabo, l. 16. c. 2. s. 4. (766) 7:303} Therefore, the Tyrians and Aradians sailed there and beyond to the coasts of India, while the Sidonians frequented the Mediterranean Sea. Hence, Homer celebrates Sidon and makes no mention of Tyre.

10. The Revolt of Edom and the Effect on Tyre

10.1 The Time of the Revolt of Edom

285. At length, in the reign of Jehoram, the king of Judah, Edom revolted from Judah and became an independent kingdom around 889 BC. {2Ch 21:8,10 2Ki 8:20,22} When this stopped the trade of Judah and Tyre on the Red Sea, the Tyrians built ships for trade on the Mediterranean Sea. They began to make long voyages to places not yet frequented by the Sidonians. Some went to the coasts of North Africa beyond the Syrtes and built Adrymentum, Carthage, Leptis, Utica and Capsa. {E108} Others journeyed to the coasts of Spain and built Carteia, Gades and Tartessus. Still others went farther to the Fortunate

Islands (Canary Islands), Britain and Thule. (Thule is possibly NW Norway. Editor.)

286. Jehoram reigned eight years from 892 to 885 BC and in the last two years of his life had a sickness in his bowels. Before that sickness, Edom revolted because of Jehoram's wicked reign. If we place that revolt about the middle of the first six years in 889 BC, it happened in the sixth year of Pygmalion the king of Tyre, and so was about fifteen years after the taking of Troy in 904 BC. Because of Edom's revolt, the Tyrians no longer had access to the Red Sea. Then they began to make long voyages on the Mediterranean Sea, for in the seventh year of Pygmalion, his sister Dido sailed to the coast of North Africa beyond the Syrtes and there built Carthage. The abandoning of the Red Sea by the Tyrians to make long voyages on the Mediterranean, coupled with the flight of the Edomites from David to the Philistines, was the basis of the tradition of the ancient Persians and the Phoenicians that the Phoenicians came originally from the Red Sea to the coasts of the Mediterranean Sea and subsequently took long voyages there. {*Herodotus, l. 1. c. 1. 1:3} {*Herodotus, l. 7. c. 89. 3:395} {E109}

10.2 Tyre's Mediterranean Voyages

287. Herodotus relates that the Phoenicians came from the Red Sea to the Mediterranean Sea. {*Herodotus, l. 7. c. 89. 3:395} They began to make long voyages with Egyptian and Assyrian merchandise. Argos was one of the places where they sold their wares. When the women came to buy goods, they seized as many as they could and took them to Egypt. Some of the women of Greece who came to buy their wares included Io, the daughter of Inachus, who was the king of Argos. {*Herodotus, l. 1. c. 5. 1:7,9} Therefore, the Phoenicians came from the Red Sea in the days of Io and her brother Phoroneus, who was then the king of Argos. It follows then that at that time David had conquered the Edomites and forced them to flee from the Red Sea around 1044 BC. Some fled into Egypt with their young king while others fled to the Philistines, their closest neighbours and the enemies of David. This flight was the basis for the Philistines to call many places Erythra in memory of their being Erythreans or Edomites and of their coming from the Erythrean Sea. Erythra was the name of a city in Ionia, Libya, Locris, Boeotia, Cyprus, Aetolia, and another in Asia Minor near Chios. Erythia Acra was a promontory in Libya, Erythraeum a promontory in Crete, and Erythros a place near Tybur. Erythini was a city or country in Paphlagonia, and the name Erythea or Erythrae was given to the island of Gades, which was populated by the Phoenicians.

288. Hence, Solinus says: {E110}

In capite Baeticae insula a continenti septingentis passibus memoratur quam Tyrii a rubro mari profecti Erytheam, Poeni sua lingua Gadir, id est sepem nominarunt. {Solinus, Polyhistor, c. 23. Edit. Salm.}

It is said in the land of Baetica [in Spain] there is an island about three quarters of a mile from the continent which the Tyrians [settled], having set out from Edom from the Red Sea. The Phoenicians in their language call it Gades.

289. Concerning a little island near it, Pliny states:

It (Gadir) was called Erythea because the original ancestors of the Carthaginians, the Tyrians, were said to have come from the Red Sea. {*Pliny, l. 4. c. 22. (120) 2:213}

10.3 The Colonies from Tyre and the Phoenicians

10.3.1 The Colonies in Greece

290. Among the Phoenicians who accompanied Cadmus into Greece, there were Arabians. {*Strabo, l. 9. c. 2. s. 3. (401) 4:281,283} {Strabo, l. 10. c. 1. s. 8. (447) 5:13} The Erythreans or the inhabitants of the Red Sea, that is, the Edomites, also accompanied Cadmus. {*Herodotus, l. 5. c. 57. 3:63} A people settled in Thrace who were circumcised and called Odomantes, that is, as some think, Edomites. Edom, Erythra and Phoenicia are names having the same meaning, the words denoting a red colour. It is probable that the Erythreans who fled from David settled in great numbers in Phoenicia, that is, on all the sea coasts of Syria from Egypt to Sidon. By calling themselves Phoenicians in the Syrian language, instead of Erythreans, they gave the name of Phoenicia to all that sea coast and to only the coastal regions. Strabo says:

For some of them say that even the Sidonians who are our neighbours are colonists from the Sidonians on Oceanus, and they actually add the reason why our Sidonians are called Phoenicians, namely, because the colour of the Persian Gulf [Red Sea] is *red*. {*Strabo, l. 1. c. 2. s. 35. (42) 1:155,157} {E111}

10.3.2 The Exploits of the Tyrian Hercules

291. When mentioning the first men who left the sea coasts to venture out into the deep and undertake long voyages, Strabo names Bacchus, Hercules (Tyrian), Jason, Ulysses and Menelaus. {*Strabo, l. 1. c. 3. s. 2. (48) 1:177} The maritime supremacy of Minos is famous. The voyages of the Phoenicians, shortly after the Trojan War, went beyond the Pillars of Hercules. They

founded cities both there and in the middle of the seacoast parts of North Africa. These Phoenicians were the Tyrians, who at that time built Carthage in North Africa, Carteia in Spain and Gades on the Gades Island outside the straits. They named the leader Hercules (Tyrian) because of his labours and success, and they also called the city Carteia by the name of Heracleia, which he built. {*Bochart, Canaan, l. 1. c. 34.} Strabo says:

> So when you sail from our sea into the exterior sea, you have this mountain [of Calpe] on your right hand; and near it, within a distance of forty stadia (five miles), is the city Carteia, an important and ancient city, which was once a naval station of the Iberians. And some further say that it was founded by Heracles, among whom is Timosthenes, who says that *in ancient times it was called Heracleia, and that its great city walls and its docks are still to be seen. {*Strabo, l. 3. c. 1. s. 7. (140) 2:15} {E112}

292. They also called their leader Melcartus, the king of Carteia, in memory of his founding and reigning over the city Carteia. Bochart writes that Carteia was at first called Melcarteia, from its founder Melcartus, and later shortened to Carteia. Melcartus means *Melec Kartha*, the *king of the city* referring to Tyre. {*Bochart, Canaan, l. 1. c. 34. p. 682.} However, since no ancient writer says that Carteia was ever called Melcarteia, or that Melcartus was king of Tyre, I think that Melcartus or Melec-cartus, was named because he was the founder and king of the city Carteia. Under Melcartus the Tyrians sailed as far as Tartessus or Tarshish, a place in the western part of Spain, between the two mouths of the Baetis River. There they found much silver, which they purchased for next to nothing. {*Aristotle, de Mirabundus Auscultationibus*} They sailed also as far as Britain before the death of Melcartus, for Pliny states:

> Tin (mss. lead) was first imported by Midacritus from the island of Cassiteris. (Cornwall and the Scilles) {*Pliny, l. 7. c. 56. (197) 2:639}

293. Bochart notes that Midacritus is a corruption of the Greek name Melcartus. {*Bochart, Canaan, l. 1. c. 39.} Britain was unknown to the Greeks long after it was discovered by the Phoenicians. {E113} After the death of Melcartus, they built a temple to him on the island of Gades. They adorned it with the sculptures of the labours of Hercules (Idean) and of his Hydra, and the horses to whom he threw Diomedes, the king of the Bistones in Thrace, to be devoured. {*Philostratus, Life of Apollonius, l. 5. c. 4. 1:471} {Photius, Bibliotheca} In this temple was the golden belt of Teucer, the son of Telamon, and the golden olive of Pygmalion bearing Smaragdine fruit.

By these consecrated gifts of Teucer and Pygmalion you may know that it was built in their days. {*Philostratus, Life of Apollonius, l. 5. c. 5. 1:473} Pomponius derives it from the times of the Trojan War. According to the Arundelian Marbles, seven years after that war around 997 BC, Telamon banished his son Teucer from home and Teucer arrived at Cyprus and built Salamis. He and his posterity reigned there until Evagoras, who was conquered by the Persians, in the twentieth year of Artaxerxes Mnemon in 385 BC. Certainly this Hercules (Tyrian) could be no older than the Trojan War because the Tyrians did not begin to sail the Mediterranean Sea until after that war. Indeed, Homer and Hesiod knew nothing of their voyages. The Hercules (Tyrian) who went to the coasts of Spain was buried in Gades. Arnobius says:

> *Tyrius Hercules sepultus in finibus Hispaniae.*
> {*Arnobius, Adversus Nationes, l. 1. c. 36. Internet}

> The grave of the Tyrian Hercules is in the country of Spain.

294. Mela, speaking of the temple of Hercules (Tyrian) in Gades, says:

> *Cur sanctum sit ossa eius ibi sepulta efficiunt.*

> Because they caused his bones to be buried in the temple.

295. Carthage paid an annual tithe to this Hercules (Tyrian) and sent their payments to Tyre. {*Bochart, Canaan, l. 1. c. 24.} {E114} Hence, it is probable that this Hercules (Tyrian) went to the coast of North Africa as well as to Spain, and his discoveries prepared the way for Dido. Orosius and others claim that he built Capsa there. {*Orosius, l. 5. c. 15. s. 8. Internet} {*Florus, l. 1. c. 36. s. 14. 1:165} {*Sallust, Jugurtha, l. 1. c. 89. s. 4. 1:327} Josephus mentions an earlier Hercules (Tyrian), to whom Hiram built a temple at Tyre, and perhaps there might be also an earlier Hercules of Tyre who established their trade on the Red Sea in the days of David or Solomon. {*Josephus, Antiquities, l. 8. c. 5. s. 3. (146) 5:649}

296. Tatian relates that among the Phoenicians emerged three ancient historians, Theodotus, Hysicrates and Mochus. They wrote their histories, which were later translated into Greek by Chaitus (or Latus). These histories show that Europa fled at the time of one of the Phoenician kings, the coming of Menelaus into Phoenicia, and the league and friendship between Solomon and Hiram. At this time, Hiram gave his daughter to Solomon and furnished him with timber for building the temple. {*Tatian, Address of Tatian to the Greeks, l. 1. c. 37. ANF2:80} Menander of Pergamus affirms this also. Josephus tells us that the *Annals of Tyre* (relating history from the

days of Abibalus and Hiram, kings of Tyre,) were extant in his days and Menander of Pergamus had translated them into Greek. These annals record Hiram's friendship to Solomon and his assistance in building the temple, and that the temple was started in the eleventh year of Hiram. {*Josephus, Against Apion, l. 1. c. 18. (116-120) 1:209,211} {*Josephus, Antiquities, l. 8. c. 2. s. 8. (55) 5:599} {*Josephus, Antiquities, l. 8. c. 5. s. 3. (146) 5:649} {*Josephus, Antiquities, l. 9. c. 14. s. 2. (283-287) 6:151} {E115}

11. The Times of Cadmus and Europa

297. By the testimony of Menander and the ancient Phoenician historians, the flight of Europa resulted in the coming of her brother Cadmus to Greece within the time of the reigns of the kings of Tyre as recorded in their annals. Therefore, this was not before the reign of Abibalus, the first of them, nor before the reign of King David, his contemporary. The voyage of Menelaus might have been after the destruction of Troy. Therefore, Solomon reigned in the times between the flight of Europa and the kidnapping of Helen. Europa and her brother Cadmus lived during the reign of David. Minos, the son of Europa, lived during the reign of Solomon and part of the reign of Rehoboam. The children of Minos—namely Androgeus his oldest son, Deucalion his youngest son, who was an Argonaut—Ariadne, who was the wife of Theseus and Bacchus, and Phaedra, who was the wife of Theseus, all lived toward the end of the reign of Solomon and in the reigns of Rehoboam, Abijah and Asa. Idomeneus, the grandson of Minos, was in his prime during the Trojan War. Hiram succeeded his father, Abibalus, in the twenty-third year of David in 1033 BC. Abibalus may have founded the kingdom of Tyre about sixteen or eighteen years earlier, around 1040 BC when Sidon was taken by the Philistines. The Sidonians fled from there under the leadership of Cadmus and other leaders to seek new homes. {E116} Thus according to the *Annals of Tyre* and the ancient Phoenician historians who followed them, Abibalus, Cadmus, Alymnus and Europa fled from Sidon about the sixteenth year of David's reign, around 1040 BC, and the Argonaut Expedition was about three generations later. This places it about three hundred years later than the time the Greeks have dated it!

12. The Colonisation of Sicily

298. Navigation in long ships with sails and one tier of oars had spread from Egypt to Phoenicia and Greece. By this the Sidonians had extended their trade to Greece and carried it on for about a hundred and fifty years. After the Tyrians were driven from the Red Sea by the Edomites, they started trading on the Mediterranean Sea with Spain, North Africa, Britain, and other remote countries. They actively traded for about a hundred and sixty years until the Corinthians began to improve navigation. They built larger ships with three tiers of oars called triremes. Thucydides says that the Corinthians were the first Greeks who built such ships. He also says that a shipwright from Corinth went to Samos about three hundred years before the end of the Peloponnesian War and built four ships for the Samians around 700 BC. Two hundred and sixty years before the end of that war in 664 BC in the 29th Olympiad, there was a naval battle between the Corinthians and the Corcyreans. This is the oldest naval battle mentioned in history. {*Thucydides, l. 1. c. 13. s. 2-4. 1:25} {E117}

299. Thucydides continues saying that the first colony, which the Greeks sent into Sicily, came from Chalcis in Euboea, under the leadership of Thucles, who founded Naxos in Sicily. The next year, Archias came from Corinth with a colony and founded Syracuse. About the same time, Lamis came to Sicily with a colony from Megara in Achaia and settled in a place called Trotilus. Later they moved from there and joined the settlement of the Chalcidians at Leontini. After he colonised Thapsus near Syracuse, Lamis died there. After his death, his followers were expelled from Thapsus and settled then at a place called Megara Hyblaea, since Hyblon, a king in Sicily, gave the land to them and led them to the site. They lived there for two hundred and forty-five years and then were expelled by Gelon, a tyrant of Syracuse. {*Thucydides, l. 6. c. 3-5. 3:187-191} Gelon was in his prime around 482 BC, about seventy-eight years before the end of the Peloponnesian War in 404 BC. Counting backwards the seventy-eight years and the two-hundred and forty-five years and adding twelve years more for the reign of Lamis in Sicily, places the founding of Syracuse around 738 BC or in the 10th Olympiad, about three hundred and thirty-five years before the end of the Peloponnesian War. Eusebius and others, place it about this time. However, it might have been twenty or thirty years later since the Greeks exaggerated the antiquity of that time. Southern Italy was called *Graecia Magna* or *Great Greece* from the colonies sent there from Sicily and Greece. {E118}

300. Thucydides relates that the Greeks began to come into Sicily almost three hundred years after the Sicels invaded that island with an army from Italy. {*Thucydides, l. 6. c. 2. s. 5. 3:185} Now suppose that it was two hundred and eighty years later, and that the founding of Syracuse was in 714 BC, three hundred and ten years before the end of the Peloponnesian war, and that the invasion of Sicily by the Sicels was five hundred and ninety years before the end of that war in 994 BC, then this would be about the twenty-second year of Solomon's reign. Hellanicus mentions that the expedition into Sicily happened in the third generation before the Trojan War, and that it was in the twenty-sixth year of the priesthood of Alcyone, priestess of Juno Argiva. Philistus of Syracuse says the expedition took place eighty years before the Trojan War in 994 BC. That war lasted ten years. {*Dionysius, l. 1. c. 22. s. 3,4. 1:71} Hence, it follows that the Trojan War and the Argonaut Expedition were later than the days of Solomon and Rehoboam and could not be much earlier than the time we have determined.

13. The Founding of the Kingdom of Macedon

301. The kingdom of Macedon was founded by Caranus and Perdiccas, who were of the family of Temenus, the king of Argos. They were banished from Argos in the reign of Phidon, the brother of Caranus. {*Herodotus, l. 8. c. 137. 4:141} Temenus was one of the three brothers who led the Heraclides into Peloponnesus and shared the conquest among themselves. He obtained Argos and his son Cisus succeeded him. The kingdom of Argos was divided among the posterity of Temenus until Phidon reunited it, expelling his relatives. {E119} Phidon grew powerful, established weights and measures in Peloponnesus, and coined silver money. After removing the Piseans and Eleans, he presided over the Olympic Games himself. {*Herodotus, l. 6. c. 127. 3:283} Soon after this he was conquered by the Eleans and Spartans. Herodotus wrote that Perdiccas was the first king of Macedon. {*Herodotus, l. 8. c. 137. 4:141} Later writers such as Livy, Pausanias and Suidas make Caranus the first king. Justin calls Perdiccas the successor of Caranus, and Solinus says that Perdiccas succeeded Caranus and was the first of that line who was called a king. It is probable that Caranus and Perdiccas were contemporaries and fled about the same time from Phidon and at first founded small kingdoms in Macedon. After the death of Caranus, these were united under Perdiccas. Herodotus says that after Perdiccas reigned Araeus, or Argaeus, Philippus, Aeropus, Alcetas, Amyntas and Alexander reigned successively. {*Herodotus, l. 8. c. 139. 4:145} Alexander was contemporary with Xerxes I the king of Persia, and died in 460 BC and was succeeded by Perdiccas who was succeeded by his son Archelaus. Thucydides states that there were eight kings of Macedon before Archelaus. {*Thucydides, l. 2. c. 100. s. 2. 1:453}

302. By calculating more than forty years each to these kings, chronologers have made Phidon and Caranus older than the Olympiads. {E120} Whereas if we calculated the average length of a reign at eighteen or twenty years each, then the length of the first seven reigns before the death of Alexander places the time of Phidon and the founding of the kingdom of Macedon under Perdiccas and Caranus, in the 46th or 47th Olympiad around 596 to 592 BC. It could hardly be earlier because Leocides, the son of Phidon, and Megacles, the son of Alcmaeon, simultaneously courted Agarista, the daughter of Clisthenes who was the king of Sicyon. {*Herodotus, l. 6. c. 127. 3:281,283} The Amphictyonic Council, by the advice of Solon, made Alcmaeon, Clisthenes and Eurolicus the king of Thessaly, commanders of their army in their war against Cirrha. The Cirrheans were conquered in year two of the 47th Olympiad in 603 BC according to the Arundelian Marbles. Therefore, Phidon and his brother Caranus were contemporary with Solon, Alcmaeon, Clisthenes and Eurolicus, and they were in their prime about the 48th and 49th Olympiads around 596 to 592 BC. They were also contemporary in their later years to Croesus because Solon talked with Croesus. Also Alcmaeon entertained and conducted the messengers whom Croesus sent to consult the oracle at Delphi, which occurred in year one of the 56th Olympiad in 556 BC according to the Arundelian Marbles. He was sent for by Croesus and rewarded with great riches. {E121}

14. The Times of Phidon and Solon

303. The chronology recorded in the Arundelian Marbles before the Persian Empire began was determined by reckoning the reign of a king to be equivalent of a generation, and there were three generations to a hundred years or more. The actual time of the successive reigns of kings should be shortened by about forty per cent. The chronology recorded in the Arundelian Marbles detailing the conquest of Media by Cyrus, in year four of the 60th Olympiad in 537 BC is more accurate if the times are reduced by about forty per cent. Hence, the Cirrheans were conquered in year two of the 47th Olympiad in 590 BC according to the Arundelian Marbles, that is, fifty-four years before the conquest of Media. Reduce this time by about forty percent to thirty-one years which is in year one of the 53rd Olympiad in 568 BC. A similar correction to the Arundelian Marbles has Alcmaeon entertaining and leading the messengers whom Croesus sent to consult the oracle at Delphi, in year one of the 58th Olympiad in 548 BC. This is four years before the conquest of Sardis by Cyrus in 544 BC. Likewise correct the Arundelian Marbles for the start of the tyranny of Pisistratus at Athens from year four of the 54th Olympiad in 560 BC to year three of the 57th Olympiad in 550 BC. Hence, Solon died in year four of the 57th Olympiad in 549 BC. This method of adjusting dates may be used by itself when there is no other way to accurately determine the dates.

If there are better ways to determine the dates, they should be used. {E122}

304. Iphitus presided both in the temple of Jupiter Olympius and in the Olympic Games, and so did his successors until the 26th Olympiad in 676 BC. {*Strabo, l. 8. c. 3. s. 33. (358) 4:105} {*Strabo, l. 8. c. 3. s. 30. (355) 4:91,93} During this time the victors were rewarded with a *tripos* or three-legged stool. When the Piseans overcame the Eleans, they began to preside over the games. They rewarded the victors with a crown and instituted the festival of Carnea to Apollo. They continued to preside until Phidon replaced them, that is, until about the time of the 49th Olympiad in 584 BC. For in the 48th Olympiad in 580 BC, the Eleans suspected Damophon, the son of Pantaleon, of plotting against them and they invaded Pisa. However, their army was prevailed upon by prayers and oaths to return home quietly again. {*Pausanias, Elis II, l. 6. c. 22. s. 3. 3:137} Later the Piseans allied themselves with several other Greek city states and attacked the Eleans but were defeated. I think that during this war, Phidon presided in the 49th Olympiad in 584 BC, for in the 50th Olympiad in 580 BC, to stop the infighting between the kings about who would preside over the games, two men were chosen by lot from the city of Elis. Their number was increased to nine in the 95th Olympiad in 400 BC and later to ten in the 97th Olympiad in 392 BC. {*Pausanias, Elis I, l. 5. c. 9. s. 4-6. 2:429} These judges were called *Hellenodicae*, meaning judges for or in the name of Greece. Pausanias says that the Eleans called in Phidon and together with him celebrated the 8th Olympiad in 748 BC, but he should have said the 49th Olympiad in 584 BC. {E123} However, Herodotus states that Phidon removed the Eleans and both may be true. {*Herodotus, l. 6. c. 127. 3:281} The Eleans might have called in Phidon against the Piseans and upon defeating them, Phidon may have refused to let the Eleans preside over the Olympic Games. The Eleans allied themselves with the Spartans and with their help overthrew the kingdom of Phidon, thus recovering their ancient right of presiding over the games.

305. Strabo states that Phidon was the tenth generation from Temenus. He was not the tenth king, for between Cisus and Phidon that family did not reign, but he was in the tenth generation from father to son, including Temenus. {*Strabo, l. 8. c. 3. s. 33. (358) 4:105} Allowing twenty-six years for each generation as calculated by the oldest son, the nine generations amount to two hundred and thirty-four years. Counting back from the 48th Olympiad in 588 BC, in which Phidon was in his prime, places the return of the Heraclides, forty-five years before the beginning of the Olympiads, around 821 BC. However, the chronologers reckon about five hundred and fifteen years from the return of the Heraclides in 1102 BC to the 48th Olympiad, and consider Phidon to be in the seventh generation from Temenus. This assumes eighty-five years per generation, which is ridiculous!

15. The Time of Draco, Solon and Cyrus

306. According to Ptolemy's Canon, Cyrus took Babylon eight years before his death in year three of the 60th Olympiad in 538 BC. Scaliger from Sosicrates determined that he took Sardis shortly before this, in year one of the 59th Olympiad or 544 BC. {E124} Croesus was then king of Sardis and reigned fourteen years and therefore began to reign in year three of the 55th Olympiad in 558 BC.

307. After Solon had made laws for the Athenians, he obliged them under oath to observe those laws until he returned from his travels. He then travelled for ten years, going to Egypt and Cyprus visiting Thales of Miletus. On his return to Athens, Pisistratus began to establish himself as the tyrant of the city. Croesus invited Solon to Sardis and before Solon visited him, Croesus had subdued all of Asia Minor as far as to the Halys River. Therefore, Solon's visit to him was likely in the latter part of his reign. Hence, we determine the time of his visit to be about the ninth year of the reign of Croesus in year three of the 57th Olympiad in 550 BC. Then the legislature of Solon would be twelve years earlier in year three of the 54th Olympiad in 562 BC. Then the laws of Draco would be ten years earlier in year one of the 52nd Olympiad in 572 BC. Plutarch quotes Phanias of Eresos as saying that Solon had visited Croesus, then he travelled to Cilicia and some other places and died in his travels. This was in the second year of the tyranny of Pisistratus. Comeas was the archon when Solon returned from his first travels to Athens. The next year Hegestratus was the archon and Solon died before the end of the year, in year three of the 57th Olympiad in 549 BC. Using this calculation places his death ten years later than Plutarch states. {*Plutarch, Lives-Solon, l. 1. c. 32. s. 2. 1:497,499} {E125}

The Summary of Conclusions

308. In the preceding sections we have documented the points by order of importance, the points foundational to the rest were dealt with first. The following is the summary of these points in chonological order. (We did not rearrange the preceding sections into chronological sequence but left them in the order Newton had written them. Editor.)

1) Europa, the sister of Cadmus, fled some days before him from Sidon and came to Crete, and

there became the mother of Minos. This happened about the thirteenth or fourteenth year of David's reign around 1042 BC.

2) The Phoenicians from Sidon, under the leadership of Cadmus and other leaders, fled from their enemies and came into Greece bringing with them writing and other arts. This happened about the fifteenth year of King David's reign around 1041 BC.

3) Sesostris and the great Bacchus, and by consequence also Osiris, were one and the same king of Egypt as Shishak. He came out of Egypt in the fifth year of Rehoboam in 971 BC to invade the countries and died twenty-three years after the death of Solomon in 951 BC.

4) The Argonaut Expedition was about forty-two years after the death of Solomon in 933 BC.

5) Troy was taken by the Greeks about seventy-one years after the death of Solomon around 904 BC.

6) The Phoenicians of Tyre were driven from the Red Sea by the Edomites about eighty-three years after the death of Solomon. Within two or three years after this, they began to make long voyages on the Mediterranean Sea, sailing to Spain and beyond around 892 to 889 BC. Their leader in these enterprises was renowned for his industry, leadership, and discoveries and was honoured with the names of Melcartus and Hercules (Tyrian).

7) The return of the Heraclides into Peloponnesus was about one hundred and fifty years after the death of Solomon around 825 BC. {E126}

8) Lycurgus, the legislator, reigned at Sparta and gave the three discs to the Olympic treasury in the first year of the 18th Olympiad in 708 BC or two hundred and sixty-seven years after the death of Solomon. The *Quinquertium* was added at that time to the Olympic Games. The Greeks began soon after this to build triremes. They sent colonies into Sicily and Italy, which gave the name of *Greater Greece* to those countries around 750 to 700 BC.

9) The first Messenian War ended about three hundred and forty-three years after the death of Solomon in year one of the 37th Olympiad in 632 BC.

10) Phidon was contemporary with Solon and presided in the Olympic Games in the 49th Olympiad in 584 BC, which was three hundred and ninety-one years after the death of Solomon.

11) Draco was archon, and made his laws in year one of the 52nd Olympiad in 572 BC, and Solon made his in year three of the 54th Olympiad in 562 BC. Solon visited Croesus in year three of the 57th Olympiad in 550 BC, or four hundred and twenty-five years after the death of Solomon.

12) Sardis was taken by Cyrus four hundred and thirty-one years after the death of Solomon in 544 BC. He captured Babylon four hundred and thirty-seven years after the death of Solomon in 538 BC. Cyrus defeated Darius at Ecbatana four hundred and thirty-eight years after the death of Solomon in 537 BC.

309. With the establishment of these periods, we have laid the foundation for building a more accurate chronology for these ancient times. What remains for completing this chronology, besides making these periods more exact, is to show how the rest of the history of Greece, Egypt, Assyria, Chaldea and Media agrees with this chronology. {E127}

Part 2 — How Early Greek History Fits within This Framework

1. The Early Chronology of Ionia

310. While Bacchus made his expedition into India, Theseus abandoned Ariadne on the island of Naxos or Dia and succeeded his father Aegeus at Athens. When Bacchus returned from India, Ariadne became his wife and accompanied him in his triumphs. This was about ten years after the death of Solomon in 965 BC. From that time eight kings reigned in Athens: Theseus, Menestheus, Demophoon, Olyntes, Aphidas, Thymoetes, Melanthus, and Codrus. Assuming that these kings reigned an average of eighteen years each, their total reigns would be one hundred and fifty-two years and end about forty-seven years before the Olympiads in 822 BC. After them, twelve archons reigned for life. Since the city state was not stable, their reigns may have lasted an average of fourteen or fifteen years each, taking up one hundred and seventy-six years, ending in year two of the 33rd Olympiad in 647 BC. After them, seven decennial archons reigned, which are usually calculated at seventy years. However, some of them died during their reign so this period may not take more than forty years, ending about year two of the 43rd Olympiad around 607 BC. This is about the time the second Messenian War began. These decennial archons were followed by annual archons, among whom were the legislators of Draco and Solon. Soon after the death of Codrus, his second son Neleus retired into Asia

Minor, not being able to endure the reign of his lame brother Medon at Athens. {E128} He was followed by his younger brothers Androcles and Cyaretus, and many others. These had the name of Ionians, from Ion the son of Xuthus, who commanded the army of the Athenians after the death of Erechtheus. They gave the name of Ionia to the country that they invaded. About twenty or twenty-five years after the death of Codrus, these new colonies, now being masters of Ionia, set up over themselves a common council called the *Panionium*. This was composed of counsellors sent from twelve of their cities: Miletus, Myus, Priene, Ephesus, Colophon, Lebedus, Teos, Clazomenae, Phocaea, Samos, Chios and Erythraea. This was how Ionia was settled.

2. The Early Chronology of Rome

311. When the Greeks and Latins were writing their chronology, there were great disputes about the antiquity of Rome. {*Dionysius, l. 1. c. 44. s. 3,4. 1:145*} The Greeks made it much older than the Olympiads. They had the following opinions concerning the founder of Rome:

1) Aeneas,

2) Romus, the son or grandson of Latinus, the king of the aborigines,

3) Romus, the son of Ulysses, or of Ascanius, or of Italus.

312. Some of the Latins at first agreed with the opinion of the Greeks who said Rome was built by Romulus, the son or grandson of Aeneas. Timaeus Siculus recorded that it was built by Romulus, the grandson of Aeneas, about a hundred years before the Olympiads around 875 BC. {E129} Noevius (the poet who was twenty years older than Ennius, served in the first Punic War, and wrote the history of that war) agrees with Timaeus. Before this, nothing certain was agreed upon. However, about one hundred and forty or fifty years after the death of Alexander the Great around 180 BC, they began to say that Rome was built a second time by Romulus in the fifteenth age after the destruction of Troy. They used the term *age* to refer to the reigns of the kings of the Latins at Alba Longa. They calculated that the first fourteen reigns lasted about four hundred and thirty-two years and the following reigns of the seven kings of Rome lasted for two hundred and forty-four years. This sums to six hundred and seventy-six years from the taking of Troy to the first consul in 508 BC. This is much too long for the course of nature. By this reckoning they placed the building of Rome in the sixth or seventh Olympiad around 756 to 749 BC. Varro placed it in the spring of the third year of the sixth Olympiad in 753 BC, and this date was generally accepted by the Romans.

313. However, this can scarcely be reconciled with the course of nature, for I do not find any instance in all history, since chronology was certain, in which seven kings, most of whom were murdered, reigned two hundred and forty-four years in continual succession. The fourteen reigns of the kings of the Latins, at twenty years each, amount to two hundred and eighty years. {E130} Using this time and counting down from the taking of Troy places the founding of Rome at the beginning of the 38th Olympiad around 627 BC. For the seven kings of Rome, four or five of whom were murdered and one deposed, we may assume an average reign of fifteen or sixteen years each. It is not unreasonable to assume they reigned for one hundred and nineteen years until they were overthrown in 508 BC. The sum of these two periods amounts to three hundred and ninety-nine years. The same number of years arises by counting the twenty-one reigns at nineteen years each. This accounts for the time between the taking of Troy and the overthrow of the kings at Rome in year one of the 68th Olympiad in 508 BC. This places the taking of Troy about sixty-nine years after the death of Solomon around 906 BC.

3. The Times of Cadmus and Europa and Their Posterity

314. When Sesostris returned from Thrace into Egypt, he left Aeetes with part of his army in Colchis to guard that pass. Phrixus and his sister Helle fled from Ino, the daughter of Cadmus, to Aeetes soon after this time, in a ship whose ensign was a golden ram. Therefore, Ino was alive in the fourteenth year of Rehoboam in 962 BC, the year in which Sesostris returned into Egypt. {E131} By consequence, her father Cadmus lived in the reign of David and not before. Cadmus was the father of Polydorus, the grandfather of Labdacus, the great-grandfather of Laius, the great-great-grandfather of Oedipus, the great-great-great-grandfather of Eteocles and Polynices. These last two sons killed each other while young in the war of the seven captains at Thebes (Greek), about six years after the Argonaut Expedition, around 928 BC. Thersander, the son of Polynices, fought at Troy. These generations are by the oldest sons, who married young. Averaging about twenty-four years to a generation, it places the birth of Polydorus about the eighteenth year of David's reign, around 1038 BC.

315. Thus Cadmus might be a young bachelor, when he came into Greece. When he first came, he sailed to Rhodes, and thence to Samothrace, an island near Thrace on the north side of Lemnos. There he married Harmonia, the sister of Jasius and Dardanus, whose marriage ceremony gave rise to the Samothracian mysteries. Polydorus was their son, who may have been born a year or two after their arrival, and Europa, the sister of Cadmus, might then have been a young woman, in the flower of her age. These generations cannot be shorter; therefore, Cadmus and his son Polydorus, were not younger than we have calculated, nor can they be much older. {E132} Otherwise, this makes Polydorus too old to be born in Europe and to be the son of Harmonia, the sister of Jasius. Therefore, Labdacus was born at the end of David's reign, around 1016 BC. Laius, the son of Labdacus, was born about the twenty-fourth year of Solomon's reign around 992 BC. Oedipus, the son of Laius, was born about the seventh year of Rehoboam's reign around 969 BC. The other alternative is that Polydorus was born at Sidon before his father came into Europe. However, his name is a Greek name, not a Phoenician name.

316. Polydorus married Nycteis, the daughter of Nycteus, who was a native of Greece. He died young and left his kingdom and young son Labdacus under the care of Nycteus. Then Epopeus, the king of Aegialea, later called Sicyon, kidnapped Antiope, the daughter of Nycteus. Nycteus declared war on him, and in a battle, Nycteus was defeated and both were wounded and died soon after. Nycteus appointed his brother Lycus regent in the kingdom, for Labdacus, the son of Polydorus and the grandson of Cadmus, was still a child under the ward of Nycteus, who entrusted this duty to Lycus. {*Pausanias, Corinth, l. 2. c. 6. s. 1,2. 1:277*} Epopeus or as Hyginus calls him, Epaphus the Sicyonian, left his kingdom to Lamedon, who soon ended the war by returning Antiope. {*Hyginus, Fabulae, l. 1. c. 7,8. 1:98,99*} When she came home, she gave birth to the twins Amphion and Zethus. When Labdacus grew up, he received the kingdom from Lycus but died shortly thereafter. He left Lycus regent in the kingdom and his young son Laius as his ward. {E133}

317. When Amphion and Zethus were about twenty years old, at the instigation of their mother Antiope, they murdered Lycus and made Laius flee to Pelops in Olympia. They seized the city of Thebes (Greek) and surrounded it with a wall. Amphion married Niobe, the sister of Pelops, and had several children by her, among whom was Chloris, the mother of Periclymenus the Argonaut. Pelops was the father of Plisthenes, Atreus and Thyestes. Agamemnon and Menelaus, the adopted sons of Atreus, fought at Troy. Aegisthus, the son of Thyestes, killed Agamemnon

the year after the taking of Troy around 904 BC. Atreus died just before Paris kidnapped Helen, which, according to Homer, was twenty years before the taking of Troy around 924 BC. Deucalion, the son of Minos, was an Argonaut. {*Homer, Iliad, l. 22. v. 355-360. 2:479*} {*Homer, Iliad, l. 24. v. 762-768. 2:619*} {*Hyginus, Fabulae, l. 1. c. 14. s. 22. 1:103*} Talus, another son of Minos, was killed by the Argonauts. Idomeneus and Meriones, the grandsons of Minos, were in the Trojan War. All these things confirm the times of Cadmus and Europa and their posterity, as noted previously. It places the death of Epopeus or Epaphus, the king of Sicyon, and the birth of Amphion and Zethus, about the tenth year of Solomon, around 1005 BC. It also places the taking of Thebes (Greek) by Amphion and Zethus and the flight of Laius to Pelops about the thirtieth year of Solomon around 985 BC. Amphion likely married the sister of Pelops the same year, and Pelops came into Greece about three or four years before that flight, or about the twenty-sixth year of Solomon around 990 BC. {E134}

4. The Times of Erechtheus and His Descendants in Attica

318. In the days of Erechtheus, the king of Athens, and Celeus, the king of Eleusis, Ceres came into Attica. She educated Triptolemus, the son of Celeus, and taught him to sow grain. She married Jasius, or Jasion, the brother of Harmonia, who was the wife of Cadmus. {*Homer, Odyssey, l. 5. v. 122-128. 1:191*} {*Diod. Sic., l. 5. c. 49. s. 1-3. 3:233*} After her death, Erechtheus was killed in a war between the Athenians and the Eleusinians. For the gift of agriculture Ceres brought to Greece, the rituals and mysteries at Eleusis were instituted to her, and in Egypt the Festival of Isis by Celeus and Eumolpus. {*Diod. Sic., l. 1. c. 29. s. 1-4. 1:95*} A sepulchre or temple was erected to her in Eleusis, and in this temple the families of Celeus and Eumolpus became her priests. This temple and the one Eurydice erected to her daughter Danae, by the name of Juno Argiva, is the first time that we find in Greece the dead being deified with temples. Sacred rites and sacrifices were dedicated to them, along with initiation rites and a succession of priests to perform them.

319. By this history it is obvious that Erechtheus, Celeus, Eumolpus, Ceres, Jasius, Cadmus, Harmonia, Asterius and Dardanus (the brother of Jasius and one of the founders of the kingdom of Troy) were all contemporary to one another and were young when Cadmus first came into Europe. {E135} Erechtheus could not be much older, because his daughter Procris talked with Minos, the king of Crete. His other daughter Orithyia was the mother of Calais and Zetes, two of the young

Argonauts. His grandson Thespis had fifty daughters who had sexual intercourse with Hercules (Idean). Erechtheus's son Orneus was the father of Peteos, the grandfather of Menestheus who fought against Troy. {*Pausanias, Corinth, l. 2. c. 25. s. 6. 1:381} Erechtheus could not be much younger because his second son, Pandion, who with the help of the Metionides, deposed his older brother, Cecrops II. Pandion was the father of Aegeus and the grandfather of Theseus. {*Pausanias, Attica, l. 1. c. 5. s. 3. 1:25} Metion, another of Pandion's sons, was the father of Eupalamus and the grandfather of Daedalus, and was older than Theseus. His daughter Creusa married Xuthus, the son of Hellen, and by him had two sons, Achaeus and Ion. Ion commanded the army of the Athenians against the Eleusinians, in the battle in which his grandfather Erechtheus was killed. This was just before the institution of the mysteries at Eleusis and before the reign of Pandion, the father of Aegeus. Erechtheus was an Egyptian and brought grain from Egypt, and for that act was appointed king of Athens. Near the beginning of his reign, Ceres came into Attica from Sicily, in quest of her kidnapped daughter, Proserpina.

320. The time for these events would be approximately as follows:

1) Hellen was contemporary to the reign of Saul and to David when David was at Hebron around 1055 BC.

2) The beginning of the reign of Erechtheus was in David's twenty-fifth year around 1031 BC.

3) The coming of Ceres into Attica was in David's thirtieth year around 1026 BC.

4) The distribution of grain by Triptolemus was about the fortieth year of David's reign, around 1016 BC. {E136}

5) The death of Ceres and Erechtheus, and the institution of the mysteries at Eleusis, was between the tenth to fifteenth year of Solomon, around 1005 to 1000 BC.

5. The Beginning of the Line of Kings Who Ruled Troy

321. Teucer, Dardanus, Erichthonius, Tros, Ilus, Laomedon and Priam reigned successively at Troy. Assuming an average length of twenty years for each king, the total time of their reigns is one hundred and forty years. Counting back from the taking of Troy, places the beginning of the reign of Teucer about the thirteenth year of the reign of King David and that of Dardanus around 1043 BC, in the days of Ceres, who married his brother Jasius. However, chronologers calculate that the last six of these kings reigned two hundred and ninety-six years, which averages to almost fifty years per king, thus beginning their reign in the days of Moses! Dardanus married the daughter of Teucer, the son of Scamander, and succeeded him, hence Teucer was about the same age as David.

322. When Sesostris returned to Egypt, his brother Danaus not only attempted to murder him, as noted previously, but also ordered his fifty daughters, who had married the sons of Sesostris, to murder their husbands. After that, Danaus, with his daughters, fled from Egypt in a long ship with fifty oars in the fifteenth year of Rehoboam around 961 BC. {E137} Danaus first came to Lindus, a town in Rhodes, and there built a temple and erected a statue to Minerva. Three of his daughters died from a plague which raged there. After that he sailed with the rest of his daughters to Argos, arriving there in the sixteenth or seventeenth year of Rehoboam around 960 to 959 BC. He contended there with Gelanor, the brother of Eurystheus for the crown of Argos. The people chose him to be their king and he reigned at Argos while Eurystheus reigned at Mycene.

323. Eurystheus was born in the same year as Hercules (Idean). Gelanor and Eurystheus were the sons of Sthenelus by Nicippe, the daughter of Pelops. Sthenelus was the son of Perseus and reigned at Argos. {*Apollodorus, Library, l. 2. c. 4. s. 5. 1:163} {*Apollodorus, Library, l. 2. c. 4. s. 6. 1:169,171} His son Danaus succeeded him at Argos who was succeeded by his son-in-law Lynceus and he by his son Abas. This is that Abas who is commonly, but erroneously, reputed to be the father of Acrisius and Praetus.

324. In the time of the Argonaut Expedition, Castor and Pollux were beardless young men and their sisters Helen and Clytemnestra were children, and their wives, Phoebe and Ilaira, were also very young. All these, with the Argonauts Lynceus and Idas, were the grandsons of Gorgophone, the daughter of Perseus, the son of Danae, the daughter of Acrisius and Eurydice. {E138} Perieres and Oebalus, the husbands of Gorgophone, were the sons of Cynortes and the grandsons of Amyclas, brother of Eurydice. Mestor or Mastor, the brother of Sthenelus, married Lysidice, another of the daughters of Pelops, and Pelops married Hippodamia, the daughter of Evarete and the granddaughter of Acrisius. Alcmena, the mother of Hercules (Idean), was the daughter of Electryo. Sthenelus, Mestor and Electryo were the brothers of Gorgophone and sons of Perseus and Andromeda. The Argonaut Aesculapius was the grandson of

Leucippus and Phlegia, and Leucippus was the son of Perieres, the grandson of Amyclas, the brother of Eurydice. Amyclas and Eurydice were the children of Lacedemon and Sparta. Capaneus, one of the seven captains against Thebes (Greek), was the husband of Euadne, who was the daughter of Iphis, the son of Elector, the grandson of Anaxagoras, the great-grandson of Megapenthes, the great-great-grandson of Praetus, who was the brother of Acrisius. From this genealogy we deduce that Perseus, Perieres and Anaxagoras were about the same age as Minos, Pelops, Aegeus and Sesostris.

325. We also know that Acrisius, Praetus, Eurydice and Amyclas, who were two generations older, were about the same age as King David and Erechtheus. We also know that the temple of Juno Argiva was built about the same time as the temple of Solomon. {E139} This temple was built by Eurydice to her daughter Danae, as noted previously. However, some say it was built by Pirasus, or Piranthus, the son or successor of Argus, and great-grandson of Phoroneus since the first priestess of that goddess was Callithea, the daughter of Piranthus. Callithea was succeeded by Alcyone about three generations before the taking of Troy, which is about the middle of Solomon's reign. During her priesthood the Sicels invaded Sicily from Italy. Later Hypermnestra, the daughter of Danaus, became the priestess of this goddess and she lived in the time before the Argonaut Expedition. Admeta, the daughter of Eurystheus, was priestess of this Juno Argiva about the times of the Trojan War. Andromeda, the wife of Perseus, was the daughter of Cepheus an Egyptian, the grandson of Belus (Egyptian). This Egyptian Belus was Ammon. {*Herodotus, l. 7. c. 61. 3:377}

326. Perseus took Andromeda from Joppa where Cepheus, who I think is a relative of Solomon's queen, lived in the days of Solomon. Acrisius and Praetus were the sons of Abas who was not the same man as Abas, the grandson of Danaus, but a much older prince, who built Abaea in Phocis. He might be the prince from whom the island Euboea was formerly called *Abantis* and its inhabitants *Abantes*. {Bochart, Canaan, l. 2. c. 13.} Apollonius Rhodius states that the Argonaut Canthus was the son of Canethus, and that Canethus was a descendant of Abas. {*Apollonius, Argonautica, l. 1. v. 77-78. 1:7} {E140} The commentator on Apollonius further states that the inhabitants of Euboea were previously called *Abantes* after the name of Abas. Therefore, this Abas lived about three or four generations before the Argonaut expedition and so might be the father of Acrisius. The ancestors of Acrisius were considered Egyptians by the Greeks and they might have come from Egypt under the leadership of Abas into Euboea and from there into Peloponnesus. I do not consider Phorbas and his son Triopas among the kings of Argos because they fled from that kingdom to the island of Rhodes. Nor do I consider Crotopus among them because he went from Argos and built a new city for himself in Megaris as Conon relates. {Conon, Narrat. 13.}

327. We said that Pelops came into Greece about the twenty-seventh year of Solomon around 989 BC. Pelops came there in the days of Acrisius, Endymion and his sons, and captured the country of Aetolia from Aetolus. {*Pausanias, Elis I, l. 5. c. 1. s. 4,5. 2:383} {*Apollodorus, Library, l. 1. c. 7. s. 6. 1:61} Endymion was the son of Aethlius, the grandson of Protogenia who was the sister of Hellen and the daughter of Deucalion. Phrixus and Helle, the children of Athamas, the brother of Sisyphus who was the son of Aeolus, the son of Hellen, fled from their step-mother Ino who was the daughter of Cadmus, to Aeetes in Colchis shortly after the return of Sesostris into Egypt in 962 BC. Jason the Argonaut was the son of Aeson, the grandson of Cretheus, the great-grandson of Aeolus, the great-great-grandson of Hellen. {E141} Calyce was the wife of Aethlius, and the mother of Endymion, and the daughter of Aeolus, and the sister of Cretheus, Sisyphus and Athamas. As a result, Cretheus, Sisyphus and Athamas were in their prime in the latter part of the reign of Solomon and in the reign of Rehoboam around 980 to 970 BC.

328. Aethlius, Aeolus, Xuthus, Dorus, Tantalus and Danae were contemporary with Erechtheus, Jasius and Cadmus. Hellen was about one generation older and Deucalion was about two generations older than Erechtheus. They could not be much older because Xuthus, the youngest son of Hellen, married Creusa who was the daughter of Erechtheus. {*Pausanias, Achaia, l. 7. c. 1. s. 1,2. 3:167} They could not be much younger because Cephalus (the oldest son of Deioneus, the grandson of Aeolus, the great-grandson of Hellen) married Procris, the daughter of Erechtheus. {*Pausanias, Attica, l. 1. c. 37. s. 6. 1:207} {*Pausanias, Phocis, l. 10. c. 29. s. 6. 4:537} Procris fled from her husband to Minos. After the death of Hellen, his youngest son Xuthus was expelled from Thessaly by his brothers Aeolus and Dorus. {*Pausanias, Achaia, l. 7. c. 1. s. 2. 1:167} He fled to Erechtheus and married Creusa, the daughter of Erechtheus, by whom he had two sons, Achaeus and Ion. Before Erechtheus died, his youngest son commanded the army of the Athenians in the war in which Erechtheus was killed. Therefore, Hellen died about one generation before Erechtheus.

6. The Founding of Corinth

329. Based on what we have said, Sisyphus built Corinth about the latter end of the reign of Solomon or the

beginning of the reign of Rehoboam around 980 to 970 BC. {*E142*} After Phrixus and Helle fled from their step-mother Ino, their father Athamas, who was an insignificant king in Boeotia, went mad and accidentally killed his son Learchus. Then Athamas' wife, Ino, drowned herself in the sea, together with her other son, Melicertus. Sisyphus instituted the Isthmian Games at Corinth in the honour of his nephew Melicertus. This likely happened soon after Sesostris had left Aeetes in Colchis about the fourteenth year of Rehoboam in 962 BC. Hence, Athamas (the son of Aeolus and the grandson of Hellen) and his wife Ino, who was the daughter of Cadmus, were alive until about the fourteenth year of Rehoboam. Sisyphus and his successors Ornytion, Thoas, Demophon, Propodas, Doridas, and Hyanthidas, reigned successively at Corinth, until the return of the Heraclides into Peloponnesus. After that the Heraclides: Aletes, Ixion, Agelas I, Prumnis, Bacchis, Agelas II, Eudamus, Aristodemus, and Telestes, reigned consecutively for about one hundred and seventy years. After the reign of the Heraclides, Corinth was governed by *pytanes* or annual archons for about forty-two years. After them, Cypselus and Periander ruled for about forty-eight years.

7. The Amphictyonic Council

330. Celeus, the king of Eleusis, who was contemporary with Erechtheus, was the son of Rharus and the grandson of Cranaus, who was the successor of Cecrops I. {*Hesychius, in Κραναος*} {*E143*} In the reign of Cranaus, Deucalion fled with his sons Hellen and Amphictyon from the flood, which inundated Thessaly. The flood was named after him, *Deucalion's Flood.* They fled into Attica where Deucalion died shortly thereafter. Pausanias says that his grave was to be seen near Athens. {*Pausanias, Attica, l. 1. c. 18. s. 8. 1:91*} His oldest son Hellen succeeded him in Thessaly. His other son Amphictyon married the daughter of Cranaus and reigned at Thermopylae and established there the Amphictyonic Council of twelve men, two from every city state in the league. Soon after this, Acrisius established a similar council at Delphi. This was likely done when Amphictyon and Acrisius were mature enough to be counsellors and could have happened in the latter half of the reign of David and the beginning of the reign of Solomon around 1020-1010 BC. Shortly after this, likely about the middle of the reign of Solomon around 995 BC, Phemonoe became the first priestess of Apollo at Delphi and uttered oracles in hexameter verse. About this time Acrisius was accidentally killed by his grandson Perseus. The council of Thermopylae included twelve city states of the Greeks, excluding Attica. Therefore, Amphictyon did not then reign at Athens. Amphictyon might

endeavour to succeed his father-in-law Cranaus, and be prevented by Erechtheus.

331. Between the reigns of Cranaus and Erechtheus, chronologers place also Erichthonius and his son Pandion. However, I take this Erichthonius and his son Pandion, to be one and the same with Erechtheus and his son and successor Pandion. {*E144*} These names are only repeated with a little variation in the list of the kings of Attica. Erichthonius was the son of Gaia and raised by Minerva. Homer called him Erechtheus. Themistius states that Erechtheus was the first who harnessed horses to a chariot. {*Themistius, Orat. 19.*} Plato alluding to the story of Erichthonius from Homer, states: {*Homer, Iliad, l. 2. v. 545-549. 1:101*}

> For fair of face is *the people of the great-hearted Erechtheus;* but you should get a view of it stripped. {*Plato, Alcibiades I, l. 1. (132A) 12:207*}

332. Therefore, Erechtheus immediately succeeded Cranaus, while Amphictyon reigned at Thermopylae. In the reign of Cranaus the poets place the flood of Deucalion. Therefore, the death of Deucalion and the reign of his sons Hellen and Amphictyon in Thessaly and Thermopylae, was but a few years, likely eight or ten, before the reign of Erechtheus.

8. The Kingdom of Arcadia

333. The first kings of Arcadia were successively Pelasgus, Lycaon, Nyctimus, Arcas, Clitior, Aepytus I, Aleus, Lycurgus, Echemus, Agapenor, Hippothous, Aepytus II, Cypselus, Holaeas, etc. {*Pausanias, Arcadia, l. 8. c. 1. s. 5. 3:349*} {*Pausanias, Arcadia, l. 8. c. 2. s. 1. 3:351*} {*Pausanias, Arcadia, l. 8. c. 3. s. 1. 3:355*} {*Pausanias, Arcadia, l. 8. c. 4. s. 1. 3:359*} {*Pausanias, Arcadia, l. 8. c. 4. s. 7,8,10. 3:361,363*} {*Pausanias, Arcadia, l. 8. c. 5. s. 1,2,4-7. 3:365,367*} Between the reigns of Lycaon and Cypselus, the Heraclides returned into Peloponnesus, as noted previously. Agapenor was one of those who courted Helen. He courted her before he reigned and after he went to the Trojan War and from there he built Paphos in Cyprus. Echemus killed Hyllus, the son of Hercules (Idean). {*E145*} Lycurgus, Cepheus, Amphidamus and Auge were the children of Aleus. He was son of Aphidas, the grandson of Arcas, the great-grandson of Callisto who was the daughter of Lycaon. {*Pausanias, Arcadia, l. 8. c. 4. s. 8. 3:363*} {*Apollonius, Argonautica, l. 1. v. 162-165. 1:13*} Auge had sexual intercourse with Hercules (Idean). Ancaeus, the son of Lycurgus, was an Argonaut. Cepheus, the uncle of Ancaeus, was his governor in that expedition, while Lycurgus stayed home to take care of his aged father Aleus, who was likely born about seventy-five years before that expedition, around 1008 BC.

334. Arcas, the grandfather of Lycurgus, might be born about the end of the reign of Saul around 955 BC and Lycaon, the grandfather of Arcas, was probably living then and died before the middle of David's reign about 1035 BC. Lycaon's youngest son Oenotrus, the Janus of the Latins, likely grew up and led a colony into Italy before the reign of Solomon about 1016 BC. Arcas introduced the cultivation of crops which he learned from Triptolemus and taught his people to make bread from it. {*Pausanias, Arcadia, l. 8. c. 4. s. 1. 3:359} Likewise Eumelus, the first king of a region later called Achaia, did the same for his people. Therefore, Arcas and Eumelus were contemporary with Triptolemus and his father Celeus, and Erechtheus, the king of Athens. Callisto was contemporary with Rharus and her father Lycaon was contemporary with Cranaus. Lycaon died before Cranaus leaving time for Deucalion's flood between their deaths.

335. The eleven kings of Arcadia, between this flood and the return of the Heraclides into Peloponnesus (that is, between the reigns of Lycaon and Cypselus) reigned for about two hundred and twenty years assuming an average reign of twenty years per king. {E146} Counting back from the return of the Heraclides places the flood of Deucalion about the fourteenth year of David's reign around 1042 BC.

9. The Early History of Crete

336. Herodotus says that the Phoenicians who accompanied Cadmus brought many kinds of learning into Greece. {*Herodotus, l. 5. c. 58. 3:63} Among those Phoenicians were men called *Curetes,* who were more skilled in the arts and sciences of Phoenicia than any other men. {*Strabo, l. 10. c. 10. s. 3-9. (464-466) 5:79-93} Some settled in Phrygia, where they were called *Corybantes.* Others settled in Crete where they were called *Idean Dactyli,* some in Rhodes where they were called *Telchines,* some in Samothrace where they were called *Cabiri.* Others settled in Euboea, where, before the smelting of iron, they worked in copper, in a city called Chalcis. Some settled in Lemnos where they assisted Vulcan, and some in Imbrus and other places. A large number of them settled in Aetolia, which was then called the country of the Curetes until the time of Aetolus.

337. Aetolus was the son of Endymion and after he had killed Apis Epaphus, the king of Sicyon, he fled there. With the help of his father, he invaded it and named it Aetolia after himself. With the assistance of these craftsmen, Cadmus found gold in the Mount Pangaeus in Thrace and copper ore at Thebes (Greek), where copper ore is still known as *cadmia.* {E147} Where they settled, they first worked in copper until the smelting of iron was invented. After that they worked in iron. When they had made themselves iron armour, they danced in it at the sacrifices with tumult and much noise with bells, pipes, drums and swords. They struck their swords against each other's armour in musical time appearing to be seized with a divine fury. This is considered the origin of music in Greece. Solinus says:

> *Studium musicum inde coeptum cum Idaei Dactyli modulos crepitu & tinnitu aeris deprehensos in versificum ordinem transtulissent.* {Solinus, Polyhistor, c. 11.}

Hence, the study of music began when the Idean Dactyli transposed the measure by jangling and clanging recognised in the order of the verses.

338. Isidorus says:

> *Studium musicum ab Idaeis Dactylis coeptum.* {Isidorus, Originum. l. 11. c. 6.}

The musical study began with the Idean Dactyli.

339. Apollo and the Muses were two generations later. Clement calls the Idean Dactyli *barbarians* meaning strangers, and says that they were reputed to be the first wise men, to whom both the Ephesian letters and the invention of musical rhymes are attributed. {*Clement, Stromata, l. 1. c. 15. ANF2:317} It seems that when the Phoenician letters ascribed to Cadmus were brought into Greece, they were brought into Phrygia and Crete at the same time by the Curetes who settled in those countries. {*Pliny, l. 7. c. 56. (192) 2:635,637} They called them Ephesian letters after the name of the city of Ephesus, where they were first taught. The Curetes, by their smelting of copper and iron to make swords, armour and edged tools for hewing and carving of wood, brought into Europe a new way of fighting. {E148} Their technology allowed Minos to build a fleet and gain dominion of the seas. The Curetes established the trades of metallurgy and carpentry in Greece, which are the foundation of the manual trades. The fleet of Minos did not have sails, and Daedalus fled from Minos by adding sails to his ship. {*Pausanias, Boeotia, l. 9. c. 11. s. 4. 4:219} Greek ships did not have sails before the flight of Daedalus and the death of Minos. Minos was killed in pursuing Daedalus to Sicily in the reign of Rehoboam. Daedalus and his nephew Talus, in the latter part of the reign of Solomon, invented the chip axe, the saw, the auger, the plumb level, the compass, the turning lathe, glue and the potter's wheel. Eupalamus, the father of Daedalus, invented the anchor. This was the beginning of the manual arts and trades in Europe.

340. The Curetes, who thus introduced letters, music, poetry, dancing and arts, and attended to the sacrifices, were no less active about religious institutions. For their skill, knowledge and mystical practices, they were accounted wise men and conjurers by the common people. {*Strabo, l. 10. c. 3. s. 19-22. (472,473) 5:111-117} In Phrygia their mysteries were about Rhea (Cretan), called *Magna Mater* or *Great Mother* and the mysteries were named from the places where she was worshipped: Cybele, Berecynthia, Pessinuntia, Dindymene, Mygdonia and Idean Phrygia. {E149}

341. In Crete and the *Terra Curetum* or the *Land of the Curetes*, the mysteries were about Jupiter Olympius, the son of the Rhea (Cretan). They say that when Jupiter (Cretan) was born in Crete, his mother Rhea (Cretan) had him raised in a cave in Mount Ida under their care. {*Strabo, l. 10. c. 3. s. 11. (468) 5:97} {*Strabo, l. 10. c. 10. s. 19. (472) 5:111} {*Diod. Sic., l. 5. c. 70. s. 2,3. 3:287} The Curetes danced about Jupiter (Cretan) in their armour, with a great noise so that his father Saturn (Cretan) might not hear him cry. When Jupiter (Cretan) was grown up, they assisted him in conquering his father and his father's friends. In memory of these deeds they instituted their mysteries. {*Lucian, On Sacrifices, l. 1. (10-13) 3:165-169} {*Apollodorus, Library, l. 1. c. 1. s. 5-7. 1:1,2} {*Apollodorus, Library, l. 1. c. 2. 1:9-15} Bochart says that they came from Palestine and thinks that they had the name of Curetes from the people among the Philistines called Crethim, or Cerethites since the Philistines conquered Sidon and mixed with the Sidonians. {Bochart, Canaan, l. 1. c. 15.} {Eze 25:16 Zep 2:5 1Sa 30:14}

342. The first two kings of Crete, who reigned after the coming of the Curetes, were Asterius and Minos. Europa was the queen of Asterius and the mother of Minos. The Idean Dactyli were her fellow countrymen and accompanied her and her brother Alymnus into Crete. They lived in an Idean cave in her reign and there raised Jupiter. They discovered the process for smelting iron and made armour. Therefore, these three, Asterius, Europa, and Minos, must be the Saturn (Cretan), Rhea (Cretan) and Jupiter of the Cretans. Minos is usually called the son of Jupiter. {E150} However, this is in relation to the fable that Jupiter in the shape of a bull, the ensign of the ship, carried away Europa from Sidon.

343. When the Phoenicians first came into Greece, they gave the name of *Jao-pater* or *Jupiter*, to every king. Thus both Minos and his father were *Jupiters*. Echemenes, an ancient author cited by Athenaeus, says that Minos was that Jupiter who kidnapped Ganymede. {*Athenaeus, l. 13. (601e) 6:243} Others say more accurately that it was Tantalus. Minos alone was that Jupiter who was most famous among the Greeks for dominion and justice. He was the greatest king in all Greece in those days, and the only legislator.

344. Plutarch relates that the people of Naxos, contrary to what others have written, pretended that there were two Minoses and two Ariadnes; the first Ariadne married Bacchus and the last one was carried away by Theseus. {*Plutarch, Lives-Theseus, l. 1. c. 20. s. 5. 1:43} Homer, Hesiod, Thucydides, Herodotus and Strabo only knew of one Minos. Homer describes him to be the son of Jupiter and Europa, and the brother of Rhadamanthus and Sarpedon. Minos was the father of Deucalion the Argonaut and the grandfather of Idomeneus who fought at Troy and was the ruler of the underworld. {*Homer, Iliad, l. 13. v. 449-454. 2:35} {*Homer, Iliad, l. 23. v. 448-451. 2:527} {*Homer, Odyssey, l. 11. v. 320-325. 1:423,425} {*Homer, Odyssey, l. 19. v. 180-183. 1:247} Herodotus has Minos, Sarpedon and Rhadamanthus, the three sons of Europa, as contemporaries with Aegeus. {*Herodotus, l. 1. c. 173. 1:217} {E151} Apollodorus and Hyginus state that Minos, the father of Androgeus, Ariadne and Phaedra, was the son of Jupiter and Europa, and the brother of Rhadamanthus and Sarpedon. {*Apollodorus, Library, l. 3. c. 1. s. 1. 1:299} {*Hyginus, Fabulae, l. 1. c. 40-42. 1:113} {*Hyginus, Fabulae, l. 1. c. 178. 1:156}

345. Lucian states that Europa, the mother of Minos, was worshipped by the name of Rhea (Cretan), in the form of a woman sitting in a chariot drawn by lions, with a drum in her hand and a crown of towers on her head like Astarte and Isis. {*Lucian, The Goddess of Surrye, l. 1. (4) 4:341} The Cretans showed the foundations of the house where this Rhea (Cretan) lived, and a cypress grove which was dedicated to her from ancient times. {*Diod. Sic., l. 5. c. 66. s. 1. 3:275} Apollonius Rhodius states that Saturn (Cretan) (while he reigned over the Titans in Mount Olympus in Crete and Jupiter was being raised by the Curetes in a cave in Crete) deceived Rhea (Cretan) and fathered a son Chiron by Philyra. {*Apollonius, Argonautica, l. 2. v. 1233-1237. 1:187} Therefore, the Saturn (Cretan) and Rhea (Cretan) were only one generation older than Chiron, and by consequence not older than Asterius and Europa, the parents of Minos, for Chiron lived until after the Argonaut Expedition and had two grandsons in that expedition. Europa came into Crete about a hundred years before that expedition, around 1033 BC.

346. Lucian says that the Cretans not only relate that Jupiter was born and buried among them but also showed his grave. {*Lucian, On Sacrifices, l. 1. (10) 3:165,167} Porphyry mentions that Pythagoras entered the Idean cave to see Jupiter's grave. {Porphyry, Life of Pythagoras} {E152} Cicero, in listing three Jupiters, says that the third was

the Cretan Jupiter, the son of Saturn (Cretan), whose grave is shown in Crete. {*Cicero, De Natura Deorum, l. 3. c. 19. (53) 19:337} Callimachus states:

Cretans are ever liars. Yet a tomb, oh Lord, for the Cretans built; but thou didst not die, for thou art for ever. {*Callimachus, Hymn to Zeus, l. 1. v. 8,9. 1:37}

347. The scholiast in commenting on Callimachus says that this was the sepulchre of Minos.

Εν Κρητη επι τωι ταφωι του Μινωος επεγεγραπτο, ΜΙΝΩΟΣ ΤΟΥ ΔΙΟΣ ΤΑΦΟΣ. τωι χρονωι δε του Μινωος απηλειφθη, ωστε περιλειφθηναι ΔΙΟΣ ΤΑΦΟΣ. εκ τουτου ουν εχειν λεγουσι Κρητες τον ταφον του Διος.

In Crete upon the tomb of Minos has been written *The grave of Minos the Jupiter.* Now the chronological time from [the days of] Minos has [long ago] passed away, so that what remains [now] is [only what looks like] *the grave of Jupiter.* From this, therefore, they have the saying *Crete, the location of Jupiter's tomb.*

10. The Saturn of Italy

348. In Crete, upon the tomb of Minos was written, *Minois Iovis Sepulchrum*: the tomb of Minos Jupiter. Over time the word *Minois* eroded away so that there remained only the words *Iovis Sepulchrum* and hence the Cretans called it the tomb of Jupiter. By Saturn (Cretan), Cicero, who was a Latin, understood this to be the Saturn of the Latins since after Saturn was expelled from his kingdom, he fled from Crete by sea and there to Italy. The poets relate this by saying that Jupiter cast him down to Tartarus, that is, into the sea. Since he was hiding in Italy, the Latins called him *Saturn*, and Italy, *Saturnia*, and *Latium*, and themselves *Latins*. Cyprian states:

The cave of Jupiter is to be seen in Crete, and his sepulchre is shown; and it is manifest that Saturn (Cretan) was driven away by him, and that from him Latium received its name, as being his lurking place. He was the first that taught to print letters; he was the first that taught to stamp money in Italy, and thence the treasury is called the treasury of Saturn (Cretan). And he also was the cultivator of the rustic life, whence he is painted as a man carrying a sickle. {*Cyprian, Vanity of Idols, Trestise 6. s. 2. ANF5:466} {E153}

349. Minutius Felix says:

This Saturn (Cretan) then, driven from Crete by the fear of his raging son, had come to Italy, and received by the hospitality of Janus, taught those unskilled and rustic men many things—as, being something of a Greek, and polished—to print letters, for instance, to coin money, to make instruments. Therefore, he preferred that his hiding place, because he had been safely hidden there, should be called *Latium*; and he gave a city, from his own name, the name of *Saturnia*. . . . His son Jupiter reigned at Crete after his father was driven out. There he died, there he had sons. To this day the cave of Jupiter is visited, and his sepulchre is shown, and he is convicted of being human by those very sacred rites of his. {*Minutius Felix, The Octavius, l. 1. c. 22. ANF4:186}

350. Tertullian also states:

So far as the question depends on the facts, I find none more trustworthy than those—that in Italy itself we have a country in which, after many expeditions, and having partaken of Attic hospitalities, Saturn (Cretan) settled, obtaining cordial welcome from Janus, or, as the Salii will have it, Janis. The mountain on which he dwelt was called *Saturnia* to this day; last of all, the whole of Italy, after having borne the name of *Oenotria*, was called *Saturnia* from him. He first gave you the art of writing, and a stamped coinage, and thence it is he who presides over the public treasury. {*Tertullian, Apology, l. 1. c. 10. ANF3:26,27}

351. Saturn (Cretan) brought into Italy writing, the coining of money, the knowledge of agriculture, making instruments, and constructing towns. Therefore, we know before he fled from Crete, writing, the coining of money, and manual arts were brought into Europe by the Phoenicians. He left Attica after agriculture was brought into Greece by Ceres. So Saturn (Cretan) could not be older than Asterius, and Europa could not be older than her brother Cadmus. {E154} Since Italy was called Oenotria before it was called Saturnia, you may know that Saturn (Cretan) came into Italy after Oenotrus, and so he was not older than the sons of Lycaon. Oenotrus led the first colony of the Greeks into Italy, Saturn (Cretan) the second, and Evander the third. The Latins know of nothing older in Italy than Janus and Saturn (Cretan). Therefore, Oenotrus was the Janus of the Latins, and Saturn (Cretan) was contemporary with the sons of Lycaon, and by consequence also with Celeus, Erechtheus, Ceres and Asterius. Ceres educated Triptolemus, the son of Celeus, in the reign of Erechtheus and then taught him and his people how to sow grain. Arcas, the son of Callisto, and the grandson of Lycaon, received grain from Triptolemus and taught his people to make bread from it. Procris, the daughter of Erechtheus, fled to Minos, who was the son of Asterius.

352. In memory of Saturn's coming into Italy by sea, the Latins coined their first money, with his head on one side and a ship on the other. Macrobius says that after Saturn disappeared, Janus erected an altar to him with sacred rites as to a god and instituted the Saturnalia and that human sacrifices were offered to him. Janus named the area he controlled *Saturnia.* {*Macrobius, Saturnalia, l. 1. c. 7. s. 24. 1:59} These sacrifices continued until Hercules (Egyptian) drove the cattle of Geryon through Italy and abolished that custom. {*E155*} We know that Janus was from the family of Lycaon since he offered human sacrifices. This behaviour agrees with what we know of Oenotrus. Dionysius Halicarnassus says that Oenotrus found in the western part of Italy a large, thinly populated region suitable for pasture and agriculture. In a certain part of it, he expelled the inhabitants and built small, numerous towns on the hills after the manner of building that was familiar to the ancients. This was the origin of towns in Italy. {*Dionysius, l. 1. c. 12. s. 1. 1:37}

11. The Olympic Games

353. Pausanias states that the people of Elis, who were the best skilled in history stated that this was the origin of the Olympic Games. Saturn (Cretan) reigned first and had a temple built to him in Olympia by the men of the Golden Age. When Jupiter was born, his mother Rhea (Cretan) gave him into the care of the Idean Dactyli, who were also called the Curetes. Afterward five of them came from Mount Ida in Crete into Elis. They were Hercules (Idean), Poeonius, Epimedes, Jasius and Ida. Hercules was also called the Idean Hercules and was the oldest of the five brothers, instituting the game of racing in memory of the war between Saturn and Jupiter. The victor was awarded an olive crown. He erected there an altar to Jupiter Olympius and called these games *Olympic.* {*E156*} {*Pausanias, Elis I, l. 5. c. 7. 2:417} {*Pausanias, Elis I, l. 5. c. 13,14. 2:451-465} {*Pausanias, Arcadia, l. 8. c. 2. 3:315-355} Some of the Eleans said that Jupiter fought here with Saturn for the kingdom while others said that Hercules (Idean) instituted these games in memory of their victory over the Titans.

354. The people of Arcadia had a tradition that the Titans fought with the gods in the valley of Bathos near the Alpheus River and the spring called Olympias. {*Pausanias, Arcadia, l. 8. c. 29. s. 1. 4:49} Before the reign of Asterius, his father Teutamus came into Crete with a colony from Olympia. {*Diod. Sic., l. 5. c. 80. s. 2. 3:3177} After the flight of Asterius, some of his friends likely retired with him into their own country, and were pursued and defeated there by Hercules (Idean). The Eleans said also that Clymenus, the grandson of Hercules (Idean), about fifty years after Deucalion's flood, came from Crete and celebrated these games again in Olympia. He erected there an altar to Juno Olympia, that is, to Europa, and another to this Hercules (Idean) and the rest of the Curetes. Clymenus reigned in Elis until he was deposed by Endymion. {*Pausanias, Elis I, l. 5. c. 8. s. 1,2. 2:419,421} {*Pausanias, Elis I, l. 5. c. 14. s. 8. 2:463} He celebrated these games again and so did Pelops, who expelled his son Aetolus. Likewise Hercules (Idean), the son of Alcmena, and Atreus, the son of Pelops, and Oxylus also celebrated these games. They might be celebrated originally in triumph for victories:

1) Hercules (Idean) after his conquest of Saturn and the Titans,

2) Clymenus after his return to the land of the Curetes (*Terra Curetum*) to reign, {*E157*}

3) Endymion after conquering Clymenus,

4) Pelops after conquering Aetolus,

5) Hercules (Idean) after he killed Augeas,

6) Atreus after repelling the invasion of the Heraclides,

7) Oxylus after the Heraclides returned into Peloponnesus.

355. This Jupiter, to whom the games were instituted, had a temple and altar erected to him in Olympia where the games were celebrated, hence the place was called Jupiter Olympius. Olympia was a place on the confines of Pisa near the Alpheus River.

12. The Origin of the Mysteries and Temples

356. On the island of Thasos, where Cadmus left his brother Thasus, the Phoenicians built a temple to Hercules Olympius. {*Herodotus, l. 2. c. 44. 1:331} This is the Hercules whom Cicero calls

> the Idean Dactyli of Mount Ida (in Crete) offer sacrifices at his (Hercules') tomb. {*Cicero, De Natura Deorum, l. 3. c. 16. (42) 19:325}

357. When the mysteries of Ceres were instituted in Eleusis by Eumolpus, there were other mysteries instituted to her and her daughter and daughter's husband, in the island of Samothrace, by the Phoenician names of *Dii Cabiri Axieros, Axiokersa* and *Axiokerses* that is, the great gods *Ceres, Proserpina* and *Pluto.* Jasius, a Samothracian, whose sister married Cadmus, was acquainted with Ceres, and both Cadmus and Jasius were initiated into these mysteries. {*Diod. Sic., l. 5. c. 48. s. 5. 3:233} {E158}

358. Jasius was the brother of Dardanus, and married Cybele the daughter of Meones, the king of Phrygia, and by her had a son Corybas. After his death, Dardanus, Cybele and Corybas went into Phrygia, and initiated the mysteries of the *Mother of the Gods* there. Cybele called the goddess after her own name and Corybas called her priests *Corybantes*. {*Diod. Sic., l. 5. c. 49. s. 3. 3:233,235} However, Dionysius says that Dardanus instituted the Samothracian mysteries, and that his wife Chryses learned about them in Arcadia. Later, Idaeus, the son of Dardanus, instituted the mysteries of the *Mother of the Gods* in Phrygia. {*Dionysius, l. 1. c. 61. s. 4. 1:203,205} {*Dionysius, l. 1. c. 68. s. 3. 1:225} This Phrygian goddess was drawn in a chariot by lions and had a *corona turrita*, a crown of towers, on her head and a drum in her hand like the Phoenician goddess Astarte. The Corybantes danced in armour at her sacrifices in a furious manner like the Idean Dactyli. Lucian says that she was the Cretan Rhea, that is, Europa the mother of Minos. {*Lucian, Dance, l. 1. (8) 5:221} Thus the Phoenicians introduced the practice of deifying dead men and women among the Greeks and Phrygians, for I find no instance of deifying dead men and women in Greece before the coming of Cadmus and Europa from Sidon. {E159}

359. From these origins it came into fashion among the Greeks to celebrate the funerals of dead parents with festivals and invocations. They offered sacrifices to their ghosts and erected magnificent sepulchres in the form of temples, with altars and statues to famous persons. They publicly honoured them in these temples. Each man might do this for his ancestors, and the cities of Greece did it for all the eminent Greeks:

1) Europa, the sister of Cadmus,

2) Alymnus, the brother of Cadmus,

3) Minos and Rhadamanthus, the nephews of Cadmus,

4) Ino, the daughter of Cadmus,

5) Melicertus, the son of Ino,

6) Bacchus, the son of Semele, the daughter of Cadmus,

7) Aristaeus, the husband of Autonoe, the daughter Cadmus,

8) Jasius, the brother of Harmonia,

9) Hercules (Idean), a Theban,

10) Alcmena, the mother of Hercules (Idean),

11) Danae, the daughter of Acrisius,

12) Aesculapius and Polemocrates, the sons of Machaon,

13) Pandion and Theseus, the kings of Athens,

14) Hippolytus, the son of Theseus,

15) Pan, the son of Penelope,

16) Proserpina,

17) Triptolemus,

18) Celeus,

19) Trophonius,

20) Castor,

21) Pollux,

22) Helen,

23) Menelaus,

24) Agamemnon,

25) Amphiaraus and his son Amphilochus,

26) Hector and Alexandra, the son and the daughter of Priam,

27) Phoroneus,

28) Orpheus,

29) Protesilaus,

30) Achilles and his mother Thetis,

31) Ajax,

32) Arcas,

33) Idomeneus,

34) Meriones,

35) Aeacus,

37) Melampus,

38) Britomartis,

39) Adrastus,

40) Iolaus, etc. {E160}

360. They deified their dead in various ways according to their abilities and circumstances and the merits of the person. Some were only in private families, as household gods or *Dii Paenates*; while others were honoured by erecting gravestones to them in public places, to be used as altars for annual sacrifices. Still others were honoured with sepulchres in the form of houses or temples. Some had mysteries, ceremonies,

sacrifices, festivals, initiations, and a succession of priests for performing those institutions in the temples and handing them down to posterity.

361. Altars might have begun to be erected in Europe a little before the days of Cadmus, for sacrificing to the old god or gods of the colonies, but temples began to be built in the days of Solomon. Aeacus, the son of Aegina, who was two generations older than the Trojan War, is by some reputed one of the first to have built a temple in Greece around 970 BC. {*Arnobius, Adversus Nationes, l. 6. c. 3. Internet} Oracles came first from Egypt into Greece about the same time, as did the custom of forming the images of the gods with their legs bound up in the shape of the mummies of Egypt.

362. Idolatry had began in Chaldea and Egypt and spread from there into Phoenicia and the neighbouring countries, long before it came into Europe. The Pelasgians propagated it in Greece by the dictates of the oracles. {E161} The countries on the Tigris and the Nile Rivers were exceedingly fertile and were the first to be inhabited by mankind after the flood of Noah. These areas were the first to become kingdoms and therefore, they were the first to worship their dead kings and queens. Hence came the gods of Laban, the gods and goddesses called Baal and Ashtaroth from the Canaanites, the demons or ghosts to whom they sacrificed, and the Moloch to whom they offered their children in the days of Moses and the judges. Every city inaugurated worship to its own founder and kings and by alliances and conquests they spread this worship. Finally, the Phoenicians and Egyptians brought the practice of deifying the dead into Europe.

363. The kingdom of Lower Egypt began to worship their kings before the days of Moses, which is expressly forbidden in the second commandment. {Ex 20:2-5} When the Shepherds invaded Lower Egypt, they stopped this worship of the former Egyptians and replaced it with the worship of their kings. Finally, the Egyptians of Coptos and Thebes, under Misphragmuthosis and his son Amosis I, expelled the Shepherds. They stopped the worship of the gods of the Shepherds and they deified their own kings and princes. They propagated the worship of twelve of them throughout their conquests. They made them more universal than the false gods of any other nation that had been before them, so much so as to be called *Dii magni maiorum gentium.* or the *Great Gods of the Greater Nations.* {E162} Sesostris conquered Thrace, and Amphictyon, the son of Prometheus, brought the twelve gods from Thrace into Greece. Herodotus states that they came from Egypt. {*Herodotus, l. 2. c. 4. 1:279} The Egyptians named their cities after these gods, as

one can tell by the Egyptian origin of the names. The Egyptians, according to Diodorus, usually say that after the reign of their Saturn and Rhea (Egyptian), then reigned Jupiter and Juno, the parents of Osiris and Isis and the grandparents of Orus and Bubaste. {*Diod. Sic., l. 1. c. 13. s. 2. 1:47}

13. The Four Ages

364. By all this it may be understood that as the Egyptians who deified their kings, began their kingdom with the reign of their gods and heroes, considered Menes the first man who reigned after their gods. Likewise, the Cretans had the ages of their gods and heroes, calling the first four ages of their deified kings and princes, the Golden, Silver, Bronze and Iron Ages.

365. Hesiod in describing these four ages of the gods and demigods of Greece, represents them to be four generations of men, each of which ended when the men then living grew old and died. He says that the fourth age ended with the wars of Thebes (Greek) and Troy. {*Hesiod, Works and Days, l. 1. v. 109-170. 1:101} Hence, there were four generations from the coming of the Phoenicians and Curetes with Cadmus and Europa into Greece, to the time of the destruction of Troy. {E163} Apollonius Rhodius says that when the Argonauts came to Crete, they killed Talus, a man who remained of those who were from the Bronze Age and guarded the pass. {*Apollonius, Argonautica, l. 4. v. 1637-1644. 1:407} Talus was reputed to be the son of Minos, and therefore the sons of Minos lived in the Bronze Age and Minos reigned in the Silver Age.

366. In the Silver Age of the Greeks, they began to plow and sow grain. It was Ceres who taught them how to do it, and she lived in the reign of Celeus, Erechtheus and Minos. Mythologists claim that Alcmena was the last woman with whom Jupiter had sexual relations. Thereby they seem to mark the end of the reign of Jupiter among mortals and the Silver Age, when Alcmena was pregnant with Hercules (Idean). Therefore, he was born about the eighth or tenth year of Rehoboam's reign, around 966 BC, and was about thirty-four years old at the time of the Argonaut Expedition in 933 BC.

367. Chiron was the son of Saturn (Cretan) and Philyra in the Golden Age when Jupiter was a child in the cave in Crete, as noted previously. This was in the reign of Asterius, the king of Crete. Therefore, Asterius reigned in Crete in the Golden Age, and the Silver Age began when Chiron was a child. If Chiron was born about the thirty-fifth year of David's reign, he would have been born in the reign of Asterius, when

Jupiter was a child in the Cretan cave around 1020 BC. {E164} He would be about eighty-eight years old at the time of the Argonaut Expedition in 933 BC, when he invented the constellations and this is possible since people do live to that age. Therefore, the Golden Age was about the same time as the reign of Asterius and the Silver Age with that of Minos. To make these ages much longer than ordinary generations, is to make Chiron live much longer than is humanly possible. This fable of the four ages seems to have been made by the Curetes in the fourth age or the Iron Age. This was likely done in memory of or to honour the following first four generations of their coming into Europe, as into a new world:

1) their country woman Europa and her husband Asterius, the Saturn (Cretan) of the Latins,

2) Europa's son Minos who was Jupiter (Cretan)

3) Europa's grandson Deucalion, who reigned until the Argonaut expedition and is sometimes considered an Argonaut

4) Europa's great-grandson Idomeneus who fought at Troy.

368. Hesiod says that he himself lived in the fifth age, the age after the taking of Troy, and therefore he lived within thirty or thirty-five years after it around 870 BC. {*Hesiod, Works and Days, l. 1. v. 174,175. 1:101} Homer was about the same age, for he lived some time with Mentor in Ithaca and learned there from him many things concerning Ulysses, with whom Mentor had been personally acquainted. {Vita Homeri Herodoto adser.} Herodotus, the oldest extant historian of the Greeks, says that Hesiod and Homer were not more than four hundred years older than himself. {*Herodotus, l. 2. c. 53. 1:341} {E165} Therefore, they lived within one hundred and ten or twenty years after the death of Solomon around 865 BC, and according to my calculations, the taking of Troy was only one generation earlier.

369. Mythologists claim that Niobe, the daughter of Phoroneus, was the first woman with whom Jupiter had sexual relations and she gave him the son Argus. He succeeded Phoroneus in the kingdom of Argos and gave his name to that city. Therefore, Argus was born in the beginning of the Silver Age, unless by Jupiter they meant Asterius. For the Phoenicians gave the name of Jupiter to every king from the time of their first coming into Greece with Cadmus and Europa, until the invasion of Greece by Sesostris and the birth of Hercules (Idean). In particular, they gave it to the father of Minos, Pelops, Lacedemon, Aeacus, and Perseus.

370. The first four ages succeeded the flood of Deucalion. Some say that Deucalion was the son of Prometheus (who had a brother named Atlas) and the grandson of Japetus. However, this was another Deucalion, for Japetus the father of Prometheus, Epimetheus and Atlas, was an Egyptian, the brother of Osiris, and lived two generations after the flood of Deucalion.

14. Summary of Major Conclusions

371. I have now taken the chronology of the Greeks as far as:

1) The beginning of writing,

2) The beginning of plowing and sowing of grain,

3) The beginning of the manufacturing of copper and iron,

4) The beginning in Europe of the trades:

4a) metallurgy,

4b) carpenters,

4c) joiners,

4d) turners,

4e) brickmakers,

4f) stonemasons,

4g) potters,

5) The beginning of the first walled cities,

6) The beginning of the building of temples,

7) The origin of oracles in Greece,

8) The beginning of navigation by the stars in long ships with sails,

9) The start of the Amphictyonic Council,

10) The first ages of Greece, the Golden, Silver, Bronze and Iron Ages,

11) The flood of Deucalion, which immediately preceded these ages.

372. Those ages could not be earlier than the discovery and use of the four metals in Greece, from which the ages had their names. The flood of Ogyges could not be older than two or three generations before the flood of Deucalion, for among such wandering people as were then in Europe, there could be no memory of things done more than three or four generations before written records.

15. The Expulsion of the Shepherds

373. The expulsion of the Shepherds from Egypt was the reason for the first migration of people from Egypt

into Greece and the building of houses and villages in Greece. This could scarcely be earlier than the days of Eli and Samuel for Manetho says that when the Shepherds were forced to abandon Abaris and leave Egypt, they went through the wilderness into Palestine and built Jerusalem around 1120 BC. {E167} I do not agree with Manetho that they were the Israelites under Moses, but rather believe that they were Canaanites. After they abandoned Abaris, they lived among the Philistines, their closest neighbours, although some of them might be conscripted by David and Solomon to help build Jerusalem and the temple.

374. Saul was appointed king to deliver Israel from the Philistines, who oppressed them. {1Sa 9:16 13:19,20} In the second year of his reign in 1094 BC, the Philistines brought into the field against him

> thirty thousand chariots, and six thousand horsemen, and people as the sand which is on the seashore for multitude. {1Sa 13:5}

375. The Canaanites obtained their horses from Egypt and yet in the days of Moses, Pharaoh only had six hundred chariots of Egypt with which he pursued Israel. {Ex 14:7} From the large army of the Philistines against Saul, and the great number of their horses, I seem to gather that the Shepherds had recently been driven from Egypt and joined the Philistines. The Shepherds might be defeated and driven from most of Egypt and confined in Abaris by Misphragmuthosis in the latter end of the days of Eli. Some would flee to the Philistines and strengthen them against Israel, in the last year of Eli in 1117 BC.

376. Some of the Shepherds might hve gone from the Philistines to Sidon, and from Sidon, migrated by sea to Asia Minor and Greece. Afterward, just before the reign of Saul, the Shepherds who still remained in Egypt might have been forced by Tethmosis or Amosis I, the son of Misphragmuthosis, to leave Abaris and retire in very large numbers to the Philistines, around 1096 BC. On these occasions several of them, as Pelasgus, Inachus, Lelex, Cecrops I and Abas, might have come with their people by sea from Egypt to Sidon and Cyprus, and from there to Asia Minor and Greece, in the days of Eli, Samuel and Saul. Thereby they would have initiated commerce by sea between Sidon and Greece before the revolt of Edom from Judah and the final coming of the Phoenicians from the Red Sea.

377. According to Pherecydes Atheniensis, Pelasgus reigned in Arcadia, and was the father of Lycaon, and he died just before the flood of Deucalion. Therefore, his father, Pelasgus, might have come into Greece about two generations earlier than Cadmus or about

eleven years after the death of Eli, around 1106 BC. Lycaon sacrificed children, therefore his father might with his people have come from the Shepherds in Egypt and perhaps from the regions of Heliopolis, where they sacrificed men until Amosis I abolished that custom. {E169} Misphragmuthosis, the father of Amosis I, expelled the Shepherds from most of Egypt and confined the rest in Abaris. After this, large numbers might have escaped to Greece, some from the regions of Heliopolis under Pelasgus, and others from Memphis and other places under other leaders. Hence, it might happen that the Pelasgians were originally very numerous in Greece, did not speak Greek, and were the instigators in bringing the worship of the dead into Greece.

16. The Kingdom of Sicyon in Greece

378. Inachus is called the son of Oceanus, perhaps because he came to Greece by sea. He might have come with his people to Argos from Egypt in the days of Eli around 1120 BC. He established himself on the Inachus River which was named after him. He left his lands to his sons Phoroneus, Aegialeus and Phegeus, in the days of Samuel, since Car the son of Phoroneus built a temple to Ceres in Megara. Therefore he was contemporary with Erechtheus. Phoroneus reigned at Argos and Aegialeus at Sicyon and founded those kingdoms and yet Aegialeus is said to be more than five hundred years older than his brother Phoroneus by some chronologers! Acusilaus, Anticlides and Plato consider Phoroneus to be the oldest king in Greece. {*Clement, Stromata, l. 1. c. 21. ANF2:324} {*Pliny, l. 7. c. 56. (194) 2:637} {*Plato, Timaeus, l. 1. (22A) 9:33} Apollodorus says Aegialeus was the brother of Phoroneus. {*Apollodorus, Library, l. 2. c. 1. s. 1. 1:129}

379. Aegialeus died without an heir and after him reigned Europs, Telchin, Apis, Lamedon, Sicyon, Polybus, Adrastus and Agamemnon. The kingdom was named after Sicyon. Herodotus says that Apis in the Greek language is Epaphus. {*Herodotus, l. 2. c. 153. 1:465} Hyginus states that Epaphus, the Sicyonian, impregnated Antiope. {*Hyginus, Fabulae, l. 1. c. 7. 1:98} The later Greeks have created two men from the two names Apis and Epaphus or Epopeus from this one person and inserted between them twelve imaginary kings of Sicyon who did nothing noteworthy and yet reigned five hundred and twenty years, each who reigned an average of forty-three years! If these imaginary kings are deleted and the two kings Apis and Epopeus are reunited into one person then Aegialeus was contemporary with his brother Phoroneus, as he ought to be, for Apis or Epopeus and Nycteus, the guardian of Labdacus, were killed in battle about the tenth year of Solomon around 1005 BC, as noted previously.

380. The first four kings of Sicyon: Aegialeus, Europs, Telchin and Apis Epaphus, would reign about seventy-one years assuming an average reign of twenty years for the first three and ten or eleven for the last king since he died in battle. Counting back from the tenth year of Solomon in 1005 BC, places the beginning of the reign of Aegialeus about the twentieth year of Saul and about that time Phoroneus began to reign in Argos around 1076 BC. Apollodorus calls Adrastus the king of Argos. {*Apollodorus, Library, l. 3. c. 6. s. 1. 1:353} However, Homer states that he reigned first at Sicyon and was in the first war against Thebes (Greek). {*Homer, Iliad, l. 2. v. 574-579. 1:103,105} {E171} Some place Janiscus and Phaestus between Polybus and Adrastus, but without any degree of certainty.

381. Lelex likely came with his colony into Laconia in the days of Eli, around 1120 BC and left his lands to his sons Myles, Eurotas, Cleson and Polycaon in the days of Samuel around 1106 BC. Myles set up a quern or hand mill to grind grain and is reputed to be the first among the Greeks who did this. However, he lived before Triptolemus and seems to have had his grain and craftsmen from Egypt. Eurotas the brother, or as some say the son of Myles, built Sparta and called it after the name of his daughter Sparta, the wife of Lacedemon and the mother of Eurydice. Cleson, who was the father of Pylas and the grandfather of Sciron, married the daughter of Pandion the son of Erechtheus, and quarrelled with Nisus, the brother of Aegeus and sons of Pandion, for the kingdom. Aeacus arbitrated the dispute in favour of Nisus. Polycaon invaded Messene at that time which was only populated by villages. He called it Messene after the name of his wife and built cities there.

382. Cecrops I came from Sais in Egypt to Cyprus and from there into Attica, likely in the days of Eli around 1121 BC. There he married Agraule, the daughter of Actaeus, and succeeded him in Attica soon after. {E172} He left his kingdom to Cranaus in the days of Saul or in the beginning of the reign of David around 1060 BC, for the flood of Deucalion happened in the reign of Cranaus.

383. Ogyges was about the same age as Pelasgus, Inachus, Lelex, and Actaeus. He reigned in Boeotia and some of his people were Leleges. Either he or his son Eleusinus built the city of Eleusis in Attica, that is, they built a few clay brick houses. In time the settlement grew into a city. Acusilaus wrote that Phoroneus was older than Ogyges, and that Ogyges lived one thousand and twenty years before the first Olympiad in 1796 BC, as noted previously! However, Acusilaus was from Argos and imagined these things to honour his country. To the ancient Greeks, anything called *Ogygian* means they are as old as the first memory of things. We have now gone back as far as possible into the history of the Greeks. Inachus might be as old as Ogyges but Acusilaus and his followers said they were seven hundred years older than the truth. Chronologers, to justify this fiction, have multiplied the numbers of the kings of Argos and Sicyon and changed several contemporary rulers of Argos into successive kings and inserted many imaginary kings into the line of the kings of Sicyon.

384. Inachus had several sons, who reigned in various parts of Peloponnesus and built towns there. {E173} His son Phoroneus built Phoronicum, which was later called Argos after Argus his grandson. Aegialeus built Aegialea, which was later called Sicyon after Sicyon the grandson of Erechtheus. Phegeus built Phegea, which was later called Psophis after Psophis, the daughter of Lycaon. These were the oldest towns in Peloponnesus. Later, Sisyphus (the son of Aeolus and grandson of Hellen) built Ephyra, which was later called Corinth. Aethlius, the son of Aeolus, built Elis. Before these, Cecrops I built Cecropia, the citadel of Athens. Lycaon built Lycosura, which was considered the oldest town in Arcadia. Each of his twenty-four sons built a town, except for the youngest. He was called Oenotrus, who grew up after his father's death, and sailed into Italy with his people. There he started the practice of building towns and became the Janus of the Latins. Phoroneus also had several children and grandchildren, who reigned in various places and built new towns, as Car, Apis, etc. Haemon, the son of Pelasgus and the father of Thessalus, reigned in Haemonia, later called Thessaly, and built towns there.

385. This division and subdivision has made great confusion in the history of the first kingdoms of Peloponnesus and by this given occasion to the vain glorious Greeks to make those kingdoms much older than they really were. {E174} However, by all the calculations mentioned previously, the first civilising of the Greeks and teaching them to live in houses and towns, and the oldest towns in Europe, could scarcely be more than two or three generations older than the arrival of Cadmus from Sidon into Greece. It is likely that the arrival of Cadmus was the result of the expulsion of the Shepherds from Egypt in the days of Eli, Samuel and Saul around 1120 BC to 960 BC. They fled to Greece in considerable numbers. However, it is difficult to correct the genealogies and chronology of the fabulous ages of the Greeks and I leave these things to be further examined.

17. The Origin of Athens

386. Before the Phoenicians introduced the deification of dead men, the Greeks had a council of elders in every town for its administration and had a place where the elders and people worshipped their god with sacrifices. When many of those towns, for their common safety, united under a common council, they erected a *prytaneum* or court in one of the towns. The council and people met there at certain times to consult about their common safety, to worship their common god with sacrifices, and to buy and sell. The Greeks called the towns where these councils met δημοι, peoples or communities, or corporation towns. {*E175*}

387. Finally, when many of these corporation towns for their common safety agreed to unite under one common council, they erected a πυροσταμειον or *prytaneum* or town hall in the corporate towns for the common council and people to meet in, to consult and worship in, to feast and buy and sell. They walled this corporate town for protection and called it την πολιν, *the city*. This I take to have been the origin of villages, market towns, cities, common councils, vestal temples, feasts and fairs in Europe. The town hall was a court with a place of worship where a perpetual fire was burning on an altar for sacrificing. From the word εσια, or *fire*, came the name *Vesta,*, which at length the people turned into a goddess, thus becoming fire worshippers like the ancient Persians. When these councils made war on their neighbours, they had a general commander to lead their armies, and he became their king.

388. Thucydides states that under Cecrops I and the ancient kings to the time of Theseus, Attica had always been divided into separate towns, each having magistrates and a town hall. They did not come together to consult with the king when there was no fear of danger, but each individually administered their own affairs and had their own council. Sometimes they even made war on the king, as the Eleusinians led by Eumolpus did against Erechtheus. {*E176*} When Theseus, a prudent and powerful man, became king, he abolished the courts and magistrates of the minor towns and compelled them all to meet in one council and town hall in Athens. {*Thucydides, l. 2. c. 15. s. 1. 1:289*} {*Plutarch, Lives-Theseus, l. 1. c. 24. 1:51,53*} Polemon, as he is cited by Strabo, says that in Attica, there were one hundred and seventy corporate towns, of which Eleusis was one. {*Strabo, l. 9. c. 1. s. 16. (396) 4:263*} Philochorus relates that when Attica was being devastated from the sea by the Carians and from land by the Boeotians, Cecrops I first consolidated one hundred and seventy towns into twelve cities, whose names were: Cecropia,

Tetrapolis, Epacria, Decelia, Eleusis, Aphydna, Thoricus, Brauron, Cytherus, Sphettus, Cephissia and Phalerus. Theseus consolidated these twelve cities to create Athens. {*Strabo, l. 9. c. 1. s. 19. (397) 4:267*}

18. The Kingdom of Argos

389. The kingdom of Argos came about in much the same manner. Pausanias states that Phoroneus, the son of Inachus, was the first who gathered the Argives into one city, who until then were scattered and lived in isolated families. They first assembled at Phoronicum, the city of Phoroneus. {*Pausanias, Corinth, l. 2. c. 15. s. 5. 1:327*} Homer calls all the places which he notes in Peloponnesus, with few exceptions, not cities but regions. The reason for this was that each of them consisted of a convention of many corporate towns, from which later larger cities were built and inhabited. {*Strabo, l. 8. c. 1. s. 3. (337) 4:23*} {*E177*} The Argives created Mantinaea in Arcadia from five towns, and Tegea from nine; and from so many was Heraea built by Cleombrotus, or by Cleonymus. So also Elis was built by the consolidation of many towns into one city.

390. The inhabitants of Arcadia consider Pelasgus the first man to inhabit their land and was their first king. He taught the unlearned people to build houses to protect them from the weather. He taught them to make clothes of skins and instead of eating any herbs and roots, which were sometimes poisonous, to eat the acorns of the beech tree. {*Pausanias, Arcadia, l. 8. c. 1. s. 4,5. 3:349*} His son Lycaon built the oldest city in all Greece. {*Pausanias, Arcadia, l. 8. c. 1. s. 1,2. 3:351*}

391. In the days of Lelex, the Spartans lived in individual villages. Therefore, the Greeks began to build houses and villages in the days of Pelasgus, the father of Lycaon, and Lelex, the father of Myles. This was about two or three generations before the flood of Deucalion and the coming of Cadmus into Greece for until then they lived in the forests and caves of the earth. The first houses were made of clay, until the brothers Euryalus and Hyperbius taught them to make and build with clay bricks. {*Pliny, l. 7. c. 56. (194) 2:637*} {*E178*} In the days of Ogyges, Pelasgus, Aezeus, Inachus and Lelex, Doxius, the son of Caelus, taught them to build houses using clay bricks and establish villages. In the days of Lycaon, Phoroneus, Aegialeus, Phegeus, Eurotas, Myles, Polycaon, and Cecrops I, and their sons, they began to consolidate the villages into corporate towns and from these into cities.

19. The Colonisation of Italy

392. When Oenotrus, the son of Lycaon, led a colony into Italy from Greece, he found that country for the most part uninhabited or lightly populated. He cleared some of it of the barbarians and built small unwalled towns contiguous to one another on the hills, which was the customary manner of habitation in use among the ancients. {*Dionysius, l. 1. c. 11,12. 1:35,37} After this, when the colony expanded and needed more land, they expelled the Sicels, surrounded many cities with walls and occupied all the territory between the two rivers of Liris and Tiber. {*Dionysius, l. 1. c. 9. s. 2. 1:29}

393. It is to be understood that those cities had their councils and town halls after the manner of the Greeks. Dionysius states that the new kingdom of Rome, as Romulus left it, consisted of thirty courts or councils in thirty towns. Each town had the sacred fire kept in the town hall of the court, for the senators who met there to perform sacred rites similar to the Greeks. {*Dionysius, l. 2. c. 7. s. 3,4. 1:33,335} {E179} When Numa, the successor of Romulus, reigned, he left various fires in their own courts and instituted one common to them all at Rome. Hence, Rome was not a single city before the days of Numa.

20. The Populating of the Mediterranean Islands

394. After navigation was greatly improved, the Phoenicians began to sail through the Mediterranean Sea navigating by the stars. It is likely that they began to discover the islands of the Mediterranean Sea and for the sake of trade to sail as far as Greece. It was not long after this that they kidnapped Io, the daughter of Inachus, from Argos. The Carians first infested the Greek seas with piracy. Then Minos, the son of Europa, assembled a powerful fleet, cleared the seas of pirates, and sent out colonies.

395. Diodorus says that the Cyclades Islands, those near Crete, were at first desolate and uninhabited. However, Minos with his powerful fleet, sent many colonies from Crete and populated many of them. {*Diod. Sic., l. 5. c. 78. s. 3,4. 3:311,312} {*Diod. Sic., l. 5. c. 84. s. 1. 3:325,327} In particular, the island of Carpathus was first settled by the soldiers of Minos. {*Diod. Sic., l. 5. c. 54. s. 4. 3:245} Syme was uninhabited until Triops arrived with a colony under Chthonius. Strongyle or Naxos was first inhabited by the Thracians in the days of Boreas around 935 BC, shortly before the Argonaut Expedition. {E180} Samos was at first deserted and inhabited only by a great number of fierce wild beasts until Macarius populated it, as he also did the islands of Chios and Cos. Lesbos was uninhabited until Xanthus sailed there with a colony. Likewise, Tenedos was uninhabited until Tennes sailed there from Troas around 915 BC, shortly before the Trojan

War. Aristaeus, who married Autonoe the daughter of Cadmus, led a colony from Thebes (Greek) into the uninhabited island of Caea. The island of Rhodes was first called Ophiusa and was full of snakes before Phorbas, a prince of Argos, went there and made it habitable by destroying the snakes. This was about the end of Solomon's reign around 975 BC. In his memory, Phorbas is commemorated in the heavens in the constellation of Ophiuchus, which is shaped like a man grasping a snake. Ammianus states concerning these islands:

Earthquakes . . . lift up the ground from far within, like a tide and force upward huge masses, as in Asia Delos came to the surface, and Hiera, Anaphe and Rhodes. . . . {*Ammianus, l. 17. c. 7. 1:349}

396. Likewise Pliny states:

The famous islands of Delos and Rhodes are recorded in history as having been born from the sea long ago, and subsequently smaller ones, Anaphe beyond Melos, Naea between Lemnos and the Dardanelles, Halone between Lebedos and Teos. . . . {*Pliny, l. 2. c. 89. (202) 1:333}

397. Diodorus says that the seven islands called the Aeolides between Italy and Sicily, were uninhabited until Lipparus and Aeolus settled there from Italy around 915 BC, shortly before the Trojan War. {*Diod. Sic., l. 5. c. 7. s. 5. 3:117} Also, Malta and Gaulus (now called Gozo), on the other side of Sicily, were first settled by the Phoenicians as was Madera outside the Strait of Gibraltar. {*Diod. Sic., l. 5. c. 12. s. 2,3. 3:129} {E181} Homer writes that Ulysses found the island of Ogygia covered with forests and uninhibited except by Calypso and her maids who lived in a cave. {*Homer, Odyssey, l. 7. v. 244-248. 1:265} It is not likely that Britain and Ireland would be populated before navigation extended beyond the Strait of Gibraltar.

21. The Inhabitants of Sicily

398. The Sicaneans were reputed to be the first inhabitants of Sicily. They built little villages or towns on hills and every town had its own king. By this means they inhabited all the country before they formed themselves into larger governments with a common king. Philistus says that they were moved into Sicily from the Sicanus River in Spain or Iberia. {*Diod. Sic., l. 5. c. 6. s. 1. 3:113} Dionysius states that they were a Spanish people who fled from the Ligures in Italy. {*Dionysius, l. 1. c. 22. s. 2. 1:69,71} He means the Ligures who opposed Hercules (Egyptian) when he returned from his expedition against Geryon in Spain, and tried to cross the Alps from Gaul into Italy. {*Dionysius, l. 1. c. 41. s. 3. 1:137}

399. The year Hercules (Egyptian) entered Italy, he made some conquests there and founded the city Croton. After the winter and the arrival of his fleet from Erythra in Spain, he sailed to Sicily and left the Sicaneans there. It was his custom to recruit into his army newly conquered people and after they had helped him in making new conquests, to reward them with new homes. {*Dionysius, l. 1. c. 44. 1:141,143} {E182} This was the Hercules (Egyptian), who had a powerful fleet, and in the days of Solomon sailed to the Strait of Gibraltar and according to his custom set up pillars there around 1004 BC. He conquered Geryon and returned to Italy and Sicily and then to Egypt. The ancient Gauls called him Ogmius and the Egyptians Nilus. Erythra and the country of Geryon were outside the Strait of Gibraltar. {Ptolemy, Hephaestus, l. 2.} Dionysius says this Hercules (Egyptian) was contemporary with Evander. {*Dionysius, l. 2. c. 1. s. 3,4. 1:315}

22. The Inhabitants of Crete

400. The first inhabitants of Crete were called Eteocretans. {*Diod. Sic., l. 5. c. 80. s. 1. 3:315} History does not say where they came from or how they got there. After them, a colony of Pelasgians arrived by ship from Greece. Shortly after this, Teutamus, the grandfather of Minos, led a colony of Dorians there from Laconia and from the territory of Olympia in Peloponnesus. These various colonies spoke different languages and lived on what grew wild. They lived quietly in caves and huts until the invention of iron tools in the days of Asterius, the son of Teutamus.

401. At length they were consolidated into one kingdom and one people by Minos, who was their first lawgiver. He built many towns and ships and introduced agriculture and in whose days the Curetes conquered his father's friends in Crete and Peloponnesus. {E183} According to Ister, the Curetes sacrificed children to Saturn (Cretan). {Porphyry, Aristotle, l. 2. s. 56.} Bochart states that the Curetes were Philistines. {Bochart, Canaan, l. 1. c. 15.} Eusebius says that Crete had its name from Cres, one of the Curetes who raised Jupiter. Whatever was the origin of the island's name, it seems to have been populated by colonies who spoke different languages until the days of Asterius and Minos. These people likely arrived about two or three generations before those two men, due to lack of navigational skills on those seas.

23. The Inhabitants of Cyprus

402. The island of Cyprus was discovered by the Phoenicians not long before this. Eratosthenes states this about Cyprus:

. . . in ancient times the plains were thickly overgrown with forests, and therefore were covered with woods and not cultivated; that the mines helped a little against this, since the people would cut down the trees to burn the copper and the silver, and that the building of the fleets further helped, since the sea was now being navigated safely, (after the Trojan War), with naval forces, but that, because they could not prevail over the growth of the timber, they permitted anyone who wished, or was able, to cut out the timber and to keep the land thus cleared as his own property and exempt from taxes. {*Strabo, l. 14. c. 6. s. 5. (684) 6:383}

403. Likewise Europe was also heavily forested. One forest was called the Hercinian and covered most of Germany and was a full nine days' journey across and more than forty days long in the days of Julius Caesar. {E184} This is in spite of the fact that the Europeans had been cutting down their forests to make room for mankind ever since the invention of iron tools in the days of Asterius and Minos.

24. Cavemen

404. This documents the stages of the first populating of Europe and its islands by sea. Before those days it seems to have been thinly populated from the northern coast of the Black Sea by Scythians who descended from Japheth. These nomads sheltered themselves from rain and wild animals in thickets and caves of the earth. Such were the caves in Mount Ida in Crete in which Minos was raised and buried, the cave of Cacus, and the Catacombs in Italy near Rome and Naples which were later turned into burying places. Similarily were the Syringes and many other caves in the sides of the mountains of Egypt, the caves of the Troglodytes between Egypt and the Red Sea and those of the Phaurusii in North Africa, mentioned by Strabo. {*Strabo, l. 17. c. 3. s. 7. (828) 8:169} The Israelites hid themselves in the caves, thickets, rocks, high places and pits from the Philistines in the days of Saul around 1094 BC. {1Sa 13:6} Nothing is extant from Europe of the history of those days.

25. The Inhabitants of Libya

405. The history of Libya was not much older than that of Europe. {E185} Diodorus states that Uranus, (who was the father of Hyperion, and grandfather of Helius and Selene), is that Ammon, who is the father of Sesostris, and was their first king. He gathered the people, who lived in scattered habitations, within the shelter of a walled city. {*Diod. Sic., l. 3. c. 56. s. 3,4. 2:263} {*Diod. Sic., l. 3. c. 57. s. 4,5. 2:265,267}

26. The Inhabitants of Media

406. Herodotus says that all Media was populated by unwalled towns until they revolted from the Assyrians in 712 BC, which was two hundred and sixty-three years after the death of Solomon. {*Herodotus, l. 1. c. 95. 1:127*} After that revolt, they set up a king over themselves and built Ecbatana with walls for his capital. This was the first walled town they had.

27. The State of Early Government

407. About seventy-four years after the death of Solomon around 901 BC, Benhadad II, the king of Syria, had thirty-two kings in his army against Ahab. {*1Ki 20:16*} When Joshua conquered the land of Canaan around 1450 BC, every city of the Canaanites had its own king, like the cities of Europe before they conquered one another. One of those kings, Adonibezek, the king of Bezek, had conquered seventy other kings shortly before the time of Joshua. {*Jud 1:7*} Therefore, towns began to be built in that land not many years before the days of Joshua for when the patriarchs wandered there in tents. They fed their flocks anywhere they pleased since the land of Phoenicia was not fully settled for lack of people. {*E186*}

408. The countries first inhabited by mankind, were in those days so thinly populated that four kings from the land of Shinar and Elam invaded and plundered the Rephaims, and the inhabitants of the countries of Moab, Ammon, Edom, and the kingdoms of Sodom, Gomorrah, Admah and Zeboim. However, they were pursued and defeated by Abraham with an armed force of only three hundred and eighteen men, the whole force which Abraham and the princes with him could raise. {*Ge 14:5-7 15-17 De 2:9,12,19-22*} Likewise, Egypt was so thinly populated before the birth of Moses that Pharaoh said of the Israelites:

> behold the people of the children of Israel are more and mightier than we. {*Ex 1:9,22*}

409. To prevent their multiplying and growing too strong, Pharaoh had their male children drowned. By these stages was the earth first populated by mankind not long before the days of Abraham. With this came the development of villages, towns and cities which grew into kingdoms. These smaller kingdoms became greater, until the rise of the kingdoms of Egypt, Assyria, Babylon, Media, Persia, Greece and Rome—the first great empires on this side of India. Abraham was the fifth generation from Peleg and all mankind lived together in Chaldea under the government of Noah and his sons until the days of Peleg. Up until this time they had one language, one society, and one religion.

Then Noah divided the earth among them. Perhaps the rebellion of Nimrod disrupted them along with the division of languages, and forced them to stop building the tower of Babel. {*E187*}

28. The Antiquity of God's Law

410. From there they spread into the various countries, which fell to their lot, carrying along with them the laws, customs and religion, under which they had lived when under the administration of Noah, his sons and grandsons. These laws were handed down to Abraham, Melchizedek, Job, and their contemporaries, and for some time were observed by the judges of the eastern countries. Job says that adultery was an heinous crime, even an iniquity to be punished by the judges. {*Job 31:11*} Concerning idolatry he says:

> If I beheld the sun, when it shined, or the moon walking in brightness; And my heart hath been secretly enticed, or my mouth hath kissed my hand: this also were an iniquity to be punished by the judge: for I should have denied the God that is above. {*Job 31:26-28*}

411. Since there was no dispute between Job and his friends about these matters, it may be presumed that they also with their countrymen were of the same religion. Melchizedek was a priest of the most high God and Abraham voluntarily paid tithes to him. He would not have done this if they had not been of the same religion. The first inhabitants of the land of Canaan seem also to have originally been of the same religion. {*E188*} They continued in it until the death of Noah and the days of Abraham for Jerusalem was anciently called Jebus, its people Jebusites, and Melchizedek was their priest and king. {*1Ch 1:4,5 Jud 1:21 2Sa 5:6*} Therefore, these nations revolted after the days of Melchizedek to the worship of false gods, as did also the posterity of Ishmael, Esau, Moab, Ammon and that of Abraham by Keturah. The Israelites themselves were very apt to revolt. Idolarty was one reason why Terah left Ur of Chaldea to go to Haran on his way to the land of Canaan. Likewise, Abraham later left Haran and went into the land of Canaan to avoid the worship of false gods, which in their days began in Chaldea and spread everywhere from there but had not yet arrived into the land of Canaan. Several of the laws and precepts in which this primitive religion consisted are mentioned in Job:

1) Not to blaspheme or curse God. {*Job 1:5*}

2) Not to worship the sun or the moon. {*Job 31:26-28*}

3) Not to kill. {*Job 31:39*}

4) Not to steal. {*Job 31:39*}

5) Not to commit adultery. {Job 31:11}

6) Not to trust in riches. {Job 31:24,25}

7) Not to oppress the poor or fatherless. {Job 31:16,17}

8) Not to curse your enemies or rejoice at their misfortunes. {Job 31:29,30}

9) Be friendly, hospitable and merciful. {Job 31:26-28}

10) Relieve the poor and needy. {Job 31:19-22}

11) Set up judges. {Job 31:28}

412. This was the morality and religion of the first ages, still called by the Jews, *The Precepts of the Sons of Noah.* {E189} This was the religion of Moses and the prophets, comprehended in the two great commandments, of *loving the Lord our God with all our heart and soul and mind, and our neighbour as ourselves.* This was the religion enjoined by Moses to the uncircumcised stranger within the gates of Israel, as well as to the Israelites. This was the primitive religion of both Jews and Christians and should be the standing religion of all nations, for it honours God and the good of mankind. Moses adds this precept of being merciful even to brute beasts, so as not to:

1) Drink their blood.

2) Cut off their flesh alive with the blood in it.

3) Kill them for the sake of their blood.

4) Strangle them.

413. They were to be killed for food and their blood drained out and spilt on the ground. {Ge 9:4 Le 17:12,13}

This law was older than the days of Moses, being given to Noah and his sons long before the days of Abraham. Therefore, the apostles and elders in the council at Jerusalem declared that the Gentiles were not obliged to be circumcised and keep the law of Moses. However they expected this law of abstaining from blood and things strangled as being an earlier law of God, imposed not on the sons of Abraham only, but on all nations, while they lived together in Shinar under the dominion of Noah. {E190} This is the same kind as the law of:

> . . . abstaining from meats offered to idols or false gods, and from fornication. {Ac 15:20}

414. So then, the oldest religion is believing that

1) the world was created and governed by one supreme God.

2) we are to love and worship him.

3) we are to honour our parents.

4) we are to love our neighbour as ourselves.

5) we are to be merciful even to brute beasts.

415. This is the oldest of all religions and the origin of writing, agriculture, navigation, music, arts and sciences, metals, smiths and carpenters. Towns and houses in Europe did not predate the days of Eli, Samuel and David around 1100 BC. Before those days the earth was so thinly populated and so overgrown with forests that mankind could not be older than is represented in the scriptures.

Chapter 2 — The Empire of Egypt

416. The ancient Egyptians boasted of a very large and lasting empire under their kings Ammon, Osiris, Bacchus, Sesostris, Hercules (Egyptian), Memnon, etc., reaching eastward to India and westward to the Atlantic Ocean. From their vanity, they have made this kingdom many thousands of years older than the world! Let us now try to amend the chronology of Egypt, by comparing the affairs of Egypt with the synchronised affairs of the Greeks and Hebrews.

1. The Identification of Bacchus, Osiris and Sesostris

1.1 Bacchus and Sesostris the Same Man

417. Bacchus, the conqueror, loved two women, Venus and Ariadne. Venus was the mistress of Anchises and Cinyras, and the mother of Aeneas, who all lived until the destruction of Troy. The sons of Bacchus and Ariadne were Argonauts and therefore the great Bacchus lived only one generation before the Argonaut Expedition. Athenaeus cites Hermippus saying that this Bacchus

1) had a powerful fleet,

2) conquered as far east as India,

3) returned in triumph,

4) led his army over the Hellespont,

5) conquered Thrace and introduced music, dancing and poetry there,

6) killed Lycurgus, the king of Thrace, and Pentheus, the grandson of Cadmus,

7) gave the kingdom of Lycurgus to Tharops, {E192}

8) gave one of his Muses, called by the Greeks Calliope, to Oeagrus the son of Tharops,

9) Oeagrus and Calliope gave birth to Orpheus,

10) Orpheus sailed with the Argonauts.

418. Therefore,

1) Bacchus was contemporary with Sesostris,

2) both were kings of Egypt,

3) both had powerful fleets,

4) both were great conquerors,

5) both conquered as far east as India and into Thrace.

Hence, Sesostris and Bacchus must be one and the same man!

1.2 Bacchus and Osiris, the Same Man

419. The ancient Greeks, who created the fables of the gods, related that Io, the daughter of Inachus, was kidnapped into Egypt and there became the Egyptian Isis. Apis, the son of Phoroneus, became the god Serapis after his death. Some said that Epaphus was the son of Io, and that Serapis and Epaphus are Osiris. Therefore, Isis and Osiris, in the opinion of the ancient Greeks who created the fables of the gods, were not more than two or three generations older than the Argonaut Expedition. Dicaearchus, as he is cited by the scholiast in Apollonius, says Isis and Osiris were two generations older than Sesostris and after their son Orus, Sesostris or Sesonchosis reigned. {*Apollonius, Argonautica, l. 4. v. 270-273. 1:313} {*Herodotus, l. 2. c. 102,103. 1:389,391} He seems to have followed the opinion of the people of Naxos, who made Bacchus two generations older than Theseus, and for that end created two Minoses and two Ariadnes, for by the consent of all antiquity Osiris and Bacchus were one and the same king of Egypt. {E193} This is affirmed by the Egyptians, as well as by the Greeks and some of the ancient mythologists, as Eumolpus and Orpheus, for they called Osiris by the names of Dionysus and Sirius respectively. {*Diod. Sic., l. 1. c. 11. s. 3,4. 1:39}

420. Osiris was the king of all Egypt and a great conqueror. He came over the Hellespont in the days of Triptolemus and subdued Thrace and killed Lycurgus. Therefore, his expedition agrees with that of the great Bacchus. Note the similarities among Osiris, Bacchus and Sesostris:

1) They lived about the same time.

2) They were kings over all of Egypt.

3) They reigned at Thebes (Egyptian) and adorned that city.

4) They were very powerful on land and sea.

5) They were great conquerors.

6) They conquered on land through Asia, as far as India.

7) They came over the Hellespont and almost lost their army there.

8) They conquered Thrace and there halted their conquests.

9) They returned back from there into Egypt.

10) They left pillars with inscriptions in the lands of their conquests.

421. Therefore, all three must be one and the same king of Egypt and this king can be none other than Sesostris for the following reasons:

1) All Egypt, including Thebes (Egyptian), Ethiopia and Libya had no common king before the expulsion of the Shepherds who reigned in Lower Egypt. {*E194*}

2) History records no conqueror of Syria, India, Asia and Thrace before Sesostris.

3) Biblical history records no Egyptian conqueror of Palestine before Sesostris.

1.3 Bacchus, Osiris and Sesostris the Same Man

422. Thymoetes was contemporary with Orpheus and wrote a poem using archaic language and letters called *Phrygia* about the actions of Bacchus. He said that Bacchus had Libyan women in his army. Among these women was Minerva who was born in Libya near the Triton River. Bacchus commanded the men and Minerva the women. {*Diod. Sic., l. 3. c. 67. s. 5. 2:309*} Diodorus calls her Myrina and says that she was the queen of the Amazons in Libya and conquered the Atlanteans and Gorgons there. {*Diod. Sic., l. 3. c. 53. s. 2. 2:253*} After this, she made a league with Horus or Orus, the son of Isis, who was sent to her by his father Osiris or Bacchus for that purpose. She journeyed through Egypt and subdued Arabia Faelix, Syria, Cilicia and came through Phrygia as part of the army of Bacchus to the Mediterranean Sea. After crossing over into Europe, she and many of her women were killed by the Thracians and Scythians under the command of Sipylus, a Scythian, and Mopsus, a Thracian whom Lycurgus the king of Thrace had banished. {*Diod. Sic., l. 3. c. 55. s. 4-10. 2:257-261*} This was that Lycurgus who opposed the crossing of Bacchus with his army over the Hellespont and was soon after conquered and killed by him. However after this, Bacchus was repelled by the Greeks under the leadership of Perseus, who killed many of his women, as Pausanias states. {*Pausanias, Corinth, l. 2. c. 20. s. 4. 1:351*} {*E195*} Perseus was assisted by the Scythians and Thracians who were commanded by Sipylus and Mopsus. This defeat together with a revolt of his brother Danaus in Egypt put a halt to his victories. When he returned home he left some of his men in Colchis and at Mount Caucasus under Aeetes and Prometheus. He left his women at the Thermodon River near Colchis, under their new queens, Marthesia and Lampeto.

423. Diodorus, speaking of the Amazons who were located at the Thermodon River, says that they lived originally in Libya. They reigned there over the Atlanteans, and invaded their neighbours and conquered as far as Europe. {*Diod. Sic., l. 3. c. 52. s. 1. 1:245,247*} {*Apollonius, Argonautica, l. 2. v. 370-357. 1:127*} Ammianus says that the ancient Amazons defeated many nations and attacked the Athenians. They were soundly defeated with heavy losses and retreated to the Thermodon River. {*Ammianus, l. 22. c. 8. s. 17-19. 2:225,227*} Justin says that these Amazons had at first (he means at their first coming to Thermodon) two queens who called themselves the daughters of Mars. They conquered part of Europe and some cities of Asia Minor in the reign of Minerva. They sent back part of their army with great plunder under their new queens. After that when Marthesia was killed, she was succeeded by her daughter Orithya and she by Penthesilea. Theseus captured and married Antiope, the sister of Orithya. {*E196*} Hercules (Idean) made war on the Amazons and in the reign of their queens, Orithya and Penthesilea, they came to the Trojan War. {*Justin, Trogus, l. 2. c. 4. s. 12-25. 1:29,30*} Therefore, the first wars of the Amazons in Europe and Asia, and their settling at the Thermodon River, were only one generation before those actions of Hercules (Idean) and Theseus. Their actions were only two generations before the Trojan War and so agree with the expedition of Sesostris. Since they warred in the days of Isis and her son Orus and were a part of the army of Bacchus or Osiris, we have here another argument for making Osiris and Bacchus contemporary with Sesostris, and all three, one and the same king as Sesostris.

2. The Errors in Manetho's 11th and 12th Dynasty

424. The Greeks consider Osiris and Bacchus to be sons of Jupiter, and the Egyptian name of Jupiter is Ammon. Manetho in his 11th and 12th dynasties, as he is cited by Africanus and Eusebius, names these four kings of Egypt, as reigning successively: {*Manetho, l. 1. fr. 31. 1:63} {*Manetho, l. 2. fr. 34. 1:67}

1) Ammenemes I,

2) Gesongeses or Sesonchoris, the son of Ammenemes I,

3) Ammenemes II who was murdered by his eunuchs,

4) Sesostris who subdued all Asia and part of Europe.

425. Gesongeses and Sesonchoris are corruptly written for Sesonchosis. The first two of these four kings, Ammenemes I and Sesonchosis, are the same as the two last, Ammenemes II and Sesostris, that is, as Ammon and Sesostris. {E197} Diodorus says that Osiris built a magnificent temple in Thebes (Egyptian) to his parents Jupiter and Juno, and two other temples to Jupiter, a larger one to Jupiter Uranus, and a smaller one to his father Jupiter Ammon, who reigned in that city. {*Diod. Sic., l. 1. c. 15. s. 1-4. 1:49,51} Thymoetes, who was mentioned previously and was contemporary with Orpheus, wrote expressly that the father of Bacchus was Ammon, a king reigning over part of Libya, that is, a king of Egypt reigning over all that part of Libya, anciently called Ammonia. {*Diod. Sic., l. 3. c. 67,68. 2:309,311} Stephanus says that all Libya was anciently called Ammonia from Ammon. {Stephanus, in Ἀμμωνια} This is that king of Egypt from whom Thebes (Egyptian) was called No-Ammon, and Ammon-No, the city of Ammon. The Greeks call it Diospolis, the city of Jupiter Ammon. Sesostris built it sumptuously and called it after his father's name, Ammon. After the name of the same king is the river called Ammon, the people called Ammonii. {*Pliny, l. 6. c. 35. (186,187) 2:477} The promontory called Ammonium in Arabia Faelix is also named after him. {Ptolemy, Hephaestus, l. 6. c. 7.}

3. The Origin of the Kingdom of Egypt

426. Lower Egypt is flooded annually by the Nile River. This area was uninhabitable until the cultivation of crops was introduced. The king, who did this and first populated the area, reigned over it, and perhaps was the king of the city called Mesir where Memphis was later built. {E198} He was likely worshipped by his subjects after his death in the form of an ox or a calf for this good deed. This city stood in the most convenient place to populate and control Lower Egypt. Since it straddled the Nile River, this might be the reason for the name of Mizraim, meaning *double straits* being given to its founder and people unless one refers the word to the *double people*, those above the delta, and those within it. This I take to be the state of Lower Egypt until the Shepherds or Phoenicians who fled from Joshua conquered it. The Ethiopians conquered them later causing them to flee into North Africa and other places. There was a tradition that some of them fled into North Africa and Augustine confirms this, by saying that the common people of North Africa when asked who they were, replied *Chanani*, that is, *Canaanites*. He says:

Interrogati rustici nostri quid sint, Punice respondentes Chanani, corrupta scilicet voce sicut in talibus solet, quid aliud respondent quam Chanaanaei? {Augustine, Romans, Exposition of the Epistle to Romans, sub. initio.}

When our peasant farmers are asked where they came from, they reply from *Chanani*, which is a corruption of the pronunciation, which they are accustomed to when asked, rather than say, *Canaanites*.

427. Procopius also states:

In that place are two columns made of white stone near by a great spring, having Phoenician letters cut in them which say in the Phoenician tongue: *We are they who fled from before the face of Joshua, the robber, the son of Nun.* {*Procopius, Vandalic War, l. 2. c. 10. (22,23) 2:289}

428. Eusebius states that these Canaanites fled from the sons of Israel and built Tripoli in Africa. {*Eusebius, Chronicles, l. 1. (11) 1:75} The Jerusalem Gemara states that the Gergesites fled from Joshua into Africa. {Jerusalem Gemara, ad tit. Shebijth. c. 6.}

429. Procopius relates their flight in this manner: {E199}

When the Hebrews had withdrawn from Egypt and had come near the boundaries of Palestine, Moses, a wise man, who was their leader on the journey, died, and the leadership was passed on to Joshua, the son of Nun, who led the people into Palestine, and, by displaying a valour in war greater than that natural to a man, gained possession of the land. And after overthrowing all the nations he easily won the cities, and he seemed to be altogether invincible. Now at that time the whole country along the sea from Sidon as far as the boundaries of Egypt was called Phoenicia. And one king in ancient times held sway over it, as is agreed by all who have written the earliest accounts of the Phoenicians. In that country there dwelt very populous tribes, the Gergesites and the

Jebusites and some others with other names by which they are called in the history of the Hebrews. Now when these nations saw that the invading general was an irresistible prodigy, they emigrated from their ancestral homes and made their way to Egypt, which adjoined their country. And finding there no place sufficient for them to dwell in, since there has been a great population in Egypt from ancient times, they proceeded to Libya. And they established numerous cities and took possession of the whole of Libya as far as the Pillars of Heracles, and there they have lived even up to my time, using the Phoenician tongue. {*Procopius, Vandalic War, l. 2. c. 10. (13,21) 2:287,289} {E201}

430. By the language and extreme poverty of the Moors as described also by Procopius, and by their not being familiar with trade and navigation, you may know that they were Canaanites originally and peopled North Africa before the merchants of Tyre came there. Manetho says these Canaanites came from the east and settled in great numbers in Lower Egypt during the reign of Tutimaeus {*Josephus, Against Apion, l. 1. c. 14. (75-81) 1:193,195} They easily seized the country, fortified Pelusium then called Auaris, and they founded a kingdom there. They reigned there for almost two hundred and sixty years. Their first six kings were named Salatis, Boeon, Apachnas, Apophis, Janias, Assis, and after them others ruled successively.

431. During this time, Upper Egypt, which was called *Thebes*, and according to Herodotus, *Aegyptus*, and in the scripture the *land of Pathros*, was under other kings, reigning perhaps at Coptos, Thebes (Egyptian), This, Syene, Pathros, Elephantis, Heracleopolis, Mesir, and other great cities, until they were conquered by the Ethiopians. {*Herodotus, l. 2. c. 1-9. 1:275-285} {Jer 44:1 Eze 29:14} In those days, cities became great by being the capitals of kingdoms. Over time, one of these kingdoms conquered the others and made a continual war upon the Shepherds. In the reign of its King Misphragmuthosis and his son Amosis I (also called Tethmosis, Tuthmosis, and Thomosis) they drove the Shepherds from Egypt and made them flee into North Africa, Syria and other places, and the king united all Egypt into one kingdom. {E202} Under their next kings, Ammon and Sesostris, the kingdom was enlarged into a great empire. This conquering people did not worship the kings of the Shepherds whom they conquered and expelled. {Manetho apud Porphyry, περι αττοχης l. 1. s. 55.} {*Eusebius, Gospel, l. 4. c. 16. (155d) 1:170} They abolished their religion of human sacrifice and, according to the customs of their times, they deified their kings who had founded their new dominion.

They began the history of their empire with the reigns and great acts of their gods and heroes. Hence, they derived their gods:

1) Ammon and Rhea (Egyptian), or Uranus and Titaea,

2) Osiris and Isis,

3) Orus and Bubaste,

4) Their secretary Thoth,

5) Their generals Hercules (Egyptian) and Pan,

6) Their admiral Japetus, Neptune or Typhon.

432. All of them were Thebans and lived after the expulsion of the Shepherds. Homer places Thebes (Egyptian) in Ethiopia, and the Ethiopians stated that the Egyptians were an Ethiopian colony led by Osiris. {*Diod. Sic., l. 3. c. 3. s. 2. 2:93} Hence, it happened that most of the laws of Egypt were the same as those of Ethiopia, and the Egyptians learned from the Ethiopians the custom of deifying their kings.

433. When Joseph entertained his brothers in Egypt in 1706 BC, they ate at a table by themselves, and he ate at another table by himself. The Egyptians who ate with him sat at another table, because the Egyptians would not eat food with the Hebrews, for that was an abomination to the Egyptians. {Ge 43:32} {E203} Later it was said concerning these Egyptians and their fellow subjects that every shepherd was an abomination to the Egyptians. {Ge 46:34} Therefore, these Egyptians who ate with Joseph were from Pharaoh's court and hence at this time Pharaoh and his court were not Shepherds but genuine Egyptians.

434. After the descent of Jacob and his sons into Egypt, Joseph lived seventy years, dying in 1635 BC, and for that time continued in favour with the kings of Egypt. Sixty-four years after his death in 1571 BC, Moses was born, and between the death of Joseph and the birth of Moses, there arose a new king over Egypt who did not know about Joseph. {Ex 1:8} However, this king of Egypt was not one of the Shepherds for he is called Pharaoh. {Ex 1:11,22} Also, Moses told his successor that if the people of Israel should sacrifice in the land of Egypt, they would sacrifice the abomination of the Egyptians before their eyes and the Egyptians would stone them. {Ex 8:26} That is, they would sacrifice sheep or oxen, contrary to the religion of Egypt. Therefore, the Shepherds did not reign over Egypt while Israel was there, but either were driven out of Egypt before Israel went down there or did not enter into Egypt until after Moses had brought Israel from Egypt. The latter must be true, if they were driven from Egypt a

little before the building of the temple of Solomon, as Manetho affirms.

435. Diodorus says that in Egypt there were formerly multitudes of strangers from various countries, who used foreign rites and ceremonies in worshipping the gods and were expelled from Egypt for that reason. Under Danaus, Cadmus, and other skilful leaders, they came into Greece and other places after great hardships. However, most of them went into Palestine (which was not far from Egypt and was uninhabited and deserted at that time) under the leadership of Moses. He was a wise and valiant man, who after he had conquered the country, among other things he built Jerusalem and the temple. {*Diod. Sic., l. 40. c. 3. s. 1-3. 12:279,281} {Photius, Bibliotheca} Diodorus here mistakens the origin of the Israelites, as Manetho had done before, confounding their exodus into the wilderness under the leadership of Moses, with the flight of the Shepherds from Misphragmuthosis and his son Amosis I into Phoenicia and North Africa. {E205} Diodorus did not know that Palestine was inhabited by Canaanites before the Israelites under Moses came there. However, he says that the Shepherds were expelled from Egypt by Amosis I, a little before the building of Jerusalem and the temple, and that after many hardships some of them came into Greece and other places, under the leadership of Cadmus and others around 1041 BC. However, most of them settled in Phoenicia next to Egypt.

436. Therefore, we think that the expulsion of the Shepherds by the kings of Thebes (Egyptian) was the reason that the Philistines became so numerous in the days of Saul. Many men came with colonies from Egypt and Phoenicia into Greece such as: Lelex, Inachus, Pelasgus, Aezeus, Cecrops I, Aegialeus, Cadmus, Phoenix, Membliarius, Alymnus, Abas, Erechtheus, Peteos and Phorbas, in the days of Eli, Samuel, Saul and David from around 1135 to 1035 BC. Some of them fled in the days of Eli from Misphragmuthosis who conquered part of Lower Egypt. Others retired from his successor Amosis I into Phoenicia, Arabia Faelix and Petraea and there intermarried with the inhabitants. However, they were shortly conquered by David and along with the Philistines fled from David by sea, under the leadership of Cadmus and others into Asia Minor, Greece and Libya to seek new homes. {E206} There they built towns, founded kingdoms, and established the religion of worshipping the dead. Some remained in Judah and were conscripted by David and Solomon in building Jerusalem and the temple. Among the foreign rites used by the strangers in Egypt in worshipping the gods was human sacrifice, for Amosis I abolished that custom at Heliopolis.

Therefore, those strangers were Canaanites, such as fled from Joshua for the Canaanites offered their children to Moloch and burned their sons and their daughters in the fire to their gods. {De 12:31} Manetho calls them Phoenician strangers.

437. After Amosis I had expelled the Shepherds and extended his kingdom over all Egypt, his son and successor Ammenemes or Ammon, by much greater conquests laid the foundation for the Egyptian Empire. By the assistance of his young son Sesostris, whom he disciplined in hunting and other laborious exercises, he conquered Arabia Faelix, Troglodytica and Libya. All Libya was anciently called Ammonia after the name of Ammon. When he died, in the temples erected to him at Thebes (Egyptian), Ammonia, and Meroe in Ethiopia, they appointed oracles to him, and made the people worship him as the god who acted through them. {E207} These are the oldest oracles mentioned in history. Hence, the Greeks imitated the Egyptians in this practice for the oracle at Dodona was the oldest in Greece and was set up by an Egyptian woman, after the example of the oracle of Jupiter Ammon at Thebes (Egyptian). {*Herodotus, l. 2. c. 52. 1:341}

4. The Origin of Navigation and Trade

438. In the days of Ammon, a body of the Edomites fled from David into Egypt with Hadad, their young king, around 1044 BC. There they introduced skills in navigation. This seems to have been the reason that the Egyptians built a fleet on the Red Sea near Coptos and might have ingratiated Hadad with Pharaoh. The Midianites and Ishmaelites, who bordered upon the Red Sea, near Mount Horeb on the south side of Edom, were merchants from the days of the patriarch Jacob. {Ge 37:28,36} By their merchandise the Midianites were rich in gold in the days of Moses. {Nu 31:50-52} In the days of the judges of Israel, because they were Ishmaelites, they had gold earrings. {Jud 8:24}

439. Therefore, in those days the Ishmaelites grew rich by trading. They carried their merchandise on camels through Petra to Rhinocolura, and from there to Egypt. This trade route came into the hands of David when he conquered the Edomites and captured the ports of Eloth and Ezion Geber on the Red Sea. {E208} This we may understand by the three thousand talents of gold of Ophir, which David gave to the temple. {1Ch 29:4} The Egyptians had the knowledge of making linen cloth and about this time they began to build long ships with sails in their port on those seas near Coptos. They mastered the skills of the Edomites and now began to observe the positions of the stars and the length of the solar year. This enabled them to know the position of the stars at any time, and to sail by them at all times when beyond the sight of the shore. This was the beginning of astronomy and navigation. Before this they had only ventured along the shore with oars in round-shaped cargo vessels, which were first invented on that shallow sea by the posterity of Abraham. They passed from island to island, guiding themselves by the sight of the islands in the day time, or by the sight of some of the stars in the night. Their old year was the luni-solar year, derived from Noah to all his posterity, for until that time it consisted of twelve thirty day months. At the end of the calendar year they added five days making the solar year of twelve months and five days or three hundred and sixty-five days.

5. The Origin of the Egyptian Solar Year

440. The ancient Egyptians imagined that Rhea (Egyptian) had secret sexual intercourse with Saturn, and Sol prayed that she might not have a child in any month nor in the year. {*E209*} Mercury was playing dice with Luna and won. For his prize he took from the lunar year the 72nd part of every day and created five days adding them to the year of three hundred and sixty days so Rhea (Egyptian) might give birth in them. The Egyptians celebrated those days as the birthdays of Rhea's five children, Osiris, Orus Senior, Typhon, Isis, and Nephthys the wife of Typhon. {*Plutarch, Moralia-Isis and Osiris, l. 1. c. 12. (355EF) 5:31,33*} {*Diod. Sic., l. 1. c. 13. s. 4,5. 1:47*} In the opinion of the ancient Egyptians, the five days were added to the luni-solar calendar year during the reign of Saturn (Egyptian) and Rhea (Egyptian), the parents of Osiris, Isis and Typhon. This happened in the reign of Ammon and Titaea, who were the parents of the Titans, or in the latter half of the reign of David, when those Titans were born around 1025 BC. By consequence, this was soon after the flight of the Edomites from David into Egypt around 1044 BC. However, the solstices had not been established yet and the beginning of this new year might not start on the vernal equinox before the time of the reign of Amenophis, the successor of Orus, the son of Osiris and Isis.

6. The Origin of Writing in Egypt, Europe and Chaldea

441. When the Edomites fled from David with their young king Hadad into Egypt, it is probable that they also carried there the use of writing. Writing was then in use among the posterity of Abraham in Arabia Petraea and on the borders of the Red Sea. {*E210*} The law was written there by Moses in a book on tables of stone long before this. Moses married the daughter of the prince of Midian and lived with

him for forty years and was taught writing by the Midianites. Job, who lived among their neighbours the Edomites, mentions the writing down of words, as used there in his days. {*Augustine, The City of God, l. 18. c. 47. NPN2:390*} {*Job 19:23,24*} There is no instance of letters for writing down sounds, being in use before the days of David, in any other country except among the posterity of Abraham. The Egyptians ascribed this invention to Thoth, the secretary of Osiris. Therefore, writing began to be in use in Egypt in the days of Thoth, that is, a little after the flight of the Edomites from David, or about the time that Cadmus brought them into Europe around 1041 BC.

442. Helladius says that a man called Oes (who appeared in the Red Sea with the tail of a fish, so they painted him as a seaman) taught the Egyptians astronomy and writing. {*Photius, Bibliotheca, c. 279.*} Hyginus says that Euhadnes, who came out of the sea in Chaldea, was the first to teach astrology (he means astronomy) to the Chaldeans. {*Hyginus, Fabulae, l. 1. c. 274. s. 16. 1:181*} Alexander Polyhistor relates from Berosus that Oannes taught the Chaldeans writing, mathematics, arts, agriculture, living in cities and the construction of temples. {*E211*} See also Eusebius' Chronicles. Several such men came there successively. Oes, Euhadnes and Oannes seem to be the same name a little varied by corruption. This name seems to have been given in common to several seamen, who came there from time to time. By consequence they were merchants and travelled those seas with their merchandise or else fled from their enemies. Hence, writing, astronomy, architecture and agriculture came into Chaldea by sea. They were carried there by seamen who frequented the Persian Gulf, and came there periodically after all those things were practised in other countries where they came from. By consequence, this happened in the days of Ammon and Sesostris, David and Solomon, and their successors, or not long before. The Chaldeans indeed made Oannes older than the flood of Xisuthrus, and the Egyptians made Osiris as old as that flood. However, I make them contemporary with each other.

443. The Red Sea had its name not from its colour, but from Edom and Erythras, the names of Esau, which signify that colour. Some say that King Erythras, meaning Esau, invented the rafts by which they navigated that sea and he was buried on an island near the Persian Gulf. {*Pliny, l. 6. c. 28. (108) 2:421*} {*Pliny, l. 7. c. 56. (206) 2:645*} Hence, it follows that the Edomites sailed that sea from the days of Esau. {*E212*} There is no need that the oldest Oannes should be older. There were boats on rivers before this time, such as the boats which carried the patriarchs over the Euphrates and

Jordan Rivers and the early peoples over many other rivers to populate the earth. They sought new homes and invaded one another's territories.

444. Patterning their design after such vessels, Ishmael and Midian, the sons of Abraham, and Esau his grandson, might build larger vessels to go to the islands on the Red Sea to search for new homes. The Edomites would slowly learn how to navigate that sea as far as to the Persian Gulf, since ships were as old, even on the Mediterranean Sea, as the days of Jacob. {*Ge 49:13 Jud 5:17*} It is likely that the merchants of that sea were not eager to reveal their arts and sciences on which their trade depended. Therefore, it seems that writing, astronomy and carpentry were invented by the merchants of the Red Sea for recording their cargoes, keeping their accounts, guiding their ships at night by the stars and building ships. They propagated these skills from Arabia Petraea into Egypt, Chaldea, Syria, Asia Minor and Europe at about the same time. {*E213*} This would be the time when David conquered and dispersed those merchants for we hear nothing of writing before the days of David, except among the posterity of Abraham. Except for the constellations mentioned by Job, who lived in Arabia Petraea among these merchants, we hear nothing of astronomy before the Egyptians under Ammon and Sesostris applied themselves to that study. Likewise, this is also true of carpentry and architecture until Solomon sent to Hiram, the king of Tyre. He wanted Hiram to supply him with such craftsmen, saying that there was no one in Israel who was as skilled at carpentry as the Sidonians.

7. The Identity of Belus

445. Diodorus says that the Egyptians sent many colonies from Egypt into other countries. Belus (Egyptian), the son of Neptune and Libya, led colonies from there into Babylonia, and established himself on the Euphrates River. There he appointed priests called Chaldeans, who were exempt from taxation and free from every kind of service to the state. These Chaldeans observed the stars after the customs of Egypt. {*Diod. Sic., l. 1. c. 28. s. 1. 1:91*} Pausanias states that the Belus of Babylon was named after an Egyptian Belus, the son of Libya. {*Pausanias, Messenia, l. 4. c. 23. s. 10. 2:303*} Apollodorus states that Belus, the son of Neptune and Libya, was a king of Egypt and the father of Aegyptus and Danaus. Therefore, Belus is the same man as Ammon. Busiris, the son of Neptune and Lisianassa [Libyanassa], the daughter of Epaphus, was the king of Egypt. {*Apollodorus, Library, l. 2. c. 1. s. 4. 1:135,137*} {*E214*} Eusebius calls this king Busiris, the son of Neptune and Libya, the daughter of Epaphus. By

these things the later Egyptians seem to have made two Beluses, the one the father of Osiris, Isis, and Neptune, the other the son of Neptune, and the father of Aegyptus and Danaus. Hence, came the opinion of the people of Naxos that there were two Minoses and two Ariadnes, the one two generations older than the other. This we have refuted. The father of Aegyptus and Danaus was the father of Osiris, Isis, and Typhon and Typhon was not the grandfather of Neptune but Neptune himself.

8. The Exploits of Sesostris

446. Sesostris was raised rigorously by his father Ammon and warred first under his father, being the *Hero* or *Hercules* of the Egyptians during his father's reign and later became their king. Under his father, while Sesostris was very young, he invaded and conquered Troglodytica around 1006 BC, and thereby secured the harbour of the Red Sea near Coptos in Egypt. Then he invaded Ethiopia and carried on his conquest south as far as to the region bearing cinnamon. His father, with the assistance of the Edomites, built a fleet on the Red Sea. He then sailed past Arabia Faelix into the Persian Gulf and beyond. {*E215*} In those countries he set up columns with inscriptions of his conquests. He set up a pillar at Dira, a promontory in the straits of the Red Sea next to Ethiopia and two pillars in India on the mountains near the mouth of the Ganges River. Dionysius states:

> *Ubi etiamnum columnae Thebis geniti Bacchi*
> *Stant extremi iuxta fluxum Oceani*
> *Indorum ultimus in montibus: ubi et Ganges*
> *Claram aquam Nyssaeam ad planitiem*
> *devolvit.*

Even where the Thebian columns of the Bacchus of the nations stand near the stream at the Indian Ocean in the highest mountains, where the Ganges rolls down the clear Nyssean water. {*Dionysius, On Imitation, v. 623.*}

447. After these conquests Sesostris invaded Libya and fought the Africans with clubs around 1004 BC. According to Hyginus, this is the reason he is painted with a club in his hand.

> Egyptians first fought with clubs; later Belus (Egyptian), the son of Neptune, fought with a sword, and *bellum* meaning *war,* is named from this. {*Hyginus, Fabulae, l. 1. c. 274. s. 22. 1:181*}

448. After the conquest of Libya, Egypt was supplied with horses from which they furnished Solomon and his friends. Sesostris prepared a fleet on the Mediterranean Sea and went west along the coast of North

Africa to explore those countries. He went as far as to the ocean and the island of Erythra or Gades in Spain as Macrobius notes from Panyasis and Pherecydes. {*Macrobius, Saturnalia, l. 5. c. 21. s. 19. 1:381} {E216} He conquered Geryon there and at the mouth of the Strait of Gibraltar set up his famous pillars. Lucan said that Sesostris made his way west and to the limits of the world. {*Lucan, l. 10. (276) 1:611} Then he returned through Spain and the southern coasts of Gaul and Italy with the cattle of Geryon. His fleet accompanied him by sea. In Sicily he settled the Sicaneans, a people whom he had brought from Spain. After his father's death he built temples to him in his conquests. Hence, it happened that Jupiter Ammon was worshipped in Ammonia (Libya), Ethiopia, Arabia, and as far east as India according to Lucan the poet.

> Though the Ethiopians and Indians and wealthy
> Arabians have no god but Jupiter Ammon. . . .
> {*Lucan, l. 9. (517,518) 1:542}

449. The Arabians worshipped only two gods, Caelus (otherwise called Ouranus or Jupiter Uranus), and Bacchus. These were Jupiter Ammon and Sesostris, as noted above. So also the people of Meroe, the capital of Ethiopia, worshipped no other gods but Jupiter and Bacchus, and had an oracle to Jupiter. {*Herodotus, l. 2. c. 29. 1:307,309} These two gods were Jupiter Ammon and Osiris, according to the Egyptian language.

450. After this Sesostris, in the fifth year of Rehoboam in 971 BC, came from Egypt with a great army of Libyans, Troglodytes and Ethiopians. {E217} He plundered the temple and subdued Judah and went on to conquer, first east into India and then west as far as Thrace for God had given him the kingdoms of those countries. {2Ch 12:2,3,8} Sesostris spent nine years on this expedition. {*Diod. Sic., l. 1. c. 55. s. 3-9. 1:193,195} Herodotus says that he set up pillars with inscriptions in all his conquests, some of which remained in Syria until the days of Herodotus. {*Herodotus, l. 2. c. 102. 1:389,391} {*Herodotus, l. 2. c. 103. 1:391} {*Herodotus, l. 2. c. 106. 1:393,395} Sesostris was accompanied by his son Orus or Apollo, and with some singing women, called the Muses, one of which was named Calliope, who was the mother of Orpheus an Argonaut. The two peaks of Mount Parnassus, which were very high, were dedicated, the one to this Bacchus, and the other to his son Apollo. {*Pausanias, Phocis, l. 10. c. 32. s. 7. 4:559} {Suidas, in Παρνασιοι} Hence, Lucan says:

> The twin peaks of Parnassus soar to heaven.
> The mountain is sacred to Phoebus and Bromios. . . . {*Lucan, l. 5. (72,73) 1:243}

451. In 962 BC, which was the fourteenth year of Rehoboam, he returned to Egypt, leaving Aeetes in Colchis and his nephew Prometheus at Mount Caucasus with part of his army to defend his conquests from the Scythians. Apollonius Rhodius and his scholiast say that Sesonchosis, the king of all Egypt, that is Sesostris, after invading all Asia and a great part of Europe, populated many cities which he captured. {E218} Aea, the metropolis of Colchis, remained ever since his days with the posterity of those Egyptians which he placed there. They preserved the pillars or tables in which all the journeys and the bounds of sea and land were described, for their use when travelling. {*Apollonius, Argonautica, l. 4. v. 270-273. 1:313} Therefore, these tables indicate the beginning of the discipline of geography.

9. The Origin of Nomes and Temples in Egypt and Other Countries

452. When Sesostris returned home, he divided Egypt into equal square parcels of land for the Egyptians. This indicates the beginning of surveying and geometry. {*Herodotus, l. 2. c. 109. 1:397,399} Jambilicus associates this division of Egypt and the beginning of geometry with the age of the gods of Egypt. {Jambilicus, Life of Pythagoras, c. 29.} Sesostris divided Egypt into thirty-six nomes or counties and dug a canal from the Nile to the capital city of each nome. He used the earth from the canal to elevate the foundation of each city. He built a temple in every city for the worship in the nome and in the temples set up oracles, some of which remained until the days of Herodotus. {*Diod. Sic., l. 1. c. 57. s. 1-4. 1:199,201} By this means the Egyptians in each nome were induced to worship the great men of the kingdom to whom the nome, the city, and the temple or grave of the god, were dedicated. {E219} Each temple had its own god, modes of worship and annual festivals. The council and people of the nome met at the temple at certain times for sacrifice, to regulate the affairs of the nome, to administer justice and to buy and sell. Sesostris and his queen were worshipped in all Egypt under the names of Osiris and Isis.

453. Sesostris made the Nile more useful by digging channels from it to all the capital cities of the nomes of Egypt. The river was consecrated to him and he was called by its names: *Aegyptus, Siris* or *Nilus*. Dionysius states that the Nile was called *Siris* by the Ethiopians and *Nilus* by the people of Siene. {Dionysius, De Situ. Orbis.} From the word *Nahal*, which signifies a torrent, that river was called Nilus. Diodorus says that Nilus was that king who constructed canals in Egypt to make the river more useful. {*Diod. Sic., l. 1. c. 63. s. 1. 1:215} In the scriptures the river is called *Shihor* or *Sihor*. {1Ch 13:5 Isa 23:3 Jer 2:18} From that word the Greeks formed the words *Siris, Sirius, Ser-Apis* and *O-Siris*. Plutarch says

that the syllable *O*, put before the word *Siris* by the Greeks, made it scarcely intelligible to the Egyptians. {*Plutarch, Moralia-Isis and Osiris, l. 1. c. 61. (375F) 5:145*}

454. We have now documented the origin of the nomes of Egypt, the religions and temples of the nomes and the cities built there by the gods and named after them. Diodorus says that Egypt is the only country in the whole inhabited world where there are many cities which were founded by the first gods, such as Jupiter, Sol, Hermes, Apollo, Pan, Eilithyia, and many more. {*Diod. Sic., l. 1. c. 12. s. 6. 1:43*} {E220} Lucian, an Assyrian, who had travelled into Phoenicia and Egypt, states that the temples of Egypt were very old, those in Phoenicia built by Cinyras as old, and those in Assyria almost as old as the former. {*Lucian, The Goddess of Surrye, l. 1. (9) 4:347,349*} This shows that the kingdom of Assyria rose up after the kingdom of Egypt as is stated in the scriptures. This also shows that the temples of Egypt then standing, were those built by Sesostris, about the same time that the temples of Phoenicia and Cyprus were built by Cinyras, Benhadad I, and Hiram. This was not the first origin of idolatry but only of the building of much more sumptuous temples than formerly to the founders of new kingdoms for the first temples were very small. Ovid says:

> Jupiter had hardly room to stand upright in his cramped shrine. {*Ovid, Fasti, l. 1. (201) 5:17*}

455. Altars were at first built without temples and this custom continued in Persia until after the days of Herodotus. In Phoenicia they had altars with little houses for eating the sacrifices much earlier and they called these the high places. Such was the high place where Samuel entertained Saul and the house of Dagon at Ashdod into which the Philistines brought the ark. {E221} Likewise so was the house of Baal, where Jehu killed the prophets of Baal, and such were the high places of the Canaanites. Moses ordered Israel to destroy the altars, images, high places and groves of the Canaanites but made no mention of their temples as he would have done had there been any in those days. {Ex 34:13 Nu 33:52 De 7:5 12:3} I find no mention of sumptuous temples before the days of Solomon. New kingdoms then began to build sepulchres to their founders in the form of sumptuous temples. Hiram built such temples in Tyre, Sesostris in all Egypt and Benhadad I in Damascus.

456. In 1042 BC, when David defeated Hadadezer who was the king of Zobah, and killed the Syrians of Damascus who came to help him, Rezon, the son of Eliadah, fled from his master Hadadezer. {2Sa 8:10 1Ki 11:23} He gathered men to himself and became their captain and reigned in Damascus over Syria. He is also called Hezion. {1Ki 15:18} His successors mentioned in history were Tabrimon, Hadad or Benhadad I, Benhadad II, Hazael, Benhadad III and Rezin, the son of Tobeah. Syria became subject to Egypt in the days of Tabrimon and recovered her liberty under Benhadad II. In the days of Benhadad III until the reign of the last Rezin, they became subject to Israel. {E222} In the third year of Ahaz, the king of Judah, Tiglathpilasser, the king of Assyria, defeated the Syrians, ending their kingdom in 740 BC. Josephus states that the Syrians until his days worshipped both Adar, that is, Hadad or Benhadad I, and his successor Hazael as gods for their benefactions and for building temples by which they adorned the city of Damascus. He says that they daily have processions in honour of these kings and the glory of their antiquity, not knowing that they are of recent origin and lived not more than eleven hundred years ago. {*Josephus, Antiquities, l. 9. c. 4. s. 6. (93,94) 6:51*} It seems these kings built sumptuous sepulchres for themselves and were worshipped in them. Justin calls the first of these two kings *Damascus*, saying that the city was named after him and that in honour of him the Syrians worshipped his wife Arathes as a goddess, using her sepulchre for a temple. {*Justin, Trogus, l. 36. c. 2. s. 2. 1:229*}

457. We have another instance of the deification of kings in the kingdom of Byblus. In the reign of Minos, the king of Crete, when Rhadamanthus the brother of Minos led colonies from Crete to the islands of Greece, he gave the islands to his captains. Rhadamanthus gave Lemnos to his nephew Thoas, or Theias or Thoantes who was the father of Hypsipyle. Thoas was a metallurgist from Crete and by consequence a disciple of the Idean Dactyli, and perhaps a Phoenician. {*Diod. Sic., l. 5. c. 79. s. 1,2. 3:313*} It was the Curetes (also called the Idean Dactyli, Telchines and Corybantes) who brought their arts and sciences from Phoenicia. {E223} Suidas says that Thoas was descended from Pharnaces, the king of Cyprus. {Suidas, in Σαρδανατταλος} Apollodorus says that Thoas was the son of Sandochus a Syrian. {*Apollodorus, Library, l. 3. c. 14. s. 3. 2:83*} Apollonius Rhodius states that Thoas gave Jason the purple cloak which the Graces had made for Bacchus. He gave it to his son Thoas, the father of Hypsipyle, and a king of Lemnos. {*Apollonius, Argonautica, l. 4. v. 421-424. 1:323*} {*Apollonius, Argonautica, l. 1. v. 621. 1:45*} Thoas married Calycopis, the daughter of Otreus the king of Phrygia. She was the mother of Aeneas. For Thoas's skill on the harp, he was called Cinyras and was said to be exceedingly beloved by Apollo or Orus. {*Homer, Odyssey, l. 8. v. 268-294. 1:291,293*} {*Homer, Hymns-To Dionysus, l. 1. (A-C) 1:27-31*} {*Homer, Hymns-To Demeter, l. 1. (1-150) 1:33-43*} {*Hesiod, Theogony, l. 1. v. 194-198. 1:19*}

458. The great Bacchus loved the wife of Thoas and being caught in bed with her in Phrygia, appeased him with wine and settled the matter by appointing him king of Byblus and Cyprus. {*Pausanias, Attica, l. 1. c. 20. 1:99} Bacchus then came over the Hellespont with his army and conquered Thrace. The poets allude to these events in feigning that Vulcan fell from heaven into Lemnos and that Bacchus appeased him with wine, and brought him back into heaven. He again fell from the heaven of the gods of Crete when he went from Crete to Lemnos to work in metals. He was brought back to heaven when Bacchus appointed him king of Cyprus and Byblus. He reigned there until a very great age, living to the times of the Trojan War and becoming very rich. {E224} After the death of his wife Calycopis, he built temples to her at Paphos and Amathus in Cyprus and at Byblus in Syria. {*Clement, Exhoration to the Heathen, c. 3. ANF2:184} {*Apollodorus, Library, l. 3. c. 14. s. 3. 1:83} {*Pindar, Pythian Ode 2, l. 1. (20-27) 1:65} {Hesychius, in Κινυραδαι} {Stephanus, in Αμαθους} {*Strabo, l. 16. c. 2. s. 18. (755) 7:263} He instituted priests to her with sacred rites and the lustful Orgia. or secret rites. From this she became known as the Dea Cypria the goddess of Cyprus and the Dea Syria the goddess of Syria. From the temples erected to her in these and other places she was also called Paphia, Amathusia, Byblia, Cytherea, Salaminia, Cnidia, Erycina and Idalia. Tacitus states:

> A more recent tradition reports that the temple (most ancient temple of Paphian Venus) was consecrated by Cinyras, and that the goddess herself, after she sprang from the sea, was wafted here. {*Tacitus, Histories, l. 2. c. 3. 2:163,165}

459. Calycopis sailed from Phrygia to the island of Cythera, and from there to Cyprus where she became queen. The Cyprians say that she was born from the sea and they painted her sailing upon a shell. Cinyras deified his son Gingris under the name of Adonis. For helping the Egyptians develop armour, it is probable that Cinyras himself was deified by his friends the Egyptians by the name of Baal Canaan, or Vulcan. Vulcan was celebrated principally by the Egyptians, and was a king according to Homer and reigned in Lemnos. Cinyras was an inventor of arts, the smelting of copper ore in Cyprus, and also tongs, hammer, crowbar and the anvil. {Clement, Exhoration to the Heathen, p. 21.} {*Pliny, l. 7. c. 56. (195) 2:637,639} He employed workmen in making armour and other things of bronze and iron and was the only king famous in history for metallurgy. {E225} He was the king of Lemnos and the husband of Venus. All these are the characteristics of Vulcan. The Egyptians about the time of the death of Cinyras, that is, in the reign of their King Amenophis, built a very sumptuous temple at Memphis to Vulcan and near it a smaller temple to Venus Hospita. She was not an Egyptian woman but a foreigner, not Helen but Vulcan's Venus. Herodotus states that the region around this temple was inhabited by Tyrian Phoenicians. {*Herodotus, l. 2. c. 112. 1:401} When Cambyses entered this temple at Memphis, he very much derided the statue of Vulcan for its small size. {*Herodotus, l. 3. c. 37. 2:49,51} Cambyses said that this statue is most like those gods which the Phoenicians call Pataeci and carry about in the prows of their ships in the form of pygmies. Bochart says of this goddess Venus Hospita:

> Phoeniciam Venerem in Aegypto pro peregrina habitam. {Bochart, Canaan, l. 1. c. 4.}

having the Phoenician Venus in Egypt for a foreign deity."

10. The Origin of Hieroglyphic Figures

460. As the Egyptians, Phoenicians and Syrians in those days deified their kings and princes, so when they came into Asia Minor and Greece, they taught those countries to do the same as we have shown previously. In those days the writing of the Thebans and Ethiopians was in hieroglyphics. This method of writing seems to have spread into Lower Egypt before the days of Moses. With this came the worship of their gods in the various shapes of birds, beasts and fishes, all of which was forbidden in the second commandment. {Ex 20:4,5} {E226} The Thebans and Ethiopians, in the days of Saul, David, Solomon and Rehoboam had conquered Egypt and the surrounding countries and built a great empire. This symbolic way of writing was the way to represent and signify their conquering kings and princes. They did not write down their names but made various hieroglyphic figures to symbolise them and their deeds. Consider the following:

1) Ammon is represented with rams' horns, to signify the king who conquered Libya, a country abounding with sheep.

2) Ammosis, the father of Ammon, is represented with a scythe, to signify that king who conquered Lower Egypt, a country abounding with grain.

3) Osiris, the son of Ammon, is represented with an ox, because he taught the conquered nations to plow with oxen.

4) Bacchus is represented with bull's horns for the same reason and with grapes because he taught the nations to plant vines, and on a tiger because he subdued India.

5) Orus, the son of Osiris, is represented with a harp to signify the prince was a highly skilled harpist.

6) Jupiter is represented on an eagle to signify the sublimity of his dominion and with a thunderbolt to represent him as a warrior.

7) Venus is represented in a chariot drawn with two doves to signify her amorous and lustful ways.

8) Neptune is represented with a trident to signify the commander of a fleet composed of three squadrons. {E227}

9) Aegeon is represented as a giant with fifty heads and a hundred hands to signify Neptune with his men in a ship of fifty oars.

10) Thoth is represented with a dog's head and wings at his cap and feet.

11) Caduceus is represented wrapped about with two snakes to signify a man of craft and an ambassador who reconciled two contending nations.

12) Pan is represented with a pipe and the legs of a goat to signify a man delighted in piping and dancing.

13) Hercules (Egyptian) is represented with pillars and a club because Sesostris set up pillars in all his conquests and fought against the Libyans with clubs.

461. According to Eudoxus, this is that Hercules (Egyptian) who was killed by Typhon. {*Athenaeus, l. 9. (392d) 4:275*} According to Ptolemy, Hephaestion was called Nilus, who conquered Geryon with his three sons in Spain and set up the famous pillars at the mouth of the Strait of Gibraltar. {*Ptolemy, Hephaestus, l. 2.*} Diodorus mentions three men named Hercules, the Egyptian, the Cretan and Greek who was the son of Alcmena. The oldest one lived among the Egyptians and after he conquered most of the world, set up the pillars in Libya. {*Diod. Sic., l. 3. c. 74. s. 4. 2:331*} Vasaeus says that Osiris, called also Dionysus, came into Spain and conquered Geryon. He was the first who brought idolatry into Spain. {*Vasaeus, Chronicles of Spain, c. 10.*} Strabo states that the Ethiopians who were called Megabars, fought with clubs. {*Strabo, l. 16. c. 4. s. 17. (776) 7:339*} Homer says some of the Greeks also fought with clubs until the time of the Trojan War. {E228}

462. From this hieroglyphic way of writing it happened that when Sesostris divided Egypt into nomes, the great men of the kingdom to whom the nomes were dedicated, were represented in their sepulchres or temples of the nomes by various hieroglyphics. For example, some were represented as an ox, a cat, a dog, a cebus, a goat, a lion, a scarabaeus, an ichneumon, a crocodile, a hippopotamus, an oxyrinchus, an ibis, a crow, a hawk or a green-leek (a type of parrot). They were worshipped in the nomes in the shape of these creatures.

11. Exaggerated Antiquities

463. Ammon, the Egyptian, conquered the Atlanteans, a people living on Mount Atlas. The Atlanteans state that Uranus was their first king and changed them from their lawless ways and settled them in towns and cities. He taught them how to cultivate fruits and store them. He reigned over most of the world and by his wife Titaea had eighteen children, among whom were Hyperion and Basilea, the parents of Helius and Selene. The brothers of Hyperion murdered him and drowned his son Helius, the Phaeton of the ancients, in the Nile River and divided his kingdom among themselves. {*Diod. Sic., l. 3. c. 56,57. 2:263-267*} The country, which bordered on the oceans, fell to the lot of Atlas, from whom the people were called Atlanteans. I understand Uranus or Jupiter Uranus, Hyperion, Basilea, Helius and Selene, to correspond to Jupiter Ammon, Osiris, Isis, Orus and Bubaste. {E229} I take the sharing of the kingdom of Hyperion among his brothers the Titans, to be the division of the earth among the gods mentioned in the poem of Solon.

464. When Solon travelled into Egypt, he talked with the priests of Sais about their history. He wrote a poem of what he had learned but did not finish it. It eventually came into the hands of Plato. {*Plato, Timaeus, l. 1 (21C) 9:31*} {*Plato, Critias, l. 1. (109DE) 9:265*} Plato relates from it that at the mouth of the Strait of Gibraltar near the pillars of Hercules there was an island called Atlantis. Its inhabitants lived nine thousand years before the days of Solon and reigned over Libya as far as Egypt and over Europe as far as the Tyrrhene Sea. Gathering forces from these countries, they invaded Egypt and Greece and whatever was contained within the pillars of Hercules or the Mediterranean Sea. They were opposed and their advance halted by the Athenians and other Greeks so that the remaining countries were not conquered. Plato continues and says that in those days after the gods had finished their conquests, they divided the whole earth among themselves into larger and smaller regions and instituted temples and sacred rites to themselves. The island of Atlantis fell to the lot of Neptune, who appointed his oldest son Atlas king of the whole island, a part of which was called Gadir. {E230} In the history of the wars between Cecrops I, Erechtheus, Erichthonius, and others before the time of Theseus, women fought along side men in similar clothes and in the same manner as Minerva. In those days the study of war was common to both men and women. By all these circumstances, the following is obvious:

1) These gods were the *Dii magni maiorum gentium,* the *Great Gods of the Greater Nations* and lived between the time of Cecrops I and Theseus.

2) The wars, which Sesostris with his brother Neptune made on the countries by land and sea, the resistance he met with in Greece and the following invasion of Egypt by Neptune, are described here.

3) The captains of Sesostris shared his conquests among themselves just as the captains of Alexander the Great did with his conquests much later.

4) They instituted temples, priests and sacred rites to themselves and caused the nations to worship them after their death as gods.

5) The island of Gadir or Gades, with all Libya, fell to the lot of him who after death was deified by the name of Neptune.

6) The time therefore when these things were done is limited by Solon to the age of Neptune, the father of Atlas.

465. Homer states that Ulysses soon after the Trojan War found Calypso, the daughter of Atlas, on the island of Ogygia, perhaps Gadir. {*Homer, Odyssey, l. 7. v. 244,245. 1:265} {E231} Therefore, the age of Neptune was only two generations before the Trojan War. This is that Neptune, who with Apollo or Orus fortified Troy with a wall in the reign of Laomedon, who was the father of Priam. Neptune had many natural children in Greece, some of which were Argonauts, and others were contemporary to the Argonauts. Therefore, he lived only one generation before the Argonaut Expedition and by consequence about four hundred years before Solon went into Egypt. However, the priests of Egypt in those four hundred years had so exaggerated the stories and antiquity of their gods as to make them nine thousand years older than Solon. They made the island of Atlantis larger than all Africa and Asia together and full of people! Since in the days of Solon this large island was not found, they pretended that it sank into the sea with all its people. So great was the vanity of the priests of Egypt in magnifying their antiquities.

12. Antaeus and Atlas are the Same Person

466. The Cretans say that after Saturn gave Neptune the dominion of the sea, Neptune was the first man to outfit a fleet. That is why the tradition has been passed along that he controls whatever is done on the sea, and why mariners honour him with sacrifices. {*Diod. Sic., l. 5. c. 69. s. 4. 3:285} Pamphos states that Neptune invented tall ships with sails. {*Pausanias, Achaia, l. 7. c. 21. s. 9. 3:295} Herodotus affirms that Neptune was first worshipped in North Africa and therefore reigned over that province. {*Herodotus, l. 2. c. 50. 1:339} His oldest son Atlas, who succeeded him, was not only king of the island of Atlantis but also reigned over a great part of Libya. He gave his name to the people called Atlanteans, the mountain of Atlas and the Atlantic Ocean. The Egyptians called the farthest parts of the earth and promontories and whatever bordered on the sea and its coastal areas by the name of *Neptys.* {*Plutarch, Moralia-Isis and Osiris, l. 1. c. 75. (381F) 5:177} (The Roman goddess Neptys was the wife of the god Neptune whose Greek equivalents are Amphitrite and Poseidon respectively. Editor.) Bochart and Arius Montanus locate the home of the Naphtuhim, a people descended from Mizraim, on the coasts of Marmorica and Byrene. {Ge 10:13} Hence, this may be the origin of the names for Neptune and his wife Neptys since the words *Neptune, Neptys* and *Naphtuhim* mean the *king, queen* and *people of the seacoasts* respectively. The Greeks say that Japetus was the father of Atlas and Bochart derives the names Japetus and Neptune from the same original root word. Neptune and his son Atlas are celebrated in the ancient fables for making war upon the gods of Egypt.

467. Lucian says that Corinth is full of fables of this war which tell of the fight of Sol and Neptune, that is, of Apollo and Python, or Orus and Typhon. {*Lucian, Dance, l. 1. (42) 5:253} Agatharcides relates how the gods of Egypt fled from the giants, until the Titans arrived and saved them by putting Neptune to flight. {Photius, Bibliotheca} Hyginus tells of the war between the gods of Egypt and the Titans led by Atlas. {*Hyginus, Fabulae, l. 1. c. 150. 1:149} {E233} The Titans are the posterity of Titaea, some of whom under Hercules (Egyptian) assisted the gods, others under Neptune and Atlas warred against them. For this reason Plutarch says the priests of Egypt hated the sea and held Neptune in contempt. {*Plutarch, Moralia-Isis and Osiris, l. 1. c. 75. (381F) 5:177} By Hercules (Egyptian), I understand here the general of the forces of Thebes (Egyptian) and Ethiopia whom the gods or great men of Egypt called in to their assistance. These fought against the Titans or great men of Libya, who had murdered Osiris and invaded Egypt. Diodorus says that when Osiris made his expedition over the world he left his relative Hercules (Egyptian) as general of his forces over all his dominions, and Antaeus as governor of Libya and Ethiopia. {*Diod. Sic., l. 1. c. 17. s. 3. 1:55} Antaeus reigned over all of North Africa to the Atlantic Ocean and built Tingis or Tangieres. Pindar says that he reigned at Irasa, a town of Libya, where Cyrene was later built and that he invaded Egypt and Thebes (Egyptian). {*Pindar, Pythian Ode 9, l. 1. (106) 1:353} Antaeus was defeated by Hercules (Egyptian) and the Egyptians near Antaea or Antaeopolis, a town of Thebes (Egyptian). Diodorus says that this town had its name from Antaeus, whom Hercules (Egyptian) killed in the days of Osiris. {*Diod. Sic., l. 1. c. 21. s. 4,5. 1:67} Hercules (Egyptian) overthrew him several times, and every time he grew stronger by recruits from Libya, his mother earth. Finally, Hercules (Egyptian) intercepted his recruits and at length killed him. {E234} In these wars Hercules (Egyptian) took the Libyan world from Atlas and made Atlas pay tribute from his golden orchard, the kingdom of North Africa. Consider the following about Antaeus and Atlas:

1) Both were sons of Neptune,

2) Both reigned over all Libya and North Africa, between Mount Atlas and the Mediterranean Sea to the Atlantic Ocean.

3) Both invaded Egypt,

4) Both fought with Hercules (Egyptian) in the wars of the gods.

468. Therefore, they are only two names for one and the same man. Even the name of Atlas in the oblique cases seems to have been compounded from the name of Antaeus and some other word, perhaps the word *Atal* preceding it. Ovid says concerning the invasion of Egypt by Antaeus that Hercules (Egyptian) said:

I deprived Antaeus of his mother's strength.

{*Ovid, Metamorphoses, l. 9. (183,184) 4:17}

469. This war between the gods and the Titans was finally settled by the intervention of Mercury. In memory of this he was said to reconcile two contending snakes by casting his ambassador's rod between them. This is what we can gather from Solon concerning the ancient state of Egypt, Libya and Greece.

470. The mythology of the Cretans differed in some things from that of Egypt and Libya. {E235} In their mythology, Caelus and Terra, or Uranus and Titaea, were the parents of Saturn (Cretan) and Rhea (Cretan) who were the parents of Jupiter and Juno. Hyperion, Japetus and the Titans were one generation older than Jupiter (Cretan). Saturn (Cretan) was expelled from his kingdom and castrated by his son Jupiter. This fable has no equivalent in the mythology of Egypt.

13. The Times after Sesostris

471. During part of the reign of Sesostris, Jeroboam I was in subjection to Egypt. He set up the gods of Egypt in Dan and Bethel after he rebelled from Judah.

3 Now for a long season Israel *hath been* without the true God, and without a teaching priest, and without law. 5 And in those times *there was* no peace to him that went out, nor to him that came in, but great vexations *were* upon all the inhabitants of the countries. 6 And nation was destroyed of nation, and city of city: for God did vex them with all adversity. {2Ch 15:3,5,6}

13.1 Orus (951–942 BC)

472. However, in the fifth year of Asa, the land of Judah had rest from war for ten years from 951 to 942 BC. Asa took away the altars of the strange gods, broke down the images and built the fortified cities of Judah with walls, towers, gates and bars. During this period of rest from war, he raised an army of five hundred and eighty thousand men. In the fifteenth year of his reign in 941 BC, he met Zerah the Ethiopian, who came out against him with an army of a million Ethiopians and Libyans. {E236} Since the way of the Libyans was through Egypt, therefore Zerah was now master of Egypt. They fought at Mareshah near Gerar, between Egypt and Judah, and Zerah was irreparably defeated. From all this I seem to gather that Osiris was killed in the fifth year of Asa in 951 BC and thereupon Egypt embroiled in civil wars. It was invaded by the Libyans and defended by the Ethiopians for a time. After ten more years it was invaded by the Ethiopians. They killed Orus, the son and successor of Osiris, drowning him in the Nile, and seizing his kingdom. These civil wars in Egypt gave the land of Judah peace for ten years. According to Manetho, Osiris or Sesostris reigned for forty-eight years. If this is true, then he began to reign about the eighteenth year of Solomon in 998 BC and Orus, his son, was drowned in the fourteenth year of Asa in 942 BC.

473. Pliny states:

Ethiopia was worn out by alternating periods of dominance and subjection in a series of wars with Egypt, having been a famous and powerful country even down to the Trojan Wars, when Memnon was king. {*Pliny, l. 6. c. 35. (182) 2:475}

474. Ethiopia served Egypt until the death of Sesostris and no longer. Herodotus states that only he ever

subjected Ethiopia. When he died, the Ethiopians became free and after ten years became the masters of Egypt and Libya under Zerah and Amenophis. {*Herodotus, l. 2. c. 110. 1:399}

475. By his victory over Zerah, Asa no longer had anything to fear from Egypt and he assembled all the people. They offered sacrifices from the plunder and entered into a covenant with an oath to seek the Lord. {E237} In lieu of the temple vessels taken away by Sesostris from Rehoboam, he brought into the house of God the things that he and his father had dedicated, silver, gold and other vessels. {2Ch 15:9-15,18}

13.2 Osarsiphus (940–927 BC)

476. When Zerah was irreparably defeated, the people of Lower Egypt revolted from the Ethiopians and called in to their assistance two hundred thousand Jews and Canaanites. {*Josephus, Against Apion, l. 1. c. 28. (262,263) 1:271} Under the command of Osarsiphus, a priest of Egypt, called Usorthon, Osorchon, Osorchor, and Hercules Egyptius by Manetho, they forced the Ethiopians, now commanded by Memnon, to retire to Memphis in 940 BC. There Memnon turned the Nile River into a new channel, built a bridge over it, fortified that pass and then returned into Ethiopia. After thirteen years in 926 BC, Memnon and his young son Ramesses came down with an army from Ethiopia, conquered Lower Egypt and drove out the Jews and Phoenicians. The Egyptian writers and their followers call this event the second expulsion of the Shepherds and confound Osarsiphus with Moses.

477. Tithonus, a handsome youth and the older brother of Priam, was carried captive into Ethiopia along with many captives by Sesostris. {E238} Before the days of Hesiod the Greeks imagined that Memnon was his son. Therefore, Memnon, in the opinion of those ancient Greeks, was one generation younger than Tithonus and was born after the return of Sesostris into Egypt, which may have been about sixteen or twenty years after the death of Solomon, around 959 to 955 BC. He is said to have lived very long and so might have died about eighty-eight years after Solomon as we reckoned above, around 887 BC. In a statue erected to his mother in Egypt, called Cissia by Aeschylus, she was represented as the daughter, the wife, and the mother of a king, and therefore he was the son of a king. {*Diod. Sic., l. 1. c. 47. s. 5. 1:169} {*Aeschylus, Libation Bearers, l. 1. v. 423,424. 1:108} This makes it probable that Zerah, whom he succeeded in the kingdom of Ethiopia, was his father.

13.3 Menes or Amenophis (926–887 BC)

478. Historians agree that Menes reigned in Egypt next after the gods, turned the river into a new channel, built a bridge over it, built Memphis and the magnificent temple of Vulcan. {*Herodotus, l. 2. c. 101. 1:389} He built Memphis opposite the place where Grand Cairo now stands, called by the Arabian historians Mesir. He built only the body of the temple of Vulcan and his successors Ramesses or Rhampsinitus, Moeris, Asychis, and Psammitichus built its western, northern, eastern and southern porticos. Psammitichus, who built the last portico of this temple, reigned about three hundred years after the victory of Asa over Zerah. {E239} It is not likely that this temple could be more than three hundred years in construction or that any Menes could be king of all Egypt before the expulsion of the Shepherds. The last of the gods of Egypt was Orus, with his mother Isis, sister Bubaste, secretary Thoth and uncle Typhon. The king who reigned next after all their deaths, turned the river into a new channel, built a bridge over it, built Memphis and the temple of Vulcan. He was Memnon or Amenophis who was called by the Egyptians Amenoph. Therefore, he is Menes for the names *Amenoph,* or *Menoph,* and *Menes* do not differ by much. From Amenoph, the city of Memphis built by Menes had its Egyptian names of *Moph, Noph, Menoph* or *Menus,* as it is still called by the Arabian historians. It was built to fortify this place against Osarsiphus.

14. The Argonaut Expedition

479. When Lower Egypt revolted under Osarsiphus then Amenophis retired into Ethiopia and Egypt was in much civil unrest. The Greeks built the ship *Argo* and sent the flower of Greek youth in it to Aeetes in Colchis and to many other princes on the coasts of the Black and Mediterranean seas. This ship was built after the pattern of the ship from Egypt with fifty oars in which Danaus with his fifty daughters had fled from Egypt into Greece a few years earlier. {E240} It was the first long ship with sails built by the Greeks and designed to send envoys to many states. This was too great an undertaking to be done without the concurrence and co-operation of the princes and states of Greece and perhaps the approval of the Amphictyonic Council for it was done by the dictates of an oracle. This council met semi-annually to discuss state affairs for the welfare of Greece. Therefore, they knew of this expedition and might have sent the Argonauts on an embassy to these princes. To conceal their mission, they might have created the fable of the golden fleece, in relation to the ship of Phrixus whose ensign was a golden ram. Probably their intentions were to spread the news to these princes of the civil disorder in Egypt and its invasion by the Ethiopians and Israelites. They hoped to persuade them to use this opportunity to revolt from Egypt and establish

independent governments and make a league with the Greeks.

480. The Argonauts went through the kingdom of Colchis by land to the Armenians, and through Armenia to the Medes. {*Strabo, l. 1. c. 3. s. 2. (48) 1:177} This would be impossible if the countries through which they passed were hostile. {E241} They also visited Laomedon, the king of the Trojans, Phineus, the king of the Thracians, Cyzicus, the king of the Doliones, and Lycus, the king of the Mariandyni. They also visited the coasts of Mysia and Taurica Chersonesus, the countries on the Tanais, the people around Byzantium, and the coasts of Epirus, Corsica, Melita, Italy, Sicily, Sardinia and Gallia on the Mediterranean Sea. From there they crossed the sea to North Africa and conferred with Euripylus, the king of Cyrene. {*Pindar, Pythian Ode 4, l. 1. (171-262) 1:283-293} Strabo states that in Armenia and Media, and the neighbouring places, there were numerous monuments to this expedition of Jason. Likewise there were monuments around Sinope and its sea coasts, the Propontis and the Hellespont, and in the Mediterranean. These envoys from the Greeks to so many nations could only be state policy on the part of the Greeks. These nations had been invaded by the Egyptians, but after this expedition we hear no more of their continuing in subjection to Egypt. {*Strabo, l. 1. c. 2. s. 10. (21) 1:75,77} {*Strabo, l. 1. c. 2. s. 38. (45) 1:165,167} {*Strabo, l. 1. c. 2. s. 39. (46) 1:167,169}

15. Exploits of Menes

481. The Egyptians originally subsisted on the fruits of the earth and the produce from the Nile River and fared well. {*Diod. Sic., l. 1. c. 43. 1:153-157} They abstained from animals and therefore hated shepherds. Menes taught them to worship the gods and offer sacrifices, and also to supply themselves with tables and couches and to use costly bedding. He introduced luxury and an extravagant lifestyle. {*Diod. Sic., l. 1. c. 45. s. 1. 1:159} {E242} About a hundred years after his death, Tnephachthus, one of his successors, cursed Menes for it and to reduce the luxury of Egypt, he inscribed his curse on the temple of Jupiter Ammon at Thebes (Egyptian). This curse diminished the fame of Menes among the Egyptians. {*Diod. Sic., l. 1. c. 45. s. 2,3. 1:159,161}

16. Egypt After the Expulsion of the Shepherds

482. The kings of Egypt who expelled the Shepherds and succeeded them, I think reigned first at Coptos, and then at Thebes (Egyptian), and later at Memphis. At Coptos, I place Misphragmuthosis and Amosis I or Thomosis who expelled the Shepherds. They abolished their custom of sacrificing men and extended the Coptic language, and the name of Αια Κοπτου or *Aegyptus* to the conquered land. Then Thebes (Egyptian) became the royal city of Ammon, and was called No-Ammon after him, and his conquest on the west of Egypt was called Ammonia. After him, Osiris, Orus, Menes or Amenophis, and Ramesses reigned in the same city of Thebes (Egyptian). Memphis and her wonders were not yet famous in Greece for Homer notes Thebes (Egyptian) as being in its glory in his days, and makes no mention of Memphis. After Menes had built Memphis, Moeris, the successor of Ramesses, embellished it making it the capital of the kingdom. This was almost two generations after the Trojan War. Cinyras was the Vulcan who married Venus, and under the kings of Egypt reigned over Cyprus and part of Phoenicia, and made armour for those kings. He lived until the times of the Trojan War. {E243} After his death Menes or Memnon might have deified him and started to build the famous temple of Vulcan in that city for his worship but not live to finish it. Manetho states that in a plain near Memphis there are many small pyramids which are said to have been built by Venephes or Enephes. I suspect that Venephes and Enephes are corruptions for the names Menephes or Amenophis, since the letters *AM* are almost worn away in some old manuscripts. After the example of these pyramids, the following kings, Moeris and his successors, built much larger ones. The plain in which they were built was the burying place of that city as appears by the mummies which are found there. Therefore, the pyramids were the sepulchral monuments of the kings and princes of that city. By these and other such works the city grew famous soon after the days of Homer who therefore lived in the reign of Ramesses.

17. The Amended King Lists of Egypt

483. Herodotus is the oldest extant historian who wrote of the antiquities of Egypt and got his material from the priests of that country. {*Herodotus, l. 2. c. 1-182. 1:275-497} Diodorus, who wrote almost four hundred years after him, also got his material from the priests of Egypt. By that time, the priests had placed many nameless kings between those whom Herodotus had placed in continuous succession. {E244} Therefore, the priests of Egypt between the time of Herodotus and Diodorus, from vanity, had greatly increased the number of their kings. What they did after the time of Herodotus, they surely began to do before his time for Herodotus states that they cited to him from their books the names of three hundred and thirty kings who reigned after Menes, but did nothing of note except for Nitocris and Moeris who were the last two of them. All these reigned at Thebes (Egyptian), until Moeris moved the capital of the empire from Thebes (Egyptian) to

Memphis. After Moeris he lists Sesostris, Pheron, Proteus, Rhampsinitus, Cheops, Chephron, Mycerinus, Asychis, Anysis, Sabacon, Anysis (a second time), Sethon, the twelve contemporary kings followed by Psammitichus, Nechus, Psammis, Apries, Amasis, and Psammenitus.

484. Before the days of Solon, the Egyptians had made their kingdom nine thousand years old. To justify this, they told Herodotus of a succession of three hundred and thirty kings reigning as many generations, that is, about eleven thousand years before Sesostris. However, the kings who reigned long before Sesostris might reign over several little kingdoms in various parts of Egypt before the rise of their united kingdom. By consequence, this would be before the days of Eli and Samuel, and we are not considering that time period. Also the number of these names may have been greatly multiplied by corruption. {E245} Some of them, such as Athothes or Thoth, the secretary of Osiris, Tosorthrus or Aesculapius a physician who invented building with square stones, and Thuor or Polybus, the husband of Acandra, were only princes in Egypt.

485. If we follow Herodotus and omit the names of those kings who did nothing of note and consider only those whose actions are recorded and who left splendid monuments of their having reigned over Egypt, such as temples, statues, pyramids, obelisks and palaces dedicated or ascribed to them, we get a much smaller list of kings. When these kings are arranged in order, we have all or almost all the kings of Egypt from the days of the expulsion of the Shepherds and the founding of the kingdom, down to the conquest of Egypt by Cambyses.

17.1 Sesostris (998–951 BC)

486. Sesostris reigned in the age of the gods of Egypt, being deified under the names of Osiris, Hercules (Egyptian) and Bacchus, as noted previously. Therefore, Menes, Nitocris, and Moeris are to be placed after him. Menes and his son Ramesses reigned next after the gods and therefore Nitocris and Moeris reigned after Ramesses. Moeris is recorded immediately before Cheops, three times in the dynasties of the kings of Egypt composed by Eratosthenes and once in the dynasties of Manetho. In the same dynasties, Nitocris is recorded after the builders of the three great pyramids. {E246} According to Herodotus, her brother reigned before her and was murdered and she revenged his death. {*Herodotus, l. 2. c. 100. 1:387,389} According to George Syncellus she built the third great pyramid and the builders of the pyramids reigned at Memphis and by consequence after Moeris. {*Syncellus, l. 1. (65) 1:83} From these things I deduce that the

kings of Egypt mentioned by Herodotus ought to be placed in this order: Sesostris, Pheron, Proteus, Menes, Rhampsinitus, Moeris, Cheops, Chephron, Mycerinus, Nitocris, Asychis, Anysis, Sabacon, Anysis (a second time), Sethon, the twelve contemporary kings followed by Psammitichus, Nechus, Psammis, Apries, Amasis and Psammenitus.

17.2 Pheron (950–941 BC)

487. Pheron was the son and successor of Sesostris. {*Herodotus, l. 2. c. 111. 1:399} He was deified under the name of Orus.

17.3 Proteus (viceroy for Amenophis) (c. 900 BC)

488. Proteus reigned in Lower Egypt when Paris sailed there, that is at the end of the Trojan War around 900 BC, according to Herodotus. {*Herodotus, l. 2. c. 114. 1:403} At that time, Amenophis was king of Egypt and Ethiopia but in his absence Proteus might have been the governor of some part of Lower Egypt under him. Homer locates Proteus in the sea coasts making him a sea god, and calls him the servant of Neptune. {*Homer, Odyssey, l. 4. v. 384-386. 1:147} Herodotus says that he rose up from among the common people, and that Proteus is the Greek translation of his name. {*Herodotus, l. 2. c. 112. 1:401} This name in Greek means only a *prince* or *president*. {E247} He succeeded Pheron and was succeeded by Rhampsinitus according to Herodotus and so was contemporary with Amenophis.

17.4 Menes or Amenophis (940–886 BC)

489. Amenophis reigned next after Orus and Isis who were the last of the gods. He first reigned over all Egypt and then over Memphis and Upper Egypt. After his conquest of Osarsiphus, who had revolted from him, he became king of all Egypt again about forty-nine years after the death of Solomon in 926 BC. He built Memphis and ordered the worship of the gods of Egypt. He built a palace at Abydus, the Memnonia at This and Susa and the magnificent temple of Vulcan in Memphis. After Tosorthrus discovered the method for building with square stones, Amenophis built the Aesculapius of Egypt. Corruptions of his name include Menes, Mines, Minaeus, Mineus, Minies, Mnevis, Enephes, Venephes, Phamenophis, Osymanthias, Osimandes, Ismandes, Imandes, Memnon and Arminon.

17.5 Rhampsinitus or Ramesses (887–861 BC)

490. Amenophis was succeeded by his son, called by Herodotus Rhampsinitus, and by others Ramses, Ramises, Rameses, Ramesses, Ramestes, Rhampses or Remphis. Emperor Constantius had the obelisk erected by this king in Heliopolis sent to Rome. It contained an inscription, which was interpreted by Hermapion, an Egyptian priest, expressing that the king was long lived, and reigned over a great part of the earth. {*Ammianus, l. 17. c. 4. s. 13-18. 1:323-329} {E248} Strabo, an eyewitness, says that in the monuments of the kings of Egypt, south of Memnonium were inscriptions on obelisks, expressing the riches of the kings, and their reigning as far as Scythia, Bactria, India and Ionia. {*Strabo, l. 17. c. 1. s. 42. (813) 8:111,113} Tacitus writes of an inscription seen at Thebes (Egyptian) by Caesar Germanicus and interpreted to him by the Egyptian priests. It said this King Ramesses had an army of seven hundred thousand men and reigned over Libya, Ethiopia, Media, Persia, Bactria, Scythia, Armenia, Cappadocia, Bithynia and Lycia. {*Tacitus, Annals, l. 2. c. 60. 3:491} Hence, the kingdom of Assyria could not yet have been established. This king was very covetous and a great collector of taxes. He was one of the richest of all the kings of Egypt and built the western portico of the temple of Vulcan. {*Herodotus, l. 2. c. 121. 1:415}

17.6 Moeris (860–839 BC)

491. Moeris, inheriting the riches of Ramesses, built the northern portico of that temple of Vulcan more sumptuously and created the Lake of Moeris with two large brick pyramids in the middle of it. The king wrote a book of surveying which gave rise to the beginning of geometry. He used this knowledge to divide Egypt into equal shares among the soldiers. {*Herodotus, l. 2. c. 101. 1:389} He is called also Maris, Myris, Meres, Marres, Smarres; and more corruptly, by changing M into A, T, B, Σ, YX, Λ, etc., resulting in names like Ayres, Tyris, Byires, Soris, Uchoreus, Lachares, Labaris, etc.

492. Diodorus places Uchoreus between Osymandias and Myris, that is, between Amenophis and Moeris. He says that he built Memphis and fortified it with a large rampart of earth, and a broad and deep trench, which was filled with the water of the Nile. He made there a vast and deep lake for holding the water of the Nile when it flooded, and he built palaces in the city. This place was so ideally located that most of the kings who reigned after him preferred it ahead of Thebes (Egyptian), and moved the court from there to this place. After this, over time the magnificence of Thebes (Egyptian) began to decline and that of Memphis to increase until Alexander the Great built Alexandria. {*Diod. Sic., l. 1. c. 50. s. 3. 1:177} These great works of Uchoreus and those of Moeris savour of one and the same genius, and were certainly done by one and the same king. They were distinguished into two by

a corruption of the name as noted previously for this Lake of Uchoreus was certainly the same as the Lake of Moeris.

17.7 Cheops (838–825 BC), Chephron (824–809 BC), Mycerinus (808–803 BC) and Nitocris (802–789 BC)

493. After the example of the two brick pyramids made by Moeris, the next three kings, Cheops, Chephron and Mycerinus built the three large pyramids at Memphis and therefore reigned in that city. Cheops closed the temples of the nomes and prohibited the worship of the gods of Egypt. No doubt he intended to be worshipped after he died. {E250} He is called also Chembis, Chemmis, Chemnis, Phiops, Apathus, Apappus, Suphis, Saophis, Syphoas, Syphaosis, Soiphis, Syphuris, Aniophis and Anoisis. He built the largest of the three pyramids which stand together. His brother Chephron or Cerpheres built the second, and his son Mycerinus built the third. This last king was famous for clemency and justice. He enclosed the dead body of his daughter in a hollow ox and caused her to be worshipped daily with perfumes. He is called also Cheres, Cherinus, Bicheres, Moscheres and Mencheres. He died before the third pyramid was finished and his sister and successor Nitocris finished it. {*Herodotus, l. 2. c. 124-135. 1:429-439} {*Diod. Sic., l. 1. c. 63,64. 1:215-223}

17.8 Asychis (788–780? BC)

494. After Nitocris, Asychis reigned and he built the eastern portico of the temple of Vulcan very splendidly. From the mud dug from the Lake of Moeris, he made a large brick pyramid among the smaller pyramids. These are the kings who reigned at Memphis and spent their time in adorning that city until the Ethiopians and the Assyrians and others revolted. Egypt lost all her empire abroad and again became divided into several small kingdoms. {*Herodotus, l. 2. c. 136. 1:439,441}

17.9 Egypt Breaks up into Four Kingdoms (780?–752 BC)

495. Egypt broke up into at least four independent kingdoms.

1) One of those kingdoms was at Memphis in Upper Egypt, under Gnephactus, and his son and successor Bocchoris. {E251} Africanus calls Bocchoris a Saite but Sais at this time had other kings. Gnephactus, otherwise called Neochabis, Technatis and Tnephachthus, cursed Menes for his luxury, and caused the curse to be recorded in the temple of Jupiter Ammon at Thebes (Egyptian). {*Diod. Sic., l. 1. c. 45. s. 2,3. 1:161} Therefore, he reigned over Thebes (Egyptian). Bocchoris sent in a wild

bull on the god Mnevis which was worshipped at Heliopolis.

2) Another of those kingdoms was at Anysis, or Hanes, under its king Anysis or Amosis. {Isa 30:4}

3) A third kingdom was at Sais, under Stephanathis, Necepsos and Nechus.

4) A fourth one was at Tanis or Zoan, under Petubastes, Osorchon and Psammis.

17.10 Sabacon (751–702 BC)

496. Egypt was weakened by these divisions and was invaded and conquered by the Ethiopians under Sabacon. He killed Bocchoris and Nechus and forced Anysis to flee. The Olympiads began in the reign of Petubastes, and the era of Nabonassar in the twenty-second year of the reign of Bocchoris according to Africanus. Therefore, the division of Egypt into many kingdoms began before the Olympiads but not more than the time of two reigns of kings before them.

17.10.1 Era of Nabonassar Established

497. After the study of astronomy was established for the use of navigation, the Egyptians, by noting the heliacal risings and settings of the stars, had determined the length of the solar year to be three hundred and sixty-five days. {E252} By other observations they had determined the solstices, and formed the fixed stars into constellations, all which was done in the reign of Ammon, Sesostris, Orus and Memnon. It may be presumed that they continued to observe the motions of the planets for they called them after the names of their gods. Necepsos or Nechepsos, the king of Sais, by the assistance of Petosiris, an Egyptian priest, invented astrology, founding it on the motions of the planets and the qualities of the men and women to whom they were dedicated.

498. In the beginning of the reign of Nabonassar, the king of Babylon, about which time the Ethiopians under Sabacon invaded Egypt, some Egyptians fled from him to Babylon around 751 BC. They introduced there the three hundred and sixty-five day year of the Egyptians, the study of astronomy and astrology. They initiated the era of Nabonassar dating it from the first year of that king's reign which was the twenty-second year of Bocchoris in 747 BC. They started the year on the same day as the Egyptians did. Diodorus says that the Chaldeans in Babylon were colonies of the Egyptians who became famous for astrology having learned it from the priests of Egypt. {*Diod. Sic., l. 1. c. 81. s. 6. 1:279} Hestiaeus, who wrote a history of Egypt, speaking of a disaster of the invaded Egyptians, says that the priests who survived this disaster, took with them the sacred vessels of Jupiter Enyalius and came to Sennaar in Babylonia. {*Josephus, Antiquities, l. 1. c. 4. (119) 4:57} {E253}

17.10.2 Checking Herodotus with the Normal Length of the Reign of Kings

499. From the fifteenth year of Asa in 941 BC in which Zerah was defeated and Menes or Amenophis began his reign, to the beginning of the era of Nabonassar in 747 BC was about two hundred years. This time period allows for about nine or ten reigns of kings at about twenty years each. There were this many reigns according to the account set down by Herodotus. Therefore, that account is the most accurate, since it is the oldest, and was received by Herodotus from the priests of Thebes (Egyptian), Memphis and Heliopolis, the three principal cities of Egypt. Also his account best agrees with the course of nature and leaves no room for the reigns of the many nameless kings which we have omitted.

500. These omitted kings reigned before Moeris and by consequence at Thebes (Egyptian) for Moeris moved the capital of the empire from Thebes (Egyptian) to Memphis. They reigned after Ramesses for Ramesses was the son and successor of Menes who reigned next after the gods. Menes built the temple of Vulcan, Ramesses added its first portico and Moeris added its northern portico. However, the Egyptians, to make their gods and kingdom look ancient, have inserted between the builders of the first and second portico of this temple, three hundred and thirty kings of Thebes (Egyptian). {E254} They suppose that these kings reigned eleven thousand years as if any temple could stand so long! This being an obvious falsehood, we have corrected it, by omitting those intervening kings who did absolutely nothing and placed Moeris who built the second portico after Ramesses who built the first portico.

17.11 Sethon or Sevechus (701–688 BC)

501. In the dynasties of Manetho, Sevechus is the successor and the son of Sabacon. He may be the Sethon of Herodotus who became the priest of Vulcan. Sabacon neglected military matters for Sabacon is that So or Sua with whom Hoshea, the king of Israel, conspired against the Assyrians, in the third year of Hezekiah in 725 BC. {2Ki 17:4} Herodotus says that Sabacon voluntarily relinquished Egypt after a long reign of fifty years and that Anysis who had fled from him, returned and reigned again in Lower Egypt after him or rather with him. Sethon reigned with Sabacon and went to Pelusium against the army of Sennacherib in 712 BC. It is thought that he won when a large number of mice ate the bowstrings of the Assyrians. In memory of this, Herodotus saw a statue of Sethon with a mouse in its hand. {*Herodotus, l. 2. c. 141. 1:447,449} A mouse was the Egyptian symbol of destruction and the mouse in the hand of Sethon means only that he overcame the Assyrians with a great destruction. {E255}

502. The scriptures say that when Sennacherib invaded Judah, he besieged Lachish and Libnah, in the fourteenth year of Hezekiah in 714 BC. The king of Judah trusted on Pharaoh, the king of Egypt, that is, on Sethon and that Tirhakah, the king of Ethiopia, who also came to fight against Sennacherib. {2Ki 18:21 19:9} This makes it probable that when Sennacherib heard that the kings of Egypt and Ethiopia were coming against him, he went from Libnah toward Pelusium to oppose them. There he was attacked by surprise in the night by both of them and was routed with as great a slaughter as if the bowstrings of the Assyrians had been eaten by mice. Some think that the Assyrians were struck by lightning or by a fiery wind which sometimes comes from the southern parts of Chaldea.

17.12 Tirhakah (687–671)

503. After this victory Tirhakah succeeded Sethon and fought westward through Libya and North Africa to the entrance of the Strait of Gibraltar. However, Herodotus says that the priests of Egypt consider Sethon the last king of Egypt. He reigned before the division of Egypt into twelve contemporary kingdoms and by consequence before the invasion of Egypt by the Assyrians.

17.12.1 Invasion of Esarhaddon

504. Esarhaddon, the king of Assyria, after he had reigned about thirty-three years over Assyria, invaded the kingdom of Babylon in 677 BC. He carried into captivity many people from Babylon, Cuthah, Ava, Hamath and Sepharvaim, placing them in the regions of Samaria and Damascus. From there they carried into Babylonia and Assyria the remainder of the people of Israel and Syria which had been left there by Tiglathpileser. This captivity was sixty-five years after the first year of Ahaz in 741 BC {Isa 7:1,8 2Ki 15:37 16:5} and by consequence in the twenty-second year of Manasseh in 677 BC. Esarhaddon sent Tartan with an army against Ashdod or Azoth, a town at that time subject to Judah, and he captured it. {2Ch 26:6 Isa 20:1}

505. After this position was secured, the Assyrians defeated the Jews, captured Manasseh and subdued Judah. In these wars, Isaiah was sawed asunder by the command of Manasseh for prophesying against him.

Then the Assyrians invaded and subdued Egypt and Ethiopia. They carried the Egyptians and Ethiopians into captivity and thereby put an end to the reign of the Ethiopians over Egypt. {Isa 7:18 8:7 10:11,12 19:23 20:4} {E257} In this war the city of No-Ammon or Thebes (Egyptian), which before this was quite prosperous, was miserably destroyed and led into captivity. {Na 3:8-10} Nahum wrote after the last invasion of Judah by the Assyrians, and therefore describes this captivity as being fresh in his memory. {Na 1:15} This and other invasions of Egypt under Nebuchadnezzar and Cambyses, put an end to the glory of that city.

506. Esarhaddon reigned over the Egyptians and Ethiopians for three years until his death in 668 BC. {Isa 20:3,4} Therefore, he invaded Egypt and ended the reign of the Ethiopians over the Egyptians in 670 BC. Thus, the Ethiopians, under Sabacon, and his successors Sethon and Tirhakah, reigned over Egypt about eighty years. Herodotus allots fifty years to the reign of Sabacon, and Africanus fourteen years to Sethon, and eighteen to Tirhakah.

507. The division of Egypt into more than one kingdom, both before and after the reign of the Ethiopians, and the conquest of the Egyptians by Esarhaddon, seems to be alluded to by the prophet Isaiah in these words: {E258}

> I will set, saith he, the Egyptians against the Egyptians, and they shall fight every one against his brother, and every one against his neighbour, city against city, and kingdom against kingdom, and the spirit of Egypt shall fail. . . . And the Egyptians will I give over into the hand of a cruel lord [viz. Esarhaddon] and a fierce king shall reign over them. . . . Surely the princes of Zoan [Tanis] are fools, the counsel of the wise councillors of Pharaoh is become brutish: how long say ye unto Pharaoh, I am the son of the ancient kings. . . . The princes of Zoan have become fools: the princes of Noph [Memphis] are deceived . . . even they that were the stay of the tribes thereof. . . . In that day there shall be a highway out of Egypt into Assyria, and the Egyptians shall serve the Assyrians. {Isa 19:2,4,11,13,23}

17.13 Twelve Contemporary Kings (670–656 BC)

508. After the death of Esarhaddon, Egypt remained subject to twelve contemporary kings, who revolted from the Assyrian Empire and reigned together fifteen years. I think this includes the three years of Esarhaddon, because the Egyptians do not count him among their kings. These dozen kings built the labyrinth

adjoining the Lake of Moeris. It was a magnificent structure, with twelve halls in it for their palaces. {*Herodotus, l. 2. c. 148-150. 1:455-461}

17.14 Psammitichus (670–617 BC), Nechus (616–601 BC), Psammis (600–595 BC), Apries (594–571 BC), Amasis (570–526 BC) and Psammenitus (525 BC)

509. Psammitichus, who was one of the twelve, conquered all the rest. {E259} He built the last portico of the temple of Vulcan, started by Menes about two hundred and sixty years earlier. {*Herodotus, l. 2. c. 152,153. 1:465} He reigned fifty-four years, including the fifteen years of his reign with the twelve kings. After him, Nechaoh or Nechus reigned for seventeen years and Psammis for six years. According to Herodotus, he was followed by Apries, Vaphres, Eraphius or Hophra, for twenty-five years; Amasis for forty-four years and Psammenitus for six months. Egypt was subdued by Nebuchadnezzar in the second last year of Hophra in 571 BC. It was in subjection for forty years, that is, almost all the reign of Amasis, a commoner set over Egypt by the conqueror. {Jer 44:30 Eze 29:12-14,17,19} The forty years ended with the death of Cyrus for he reigned over Egypt and Ethiopia. {*Xenophon, Cyropaedia, l. 8. c. 6. s. 21. 6:421} Therefore, at that time those nations recovered their liberty. However, after four or five more years, they were invaded and conquered by Cambyses in 525 BC. From that time they have almost always been in servitude, as the prophets predicted.

510. The reigns of Psammitichus, Nechus, Psammis, Apries, Amasis and Psammenitus, as recorded by Herodotus, amount to one hundred and forty-five years and six months. {E260} This was the number of years in which the dominion of the Ethiopians over Egypt came to an end, in 670 BC to the year when Cambyses invaded Egypt and ended that kingdom in 525 BC. This is a good argument that Herodotus was honest and faithful in his history and has given a good account of the antiquities of Egypt. He consulted with the priests of Egypt at Thebes, Memphis and Heliopolis, and with the Carians and Ionians who were inhabiting Egypt, in order to prepare his history of Egypt. The Carians and Ionians had been in Egypt from the time of the reign of the twelve contemporary kings.

18. The Obelisks and the Extent of Egypt

511. Pliny says that the Egyptian obelisks were made from stone dug near Syene in Thebes (Egyptian). The first obelisk was made by Mitres, who reigned in Heliopolis, that is, by Mesphres the predecessor of Misphragmuthosis. Afterward, others were built by later kings. {*Pliny, l. 36. c. 13,14. (63-71) 10:49-57}

1) Sochis, that is, Sesochis, or Sesostris made four, each forty-eight cubits high.

2) Ramises, that is, Ramesses, made two, one hundred and forty cubits and another one hundred and twenty cubits high.

3) Zmarres, that is, Moeris, made one forty-eight cubits high.

4) Eraphius, or Hophra or Phius, made one forty-eight cubits high.

5) Nectabis or Nectenabis made one eight cubits high.

512. Therefore, Mesphres extended his dominion over all Upper Egypt from Syene to Heliopolis. {E261} After Mesphres, reigned Misphragmuthosis, Amosis I, Ammon and Sesostris reigned who created the first great empire in the world. These four, Amosis I, Ammon, Sesostris and Orus reigned in the four ages of the great gods of Egypt. Amenophis was the Menes who reigned next after them. He was succeeded by Ramesses and Moeris, and some time later by Hophra.

19. Correcting the Egyptian King List of Diodorus Siculus

513. Diodorus recites the same kings of Egypt as Herodotus, but in a more confused order, and repeats some of them twice, or more often, under various names, and omits others. His kings are these: Jupiter Ammon and Juno, Osiris and Isis, Horus, Menes, Busiris I, Busiris II, Osymandias, Uchoreus, Myris, Sesoosis I, Sesoosis II, Amasis, Actisanes, Mendes or Marrus, Proteus, Remphis, Chembis, Chephron, Mycerinus or Cherinus, Tnephachthus, Bocchoris, Sabacon, twelve contemporary kings, Psammitichus,...Apries, Amasis. {*Diod. Sic., l. 1. c. 45-65. 1:159-223}

514. I take Sesoosis I and Sesoosis II, Busiris I and Busiris II to be the same kings as Osiris and Orus. Osymandias is the same king as Amenophis or Menes. Amasis and Actisanes, an Ethiopian who conquered him, is the same king as Anysis and Sabacon in Herodotus. Uchoreus, Mendes, Marrus, and Myris, are only variations of the names for the same king. {E262} Hence, the catalogue of Diodorus is reduced to this: Jupiter Ammon and Juno; Osiris, Busiris I or Sesoosis I, and Isis; Horus, Busiris II or Sesoosis II; Menes, or Osymandias; Proteus; Remphis or Ramesses; Uchoreus, Mendes, Marrus, or Myris; Chembis or Cheops; Chephron; Mycerinus;...Tnephachthus; Bocchoris; Amasis, or Anysis; Actisanes, or Sabacon;... twelve contemporary kings; Psammitichus;...Apries; Amasis. To this list, if in their proper places you insert

Nitocris, Asychis, Sethon, Nechus and Psammis you will have the catalogue of Herodotus.

515. The dynasties of Manetho and Eratosthenes seem to be filled with many names of kings that Herodotus omitted. If any appear to have reigned in Egypt after the expulsion of the Shepherds and were different from the kings described above, they may be inserted in their proper places.

516. Egypt was conquered by the Ethiopians under Sabacon around 751 BC, about the beginning of the era of Nabonassar or perhaps three or four years before, that is, about three hundred years before Herodotus wrote his history. About eighty years after that conquest, it was conquered again by the Assyrians under Esarhaddon in 670 BC. {*E263*} The history of Egypt, as recorded by Herodotus from the time of the Assyrian conquest, is correct with respect to the number, order and names of the kings and as to the length of their reigns. Therefore, he is now followed by historians, since he is the only author who has given so accurate a history of Egypt for that interval of time.

20. Conclusion

517. If the history of Herodotus of the earlier times is less accurate, it is because the archives of Egypt suffered much during the reigns of the Ethiopians and Assyrians. It is not likely that the priests of Egypt, who lived two or three hundred years after the days of Herodotus, could correct this. On the contrary, after Cambyses had carried away the records of Egypt, the priests were daily feigning new kings, to make their gods and nation look more ancient. This is obvious by comparing Herodotus with Diodorus and both of them with what Plato relates from the poem of Solon. This poem makes the wars of the great gods of Egypt against the Greeks, to have been in the days of Cecrops I, Erechtheus and Erichthonius and a little before those of Theseus. These gods at that time instituted temples and sacred rites to themselves. {*E264*} Therefore, I have chosen to rely upon the accounts related to Herodotus by the priests of Egypt in those days and corrected by the poem of Solon. This makes these gods of Egypt no older than Cecrops I and Erechtheus. Their successor Menes is no older than Theseus and Memnon, and the temple of Vulcan was not more than two hundred and eighty years in construction. It is foolish to correct Herodotus by Manetho, Eratosthenes, Diodorus, and others who lived after the priests of Egypt had corrupted their antiquities much more than they had done in the days of Herodotus.

Chapter 3 — The Assyrian Empire

1. Introduction

518. Just as the gods or ancient deified kings and princes of Greece, Egypt and Syria of Damascus, have been made much older than the truth, so have those of Chaldea and Assyria. Diodorus says that to the time when Alexander the Great entered Asia, the Chaldeans reckoned four hundred and seventy-three thousand years since they first began to observe the stars around 473300 BC! {*Diod. Sic., l. 2. c. 31. s. 9,10. 1:455,457}

2. The Creative History of Ctesias

519. Ctesias, and the ancient Greek and Latin writers who copy from him, have made the Assyrian Empire as old as 2280 BC, which is within sixty or seventy years of Noah's flood. They list the names of all the kings of Assyria from Belus (Assyrian) and his feigned son Ninus, to Sardanapalus the last king of that kingdom. However, the names of his kings, except for two or three, have no similarity with the names of the Assyrians mentioned in scripture. The Assyrian kings were usually named after their gods, Bel or Pul, Chaddon, Hadon, Adon or Adonis, Melech or Moloch, Atsur or Assur, Nebo, Nergal and Merodach. {E266} The names of the kings were either the names of their gods or compounded with the names of one of their gods. Consider these examples: Pul, Tiglath-Pul-Assur, Salman-Assur, Adra-Melech, Shar-Assur, Assur-Hadon, Sardanapalus or Assur-Hadon-Pul, Nabonassar or Nebo-Adon-Assur, Bel Adon, Chiniladon or Chen-El-Adon, Nebo-Pul-Assur, Nebo-Chaddon-Assur, Nebuzaradon or Nebo-Assur-Adon, Nergal-Assur, Nergal-Shar-Assur, Labo-Assur-dach, Sheseb-Assur, Beltes-Assur, Evil-Merodach, Shamgar-Nebo, Rabsaris or Rab-Assur, Nebo-Shashban and Mardocempad or Merodach-Empad.

520. These were genuine Assyrian names but the names of Ctesias are foreign to this except for Sardanapalus, whose name he had found in Herodotus. Ctesias makes Semiramis as old as the first Belus (Assyrian) but Herodotus says that she was only five generations older than the mother of Labynitus. {*Herodotus, l. 1. c. 184. 1:229} He says that the city of Ninus was founded by a man of the same name and Babylon by Semiramis.

However, either Nimrod or Asshur founded those and other cities, without giving their own name to any of them.

521. Ctesias makes the Assyrian Empire continue for about thirteen hundred and sixty years, whereas Herodotus says that it lasted only five hundred and twenty years. However, even the numbers of Herodotus concerning those ancient times are much too long. {*Herodotus, l. 1. c. 95. 1:127} Ctesias says Nineveh was destroyed by the Medes and Babylonians, three hundred years before the reign of Astibares and Nebuchadnezzar who actually destroyed it. He records the names of seven or eight imaginary kings of Media, between the destruction of Nineveh and the reigns of Astibares and Nebuchadnezzar. {E267} This makes the Median Empire, erected upon the ruins of the Assyrian Empire, to last three hundred years, whereas in fact, it lasted only seventy-four years from 610 BC to 537 BC. The true empire of the Assyrians as described in the scripture, whose kings were Pul, Tiglathpileser, Shalmaneser, Sennacherib, Esarhaddon, etc. Ctesias does not even mention this even though this time period was much closer to his times. All this shows that he was ignorant of the history of the Assyrians. Yet there is a grain of truth in some of his stories, namely:

1) Nineveh was destroyed by the Medes and Babylonians,

2) Sardanapalus was the last king of the Assyrian Empire,

3) Astibares and Astyages were kings of the Medes.

However, Ctesias has made all things much too old and from vain glory taken too much liberty in creating names and stories to please his readers.

3. The Early History of Assyria

522. When the Jews had recently returned from the Babylonian captivity, they confessed their sins in this manner:

> Now therefore our God . . . let not all the trouble seem little before thee that hath come

upon us, on our kings, on our princes, and on our priests, and on our prophets, and on our fathers, and on all thy people, since the time of the kings of Assyria, unto this day. {Ne 9:32} {E268}

523. They meant since the time of the Assyrian kingdom or since the rise of that empire. Therefore, the Assyrian Empire arose when the kings of Assyria began to afflict the inhabitants of Israel, which was in the days of Pul. He and his successors afflicted Israel and conquered the nations around them. Upon the ruins of many small and ancient kingdoms, they erected their empire conquering the Medes as well as other nations. Concerning these conquests, Ctesias says not a word, not even mentioning the names of the conquerors or that there was an Assyrian Empire at that time. He thinks that the Median Empire existed at that time and that the Assyrian Empire had ended more than two hundred and fifty years before the Median Empire actually began!

4. The Unknown Empire

524. However, we must allow that Nimrod founded a kingdom at Babylon and perhaps extended it into Assyria. This kingdom was small when compared with the later empires. His empire was confined to the fertile plains of Chaldea, Chalonitis and Assyria, which were watered by the Tigris and Euphrates Rivers. If it had been larger, it did not last long for it was the custom in those early times for every father to divide his territories among his sons. Although Noah was king of all the world, Ham was king of all Africa and Japheth of all Europe and Asia, they left no standing kingdoms. {E269}

525. After the days of Nimrod, we hear no more of an Assyrian Empire until the days of Pul. The four kings, who in the days of Abraham invaded the southern coast of Canaan, came from the countries where Nimrod had reigned. Perhaps they were some of his posterity who had shared his conquests. In the time of the judges of Israel, Mesopotamia was under its own king. {Jud 3:8} The king of Zobah reigned on both sides of the Euphrates River until David conquered him. {2 Sa 8:3 10:8,13} The kingdoms of Israel, Moab, Ammon, Edom, Philistia, Sidon, Damascus and Hamath the Great, were subject to other kings than the Assyrians until the days of Pul and his successors. Likewise was the house of Eden, {Am 1:5 2 Ki 19:12} Haran or Carrhae, {Ge 12:4,5 2 Ki 19:12} and Sepharvaim in Mesopotamia and Calneh near Bagdad were under their own kings. {Ge 10:10 Isa 10:9 2 Ki 17:31}

526. Sesostris and Memnon were great conquerors and reigned over Chaldea, Assyria and Persia, but in their histories there is not a word of any opposition made to them by an existing Assyrian Empire. On the contrary, Susiana, Media, Persia, Bactria, Armenia, Cappadocia, etc., were conquered by them, and continued subject to the kings of Egypt until after the long reign of Ramesses, the son of Memnon, as we noted previously. {E270} Homer mentions Bacchus and Memnon as kings of Egypt and Persia but knew nothing of an Assyrian Empire.

5. Biblical Prophecies about the Assyrian Empire

527. Jonah prophesied when the Syrian king was afflicting Israel. This was in the first part of the reign of Jehoahaz and the latter part of the reign of Joash. They were kings of Israel and Judah respectively around 850 BC. I think this was in the reign of Moeris, the successor of Ramesses, the king of Egypt, and about sixty years before the reign of Pul around 790 BC. Nineveh was then a city of large extent but full of pastures for cattle, so that it contained only about one hundred and twenty thousand people. It was not yet grown so great and powerful as not to be terrified at the preaching of Jonah, and to fear being invaded by its neighbours, and ruined within forty days. It had some time before thrown off the yoke of Egypt and had its own king who was not yet called the king of Assyria but only the king of Nineveh. {Jon 3:6,7} The king's proclamation for a fast was not published in various nations nor in all Assyria, but only in Nineveh and perhaps its daughter villages. However, soon after this, the dominion of Nineveh was established at home and ruled over all Assyria properly so called. When this kingdom began to make war on the neighbouring nations, its kings were no longer called the kings of Nineveh but began to be called the kings of Assyria. {E271}

528. Amos prophesied in the reign of Jeroboam II, the son of Jehoahaz, the king of Israel, soon after Jeroboam II had subdued the kingdoms of Damascus and Hamath around 810 to 800 BC, that is, about ten or twenty years before the reign of Pul. He rebukes Israel's pride over those conquests, saying:

> Ye which rejoice in a thing of nought, which say, have we not taken to us horns by our strength? But behold I will raise up against you a nation, oh house of Israel, saith the Lord the God of Hosts, and they shall afflict you from the entering in of Hamath unto the river of the wilderness. {Am 6:13,14}

529. God here threatens to raise up an unknown nation against Israel. The military actions of the Assyrian Empire revealed who this nation was. In the prophesies of Isaiah, Jeremiah, Ezekiel, Hosea, Micah, Nahum, Zephaniah and Zechariah, which were written after the kingdom was mature, this empire is publicly named on all occasions. However, Amos makes no mention of the empire although the captivity of Israel and Syria is the subject of his prophecy. Israel would be often threatened by this empire. He only says in general terms that Syria would go into captivity to Kir and that Israel, notwithstanding her present greatness, should go into captivity beyond Damascus. God would raise up a nation to afflict them. {E272} This means that he would raise up above them from a lower condition, a nation whom they had not yet feared for so the Hebrew word קום signifies when applied to men. {Am 5:2 2Sa 12:11 Ps 113:7 Jer 10:20 50:32 Hab 1:6 Zec 11:16} Since Amos does not name the Assyrians when writing his prophecy, they were a minor power in the world but were to be raised up later against Israel. By consequence, they rose up in the days of Pul and his successors for after Jeroboam II had conquered Damascus and Hamath, his successor Menahem destroyed Tiphsah with its territories on the Euphrates River because they did not surrender to him. {2Ki 15:16} This happened around 773 BC. Therefore, Israel continued in its greatness until Pul, who had probably grown formidable by some victories, which caused Menahem to buy his peace. Therefore, Pul reigned shortly after the prophecy of Amos around 790 BC, and was the first on record who began to fulfil the prophecies of Amos. Pul may be justly considered the first conqueror and founder of this empire since God stirred up the spirit of Pul and the spirit of Tiglathpileser, the kings of Assyria. {1Ch 5:26}

530. The same prophet Amos, in prophesying against Israel, threatens them in this manner with what had recently happened to other kingdoms, saying:

> Pass ye unto Calneh and see, and from thence go ye to Hamath the great, then go down to Gath of the Philistines: *be they* better than these kingdoms? {Am 6:2} {E273}

6. The Establishing of the Empire

531. The Assyrians had not yet conquered these kingdoms except for Calneh or Chalonitis on the Tigris River between Babylon and Nineveh. Uzzah, the king of Judah, had recently conquered Gath, and Jeroboam II, the king of Israel, had taken Hamath. {2Ch 26:6 2Ki 14:25} The prophet, in threatening Israel with the Assyrians, notes the desolations made by other nations and makes mention of no other conquest of the Assyrians than that of Chalonitis near Nineveh. This is a good reason to think that the king of Nineveh was now beginning his long series of conquests, which happened a few years later.

532. About seven years after the captivity of the ten tribes, when Sennacherib warred in Syria in 714 BC, he sent this message to the king of Judah:

> Behold, thou hast heard what the kings of Assyria have done to all lands by destroying them utterly, and shalt thou be delivered? Have the gods of the nations delivered them which my fathers have destroyed, as Gozan and Haran and Reseph, and the children of Eden which were in [the kingdom of] Thelasar? Where is the king of Hamath, and the king of Arpad, and the king of the city of Sepharvaim, and of Hena and Ivah? {2Ki 19:11-13} {E274}

533. Isaiah introduces the king of Assyria boasting:

> Are not my princes altogether as kings? Is not Calno [or Calneh] as Carchemish? Is not Hamath as Arpad? Is not Samaria as Damascus? As my hand hath found the kingdoms of the idols, and whose graven images did excel them of Jerusalem and of Samaria; shall I not as I have done unto Samaria and her idols, so do to Jerusalem and her idols? {Isa 10:8-11}

534. All this desolation is recited again as recent history to terrify the Jews. These kingdoms reach to the borders of Assyria and to show the size of the conquests, they are called all lands, that is, all around Assyria. It was the custom of the kings of Assyria, for preventing the rebellion of recently conquered peoples, to enslave and transplant those of various countries into one another's lands and intermix them. Thus, it appears that Halah, Habor, Hara, Gozan and the cities of Media were transplanted into Galilee and Samaria. {1Ch 5:26 2Ki 16:9 17:6,24 Ezr 4:9} Also Kir was transplanted into Damascus which itself was also transplanted elsewhere. Part or all of Babylon, Cuth or Sepharvaim and the Dinaites, the Apharsachites, the Tarpelites, the Archevites, the Dehavites, the Elamites or Persians, were led captive by Esarhaddon and his predecessors into Samaria. All were conquered by the Assyrians not long before Israel was conquered. {E275}

7. The Extent of the Empire

535. On the west and south side of the Assyrian Empire these kingdoms were conquered:

1) The kingdoms of Mesopotamia whose royal seats were Haran or Carrhae.

2) Carchemish or Circutium.

3) Sepharvaim, a city on the Euphrates River between Babylon and Nineveh, which was called Sipparae by Berosus, Abydenus by Alexander Polyhistor, and called Sipphara by Ptolemy.

4) The kingdoms of Syria seated at Samaria, Damascus, Gath, Hamath, Arpad and Reseph, a city placed by Ptolemy near Thapsacus.

536. On the south and south-east side were the following kingdoms:

1) Babylon.

2) Calneh or Calno, a city which was founded by Nimrod where Bagdad now stands. It gave the name of Chalonitis to a large region under its government.

3) Thelasar or Talatha, a city of the children of Eden, located by Ptolemy in Babylonia, on the common stream of the Tigris and Euphrates Rivers.

4) The Archevites at Areca or Erech, a city built by Nimrod on the east side of Pasitigris, between Apamia and the Persian Gulf.

5) The Susanchites at Cuth or Susa, the metropolis of Susiana.

537. On the east side were the following kingdoms:

1) Elymais and some cities of the Medes.

2) Kir, a city and large region of Media, between Elymais and Assyria, called Kirene by the Chaldee paraphrase and Latin interpreter, and Carine by Ptolemy. {Isa 22:6}

538. On the north-east side were the following kingdoms:

1) Habor or Chaboras, a mountainous region between Assyria and Media. {E276}

2) The Apharsachites or men of Arrapachitis, a region originally populated by Arphaxad, and located by Ptolemy at the base of the mountains next to Assyria.

539. On the north side between Assyria and the Gordyean mountains were the following kingdoms:

1) Halah or Chalach, the metropolis of Calachene.

2) Gozan on the Caspian Sea, called Gauzania by Ptolemy.

540. Thus these new conquests extended in every direction from the province of Assyria to considerable distances and made up that large empire. Well might the king of Assyria boast how his armies had destroyed all lands. All these nations had until now their various gods and each accounted his god the god of his own land and its defender against the gods of the neighbouring countries, and particularly against the gods of Assyria. {2Ki 17:24,30,31 18:33-35 2Ch 32:15} Therefore, they were never until now united under the Assyrian kingdom, especially since the king of Assyria did not boast of their being conquered by the Assyrians more often than once. Since these were small kingdoms, the king of Assyria easily subdued them for Sennacherib said to the Jews: {E277}

> Know ye not what I and my fathers have done unto all the people of other lands? . . . for no god of any nation or kingdom was able to deliver his people out of mine hand, and out of the hand of my fathers: how much less shall your God deliver you out of mine hand? {2Ch 32:13,15}

541. Therefore, he and his fathers Pul, Tiglathpileser and Salmanasser, were the great conquerors and with a tide of victories, had recently conquered all the kingdoms around Assyria establishing this empire.

8. Impact on Israel

542. Between the reigns of Jeroboam II and his son Zachariah, there was an interregnum of about eleven years in the kingdom of Israel from 784 to 773 BC. During this interregnum or shortly thereafter, the prophet Hosea mentions the king of Assyria by the name of Jareb and another conqueror by the name of Shalman. {Ho 5:13 10:6,14} Perhaps *Shalman* might be the first part of the name of Shalmaneser, and *Iareb*, or *Irib*, (for it may be read both ways), the last part of the name of his successor Sennacherib. Whoever these princes were, it appears they did not reign before Shalmaneser. Pul or Belus (Assyrian) seems to be the first who carried on his conquests beyond the province of Assyria. He conquered Calneh with its territories in the reign of Jeroboam II. {Am 1:1 6:2 Isa 10:8,9} He invaded Israel in the reign of Menahem but did not remain for Menahem bought him off for a thousand talents of silver. {2Ki 15:19} {E278} Therefore, in his reign the kingdom of Assyria had advanced west of the Tigris River, for Pul was a great warrior. He seems to have conquered Haron, Carchemish, Reseph, Calneh and

Thelasar and might have founded or enlarged the city of Babylon, rebuilding the old palace.

9. Kings of Assyria

9.1 Pul or Belus (c. 790–748 BC)

9.1.1 The Founding of Babylon

543. Herodotus says that one of the gates of Babylon was called the gate of Semiramis. {*Herodotus, l. 3. c. 155. 2:189} She finished building the walls of the city and the temple of Belus (Assyrian) and she was five generations older than Nitocris, the mother of Labynitus or Nabonnedus, the last king of Babylon. {*Herodotus, l. 1. c. 184. 1:229} Therefore, Semiramis lived four generations or about one hundred and thirty-four years before Nebuchadnezzar and by consequence in the reign of Tiglathpileser, the successor of Pul. The followers of Ctesias say that she built Babylon and was the widow of the son and successor of Belus (Assyrian), the founder of the Assyrian Empire. That is, she was the widow of one of the sons of Pul. However, Berosus, a Chaldean, blames the Greeks for ascribing the building of Babylon to Semiramis. {*Josephus, Against Apion, l. 1. c. 24. (142) 1:219,221} Other authors ascribe the building of this city to Belus (Assyrian) himself, that is, to Pul. Curtius says:

> Semiramis had founded it (Babylon), not, as many have believed, Belus (Assyrian), whose palace is still pointed out. {*Curtius, l. 5. c. 1. (24) 1:335} {E279}

> Babylon, whose walls Semiramis built with bitumen (for the ancient king Belus (Assyrian) built the citadel). . . . {*Ammianus, l. 23. c. 6. s. 23. 3:363}

544. Abydenus, who took his history from the ancient monuments of the Chaldeans, writes:

> It is said that all was originally water, and called a sea. But Belus (Assyrian) put a stop to this, and assigned a district to each, and surrounded Babylon with a wall; and at the appointed time he disappeared. And afterwards Nebuchadnezzar built the wall which remained to the time of the Macedonian Empire, and was furnished with gates of brass. {*Eusebius, Gospel, l. 9. c. 41. (457bc) 1:485}

545. Dorotheus, an ancient poet from Sidon as cited by Julius Firmicus, says:

> The ancient city Babylon [was] built by the Tyrian Belus. . . .

546. That is, by the Syrian or Assyrian Belus for in ancient times the words Tyrian, Syrian and Assyrian were used interchangeably.

547. Herennius says that Babylon was built by the son of Belus (Assyrian) and this son might be Nabonassar. {Stephanus, in βαρ} After the conquest of Calneh, Thelasar and Sipparae, Belus (Assyrian) might have seized Chaldea and begin to build Babylon. He may have bequeathed it to his younger son for all the kings of Babylon in the Canon of Ptolemy are called Assyrians and Nabonassar is the first of them. Abydenus says that Nebuchadnezzar thought he descended from Belus (Assyrian), that is, from the Assyrian Pul. {*Eusebius, Gospel, l. 9. c. 41. (456d) 1:484} {E280} Isaiah states that the Assyrians built Babylon:

> Behold, saith he, the land of the Chaldeans: This people was not till the Assyrian founded it for them that dwell in the wilderness: [that is, for the Arabians.] They set up the towers thereof, they raised up the palaces thereof. . . . {Isa 23:13}

548. Therefore, from all this it seems that Pul founded the walls and the palaces of Babylon and left the city with the province of Chaldea to his younger son Nabonassar. He finished what his father began and built the temple of Jupiter Belus to his father. Semiramis lived in those days and was the queen of Nabonassar because Herodotus says that one of the gates of Babylon was called the gate of Semiramis. {*Herodotus, l. 3. c. 155. 2:189}

9.2 Tiglathpileser (747–730 BC)

549. Since, it is doubtful that Semiramis continued to reign there after her husband Pul died, it is most likely that Pul's older son Tiglathpileser succeeded him at Nineveh and at the same time he left Babylon to his younger son Nabonassar. Tiglathpileser, the second king of Assyria, warred in Phoenicia and captured Galilee with its two and a half tribes in the days of Pekah, the king of Israel around 747 to 741 BC. He transplanted them into Halah, Habor, Hara and to the Gozan River. These places lay on the western borders of Media between Assyria and the Caspian Sea. {2Ki 15:29 1Ch 5:26} {E281} In 741 BC Tiglathpileser came to the assistance of Ahaz, the king of Judah, against the kings of Israel and Syria. He overthrew the kingdom of Syria, which had been seated at Damascus ever since the days of King David. He transplanted the Syrians into Kir in Media, as Amos had prophesied, and placed other nations in the regions of Damascus. {2Ki 15:37 16:5,9 Am 1:5} {*Josephus, Antiquities, l. 9. c. 13. s. 1. (259) 6:137} Hence, it seems that the Medes were conquered before this time and that the Assyrian Empire had now grown great for the God of Israel stirred up the spirit of Pul and Tiglathpileser, the kings of Assyria to make war. {1Ch 5:26}

9.3 Salmanasser or Shalmaneser (729–720 BC)

550. The *Annals of Tyre* relate that Salmanasser or Shalmaneser, (also called Enemessar by Tobit), invaded all Phoenicia, captured the city of Samaria and transplanted Israel into Chalach and Chabor, by the Gozan River in the cities of the Medes. {*Josephus, Antiquities, l. 9. c. 14. s. 2,3. (284-288) 6:151,153} {APC Tob 1:13} Hosea seems to say that he captured Beth-Arbela. His successor Sennacherib said that his fathers had conquered also Gozan, Haran or Carrhae, Reseph or Resen, the children of Eden and Arpad or Aradus. {2Ki 19:12,13}

9.4 Sennacherib (719–710 BC)

551. Sennacherib the son of Salmanasser, toward the end of the fourteenth year of Hezekiah in 714 BC, invaded Phoenicia and took several cities of Judah and attempted to conquer Egypt. That war took three years. {Isa 20:3-6} {E282} At that time, Merodach Baladan or Mardocempad, the king of Babylon sent an embassy to Hezekiah, the king of Judah in his fifteenth year in 713 BC. {Isa 38:5,6 2Ki 20:6 Isa 39:1,2} Sethon or Sevechus, the king of Egypt, and Tirhakah, the king of Ethiopia, opposed Sennacherib. Initially, they defeated the Assyrians in 712 BC. It may have been a surprise attack by Sethon and Tirhakah, because the Egyptians in memory of this event erected a statue to Sethon. He is holding in his hand a mouse which is the Egyptian symbol of destruction. {*Herodotus, l. 2. c. 141. 1:447} I think at this time the Medes revolted from him. Later in 710 BC, Sennacherib returned victorious from Egypt with many captives and besieged Jerusalem. {Na 3:10 Isa 20:5,6} An angel struck Sennacherib's army and in one night he lost one hundred and eighty-five thousand men. Some say it was by a plague, or perhaps by lightning, or a fiery wind which sometimes blows in the neighbouring deserts but this was most likely a supernatural act by God. {2Ki 19:35} After this defeat, Sennacherib quickly returned to Nineveh and his kingdom became troubled so that Tobit could not go into Media. {APC Tob 1:15} Soon after this, he was murdered by two of his sons who fled into Armenia and his son Esarhaddon succeeded him. {2Ki 19:36,37}

9.5 Esarhaddon (709–668 BC)

552. Esarhaddon, called Sarchedon by Tobit, Asordan by the LXX, and Assaradin in Ptolemy's Canon, began his reign at Nineveh in 710 BC. {APC Tob 1:21} {2Ki 19:37} {LXXE 2Ki 19:37} {Ptolemy, Canon} In 680 BC Esarhaddon

captured Babylon then he carried the remainder of the Samaritans into captivity in 677 BC. {E283} He populated Samaria with captives brought from various parts of his kingdom: the Dinaites, the Apharsachites, the Tarpelites, the Apharsites, the Archevites, the Babylonians, the Susanchites, the Dehavites and the Elamites. {Ezr 4:2,9} Therefore, he reigned over all these countries.

553. Pekah and Rezin kings of Samaria and Damascus, invaded Judah in the first year of Ahaz in 741 BC. Sixty-five years after this invasion, that is, in the twenty-second year of Manasseh in 677 BC, Samaria ceased to be a separate people and was led into captivity. {Isa 7:8} Then Esarhaddon invaded Judah, captured Ashdod, and carried Manasseh captive to Babylon. {Isa 20:1,3,4} Manasseh was released soon after and returned home and fortified Jerusalem. His captivity did not last long because no mention is made of it in the book of Kings. {2Ki 21:1-18} Esarhaddon also conquered Egypt, Thebes (Egyptian) and Ethiopia above Thebes. By this war he seems to have put an end to the reign over Egypt by Ethiopia, around 670 BC.

554. In the reign of Sennacherib and Esarhaddon, the Assyrian Empire seems to have reached its greatest height. It ruled under one king: Assyria, Media, Apolloniatis, Susiana, Chaldea, Mesopotamia, Cilicia, Syria, Phoenicia, Egypt, Ethiopia and part of Arabia. It reached east to Elymais and Paraetacene, a province of the Medes. If Chalach and Chabor are Colchis and Iberia (as some think and as may seem probable from the circumcision used by those nations until the days of Herodotus) we are also to add these two provinces, along with the two Armenia's, Pontus and Cappadocia, as far as to the Halys River. {E284} Herodotus says that the people of Cappadocia as far as to that river were called Syrians by the Greeks, both before and after the days of Cyrus and that the Assyrians were also called Syrians by the Greeks. {*Herodotus, l. 1. c. 72. 1:87,89} {*Herodotus, l. 7. c. 63. 3:379}

555. However, the Medes revolted from the Assyrians in the latter end of the reign of Sennacherib. I think it happened after the initial defeat of his army near Egypt in 712 BC. Later in 710 BC in Judah, God sent an angel which destroyed his army in one night. At that time the estate of Sennacherib was troubled, so that Tobit could not go into Media as he had done before. {APC Tob 1:15} Some time later, Tobit advised his son to go into Media where he might expect peace while Nineveh, according to the prophecy of Nahum, should be destroyed.

556. Ctesias writes that Arbaces, a Mede, was admitted to see Sardanapalus in his palace and observed his

voluptuous life among women. He revolted with the Medes, and in conjunction with Belesis, a Babylonian, overcame Sardanapalus causing him to burn his palace and himself. However, he is contradicted by other better historians. For Duris and many others wrote that when Arbaces was admitted into the palace of Sardanapalus and saw his effeminate lifestyle, he murdered him. {*Athenaeus, l. 12. (528,529) 5:387,389} Cleitarchus says that Sardanapalus died of old age after he had lost control of Syria when the western nations revolted from him. {E285} Herodotus says that the Medes revolted first and defended their liberty by force against the Assyrians but did not conquer them. After their first revolt in 712 BC they had no king, but after some time, set up Dejoces over them in 710 BC and built Ecbatana for his residence in 708 BC. Dejoces reigned only over Media, and had a peaceable reign of fifty-three years, dying in 657 BC. His son and successor Phraortes made war upon his neighbours and conquered Persia. The Syrians and other western nations had finally revolted from the Assyrians, following the example of the Medes. After the revolt of the western nations, Phraortes invaded the Assyrians, but was killed by them in that war in 635 BC. He had reigned twenty-two years and was succeeded by Astyages. {*Herodotus, l. 1. c. 95-103. 1:127-133}

9.6 Saosduchinus (667–648 BC)

557. Esarhaddon seems to be the Sardanapalus who died of old age after the revolt of Syria, for the name Sardanapalus is derived from Esarhaddon-Pul. Sardanapalus was the son of Anacyndaraxis, Cyndaraxis, or Anabaxaris, the king of Assyria. {*Athenaeus, l. 12. (529,530) 5:391} This name seems to have been corruptly written for Sennacherib, the father of Esarhaddon. Sardanapalus built Tarsus and Anchiale in one day and therefore reigned over Cilicia before the revolt of the western nations. {E286} If he is the same king as Esarhaddon, he was succeeded by Saosduchinus in 668 BC. Also, the Egyptians, after the Assyrians had harassed Egypt and Ethiopia for three years, were set at liberty and continued under twelve contemporary kings of their own nation, as noted before. {Isa 20:3,4} The Assyrians invaded and conquered the Egyptians in the first of the three years and reigned over them for two more years. These two years are the interregnum which Africanus, from Manetho, places before the reign of these twelve kings. The Scythians of Touran or Turquestan beyond the Oxus River began to raid Persia in those days. One of their raids might have triggered the revolt of the western nations.

9.7 Chyniladon or Nabuchodonosor (647–626 BC)

558. In 648 BC after a reign of twenty years, Chyniladon succeeded Saosduchinus at Babylon. I think

he also ruled at Nineveh for I take Chyniladon to be that Nabuchodonosor who is mentioned in the book of Judith, for the history of that king suits best with these times. {APC Jdt 1:1} Nabuchodonosor, the king of the Assyrians who reigned at the large city of Nineveh, in the twelfth year of his reign in 636 BC, made war upon Arphaxad king of the Medes. {E287} The Medes were abandoned by a defection of the auxiliary nations of Cilicia, Damascus, Syria, Phoenicia, Moab, Ammon and Egypt. Without their help Nabuchodonosor routed the army of the Medes. The next year in 635 BC, Arphaxad perished in the siege of Nineveh. Arphaxad is said to have built Ecbatana and therefore was either Dejoces or his son Phraortes who might have finished the city founded by his father. Herodotus tells the same story of a king of the Assyrians who routed the Medes killing their King Phraortes. He adds that during this war the Assyrians were left alone by the defection of its allies but were otherwise in good condition. {*Herodotus, l. 1. c. 102. 1:133} Therefore, Arphaxad was the Phraortes of Herodotus, and by consequence was killed near the beginning of the reign of Josiah around 635 BC.

559. This war was made after Phoenicia, Moab, Ammon and Egypt had been conquered and revolted and by consequence after the reign of Esarhaddon who conquered them. {APC Jdt 1:7-9} It was made after the Jews had recently returned from captivity, *and the vessels, the altar and the temple were sanctified after being profaned.* {APC Jdt 4:3} This happened soon after their king Manasseh had been carried captive to Babylon by Esarhaddon in 677 BC. Some change in the Assyrian Empire occasioned their release from that captivity. {E288} They repaired the altar and restored the sacrifices and worship of the temple. {2Ch 33:11,16} In the Greek version of the book of Judith it is said that *the temple of God was cast to the ground* but this is not said in Jerome's Latin version. {APC Jud 5:18} {Vulgate APC Jud 5:22} Also in the Greek version it is said that *the vessels, the altar and the house were sanctified after being profaned.* {APC Jdt 4:3 16:20} In both versions of the Apocrypha the temple is presented as standing. {APC Jdt 4:11} {Vulgate APC Jud 4:7}

560. After this war, in the thirteenth year of his reign in 635 BC, Nabuchodonosor king of Assyria, according to the version of Jerom's Apocrypha, sent his captain Holofernes with a great army to avenge himself on all the western countries because they had disobeyed his commands. (The Greek Apocrypha has *eighteenth* instead of *thirteenth* year which causes historical contradictions. Editor.) Holofernes had an army of twelve thousand cavalry and one hundred and twenty thousand foot soldiers from the Assyrians, Medes and Persians. He conquered Cilicia, Mesopotamia, Syria, Damascus, part of Arabia, Ammon, Edom and Madian. Then he came against Judah when the government was in the hands of the high priest and ancients of all the people of Israel. {APC Jud 4:8 7:23} By consequence this was not in the reign of Manasseh or Amon but when Josiah was still young around 635 BC. {E289} In times of prosperity the children of Israel were apt to go after false gods and in times of affliction to repent and return to the Lord. So Manasseh a very wicked king, repented after being captured by the Assyrians. When he was released from captivity, he restored the worship of the true God. We are told:

> Josiah in the eighth year of his reign, while he was yet young, began to seek after the God of David his father: and in the twelfth year he began to purge Judah and Jerusalem from the high places, and groves, and the carved images and the molten images. {2Ch 34:3}

561. We may understand that these acts of religion were occasioned by impending dangers or escapes from danger. When Holofernes came against the western countries and plundered them, then the Jews were terrified and fortified Judah. They cried to God with great fervency and put on sackcloth and put ashes on their heads. They cried to the God of Israel that He would not give their wives and children and cities for a prey and the temple to be profaned. The high priest and all the priests put on sackcloth and ashes and offered daily burnt offerings with vows and free gifts of the people. {APC Jud 4:12-14} Then began Josiah to seek after the God of his father David. {E290} After Judith had killed Holofernes and the Assyrians had fled, then the Jews who had pursued them returned to Jerusalem. They worshipped the Lord and offered burnt offerings and gifts, and continued feasting before the sanctuary for three months. {APC Jud 16:18,20} Then Josiah purged Judah and Jerusalem from idolatry. Hence, it seems to me that the eighth year of Josiah, which was 634 BC, aligned with the fourteenth or fifteenth year of Nabuchodonosor. The thirteenth year of Nabuchodonosor, in which Phraortes was killed, was the seventh of Josiah in 635 BC. Phraortes reigned twenty-two years according to Herodotus. Therefore he succeeded his father Dejoces about the forty-third year of Manasseh in 656 BC and was killed by the Assyrians and succeeded by Astyages in 635 BC. Dejoces reigned fifty-three years according to Herodotus and these years began in the eighteenth year of Hezekiah around 710 BC. It is probable that the Medes did not make him king for a couple of years after their revolt. Then according to all this

reckoning, the reign of Nabuchodonosor agrees with that of Chyniladon which makes it probable that they were two names for the same king.

562. Soon after the death of Phraortes, the Scythians under Madyes or Medus invaded Media and defeated the Medes in battle in 634 BC. From there they went toward Egypt but were met in Phoenicia by Psammitichus who bought them off. {E291} They returned and reigned over a great part of Asia. {*Herodotus, l. 1. c. 103-105. 1:135,137} {Stephanus, in Παρθυαιοι} After twenty-eight years they were expelled in 607 BC. Many of their princes and commanders were killed at a feast held by Cyaxeres the Mede, the successor of Astyages. This feast took place a few years after the destruction of Nineveh by the Medes and the Chaldeans. The rest of the Scythians were forced to retire from Asia.

10. The End of the Empire

563. According to Alexander Polyhistor, in 626 BC Nabopolassar the commander of the forces in Chaldea of Chyniladon, the king of Assyria, revolted from him, and became king of Babylon. {*Eusebius, Chronicles, l. 1. (46) 1:170} {*Syncellus, l. 1. (249) 1:306} Chyniladon was either then, or soon after, succeeded at Nineveh by the last king of Assyria, called Sarac by Polyhistor. In time Nebuchadnezzar, the son of Nabopolassar, married Amyite, the daughter of Astyages and the sister of Cyaxeres. This marriage cemented an alliance between the two families and they conspired against Assyria.

564. When Nabopolasser was growing old, his son Nebuchadnezzar and Cyaxeres led their armies of the two nations against Nineveh, killed Sarac, destroyed Nineveh and shared the Assyrian Empire. The Jews attribute this victory to the Chaldeans while the Greeks attribute it to the Medes. However Tobit, Alexander Polyhistor, Josephus and Ctesias give the credit to both. {E292} It was the start of the great successes of Nebuchadnezzar and Cyaxeres and laid the foundation of the two collateral empires of the Babylonians and Medes, which were branches of the Assyrian Empire. This time marks the fall of the Assyrian Empire around 610 BC.

565. In the reign of Josiah when Zephaniah prophesied, Nineveh and the kingdom of Assyria were still standing and their fall was predicted by that prophet. {Zep 1:1 2:13} Pharaoh Necho, the king of Egypt, the successor of Psammitichus, went up against the king of Assyria to the Euphrates River to fight against Carchemish or Circutium, and on his way there he killed Josiah in 610 BC. {2Ki 23:29 2Ch 35:20} Therefore, the last king

of Assyria was still alive. In the third and fourth year of Jehoiakim the successor of Josiah, after the two conquerors captured Nineveh and finished their war in Assyria, they advanced westward. They led their forces against the king of Egypt as an invader of their right of conquest and they defeated him at Carchemish in 607 BC. {2Ki 24:7 Jer 46:2} They took from him whatever he had recently taken from the Assyrians. Therefore, we cannot err by more than a year or two, if we refer to the final destruction of Nineveh, and fall of the Assyrian Empire, to the first year of Jehoiakim in 610 BC. {E293} Sarac, the name of the last king, might perhaps be contracted from Sarchedon, since this name was from Esarhaddon, Esarhaddon-Pul or Sardanapalus.

566. During the Assyrian Empire, Persia was divided into several kingdoms. Among other kingdoms was Elam which flourished in the days of Hezekiah, Manasseh, Josiah and Jehoiakim, the kings of Judah but it fell in the days of Zedekiah. {Jer 25:25 49:34 Eze 32:24} This kingdom seems to have been powerful and to have had wars with the king of Touran or Scythia beyond the Oxus River with various successes. It was finally conquered either by the Medes and Babylonians or one of them. For while Nebuchadnezzar warred in the west, Cyaxeres recovered the Assyrian provinces of Persia and Parthia. We will consider later whether the Pischdadians, whom the Persians consider to have been their oldest kings, were kings of the kingdom of Elam, or of the Assyrians, and whether Elam was conquered by the Assyrians at the same time with Babylonia and Susiana in the reign of Esarhaddon and revolted soon after.

CHAPTER 4

The Empires of the Babylonians and the Medes

1. Introduction

567. After the fall of the Assyrian Empire the kingdoms of the Babylonians and Medes became great and powerful. The reigns of the kings of Babylon are stated in Ptolemy's Canon. To understand his work you must note that every king's reign in that canon began with the first month of Thoth in his reign, that is, accession dating. From that canon we see that

1) Esarhaddon died in 668 BC after reigning for thirteen years over Babylon.

2) Saosduchinus died in 648 BC after reigning for twenty-one years.

3) Chyniladon died in 626 BC after reigning for twenty-two years.

4) Nabopolassar died in 605 BC after reigning for twenty-one years.

5) Nebuchadnezzar died in the year 562 BC after reigning for forty-three years.

568. All these kings, and some others mentioned in the canon, reigned successively over Babylon, and this last king died in the thirty-seventh year of Jeconiah's captivity, {2Ki 25:27} and therefore, Jeconiah was captured in 599 BC. {E295}

2. The Times of Jehoiakim, Zedekiah and Nebuchadnezzar

569. This captivity was in the eighth year of Nebuchadnezzar's reign and the eleventh of Jehoiakim's for: {2Ki 23:36 24:12}

1) The first year of Nebuchadnezzar's reign was the fourth of Jehoiakim's. {Jer 25:1}

2) Jehoiakim reigned for eleven years before this captivity and Jeconiah for three months, ending with the captivity. {2Ki 23:36 24:8,12 2Ch 36:5,9,10}

3) The tenth year of Jeconiah's captivity was the eighteenth year of Nebuchadnezzar's reign. {Jer 32:1}

4) The eleventh year of Zedekiah, in which Jerusalem was taken, was the nineteenth year of Nebuchadnezzar. {Jer 52:1,5,12}

570. Therefore, Nebuchadnezzar's first regal year was 606 BC, that is, two years before the death of his father Nabopolassar who made him viceroy some time after the Babylonian New Year of 607 BC and before the next New Year in 606 BC. Jehoiakim succeeded his father Josiah in 610 BC, which was his first regal year, and Jerusalem was taken and the temple burned in 588 BC, which is about twenty-two years after the destruction of Nineveh.

571. The reign of Darius Hystaspes over Persia, by Ptolemy's Canon and the consent of all chronologers, and by several eclipses of the moon, began in 521 BC.

> In the fourth year of King Darius, in the fourth day of the ninth month, which is the month Chisleu, when the Jews had sent unto the house of God,...saying, should I weep in the fifth month as I have done these so many years? Then the word of the Lord of hosts came unto me (Zechariah), saying, Speak to all the people of the land, and to the priests, saying, when ye fasted and mourned in the fifth and seventh month, even those seventy years, did ye at all fast unto me? {Zec 7:1-5}

572. Count back seventy years from the time when they fasted in the fifth month for the burning of the temple, and in the seventh for the death of Gedaliah. Then the burning of the temple and the murder of Gedaliah, falls on the fifth and seventh Jewish months in 588 BC as noted above.

573. As the astronomers of Chaldea counted the reigns of their kings by the years of Nabonassar, beginning with the month of Thoth, so the Jews, as their writers say, counted the reigns of theirs by the years of Moses, beginning every year with the month of Nisan. For if any king began his reign a few days before this month began, it was not reckoned to him and the beginning of this month was accounted the beginning of the first year of his reign. According to this reckoning the first year of Jehoiakim began with the month of Nisan in 610 BC although his reign may have begun as much as five or six months earlier. {E297} The fourth year of Jehoiakim, which was in the first year of Nebuchadnezzar, according to the reckoning of the Jews, began with the month Nisan in 607 BC. The first year of Jeconiah's captivity was in the eighth year of Nebuchadnezzar, beginning in the month Nisan in 599 BC. The ninth year of Zedekiah, which was in the seventeenth year of Nebuchadnezzar, began with the month Nisan in 590 BC. In that year Nebuchadnezzar invaded Judah and its cities, and in the tenth day of the tenth month of that year he and his army besieged Jerusalem. {2Ki 25:1 Jer 34:1 39:1 42:4} From this time to the tenth month in the second year of Darius Hystaspes are just seventy years, and accordingly

> upon the four and twentieth day of the eleventh month of the second year of Darius, the word of the Lord came unto Zechariah,...then the angel of the Lord said, Oh Lord of hosts, how long wilt thou not have mercy on Jerusalem, and on the cities of Judah, against which thou hast had indignation, these threescore and ten years. {Zec 1:7,12}

574. Hence, in the ninth year of Zedekiah in 590 BC, Jerusalem and the cities of Judah were attacked. {E298} The eleventh year of Zedekiah, and the nineteenth of Nebuchadnezzar, in which the city was taken and the temple burned, commenced with the month Nisan in 588 BC. By all these means the years of Jehoiakim, Zedekiah, and Nebuchadnezzar seem to be sufficiently determined, and thereby the chronology of the Jews in the Old Testament is connected with the rest of secular history.

3. The Kingdom of Babylon

3.1 The Kings of Babylon

3.1.1 Nebuchadnezzar (604–562 BC)

575. At the end of the reign of Josiah in 610 BC, Pharaoh Necho, the successor of Psammitichus, came with a large army from Egypt against the king of Assyria. {2Ki 23:29-37} When he was denied passage through Judah, he defeated the Jews at Megiddo or Magdolus before Egypt and killed Josiah their king. He continued and marched to Carchemish or Circutium, a town of Mesopotamia on the Euphrates River. {E299} After he captured it and other cities of Syria, he sent Jehoahaz, the new king of Judah, to Riblah or Antioch in irons. He made Jehoiakim the king in the place of Josiah and levied a tribute on the kingdom of Judah. In the meantime the king of Assyria was besieged and conquered. Assuerus, the king of the Medes, and Nebuchadnezzar, the king of Babylon, destroyed Nineveh. As victors they were entitled to the countries belonging to the king of Assyria and they led their victorious armies against the king of Egypt who had seized some of these countries.

576. Nebuchadnezzar was assisted by Astibares, that is, by Astivares, Assuerus, Acksweres, Axeres, or Cy-Axeres, the king of the Medes, in the third year of Jehoiakim. They came with an army of Babylonians, Medes, Syrians, Moabites and Ammonites to the number of ten thousand chariots, one hundred and eighty thousand foot soldiers and one hundred and twenty thousand cavalry. They subdued Samaria, Galilee, Scythopolis, and the Jews in the region of Galeed and besieged Jerusalem. {*Eusebius, Gospel, l. 9. c. 39. (454cd) 1:482} {2Ki 25:2,7 Da 1:1} They captured King Jehoiakim alive and bound him in chains for a time. {Da 1:2 2Ch 36:6} They carried the king, Daniel and other people to Babylon along with part of what gold, silver and brass they found in the temple. In 607 BC, the fourth year of Jehoiakim, they routed the army of Pharaoh Necho at Carchemish. {E300} They took from the king of Egypt whatever pertained to him from the river of Egypt to the Euphrates River. {Jer 46:2} Berosus called this king of Egypt the *satrap* of Egypt, Coele Syria and Phoenicia. {*Josephus, Antiquities, l. 10. c. 11. (220) 6:279} This victory over him ended his rule over these recently acquired areas and was the start of the reign of Nebuchadnezzar there. The small kingdom of Babylon became a powerful empire by its conquests over Assyria and Syria.

577. While Nebuchadnezzar was in Syria, his father Nabopolassar died in 605 BC after he reigned for twenty-one years. When Nebuchadnezzar heard the news, he settled his affairs in Egypt and the other countries and returned to Babylon. He left the captives and his army with his officials who were to follow him later. After this he divided his time between war and peace. He conquered Sittacene, Susiana, Arabia, Edom, Egypt and some other countries. He adorned the temple of Jupiter Belus with the plunder that he had taken. Berosus relates that he fortified Babylon with magnificent walls and gates and built stately palaces and the hanging gardens. {*Josephus, Antiquities, l. 10. c. 11. (221-226) 6:281,283} Among other things, he cut the new rivers Naarmalcha and Pallacopas upstream from Babylon, and built the city of Teredon. {E301}

578. Judah was not in servitude to the king of Babylon. It was invaded and conquered in the third and fourth

year of Jehoiakim, and Jehoiakim served him for three years and then rebelled in 604 BC. {2Ki 24:1} While Nebuchadnezzar and the army of the Chaldeans continued in Syria, Jehoiakim was under control. Nebuchadnezzar sent and besieged Jerusalem. Thereupon at the end of Jehoiakim's eleventh year in the spring of 599 BC, Nebuchadnezzar captured Jeconiah, the son and successor of Jehoiakim. He plundered the temple and carried away to Babylon the princes, craftsmen, smiths and all that were fit for war. {2Ki 24:12,14 2Ch 36:10} Only the poorest people remained in the land. {2Ki 24:17 Eze 17:13,16,18} He appointed Zedekiah as their king and bound him with an oath to serve the king of Babylon. Jehoiakim's reign officially ended in the spring at the end of his eleventh year before the month Nisan, which started the Jewish New Year in 599 BC. Zedekiah was not made the new king until shortly after the Jewish New Year so 599 BC did not count as his first year.

579. Notwithstanding his oath, Zedekiah revolted and made an alliance with the king of Egypt. {Eze 17:15} Therefore, in the ninth year of Zedekiah in 590 BC, Nebuchadnezzar invaded Judah and its cities. {E302} In the tenth Jewish month of that year he besieged Jerusalem again. In the eleventh year of Zedekiah in 588 BC in the fourth and fifth months, after a siege of about eighteen months, he took and burned the city and the temple. {2Ki 25:1,2,8 Jer 32:1 39:1,2}

580. After he was appointed king by his father, Nebuchadnezzar reigned over Phoenicia and Coele Syria for forty-five years, and after the death of his father for forty-three years. {Ptolemy, Canon} {*Josephus, Antiquities, l. 10. c. 11. (219) 6:279} He lived for thirty-seven years after the captivity of Jeconiah. {2Ki 25:27}

3.1.2 Evilmerodach (561–560 BC)

581. His son Evilmerodach succeeded him and is also called Iluarodamus in Ptolemy's Canon. Jerome states that Evilmerodach reigned seven years in his father's lifetime from 569 to 563 BC, while his father ate grass with oxen. {Jerome, on Isa 14:19} After his father's restoration, he was imprisoned with Jeconiah, the king of Judah until the death of his father, and then succeeded his father on the throne. In the fifth year of Jeconiah's captivity in 595 BC, Belshazzar was next in power to his father Nebuchadnezzar and was designated to be his successor. {APC Bar 1:2,10-12,14} Therefore, Evilmerodach was even then in disgrace. When he came to the throne he brought his friend and companion Jeconiah out of prison on the twenty-seventh day of the twelfth month. {2Ki 25:27,29} Thus Nebuchadnezzar died at the end of the winter in 562 BC.

582. Evilmerodach reigned for two years after his father's death. Because of his lust and wicked behaviour he was murdered by his brother-in-law Neriglissaros, or Nergalassaros, in 560 BC according to Ptolemy's Canon.

3.1.3 Neriglissaros (559–556 BC), Laboasserdach (9 months 556 BC)

583. Neriglissaros, in the name of his young son Labosordachus or Laboasserdach, the grandson of Nebuchadnezzar by his daughter, reigned four years, according to Ptolemy's Canon and Berosus, including the short reign of Laboasserdach alone. According to Berosus and Josephus, Laboasserdach reigned nine months after the death of his father. {*Josephus, Antiquities, l. 10. c. 11. (231,232) 6:287} For his wickedness he was murdered at a feast by the conspiracy of his friends with Nabonnedus a Babylonian, to whom by consent they gave the kingdom. These nine months are not listed separately in Ptolemy's Canon.

3.1.4 Labynitus or Belshazzar (555–538 BC)

584. According to Ptolemy's Canon, Nabonnedus, or Nabonadius began his reign in 555 BC, and reigned eighteen years until the midsummer of 538 BC when Cyrus conquered him and captured Babylon.

585. Herodotus calls this last king of Babylon, Labynitus, and says that he was the son of a former Labynitus, and of Nitocris an eminent queen of Babylon. {*Herodotus, l. 1. c. 188. 1:235} By the father he seems to mean that Labynitus who was the king of Babylon when the great eclipse of the sun predicted by Thales put an end to the five years of war between the Medes and Lydians in 585 BC. {*Herodotus, l. 1. c. 74. 1:91} This king was Nebuchadnezzar. Daniel calls the last king of Babylon Belshazzar, and says that Nebuchadnezzar was his father. {Da 5:2} {E304} Josephus calls the last king of Babylon Naboandelos by the Babylonians and he reigned seventeen years. {*Josephus, Antiquities, l. 10. c. 11. s. 2. (231) 6:287} {*Josephus, Antiquities, l. 10. c. 11. s. 4. (248) 6:295} Therefore, he is the same king of Babylon as Nabonnedus or Labynitus. This is more agreeable to the scriptures than to make Nabonnedus a stranger to the royal line since all nations were to serve Nebuchadnezzar and his posterity:

> And all nations shall serve him, and his son, and his son's son, until the very time of his land come: and then many nations and great kings shall serve themselves of him. {Jer 27:7}

586. Belshazzar was born and lived in royalty before the fifth year of Jeconiah's captivity, which was the twelfth

year of Nebuchadnezzar's reign in 595 BC. Therefore, he was more than thirty-four years old at the time of the death of Evilmerodach in 560 BC, and so could only be none than Nabonnedus, for Laboasserdach, the grandson of Nebuchadnezzar, was a child when he reigned.

3.2 Queens of Babylon

587. Herodotus says that there were two famous queens of Babylon, Semiramis and Nitocris and that the latter was more skilful. She noted that after the kingdom of Media had subdued many cities including Nineveh, it was becoming great and powerful. She intercepted and fortified the passes from Media into Babylonia. She made the river, which before was straight, very crooked with large bends so that it might be more calm and less apt to overflow. On the side of the river above Babylon, in imitation of the Lake of Moeris in Egypt, she dug a circular lake forty miles in diameter to hold the water of the river and keep it for irrigation. She also built a bridge over the river in the middle of Babylon, turning the river into the lake until the bridge was built. {*Herodotus, l. 1. c. 184-186. 1:229-233} Philostratus says she made a tunnel under the river six feet wide. He means an arched vault over which the river flowed and under which they might walk under the river. He calls her Μηδεια, a Mede. {*Philostratus, Life of Apollonius, l. 1. c. 25. 1:75}

588. Berosus states that Nebuchadnezzar built a hanging garden on arches, because his wife was a Mede and delighted in the mountainous scenery of Media but not in the plains of Babylonia. She was Amyite, the daughter of Astyages, and the sister of Cyaxeres, both kings of the Medes. Nebuchadnezzar married her for an alliance between the two families against the king of Assyria. Nitocris might be another woman, who in the reign of her son Labynitus, a voluptuous and vicious king, took care of his affairs. To secure his kingdom against the Medes, she did the works mentioned previously. This is the queen mentioned in Daniel. {Da 5:10} {E306}

3.3 The Capture of Babylon

589. Josephus relates from the Tyrian records the following kings who reigned at Tyre:

1) Nebuchadnezzar besieged Ithobalus king of Tyre for thirteen years from 585 to 573 BC, after which Ithobalus was killed. {Eze 28:8-10}

2) Baal reigned for ten years from 572 to 563 BC.

3) Ecnibalus reigned for two months and Chelbes for ten months from 563 to 562 BC.

4) Abbar reigned for three months in 562 BC.

5) Mytgonus and Gerastratus reigned for six years from 562 BC to 557 BC.

6) Balatorus reigned for one year in 556 BC.

7) Merbalus reigned for four years from 555 to 552 BC.

8) Hirom reigned for twenty years from 551 to 532 BC.

590. The records of Tyre say that in the fourteenth year of Hirom in 538 BC, Cyrus began to reign in Babylonia. {*Josephus, Against Apion, l. 1. c. 21. (156-159) 1:225,227} Therefore, the siege of Tyre began forty-eight years and a few months before the reign of Cyrus in Babylonia in 585 BC. It began when Jerusalem had been recently captured and burned along with the temple. {Eze 26} By consequence, it was after the eleventh year of Jeconiah's captivity in 588 BC, and therefore the reign of Cyrus in Babylonia began after 540 BC. The seige ended before the twenty-eighth year of Jeconiah's captivity in 572 BC. {Eze 29:17}

591. Therefore, the reign of Cyrus in Babylonia began before 537 BC. By this argument, the first year of Cyrus in Babylonia was one of the two intermediate years of 539 or 538 BC. Cyrus invaded Babylonia in 539 BC. {E307} Babylon held out and the next year was taken when Cyrus diverted the Euphrates River and entered the city through its empty channel in 538 BC. By consequence, this was after the midsummer since by the melting of the snow in Armenia, the river overflows yearly in the beginning of summer but in the heat of summer it becomes shallow. {Jer 51:39,57} {*Herodotus, l. 1. c. 189-191. 1:235-241} {*Xenophon, Cyropaedia, l. 7. c. 5. s. 9-19. 6:265-269}

And that night was the king of Babylon slain, and Darius the Mede, (or king of the Medes,) took the kingdom, being about threescore and two years old. {Da 5:30,31} {*Josephus, Antiquities, l. 10. c. 11. s. 4. (248)6:295}

592. Hence, Babylon was taken a month or two after the summer solstice, in 538 BC as Ptolemy's Canon states.

4. The Kingdom of the Medes

593. The kings of the Medes before Cyrus were Dejoces, Phraortes, Astyages, Cyaxeres and Darius. The first three reigned before the kingdom became great and the last two were great conquerors and founded the empire. Aeschylus, who lived in the reigns of Darius Hystaspes and Xerxes I, and died in the 76th

Olympiad around 476 BC, introduces Darius Hystaspes complaining of those who persuaded his son Xerxes I to invade Greece.

> They have done a work
> The greatest, and most memorable, such as never happened,
> For it has emptied the falling of Susa:
> From the time that King Jupiter granted this honour,
> That one man should reign over all fruitful Asia,
> Having the imperial sceptre.
> For he that first led the army was a Mede;
> The next, who was his son, finished the work,
> For prudence directed his soul;
> The third was Cyrus, a happy man, etc. {*Aeschylus, Persians, l. 1. v. 759-769. 1:247}

594. The poet here attributes the founding of the Medo-Persian Empire to the two immediate predecessors of Cyrus. The first man was a Mede and the second was his son Darius the Mede, who was the immediate predecessor of Cyrus according to Daniel. {Da 6:28} {E309} Therefore, the first was the father of Darius, that is, Achsuerus, Assuerus, Oxyares, Axeres, Prince Axeres or Cy-Axeres for the word *Cy* means *a prince*. Daniel states that Darius was the son of Achsuerus or Ahasuerus, (as the Masoretes erroneously call him), of the seed of the Medes, that is, of the seed royal. {Da 9:1} This is that Assuerus who together with Nebuchadnezzar took and destroyed Nineveh, according to Tobit. {APC Tob 14:15} The Greeks attribute this to Cyaxeres and by Eupolemus to Astibares, a name perhaps corruptly written for Assuerus. By this victory over the Assyrians and the overthrow of the empire, whose capital was Nineveh and the ensuing conquests of Armenia, Cappadocia and Persia, he began to extend his reign over all Asia. His son Darius the Mede finished the work by conquering the kingdoms of Lydia and Babylon. The third king was Cyrus, who had great successes under and against Darius and as a result, ruled a large and peaceful empire.

4.1 The Confounding of Astyages with Cyaxeres

595. According to Cicero, Cyrus lived seventy years and according to Ptolemy's Canon, he reigned nine years over Babylon. Therefore, he was sixty-one years old when he captured Babylon and Darius the Mede was sixty-two years old. {Da 5:31} Hence, Darius was two generations younger than Astyages, the grandfather of Cyrus. {E310} According to Herodotus and Xenophon, Astyages gave his daughter Mandane to Cambyses, a prince of Persia, and by them Astyages became the grandfather of Cyrus. {*Herodotus, l. 1. c. 107,108. 1:139} {*Xenophon, Cyropaedia, l. 1. c. 2. s. 1. 5:11,13} According to

Xenophon, Cyaxeres was the son of Astyages and gave his daughter to Cyrus. {*Xenophon, Cyropaedia, l. 1. c. 4. s. 9. 5:53} Xenophon says that this daughter was very beautiful and used to play with Cyrus when they were both children, and she said she would marry him. {*Xenophon, Cyropaedia, l. 8. c. 5. s. 19. 6:403} {*Xenophon, Cyropaedia, l. 8. c. 5. s. 28. 6:409} Therefore, they were about the same age. Xenophon says that Cyrus married her after the taking of Babylon but by that time she would be an old woman. It is more likely that he married her while she was young and beautiful and he was a young man for he was the brother-in-law of Darius the Mede and led the armies of the kingdom until he revolted from Darius. So then Astyages, Cyaxeres and Darius reigned successively over the Medes. Cyrus was the grandson of Astyages and married the sister of Darius and succeeded him on the throne.

596. Therefore, Herodotus has inverted the order of the kings Astyages and Cyaxeres. He makes Cyaxeres to be the son and successor of Phraortes, and the father and predecessor of Astyages, the father of Mandane, and the grandfather of Cyrus. {E311} He states that Astyages married Ariene, the daughter of Alyattes who was the king of Lydia, and was at length taken prisoner and deprived of his kingdom by Cyrus. {*Herodotus, l. 1. c. 73. 1:89} Pausanias copied the mistake of Herodotus by saying that Astyages, the son of Cyaxeres, reigned in Media in the days of Alyattes the king of Lydia. Cyaxeres had a son who married Ariene, the daughter of Alyattes. However, his son was not the father of Mandane and the grandfather of Cyrus but the same age as Cyrus. His true name is preserved in the name of the coins called *Darics,* after the conquest of Croesus by his general Cyrus. Darius coined these from the gold and silver coins of the conquered Lydians. Therefore, his name is Darius as he is called by Daniel for Daniel says that this Darius was a Mede and that his father's name was Ahasuerus, that is, Axeres or Cyaxeres, as noted previously. {Da 9:1} Therefore, consider:

1) Cyaxeres had a long reign.

2) No author mentions more kings of Media than one called Astyages.

3) Aeschylus who lived in those days only knew of two great kings of Media and Persia, the father and the son, both older than Cyrus.

597. It seems most likely then:

1) Astyages, the father of Mandane and the grandfather of Cyrus, was the father and predecessor of Cyaxeres.

2) The son and successor of Cyaxeres was called Darius. {E312}

598. According to Herodotus, Cyaxeres reigned for forty years and his successor Astyages for thirty-five. {*Herodotus, l. 1. c. 106,107. 1:137,139} {*Herodotus, l. 1. c. 130. 1:169} Xenophon states that Cyrus reigned for seven years. {*Xenophon, Cyropaedia, l. 8. c. 7. s. 1. 6:423} Cyrus died in 530 BC according to Ptolemy's Canon. Phraortes was killed in 635 BC. His son Astyages reigned for thirty-five years and died in 600 BC. His son Cyaxeres reigned for forty years and died in 560 BC. Therefore, his son Darius the Mede reigned from 559 to 537 BC for twenty-three years.

4.2 Cyaxeres the Warrior

599. Of all the kings of the Medes, Cyaxeres was the greatest warrior. Herodotus says that he was much more valiant than his ancestors. He was the first who divided the kingdom into provinces and reduced the irregular and undisciplined forces of the Medes into discipline and order. {*Herodotus, l. 1. c. 103. 1:133,135} Therefore, by the testimony of Herodotus, he was that king of the Medes whom Aeschylus says was the first conqueror and founder of the empire. {*Aeschylus, Persians, l. 1. v. 765. 1:247} Herodotus represents him and his son to have been the two immediate predecessors of Cyrus, erring only in the name of the son.

600. Astyages did nothing glorious and in the beginning of his reign a large body of Scythians commanded by Madyes, invaded Media and Parthia in 634 BC. They reigned there for about twenty-eight years. Finally, his son Cyaxeres outwitted them and killed their leaders at a feast in 607 BC. The remaining Scythians fled into Parthia. {*Herodotus, l. 1. c. 103-106. 1:133-139} {E313} Shortly before this, Cyaxeres in conjunction with Nebuchadnezzar, had invaded and conquered the kingdom of Assyria and destroyed Nineveh in 610 BC.

4.3 Expansion of the Babylonian Empire Westward

601. The fourth year of Jehoiakim the Jews reckon to be the first of Nebuchadnezzar. They date his reign from his being made viceroy with his father or from the month Nisan preceding, when the victors had recently shared the empire of the Assyrians. In following up on this great victory, they invaded Syria and Phoenicia and were ready to invade the other nations around there. God threatened that

> he would take all the families of the north, (that is the armies of the Medes, and Nebuchadnezzar the king of Babylon), and bring them against Judah, and against the nations round about, and

utterly destroy those nations, and make them an astonishment and lasting desolations,...and cause them all to drink the wine cup of his fury. ... {Jer 25:9,15 Newton's paraphrase}

602. In particular, Jeremiah names the kings of Judah, Egypt, Edom, Moab, Ammon, Tyre, Sidon, the isles of the sea, Arabia, Zimri, and all the kings of Elam, all the kings of the Medes, all the kings of the north and the king of Sheshach. God says then:

> ... and that after seventy years, he would also punish the king of Babylon. {Jer 25:12} {E314}

603. In numbering the countries which should suffer, Jeremiah omits the Assyrians since they had already been conquered, and names the kings of Elam or Persia, and Sheshach or Susiana, as distinct from those of the Medes and Chaldeans. Therefore, Persia was not yet subdued by the Medes, nor the king of Susiana by the Chaldeans. By the punishment of the king of Babylon, he means the conquest of Babylon by the Medes. By the punishment of the Medes, he seems to mean the conquest of the Medes by Cyrus.

604. After this, in the beginning of the reign of Zedekiah, that is, in the ninth year of Nebuchadnezzar in 598 BC, God threatened that He would give the kingdoms of Edom, Moab, Ammon, Tyre and Sidon into the hand of Nebuchadnezzar, the king of Babylon. God says:

> And all nations shall serve him (Nebuchadnezzar), and his son, and his son's son, until the very time of his land come: and then many nations and great kings shall serve themselves of him. {Jer 27:7}

4.4 Persian Conquest by Media Predicted

605. And at the same time God thus predicted the approaching conquest of the Persians by the Medes and their confederates:

> Thus saith the LORD of hosts; Behold, I will break the bow of Elam, the chief of their might. And upon Elam will I bring the four winds from the four quarters of heaven, and will scatter them toward all those winds; and there shall be no nation whither the outcasts of Elam shall not come. For I will cause Elam to be dismayed before their enemies, and before them that seek their life: and I will bring evil upon them, *even* my fierce anger, saith the LORD; and I will send the sword after them, till I have consumed them: And I will set my throne in Elam, and will

destroy from thence the king and the princes, saith the LORD. But it shall come to pass in the latter days, *that* I will bring again the captivity of Elam, saith the LORD. {*Jer 49:35-39*}

606. Therefore, the Persians before this were a free nation under their own king. However, soon after this they were invaded, subdued, captured and dispersed into the surrounding nations. They continued in servitude until the reign of Cyrus. Since the Medes and Chaldeans did not conquer the Persians until after the ninth year of Nebuchadnezzar or 598 BC, it raises the question as to what that active warrior Cyaxeres did after the taking of Nineveh.

4.5 Cyaxeres and the Scythians

607. When Cyaxeres drove out the Scythians in 607 BC, some of them made peace with him and stayed in Media. Daily they presented to him some of the venison which they took in hunting. Many years later, it happened one day that they caught nothing and Cyaxeres in a passion treated them very roughly and despitefully. {*E316*} They greatly resented this and soon after killed one of the children of the Medes, dressed it like venison and presented it to Cyaxeres. Then they fled to Alyattes, the king of Lydia which caused a five year war between the kings of Cyaxeres and Alyattes from 590 to 585 BC. {**Herodotus, l. 1. c. 73. 1:89,91*}

608. By this I assume that the kingdoms of the Medes and Lydians were now adjacent and Cyaxeres, soon after the conquest of Nineveh, had seized the lands belonging to the Assyrians as far west as to the Halys River. In the sixth year of this war, in the midst of a battle between the two kings, there was a total eclipse of the sun as predicted by Thales. This eclipse happened on the 28th of May in 585 BC, forty-seven years before the taking of Babylon. {**Pliny, l. 2. c. 9. (53) 1:203*} This eclipse ended the war and the two kings made peace by the mediation of Nebuchadnezzar, the king of Babylon, and Syennesis, the king of Cilicia. The peace was ratified by a marriage between Darius, the son of Cyaxeres and Ariene, the daughter of Alyattes. {**Herodotus, l. 1. c. 74. 1:91,93*} Therefore, Darius was fifteen or sixteen years old at the time of this marriage for he was sixty-two years old when Babylon was captured. {*E317*}

4.6 Predictions about the Conquests of Babylon and Media

609. In the eleventh year of Zedekiah's reign, the year in which Nebuchadnezzar took Jerusalem and destroyed the temple in 588 BC, Ezekiel compared the kingdoms of the east to trees in the garden of Eden and notes that the kings of the Medes and Chaldeans conquered them. He says:

> Behold, the Assyrian was a cedar in Lebanon with fair branches,...his height was exalted above all the trees of the fields,...and under his shadow dwelt all great nations,...not any tree in the garden of God was like unto him in his beauty:...but I have delivered him into the hand of the mighty one of the heathen,...I made the nations to shake at the sound of his fall, when I cast him down to the grave with them that descend into the pit: and all the trees of Eden, the choice and best of Lebanon, all that drink water, shall be comforted in the nether parts of the earth: they also went down into the grave with him, unto them that be slain with the sword, and they that were his arm, that dwelt under his shadow in the midst of the heathen. {*Eze 31:3-17*}

610. The next year in 587 BC Ezekiel in another prophecy thus enumerates the principal nations whom the conquering sword of Cyaxeres and Nebuchadnezzar had subdued and slaughtered.

> Asshur is there and all her company, (viz. in hades or the lower parts of the earth, where the dead bodies lay buried,) his graves are about him, {*E318*} all of them slain, fallen by the sword, which caused their terror in the land of the living. There is Elam, and all her multitude round about her grave, all of them slain, fallen by the sword, which are gone down uncircumcised into the nether parts of the earth, which caused their terror in the land of the living: yet have they borne their shame with them that go down into the pit...There is Mesheck, Tubal, and all her multitude (the Scythians,) her graves are round about him: all of them uncircumcised, slain by the sword, though they caused their terror in the land of the living...There is Edom, her kings, and all her princes, which with their might are laid by them that were slain by the sword...There be the princes of the north all of them, and all the Sidonians, with which their terror are gone down with the slain. {*Eze 32:22-30*}

4.7 Conquests of Media

611. Here by the princes of the north I understand those to be on the north of Judah, and chiefly the princes of Armenia and Cappadocia, who died in the wars which Cyaxeres made against those countries after the taking of Nineveh. Elam or Persia was conquered by the Medes, and Susiana by the

Babylonians, after the ninth year in 598 BC, and before the nineteenth year of Nebuchadnezzar in 588 BC. Therefore, we are reasonably close if we place these conquests in the twelfth or fourteenth year of Nebuchadnezzar around 594 BC. From 588 to 586 BC, this king invaded and conquered Judah, Moab, Ammon, Edom, the Philistines and Sidon. {*Jer 27:3,6 Eze 21:19,20 25:2,8} The next year, he besieged Tyre and after a siege of thirteen years from 585 to 572 BC, and then he took it in the thirty-fifth year of his reign in 572 BC. {Eze 26:2 29:17,19} He then invaded and conquered Egypt, Ethiopia and Libya. {Eze 29:19 30:4,5} About eighteen or twenty years after the death of this king, Darius the Mede conquered the kingdom of Sardis around 544 BC. After five or six more years he invaded and conquered the empire of Babylon in 538 BC, thereby finishing the work of extending the Medo-Persian Empire over all Asia, as Aeschylus says. {*Aeschylus, Persians, l. 1. v. 763-765. 1:247}

612. Darius coined a great number of pure gold coins called *Darics*, or *Stateres Darici*. Suidas, Harpocration, and the scholiast of Aristophanes say that these were coined not by the father of Xerxes I, but by an earlier Darius, by Darius the first who was the first king of the Medo-Persian Empire. {Suidas, in Δαρεικος & Δαρεικους} {Harpocration, in Δαρεικος} {*Aristophanes, Birds Εκκλησιαζουστον, l. 1. (598-600) 3:103} They were stamped on one side with the figure of an archer who was crowned with a spiked crown, had a bow in his left hand, and an arrow in his right, and was clothed with a long robe. I have seen one of them in gold and another in silver. {E320} They were of the same weight and value with the Attic stater or piece of gold money weighing two Attic drachms.

613. Darius seems to have learned the art and use of money from the conquered kingdom of the Lydians. He recoined their gold, for the Medes had no money before they conquered the Lydians. Herodotus says that when Croesus was preparing to invade Cyrus, a certain Lydian called Sandanis advised him that he was preparing an expedition against a nation who was clothed with leather breeches. Their food was not what they desired but what their barren country afforded. They drank no wine but water only. They ate no figs nor other good food. They had nothing to lose but might gain much from the Lydians. Herodotus says that the Persians had nothing rich or valuable before they conquered the Lydians. {*Herodotus, l. 1. c. 71. 1:87} Isaiah says that the Medes did not regard silver nor delighted in gold. {Isa 13:17} However, the Lydians and Phrygians were exceedingly rich, even to a proverb for Pliny says:

Midas and Croesus had already possessed wealth without limit, and after conquering Asia Minor, Cyrus had already found booty consisting of twenty-four thousand pounds weight of gold, besides vessels and articles made of gold, including a throne, a Platanus tree and a vine. And by this victory he carried off five hundred thousand talents of silver and the wine bowl of Semiramis, which weighed fifteen talents. The Egyptian talent according to Varro amounts to eighty pounds of gold. {*Pliny, l. 33. c. 15. (51,52) 9:43} {E321}

614. Darius appears to have coined all this gold and silver into *Darics*. Herodotus says the Lydians were the first who minted gold and silver and Croesus minted innumerable gold coins called *Croesei*. {*Herodotus, l. 1. c. 94. 1:123} It was not reasonable that the coins of the kings of Lydia should remain in circulation after the overthrow of their kingdom. Therefore, Darius recoined it with his own effigies but without altering the current weight and value. He reigned then from before the conquest of Sardis until after the conquest of Babylon. Since the cup of Semiramis was preserved until Darius conquered Croesus, it is not probable that she could be older than Herodotus claims.

615. This conquest of the kingdom of Lydia made the Greeks fear the Medes, for Theognis, who lived at Megara in the very times of these wars, writes:

Let us drink, talking pleasant things with one
    another,
Not fearing the war of the Medes. {*Theognis, Elegiac
    Poems, l. 1. (761,762) 1:285}

616. Later he says: {E322}

Thou Apollo drive away the injurious army of
    the Medes
From this city, that the people may with joy
Send thee choice hecatombs in the spring,
    Delighted with the harp and cheerful feast-
    ing,
And choruses of praise and acclamations about
    thy altar.
For truly I am afraid, beholding the folly
And sedition of the Greeks, which corrupts
    the people:
But thou Apollo,
Being propitious, keep this our city. {*Theognis,
    Elegiac Poems, l. 1. (773-781) 1:287}

617. The poet says later that internal discord had destroyed Magnesia, Colophon and Smyrna, cities of Ionia and Phrygia, and would destroy the Greeks.

This is as much as to say that the Medes had already conquered those cities.

618. Therefore, the Medes reigned until the taking of Sardis and later according to Xenophon and the scriptures. They reigned until the taking of Babylon, for Xenophon says that after the taking of Babylon, Cyrus went to the king of the Medes at Ecbatana and succeeded him in the kingdom. {*Xenophon, Cyropaedia, l. 8. c. 5. s. 1. 6:395} {*Xenophon, Cyropaedia, l. 8. c. 6. s. 22. 6:421} Jerome says that Babylon was taken by Darius the king of the Medes and his brother-in-law Cyrus. {Jerome, Da 5} The scriptures state that Babylon was destroyed by a nation from the north, {Jer 50:3,9,41} by the kingdoms of Ararat Minni or Armenia, and Ashchenez or Phrygia Minor, {Jer 51:27} by the Medes, {Isa 13:17,19} by the kings of the Medes and its captains and rulers and all the land of their dominion. {Jer 51:11,28}

619. The kingdom of Babylon was numbered and finished and broken and given to the Medes and Persians, {Da 5:26,28} first to the Medes under Darius, and then to the Persians under Cyrus. Darius reigned over Babylon like a conqueror, not observing the laws of the Babylonians, but introducing the immutable laws of the conquering nations, the Medes and Persians. {Da 6:8,12,15} {E324} During his reign, the Medes are set before the Persians, {Da 6:8,12,15 5:28 8:20} just as the Persians were later set before the Medes in the reign of Cyrus and his successors. {Es 1:3,14,18,19 Da 10:1,20 11:2} This shows that in the reign of Darius, the Medes were most prominent.

620. We also know by the great number of provinces in the kingdom of Darius that he was king of the Medes and Persians for after the conquest of Babylon, he set over the whole kingdom a hundred and twenty princes. {Da 6:1} Later when Cambyses and Darius Hystaspes had added some new territories, the whole number of provinces increased only to one hundred and twenty-seven provinces.

5. Extent of the Babylonian Empire

621. The extent of the Babylonian Empire was much the same as the Assyrian Empire after the revolt of the Medes. Berosus says that Nebuchadnezzar held Egypt, Syria, Phoenicia and Arabia. Strabo adds Arbela to the territories of Babylon and says that Babylon was anciently the metropolis of Assyria. {*Strabo, l. 16. c. 1. s. 3. (737) 7:195} He then goes on to describe the extent of this empire. He says next to Persia and Susiana are the Assyrians for so they call Babylonia, and most of the region around it. Part of this region is Arturia, which contains Ninus or Nineveh, Apolloniatis, the Elymeans, the Paraetacae, Chalonitis by Mount Zagrus, the plains near Ninus, and also Dolomene, Calachene, Chazene, Adiabene, and the tribes of Mesopotamia near the Gordyeans. {E325} It contains the Mygdones around Nisibis as far as Zeugma on the Euphrates River, as much of the country on the far side of the Euphrates River, which is inhabited by the Arabians and Syrians properly so called who extend as far as Cilicia, Phoenicia, Libya, the Egyptian Sea and the Gulf of Issus. {*Strabo, l. 16. c. 1. s. 1. (737) 7:193}

622. Berosus describes the extent of Babylonia as being bounded on the north by Armenia and Media to Mount Zagrus, on the east by Susa and Elymais and Paraetacene, on the south by the Persian Gulf and Chaldea and on the west by the Arabians called the Scenitae as far as Adiabene and Gordyea. {*Strabo, l. 16. c. 1. s. 8. (739) 7:203} Later when speaking of Susiana and Sittacene, a region between Babylon and Susa, and of Paraetacene, Cossaea and Elymais, and of the Sagapeni and Siloceni, two little adjoining provinces, he concludes that these are the countries which lived east of Babylonia. To the north are Media and Armenia, and on the west are Adiabene and Mesopotamia. Most of Adiabene is a plain which is part of Babylonia and in some places it borders on Armenia. The Medes, Armenians and Babylonians warred frequently. {*Strabo, l. 16. c. 1. s. 17,18. (745) 7:219-223}

623. When Cyrus took Babylon, he changed the kingdom into a satrap or province by which the boundaries were known long afterward. {E326} By this means Herodotus estimates the size of this kingdom in proportion to that of the Persians. He states that every region over which the king of Persia reigned in his days was parcelled out for the provisioning of himself and his army, besides the tribute. Babylonia supplied him for four months of the year and all the rest of Asia for eight months. Hence, the wealth of the region is equivalent to one third of Asia and its governorship (which the Persians call a satrap), is by far the best of all the provinces. {*Herodotus, l. 1. c. 192. 1:214}

624. Babylon was a fifteen-mile-square city, surrounded first by a broad and deep ditch and then with a wall eighty-five feet thick and three hundred and forty feet high. The Euphrates River flowed through the middle of it to the south, a few miles on this side of the Tigris River. In the middle of one section of the city, Nebuchadnezzar built his new palace. In the middle of the other half stood the temple of Jupiter Belus with the old palace between that temple and the river. {*Herodotus, l. 1. c. 178-181. 1:223-225} This old palace was built by the Assyrians according to Isaiah.

{*Isa 23:13*} By consequence, it was built by Pul and his son Nabonassar as noted previously. They founded the city for the Arabians and built its towers and palaces. {*E327*}

6. Origin of the Chaldeans

625. Around that time in 751 BC, Sabacon, the Ethiopian, invaded Egypt and forced great numbers of Egyptians to flee from him into Chaldea. They brought with them their knowledge of astronomy, astrology, architecture and their three hundred and sixty-five day year. This year was the basis for the era of Nabonassar. The practice of observing the stars began in Egypt in the days of Ammon, as noted previously. His son Sesostris propagated this knowledge into North Africa, Europe, and Asia by his conquests. Then Atlas formed the celestial sphere for the Libyans and Chiron did the same for the Greeks. The Chaldeans also made a celestial sphere of their own. However, astrology was invented in Egypt shortly before the time of Sabacon by Necepsos or Nechepsos, one of the kings of Lower Egypt, and Petosiris his priest. It was propagated from there into Chaldea, where Zoroaster, the legislator of the Magi, learned them. Paulinus says:

Quique magos docuit mysteria vana Necepsos:

Also, he (Zoroaster) taught the Magi the vain mysteries of Necepsos.

626. Diodorus states that the Chaldeans themselves say that they are Egyptian colonies in Babylonia, and enjoy the fame that they have for their astrology because they learned that science from the Egyptian priests. {**Diod. Sic., l. 1. c. 81. s. 6. 1:279*}

627. By the influence of the same colonies, the temple of Jupiter Belus in Babylon seems to have been erected in the form of the Egyptian pyramids. {*E328*} This temple was a solid tower or pyramid with a square base about six hundred and sixty feet long and high. It went up in seven indentations which made it appear like eight towers standing one on top of another and growing less and less to the top. In the eighth tower was a temple with a couch and a golden table, kept by a woman, after the manner of the Egyptians in the temple of Jupiter Ammon at Thebes (Egyptian). Above the temple was a place for observing the stars. They ascended to its top by steps on the outside. The bottom was surrounded with a court and the square court with a building was about thirteen hundred feet long. {**Herodotus, l. 1. c. 181. 1:225,227*}

628. The Babylonians were extremely addicted to sorcery, enchantments, astrology and divinations, {*Isa 47:9,12,13 Da 2:2 5:11*} and to the worship of idols, {*Jer 50:2,40*} and to feasting, wine and women.

Nothing is more corrupt than the habits of that city, nothing more inclined to arouse and attract dissolute desires. Fathers and husbands allow their children and wives to prostitute themselves to their guests, provided a price is paid for their shame. Jovial festivals throughout all Persia are dear to the kings and their courtiers; but the Babylonians in particular are lavishly devoted to wine and the accompanying drunkenness. The women who take part in these feasts are in the beginning modestly attired, then they take off their outer garments one by one and gradually disgrace their modesty, at last—with due respect to your ears—they throw aside the inmost coverings of their bodies. This shameful conduct is not confined to courtesans, but is practised by matrons and maidens, with whom the baseness of prostitution is regarded as courtesy. {**Curtius, l. 5. c. 1. (36-38) 1:339,341*}

629. This lewdness of their women, coloured over with the name of civility, was encouraged even by their religion. For it was the custom for their women once in their life to sit in the temple of Venus for the immoral use by strangers. They called this temple *Succoth Benoth,* the *Temple of Women.* Once any woman sat there she had to stay until some stranger threw money into her bosom, took her away and had sexual relations with her. Since the money was for sacred uses, she was obliged to accept it no matter how little the amount and go with the stranger.

7. End of the Median Empire

630. The Medes conquered the Persians about the middle of the reign of Zedekiah around 594 BC. The Persians continued in subjection under the Medes until the end of the reign of Darius the Mede from around 594 BC to 537 BC. Cyrus, who was of the royal family of the Persians, might have been a satrap of Persia and commanded a part of the army under Darius but was not yet an absolute and independent king. However, soon after the taking of Babylon, when he had a victorious army at his devotion and after Darius returned to Media from Babylon, Cyrus and the Persians under him revolted from Darius. {*E330*} Harpagus, a Mede, instigated this revolt. Xenophon calls him Artagerses and Artabazus and he had helped Cyrus conquer Croesus and Asia Minor. Darius had offended him. Harpagus was sent with an army against Cyrus, and in the midst of a battle defected with part of the army to Cyrus. Darius raised a new army and the two armies fought again. {*Herodotus, l. 1. c. 123-129. 1:163-169} {Suidas, in Αρισταρχος.} {*Xenophon, Cyropaedia, l. 7. c. 1. s. 22. 6:215} {*Xenophon, Cyropaedia, l. 8. c. 3. s. 25. 6:361}

631. According to Strabo, this last battle was fought at Persepolis or Pasargadae in Persia, and Darius the Mede was beaten and taken prisoner by Cyrus. This victory transferred the empire to the Persians from the Medes. {*Strabo, l. 15. c. 3. s. 8. (730) 7:169} Xenophon calls the last king of the Medes Cyaxeres and Herodotus calls him Astyages, the father of Mandane. However, these kings were dead before this time and Daniel states that Darius was the true name of the last king. Herodotus relates that the last king was conquered by Cyrus in the manner previously described. {*Herodotus, l. 1. c. 123-129. 1:163-169} Further, the *Darics* coined by the last king testify to the fact that his name was Darius.

632. This victory over Darius the Mede likely happened in 537 BC, about the year after the taking of Babylon, for the reign of Nabonnedus the last king of the Chaldeans, whom Josephus calls Naboandelos and Belshazzar, ended in 538 BC eight years before the death of Cyrus, according to Ptolemy's Canon.

{*Josephus, Antiquities, l. 10. c. 11. s. 1. (232) 6:287} {E331} After the kingdom of the Medes was transferred to the Persians, Cyrus reigned only seven years from 536 to 530 BC. {*Xenophon, Cyropaedia, l. 8. c. 6. s. 22. 6:421} He spent the seven winter months yearly at Babylon and the three spring months yearly at Susa, and the two summer months at Ecbatana. He came the seventh time into Persia and died there in the spring and was buried at Pasargadae or Persepolis. {*Xenophon, Cyropaedia, l. 8. c. 7. s. 1. 6:423} By Ptolemy's Canon and the common consent of all chronologers, he died in 530 BC and therefore conquered Darius in 537 BC seventy-three years after the destruction of Nineveh in 610 BC.

633. The first time Cyrus defeated Darius the Mede was in 537 BC. He revolted from Darius and became king of the Persians, either the same year, or in the end of the previous year. At his death he was seventy years old according to Herodotus, and therefore he was born in 599 BC. Mandane his mother was the sister of Cyaxeres, who was a young man at that time. She was also the sister of Amyite, the wife of Nebuchadnezzar. Cambyses, the father of Cyrus, was from an old royal family of the Persians.

CHAPTER 5 A Description of the Temple of Solomon

634. (The cubit was about 21.5 or almost 22 inches long, and was called the sacred cubit of the Jews, which was a hand breadth, or the sixth part of its length larger than the common cubit. Newton.)

635. The Babylonians destroyed the temple of Solomon in 588 BC. We describe that building in this chapter.

636. This temple looked eastward and stood in a square area called the separate place. {*Eze 41:13,14*} The altar stood before the temple in the centre of another square area called the inner court or the *Priests' Court*. {*Eze 40:47*} These two square areas were separated by only a marble rail and made an area two hundred cubits long from west to east and one hundred cubits wide. This area was surrounded on the west with a wall and on the other three sides with a pavement fifty cubits wide, on which stood the buildings for the priests with cloisters beneath them. {*Eze 40:29,33,36*} The pavement was bounded on the inside with a marble rail before the cloisters. The whole of this made an area two hundred and fifty cubits long from west to east and two hundred cubits wide. It was surrounded with an outer court, called also the *Great Court*, or the *People's Court*, which was a hundred cubits wide on every side. {*Eze 40:19,23,27 2Ki 21:5 2Ch 4:9*} {*E333*} Solomon built only two courts and the outer court was about four cubits lower than the inner one. It was surrounded on the west with a wall and on the other three sides with a pavement fifty cubits wide on which stood the buildings for the people. {*Eze 40:15,17,21 1Ch 28:12*} All of this composed the sanctuary and made a square area five hundred cubits on each side. {*Eze 40:5 42:20 45:2*} It was surrounded with a walk called the *Mountain of the House*. This walk was fifty cubits wide, and was surrounded with a wall six cubits wide. The wall was six cubits high and six hundred cubits long on each side.

637. The altar stood in the centre of the whole structure. In the buildings of both courts opposite the middle of the altar, eastward, southward and northward, were gates {*2Ki 21:5 Eze 40*} These were twenty-five cubits wide between the buildings and forty cubits long. They had porches ten cubits wide looking toward the *Altar Court* which made the whole length of the gates fifty cubits across the pavements. {*E334*} Every gate had two doors one at either end ten cubits wide and

twenty high with posts and thresholds six cubits wide. Within the gates was an area twenty-eight cubits long between the thresholds and thirteen cubits wide. On either side of this area there were three posts, each six cubits square and twenty cubits high with arches five cubits wide between them. All these posts and arches filled the twenty-eight cubits in length between the thresholds. Their width totalled thirteen cubits which made the whole width of the gates twenty-five cubits wide. These posts were hollow and had rooms in them with narrow windows for the porters. The entrance step was a cubit wide. The walls of the porches were six cubits thick and were also hollow for various uses. (Figure 1) At the east gate of the *People's Court*, called the *King's Gate*, were six porters. At the south gate and the north gate there were four porters each. {*1Ch 26:17*} The people went in and out at the south and north gates. {*Eze 46:8,9*} The east gate was opened only for the king and in this gate he ate the sacrifices. {*Eze 44:2,3*}

638. There were also four gates or doors in the western wall of the *Mountain of the House*. Of these {*1Ch 26:15-18*} the most northern, called *Shallecheth*, or the *Gate of the Causeway*, led to the king's palace. The valley between the two buildings was filled with a causeway. The next gate, called *Parbar*, led to Millo. {*E335*} Of the third and fourth gates, called *Asuppim*, one led to Millo, the other to the city of Jerusalem. There were steps down into the valley and up again into the city. Four porters were at the gate called *Shallecheth*. Six porters were at the other three gates, two at each gate. The house of the porters, who had the charge of the north gate of the *People's Court*, had also the charge of the gates called *Shallecheth* and *Parbar*. The house of the porters who had the charge of the south gate of the *People's Court*, had also the charge of the other two gates called *Asuppim*.

639. They came through the four western gates into the *Mountain of the House*, and went up from there to the gates of the *People's Court* by seven steps and from there to the gates of the *Priests' Court* by eight steps. {*Eze 40:22,26,31,34,37*} The arches in the sides of the gates of both courts led into cloisters under a double building, supported by three rows of marble pillars. These butted directly on the centres of the square posts and ran along from there on the pavements toward the corners of the courts. {1Ki 6:36 7:12 Eze 40:17,18} The centres of the pillars in the middle row were eleven cubits from the centres of the pillars in the other two rows on each side. {E336} Where the building joined to the sides of the gates, the pillars were three cubits in diameter and their bases four cubits and a half square. The gates and buildings of both courts were similar and faced their courts. {Eze 40:19,31,34,37}

640. The cloisters of all the buildings and the porches of all the gates faced toward the altar. The row of pillars behind the cloisters adhered to marble walls, which bounded the cloisters and supported the buildings. These buildings were three storeys high above the cloisters. Each storey was supported by a row of cedar beams or pillars of cedar, standing above the middle row of the marble pillars. {1Ki 6:36 7:12} The buildings on either side of each gate of the *People's Court*, were one hundred and eight-seven and a half cubits long. They were distinguished into five rooms on a floor, running in length from the gates to the corners of the courts. There were thirty rooms to a storey, (where the people ate the sacrifices), or thirty porticos, each containing three rooms, a lower, a middle and an upper. {Eze 40:17}

641. Every portico was thirty-seven and a half cubits long and was supported by four pillars in each row. The base of a pillar was four and a half cubits square, and the distance between their bases was six and half cubits. The distance between the centres of the pillars was eleven cubits. {E337} Where two porticos joined, there the bases of their pillars joined. The centres of those two pillars were only four and a half cubits from each another. Perhaps to strengthen the building, the space between the centres of these two pillars in the front was filled up with a marble column four and a half cubits square with the two pillars standing half out on each side of the square column.

642. At the ends of these buildings, in the four corners of the *People's Court*, were little courts fifty cubits square on their outside walls. Their purpose was for staircases to the buildings and kitchens to bake and boil the sacrifices for the people. The kitchen was thirty cubits wide, and the staircase was ten cubits wide. {Eze 41:21,22} The buildings on each side of the gates of the *Priests' Court* were also thirty seven and a half cubits long. Each contained one great room in a storey, subdivided into smaller rooms for the senior officers of the temple and the leaders of the priests. In the southeast and northeast corners of this court, at the ends of the buildings, were kitchens and staircases for the senior officers and perhaps rooms for storing wood for the altar.

643. In the eastern gate of the *People's Court*, sat the *Court of Judicature*, which was composed of twenty-three elders. The eastern gate of the *Priests' Court*, with the buildings on each side, was for the high priest and his deputy, the Sagan, and for the Sanhedrin or *Supreme Court of Judicature*, composed of seventy elders. {E338} The building or portico on the eastern side of the southern gate, was for the priests who had the oversight of the charge of the sanctuary with its treasuries. {Eze 40:45} These were, first, two *Catholikim*, who were chief treasurers and secretaries to the high priest, and examined, stated and prepared all acts and accounts to be signed and sealed by him. Then there were seven *Amarcholim*, who kept the keys of the seven locks of each gate of the sanctuary and also of the treasuries. They had the oversight, direction and appointment of all things in the sanctuary. Then three or more *Gisbarim*, or junior treasurers, or receivers, who kept the holy vessels and the public funds. They received or dispensed of such sums as were brought in for service of the temple and kept a record of their transactions. All these, with the high priest, composed the Supreme Council for managing the affairs of the temple.

644. The sacrifices were killed on the northern side of the altar and flayed, cut in pieces and salted in the northern gate of the temple. {Eze 40:39,41,42,46} Therefore, the building or portico on the eastern side of this gate was for the priests who had the oversight of the charge of the altar and the daily service. {E339} These officers were:

1) The officer who received the people's money for purchasing things for the sacrifices and gave out tickets for the same.

2) The officer who exchanged the tickets for wine, flour and oil.

3) The officer over the lots, by which each priest who attended to the altar had his duty assigned.

4) The officer who exchanged the tickets for the doves and pigeons.

5) The officer who administered to the physical needs of the priests attending the altar.

6) The officer who was in charge of the water.

7) The officer in charge of the schedule who called the priests or Levites to their ministries.

8) The officer who opened the gates in the morning to begin the service and shut them in the evening when the service was done. He received the keys from the *Amarcholim* and returned them when he had finished his duty.

9) The officer who checked the night watches.

10) The officer who used a cymbal to summon the Levites to their stations for singing.

11) The officer who appointed the hymns and set the tune.

12) The officer who took care of the showbread.

13) The officers who took care of the perfume, the veil and the wardrobe of the priests.

645. The portico on the western side of the south gate, (Figure 2.) and that on the western side of the north gate, were for the princes of the twenty-four courses of the priests, one portico for twelve of the princes, and the other portico for the other twelve. {E340} On the pavement on either side of the *Separate Place* were other buildings without cloisters. These were for the twenty-four courses of the priests to eat the sacrifices, and lay up their garments and the most holy things. {Eze 42:1-4,6,8,13,14} Each pavement was a hundred cubits long and fifty cubits wide. They had buildings on each of its sides twenty cubits wide, with a walkway ten cubits wide between them. The building which bordered on the *Separate Place* was a hundred cubits long and the one next to the *People's Court* was fifty cubits long and the other one, fifty cubits on the west. It was used for a staircase and a kitchen. {Eze 41:19,20} These buildings were three storeys high, and the middle storey was narrower in the front than the lower storey, and the upper storey still narrower, to allow for room for galleries. {Eze 42:5,6} Each building had galleries in front of them. Under the galleries were closets for storing the holy things and the garments of the priests. These galleries faced toward the walkway which ran between the buildings.

646. Ten steps went up from the *Priests' Court* to the porch of the temple. The house of the temple was twenty cubits wide and sixty long on the inside. The outside dimensions were thirty cubits wide and seventy cubits long. {E341} Including the treasure rooms, which were twenty cubits wide on three sides of the house, the building was seventy cubits wide and ninety cubits long. {1Ki 6:2 Eze 41:2,4,12-14} If the porch was included, the temple was one hundred cubits long. {1Ki 6:3 Eze 41:13}

647. The treasure rooms were built of cedar between the wall of the temple and another outside wall. They were built in two rows, three storeys high. Each door opposite the door on the other side of the walkway opened into a walkway or gallery which ran along between them. {Eze 41:6,11} The gallery was five cubits wide on each storey so that the width of the rooms on each side of the gallery, including the width of the wall to which they adjoined, was ten cubits. The entire width of the gallery, rooms and both walls was twenty-five cubits. The rooms were five cubits wide on the lower storey, six cubits wide on the middle storey, and seven cubits wide on the upper storey, for the wall of the temple was built with retractions of a cubit to rest the timber on. {1Ki 6:6} Ezekiel represents the rooms a cubit narrower, and the walls a cubit thicker than they were in Solomon's temple and there were thirty rooms to a storey. {Eze 41:6} The porch of the temple was one hundred and twenty cubits high, and its length from south to north equalled the width of the house. {2Ch 3:4} {E342} The house was three storeys high which made the height of the holy place ninety cubits and the height of the most holy place was sixty cubits. The upper rooms were treasure rooms. They went up to the middle room by winding stairs in the southern corner of the house and from the middle into the upper storeys. {1Ki 6:8}

648. Some time after this temple was built, the Jews added a new court, on the eastern side of the *Priests' Court* before the king's gate. In it they built a canopy for use on the sabbath. {2Ch 20:5 2Ki 16:18} Ezekiel measured this court but its dimensions may be deduced from those of the women's court in the second temple. Zerubbabel, by the commissions of Cyrus and Darius Hystaspes, built another court in the same area except the outer court, which was left open to the Gentiles. This temple was sixty cubits square and only two storeys high. {Ezr 6:3,4} It had only one row of treasure rooms around it.

649. On either side of the *Priests' Court* were double buildings for the priests, built on three rows of marble pillars in the lower storey, with a row of cedar beams or pillars in the upper storeys. The cloister in the lower storey looked toward the *Priests' Court* and the *Separate Place*. The *Priests' Court*, with their buildings on the north and south sides, and the *Women's Court*, at the east end, took up an area three hundred cubits long and two hundred cubits wide. The altar was placed in the centre of the whole area. The *Women's Court* was so named, because the women came into it as well as the men. There were galleries for the women and the men worshipped on the ground below. In this state the second temple continued throughout all the reign of the Persians but later was altered in the days of Herod.

650. This description of the temple was taken primarily from Ezekiel's vision based on the ancient Hebrew copy followed by the LXX which differs in some readings from the modern Hebrew copy. I appended the part of Ezekiel's vision, which relates to the outer court, as I have deduced it by comparing the present Hebrew and LXX.

Figure 1 — A Description of Solomon's Temple

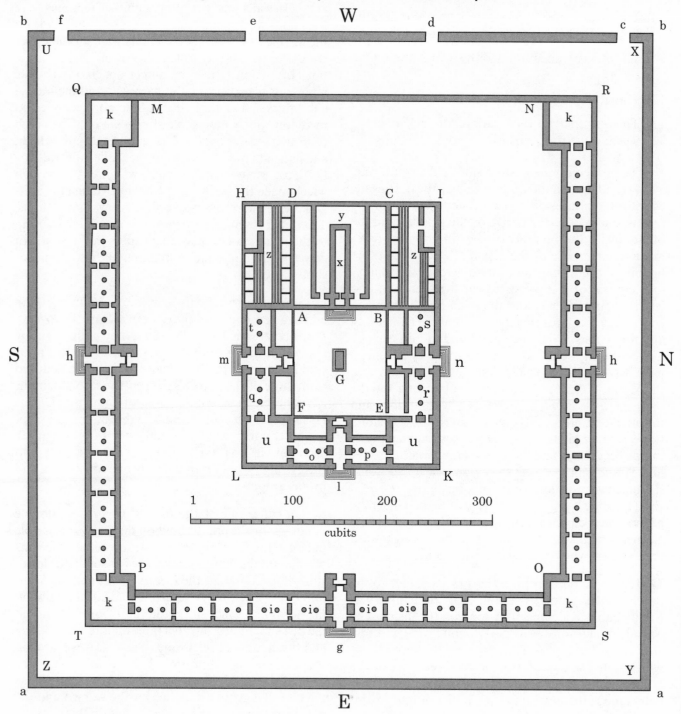

Ezekiel 40:5–23

Eze. 40:5, The New Temple—Figure 1

There was a wall (aabb) all around the outside of the temple at the distance of fifty cubits (almost 90') from it {E344}. In the man's hand was a measuring rod six sacred cubits long (129" or 10' 9"), each being a standard cubit plus a handbreadth (21.5 inches). He measured the wall to be one rod wide and one rod high (10' 9"feet by 10' 9" feet).

Eze. 40:6–16, The Eastern Gate of the Temple—Figure 3

Then he came to the gate of the temple which faced east (gate g on Figure 1), and he went up its seven steps (AB) and measured the gate's

118

Figure 1 — A Description of Solomon's Temple

ABCD	The *Separate Place* where the temple was built
ABEF	The *Priests' Court*
G	The Altar
DHLKICEFD	A pavement surrounding three sides of the *Priests' Court* and on which stood the buildings for the priests and the adjoining cloisters below them
MNOP	The *People's Court*
MQTSRN	The pavement surrounding three sides of the *People's Court* on which stood the buildings for the people with the cloisters below them
UXYZ	The *Mountain of the House*
aabb	A wall enclosing the entire temple complex
c	The gate called Shallecheth
d	The gate called Parbar
ef	The two gates called Asuppim
g	The east gate of the *People's Court* called the *King's Gate*
hh	The north and south gates of the *People's Court*
iiii &c.	The thirty rooms over the cloisters of the *People's Court* where the priests ate the sacrifices
kkkk	The four small courts serving for staircases and kitchens for the people
l	The eastern gate of the *Priests' Court* above which the Sanhedrin met
m	The southern gate of the *Priests' Court*
n	The northern gate of the *Priests' Court* where the sacrifices where prepared
opqrst	The buildings above the cloisters for the priests. These were six large subdivided rooms on each storey
op	The rooms for the high priest and his deputy, the Sagan
q	The room for the overseers of the sanctuary and treasury
r	The room for the overseers of the altar and the sacrifice
st	The rooms for the princes of the twenty-four courses of priests
uu	The two courts containing the staircases and the kitchens for the priests
x	The house or temple (along with the treasure rooms "y" and the buildings "zz" on each side of the *Separate Place*), described in detail in the next diagram

threshold (CDcd) to be one rod wide (10′ 9″). The gatekeepers' little rooms (EFG, efg) were one rod square (10′ 9″). The arched passage between the little rooms (FH, fh) was five cubits wide (almost 9′). The second little room (HIK, hik) was a rod square (10′ 9″), and separated from the adjoining rooms by an arched passage (FH, IL, fh, il) five cubits wide (almost 9′). The third little room (LMN, lmn) was also a rod square (10′ 9″). The inner gate's threshold (OPpo) next to its porch was one rod long (10′ 9″). He measured the inner gate's porch (QRrq) to be eight cubits wide (14′ 4″). Its posts (ST, st) were two cubits wide (3′ 7″). The inner gate's porch (QRqr) faced inward toward the inner court. The little rooms (EFG, HIK, LMN, efg, hik, lmn) faced out toward the east— three on each side of the gate opening into the hall (EMme). Each of these six rooms and its adjacent posts were the same dimensions. The door of the entrance gate (Cc, Dd) was ten

Figure 2 — A Description of the Inner Court and Buildings for the Priests in Solomon's Temple

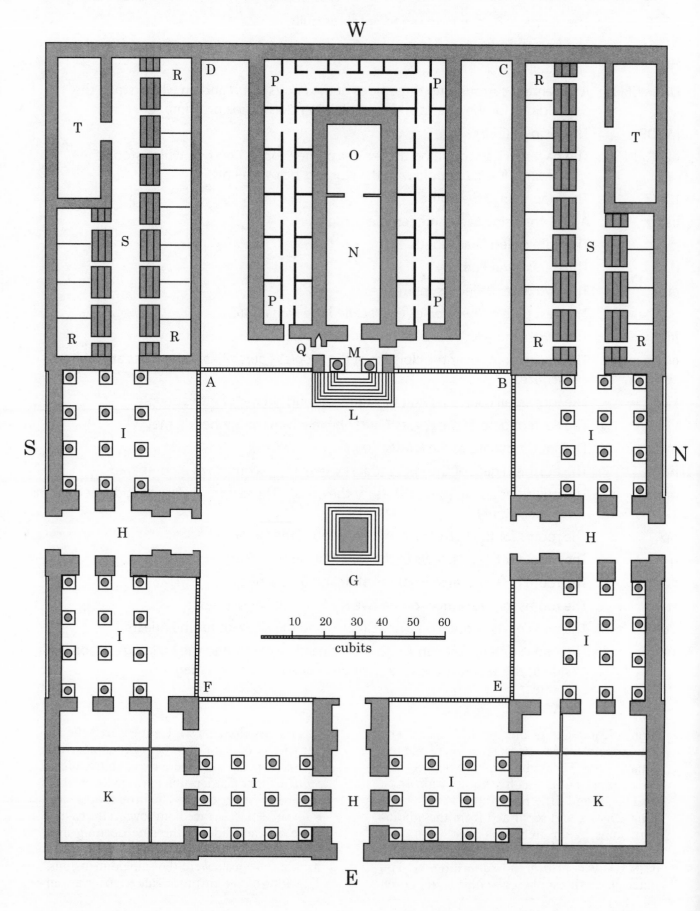

Figure 2—A Description of the Inner Court and Buildings for the Priests in Solomon's Temple

ABCD	The *Separate Place*
ABEF	The *Inner Court or the Priests' Court*, separated from the *Separate Place* and the pavement on the other three sides by a marble railing
G	The Altar
HHH	The east, south and north gates of the *Priests' Court*
III &c.	The cloisters supporting the buildings for the priests
KK	The two courts containing the staircases and kitchens for the priests
L	The ten steps to the porch of the temple
M	The porch of the temple
N	The Holy Place
O	The most Holy Place
PPPP	The thirty treasure rooms, in two rows, opening into a gallery, door opposite door, and surrounding the Holy and the most Holy Places on three sides
Q	The stairs leading to the middle room
RRRR &c.	The buildings for the twenty-four *Priests' Courts* on the pavement on either side of the *Separate Place*. These buildings where three storeys high outside the cloisters, but the upper storeys were narrower than the lower ones. This made room for the galleries in front of them. There were twenty-four rooms on each storey and they opened onto a narrow walk or hall SS between the buildings.
TT	The two courts in which were the kitchens for the priests of the twenty-four courts

cubits wide (almost 18'). The width of the gate between the six little rooms (Ed, Ff) was thirteen cubits (23' 4"). The six little rooms (EFG, HIK, LMN, efg, hik, lmn) were inset one cubit (21.5") from the hall (EMme) {E345}, and had an outside measurement of six cubits square (10' 9"). He measured the entire width of the gate, from the farther wall of one little room to the farther wall of its opposite little room (Gg, or Kk, or Nn), and it was twenty-five cubits across (almost 45'). The doors (FH, HI, LM, fh, hi, lm) of the rooms opened into the hall (EMme). He measured the height of the posts (EF, HI, LM, ef, hi, lm) to be twenty cubits high (almost 36 feet). All around the posts there were gates or arched passages (FH, IL, fh, il). The distance from the eastern side of the entrance gate (Cc) to the western side of the porch of the inside gate (Tt) was fifty cubits (almost 90'). There were narrow windows on each of the outside walls of the six little rooms (EFG, HIK, LMN, efg, hik, lmn). Each post (EF, HI, LM, ef, hi, lm) was decorated with palm trees.

Eze. 40:17–19, The Outer Court—Figure 1

Then he brought me through the gate (g) into the outer court of the temple (MNOP). The court was paved with stones and surrounded by thirty rooms (iiii), ten on each side except for the west side. There were five rooms on each side of each of the three gates (ghh) {E346}. The court was a hundred cubits wide (almost 180') between the stairs of its gates (hm, hn, gl).

Eze. 40:20–23, The Northern Gate—Figure 1

He brought me to the north gate (h) which was similar in design and size to the eastern gate (g). It was fifty cubits long and twenty-five cubits wide (almost 90' by 45'). It also had three little rooms on each of its sides with accompanying posts. These were the same size and layout as those in the eastern gate. Its windows, porch and palm trees were similar to those in the eastern gate. It also had stairs with seven steps to enter the gate. From the end of the gate to the stairs (m) was one hundred cubits (almost 180').

Figure 3—An Individual Description of One of the Gates of the *People's Court*, with Part of the Adjoining Cloister

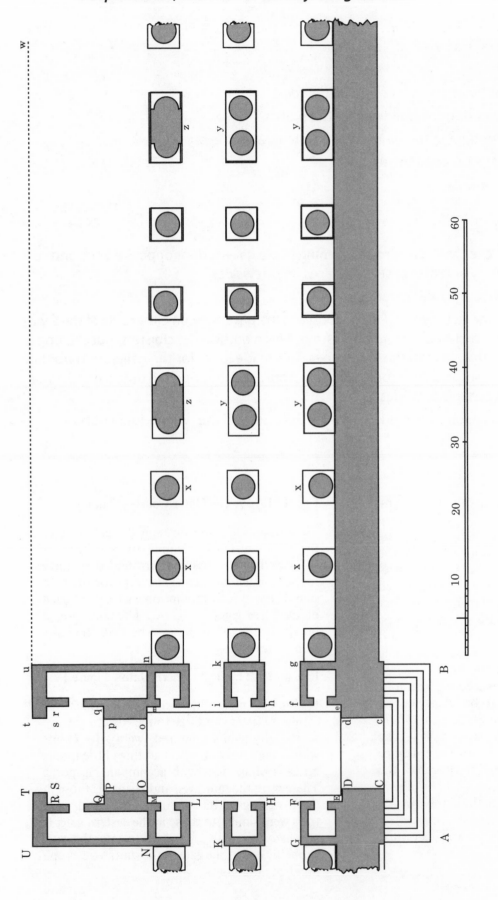

AB—Stairs leading to the entrance gate

CDdc—Threshold of the entrance gate

Cc, Dd—Door of the entrance gate

EMme—Hall of the gate

EFG, efg—Gatekeeper's room

FH, IL, fh, il—Arched passage between the rooms

HIK, hik—Second little room

LMN, lmn—Third little room

OPpo- Threshold of the inner gate

QRrq—Porch of the inner gate

ST, st—Post for the inner gate

uw—The inner edge of the pavement around three sides of the *People's Court*

xxx &c.—The pillars of the cloister supporting the buildings for the people

yyyy—Double pillars where the two porticos joined and whose intersection before "z" was never filled up with a square column of marble

zz—Large supporting pillar.

CHAPTER 6 The Persian Empire

1. A List of Persian Kings

1.1 Cyrus (536–530 BC) and Cambyses (529–522 BC)

651. After Cyrus had established the kingdom of the Persians and reigned for seven years, he was succeeded by his son Cambyses. He reigned for seven years and five months and in the three last years of his reign he subdued Egypt. He was succeeded by Mardus, or Smerdis the Magus, who pretended to be Smerdis, the brother of Cambyses.

1.2 Smerdis (522 BC)

652. Smerdis reigned for seven months and when he was exposed in the eighth month, he was killed along with a great number of the Magi, which is the name the Persians gave to their priests. They called this day the slaughter of the Magi which they annually observed in remembrance of that event. Maraphus and Artaphernes reigned for only a few days.

1.3 Darius Hystaspes (521—85 BC)

653. After them Darius (the son of Hystaspes and the grandson of Arsamenes, of the family of Achaemenes, a Persian) was chosen king because his horse neighed first. Before he reigned his name was Ochus. {*Valerius Maximus, l. 9. c. 2. ext. 6. 2:317*} He seemed on this occasion to have reformed the constitution of the Magi, making his father Hystaspes their high priest or *Archimagus.* {*E348*} Porphyry states that the Magi were the most venerable men among the Persians and that Darius, the son of Hystaspes, wrote on the monument of his father, among other things, that he had been the high priest of the Magi. {*Porphyry, De Abstinentia, l. 4.*} Zoroaster assisted Darius Hystaspes in reforming the Magi. The Persians at that time said that Zoroaster lived in the same region as Hystaspes. {*Agathias, l. 2. c. 24. s. 6. Internet*} Apuleius states:

> *Pythagoram, aiunt, inter captivos Cambysae Regis [ex Aegypto Babylonem abductos] doctores habuisse Persarum Magos, et praecipue Zoroastrem, omnis divini arcani antistitem.*

They say that between the captivity of Pythagorus by King Cambyses [having been abducted from Egypt to Babylon], the Persian instructors, the Magi and especially Zoroaster taught Pythagorus all sacred secrets of the master.

654. When Zoroaster lived at Babylon, he seemed to have borrowed his skill from the Chaldeans, for he was skilled in astronomy and used their year. Curtius says:

> Next came the Magi, chanting their traditional hymn. These were followed by three hundred and sixty-five young men clad in purple robes, equal in number to the days of the whole year.
>
> {*Curtius, l. 3. c. 3. (10) 1:83*}

655. Ammianus adds this:

> To the science of this (the purest worship of the gods), derived from the secret lore of the Chaldeans, in ages long past the Bactrian Zoroaster made many contributions, and after him the wise King Hystaspes, the father of Darius.
>
> {*Ammianus, l. 23. c. 6. s. 32. 2:367*}

656. Since Zoroaster lived in various places, he is considered a Chaldean, an Assyrian, a Mede, a Persian and a Bactrian. Suidas calls him a Medo-Persian and says that he was the most skilful of astronomers and was the author of the name *Magi.* {*Suidas, in* Ζωροαστρης} He undoubtedly received his skill in astronomy from the Chaldeans but Hystaspes travelled into India, to be instructed by the Gymnosophists. {*E349*} These two combined their skill and authority and instituted a new set of priests or Magi. They instructed them in such ceremonies and mysteries of religion and philosophy as they thought fit to establish for the empire. These in turn instructed others until they became a great number. Suidas says that Zoroaster was the author of the name of the *Magi.* Elmacinus states that he reformed the religion of the Persians, which before was divided into many sects. Agathias says that he introduced the religion of the Magi among the Persians, changing their ancient sacred rites. {*Agathias, l. 2. c. 24. s. 6. Internet*} Ammianus states:

> According to Plato, the most eminent author of lofty ideas, magic, under the mystic name

of *hagistia*, is the purest worship of the gods. To the science of this, derived from the secret lore of the Chaldeans, in ages long past the Bactrian Zoroaster made many contributions, and after him the wise King Hystaspes, the father of Darius. 33. When Zoroaster had boldly made his way into the unknown regions of Upper India, he reached a wooded wilderness, whose calm silence the lofty intellects of the Brahmins control. From their teaching he learned as much as he could grasp of the laws regulating the movements of the earth and the stars, and of the pure sacrificial rites. Of what he had learned he communicated something to the understanding of the Magi, which they, along with the art of divining the future, hand on from generation to generation to later times. 34. From that time on for many ages down to the present a large class of men of one and the same descent have devoted themselves to the service of the gods. The Magi also say (if it is right to believe them) that they guard on ever-burning braziers a fire sent down from heaven in their country, and that a small portion of it, as a good omen, used to be carried before the kings of Asia. 35. The number of Magi of this origin in old times was very small, and the Persian potentates made regular use of their services in the worship of their gods. And it was sin to approach an altar, or touch a sacrificial victim, before one of the Magi, with a set form of prayer, poured the preliminary libations. But they gradually increased in number and became a strong clan, with a name of their own; they possessed country residences, which were protected by no great walls, and they were allowed to live in accordance with their own laws, and through respect for religion were held in high esteem." {*Ammianus, l. 23. c. 6. s. 32-35. 2:367,369}

657. Hence, this empire was first composed of many nations, each having its own religion. Hystaspes and Zoroaster collected what they conceived to be the best from these and established it by law. They taught it to others until their disciples became numerous enough for the priesthood of the whole empire. Instead of those various old religions, they set up their own institutions for the whole empire, in much the same way that Numa conceived and instituted the religion of the Romans. This religion of the Persian Empire was based partly on the institutions of the Chaldeans, in which Zoroaster was well skilled, and partly of the institutions of the ancient Brahmins. {E351} These are supposed to derive even their name from the Abrahamans, or sons of Abraham, who were born by his second wife Keturah and instructed by their father in the worship of ONE GOD without images. They were sent into the east where Hystaspes was instructed by their successors. About the same time with Hystaspes and Zoroaster, lived also Ostanes, another eminent man of the Magi. Pliny places him under Darius Hystaspes and Suidas makes him the follower of Zoroaster. He came into Greece with Xerxes I and seems to be the Otanes of Herodotus, who exposed Smerdis and headed the conspiracy against him. For that service he was honoured by the conspirators and exempted from the authority of Darius. {*Herodotus, l. 3. c. 68-71. 2:89}

658. In the sacred commentary of the Persian rites these words are ascribed to Zoroaster:

> And god has the head of a hawk. He is the first, incorruptible, eternal, uncreated, without parts, most unlike (all else), the controller of all good, who cannot be bribed, the best of all the good, the wisest of all wise; and he is also a father of good laws and justice, self-taught, natural, and perfect, and wise, and the sole author of the sacred power of nature. {*Eusebius, Gospel, l. 1. c. 10. 1:47}

659. This was also taught by Ostanes, in his book called *Octateuchus*. This was the ancient god of the Persian Magi, and they worshipped him by keeping a perpetual fire for sacrifices on an altar in the centre of a round area surrounded by a ditch. There was no temple in the place and they did not worship the dead or any images. However, in a short time they apostatised from the worship of this eternal, invisible God, to worship the sun, the fire, dead men and images, like the Egyptians, Phoenicians and Chaldeans had done before them. From these superstitions, and the pretending to tell the future, the words *Magi* meaning *priests*, *Magia* meaning the *religion of the Persians*, obtained a bad reputation.

660. Darius Hystaspes or Darab, began his reign in the spring of 522 BC, in the fifteenth year of the empire of the Persians, and reigned for thirty-six years by the unanimous consent of all chronologers. His accession year was 522 BC and his first regal year was 521 BC. {E353} In the second year of his reign, the Jews began to build the temple, by the prophesying of Haggai and Zechariah, and finished it in the sixth year. He fought the Greeks at Marathon in October of 490 BC, ten years before the battle at Salamis in 480 BC. He died in the fifth year after the battle at Marathon at the end of the winter or beginning of the spring in 485 BC. The years of Cambyses and Darius are determined by three eclipses of the moon recorded by Ptolemy,

so that they cannot be disputed. By those eclipses and the prophecies of Haggai and Zechariah compared together, it is obvious that the years of Darius began after the 24th day of the eleventh Jewish month and before the 25th day of April, and by consequence in March or April.

1.4 Xerxes I (484–465 BC)

661. Xerxes I, Achschirosch, Achsweros or Oxyares, succeeded his father Darius, and spent at least five years preparing for his expedition against the Greeks. This expedition happened during the time of the Olympic Games. It was in the beginning of the first year of the 75th Olympiad in 480 BC, when Callias was the archon at Athens; as all chronologers agree. The great number of people which he took from Susa to invade Greece, made Aeschylus the poet say:

It emptied the falling city of Susa. {*Aeschylus, Persians, l. 1. v. 761. 1:247}

662. His army took about a month to cross the Hellespont at the end of the fourth year of the 74th Olympiad or 480 BC. The battle at Salamis happened in autumn, three months later on the 16th day of the month Munychion on the full moon. This was shortly after an eclipse of the moon, which happened on October 2nd. Therefore, his first year began in the spring of 485 BC. He reigned almost twenty-one years by the consent of all writers, and was murdered by Artabanus, the captain of his guards near the end of the winter of 464 BC.

1.5 Artabanus (465 BC)

663. Artabanus reigned seven months. When suspected of treason against Xerxes I, he was killed by Artaxerxes Longimanus, the son of Xerxes I.

1.6 Artaxerxes Longimanus (464–425 BC)

664. Artaxerxes Longimanus began his sole reign in the autumn half of the year between the fourth and ninth Jewish months, {Ne 1:1 2:1 5:14 Ezr 7:7,8,9} and his 20th year fell on the 4th year of the 83rd Olympiad or 445 BC as Africanus states. {Jerome, Da 8} Therefore, his first year began within a month or two of the autumnal equinox of 464 BC. However, he was made viceroy with his father in 474 BC from which we count his regal years. Thucydides relates that the news of the death of Artaxerxes came to Athens in the winter, in the seventh year of the Peloponnesian War in 425 BC. {*Thucydides, l. 4. c. 50. s. 3. 2:299} {E355} By Ptolemy's Canon, he reigned forty-one years as sole king, including the reign of his predecessor Artabanus, and died about the middle of the winter in 425 BC. The Persians now call

him Ardschir Diraz and Bahaman while the oriental Christians call him Artahascht.

1.7 Xerxes II, Sogdianus, Darius Nothus (424–405 BC)

665. After the death of Artaxerxes Longimanus, Xerxes II reigned for two months followed by Sogdianus for seven months. Darius Nothus, the bastard son of Artaxerxes, succeeded him in 424 BC and reigned nineteen years and seven or eight months. He died in the summer before the end of the Peloponnesian War and in the same Olympic year, and by consequence in July or August 405 BC. The thirteenth year of his reign in the winter coincided with the twentieth year of the Peloponnesian War. The years of that war are well established and agreed on by all chronologers. The war began in the spring of 431 BC, lasting twenty-eight years and ended in April of 404 BC.

1.8 Artaxerxes Mnemon (404–359 BC), Artaxerxes Ochus (358–338 BC), Arses or Arogus (337–336 BC), Darius Codomannus (335–331 BC)

666. The next king was Artaxerxes Mnemon, the son of Darius Nothus and he reigned for forty-six years and died in 359 BC. After him reigned Artaxerxes Ochus for twenty-one years to 338 BC and was succeeded by Arses or Arogus who reigned for two years to 336 BC. The last king, Darius Codomannus, reigned for four years until the battle of Gaugamela by which the empire was lost to the Greeks on October 2, 331 BC. Darius was not murdered until a year and some months later. {E356}

2.0 The Corrupted Jewish Version of Persian History

667. We have derived this chronology from the Greek and Latin writers for the Jews know nothing more of the Babylonian and Medo-Persian Empires than what they have from of the books of the Old Testament of the Bible. Therefore, they allow for no more kings, nor years of kings than they can find in those books. The only kings they know of are Nebuchadnezzar, Evilmerodach, Belshazzar, Darius the Mede, Cyrus, Ahasuerus or Cambyses, and Darius the Persian. The last Darius they consider to be the Artaxerxes, in whose reign Ezra and Nehemiah came to Jerusalem for they consider Artaxerxes a common name of the Persian kings. They say that Nebuchadnezzar reigned for forty-five years {2Ki 25:27} and Belshazzar for three years. {Da 8:1} Therefore, Evilmerodach reigned for twenty-three years, thus making up the seventy years of captivity. They exclude the first year of Nebuchadnezzar, in which they say the prophecy of the seventy years was given. They assign one year, or at most two years, to Darius the Mede. {Da 9:1} They allow for three incomplete years for Cyrus. {Da 10:1} To Ahasuerus, they assign twelve years until the casting of Pur, {Es 3:7} one year more until the Jews killed their enemies, {Es 9:1} and one year more until Esther and Mordecai wrote the second letter for the keeping of Purim. {Es 9:29} Hence, his reign sums to only fourteen years. {E357}

668. To Darius the Persian they allot thirty-two or rather thirty-six years. {Ne 13:6} Hence, according to their reckoning, the Persian Empire from the time of the building of the temple in the second year of Darius Hystaspes lasted only thirty-four years until Alexander the Great overthrew it. Thus the Jews so reckon in their greater chronicle, Seder Olam Rabbah, which was compiled by Rabbi Yose ben Halafta who died in 160 AD. Josephus, from the biblical and other books, reckons only these kings of Persia: Cyrus, Cambyses, Darius Hystaspes, Xerxes I, Artaxerxes, and Darius. He confounds this Darius, who was Darius Nothus, with Darius Codomannus whom Alexander the Great overthrew. By means of this reckoning, he makes Sanballat and Jaddua alive when Alexander the Great overthrew the Persian Empire. Thus all the Jews conclude the Persian Empire with the kings of Artaxerxes Longimanus and Darius Nothus. They allow for no more kings of Persia than those mentioned in the books of Ezra and Nehemiah. They refer to the reigns of this Artaxerxes, and this Darius, whenever they find similar names in profane history. They consider Artaxerxes Longimanus, Artaxerxes Mnemon and Artaxerxes Ochus, to be one and the same king as Artaxerxes. Likewise they consider Darius Nothus and Darius Codomannus to be the same man. Similarily they reckon Jaddua and Simeon Justus to be one and the same high priest. {E358}

669. The Jews who took Herod for the messiah were called Herodians. They seemed to justify their opinion based on the seventy weeks of years which they found between the reign of Cyrus and that of Herod. When this proved false, they applied Daniel's prophecy to Theudas and Judas of Galilee and finally to Bar Kokhab, for they seemed to have adopted this abridged version of the kings of Persia. Since their accounts are most inaccurate, it was necessary to use the records of the Greeks, Latins and Ptolemy's Canon for establishing the times of the kings of this empire. When this is done, we have a better understanding of the history of the Jews as recorded in the books of Ezra and Nehemiah. This history has been misunderstood by them and needs further development. First, we shall state the history of the Jews under Zerubbabel, in the reigns of Cyrus, Cambyses and Darius Hystaspes.

3.0 The Correct History of the Jews Under Cyrus, Cambyses and Darius Hystaspes

670. This history is contained in Ezra 1:1-4:4, Nehemiah 7:5-12:9. Nehemiah copied all this from the chronicles of the Jews written before his days. {E359} This appears by reading these passages and considering that the priests and Levites who sealed the covenant on the twenty-fourth day of the seventh month in Nehemiah 8:14 9:1 10:1-27 were the very same priests as those who returned from the captivity in the first year of Cyrus in 536 BC. {Ne 12:1-26}

671. This is seen by the comparison of their names in the chart on the following page.

672. The Levites Jeshua, Kadmiel, and Hodaviah or Judah, mentioned here are considered leaders among the people who returned with Zerubbabel. {Ezr 2:40} They assisted in laying the foundation of the temple, {Ezr 3:9} in reading the law and making and sealing the covenant. {Ne 8:7 9:5 10:9,10}

673. Therefore, when the books of Ezra and Nehemiah are compared, the history of the Jews under Cyrus, Cambyses and Darius Hystaspes can be deduced. {E361} They returned from captivity under Zerubbabel in the first year of Cyrus with the holy vessels and a commission to build the temple. They came to Jerusalem and Judah, each to his city, and lived in their cities until the seventh month. Then they went to Jerusalem and first built the altar. On the first day of the seventh month, they began to offer the daily burnt offerings and to read in the book of the law. They kept a solemn fast and sealed a covenant.

674. After this, the rulers of the people lived in Jerusalem and the rest of the people cast lots. One in ten was to live in Jerusalem and the rest in the cities of Judah. In the second year and second month of their coming, which was five years before the death of Cyrus, they laid the foundation of the temple in 535 BC. However, the adversaries of Judah interrupted their building and hired counsellors against them during all the days of Cyrus and to the reign of Darius Hystaspes. However, in the second year of his reign, by the prophesying of Haggai and Zechariah, they returned to the work. By a new decree from Darius, they finished it on the third day of the month Adar in the sixth year of his reign in 515 BC. They kept the dedication with joy, and the passover, and feast of unleavened bread.

675. This Darius was not Darius Nothus but Darius Hystaspes, as I deduce by considering that the second

The Priests Who Returned	The Priests Who Sealed
Nehemiah {Ezr 2:2}	Nehemiah {Ne 10:1}
Seraiah {Ne 12:1}	Seraiah {Ne 10:2}
*	Azariah {Ne 10:2}
Jeremiah {Ne 12:1}	Jeremiah {Ne 10:2}
Ezra {Ne 12:1}	Ezra {Ne 8:1}
*	Pashur {Ne 10:3}
Amariah {Ne 12:2}	Amariah {Ne 10:3}
Malluch or Melicu {Ne 12:2,14}	Malchijah {Ne 10:3}
Hattush {Ne 12:2}	Hattush {Ne 10:4}
Shechaniah or Shebaniah {Ne 12:3,14}	Shebaniah {Ne 10:4}
*	Malluch {Ne 10:4}
Rehum or Harim {Ne 12:3,15}	Harim {Ne 10:5}
Meremoth {Ne 12:3}	Meremoth {Ne 10:5}
Iddo {Ne 12:4}	Obadiah or Obdia {Ne 10:5}
*	Daniel {Ne 10:6}
Ginnetho or Ginnethon {Ne 12:4,16}	Ginnethon {Ne 10:6} {E360}
*	Baruch {Ne 10:6}
*	Meshullam {Ne 10:7}
Abijah {Ne 12:4}	Abijah {Ne 10:7}
Miamin or Miniamin {Ne 12:5,17}	Mijamin {Ne 10:7}
Maadiah {Ne 12:5}	Maaziah {Ne 10:8}
Bilgah {Ne 12:5}	Bilgai {Ne 10:8}
Shemajah {Ne 12:6}	Shemajah {Ne 10:8}
Jeshua {Ne 12:8}	Jeshua {Ne 10:9}
Binnui {Ne 12:8}	Binnui {Ne 10:9}
Kadmiel {Ne 12:8}	Kadmiel {Ne 10:9}
Sherebiah שרביה {Ne 12:8}	Shebaniah שבניה {Ne 10:10}
Judah or Hodaviah {Ne 12:8 Ezr 2:40,3:9} Ωδουια {LXX Ezr 2:40}	Hodijah {Ne 10:10}

year of his reign in 520 BC was seventy years from the invasion of Jerusalem and the cities of Judah by Nebuchadnezzar in the ninth year of Zedekiah in 590 BC. {Zec 1:12 Jer 34:1,7,22 39:1} The fourth year of this Darius in 518 BC was seventy years from the burning of the temple in the eleventh year of Zedekiah in 588 BC. {Zec 7:5 Jer 42:12} This is only true for Darius Hystaspes for in his second year there were still men living who had seen the first temple. {Hag 2:3} However, the second year of Darius Nothus in 422 BC was one hundred and sixty-six years after the desolation of the temple and city in 588 BC.

Further, if the finishing of the temple was deferred to the sixth year of Darius Nothus in 418 BC, then Jeshua, the high priest, and Zerubbabel the leader of the people must have held these offices for at least a hundred and nineteen years together. This does not even consider the time they lived before this, which is surely too long!

676. In the first year of Cyrus in 536 BC, the chief priests were Seraiah, Jeremiah, Ezra, Amariah, Malluch, Shechaniah, Rehum, Meremoth, Iddo, Ginnetho, Abijah, Miamin, Maadiah, Bilgah,

Shemajah, Joiarib, Jedaiah, Sallu, Amok, Kilkiah and Jedaiah. {E363} These were priests in the days of Jeshua, and the oldest sons of them all, Merajah the son of Seraiah, Hananiah the son of Jeremiah, Meshullam the son of Ezra, etc., were chief priests in the days of Joiakim, the son of Jeshua. {Ne 12:1-26} Therefore, the high priesthood of Jeshua was ordinary in length.

4. The Correct History of the Jews Under Xerxes I and Artaxerxes Longimanus

677. I have now outlined the history of the Jews in the reigns of Cyrus, Cambyses, and Darius Hystaspes. It remains that we detail their history in the reigns of Xerxes I and Artaxerxes Longimanus for I place the history of Ezra and Nehemiah in the reign of Artaxerxes Longimanus, and not in that of Artaxerxes Mnemon.

4.1 The Jewish High Priests During the Persian Empire

678. During all the Persian Empire until the last Darius mentioned in scripture, whom I take to be Darius Codomannus, there were only six high priests in continual succession of father and son. These are Jeshua, Joiakim, Eliashib, Joiada, Jonathan, Jaddua. The seventh high priest was Onias the son of Jaddua, the eighth was Simeon Justus, the son of Onias, and the ninth was Eleazar the younger brother of Simeon Justus.

679. Now, we may consider an average of twenty-seven or eight years to a generation by the oldest sons of a family from one generation to the next. {E364} If this is the case and we allow thirty years to a generation, then we may further suppose that Jeshua, on the return of the captivity in the first year of the Persian Empire, was about thirty or forty years old. The high priests would be of that age and be as follows:

1) Jeshua in the return of the captivity in the first year of the Persian Empire,

2) Joiakim in the sixteenth year of Darius Hystaspes,

3) Eliashib in the tenth year of Xerxes I,

4) Joiada in the nineteenth year of Artaxerxes Longimanus (as sole king),

5) Jonathan in the eighth year of Darius Nothus,

6) Jaddua in the nineteen year of Artaxerxes Mnemon,

7) Onias in the third year of Artaxerxes Ochus,

8) Simeon Justus two years before the death of Alexander the Great.

680. This reckoning agrees with the course of nature and perfectly well with history for this Eliashib might be high priest, and have grandsons, before the seventh year of Artaxerxes Longimanus. {Ezr 10:6} Without exceeding the age which many old men attain to, he may continue to be the high priest until after the thirty-second year of that king. {Neh 13:6,7} His grandson Johanan or Jonathan, might have a room in the temple in the seventh year of that king {Ezr 10:6} and be the high priest before Ezra recorded a list of the sons of Levi in the book of Chronicles. {Neh 12:23} In his high priesthood, he might slay his younger brother Jesus in the temple, before the end of the reign of Artaxerxes Mnemon. {*Josephus, Antiquities, l. 11. c. 7. s. 1. (298) 6:459} {E365}

681. Jaddua might be high priest before the death of Sanballat, {*Josephus, Antiquities, l. 11. c. 7. s. 2. (302) 6:461} and before the death of Nehemiah, {Neh 12:22} and also before the end of the reign of Darius Nothus. Thereby, he might be the basis for Josephus and the later Jews, who mistook this king for the last Darius, to arrive at the opinion that Sanballat, Jaddua, and Manasseh the younger brother of Jaddua, lived until the end of the reign of the last Darius. {*Josephus, Antiquities, l. 11. c. 7,8. (297-347) 6:457-483} Then this Manasseh might marry Nicaso, the daughter of Sanballat, and for that offence be expelled by Nehemiah, before the end of the reign of Artaxerxes Longimanus. {Neh 13:28} {*Josephus, Antiquities, l. 11. c. 7,8. (297-347) 6:457-483} At that time, Sanballat might be governor of Samaria and in the reign of Darius Nothus, or soon after, build the temple of the Samaritans in Mount Gerizim for his son-in-law Manasseh, the first high priest of that temple. {*Josephus, Antiquities, l. 11. c. 8. s. 2. (309-312) 6:463,465}

682. Simeon Justus might be high priest when the Persian Empire was invaded by Alexander the Great, as the Jews think. {Joma, fol. 69. 1.} {Liber Juchasis. R. Gedaliah, etc.} For that reason he might be mistaken by some of the Jews for the same high priest with Jaddua and be dead some time before the book of Ecclesiasticus was written in Hebrew at Jerusalem, by his grandfather. {E366} In 247 BC a copy of the book was found in Egypt and there translated into Greek. {APC Sir 50:27 1:1 Prologue} Eleazar, the younger brother and successor of Simeon, might also cause the law to be translated into Greek in the beginning of the reign of Ptolemy Philadelphus. {*Josephus, Antiquities, l. 12. c. 2. s. 1. (11,12(7:9} Onias, the son of Simeon Justus, who was a child at his father's death, and hence was born when his father was old, might be so old in the reign of Ptolemy Euergetes, as to have his follies excused to that king, by saying that he had grown childish with old age. {*Josephus, Antiquities, l. 12. c. 4. s. 3. (172) 7:91}

683. In this manner, the actions of all these high priests agree with the reigns of the kings without any straining from the normal course of nature. According to this reckoning, the days of Ezra and Nehemiah occurred within the reign of the first Artaxerxes, for Ezra and Nehemiah lived in the high priesthood of Eliashib. {Ezr 10:6 Neh 3:1 13:4,28} However, if Eliashib, Ezra and Nehemiah are placed in the reign of the second Artaxerxes, since they lived beyond the thirty-second year of Artaxerxes which was 373 BC, {Neh 13:28} there must be at least one hundred and sixty years allotted to the three first high priests and only four or five years to the remaining high priests. {E367} This is much too artificial, for the high priesthoods of Jeshua, Joiakim, and Eliashib were ordinary in length.

684. Jeshua's priesthood was within one generation of the chief priests and that of Joiakim with the next generation, as we have shown already. Eliashib's occurred within the third generation for at the dedication of the wall, Zechariah, the son of Jonathan and the grandson of Shemaiah, was one of the priests. {Neh 12:35} Jonathan and his father Shemaiah, were contemporaries with Joiakim and his father Jeshua. {Neh 12:6,18} I observe further that in the first year of Cyrus, Jeshua, and Bani, or Binnui, were chief fathers of the Levites. {Neh 7:7,15 Ezr 2:2,10 3:9} Jozabad, the son of Jeshua, and Noadiah, the son of Binnui, were chief Levites in the seventh year of Artaxerxes, when Ezra came to Jerusalem in 467 BC. {Ezr 7:8 8:33} Hence, this Artaxerxes began his reign before the end of the second generation and that he reigned in the time of the third generation is confirmed by two more examples. Meshullam, the son of Berechiah and the grandson of Meshezabeel, and Azariah, the son of Maaseiah and the grandson of Ananiah, were fathers of their houses at the repairing of the wall. {Neh 3:4,23} {E368} Their grandfathers, Meshezabeel and Ananiah, subscribed to the covenant in the reign of Cyrus. {Neh 10:21,23} Yet Nehemiah, this same Nehemiah the son of Hachaliah, was the Tirshatha, and also subscribed to it. {Neh 10:1 8:9 Ezr 2:2,63} Therefore, in the thirty-second year of Artaxerxes Mnemon in 373 BC, he would have been more than one hundred and eighty years old, which is far too old! The same may be said of Ezra, if he was that priest and scribe who read the law. {Neh 8:1-3} He is the son of Seraiah, the grandson of Azariah, the great-grandson of Hilkiah, the great-great-grandson of Shallum, etc. {Ezr 7:1} This Seraiah died in captivity after the burning of the temple. {1Ch 6:14 2Ki 25:18} From the time of his death to the twentieth

year of Artaxerxes Mnemon in 385 BC, is more than two hundred years. This is much too old for Ezra!

4.2 Untangling the Chronology in the Book of Ezra

685. I consider further that Cyrus, *, Darius, Ahasuerus, and Artaxerxes, are named as successors to one another. {Ezr 4:5-7} These names correspond to Cyrus, *, Darius Hystaspes, Xerxes I and Artaxerxes Longimanus and to no other kings of Persia. Some think this Artaxerxes is not the successor, but the predecessor of Darius Hystaspes and fail to realise that in his reign the Jews were busy in building the city and the wall. {Ezr 4:12} By consequence, they had finished the temple before this time. {E369} Ezra describes first how the people of the land hindered the building of the temple all the days of Cyrus, and further, until the reign of Darius. Later after the temple was built, he describes how they hindered the building of the city in the reign of Ahasuerus and Artaxerxes, and then returns to the story of the temple in the reign of Cyrus and Darius Hystaspes.

686. This is confirmed by comparing the book of Ezra with the book of I Esdras in the Apocrypha. If you omit in the book of Ezra the story of Ahasuerus and Artaxerxes Longimanus {Ezr 4} and you omit in the book of I Esdras the same story of Artaxerxes and the one of the three wise men, {APC 1Es 2:16-4:63} the two books agree. Therefore, the book of I Esdras, if you exclude the story of the three wise men, was originally copied from the authentic writings of the Bible. In the book of Ezra the story of Artaxerxes and Ahasuerus, interrupts the story of Darius Hystaspes but does not interrupt it in the book of I Esdras. There it is inserted into the story of Cyrus between the first and the second chapter of Ezra. All the rest of the story of Cyrus and that of Darius Hystaspes, is told in the book of I Esdras in chronological order, without any interruption.

687. So the Darius, which in the book of Ezra precedes Ahasuerus and Artaxerxes, and the Darius which in the same book follows them, is, by the book of I Esdras, one and the same Darius. {E370} Therefore, I take the book of I Esdras to be the best interpreter of the historical sequence of the events in the book of Ezra. Hence, the Darius mentioned between Cyrus and Ahasuerus, is Darius Hystaspes. Therefore, Ahasuerus and Artaxerxes who succeeded him, are Xerxes I and Artaxerxes Longimanus. The Jews who came up from Artaxerxes to Jerusalem, and began to build the city and the wall, are Ezra with his companions. {Ezr 4:13} When we understand this, the history of the Jews in the reign of these kings will be as follows.

4.3 Building the Wall of Jerusalem

(Dates of regal years for Artaxerxes are from the time he was appointed viceroy with his father in 474 BC. Editor.)

688. After the temple was built and Darius Hystaspes was dead, the enemies of the Jews in the beginning of the reign of his successor Ahasuerus or Xerxes I, wrote to him an accusation against them. {*Ezr 4:6*} In the seventh year in 467 BC of his successor Artaxerxes, Ezra and his companions went up from Babylon with offerings and vessels for the temple. They had the authority to take from the king's treasury whatever was necessary for sacrifices in the temple. {*Ezr 7:1,7,12-24*} This assumes that the temple was finished, according to the command of Cyrus, and Darius and Artaxerxes, the kings of Persia. {*Ezr 6:14*} Their commission was also to set magistrates and judges over the land and thereby establish a new government over the region. {*E371*} They convened a great council or Sanhedrin to separate the people from foreign wives. They were also encouraged to attempt the building of Jerusalem with its wall. Hence, Ezra said in his prayer:

> God had extended mercy unto them in the sight of the kings of Persia, and given them a reviving to set up the house of their God, and to repair the desolations thereof, and to give them a *wall* in Judah, even in Jerusalem. {*Ezr 9:9*}

689. When they began to repair the wall, their enemies wrote against them to Artaxerxes Longimanus and said:

> Be it known unto the king, that the Jews which came up from thee to us, are come unto Jerusalem, building the rebellious and the bad city, and have set up the walls thereof, and joined the foundations, etc. {*Ezr 4:12*}

690. The king wrote back that the Jews should cease and the city not be built, until another command should be given from him. Thereupon their enemies

> went up to Jerusalem, and made them cease by force and power; {*Ezr 4:23*}

691. In the twentieth year of the king in 454 BC, Nehemiah heard that the Jews were in great affliction and distress, and that the wall of Jerusalem which Ezra had recently repaired, was broken down and its gates burned. He obtained permission from the king to go and build the city and the governor's house. {*Neh 1:3 2:6,8,17*} {*E372*} He arrived at Jerusalem the same year and remained as governor for twelve years until 442 BC and rebuilt the wall. Although he was opposed by Sanballat, Tobiah and Geshem, he persisted in the work with great resolution and patience until the breaches in the wall were repaired. Then Sanballat and Geshem sent messengers to him five times to hinder him from setting up the doors for the gates. However, each time, he persisted in the work until the doors were also set up.

692. In just fifty-two days the wall and the gates were finished in the twenty-fifth day of the sixth month, which was Elul. {*Ne 6:15*} (According to Josephus, Nehemiah did not arrive until the twenty-fifth year of the king, and the wall was not completed until the twenty-eighth year of the king, in the ninth month. {**Josephus, Antiquities, l. 11. c. 5. s. 8. (179,180) 6:401*} His account contradicts the scriptures.) The breaches were repaired and they began to work on the gates. While the timber for the gates was being seasoned, they repaired the breaches of the wall. When he had set up the gates, he dedicated the wall with great solemnity, and appointed officers

> over the rooms for the treasure, for the offerings, for the firstfruits, and for the tithes, to gather into them out of the fields of the cities, the portions appointed by the law for the priests and Levites; and the singers and the porters kept the ward of their God. {*Ne 12:44,45*} {*E373*}

693. However, there were few people in the city and the houses were unbuilt and this is how he left Jerusalem in the thirty-second year of the king in 442 BC. {*Neh 7:1,4*} After some time, he returned from the king and corrected the abuses that had happened in his absence. {*Neh 13*} In the meantime the genealogies of the priests and Levites were recorded in the book of the I Chronicles, in the days of Eliashib, Joiada, Jonathan, and Jaddua, until the reign of the next Darius Nothus, whom Nehemiah calls Darius the Persian. {*Neh 12:11,22,23*} Hence, it follows that Nehemiah was governor of the Jews until the reign of Darius Nothus in 423 BC. And here ends the biblical history of the Jews.

5. The History of the Persian Empire according to the Persians

694. The histories of the Persians now extant in the east, claim that the Pischdadians and Kaianides were the oldest dynasties of the kings of Persia and that the dynasty of the Kaianides was immediately followed by the Pischdadians. They derive the name Kaianides from the word *Kai,* which, they say in the old language of the Persians signified a *giant* or *great king.* They call the first four kings of this dynasty, Kai-Cobad, Kai-Caus, Kai-Cosroes, and Lohorasp. {*E374*} By Lohorasp they mean Kai-Axeres, or Cyaxeres for they say that Lohorasp was the first of their kings who introduced martial discipline into their armies. Herodotus affirms the same thing of Cyaxeres. {*Herodotus, l. 1. c. 103. 1:133,135} Further, the ancient histories state that Lohorasp went eastward and conquered many provinces of Persia. One of his generals, whom the Hebrews call Nebuchadnezzar, the Arabians Bocktanassar, and others Raham and Gudars, went westward, and conquered all Syria and Judah, and took the city of Jerusalem and destroyed it. They seem to call Nebuchadnezzar the general of Lohorasp, because he assisted him in some of his wars.

695. The fifth king of this dynasty, they call Kischtasp, and by this name mean sometimes Darius the Mede, and sometimes Darius Hystaspes. They say that he was contemporary to Ozair or Ezra, and to Zaradust or Zoroaster, the legislator of the Ghebers or fire worshippers of India and he established his teachings throughout all Persia. Here they take him for Darius Hystaspes. They also say that he was contemporary with Jeremiah and Daniel, and that he was the son and successor of Lohorasp. Here they take him for Darius the Mede.

696. They call the sixth king of the Kaianides, Bahaman or Ardschir Diraz, that is, Artaxerxes Longimanus, so named from the great extent of his empire. {E375} However, they say that Bahaman went westward into Mesopotamia and Syria. There he conquered Belshazzar, the son of Nebuchadnezzar, and gave the kingdom to Cyrus his lieutenant-general over Media. Here they take Bahaman for Darius the Mede. Following Ardschir Diraz, they place Homai, a queen and the mother of Darius Nothus, although really she did not reign. They call the two next and last kings of the Kaianides, Darab, the bastard son of Ardschir Diraz, and Darab who was conquered by Ascander Roumi. That is Darius Nothus and Darius Codomannus who was conquered by Alexander the Great. The kings between these two Darius's they omit, as they also do for Cyrus, Cambyses and Xerxes I.

697. Therefore, the dynasty of the Kaianides was that of the Medes and Persians, beginning with the defection of Media from the Assyrians near the end of the reign of Sennacherib. It ended with the conquest of Persia by Alexander the Great. However, their account of this dynasty is very imperfect, some kings are omitted, and others being confounded with one another. Their chronology of this dynasty is still much worse. They assign one hundred and twenty years to the reign of the first king, one hundred and fifty years to the second, sixty years to the third, one hundred and twenty years to the fourth and fifth and one hundred and twelve years to the sixth king. {E376}

698. Hence, the dynasty of the Kaianides is the kingdom of the Medes and Persians. The kingdom of the Pischdadians, which immediately preceded it, must be that of the Assyrians. According to the oriental historians this was the oldest kingdom in the world. Some of its kings lived a thousand years each and one of them reigned for five hundred years, another for seven hundred years, and another for a thousand years.

6. Conclusion

699. We need not then wonder that the Egyptians have made the kings in the dynasty of their monarchy, which was located at Thebes (Egyptian) in the days of David, Solomon, and Rehoboam, so very ancient and so long lived. The Persians have done the same with their kings, who began to reign in Assyria two hundred years after the death of Solomon. The Syrians of Damascus have done likewise to their kings Hadar and Hazael, who reigned a hundred years after the death of Solomon. They worshipped them as gods and boasted of their antiquity, ignorant that they were of recent origin as Josephus states.

700. While all these nations have exaggerated their antiquities so much, we need not wonder that the Greeks and Latins have made their first kings a little older than the truth!

> For who does not know history's first law to be that an author must not dare to tell anything but the truth? And its second that he must be bold to tell the whole truth? That there must be no suggestion of partiality anywhere in his writings? Nor of malice? {*Cicero, De Oratore, l. 2. c. 15. 3:243,254}

FINIS

BIBLIOGRAPHY

We would give our eyeteeth to have all the books Newton referred to in preparing this work. We understand that as he kept refining this work, he kept deleting footnotes. Even so there are almost six hundred footnotes in this work.

We have gone through and prepared a bibliography. We have used the history books published by the Loeb Classical Library as the basis for most of this work. These are serious history books written for dedicated scholars. They have the Greek or Latin of the original writer with an English translation. They also note all textual problems. Wherever possible, Newton's footnotes were updated to reflect books published by Loeb.

All footnotes in the text are delimited by {…}. They follow this simple format.

{*Pliny, Natural History, l. 9. c. 23. (56) 3:201}

where:

* — reference verified. No "*" means we could not locate the reference because we did not have the book or we did not have time to track it down.
Pliny — name of author
Natural History - title of book
l. 9. — Book 9 in original author's series (l. = Latin for *liber*)
c. 23. — Chapter 23 in original author's series
(56) — Modern reference number in the original text.
Not all writers are so indexed, e.g., Herodotus 3:201 — Loeb Series, book 3, page 201

Note that some of the original writers did not use chapter breaks, In that case the footnote would have no chapter reference.

The writings of Josephus deserve special mention. We have cross indexed it with Loeb edition and included the new indexing system for it so you can readily cross index it with the Hendrickson reprint of Whiston's English version. For reasons unknown, the chapter and section numbers vary between these two publishers. We followed Loeb for the references.

{*Josephus, Jewish War, l. 6. c. 9. s. 3. (420) 4:299}

The number in (…) is the key to Hendrickson's edition and all other editions that follow the Greek text. Each of Josephus' books are numbered from the beginning with a reference number in the text. This reference in the above example is found in book 6 number 420. The Greek text also identifies this as chapter nine section 3. This scheme has the advantage of universality in that it is not tied to any page numbers for a given publisher.

In the bibliography, works published by Loeb are indicated by a *LCL* (Loeb Classical Library) and no further publisher information is noted. These are all published by Harvard University Press at Cambridge, Massachusetts. The Loeb reference numbers follow the books by that author are listed after the reference.

Format of the bibliography is, author name, book title, publisher information. Note special abbreviations:

ANF - Anti-Nicene Fathers

This series of the early church writers was published by Hendrickson in 1994.

Authors Cited

Books marked with a "*" refer to ones we did not have copies of and hence could not check the reference. This list is only partial. Newton mentioned many authors in passing but did not give references to their works. Likewise the counts represent a lower bound for the actual number of citations from a writer. Again Newton mentioned cited authors without giving the reference. Since the total work has over fourteen thousand quotes, we are not surprised Newton did not document them all. Most modern history books only document a fraction of the authors they cite. These original writers account for more than ninety-eight percent of the footnotes!

Aeschylus: 525-456 BC?, OCD p. 26. [Count 5]
    Libation Bearers (LCL 146)
    Persians (LCL 145)
Agathias: c. 523-580 AD, OCD p. 36. [Count 2]
    Internet
Ammianus Marcellinus, OCD p.73. c. 330-390 AD [Count 6]
    History (LCL 300,315)
Apollodorus of Athens: c. 180-120 BC, OCD p. 124. [Count 14]
    Library (LCL 121,122)

Apollonius Rhodius: c. 2nd century AD, OCD p. 124. [Count 10]
    Argonautica (LCL 001)
Appian of Alexandria: c. 1nd century AD, OCD p. 12
    .[Count 1]
    Punic Wars (LCL 002)
Aristophanes: c. 460-386 BC, OCD p. 163. [Count 1]
    Birds (LCL 179)
Arnobius: c. 300 AD, OCD 174. [Count 2]
    Adversus Nationes, Internet
Arrian: c. 86-160 AD, OCD p. 175. [Count 1]
    Anabasis of Alexander, (LCL 236)
Aristotle: 384-322 BC, OCD p. 165 [Count 1]
    de Mirabundus Auscultationibus
Athenaeus: c. 200 AD, OCD p. 202 [Count 9]
    Deipnosophistae (LCL 204, 208, 224, 235, 274, 327, 345)
Augustine: 354-430 AD, OCD p. 215 [Count 2]
    Prologue to Romans*
    The City of God (NPNF Book 2)
Callimachus of Cyrene: c. 3rd century BC [Count 1]
    Hymn (LCL 129)
Censorinus: 3rd century AD, OCD p. 308. [Count 2]
    De Die Natali
Cicero, Tullius: 106 - 43 BC, OCD p. 1558-1564 [Count 8]
    Against Verres II (LCL 221)
    De Natura Deorum (LCL 268)
    De Oratore (LCL 348)
Clement of Alexandria: c. 200 AD, OCD p. 344. [Count 5]
    Exhoration to the Heathen (ANF Book 2)
    Stromata (ANF Book 2)
Columella, Lucius Junius Moderatus: c. 50 AD., OCD p. 367
    [Count 1]
    De Re Rustica (LCL 407)
Curtius, Quintus: 1st or 2nd century AD, OCD p. 416 [Count 3]
    History of Alexander (LCL 368)
Cyprian: c. 200-258 AD, OCD p. 419. [Count 1]
    Vanity of Idols (ANF Book 5)
Diodorus Siculus: 1st century BC, OCD p. 472,473 [Count 61]
    Bibliotheca (LCL 279, 303, 340, 375, 384, 399, 389, 422,
    377, 390, 409, 423)
Diogenes Laertius: 3rd century AD, OCD p. 474,475 [Count 6]
    Lives of Eminent Philosophers (LCL 184, 185)
Dionysius of Halicarnassus: c. 1st century BC, OCD p. 478
    [Count 16]
    Roman Antiquities (LCL 319, 347)
    De Situ. Orbis*?
    On Imitation*?
Eusebius: c. 260-339 AD, OCD p. 575,576 [Count 7]
    Chronicles, Latin copy,
    Preparation for the Gospel, E.H. Clifford, Baker Book
    House, 1981
Florus: c. 2nd century AD?, OCD p. 602 [Count 1]
    Abridgement of all the Wars over 1200 years (LCL 231)
Geminus: c. 50 AD, OCD p. 628 [Count 2]
    Introduction to the Phenomena, James Evans and J.
    Lennart Berggren, 2006
Harpocration, 2nd century AD, OCD p. 667 [Count 1]
    In Δαρεικος
Herodotus: 5th century BC, OCD p. 696-698 [Count 92]
    The Histories (LCL 117, 118, 119, 120)
Hesiod: 9th century BC, OCD p. 700 [Count 8]
    Theogony (LCL 057)
    Works and Days (LCL 057)

Hesychius: 5th century AD, OCD p. 701 [Count 2]
    Dictionary*
Hipparchus: 2nd century BC, OCD p. 708. [Count 2]
    ad Phaenom.*
Homer: 9th century BC, OCD p. 718-720 [Count 17]
    Hymns (LCL 496)
    Illiad (LCL 170,171)
    Odyssey (LCL 104,105)
Hyginus: 2nd century AD, OCD p. 735 [Count 11]
    Fabulae, Apollodorus' Library and Hyginus' Fabulae,
    2007
Isidorus: c. 600-636 AD, OCD p. 768 [Count 1]
    Originum*
Josephus: 37/38 - 94? AD, OCD p. 798,799 [Count 33]
    Against Apion (LCL 186) (Loeb Book 1)
    Antiquities, (LCL 242, 281, 326, 365, 410, 433, 456) (Loeb
    Book 4-10)
Julian the Apostate: 331-361 AD, OCD p. 800,801 [Count 1]
    Orations (LCL 013)
Justin: 2nd-4th century AD?, OCD p. 802 [Count 3]
    History of Pompeius Trogus, Yardley, 1994
Lucan: 39-65 AD, OCD p. 94,95 [Count 3]
    The Civil War (LCL 220)
Lucian: c. 120 AD, OCD p. 886 [Count 6]
    On Sacrifices (LCL 130)
    The Goddess of Surrye (LCL 162)
    Dance (LCL 302)
Macrobius: 4th century AD, OCD p. 906,907 [Count 2]
    Saturnalia, P. Davies, 1969
Manetho: c. 280 BC, OCD p. 917 [Count 2]
    Text reconstructed from other authors (LCL 350)
Minutius Felix: c. 200-240 AD, OCD 988 [Count 1]
    The Octavius
Nonnus: c. 450-470, OCD p. 1048 [Count 1]
    Dionysiaca (LCL 344)
Orosius: c. 414 AD, OCD p. 1078 [Count 1]
    Histories against the Pagans, (Internet-Latin)
Ovid: 43 BC - 17 AD, OCD p. 1084-1087 [Count 2]
    Fasti (LCL 253)
    Metamorphoses (LCL 042)
Pausanias: c. 150 AD, OCD p. 1129 [Count 48]
    Attica; Corinth (LCL 93)
    Laconia; Messenia; Elis I (LCL 188)
    Ellis II; Achaia; Arcadia (1-21) (LCL 272)
    Arcadia (22-54); Boeotia; Phocis (LCL 297)
Philostratus: 1st century AD, OCD p. 1171 [Count 3]
    Life of Apollonius (LCL 16)
Photius: c. 810-893 AD, OCD p. 1175 [Count 4]
    Bibliotheca*, R. Henry, 1957-1977
Pindar: 5th century BC, OCD p. 1183 [Count 3]
    Pythian Ode (LCL 56)
Plato: c. 429-347 BC, OCD p. 1190 [Count 5]
    Critias; Timaeus (LCL 234)
    Alcibiades I; Minos (LCL 201)
Pliny the Elder: 23/24 - 79 AD, OCD p. 1197,1198 [Count 20]
    Natural History (LCL 330, 352, 353, 370, 371, 392, 393,
    418, 394, 419)
Plutarch: 50 - 120 AD, OCD p. 1200,1201 [Count 23]
    Moralia,
        The Oracles at Delphi (LCL 306)
        Isis and Osiris (V) (LCL 306)
        On Music (XIV) (LCL 427, 470)

Parallel Lives,
    Lycurgus and Numa (I) (LCL 046)
    Theseus and Romulus (I) (LCL 046)
    Solon and Publicola (I) (LCL 046)
Polybius: c. 200-118 BC, OCD p. 1209-1211 [Count 1]
    Histories (LCL 159)
Porphyry, 234-c. 305 AD, OCD 1126,1127 [Count 5]
    Aristotle*
    De Abstinentia*
    Isagoge*
    Life of Pythagoras*
    Manetho citation*
Procopius: c. 6th century AD, OCD p. 1251 [Count 2]
    Vandalic War (LCL 081)
Ptolemy, Claudius: 70-161 AD, OCD p. 1273-1275 [Count 5]
    Hephaestus*
    Canon of Kings*
Sallust: 86-35 BC, OCD p. 1348 [Count 1]
    Jugurtha (LCL 116)
Simplicius: 6th century AD, OCD p. 1409,1410 [Count 1]
    De Caelo* (Latin for, *About the Heavens*), R. Sorabji,
      1987, *The Ancient Commentators of Aristotle*
Solinus, Julius: c. 200 AD, OCD p. 786 [Count 3]
    Die Collectanea Rerum Memorabilium*, H. Walter, 1968
Strabo: 64 BC - 21 AD, OCD p. 1447 [Count 35]
    Geography (LCL 49, 50, 182, 196, 211, 223, 241, 267)
Suidas: (name of a lexicon not an author), c. 980 AD, OCD
    p. 1451 [Count 7]
    English translation*, Byzantine Humanism, 1986
Syncellus: c. 790 AD [Count 3]
    Chronography, Adler and Tuffin, 2002
Tacitus: 56 - 118? AD, OCD p. 1469-1471 [Count 2]
    Histories and Annals (LCL 249, 312)
Tatian: c. 172 AD, OCD p. 1477 [Count 1]
    Address of Tatian to the Greeks (ANF Book 2)
Tertullian: c. 160 - c. 240 AD, OCD p. 1487 [Count 1]
    Apology (ANF Book 3)
Themistius: 4th century AD, OCD p. 1497 [Count 1]
    Oration*
Theognis: c. 550-540 BC, OCD p. 1503 [Count 2]
    Greek Elegiac Poetry (LCL 258)
Thucydides: c. 455 - c. 400 BC, OCD p. 1516,1517 [Count 8]
    History (LCL 108, 109, 110)
Valerius Maximus: 1st century AD, OCD p. 1579 [Count 1]
    History (LCL 493)
Virgil: 70-19 BC, OCD p. 1602-1607 [Count 2]
    Aeneid (LCL 063, 064)
Xenophon: 430-360? BC, OCD p. 1628-1631 [Count 15]
    Cyropaedia (LCL 051, 052)

The following authors are not listed in the Oxford Classical Dictionary, and we think they wrote after the classical period or lived about the time of Newton.

Bochart: [Count 8]
    Canaan or Sacred Geography*
Castel: [Count 1]
    Moph*
Conon: [Count 2]
    Narrat.*

Jambilicus: [Count 1]
    Life of Pythagoras*
Jerusalem Gemara: [Count 1]
Joma:* [Count 1]
Juchasis. R. Gedaliah:* [Count 1]
Petavius: 1583-1652 AD [Count 2]
    Doct. Temp.*
    Var. Dist.*
Stephanus Byzantinus: [Count 5]
    de Urbibus*
Theodorus of Gaza: 1400-1475 AD [Count 1]
    Concerning the Months*
Vasaeus: [Count 1]
    Chronicles of Spain
Vita Homeri Herodoto adser: [Count 1]

Works used in revising this work that were not part of the Loeb collection:

Apollodorus' Library and Hyginus' Fabulae, Translated by R. Scott Smith and Stephen M. Trzaskoma, Hackett Publishing Company, Indianapolis, IN, 2007

Censorius, The Birthday Book, (De Die Natali) Translated by Holt N. Parker, University of Chicago Press, Chicago, IL, 2007

Eusebii Pamphii Chronicli Canones, Johannes Knight Fotheringham, 1923 *Geminos's Introduction to the Phenomena*, James Evans and J. Lennart Berggren, Princeton University Press, Princeton, NJ, 2006

History of Pompeius Trogus, Justin, Translated by J.C. Yardley, Scholar's Press, Atalianta, GA, 1994

Saturnalia, Translated by Percival Vaughan Davies, Columbia University Press, New York, 1969

The Chronography of George Synkellos Translated by William Adler and Paul Tuffin, Oxford University Press, Oxford, UK, 2002

Other works used by the authors in preparing this edition:

Oxford English CD-ROM Dictionary (OED), Second Edition 1994

Oxford Classical Dictionary (OCD), Third Edition, 1996

Oxford Latin Dictionary (OLD), 1996 Edition

Jones, Floyd: *Chronology of the Old Testament*, 2005, Master Books, P.O. Box 726, Green Forest, AR, 72638

Ussher, James: *Annals of the World*, 2003, Master Books, P.O. Box 726, Green Forest, AR, 72638

Websites:

1) Google searches were invaluable.
2) http://en.wikipedia.org.
3) http://homepage.mac.com/cparada/GML/Sicyon.html

Newton referred to many other writers but did not give the exact reference. We usually omitted these writers from this bibliography.

Biblical Book Name Abbreviations

Book	Abbreviation
Genesis	Ge
Exodus	Ex
Numbers	Nu
Judges	Jud
1 Samuel	1Sa
2 Samuel	2Sa
1 Kings	1Ki
2 Kings	2Ki
1 Chronicles	1Ch
2 Chronicles	2Ch
Ezra	Ez
Nehemiah	Ne
Esther	Es
Job	
Song of Solomon	So
Isaiah	Isa
Jeremiah	Jer
Ezekiel	Eze
Daniel	Da
Hosea	Ho

Amos	Am
Nahum	Na
Zephaniah	Zep
Haggai	Hag
Zechariah	Zec
Acts	Ac

Apocryphal Book Name Abbreviations

The following books are from the Apocrypha:

Book	Abbreviation
1 Esdras	1Es
Tobit	Tob
Judith	Jdt
Ecclesiasticus (Sirach)	Sir
Baruch	Bar

Citations from the Oxford Apocrypha noted as *APC*, which follows the Greek text. Citations from Jerome's Latin Vulgate Apocrypha are noted as *VulgateAPC*.

APPENDIX A   Kings of the Ancient Empires

Kings of Egypt

Most dates are taken from the shorter chronology, unless more accurate *guesses* exist elsewhere. Egyptian chronology is very difficult and this is the best Newton could do with the limited data we possess. For the period from Sesostris to Psammenitus, covering four hundred and seventy-four years ruled by about twenty-two kings, Manetho expands to almost twenty-eight hundred years and one hundred and forty kings spread through twenty dynasties! Such was the creative imagination of the Egyptian priests. Hence, Manetho king lists are almost useless but that is what most modern scholars rely on. I seriously doubt if their conjectures are superior to Newton careful work on this subject. Some alias names for a king follow the king's name and are surrounded by brackets. See the *Alias List* in Appendix D for a more complete list of alias names.

DS = Diodorus Siculus

Shepherd Kings (c. 1450-1100 BC)
Salatis, Boeon, Apachnas, Apophis, Janias, Assis, etc. (first six kings)

First expulsion of the Shepherds
    Mephres (c. 1121-1095 BC) (28 years)
    Misphragmuthosis (c. 1094-1067 BC) (28 years)
    Amosis I (Tethmosis) (c. 1066-1037 BC) (30 years)

Ammon (Jupiter Ammon) (1036-999 BC) (38 years)
Sesostris (Belus, Osiris, Shishak, Bacchus, Egyptian Hercules) (998-951 BC) (48 years)
Pheron (Orus) (950-941 BC) (9 years)
Menes (Amenophis, Osymandias (DS)) (940-888 BC) (53 years)
    Osarsiphus (940-927 BC) (14 years) (Usurped Lower Egypt)
    Second expulsion of the Shepherds (c. 926 BC)
    viceroy Proteus (c. 900 BC)
    - built the temple of Vulcan
Rhampsinitus (Ramesses) (887-861 BC) (28 years)
    - built the western portico on the temple of Vulcan
Moeris (Myris DS) (860-839 BC) (22 years)
    - built the northern portico on the temple of Vulcan
Cheops (838-825 BC) (14 years)
    - built the great pyramid
Chephron (824-809 BC) (16 years)

    - built the second large pyramid
Mycerinus (808-803 BC) (6 years)
    - built the third large pyramid
Nitocris (802-789 BC) (14 years)
Asychis (788-780? BC) (9 years) (Lower Egypt)
    - built the eastern portico on the temple of Vulcan
    - built large brick pyramid beside Lake Moeris
At least Four Kingdoms (780?-752 BC) (29 years)
    1) Upper Egypt
        1a) Gnephactus
        1b) Bocchoris
    2) At Hanes
        2a) Anysis or Amosis
    3) At Sais
        3a) Stephanathis
        3b) Necepsos
        3c) Nechus
    4) At Tanis or Zoan
        4a) Petubastes
        4b) Osorchon
        4c) Psammis
Sabacon (751-702 BC) (50 years)
Anysis (717? BC) (a second time)
Sethon (Sevechus) (701-688 BC) (14 years) (likely viceroy with Sabacon before this time)
Tirhakah (687-671 BC) (18 years)
Twelve Contemporary Kings (670-656 BC) (15 Years)
Psammitichus (670-617 BC) (54 years including 15 years as a petty king)
    - built the southern portico on the temple of Vulcan
Nechus (Necho) (616-601 BC) (16 years)
Psammis (600-595 BC) (6 years)
Apries (Pharaoh Hophra) (594-571 BC) (25 years)
Amasis (570-526 BC) (45 years)
Psammenitus (525 BC) (6 months)

Kings of the Assyrian Empire

*Pul (c. 790-748 BC) (c. 44 years)
Tiglathpilasser (747-730 BC) (18 years)
Salmanasser (729-720 BC) (10 years)
Sennacherib (Anacyndaraxis) (719-710 BC) (10 years)
Esarhaddon (Esarhaddon-Pul, Sardanapalus, Assaradin) (709-668 BC) (42 years)
Saosduchinus (667-648 BC) (20 years)
Kineladanos (Nabuchodonosor, Sarac, Saracen) (647-626 BC) (22 years)

*Modern scholars confound Pul and Tiglathpilasser and think they are the same person. This is the result of Edwin Thiele's misunderstanding of biblical and Assyrian chronology.

Kings of the Medes

Dejoces (709-657 BC) (53 years) {*Herodotus, l. 1. c. 102. 1:133}
Phraortes (656-635 BC) (22 years) {*Herodotus, l. 1. c. 102. 1:133}
Astyages (634-600 BC) (35 years) {*Herodotus, l. 1. c. 130. 1:169}
Cyaxeres (599-560 BC) (40 years) {*Herodotus, l. 1. c. 107. 1:139}
Darius the Mede (559-537 BC) (23 years)

The Medes likely revolted in 712 BC but may not have appointed a king until sometime after the month of Thoth in 710 BC. Darius was defeated in 537 BC and effectively lost the empire to Cyrus. However, later that year he gathered a second army and was defeated and captured, thus ending his rule.

Kings of Babylon

Nabonassar (747-734 BC) (14 years)
Nadius (733-732 BC) (2 years)
Chinziros and Poros (731-727 BC) (5 years)
(Jugaeus, Julaeus) (726-722 BC) (5 years)
Mardokempados (Merodach Baladan) (721-710 BC) (12 years)
Arkeanos (709-705 BC) (5 years)
Interregnum (704,703) (2 years)
Belibos (702-700 BC) (3 years)
Aparanadios (699-694 BC) (6 years)
Regebelos (693 BC) (1 year)
Mesisimordakos (692-689 BC) (4 years)
Interregnum (688-681 BC) (8 years)
Assyrian kings:
    Esarhaddon (Assaradin) (680-668 BC) (13 years)
    Saosduchinus (667-648 BC) (20 years)
    Kineladanos (Nabuchodonosor, Chyniladon) (647-626 BC) (22 years)
Babylonian kings:
Nabopolassar (625-605 BC) (21 Years)
Nebuchadnezzar (606-562 BC) (45 years) (viceroy for 20 months)
Evilmerodach (Iluarodamus) (561-560 BC) (2 years)
Neriglissaros (Nergalassaros) (559-556 BC) (4 years)
*Laboasserdach (556 BC 9 months)
Nabonadius (Labynitus, Naboandelos, Nabonnedus, Belshazzar) (555-538 BC) (18 years)

*Omitted in Ptolemy's Canon

Kings of Medo-Persian Empire

Darius the Mede (537 BC) (1 year)
Cyrus (536-530 BC BC) (7 years)
Cambyses (529-522 BC) (8 years)
Magus (Smerdis Impersonator) (522 BC) (7 months)
Darius Hystaspes (521-485 BC) (37 years)
Xerxes I (484-465 BC) (21 years)
Artaxerxes Longimanus (464-425 BC) (40 years) (viceroy 474-465 BC)
*Xerxes II (424 BC) (2 months)
*Secundianus (Sogdianus) (424 BC) (7 months)
Darius Nothus (424-405 BC) (20 years)
Artaxerxes Mnemon (404-359 BC) (46 years)
Artaxerxes Ochus (358-338 BC) (21 years)
Arses or Arogus (337-336 BC) (2 years)
**Darius Codomannus (335-331 BC) (5 years)

*Omitted in Ptolemy's Canon
**Ptolemy's Canon only allows 4 years for his rule

Appendix B — The Period of Nabonassar

The following table shows the drift in the *Period of Nabonassar* because it was based on a three hundred and sixty-five day year. The Egyptians, who fled from Sabacon, introduced their astrology and astronomy to Babylon, and founded the era of Nabonassar in Egyptian years. Originally when the Egyptians established this year, the month of Thoth, the first month in their year, started on the vernal equinox around 887 BC. Every four years the Egyptian month of Thoth drifts back one day from the start of the vernal equinox.

The kings of Babylon and Medo-Persia used accession dating. To determine number of years a king reigned, you count the number of New Years celebrated in his reign, which correspond to the first day of the month Thoth. Hence the Julian date for the first day of the month of Thoth is important. The months he reigned before his first New Year are not counted as a year of his reign. The entire year in which he died is considered part of his reign when determining the number of years he ruled. For Cambyses to have started to reign in 529 BC, implies that Cyrus died sometime between January 3, 530 BC and January 2, 529 BC. If he had died on January 3, 529 BC that year would be counted to both Cyrus and Cambyses which means that Cyrus reigned eight years not seven as Xenophon states. {*Xenophon, Cyropaedia, l. 8. c. 6. s. 22. 6:421} Therefore, Cyrus died sometime before January 3, 529 BC. Xenophon said it was in the spring so it must have been the spring of 530 BC. {*Xenophon, Cyropaedia, l. 8. c. 7. s. 1. 6:423} Therefore, Cambyses would start to reign sometime in 530 BC after the death of Cyrus but his first regal year would commence on January 3, 529 BC. The accession system has the happy result of making cardinal and ordinal numbers for a king's reign the same.

First day of the month of Thoth based on the Julian calendar without the calendar corrections introduced by Pope Gregory for leap years that are century years.

February 26, 747 BC	February 6, 667 BC	January 17, 587 BC
February 25, 743 BC	February 5, 663 BC	January 16, 583 BC
February 24, 739 BC	February 4, 659 BC	January 15, 579 BC
February 23, 735 BC	February 3, 655 BC	January 14, 575 BC
February 22, 731 BC	February 2, 651 BC	January 13, 571 BC
February 21, 727 BC	February 1, 647 BC	January 12, 567 BC
February 20, 723 BC	January 31, 643 BC	January 11, 563 BC
February 19, 719 BC	January 30, 639 BC	January 10, 559 BC
February 18, 715 BC	January 29, 635 BC	January 9, 555 BC
February 17, 711 BC	January 28, 631 BC	January 8, 551 BC
February 16, 707 BC	January 27, 627 BC	January 7, 547 BC
February 15, 703 BC	January 26, 623 BC	January 6, 543 BC
February 14, 699 BC	January 25, 619 BC	January 5, 539 BC
February 13, 695 BC	January 24, 615 BC	January 4, 535 BC
February 12, 691 BC	January 23, 611 BC	January 3, 531 BC
February 11, 687 BC	January 22, 607 BC	January 2, 527 BC
February 10, 683 BC	January 21, 603 BC	January 1, 523 BC
February 9, 679 BC	January 20, 599 BC	December 31, 519 BC
February 8, 675 BC	January 19, 595 BC	December 30, 515 BC
February 7, 671 BC	January 18, 591 BC	December 29, 511 BC

December 27, 507 BC

December 26, 503 BC

December 25, 499 BC

December 24, 495 BC

December 23, 491 BC

December 22, 487 BC

December 21, 483 BC

December 20, 479 BC

December 19, 475 BC

December 18, 471 BC

December 17, 467 BC

December 16, 463 BC

December 15, 459 BC

December 14, 455 BC

December 13, 451 BC

December 12, 447 BC

December 11, 443 BC

December 10, 439 BC

December 9, 435 BC

December 8, 431 BC

December 7, 427 BC

December 6, 423 BC

December 5, 419 BC

December 4, 415 BC

December 3, 411 BC

December 2, 407 BC

December 1, 403 BC

November 30, 399 BC

November 29, 395 BC

November 28, 391 BC

November 27, 387 BC

November 26, 383 BC

November 25, 379 BC

November 24, 375 BC

November 23, 371 BC

November 22, 367 BC

November 21, 363 BC

November 20, 359 BC

November 19, 355 BC

November 18, 351 BC

November 17, 347 BC

November 16, 343 BC

November 15, 339 BC

November 14, 335 BC

November 13, 331 BC

November 12, 327 BC

November 11, 323 BC

November 10, 319 BC

November 9, 315 BC

November 8, 311 BC

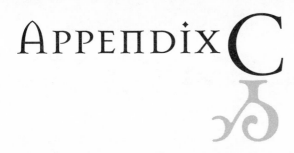

Appendix C   Glossary of Terms

Argo Navis: Argo Navis is the only constellation from Ptolemy's original list of 48 constellations that is no longer officially recognised. Due to its large size, it was split into four constellations by Nicolas Louis de Lacaille: Carina (the keel), Puppis (the poop deck), Pyxis, (the compass), and Vela (the sails). This new version was introduced in the star catalog *Caelum Australe Stelliferum* in 1763, which was published after de Lacaille's death.

Accession year: This was the year a king came to the throne and was not normally considered the first year of his reign.

Accession year system: This computes the length of a king's reign based on the number of Jewish New Years that happened during his reign. If a king reigned only a week before and a week after the New Year, he would be said to reign one year because exactly one Jewish New Year occurred in his reign. Both the Talmud and the Mishnah specify this is the normal way to calculate the length of a king's reign. This system was the normal way kings counted their years of reign. If a king had no Jewish New years in his reign, the length of his reign was normally given in months. The *Accession Year System* is also called *Postdating* by some writers.

Colure: Colure, in astronomy, is either of the two principal meridians of the celestial sphere, one of which passes through the poles and the two solstices, the other through the poles and the two equinoxes; hence designated as solstitial colure and equinoxial colure, respectively.

Colure of the Equinoxes: The great circle passing through the poles of the equator, and intersecting the ecliptic in the equinoxes in an angle of 66.5°, the complement of the angle of the sun's greatest declination.

Colure of the Solstices: The great circle passing through the same poles, and cutting the ecliptic at right angles in the solstices.

Equinox: An equinox in astronomy is that moment in time (not a whole day) when the centre of the Sun can be observed to be directly above the Earth's equator, occurring around March 20 and September 23 each year. More technically, at an equinox, the Sun is at one of two opposite points on the celestial sphere where the celestial equator (i.e., declination 0) and ecliptic intersect. These points of intersection are called equinoctial points—the vernal point and the autumnal point. By extension, the term equinox may be used to denote an equinoctial point.

Non-Accession year system: The remainder of the previous king's year is counted as the first year of his successor and also counted as the last year of the previous king. If a king reigned only a week before and a week after the New Year, he would be said to reign two years when using this system. This system was not normally used, so think of it as non-standard. Only when you plot out the actual reigns, can you determine if this system was used. The *Non-Accession Year System* is also called *Antedating* by some writers.

Primitive Sphere: The sphere which was used before the motions of the equinoxes and solstices were known.

Solace: Solstices occur twice a year, when the tilt of the Earth's axis is oriented directly towards or away from the Sun, causing the Sun to appear to reach its northernmost and southernmost extremes. The name is derived from the Latin *sol* (sun) and *sistere* (to stand still), because at the solstices, the Sun stands still in declination; that is, its apparent movement north or south comes to a standstill.

Viceroy: This position is considered to be defacto king. The viceroy's father was still alive, but the viceroy was running the kingdom. There were two reasons why a king made his son viceroy. First, the father was going to war and wanted to make sure of a smooth transition in case he was killed. Secondly, the father was in ill health and not able to manage the kingdom any more. Most viceroyships were rather short and occurred a year or so before the death of the king. According to the Talmud and the Mishnah (see Virtual Jerusalem website), the viceroy always counted his first year as king when he became viceroy, not the sole king. Ussher found no exceptions to this rule. Since appointing a viceroy was usually a planned choice, the logical time to do this would be at the start of the Jewish New Year in Nisan.

APPENDIX D — Gleanings from Archbishop Ussher

The following material was taken from Archbishop Ussher's *Annals of the World*. Paragraph numbers relate to the updated edition published by Master Books. The first extract relates to the husband of Esther. The second impacts the dating of events in the reign of Artaxerxes, and has direct implications on the time of the events in Ezra and Nehemiah. It also defines the correct starting time of Daniel's *Seventy Weeks* to be 454 BC. Newton did not discuss who Esther's husband was, and he appears to have been unaware of Ussher's findings on the dating of Artaxerxes. When we updated Newton's work, we corrected Newton's error relating to the dating of Artaxeres.

Since these errors relating to Esther and Artaxerxes have gained such a strong foothold in biblical circles in recent times, we thought it best to include this information from Ussher.

Who Was Esther's Husband?

701. When Artaphernes made peace, he surveyed their country in parasangs, (a Persian measure of length containing thirty furlongs or almost four miles), and formed divisions. On each division he imposed a tribute which was paid yearly to the king. The rate remained constant until at least the time of Herodotus. {*Herodotus, l. 6. c. 42. 3:189*} That rate was first levied when Darius became king and he imposed it on all his empire. {*Herodotus, l. 3. c. 89,90. 2:117,119*} This was before Darius was master of the islands. {*Herodotus, l. 3. c. 96. 2:123*} According to Herodotus, we note that, to facilitate taxing, Darius now reduced the one hundred and twenty-seven provinces mentioned in Esther down to twenty, yet the bounds of that empire were still the same, stretching from India to Ethiopia. One side had been conquered by Cambyses and the other by Darius. Concerning the revenue from India, Herodotus stated: {*Herodotus, l. 3. c. 94. 2:123*}

> Since the Indians were the most populous nation, more than all other men living that we know, they paid far more tribute than any other nation did, that is three hundred and sixty talents of gold dust and this was the twentieth province. *[E119]*

702. Since we find that when Darius was made king he did not control India, as is evident even from Herodotus himself {*Herodotus, l. 4. c. 44. 2:245*}, it is therefore likely that when the tax rate was set by Artaphernes in Ionia, a similar tax was imposed all over the kingdom by the governors of each of the provinces. *[L170]*

703. It should therefore be considered whether this refers to the time which was spoken of in Esther: {*Es 10:1-3*}

> After this, the king Ahasuerus imposed a tribute upon the land and isles of the sea.

704. That is, this refers to the very time when King Ahasuerus made all the earth and all the islands of the sea pay tribute. For, as Thucydides stated (and Plato confirmed this {*Plato, Menexenus*}) Darius subdued all the islands lying in the Aegean Sea by means of his Phoenician fleet. {*Thucydides, l. 1. c. 16. 1:31*} Diodorus Siculus stated that they were all lost again by his son Xerxes immediately after his defeat in Greece. {*Diod. Sic., l. 11. c. 36,37. 4:221,223*} {*Diod. Sic., l. 12. c. 1. 4:375*} It was after the twelfth year of his reign that the scriptures stated that Ahasuerus imposed this tribute upon the isles. {*Es 3:7 10:1*} For in the war of Xerxes against Greece, all the islands which lay between the Cyanean Isles and the two forelands of Triopium in Cnidos and of Sumium in Attica sent him ships. Diodorus Siculus stated that his successors held none of these isles at all except for Cyprus and Clazomene, which was at that time a small and poor island. {*Diod. Sic., l. 12. c. 3,4. 4:379-383*} {*Thucydides, l. 8. c. 14. 4:213*} {*Thucydides, l. 8. c. 31. 4:243*} {*Plutarch, Cimon, l. 1. c. 13. s. 4. 2:445*} {*Livy, l. 33. c. 20. 9:331*} This is demonstrated by the tenor of Antalcidas' peace, as recorded by Xenophon. {*Xenophon, Hellenica, l. 5. c. 1. s. 31. 2:21*} This seems to me to be a good argument for believing that the Ahasuerus mentioned in Esther is none other than Darius. For this and other similar impositions laid upon the people, the Persians used to call him *a crafty merchant* or *huckster*, as Herodotus noted of him. Under Cyrus and Cambyses, his two predecessors, there was no mention of any tribute charged upon the subjects but that they only brought the king presents. {*Herodotus, l. 3. c. 89. 2:117*} Strabo stated: {*Strabo, l. 15. c. 3. s. 21. 7:185*}

The first that ever brought up paying of tribute was Darius the Long-armed.

705. Strabo mistook the surname of Artaxerxes, the grandchild, and gave it to the grandfather. He also said:

for before him, men paid their kings from what every country yielded, as grain, horses....

706. Polyaenus stated: {*Polyaenus, Strategmata, l. 7.*}

Darius was the first that ever imposed a tribute upon the people. Nevertheless, to make it more palatable to them, he had his officers set the rate first. When they imposed a very heavy tax, he took off one half of it which they willingly paid and took it for a great favour, too, from the king's hand.

707. This story is also mentioned by Plutarch. {*Plutarch, Sayings of Kings and Commanders (172f) 3:13*}

When Was Artaxerxes Made King?

3531a AM, 4240 JP, 474 BC

708. Artaxerxes was made viceroy with his father Xerxes in the twelfth year of Xerxes' reign. This time marks the first year of Artaxerxes reign. Ptolemy's Canon does not record viceroy relationships hence starts Artaxerxes reign nine years later when his father died. (Since the time when Ussher wrote his document, this new information has come to light from archaeology. We are thankful for Dr. Floyd Jones for finding the exact source of this information. Editor.) Savile wrote the following: {*B. W. Savile, "Revelation and Science," Journal of Sacred Literature & Biblical Record, Series 4 (London: Williams and Norgate Pub. April 1863), p. 156.*}

It is satisfactory to know that the idea entertained by Archbishop Ussher of dating the commencement of Artaxerxes' reign nine years earlier than the canon of Ptolemy allows, grounded upon what Thucydides says of Themistocles' flight to Persia, has been confirmed by hieroglyphic inscriptions in Egypt, showing that Artaxerxes was associated with his father in the twelfth year of Xerxes reign, so that there ought to be no longer any doubt respecting that famous prophecy of Daniel, so far as at least regards the crucifixion.

3531b AM, 4241 JP, 473 BC

709. Eusebius noted that in the fourth year of this 76th Olympiad (which we are now documenting), Themistocles fled to the Persians. {*Eusebius, Chronicles, l. 1. 1:191*} This agreed with the account of Thucydides, who placed the coming of Themistocles to Artaxerxes between the siege of Naxos {*Thucydides, l. 1. c. 137. s. 2. 1:233*} and that famous victory over the Persians at the mouth of the Eurymedon River by Cimon, the Athenian. {*Thucydides, l. 1. c. 98-100. 1:165,167*} He took the beginning of the reign of Artaxerxes to have happened at the same time, because he said that Themistocles sent letters to Artaxerxes when he had recently been crowned king, desiring his favour and offering him his service against the Greeks. {*Thucydides, l. 1. c. 137. s. 4. 1:233*} From this we may fully discern that the true beginning of Artaxerxes' reign was almost a full nine years earlier than it is commonly said to have been. (For a more exhaustive treatment of this chronological detail refer to the readily available commentary of Albert Barnes on Daniel chapter nine verse twenty-four. Barnes drew most of his material from Henstenberg's work entitled *Christology of the Old Testament*. Editor.)

The following list contains 622 names for which there are 1034 alias names. This list illustrates one of the major problems in working with ancient history—many of the important characters have multiple names. Different historians, old and modern, transliterate the ancient names differently, helping to add to the confusion. Some of the names are completely different for the principal name but are all the same person. Consider the following two modern English examples of the totally different names for the same person:

a) Robert and Bob
b) Richard and Dick

This list is given without context or qualifications and helps explain seeming contradictions found in the descriptions for the exhaustive index.

Abantes <=> Euboea
Abaris <=> Pelusium
Abydenus <=> Sepharvaim
Achschirosch <=> Xerxes I
Achsuerus <=> Ahasuerus, Assuerus, Axeres, Cy-Axeres,
    Cyaxeres, Oxyares
Achsweros <=> Xerxes I
Acksweres <=> Astibares
Actisanes <=> Sabacon
Adar <=> Benhadad I, Hadad
Adon <=> Adonis
Adonis <=> Adon, Gingris
Aegialea <=> Sicyon
Aegyptus <=> Nile River, Sesostris, Upper Egypt
Aesculapius <=> Tosorthrus
Ahasuerus <=> Achsuerus, Cambyses, Cyaxeres, Xerxes I
Aidoneus <=> Orcus
Alexander the Great <=> Ascander Roumi
Amasis <=> Anysis
Amathusia <=> Calycopis, Venus
Amazons <=> Daughters of Mars
Amenoph <=> Amenophis, Memphis
Amenophis <=> Amenoph, Arminon, Enephes, Imandes,
    Ismandes, Memnon, Menephes, Menes, Minaeus, Mines,
    Mineus, Minies, Mnevis, Osimandes, Osymandias,
    Osymanthias, Phamenophis, Venephes
Ammenemes I <=> Ammenemes II, Ammon
Ammenemes II <=> Ammenemes I, Ammon
Ammon River <=> Nile River
Ammon-No <=> Thebes (Egyptian)

Ammon <=> Ammenemes I, Ammenemes II, Belus
    (Egyptian), Caelus, Jupiter (Egyptian), Jupiter Ammon,
    Jupiter Uranus, Uranus
Ammonia <=> Libya
Amosis I <=> Tethmosis, Thomosis
Amosis II <=> Anysis
Amphitrite <=> Neptys
Anabaxaris <=> Anacyndaraxis
Anacyndaraxis <=> Anabaxaris, Cyndaraxis, Sennacherib
Aniophis <=> Cheops
Anoisis <=> Cheops
Antaea <=> Antaeopolis
Antaeopolis <=> Antaea
Antaeus <=> Atlas
Antinous <=> Delton
Anysis <=> Amasis, Amosis II, Hanes
Apappus <=> Cheops
Apathus <=> Cheops
Apis Epaphus <=> Apis, Epopeus
Apis <=> Apis Epaphus, Epaphus, Serapis
Apollo <=> Orus, Phoebus, Sol
Apries <=> Eraphius, Hophra, Vaphres
Arabians <=> Scenitae
Aradus <=> Arpad, Arphad, Arvad
Araeus <=> Argaeus
Ararat Minni <=> Armenia
Ardschir Diraz <=> Artaxerxes Longimanus
Areca <=> Erech
Argaeus <=> Araeus
Argos <=> Phoronicum
Armais <=> Danaus
Armenia <=> Ararat Minni
Arminon <=> Amenophis
Arogus <=> Arses
Arpad <=> Aradus
Arphad <=> Aradus
Arphaxad <=> Dejoces, Phraortes
Arses <=> Arogus
Artabazus <=> Harpagus
Artagerses <=> Harpagus
Artahascht <=> Artaxerxes Longimanus
Artaxerxes Longimanus <=> Ardschir Diraz, Artahascht,
    Artaxerxes, Bahaman, Darius Hystaspes, Darius the
    Persian
Artaxerxes Mnemon <=> Artaxerxes
Artaxerxes Ochus <=> Artaxerxes
Artaxerxes <=> Artaxerxes Longimanus, Artaxerxes Mnemon,
    Artaxerxes Ochus
Arvad <=> Aradus
Ascander Roumi <=> Alexander the Great
Ashchenez <=> Phrygia
Ashdod <=> Azoth

Asordan <=> Esarhaddon
Assaradin <=> Esarhaddon
Asshur <=> Assyria
Assuerus <=> Achsuerus, Astibares, Cyaxeres
Assur <=> Atsur
Assyria <=> Asshur, Babylonia
Assyrian <=> Syrian, Tyrian
Assyrians <=> Syrians
Asterius <=> Jupiter, Saturn (Cretan)
Astibares <=> Acksweres, Assuerus, Astivares, Axeres, Cy-Axeres
Astivares <=> Astibares
Astraea <=> Isis
Athens <=> Cecropia
Athothes <=> Thoth
Atlas <=> Antaeus
Atsur <=> Assur
Auaris <=> Pelusium
Axeres <=> Achsuerus, Astibares, Cyaxeres
Ayres <=> Moeris
Azoth <=> Ashdod
Baal Canaan <=> Vulcan
Babylonia <=> Assyria
Bacchus <=> Bromios, Cretan Bacchus, Dionysus, Orpheus, Osiris, Semele, Sesostris, Shishak, The Great
Bahaman <=> Artaxerxes Longimanus, Darius the Mede
Bani <=> Binnui
Basilea <=> Isis
Belshazzar <=> Labynitus, Naboandelos, Nabonnedus
Belus (Assyrian) <=> Pul
Belus (Egyptian) <=> Ammon, Busiris, Sesostris
Benhadad I <=> Adar, Hadad
Benhadad II <=> Hadad
Bicheres <=> Mycerinus
Big Dipper <=> Plaustrum
Binnui <=> Bani
Bocktanassar <=> Nebuchadnezzar
Boeotia <=> Cadmeis
Bou Sihor <=> Busiris
Bou Siris <=> Busiris
Bromios <=> Bacchus
Bubaste <=> Selene
Busiris I <=> Osiris
Busiris II <=> Orus
Busiris <=> Belus (Egyptian), Bou Sihor, Bou Siris, Sesostris
Byblia <=> Calycopis, Venus
Byires <=> Moeris
Cabiri <=> Curetes
Cadis <=> Ogygia
Cadmeis <=> Boeotia
Caelus <=> Ammon, Heaven, Jupiter Ammon, Jupiter Uranus, Ouranus, Uranus
Cales <=> Ogygia
Calneh <=> Calno, Chalonitis
Calno <=> Calneh
Calycopis <=> Amathusia, Byblia, Cnidia, Cytherea, Dea Cypria, Dea Syria, Erycina, Idalia, Paphia, Salaminia, Venus
Cambyses <=> Ahasuerus
Canary Islands <=> Fortunate Islands
Carchemish <=> Circutium
Caria <=> Phoenicia
Carians <=> Legates

Carine <=> Kir
Carrhae <=> Haran
Carteia <=> Heracleia, Melcarteia
Carthadas <=> Carthage
Carthage <=> Carthadas
Cassiteris <=> Cornwall, Scilles
Cecropia <=> Athens
Cerethites <=> Crethim
Cerpheres <=> Chephron
Chabor <=> Iberia
Chaboras <=> Habor
Chaitus <=> Latus
Chalach <=> Colchis, Halah
Chalonitis <=> Calneh
Charilaus <=> Charillus
Charillus <=> Charilaus
Chelae <=> Scorpio
Chembis <=> Cheops
Chemmis <=> Cheops
Chemnis <=> Cheops
Cheops <=> Aniophis, Anoisis, Apappus, Apathus, Chembis, Chemmis, Chemnis, Phiops, Saophis, Soiphis, Suphis, Syphaosis, Syphoas, Syphuris
Chephron <=> Cerpheres
Cheres <=> Mycerinus
Cherinus <=> Mycerinus
Chiron <=> Sagittarius
Chyniladon <=> Nabuchodonosor
Cinyras <=> Thoas, Vulcan
Circutium <=> Carchemish
City of Jupiter Ammon <=> Diospolis
Cleombrotus <=> Cleonymus
Cleonymus <=> Cleombrotus
Cnidia <=> Calycopis, Venus
Colchis <=> Chalach
Corinth <=> Ephyra
Cornwall <=> Cassiteris
Corybantes <=> Curetes, Priests of Cybele
Cretan Bacchus <=> Bacchus
Crethim <=> Cerethites, Curetes
Curetes <=> Cabiri, Corybantes, Crethim, Idean Dactyli, Philistines, Telchines
Cush <=> Sepharvaim
Cuth <=> Susa
Cy-Axeres <=> Achsuerus, Astibares
Cy <=> Prince
Cyaxeres <=> Achsuerus, Ahasuerus, Assuerus, Axeres, Kai-Axeres, Lohorasp
Cybele <=> Mother of the Gods
Cyndaraxis <=> Anacyndaraxis
Cytherea <=> Calycopis, Venus
Damascus <=> Hadad
Danaus <=> Armais
Darab the Bastard <=> Darius Nothus
Darab <=> Darius Codomannus, Darius Hystaspes, Darius Nothus
Darics <=> Stateres Darici
Darius Codomannus <=> Darab, Darius Nothus
Darius Hystaspes <=> Artaxerxes Longimanus, Darab, Darius the Mede, Kischtasp, Ochus
Darius Nothus <=> Darab the Bastard, Darab, Darius Codomannus
Darius the Mede <=> Bahaman, Darius Hystaspes, Kischtasp

Darius the Persian <=> Artaxerxes Longimanus
Darius <=> Kischtasp, Lohorasp
Dathnis <=> Tahaphenes
Daughter of Sidon <=> Tyre
Daughters of Mars <=> Amazons
Dea Cypria <=> Calycopis, Venus
Dea Syria <=> Calycopis, Venus
Dejoces <=> Arphaxad
Delton <=> Antinous
Dia <=> Naxos
Dido <=> Elissa
Dionysus <=> Bacchus, Osiris, Sesostris
Diospolis <=> City of Jupiter Ammon
Edom <=> Erythra, Erythras, Phoenicia
Edomites <=> Erythreans, Odomantes
Egyptus <=> Sesostris
Elam <=> Persia
Elamites <=> Persians
Elissa <=> Dido
Enemessar <=> Salmanasser, Shalmaneser
Enephes <=> Amenophis
Epaphus <=> Apis, Epopeus, Osiris
Ephesian Letters <=> Phoenician Letters
Ephyra <=> Corinth
Epopeus <=> Apis Epaphus, Epaphus
Equestris <=> Neptune
Eraphius <=> Apries, Hophra
Erech <=> Areca
Erechtheus <=> Erechthonius, Erichthonius
Erechthonius <=> Erechtheus
Erichthonius <=> Erechtheus
Eridanus <=> Nile River
Erycina <=> Calycopis, Venus
Erythea <=> Gades Island, Gadir
Erythra <=> Edom, Gades Island
Erythrae <=> Gades Island
Erythras <=> Edom, Esau
Erythreans <=> Edomites
Esarhaddon-Pul <=> Esarhaddon, Sarchedon
Esarhaddon <=> Asordan, Assaradin, Esarhaddon-Pul,
    Sarchedon, Sardanapalus
Esau <=> Erythras
Ethiopians <=> Megabars
Euboea <=> Abantes
Europa <=> Juno Olympia, Rhea (Cretan)
Eurycrates <=> Eurycratidas
Eurycratidas <=> Eurycrates
Evilmerodach <=> Iluarodamus
Ezra <=> Ozair
Fortunate Islands <=> Canary Islands
Gades Island <=> Erythea, Erythra, Erythrae, Gadir
Gadir <=> Erythea, Gades Island, Ogygia
Gate of the Causeway <=> Shallecheth
Gaulus <=> Gozo
Gauzania <=> Gozan
Genealogus <=> Pherecydes
Gesongeses <=> Sesonchoris, Sesonchosis
Gingris <=> Adonis
Ginnetho <=> Ginnethon
Ginnethon <=> Ginnetho
Gnephactus <=> Neochabis, Technatis, Tnephachthus
Gozan <=> Gauzania
Gozo <=> Gaulus

Great Bear <=> Ursa Major
Great Court <=> People, People's Court
Great Mother <=> Magna Mater
Gudars <=> Nebuchadnezzar
Habor <=> Chaboras
Hadad <=> Adar, Benhadad I, Benhadad II, Damascus
Haemonia <=> Thessaly
Halah <=> Chalach
Hanes <=> Anysis
Haran <=> Carrhae
Harim <=> Rehum
Harpagus <=> Artabazus, Artagerses
Heaven <=> Caelus
Helius <=> Orus, Phaeton
Hephaestion <=> Hercules (Egyptian), Nilus, Sesostris
Heracleia <=> Carteia
Heracles <=> Hercules (Tyrian), Hercules
Hercules (Egyptian) <=> Hephaestion, Nilus, Ogmius,
    Sesostris
Hercules (Idean) <=> Hercules Olympius
Hercules (Tyrian) <=> Heracles, Melcartus
Hercules Egyptius <=> Osarsiphus
Hercules Olympius <=> Hercules (Idean)
Hercules <=> Heracles, Sesostris
Hero <=> Sesostris
Hezion <=> Rezon
Hodaviah <=> Hodijah, Judah
Hodijah <=> Hodaviah
Hophra <=> Apries, Eraphius, Phius
Horus <=> Orus
Hyperion <=> Osiris, Sesostris
Iberia <=> Chabor
Idalia <=> Calycopis, Venus
Iddo <=> Obadiah, Obdia
Idean Dactyli <=> Curetes
Iluarodamus <=> Evilmerodach
Imandes <=> Amenophis
Inachus <=> Jasius
Io <=> Isis
Isis <=> Astraea, Basilea, Io
Ismandes <=> Amenophis
Italy <=> Oenotria, Saturnia
Jaddua <=> Simeon Justus
Janis <=> Janus
Janus <=> Janis, Oenotria, Oenotrus
Japetus <=> Neptune, Python, Typhon
Jareb <=> Shalman
Jasion <=> Jasius
Jasius <=> Inachus, Jasion
Jebus <=> Jerusalem
Jerusalem <=> Jebus
Johanan <=> Jonathan
Jonathan <=> Johanan
Judah <=> Hodaviah
Juno Olympia <=> Europa
Jupiter (Cretan) <=> Minos
Jupiter (Egyptian) <=> Ammon
Jupiter Ammon <=> Ammon, Caelus, Jupiter Uranus, Uranus
Jupiter Uranus <=> Ammon, Caelus, Jupiter Ammon
Jupiter <=> Asterius
Kai-Axeres <=> Cyaxeres
Kai <=> Lohorasp
Kaianides <=> Persians

Kir <=> Carine, Kirene
Kirene <=> Kir
Kischtasp <=> Darius Hystaspes, Darius the Mede, Darius
Labaris <=> Moeris
Laboasserdach <=> Labosordachus
Labosordachus <=> Laboasserdach
Labynitus <=> Belshazzar, Nabonnedus, Nebuchadnezzar
Lachares <=> Moeris
Lake of Moeris <=> Uchoreus (Lake of)
Lake of Uchoreus <=> Moeris (Lake of)
Land of the Curetes <=> Terra Curetum
Latus <=> Chaitus
Legates <=> Carians
Libya <=> Ammonia, Libyanassa
Libyanassa <=> Libya, Lisianassa
Lisianassa <=> Libyanassa
Lohorasp <=> Cyaxeres, Darius, Kai
Ma-sors <=> Sesostris, Valiant
Maadiah <=> Maaziah
Maaziah <=> Maadiah
Madyes <=> Medus
Magdolus <=> Megiddo
Magi <=> Priests
Magia <=> Religion of the Persians
Magna Mater <=> Great Mother
Malchijah <=> Malluch
Malluch <=> Malchijah, Melicu
Manphtha <=> Memphis
Mardocempad <=> Merodach Baladan
Mardus <=> Smerdis
Maris <=> Moeris
Marres <=> Moeris
Marrus <=> Mendes, Myris, Uchoreus
Mars <=> Sesostris, Valiant
Mastor <=> Mestor
Mavors <=> Sesostris, Valiant
Medus <=> Madyes
Megabars <=> Ethiopians
Megiddo <=> Magdolus
Melcarteia <=> Carteia
Melcartus <=> Hercules (Tyrian), Melec Kartha, Melec-cartus, Midacritus
Melec Kartha <=> Melcartus
Melec-cartus <=> Melcartus
Melech <=> Moloch
Melicu <=> Malluch
Memnon <=> Amenophis
Memphis <=> Amenoph, Manphtha, Menoph, Menus, Mesir, Moph, Noph
Mencheres <=> Mycerinus
Mendes <=> Marrus, Myris, Uchoreus
Menephes <=> Amenophis
Menes <=> Amenophis
Menoph <=> Memphis
Menus <=> Memphis
Meres <=> Moeris
Merodach Baladan <=> Mardocempad
Mesir <=> Memphis
Mesphres <=> Mitres
Mestor <=> Mastor
Miamin <=> Mijamin, Miniamin
Midacritus <=> Melcartus
Mijamin <=> Miamin

Minaeus <=> Amenophis
Minerva <=> Myrina
Mines <=> Amenophis
Mineus <=> Amenophis
Miniamin <=> Miamin
Minies <=> Amenophis
Minos <=> Jupiter (Cretan)
Mitres <=> Mesphres
Mnevis <=> Amenophis
Moeris (Lake of) <=> Lake of Uchoreus
Moeris <=> Ayres, Byires, Labaris, Lachares, Maris, Marres, Meres, Myris, Smarres, Soris, Tyris, Uchoreus, Zmarres
Moloch <=> Melech
Moph <=> Memphis
Moscheres <=> Mycerinus
Mother of the Gods <=> Cybele
Mycerinus <=> Bicheres, Cheres, Cherinus, Mencheres, Moscheres
Myrina <=> Minerva
Myris <=> Marrus, Mendes, Moeris, Uchoreus
Naboandelos <=> Belshazzar, Nabonnedus
Nabonadius <=> Nabonnedus
Nabonnedus <=> Belshazzar, Labynitus, Naboandelos, Nabonadius
Nabuchodonosor <=> Chyniladon
Naxos <=> Dia, Strongyle
Nebuchadnezzar <=> Bocktanassar, Gudars, Labynitus, Raham
Necepsos <=> Nechepsos
Nechaoh <=> Nechus
Nechepsos <=> Necepsos
Nechus <=> Nechaoh
Nectabis <=> Nectenabis
Nectenabis <=> Nectabis
Neochabis <=> Gnephactus
Neptune <=> Equestris, Japetus, Poseidon, Python, Typhon
Neptys <=> Amphitrite
Nergalassaros <=> Neriglissaros
Neriglissaros <=> Nergalassaros
Nile River <=> Aegyptus, Ammon River, Eridanus, Nilus, O-Siris, Ser-Apis, Shihor, Sihor, Siris
Nilus <=> Hephaestion, Hercules (Egyptian), Nile River, Sesostris
Nineveh <=> Ninus
Ninus <=> Nineveh
No-Ammon <=> Thebes (Egyptian)
Noph <=> Memphis
O-Siris <=> Nile River
Obadiah <=> Iddo
Obdia <=> Iddo
Oceanus <=> Thrace
Ochus <=> Darius Hystaspes
Odomantes <=> Edomites
Oenotria <=> Italy, Janus, Saturnia
Oenotrus <=> Janus
Ogmius <=> Hercules (Egyptian)
Ogygia <=> Cadis, Cales, Gadir
Oh Siris <=> Osiris
Ophiusa <=> Rhodes
Orcus <=> Aidoneus
Orpheus <=> Bacchus, Sirius
Orus <=> Apollo, Busiris II, Helius, Horus, Phaeton, Pheron, Sesoosis II

Osarsiphus <=> Hercules Egyptius, Osorchon, Osorchor,
  Usorthon
Osimandes <=> Amenophis
Osiris <=> Bacchus, Busiris I, Dionysus, Epaphus, Hyperion,
  Oh Siris, Sesoosis I, Sesostris, Shishak, Sirius
Osorchon <=> Osarsiphus
Osorchor <=> Osarsiphus
Ostanes <=> Otanes
Osymandias <=> Amenophis
Osymanthias <=> Amenophis
Otanes <=> Ostanes
Ouranus <=> Caelus
Oxyares <=> Achsuerus, Xerxes I
Ozair <=> Ezra
Paphia <=> Calycopis, Venus
Pasargadae <=> Persepolis
Pathros <=> Upper Egypt
Pelusium <=> Abaris, Auaris
People <=> Great Court
People's Court <=> Great Court
Persepolis <=> Pasargadae
Persia <=> Elam
Persians <=> Elamites, Kaianides
Phaeton <=> Helius, Orus
Phamenophis <=> Amenophis
Phegea <=> Psophis
Pherecydes <=> Genealogus
Pheron <=> Orus
Philistines <=> Curetes
Phiops <=> Cheops
Phius <=> Hophra
Phoebus <=> Apollo
Phoenicia <=> Caria, Edom
Phoenician Letters <=> Ephesian Letters
Phoenicians <=> Shepherds
Phoronicum <=> Argos
Phraortes <=> Arphaxad
Phrygia <=> Ashchenez
Piranthus <=> Pirasus
Pirasus <=> Piranthus
Plaustrum <=> Big Dipper
Polybus <=> Thuor
Poseidon <=> Neptune
Priests of Cybele <=> Corybantes
Priests <=> Magi
Prince <=> Cy
Psophis <=> Phegea
Pul <=> Belus (Assyrian)
Python <=> Japetus, Neptune
Raham <=> Nebuchadnezzar
Rameses <=> Ramesses
Ramesses <=> Rameses, Ramestes, Ramises, Ramses,
  Remphis, Rhampses, Rhampsinitus
Ramestes <=> Ramesses
Ramises <=> Ramesses
Ramses <=> Ramesses
Rehum <=> Harim
Religion of the Persians <=> Magia
Remphis <=> Ramesses
Resen <=> Reseph
Reseph <=> Resen
Rezon <=> Hezion
Rhampses <=> Ramesses

Rhampsinitus <=> Ramesses
Rhea (Cretan) <=> Europa
Rhea (Egyptian) <=> Titaea
Rhodes <=> Ophiusa
Sabacon <=> Actisanes, So, Sua
Sagittarius <=> Chiron
Salaminia <=> Calycopis, Venus
Salmanasser <=> Enemessar, Shalmaneser
Sanhedrin <=> Supreme Court of Judicature
Saophis <=> Cheops
Sarac <=> Sarchedon
Sarchedon <=> Esarhaddon-Pul, Esarhaddon, Sarac,
  Sardanapalus
Sardanapalus <=> Esarhaddon, Sarchedon
Saturn (Cretan) <=> Asterius
Saturnia <=> Italy, Oenotria
Scenitae <=> Arabians
Scilles <=> Cassiteris
Scorpio <=> Chelae
Scythia <=> Touran
Selene <=> Bubaste
Semele <=> Bacchus
Sennacherib <=> Anacyndaraxis
Sepharvaim <=> Abydenus, Cush, Sipparae, Sipphara
Ser-Apis <=> Nile River
Serapis <=> Apis
Sesac <=> Sesostris
Sesach <=> Sesostris
Sesoch <=> Sesostris
Sesochis <=> Sesostris
Sesochris <=> Sesostris
Sesonch <=> Sesostris
Sesonchis <=> Sesostris
Sesonchoris <=> Gesongeses, Sesonchosis
Sesonchosis <=> Gesongeses, Sesonchoris, Sesostris
Sesoos <=> Sesostris
Sesoosis I <=> Osiris
Sesoosis II <=> Orus
Sesoosis <=> Sesostris
Sesost <=> Sesostris
Sesostris <=> Aegyptus, Bacchus, Belus (Egyptian), Busiris,
  Dionysus, Egypt, Hephaestion, Hercules (Egyptian),
  Hercules, Hero, Hyperion, Ma-sors, Mars, Mavors, Nilus,
  Osiris, Sesac, Sesach, Sesoch, Sesochis, Sesochris, Sesonch,
  Sesonchis, Sesonchosis, Sesoos, Sesoosis, Sesost, Sethon,
  Sethosis, Shishak, Sihor, Siris, Sochis
Sethon <=> Sesostris, Sevechus
Sethosis <=> Sesostris
Sevechus <=> Sethon
Shallecheth <=> Gate of the Causeway
Shalman <=> Jareb
Shalmaneser <=> Enemessar, Salmanasser
Shebaniah <=> Shechaniah, Sherebiah
Shechaniah <=> Shebaniah
Shepherds <=> Phoenicians
Sherebiah <=> Shebaniah
Sheshach <=> Susiana
Shihor <=> Nile River
Shishak <=> Bacchus, Osiris, Sesostris
Sicyon <=> Aegialea
Sidonians <=> Tyrians
Sihor <=> Nile River, Sesostris, Sirius
Simeon Justus <=> Jaddua

Sipparae <=> Sepharvaim
Sipphara <=> Sepharvaim
Siris <=> Nile River, Sesostris
Sirius <=> Orpheus, Osiris, Sihor
Smarres <=> Moeris
Smerdis <=> Mardus
So <=> Sabacon
Sochis <=> Sesostris
Soiphis <=> Cheops
Sol <=> Apollo
Soris <=> Moeris
Stateres Darici <=> Darics
Strongyle <=> Naxos
Sua <=> Sabacon
Succoth Benoth <=> Temple of Women
Suphis <=> Cheops
Supreme Court of Judicature <=> Sanhedrin
Susa <=> Cuth
Susiana <=> Sheshach
Syphaosis <=> Cheops
Syphoas <=> Cheops
Syphuris <=> Cheops
Syrian <=> Assyrian, Tyrian
Syrians <=> Assyrians
Tahaphenes <=> Dathnis
Talatha <=> Thelasar
Tangieres <=> Tingis
Tanis <=> Zoan
Tarshish <=> Tartessus
Tartessus <=> Tarshish
Technatis <=> Gnephactus
Telchines <=> Curetes
Temple of Women <=> Succoth Benoth
Terra Curetum <=> Land of the Curetes
Terra <=> Titaea
Tethmosis <=> Amosis I
Thammuz <=> Timaeus
Thamus <=> Timaeus
The Great <=> Bacchus
Thebes (Egyptian) <=> Ammon-No, No-Ammon, Upper
    Egypt

Theias <=> Thoas
Thelasar <=> Talatha
Thessaly <=> Haemonia
Thoantes <=> Thoas
Thoas <=> Cinyras, Theias, Thoantes, Vulcan
Thomosis <=> Amosis I
Thoth <=> Athothes
Thrace <=> Oceanus
Thuor <=> Polybus
Timaeus <=> Thammuz, Thamus
Tingis <=> Tangieres
Titaea <=> Rhea (Egyptian), Terra
Tnephachthus <=> Gnephactus
Tosorthrus <=> Aesculapius
Touran <=> Scythia, Turquestan
Turquestan <=> Touran
Typhon <=> Japetus, Neptune
Tyre <=> Daughter of Sidon
Tyrian <=> Assyrian, Syrian
Tyrians <=> Sidonians
Tyris <=> Moeris
Uchoreus (Lake of) <=> Lake of Moeris
Uchoreus <=> Marrus, Mendes, Moeris, Myris
Upper Egypt <=> Aegyptus, Pathros, Thebes (Egyptian)
Uranus <=> Ammon, Caelus, Jupiter Ammon
Ursa Major <=> Great Bear
Usorthon <=> Osarsiphus
Valiant <=> Ma-sors, Mars, Mavors
Vaphres <=> Apries
Venephes <=> Amenophis
Venus <=> Amathusia, Byblia, Calycopis, Cnidia, Cytherea,
    Dea Cypria, Dea Syria, Erycina, Idalia, Paphia, Salaminia
Vulcan <=> Baal Canaan, Cinyras, Thoas
Xerxes I <=> Achschirosch, Achsweros, Ahasuerus, Oxyares
Zaradust <=> Zoroaster
Zmarres <=> Moeris
Zoan <=> Tanis
Zoroaster <=> Zaradust

This list contains 2,251 entries with 10,184 descriptions and includes an exhaustive index of every proper noun in the body of the work. It pulls together facts about individuals into one place and ends up being a mini bibliography of many of the people in this work. To some, this index may seem like overkill. However, better to have too much rather than too little. I could not begin to count the hours I have wasted because of the poor indices in some of the Loeb series, especially their edition of Pliny's *Natural History*. Names preceded by an @ indicate the name has one or more alias names. This is only used when it is not clear from the context that the name has an alias. Resolve seemingly contradictory facts by checking the actual context for the entry in the body of the work.

ruled in @Colchis until the time of the Argonaut Expedition 227; visited by the Argonauts 479

Aegeon: hieroglyphic representation of 460

Aegeus: adopted son of Pandion 228; 319; brother of Nisus 381; father of Euryleon 208; father of Theseus 228; 278; 310; 319; about the same age as Perseus, Perieres and Anaxagoras 324; contemporary with @Minos, Sarpedon and Rhadamanthus 344; died about the time Theseus made an expedition into Crete 278; king in Attica (990 BC) 45; succeeded by his son Theseus as king of @Athens 310

Aegialea: built by Aegialeus and later called @Sicyon 384; 20; ruled by @Epopeus 316

Aegialeus: brother of Phoroneus 378; 379; son of @Inachus 378; 384; 20; built @Aegialea 384; 20; came with a colony into Greece 436; chronologers made him three hundred years older than his brother Phoroneus 10; died without children 379; first king of @Sicyon 204; 378; 380; in his times towns began to be consolidated into cities 391; succeeded by Europs in @Sicyon 379

Aegina: daughter of Asopus (1030 BC) 31; 361; mother of Aeacus (1030 BC) 31; 361

Aegineta: king of Arcadia 204

Aegisthus: son of Thyestes 317; killed Agamemnon the year after the taking of Troy 317

Aegyptus: brother of @Danaus 445; brother of @Isis 445; brother of @Osiris 445; brother of @Typhon 445; son of Belus 445; another name for Sesostris 230; 453; deified name of Sesostris 273

Aegyptus: another name for Upper Egypt 431; name applied to the enlarged kingdom of Misphragmuthosis and Amosis I 482

Aegyptus: another name for the Nile River 453

Aelus: son of Hellen (1039 BC) 29

Aeneas: father or grandfather of Romulus 312; son of @Calycopis according to Homer 457; son of @Venus 278; 417; lived in the time of @Dido (883 BC) 96; thought to have founded Rome 311

Aeolic Migration: occurred (844 BC) 100

Aeolides: name of the seven islands between @Italy and Sicily 397; settled by a colony led by Lipparus and Aeolus 397

Aeolus: brother of Calyce 327; brother of Dorus 328; brother of Xuthus 328; father of Aethlius 384; father of Athamas 327; 329; father of Deioneus 328; father of Sisyphus 327; 384; 51; father of Hellen 327; 328; 329; 384; 51; expelled Procris from @Thessaly 328; helped settle the Aeolides islands 397; led a colony into Greece (1121 BC) 14

Aepytus I: king of Arcadia 333

Aepytus II: king of Arcadia 333

Aeropus: king in Macedon 301

Aeschylus: describes the expedition of @Xerxes I against Greece 661; Greek writer 217; introduces @Darius Hystaspes complaining about his son @Xerxes I 593; only knows of two great kings of Media and @Persia: Astyages and @Cyaxeres 596; states @Cyaxeres was the first conqueror and founder of the empire of the Medes 599; states that @Darius the Mede finished extending the Medo-Persian Empire over all Asia 611; states that @Memnon's mother was called Cissia 477

Aesculapius: grandson of Leucippus 324; grandson of Phlegia 324; son of Machaon 359; an Argonaut 223; 324; 75; deified (927 BC) 80; Greeks built a temple to him 359; Hippocrates lived eighteen generations after him 223

Aesculapius: another name for Tosorthrus 484

Aesculapius: name of the temple in Egypt built by @Amenophis 489

Aeson: father of Jason 327; son of Cretheus 327

Aethlius: father of Endymion 30; 220; 327; grandson of Deucalion 30; husband of Calyce 327; son of Aeolus 384; son of Protogenia 327; built Elis 384; 30; contemporary with @Erechtheus, @Jasius and Cadmus 328

Aethra: mother of Theseus 229; captured by Castor and Pollux 229

Aetolia: country captured by Pelops from Aetolus 327; 46; country where the city of @Erythra was located 287; name given to this country of the @Curetes in Achaia (1006 BC) 39; named after Aetolus 337; settled by the @Curetes 336

Aetolians: under Oxylus they recovered Elis 220

Aetolus: father of Clydon 39; father of Pleuron 39; grandson of Aethlius 220; husband of Pronoe 39; son of Endymion 39; 220; 337; 354; 46; captured the country and named it Aetolia after himself 337; expelled from Aetolia by Pelops 354; fled into the country of the @Curetes

(1006 BC) 39; lost the country of Aetolia to Pelops 327; many @Curetes settled in Aetolia until his time 336

Aezeus: in his time Greeks started to build houses and villages 391; led a colony into Greece 436; 14

Africa: Atlantis was imagined to be larger than it (896 BC) 91; 465; ruled by Ham 524

Africans: fought with clubs against @Sesostris 66; 447

Africanus: allocates fourteen years to the reign of @Sethon and eighteen to Tirhakah 506; calls Bocchoris a Saite 495; copied the errors of Mathetho relating to @Ammon 424; documents a two year Egyptian interregnum when the country was invaded by the @Assyrians 557; thought the twentieth year of @Artaxerxes Longimanus was 445 BC 664

Agamemnon: adopted son of Atreus 317; father of Orestes 222; fought at Troy 317; Greeks built a temple to him 359; killed by Aegisthus 317; king of Mycene (924 BC) 83

Agamemnon: king of @Sicyon 379

Agapenor: built Paphos according to Pausanias 333; king of Arcadia 333

Agarista: daughter of Clisthenes (570 BC) 156; 302; courted by Leocides and Megacles (570 BC) 156; 302

Agasicles: Spartan king descended from Procles 209

Agatharcides: records how the gods of Egypt fled from the giants 467

Agelas: descended from the Heraclides 329; king of @Corinth 329

Agesilaus: Lycurgus published his laws during his reign 218; Spartan king descended from the family of Eurysthenes 204

Agis: Spartan king descended from the family of Eurysthenes 204

Agraule: daughter of Actaeus 382; wife of Cecrops I 382

Ahab: attacked by @Benhadad II who had thirty-two kings in his army 407

Ahasuerus: another name for Xerxes I 688; name Daniel gave to Cyaxeres 596

Ahasuerus: father of @Darius the Mede 594; another name for Achsuerus given by Masoretes 594

Ahasuerus: name the Jews gave to Cambyses who was the second king of the Persian Empire 667

Ahasuerus: his story interrupts the account of @Darius Hystaspes in @Ezra 687; Jewish name for Xerxes I who was the son of @Darius Hystaspes 685; omit his story in @Ezra to make that book match I Esdras 686

Ahaz: final captivity of Israel happened sixty-five years after the first year of his reign 504; in his third year Tiglathpilasser captured Syria 456; Pekah and Resin invaded his kingdom 553; Tiglathpileser assisted him against Israel and Syria 549

Aidoneus: another name for Orcus 229

Ajax: Greeks built a temple to him 359

Alba Longa: term *age* used to refer to each Latin king who reigned here 312

Alcaeus: Greek artist 217

Alcamenes: Spartan king descended from the family of Eurysthenes 204

Alcetas: king in Macedon 301

Alcinous: father of Nausica 256; king of the Pheaces on the island of Corcyra 256

Alcmaeon: father of Megacles 302; commanded the forces of the Amphictyons against Cirrheans 302; 156; contemporary with Phidon 156; entertained and conducted the messengers whom Croesus sent to consult the oracle at Delphi 302; 303

Alcman: Greek artist 217

Alcmena: daughter of Electryo 54; 324; 354; granddaughter of Andromeda (974 BC) 54; granddaughter of Perseus 54; mother of @Hercules (Idean) 324; 354; 359; 366; 461; Greeks built a temple to her 359; last woman @Jupiter (Cretan) had sexual relations with 366

Alcyone: priestess of Juno Argiva when the invasion of Sicily happened 300; second priestess to Juno Argiva 325

Aletes I: contemporary of Cypselus 221; descended from the Heraclides 329; king of @Corinth 329; returned with the Heraclides 221

Aletes II: descended from the Heraclides 329; king of @Corinth 329

Aleus: father of Ague 333; father of Amphidamus 333; father of Cepheus 333; father of Lycurgus 333; son of Aphidas 333; king of Arcadia 333

Alexander: contemporary of @Xerxes I 301; 302; king of Macedon 301; 302

Alexander Polyhistor: attributes the destruction of the @Assyrian Empire to the Chaldeans and the Medes 564; called @Sepharvaim by the name of @Abydenus 535; documents that Nabopolassar revolted from @ Assyria 563; documents that Oannes taught the Chaldeans 442

Alexander the Great: son of Philip of Macedon 1; 197; after his death history was recorded by generations 2; Babylon said to be founded nineteen hundred and three years before his time 194; built Alexandria in Egypt 492; Chaldeans told him they were observing the stars for almost five hundred thousand years before his time 518; conquered @ Darius Codomannus 696; conquered and ended the Persian Empire and the dynasty of the @Kaianides 697; conquered Persian Empire near Gaugamela (331 BC) 190; European history written hundreds of years after his death 202; his captains divided his empire 464; his death began the era of Philip 247; his kingdom broke up into four kingdoms when he died 205; Jews thought the Persian Empire only lasted about forty years until his time 668; Rome was sacked sixty-seven years before his death 7; 201; Simon Justus died two years before his death 679; Simon Justus the high priest lived during his time 682

Alexandra: brother of Hector 359; daughter of Priam 359; Greeks built a temple to her 359

Alexandria: built by @Alexander the Great in Egypt 492

Alpha: letter used by astronomers to indicate the brightest star in a constellation 249

Alpheus River: Arcadian tradition that the gods fought there 354; near Olympia 355

Alps: @Hercules (Egyptian) attempted to cross over into @Italy from Gaul 398

Altar Court: court in Solomon's temple containing the altars 637

Altis: location of Olympic treasury 215

Alyattes: father of Ariene (585 BC) 151; 596; attacked by @Cyaxeres (590 BC) 149; king of Lydia 149; made a peace treaty with @Cyaxeres and sealed it with the marriage of his daughter Ariene to @Darius the Mede 608; Scythians fled to him after cooking one of the children of the Medes for @Cyaxeres' dinner 607

Alymnus: brother of @Europa 342; brother of Cadmus 359; accompanied @Europa into Crete along with the Idean Dactyli 342; came with a colony into Greece 436; fled from Sidon to Greece 297; Greeks built a temple to him 359

Amarcholim: seven men who kept the keys to the sanctuary of the temple at @Jerusalem 643; 644

Amariah: priest who returned with @Ezra and Nehemiah in the first year of Cyrus 671; 676

Amasis: king of Egypt 510; king of Egypt according to Herodotus 483; king of Egypt according to Herodotus and Newton 486; name Diodorus gave to Anysis in the Egyptian king list of Herodotus 514; reigned for forty-four years in Egypt after @Apries 509; ruled Egypt 193; two different kings of Egypt according to Diodorus with the same name 513

Amathus: location of the temple in Cyprus to the deified @Calycopis (930 BC) 78; 458

Amathusia: another name for Calycopis or Venus (930 BC) 78; 458

Amazons: called themselves the *Daughters of Mars* 273; commanded by @Minerva 422; conquered part of Europe and some cities of Asia 423; left by @Sesostris at the Thermodon River under the command of Marthesia and Lampeto (962 BC) 60; originated from @Libya 423; part of the army of @Bacchus 422; reigned over the Atlanteans 423; transplanted from @Thrace by @Sesostris to the Thermodon River 273

Amenoph: also called Memphis 275; city built by @Amenophis 275; Egyptian name for Amenophis 478

Amenophis: father of @Ramesses 490; 93; possible son of Zerah 275; son of @Isis 440; son of @Osiris 440; son of Tithonus according to the Greeks (887 BC) 95; another name for Menes 68; 478; began to reign in the fifteenth year of Asa after Zerah his father was defeated by Asa 499; built Memnonia in @Susa (909 BC) 86; built small pyramids in Cochome (901 BC) 89; built the temple of @Vulcan in @Memphis 459; 85; called Memnon by the Greeks 86; did not leave @Susa for the Trojan War (904 BC) 87; died in Egypt and did not come to the Trojan War 247; Diodorus placed @Uchoreus after this king 492; Egypt in civil disorder while he was in Ethiopia 276; his sepulchre contained a circle of three hundred and sixty-five parts to correspond to the days of the year 246; invaded Lower Egypt with his army from Ethiopia and conquered @Osarsiphus (926 BC) 81; king of Egypt and Ethiopia 488; reigned after @Orus and @Isis who were the last of the gods 489; reigned after

the four ages of the gods in Egypt 512; reigned during the Trojan War 270; reigned in @Thebes (Egyptian) 482; retired into Ethiopia when @ Osarsiphus revolted from him in Egypt 479; ruled Egypt and @Libya 474; same as Diodorus' king Osymandias 514; solar year not introduced before his reign (887 BC) 94; solstices and equinoxes not established until his reign 440; succeeded by his son @Ramesses 490; 93; with his @ Ethiopians he retreated from Lower Egypt (940 BC) 69

Ammenemes I: father of @Gesongeses 424; king of Egypt according to Mathetho 424; same king as Ammenemes II and Ammon 425; 437

Ammenemes II: son of @Gesongeses according to Mathetho 424; same king as Ammenemes I and Ammon 425

Ammon: father of @Bacchus 425; father of @Isis (1030 BC) 93; father of @Orus Senior (1030 BC) 93; father of @Osiris (1030 BC) 93; father of @Sesostris 405; 446; 40; 39; 66; father of @Typhon (1030 BC) 93; father of Nephthe (1030 BC) 93; father of the Titans 440; husband of @Titaea 440; husband of Rhea (Egyptian) 431; @Thebes (Egyptian) dedicated to him by his son (998 BC) 44; another name for Uranus 405; another name is Jupiter (Egyptian) 424; appointed Cepheus the king of Joppa (1010 BC) 38; called Caelus by the @Arabians 449; called Jupiter Uranus by the @Arabians 274; captured Gezer from the Canaanites and gave it to his daughter, Solomon's wife (1012 BC) 37; civilised @ Libya after conquering it (1030 BC) 31; conquered the Atlanteans who lived on Mount @Atlas 463; deified and temples built to him at @ Thebes (Egyptian), @Ammonia and Meroe in Ethiopia 437; deified by the Egyptians 431; during his reign Thebans began to study navigation and astronomy 246; Egyptian astronomical discoveries were made during his reign 497; Egyptians knew nothing of astronomy before his time 444; enlarged Egypt into a great empire 431; first king of @ Libya 405; first king of a united Egypt 231; five extra days added to the year during his reign (1030 BC) 93; five gods or sons born to him in his reign 245; hieroglyphic representation of 460; his children were about the same age as @Sesostris 273; in his time writing, astronomy, architecture and agriculture came into Chaldea 442; king of Egypt 31; king of Egypt who established the Egyptian Empire 416; Manetho incorrectly called him by the names of two kings Ammenemes I and Ammenemes II 425; received the @Edomites and their King @Hadad who were fleeing from David 438; reign of the @Shepherds ended one or two generation before him 248; reigned during the four ages of the great gods of Egypt 512; reigned in @Thebes (Egyptian) 482; same man as Belus (Egyptian) 445; science of astronomy began in his days 625; Solomon married his daughter (1015 BC) 35; succeeded Amosis I as king of Egypt 512; trained his son @Sesostris rigorously 446

Ammon: name of city @Sesostris built and named after his father 425

Ammon: abandoned the Medes when the @Assyrians attacked the Medes 558; conquered by @Esarhaddon 559; conquered by @ Nebuchadnezzar 602; 604; 611; conquered by Holofernes 560; country defeated by David 271; 272; country plundered by four kings from the land of Shinar and @Elam 408; had its own king until it was conquered by the @Assyrians 525; his posterity worshipped false gods 411; revolted from @Assyria 559

Ammon River: another name for the Nile River 425

Ammonia: ancient name of Libya 482; 31; location of temples erected to the deified @Ammon 437; location of the temple and oracle @Sesostris dedicated to his father (998 BC) 44; name of ancient Libya according to Stephanus 425; name of the land west of Egypt 482; named after @ Ammon (1030 BC) 31; worshipped @Jupiter @Ammon 448

Ammonii: name for the inhabitants of @Thebes (Egyptian) 425

Ammonites: allied with other countries but defeated by David 271; assisted @Nebuchadnezzar in his conquests 576

Ammonium: name of a promontory in Arabia Faelix named after @ Ammon 425

Ammon-No: another name for Thebes (Egyptian) meaning the people or city of @Ammon (998 BC) 44; 425

Ammosis: hieroglyphic representation of 460

Amok: chief priest in the first year of Cyrus 676

Amon: father of Josiah 560; son of Manasseh 560; Holofernes invaded the western countries after his reign 560

Amos: @Assyrian Empire unknown to him 529; prophesied of the deportation of the @Syrians 549; rebuked Israel's pride over its recent conquests 528; threatened Israel with the same destruction that happened to the surrounding countries 530

Amosis I: son of Misphragmuthosis 376; 377; abolished religion of the @Shepherds 363; abolished the Phoenician custom in Heliopolis of sacrificing men and drove the @Shepherds from @Abaris (1066 BC) 21; deified Egyptian kings and princes 363; expelled the @Shepherds 437; extended his kingdom over all Egypt 437; forced the @Shepherds to flee from Egypt 431; 435; 436; forced the remaining @Shepherds to retire to the @Philistines 376; reigned during the four ages of the great gods of Egypt 512; reigned in Coptos 482; succeeded Misphragmuthosis as the king of Egypt 512

Amosis II: another name for Anysis (788 BC) 109; reigned over a small kingdom in Egypt at @Anysis 495

Amphiaraus: father of Amphilochus 359; Greeks built a temple to him 359

Amphictyon: brother of Hellen 330; 41; son of Deucalion 330; 41; fled with his father Deucalion from the flood in @Thessaly to Attica 330; reigned at Thermopylae a few years before the reign of @Erechtheus 332; set up the first Amphictyonic Council in Greece (1003 BC) 41

Amphictyon: son of Prometheus 363; brought the twelve gods from @Thrace into Greece 363; brought the twelve gods of Egypt into Greece (959 BC) 62; entertained @Bacchus (962 BC) 41; entertained @Sesostris in Greece (962 BC) 60

Amphictyonic Council: appointed Alcmaeon, Clisthenes and Eurolicus as the commanders of their army in their war against Cirrha 302; approved of the Argonaut Expedition 479; captured Cirrha (570 BC) 156; established at Thermopylae by Amphictyon 330; established in Greece 371; first set up at Thermopylae by the Greeks under Amphictyon (1003 BC) 41; made war on the Cirrheans 156

Amphidamus: son of Aleus 333

Amphilochus: son of Amphiaraus 359; Greeks built a temple to him 359

Amphion: husband of Niobe 317; son of Antiope 316; 317; 39; twin brother of Zethus 316; 317; 39; helped Zethus kill Lycus 317; 47

Amphitrite: Greek name for the Roman god called Neptys 466

Amyclas: brother of Eurydice 324; daughter of Eurystheus 325; father of Cynortes 324; father of Evarete 324; father of Perieres 324; son of Lacedemon 324; son of Sparta 324; lived about the time of King David and @Erechtheus 325

Amyite: daughter of Astyages 563; 588; sister of @Cyaxeres 563; 588; 633; sister to Mandane 633; wife of @Nebuchadnezzar 563; 588; 633

Amymone: daughter of @Danaus 228; mother of Nauplius 228

Amyntas: king in Macedon 301

Anabaxaris: another name for Anacyndaraxis 557

Anacreon: Greek artist 217

Anacyndaraxis: father of @Sardanapalus 557; another name for Sennacherib (710 BC) 121; king of @Assyria 557

Ananiah: father of Maaseiah 684; grandfather of Azariah 684; returned from exile during the reign of Cyrus 684

Anaphe: island formed in the sea by an earthquake 395; island located beyond Melos 396

Anaxagoras: father of Elector 324; son of Megapenthes 324; about the same age as @Minos, Pelops, Aegeus and @Sesostris 324

Anaxander: Spartan king descended from the family of Eurysthenes 204; 209

Anaxandrides: Spartan king descended from the family of Eurysthenes 204; 209

Anaxilas: Spartan king descended from Procles 209

Anaximenes: from Lampsacus and wrote in prose 196

Ancaeus: son of Lycurgus 333; an Argonaut 333

Anchiale: city built in a day by @Esarhaddon (710 BC) 121; 557

Anchises: husband of @Venus 417

Andraemon: father of @Thoas 220; both he and @Hercules (Idean) married two sisters 220

Androcles: brother of Medon 310; brother of Neleus

Androgeus: brother of Ariadne 344; brother of Phaedra 344; oldest son of @Minos 297; son of @Minos 278; 344; 49; killed by the Athenians (984 BC) 49; murdered at the age of twenty-two 278; murdered from envy after he won the Athenaea games at @Athens 277

Andromeda: daughter of Cepheus 325; mother of @Mestor 324; mother of Electryo 324; mother of Gorgophone 324; mother of Sthenelus 324; wife of Perseus 324; 325; 54; constellation named after her 254; left Joppa with Perseus in the days of Solomon 326; 43

Aniophis: another name for Cheops 493

Anoisis: another name for Cheops 493

Antaea: town in @Thebes (Egyptian) where @Hercules (Egyptian) defeated @Antaeus 467

Antaeopolis: another name for the town of Antaea in @Thebes (Egyptian) 467

Antaeus: son of @Japetus (951 BC) 66; son of @Neptune 467; defeated by @Hercules (Egyptian) in the town of @Antaea 467; defeated by @Orus (951 BC) 66; invaded Egypt 468; reigned over all of North Africa to the Atlantic Ocean 467; ruled the city of Irasa (633 BC) 139; same man as Atlas 467; 468

Anticlides: thought Phoroneus to be the oldest king in Greece 378

Antinous: constellation created long after the Argonaut Expedition 255

Antioch: location where Pharaoh Necho may have sent Jehoahaz in irons 575

Antiochus: king of Messene 204

Antiochus Soter: successor of @Alexander the Great in Syria 205

Antiope: daughter of Marthesia 423; daughter of Nycteus (1006 BC) 39; mother of Amphion 317; 39; mother of Zethus 317; 39; sister of Orithya 423; wife of Theseus 423; an Amazon 423; became pregnant by @Apis @Epaphus the Sicyonian 379; instigated her sons Amphion and Zethus to murder Lycus 317; kidnapped by @Epopeus the king of @Aegialea 316

Antissus: father of Melas 221; descended from Gonussa 221

Anysis: forced to flee the Ethiopian invasion by @Sabacon (751 BC) 113; king in Egypt at @Anysis or @Hanes (788 BC) 109; king of Egypt according to Herodotus and Newton 486; king of Egypt according to Herodotus who reigned twice 483; name Herodotus gave to Amasis in the Egyptian king list of Diodorus 514; reigned a second time in Lower Egypt after @Sabacon voluntarily relinquished Egypt 501

Anysis: capital of the kingdom of @Anysis (788 BC) 109; 495; 496

Apachnas: name of a Canaanite king who reigned in Lower Egypt after Joshua expelled the Canaanites (1445 BC) 13; 430

Apamia: city of @Areca located between this place and the Persian Gulf 536

Apappus: another name for Cheops 493

Apathus: another name for Cheops 493

Apharsachites: inhabitants of the kingdom of Arrapachitis 538; transplanted by @Esarhaddon to Samaria 534; 552

Apharsites: transplanted by @Esarhaddon to Samaria 552

Aphidas: father of Aleus 333; son of Arcas 333; early Athenian king 310

Aphydna: one of twelve cities where Cecrops I resettled a number of smaller towns 388

Apis: incorrectly thought to be a different king then Apis Epaphus 10

Apis: town built by the children of Phoroneus in @Italy 384

Apis: son of Phoroneus 419; became the god Serapis after his death 419

Apis Epaphus: son of Phroroneus (1006 BC) 39; fourth king of @Sicyon 380; guardian of Labdacus 379; impregnated Antiope 379; incorrectly thought to be the name of two kings, Apis and Epopeus 10; killed (1006 BC) 39; killed by Aetolus 337; killed in the tenth year of the reign of Solomon 379; king of @Sicyon 10

Apocrypha: contains the book of I Esdras which almost parallels @Ezra 686

Apollo: Greeks supplicated to drive away the Medes 616; his first priestess was Phemonoe at Delphi 330; loved @Thoas for his skill with the harp 457; Piseans instituted the festival of Carnea to him 304

Apollo: son of @Bacchus 450; son of @Neptune 465; another name for Orus 450; fought in the war of the gods in Egypt 467; founded a city in Egypt 454; god of Egypt 454; helped his father @Neptune fortified the walls of Troy 465; lived two generations later than the Idean Dactyli 339

Apollo: name of one peak of Mount Parnassus 450

Apollodorus: computed times by the reign of the kings of Sparta 11; copied the history of Eratosthenes 197; documents that @Minos was the son of @Jupiter and @Europa 344; followed the history of Eratosthenes 2; 3; followed Thucydides and documented that the return of the Heraclides was eighty years after the Trojan War 203; incorrectly thought that Adrastus was the king in @Argos 380; mistakenly thought Lycurgus was much older than the first Olympiad 198; 199; states that @Cinyras married Metharme the daughter of Pygmalion and built Paphos 225; states that @Thoas was the son of Sandochus a @Syrian 457; states that Aegialeus was the brother of Phoroneus 378; states that Belus, the son of @Neptune and @Libya, was a king of Egypt and the father of @Aegyptus and @Danaus 445

Apolloniatis: part of the @Assyrian Empire at its height 554; part of the Babylonian Empire 621

Apollonius Rhodius: states that @Isis and @Osiris were two generations older than @Sesostris 419; states that @Sesostris populated many cities he captured 451; states that @Thoas gave Jason the purple cloak which the Graces made for @Bacchus 457; states that Canthus was the son of Canethus 326; states that Saturn (Cretan) fathered a son @Chiron by Philyra 345; states that the Argonauts killed Talus a survivor from the Bronze Age 365

Apophis: name of a Canaanite king who reigned in Lower Egypt after Joshua expelled the Canaanites (1445 BC) 13; 430

Apries: also called Vaphres, Eraphius or Hophra 509; in the reduced king list of Diodorus 514; king of Egypt 510; king of Egypt according to Diodorus 513; king of Egypt according to Herodotus 483; king of Egypt according to Herodotus and Newton 486; reigned for twenty-five years after Psammis died 509

April: month the Peloponnesian War ended 665; possible month @Darius Hystaspes started to reign 660

Aquarius: constellation is related to Ganymede 254; constellation of the Zodiac 249; solstice colure had drifted into this constellation by 1689 AD 261

Aquila: constellation is related to Ganymede's eagle 254

Arabia: conquered by @Nebuchadnezzar 602; conquered by Holofernes 560; 577; part of the @Assyrian Empire at its height 554; part of the Babylonian Empire 621; worshipped @Jupiter @Ammon 448

Arabia Faelix: @Sesostris sailed passed it on his way to the Persian Gulf 446; conquered by @Ammon and @Sesostris 437; conquered by @Bacchus and @Minerva 422; conquered by @Sesostris 273; 274; contained promontory called Ammonium after @Ammon 425; invaded by @Sesostris who set up pillars at the mouth of the Red Sea (1006 BC) 39; location of the temple and oracle erected by @Sesostris (998 BC) 44; one place the @Shepherds fled to from Amosis I 436

Arabia Petraea: home of Job and Edomite merchants 444; one place the @Shepherds fled to from Amosis I 436; writing used here by Abraham's descendants 441

Arabians: @Assyrians built Babylon for them 547; 624; accompanied Cadmus into Greece 290; call @Memphis @*Menus* (912 BC) 85; called @Nebuchadnezzar by the name of @Bocktanassar 694; called @Sesostris @*Bacchus (Dionysus) the Great* (951 BC) 66; named @Ammon and @Sesostris, @Jupiter @Uranus, @Dionysus and @Bacchus 274; some lived on the far side of the Euphrates River 621; some lived on the west side of Chaldea and were called the Scenitae 622; started their year on the vernal equinox 243; their historians called @Memphis by various names 478; worshipped @Jupiter @Ammon 448; worshipped only two gods, @Caelus (Jupiter Ammon) and @Bacchus (Dionysus) 273; 449

Aradians: assisted Solomon with his Red Sea fleet (1013 BC) 36; sailed into the Persian Gulf and beyond to the coasts of India 284

Aradus: another name for Arphad 550; built by men fleeing from Sidon according to Strabo 280; built by the @Sidonians (1044 BC) 25; displaced by the @Edomites fleeing from David (1044 BC) 25; founded by fleeing @Sidonians after their city was captured by the @Philistines 282; its merchants colonised islands in the Persian Gulf 284; some @Sidonians fled here 283

Aradus: colony on an island in the Persian Gulf founded by the @Tyrians and Aradians (1013 BC) 36; island in the Persian Gulf containing temples like those of the @Phoenicians 284

Araeus: king in Macedon 301

Ararat Minni: another name for Armenia 618

Arathes: wife of @Hadad 456; 99; @Syrians worshipped at her sepulchre using it as a temple 456; deified and worshipped by the @Syrians (852 BC) 99

Aratus: lived about a hundred years after Eudoxus 250; mentioned the constellation of Aries or @Delton 255

Arbaces: disgusted after seeing the decadent lifestyle of @Sardanapalus 556

Arbela: part of the Babylonian Empire 621

Arcadia: husband of Chryses 358; Dardanus instituted the Samothracian mysteries in @Phrygia after his wife Chryses learned about them here 358; first ruled by Pelasgus 377; first settled by Pelasgus who civilised its inhabitants 390; hold a tradition that the gods and the Titans fought near the Alpheus River 354; its oldest town was Lycosura built by Lycaon 384; location of the town of Mantinaea created by the Argives from five towns 389; ruled by eleven kings from the flood of Deucalion to the return of the Heraclides 335; ruled by Lycaon 377; ruled by many kings 333; ruled by nine kings from the return of the Heraclides to the end of the first Messenian War (825-633 BC) 102; 204; 207; ruled by Nyctimus (1042 BC) 27; ruled first by Pelasgus 333

Arcadians: original kingdom consisted of many small towns (1076 BC) 20

Arcas: father of Aphidas 333; grandfather of Lycurgus 334; son of Callisto 254; 333; 351; 34; born about the end of the reign of Saul 334; contemporary with Triptolemus, Eumelus, Celeus and @Erechtheus 334; Greeks built a temple to him 359; he and his mother Callisto associated with the constellations of @Ursa Major and Arctophylax (Bootes) 254; king of Arcadia 333; received grain and learned agriculture from Triptolemus 351; 34; taught his people to make bread from grain 351

Archander: son of Achaeus 228; husband of a daughter of @Danaus 228

Archelaus: Spartan king descended from the family of Eurysthenes 204

Archelaus: king in Macedon 301

Archevites: located on the south and south-east side of the @Assyrian Empire 536; transplanted by @Esarhaddon to Samaria 534; 552

Archias: son of Evagetus 118; 299; built Syracuse in Sicily (719 BC) 118; 299; led a colony from @Corinth into Sicily 118; 299

Archidamus I: Spartan king descended from Procles 209

Archilites: son of Achaeus 228; husband of a daughter of @Danaus 228

Archilochus: Greek artist 217

Archimagus: name of the high priest of the @Magi 653

Arctophylax: constellation is related to Callisto and her son Arcas 254; its left hand and the middle of the body of the constellation each contain a star that pass through the colure of the equinoxes 251

Arcturus: method for determining its position on the sphere of @Chiron 264; rose sixty days after the winter solstice in the time of Hesiod 268

Ardalus: Greek musician 217

Ardschir Diraz: name the @Persians called Artaxerxes Longimanus 664; 696

Areca: also called Erech 536; city of the Archevites 536

Argaeus: another name for Araeus 301

Argives: created city of @Phoronicum by consolidating many families 389; original kingdom consisted of many small towns (1076 BC) 20

Argo: first long ship built by the Greeks 256; patterned after the long ship, which @Danaus sailed to Greece (935 BC) 73; 228; sent to Aeetes in @Colchis and to many other princes on the coasts of the Black and Mediterranean seas 479; ship commissioned by Greeks to sail on the Black and Mediterranean seas (936 BC) 72; ship used in the Argonaut Expedition by the Greek embassy to persuade countries to revolt from Egypt 276

Argo: constellation containing a star between its poop deck and its mast that passes through the colure of the solstices 252; constellation contains a star used to define the colure of the solstices 261; constellation shaped like the ship *Argo* that was used on the Argonaut Expedition 253

Argonaut Expedition: @Bacchus lived one generation before 417; @Chiron about eighty-eight years old at the time of 367; after this expedition astronomy was dormant until revived by Thales 265; at that time, Castor and Pollux were very young men 324; Boreas lived at the time of 395; civil wars in Egypt and this expedition destroy Egyptian Empire (940 BC) 69; commissioned by Greeks to persuade countries to revolt from Egypt 276; constellations of @Antinous and Bernices Coma were created long after the expedition 255; dated five different ways 270; during the time of, the cardinal points of the equinoxes and solstices were in the middle of the constellations of Aries, Cancer, @Chelae (Scorpio) and Capricorn 256; Eteocles and Polynices killed about ten years after this expedition 314; from its time the equinoxes had gone back eleven degrees by the time of Hipparchus 267; from its time until 1689 AD the colures have drifted 36° 29' 263; happened a generation before the Trojan War 11; happened about five hundred years before the Peloponnesian War (933 BC) 75; Hypermnestra, the daughter of @Danaus, lived in the time of 325; in 1689 AD the equinox had gone back 36° 44' from where it was at the time of this expedition 257; its time determined by the colures 260; many constellations named after individuals on this expedition 254; method for determining the location of stars during its time 264; occurred about 933 BC 308; 366; occurred about forty-two years after the death of Solomon 266; occurred about forty-two years after the death of Solomon based on astronomical calculations 269; occurred about thirty years after @Sesostris left Prometheus on Mount Caucasus 233; occurred after the time of Solomon and Rehoboam 300; occurred one generation after @Bacchus 278; occurred one generation before the Trojan War 222; occurred one generation later than the expedition of @Sesostris 227; 232; occurred two generations after the time of @Neptune 465; occurred two or three generations after @Isis and @Osiris lived 419; occurred while Theseus was imprisoned by @Aidoneus 229; sphere of the constellations made its use 253; used celestial sphere of @Chiron for navigation (935 BC) 73

Argonauts: included @Aesculapius 223; 324; included @Hercules (Idean) 223; included @Orpheus 417; 450; included Calais 319; included Canthus 326; included Castor 324; included Deucalion 297; 317; 344; included Eurymedon 227; 277; included Idas 324; included Jason 327; included Lycurgus 333; included Lynceus 324; included Periclymenus 317; included Phlias 227; 277; included Pollux 324; included some of the sons of @Neptune 465; included the grandsons of @Chiron 345; included the sons of @Bacchus and Ariadne 417; included Zetes 319; killed Talus, a man from the Bronze Age 365; 75; may have given the pattern of the sphere of @Chiron to Nausica 256; most of the ancient constellations relate to them 255; several were fathers of sons who were captains in the Greek war against Troy 270; visited many countries to instigate a rebellion against Egypt 479; 480

Argos: @Inachus led a colony here from Egypt 378; @Phoenicians traded here 287; founded by Phoroneus who consolidated many families into one city 389; home of Acusilaus 383; its chronology was greatly distorted by historians 383; its first eight kings said to have ruled three hundred and seventy-one years 204; location of a temple the Greeks built to @Bacchus 278; location of the kidnapping of @Io 394; named after Argus the grandson of Phoroneus 384; originally called Phoronicum and built by Phoroneus 384; 20; Phorbas and his son Triopas fled from here to @Rhodes 326; Phoroneus began to reign here around the twentieth year of Saul 380; Phoroneus drove out the @Telchines from here 283; ruled by @Danaus 322; ruled by @Danaus and his son-in-law Lynceus 323; ruled by Phorbas 395; ruled by Phoroneus and his grandson Argus 369; ruled by the family line of Temenus 301

Argus: grandson of Phoroneus 369; 384; son of @Jupiter (Cretan) 369; son of Niobe 369; @Argos named after him 384

Argus: son of @Danaus 228; built the ship Argo 228

Argus: father of @Pirasus 325

Ariadne: common-law wife of Glaucus 277; daughter of @Minos 227; 277; 344; mother of Eurymedon 227; 277; mother of Phlias 227; 277; sister of Androgeus 344; sister of Phaedra 344; wife of @Bacchus 6; 227; 277; 278; 297; 310; 417; wife of @Sesostris (962 BC) 60; wife of Theseus 277; 297; abandoned by her husband Theseus on the island of @Naxos 277; accompanied @Bacchus on his triumphs 310; died just before he returned to Egypt 278; her crown associated with the constellation of Corona Bornealis 254; her sons were Argonauts 417; lived during the reigns of Solomon and Rehoboam 297

Ariadnes: chronologers invented two women with the same name to reconcile their chronology 6; 344; 419; 445

Ariene: daughter of Alyattes (585 BC) 151; wife of @Darius the Mede 608; 151; wife of @Darius the Mede not Astyages as Herodotus thought 596; married @Darius the Mede to ratify a peace treaty 608

Aries: at the time of the Argonaut Expedition the colure of the equinox cut through this constellation 257; back of the constellation contains a star that passes through the colure of the equinoxes 251; constellation shaped like a golden ram, the ensign of the ship in which Phrixus fled to @Colchis 253; contained stars on the colure for the equinoxes 259; contains same longitude as Pleiades 265; method for determining the position of stars in this constellation on the sphere of @Chiron 264; old constellation mentioned by Aratus 255; related to the Argonaut Expedition 255; vernal equinox in this constellation moved back with time 267; vernal equinox was in the middle of this constellation at the

time of the Argonaut Expedition 256; Zodiac constellation of the vernal equinox at the time of the Argonaut Expedition (935 BC) 73; 249; 250

Arion: Greek artist 217

Aristaeus: husband of Autonoe 395; Greeks built a temple to him 359; led a colony from Thebes (Greek) to the island of Caea 395

Aristagiton: helped Harmodius murder Hipparchus (513 BC) 171

Aristarchus: Greek astronomer who wrote in prose 196

Aristillus: Greek astronomer who wrote in prose 196

Aristodemus: brother of Temenus 222; brother-in-law of Theras 208; father of Cresphontes 222; father of Eurysthenes 208; 209; 218; 222; father of Procles 208; 209; 218; 222; son of Aristomachus 222; king of Sparta 222; led the Heraclides into Peloponnesus for the fifth time 222

Aristodemus: descended from the Heraclides 329; king of @Corinth 329

Aristodemus: king of Messene 204

Aristomachus: father of Aristodemus 222; father of Cresphontes 222; father of Temenus 222; son of Cleodius 222; killed in the fourth attempt of the Heraclides to return 222

Ariston: Spartan king descended from Procles 209

Aristophanes: says that @Darius the Mede recoined the gold coins of Sardis into @Darics 612

Aristotle: incorrectly thought Lycurgus and Iphitus established the Olympic truce 3; incorrectly thought Lycurgus lived at the time of the first Olympiad 199; incorrectly thought Lycurgus was the companion of Iphitus in restoring the Olympic Games 214; made Lycurgus to live a hundred years older before he really did 4; mistakenly thought the name of Lycurgus on an Olympic discus proved that he founded the games with Iphitus 198; teacher of Callisthenes 194; thought Lycurgus was as old as Iphitus (708 BC) 122; wrote the book called *Physical Acroasis* 243

Arius Montanus: historian who located the home of the Naphtuhim on the coasts of Marmorica and Byrene 466

Armais: another name for Danaus 230

Armenia: captured by @Cyaxeres and added to the Median Empire 594; conquered by @Sesostris and @Memnon 526; contained numerous monuments to the Argonaut Expedition 480; invaded and helped destroy Babylon 618; its melting snow causes the Euphrates River to flood at the beginning of summer 591; its princes died in the wars with @Cyaxeres 611; on the northern boundary of @Babylonia 622; part of the @Assyrian Empire at its height 554; place @Sennacherib's two sons fled after murdering their father 551; ruled by @Ramesses 490; seized by @Cyaxeres from the @Assyrians (607 BC) 144

Armenians: visited by the Argonauts 480; warred frequently with the Babylonians and the Medes 622

Arminon: another name for Amenophis 489

Arnobius: states that @Hercules (Tyrian) was buried in Spain 293

Arogus: another name for Arses 666; ruled the Persian Empire (338 BC) 188

Arpad: another name for the city of Aradus 284; conquered by @Sennacherib 550; its king conquered by @Assyria 532; 533; on the west and south side of the @Assyrian Empire 535

Arphaxad: may be another name for Dejoces or his son Phraortes 558; populated the region of Arrapachitis 538

Arrapachitis: region in the north-east part of @Assyria 538

Arsamenes: father of Hystaspes 653

Arses: king of the Persian Empire 666; ruled for two years 666

Artabanus: his reign was not noted in Ptolemy's Canon 664; killed by Artaxeres Longimanus for treason 663; murdered @Xerxes I 662; 663; reigned for seven months 663

Artabazus: another name for Harpagus 630

Artagerses: another name for Harpagus 630

Artahascht: name Christians called Artaxerxes Longimanus 664

Artaphernes: king of @Persia for a few days after @Smerdis was killed 652

Artaxerxes: Jews think Artaxerxes Longimanus, Artaxerxes Mnemon and Artaxerxes Ochus are one and the same king called @Artaxerxes 668

Artaxerxes: common name the Jews gave to all Persian kings 667

Artaxerxes Longimanus: father of his bastard son @Darius Nothus 665; father of Xerxes II 665; son of @Xerxes I (474 BC) 176; son of Xerxes I 663; @Ezra and Nehemiah lived during his reign 677; 683; 684; another name the Jews thought for Artaxerxes 668; became sole king of the Persian Empire (465 BC) 178; became viceroy with his father @Xerxes

I (474 BC) 176; called Ardschir Diraz, Bahaman and Artahascht 664; called Bahaman or Ardschir Diraz by the @Persians 696; during his reign @Ezra left Babylon with offerings and vessels for the temple 688; during his reign Nehemiah expelled Manasseh from the priesthood for marrying Nicaso, the daughter of Sanballat 681; Eliashib was the high priest during the first part of his reign 680; enemies complained to him about the Jews repairing the walls at @Jerusalem 689; his story interrupts the account of @Darius Hystaspes in @Ezra 687; Jews thought he was Darius Hystaspes 667; Joiada became the high priest in the nineteenth year of his reign 679; killed Artabanus for treason and for murdering his father @Xerxes I 663; omit his story in @Ezra to make that book match I Esdras 686; successor not predecessor of @Darius Hystaspes as some incorrectly think 685

Artaxerxes Mnemon: son of @Darius Nothus 666; @Ezra and Nehemiah did not live during his reign 677; 683; 684; @Jaddua became the high priest in the nineteenth year of his reign 679; another name the Jews thought for Artaxerxes 668; conquered Cyprus 293; during his reign @Johanan murdered Jesus in the temple 680; king of the Persian Empire 666; ruled for forty-six years 666; ruled the Persian Empire (404 BC) 186

Artaxerxes Ochus: another name the Jews thought for Artaxerxes 668; king of the Persian Empire 666; Onias became the high priest in the third year of his reign 679; ruled for twenty-one years 666; ruled the Persian Empire (359 BC) 187

Arturia: part of the Babylonian Empire 621

Arundelian Marbles: do not use dating by Olympiads but date relative to time of writing 197; its chronology computed by allowing three kings to reign for at least one hundred years 303; state that Telamon banished his son Teucer from home and Teucer arrived at Cyprus and built Salamis 293; state that Teucer came to Cyprus seven years after the destruction of Troy and built Salamis 225; state that the Cirrheans were conquered in year two of the 47th Olympiad 302; written about sixty years after the death of @Alexander the Great 1

Arvad: another name for the city of Aradus 284

Asa: @Sesostris murdered in the fifth year of his reign 273; 275; children of @Minos alive during his reign 297; defeated @Ethiopians under Zerah 499; 68; free from Egyptian control after the murder of @Sesostris (951 BC) 66; freed from Egypt after he defeated Zerah 475; 478; in his fifth year his kingdom had peace for ten years 472

Ascalonians: captured the city of Sidon 279

Ascander Roumi: another name for Alexander the Great 696

Ascanius: possible father of Romus 311

Ashchenez: another name for Phrygia 618

Ashdod: attacked and captured by Tartan 504; captured by @Esarhaddon 553; location of the house of Dagon where the @Philistines brought the ark 455

Ashtaroth: goddess of Laban and the Canaanites 362

Asia: @Cyaxeres began to extend his kingdom over it 594; @Osiris, @Bacchus and @Sesostris conquered as far east as India 420; @Sesostris introduced the knowledge of observing the stars here 625; Atlantis was imagined to be larger than it 465; 91; conquered by Cyrus 1; first conquered by @Sesostris 421; 424; inhabited before this time by wandering peoples (1121 BC) 14; its kings carried the fire from the @Magi for good luck 656; its people began their year on the autumnal equinox 243; large part of it ruled by the Scythians for twenty-eight years 562; Lycurgus travelled through 216; Lycurgus, brought the poems of Homer from here into Greece (710 BC) 121; many of its cities populated by @Sesostris 451; part of the Medo-Persian Empire 611; ruled by @Darius the Mede 593; ruled by Japheth 524; supplied the armies of Cyrus for eight months of the year 623; to the time when @Alexander the Great entered, the Chaldeans claimed to have been observing the stars for four hundred and seventy-three thousand years 518

Asia Minor: @Sesostris returned through here on his way back to Egypt (962 BC) 60; Cadmus with his brothers led colonies of @Sidonians here 282; city of @Erythra located in near Chios 287; conquered by Cyrus with the help of @Harpagus 630; controlled by Croesus as far east as the Halys River 307; custom of deifying the dead introduced here by the Egyptians, @Phoenicians and @Syrians 460; Cyrus found much wealth here 613; destination the @Shepherds and @Philistines fled to when defeated by David 436; off its coast the islands of Delos, Hiera, Anaphe and @Rhodes emerged for the sea 395; one place the @Edomites

propagated their skills to 444; settled by colonies of @Phoenicians and @Syrians fleeing from Sidon and from David (1041 BC) 28; some of its cities were conquered by @Minerva, the queen of the @Amazons 423; some of the @Shepherds accompanied Sidonian colonies here 376; sons of Codrus fled here to escape the rule of their brother Medon 310

Asopus: father of Aegina (1030 BC) 31

Asordan: name of Esarhaddon according to LXX 552

Assaradin: name of Esarhaddon according to Ptolemy's Canon 552

Asshur: another name for Assyria 610

Asshur: founded cities without naming them after himself 520

Assis: name of a Canaanite king who reigned in Lower Egypt after Joshua expelled the Canaanites (1445 BC) 13; 430

Assuerus: another name for Achsuerus or Cyaxeres 594; another name for Astibares 576; helped @Nebuchadnezzar destroy @Nineveh 575; king of the Medes 575

Assur: name of an @Assyrian god also called Atsur 519

Assur-Hadon: example of an @Assyrian name compounded with the name of one of the @Assyrian gods 519

Assur-Hadon-Pul: example of an @Assyrian name compounded with the name of one of the @Assyrian gods 519

Assyria: @Esarhaddon transplanted the Israelites and the @Syrians here 504; @Habor was a mountainous region between it and Media 538; age of its kingdom was greatly exaggerated 194; another name for Babylonia 621; attacked by Pharaoh Necho at the end of the reign of Josiah 575; Babylon its ancient metropolis 621; bequeathed to Tiglathpileser by @Pul 549; border enlarged to the Tigris River by @Pul 542; conquered all the kingdoms around it 541; conquered by @Cyaxeres and @Nebuchadnezzar 600; conquered by @Sesostris and @Memnon 526; conquered by Babylon 576; Ctesias created a list of imaginary kings to justify its antiquity 8; developed from villages, towns and cities which grew into the kingdom 409; did not exist during the time of @Ramesses, the son of @Amenophis 490; empire thought to be almost as old as Noah's flood 519; exaggerated their history 518; 699; Ezekiel relates a parable about it 609; foundation laid on which to build a more exact chronology for it 309; Isaiah predicted that there would be a highway out of Egypt into @Assyria 507; Isaiah recorded the boasts of its king 533; its borders reached to @Judah 534; its king boasted of its conquests 540; its kingdom still stood when Zephaniah prophesied 565; its kings invaded the Jews 522; its province part of the @Assyrian Empire at its height 554; its temples almost as old as those in Egypt 454; opposed by an alliance of the Medes and Chaldeans 588; part of the kingdom of Nimrod 524; ruled by @Anacyndaraxis 557; ruled by @Chyniladon and its last king @Sarac according to Polyhistor 563; ruled by @Nabuchodonosor 560; ruled by @Nineveh after the time of Jonah 527; ruled by @Pul and Tiglathpileser 529; 114; ruled by @Salmanasser (721 BC) 117; ruled by @Sardanapalus 557; ruled by @Sennacherib (719 BC) 118; ruled by Saosduchinus (647 BC) 135; ruled by Tiglathpileser 456; ruled by Tiglathpileser (740 BC) 115

Assyrian: Ctesias used mainly bogus foreign king names for its kings 520; nationality of all the kings of Babylon according to the Canon of Ptolemy 547; nationality of Lucian 454; one nationality attributed to @Zoroaster since he lived here for a while 656; used interchangeably with the words Tyrian and Syrian 546

Assyrian Empire: @Persia divided into several kingdoms 566; after the Medes revolted it was about the same size as the Babylonian Empire 621; Babylonians and the Medes became powerful after its fall 567; became great before it conquered Israel 549; controlled many countries after the fall of Israel 532; Ctesias incorrectly thought it lasted thirteen hundred and sixty years 521; destroyed in the first year of Jehoiakim 565; divided between @Cyaxeres and @Nebuchadnezzar (610 BC) 143; divided between the Chaldeans and the Medes 564; Egypt revolted from 508; extended in every direction from the province of @Assyria to considerable distances 540; extended west to the Hales River 608; founded by @Pul 523; 543; 108; founded by @Pul and his successors 525; founded by @Pul and Tiglathpileser 8; list of kingdoms on its east side 537; list of kingdoms on its north side 539; list of kingdoms on its north-east side 538; list of kingdoms on its west and south side 535; lost provinces of @Armenia, Pontus and Cappadocia to @Cyaxeres (607 BC) 144; Medes revolted from (712 BC) 120; Nabopolassar revolted from the @Assyrian Empire (625 BC) 141; reached its greatest extent in the days of @Sennacherib and @Esarhaddon 554; ruled in Babylon (625 BC) 141; Samaritans came from its various regions 243; some internal change occasioned the release of Manasseh 559; Syria, @Phoenicia and Egypt revolted from the @Assyrian Empire (668 BC) 130; unknown to Amos when he wrote 529; unknown to Homer 526

Assyrians: attacked by Media when abandoned by its allies 558; built Babylon for the @Arabians 624; called Syrians by the Greeks during the time of Cyrus 554; conquered by @Cyaxeres and @Nebuchadnezzar 594; conquered Egypt under @Esarhaddon 516; conquered many countries 525; conquered many kingdoms recent to their invasion of @Judah 540; Ctesias is ignorant of their history 521; defeated by @Nebuchadnezzar 601; defeated by the Egyptians and @Ethiopians at @Pelusium 501; 502; 503; defeated the Jews, captured Manasseh and subdued @Judah 505; destroyed much of the Egyptian archives 517; fled from Judith when he killed Holofernes their leader 561; founded Babylon for the @Arabians 547; harassed Egypt and Ethiopia for three years 557; in the time of Amos only @Calneh conquered by them 531; invaded by the Scythians (634 BC) 138; Isaiah predicted that Egypt would be subject to them 507; killed @Phraortes the king of the Medes 598; killed @Phraortes, the king of the Medes (635 BC) 137; lost @Carchemish toward the end of their empire 565; lost provinces of @Persia and Parthia to @Cyaxeres 566; Media revolted from them 406; 555; 697; Media was the first to revolt from them 556; not directly mentioned in the book of Amos 529; omitted by Jeremiah in the list of countries that would suffer 603; revolted from the kings at @Memphis 494; ruled by the dynasty of the Pischdians 698; sold merchandise to the @Phoenicians 287; supplied soldiers for the army of Holofernes 560; transplanted its conquered peoples 534; used a luni-solar year 243

Astarte: Phoenician goddess with a crown of towers on her head and a drum in her hand 345; 358

Asterius: father of @Minos 342; 37; husband of @Europa 342; 345; 351; 367; son of Teutamus 354; 400; another name for Saturn (Cretan) 345; 351; 367; before he ruled in Crete his father Teutamus brought a colony to Crete 354; before him the inhabitants of Crete spoke different languages 401; contemporary with @Erechtheus, Celeus, Eumolpus, Ceres, @Jasius, Cadmus, Harmonia and Dardanus 319; contemporary with Saturn (Cretan) 345; 351; during his reign the Cretans invented iron tools 400; expelled from Crete by his son @Minos (1012 BC) 37; first king of Crete 342; iron tools invented in his time 403; lived in the Golden Age 367; possible name for Jupiter 369; ruled Crete 367; same man as Saturn (Cretan) 342

Astibares: assisted @Nebuchadnezzar in his conquests 576; assisted @Nebuchadnezzar in the conquest of @Nineveh according to Eupolemus 594; king of Media 521

Astivares: another name for Astibares 576

Astraea: another name for Isis 67

Astyages: father of @Cyaxeres 562; 563; 588; 596; 597; 598; 147; father of Amyite 563; 588; father of Mandane 596; 597; 147; grandfather of Cyrus 596; 597; 147; son of @Phraortes 556; 561; 598; Herodotus and Xenophon confounded him with his son @Cyaxeres 595; in the beginning of his reign the Scythians invaded Media 600; incorrectly is thought to be the last king of Media by Herodotus 631; king of Media 521; 561; reigned for thirty-five years 598; succeeded @Phraortes as the king of the Medes (635 BC) 137; third king of Media 593

Asuppim: name of the temple gate that led to @Jerusalem 638

Asychis: added the eastern portico to the temple of @Vulcan 9; 109; 478; 494; built a large brick pyramid (788 BC) 109; king of Egypt according to Herodotus 483; king of Egypt according to Herodotus and Newton 486; omitted in the king list of Diodorus but in the list of Herodotus 514; ruled Egypt 109

Atal: part of the name from which the name @Atlas was derived 468

Athamas: brother of Calyce 327; brother of Sisyphus (976 BC) 52; father of Helle (976 BC) 52; father of Learchus 329; father of Phrixus (976 BC) 52; grandson of Hellen 329; husband of Ino 329; 52; son of Aeolus 327; 329; lived until the time of Rehoboam 329; went mad and accidentally killed his son Learchus 329

Athenaea: games held at @Athens every four years 277

Athenaeus: states that @Minos was that @Jupiter who kidnapped Ganymede 343; states that Lycurgus was contemporary with Terpander the musician 213

Athenians: @Pherecydes wrote their history 197; built three hundred and sixty statues to Demetrius Phalereus 240; defeated the @Amazons 423; first annual archon was Creon (607 BC) 144; first decennial archon was Charops (647 BC) 135; Ion commanded their army 310; its archon Draco made laws for them (572 BC) 154; killed Androgeus (984 BC) 49; lost the war with @Minos and were compelled to send him eight young men and eight virgins every eight years 277; opposed the advance of the Atlanteans 464; original kingdom consisted of many small towns (1076 BC) 20; ruled by @Erechtheus 328; sent an army under Ion against the Eleusinians 319; Solon made some of their laws 307; waged war with the Eleusinians in which their King @Erechtheus was killed 318; waged war with the Spartans (804 BC) 105

Athens: Callias an archon of 661; Ceres came into Attica during the reign of its King @Erechtheus 318; Harmodius and Aristagiton murdered Hipparchus here (513 BC) 171; heard of the news of the death of @Artaxerxes Longimanus in the winter, in the seventh year of the Peloponnesian War 664; its citadel called @Cecropia 384; location of central council for smaller towns 388; location of the Athenaea games, which were held every four years 277; made @Erechtheus king for his bringing grain from Egypt to them 319; near the grave of Deucalion 330; not present at first Amphictyonic Council and not ruled by Amphictyon (1003 BC) 41; originally called Cecropia (1076 BC) 20; ruled by @Erechtheus 228; 334; ruled by Demophoon (903 BC) 88; ruled by Menestheus, the great-grandson of @Erechtheus (927 BC) 80; ruled by Pandion and Theseus 359; ruled by Pisistratus the tyrant 303; ruled by the tyrant Pisistratus (550 BC) 161; ruled by Theseus 310; Solon died, when Hegestratus was its archon (549 BC) 162; Solon excluded himself from the city for ten years 307; Solon their legislator (562 BC) 157; some used its archons to organise their history 1; times of its archons used to organise history 197

Athothes: another name for Thoth 484

Atlanteans: conquered by @Ammon 463; conquered by @Minerva the queen of the @Amazons 422; 423; lived on Mount @Atlas 463; named after @Atlas the son of @Neptune 466; ruled by the Atlantians 422; 423

Atlantic Ocean: named after @Atlas the son of @Neptune 466; Ulysses sailed into it (896 BC) 91; western boundary of the Egyptian Empire 416; western boundary of the kingdom of @Antaeus 467

Atlantis: heavily populated 465; huge island near the Strait of Gibraltar 464; imagined to be larger than Africa and Asia 465; 91; ruled @Libya as far as to Egypt 464; ruled by @Atlas the son of @Neptune 466

Atlas: brother of Epimetheus 370; brother of Prometheus 370; daughter of @Neptys 466; father of Calypso 465; 91; son of @Japetus according to the Greeks 466; son of @Neptune 464; 466; 467; another name for Antaeus the son of @Japetus (951 BC) 66; appointed king of Atlantis by his father @Neptune 464; compounded from the name of @Antaeus and the word *Atal* 468; formed the celestial sphere for the Libyans 625; his country bordered the ocean 463; island of Atlantis named after him (896 BC) 91; led Libyans against Egypt 275; led the Titans against the gods of Egypt 467; made war on the gods of Egypt 466; ruled Atlantis 466; same man as Antaeus 467

Atlas (Mount): border of the lands ruled by @Antaeus and @Atlas 467; home of the Atlanteans 463

Atreus: adoptive father of Agamemnon 317; adoptive father of Menelaus 317; 83; son of Pelops 317; 80; died (924 BC) 83; repelled the invasion of the Heraclides 354; ruled Mycene (927 BC) 80

Atsur: name of an @Assyrian god also called Assur 519

Attica: agriculture brought to @Italy from here 351; Ceres arrived here looking for her kidnapped daughter Proserpina 319; 320; 32; Ceres came there in the days of @Erechtheus the king of @Athens and Celeus the king of Eleusis 318; Cranaus, the successor of Cecrops I, reigned here (1041 BC) 28; Deucalion fled here with his sons Hellen and Amphictyon from the flood in @Thessaly 330; divided into separate towns in the days of Cecrops I and Theseus 388; extraneous names in its king list 331; location of the city of @Cecropia or @Athens (1076 BC) 20; location of the city of Eleusis 383; 20; partly ruled by Cranaus and Amphictyon (1003 BC) 41; ruled by @Erechtheus (1031 BC) 30; ruled by Aegeus (990 BC) 45; ruled by Cecrops I in the days of Eli 382; ruled by Cecrops II (1002 BC) 42; ruled by Pandion

(1001 BC) 43; started their year on the summer solstice 243; united by Theseus who ruled there (965 BC) 57

Atymnus: led a colony of @Phoenicians and @Syrians fleeing from Sidon and from David (1041 BC) 28; 283

Auaris: ancient name for Pelusium 430

Auge: daughter of Aleus 333; had sexual intercourse with @Hercules (Idean) 333

Augeas: killed by @Hercules (Idean) 354

Augustine: states original inhabitants of North Africa were Canaanites 426

Auriga: constellation was one of the charioteers of @Erechthonius 254

Autonoe: daughter of Cadmus 359; wife of Aristaeus 395

Ava: transplanted by @Esarhaddon into the regions of Samaria and @Damascus 504

Axeres: another name for Achsuerus 594; another name for Astibares 576; another name for Cyaxeres 596

Ayres: corruption of the name Moeris 491

Azariah: son of Maaseiah 684; helped Nehemiah repair the wall of @Jerusalem 684; priest who returned with @Ezra and Nehemiah in the first year of Cyrus 671

Azariah: father of Seraiah 684; son of Hilkiah 684

Azoth: another name for Ashdod 504; fortified by the @Edomites against David (1044 BC) 25; 271; 281; fortified for the @Philistines by a prince of @Edom who fled from David 282

Baal: god of Laban and the Canaanites 362; Jehu killed its prophets 455

Baal: king of @Tyre 589

Baal Canaan: another name for the Egyptian god Vulcan (912 BC) 85; 459

Babel (Tower of): building of disrupted by the division of languages 409

Babylon: @Darius the Mede finished capturing its kingdom 594; @Darius the Mede left here for Media 630; @Darius the Mede reigned until after its fall 614; @Darius the Mede was defeated by Cyrus after the city was taken 632; @Esarhaddon carried Manasseh captive here 553; 128; @Nebuchadnezzar returned here when his father Nabopolassar died 577; became great by conquering @Assyria and Syria 576; bequeathed to Nabonassar by @Pul 549; border of the kingdom of @Calneh 531; built by Belus (Tyrian) 545; capital of Nabopolassar after he revolted from the king of @Assyria (625 BC) 141; capital of the Babylonian Empire 621; capital of the kingdom of Nimrod 524; captured by @Darius the Mede and his brother-in-law Cyrus 618; captured by @Esarhaddon 552; captured by Cyrus 306; 308; 164; captured when @Darius the Mede was sixty-two years old 608; captured when Cyrus diverted the Euphrates River and entered the city through its empty channel 591; Chaldeans boasted that the city was founded nineteen hundred and three years before @Alexander the Great 194; Chaldeans priests instituted there by an Egyptian colony (951 BC) 66; changed to a satrap when Cyrus captured it 623; completed by Nabonassar 548; conquered by the Medes and @Persians 619; Ctesias claimed the city was founded by Semiramis 520; described by Herodotus 624; developed from villages, towns and cities which grew into the kingdom 409; did not conquer @Judah before the reign of Jehoiakim 578; during the reign of @Artaxerxes Longimanus @Ezra left here with offerings and vessels for the temple 688; Egyptian priests introduced the Egyptian three hundred and sixty-five day year here 498; founded by @Belus (Assyrian) according to @Abydenus 544; founded by the @Assyrians for the @Arabians 547; home of @Zoroaster 654; invaded by @Esarhaddon (681 BC) 127; its king @Nebuchadnezzar destroyed @Nineveh 575; its kings are listed in Ptolemy's Canon 567; its last king was called @Belshazzar, @Labynitus, @Naboandelos or @Nabonnedus by various historians 585; its people transplanted by @Esarhaddon to Samaria 534; its walls, gates and temple of @Belus (Assyrian) built by Semiramis 543; Jeconiah was held captive here for thirty-seven years 568; Jeremiah predicted their attack on @Judah 601; located on the south and south-east side of the @Assyrian Empire 536; location of the captivity of Manasseh 559; location of the temple of @Jupiter Belus 627; may have been enlarged by @Pul 542; Nabonassar succeeded @Pul here (747 BC) 114; near @Sepharvaim 535; Nitocris was the mother of its last king 8; punished when its king was conquered by the Medes 603; Pythagorus was abducted here from Egypt by King @Cambyses 653; regions of @Susiana and Sitacene lay between @Susa and here 622; ruled by @Chyniladon and Saosduchinus 558; ruled by @Merodach Baladan 551; ruled by @Nabonadius (555 BC) 160;

ruled by @Nabonnedus when it fell 584; ruled by @Nebuchadnezzar 604; ruled by eighteen kings for two hundred and nine years 205; ruled by Nabopolassar after he revolted from @Assyria 563; ruled by two famous queens Semiramis and Nitocris 587; ruled nine years by Cyrus according to Ptolemy's Canon 595; Samaritans who came from here used a luni-solar year 243; some of its inhabitants were transplanted by @Esarhaddon into the regions of Samaria and @Damascus 504; taken a month or two after the summer solstice 592; their punishment after seventy years was predicted by Jeremiah 602; worshipped a god called Belus 445

Babylonia: @Esarhaddon transplanted the Israelites and the @Syrians here 504; Berosus describes the extent of 622; colonised by an Egyptian colony led by Belus 445; conquered by the @Assyrians 566; Cyrus captured and ruled it in the fourteenth year of the @Tyrian King Hirom 590; Egyptian priests fled here bringing sacred vessels of @Jupiter Enyalius 498; founded by Egyptian colonies 626; invaded by Cyrus 591; its passes to Media fortified by Nitocris 587; part of the Babylonian Empire 621; supplied the armies of Cyrus for four months of the year 623; territory fairly flat 588; Tigris and Euphrates River flowed through it 536

Babylonian: its month names used by Samaritans 243; nationality of @Nabonnedus 583; nationality of Belesis 556

Babylonian Captivity: Jews confessed their sins after they were freed 522

Babylonian Empire: after its conquest, @Darius the Mede ruled over its hundred and twenty provinces 620; conquered by @Darius the Mede 611; its extent was described by Berosus 621; Jews only knew about it from what they had in their scriptures 667

Babylonian New Year: @Nebuchadnezzar made viceroy after it 570

Babylonians: @Persia and @Susiana were not part of their empire immediately after the capture of @Nineveh 603; assisted by the Medes in conquering the western nations 576; became powerful after the @Assyrian Empire fell 567; conquered @Susiana 611; destroyed @Nineveh 521; destroyed the temple of Solomon in 588 BC 635; its empire coexisted along with the empire of the Medes 564; laws not observed by @Darius the Mede 619; lived an extremely debauched lifestyle 628; may have conquered @Elam 566; their last king was called @Belshazzar, @Labynitus, @Naboandelos or @Nabonedus by various historians 585; their three hundred and sixty-five day year used by the @Persians 247; transplanted by @Esarhaddon to Samaria 552; used a luni-solar year 243; warred frequently with the Medes and the Armenians 622

Bacchis: descended from the Heraclides 329; king of @Corinth 329

Bacchus: father of @Apollo 450; father of Eurymedon 227; 277; father of Phlias 227; 277; husband of Ariadne 227; 277; 278; 297; 310; 344; son of @Ammon 425; also called Cretan Bacchus 278; also called Sesostris 227; 526; another name for Osiris 274; appeased @Thoas with wine 458; appointed @Thoas king over Byblus and Cyprus 458; Arabian name of the god who was Sesostris 449; armies strengthened by men from Sidonian colonies 282; called *Bacchus the Great* by the @Arabians (951 BC) 66; caught in bed with @Venus 278; chronologers incorrectly made him as old as @Io 6; contemporary with @Osiris and @Sesostris 423; deified name for Sesostris 486; Dicaearchus incorrectly made him two generations older than Theseus 419; did similar feats as @Osiris and @Sesostris 420; entertained by Amphictyon (1003 BC) 41; erected columns in India by the Ganges River 446; exploits of 422; Graces made a purple cloak for him 457; Greeks thought he was the son of @Jupiter 424; hieroglyphic representation of 460; his asses are related to the constellation of Cancer the Crab 254; his sons by Ariadne were Argonauts 417; in the Arabian language the name means *The Great* 273; king of Egypt who established the Egyptian Empire 416; lived during the reigns of Solomon and Rehoboam 297; lived one generation before the Argonaut Expedition 417; loved @Venus and Ariadne 417; loved and seduced the wife of @Thoas (Calycopis or Venus) 458; married Ariadne when he returned from India 310; same man as Sesostris 418; same man as Sesostris, Shishak and Osiris 308; undertook long voyages on the sea 291

Bacchus: name of one peak of Mount Parnassus 450

Bacchus: son of @Semele 359; Greeks built a temple to him 359; name @Orpheus gave to his son Semele when he deified him (938 BC) 71

Bactria: conquered by @Sesostris and @Memnon 526; original home of @Zoroaster 655; ruled by @Ramesses 490

Bactrian: one nationality attributed to @Zoroaster since he lived here for a while 656

Baetica: land in Spain 288

Baetis River: river in Spain 292

Bagdad: near the location of the ancient city of @Calneh 525; 536

Bahaman: name @Persians called Artaxerxes Longimanus 664; 696

Balatorus: king of @Tyre 589

Bani: chief father of the Levites 684

Bar Kokhab: false messiah the Jews created to avoid accepting Jesus as fulfilling Daniel's seventy weeks 669

Baruch: priest who returned with @Ezra and Nehemiah in the first year of Cyrus 671

Basilea: mother of @Helius 463; mother of @Selene 463; another name for Isis 463

Bathos: valley in which the gods fought the Titans 354

Bathsheba: committed adultery with David 271

Battus: built Cyrene on the site of the city of Irasa (633 BC) 139

Bayer: created a star catalogue 259; 261; indicated the brightness of the stars in the constellations using Greek letters 259; 261

Bel: name of an @Assyrian god 519

Belesis: Ctesias thought he assisted Arbaces in deposing @Sardanapalus 556

Bellerophon: his horse is related to the constellation of Pegasus 254

Belshazzar: son of @Nebuchadnezzar 581; @Persians thought he was conquered by @Bahaman or @Ardschir Diraz 696; born before the fifth year of Jeconiah's captivity 586; king of Babylon that the Jews knew about 667; last king of Babylon according to Daniel 585; name Josephus called Nabonnedus 632; next in succession after @Nebuchadnezzar 581

Beltes-Assur: example of an @Assyrian name compounded with the name of one of the @Assyrian gods 519

Belus (Assyrian): father of Nabonassar 547; another name for Pul 542; 543; Ctesias claimed Semiramis was as old as him 520; first king of @Assyria 519; founded Babylon according to @Abydenus 544; founder of Babylon 546

Belus (Babylonian): named after the Egyptian Belus according to Pausanias 445

Belus (Egyptian): father of @Aegyptus 445; father of @Danaus 445; father of @Isis 445; father of @Osiris 445; grandfather of Cepheus 325; son of @Libya 445; son of @Neptune 445; 447; another name for Ammon 325; 445; Chaldeans called Sesostris by this name 273; established the Chaldean priesthood (951 BC) 66; fought with a sword 447; led an Egyptian colony to Babylon 66

Belus (Tyrian): built Babylon 545

Benhadad I: also called Hadad 456; built temples 454; 455; king of Syria 456

Benhadad II: also called Hadad (895 BC) 92; fought Ahab with thirty-two kings in his army 407; ruled Syria 407; 456; 92

Benhadad III: ruled Syria 456; subject to Israel 456

Berechiah: father of Meshullam 684; son of Meshezabeel 684

Berecynthia: mysteries of the goddess the *Great Mother* were observed here 340

Bernices Coma: constellation created long after the Argonaut Expedition 255

Berosus: blames the Greeks for ascribing the building of Babylon to Semiramis 543; calls @Sepharvaim by the name of @Sipparae 535; calls Pharaoh Necho the *satrap* of Egypt, Coele Syria and @Phoenicia 576; describes the extent of @Babylonia 622; describes the extent of the Babylonian Empire 621; states @Nebuchadnezzar fortified Babylon with magnificent walls and gates and built stately palaces and the hanging gardens 577; states that @Laboasserdach reigned nine months after the death of his father 583; states that @Nebuchadnezzar built a hanging garden for his Median wife 588; states that Oannes taught the Chaldeans 442; states that the Babylonians celebrated the festival called *Sacaea* on the sixteenth day of the month Loos 243

Beta: letter used by astronomers to indicate the second brightest star in a constellation 249

Beth-Arbela: conquered by @Sennacherib 550

Bethel: Jeroboam I set up the gods of Egypt here 471

Bezek: city in Canaan ruled by Adonibezek 407

Bicheres: another name for Mycerinus 493

Big Dipper: another name for the constellation of Plaustrum 254

Bilgah: priest who returned with @Ezra and Nehemiah in the first year of Cyrus 671; 676

Bilgai: priest who returned with @Ezra and Nehemiah in the first year of Cyrus 671

Binnui: another name for Bani 684; priest who returned with @Ezra and Nehemiah in the first year of Cyrus 671

Bistones: city in @Thrace ruled by Diomedes 293

Bithynia: home of Hipparchus 250; ruled by @Ramesses 490; some @Sidonians fled here 283

Black Sea: countries around it received Greek envoys to incite them to revolt from Egypt 276; Greeks sent out envoys to countries around it 256; its far side inhabited by wandering peoples before this time (1121 BC) 14; north coast thinly populated by Scythians 404; ship *Argo* sailed here 479; 72

Bocchoris: son of @Gnephactus 495; burned alive by @Sabacon (751 BC) 113; his twenty-second year was the first year of Nabonassar 498; in the reduced king list of Diodorus 514; king in @Upper Egypt after @Gnephactus (788 BC) 109; king of Egypt according to Diodorus 513; ruled at @Memphis but incorrectly was called a Saite by Africanus 495; ruled at @Memphis but was incorrectly called a Saite by Africanus 496

Bochart: locates the home of the Naphtuhim on the coasts of Marmorica and Byrene 466; notes that the Egyptians had the Phoenician @Venus in Egypt for a foreign deity 459; says that @Midacritus is a corruption of a Greek name @Melcartus 293; says that the @Curetes in Crete came from Palestine and had their name from the @Crethim 341; states that @Carteia was at first called @Melcarteia, from its founder @Melcartus and later shortened to @Carteia 292; states the @Curetes were @Philistines 401

Bocktanassar: Arabian name for Nebuchadnezzar 694

Boeon: name of a Canaanite king who reigned in Lower Egypt after Joshua expelled the Canaanites (1445 BC) 13; 430

Boeotia: country where the city of @Erythra was located 287; its king Nycteus was killed (1006 BC) 39; new name for Cadmeis (844 BC) 100; ruled by Athamas 329; ruled by Ogyges 383

Boeotians: attacked Attica by land 388; captured @Cadmeis (844 BC) 100

Bootes: modern name for the constellation Arctophylax 251; 254

Boreas: @Naxos first settled in his days 395

Bou Sihor: Greeks derive name of Busiris from this name 273

Bou Siris: lament Greeks heard from the Egyptians, which they thought was the name Busiris (951 BC) 66

Brahmins: people in India who taught @Zoroaster 656; Persian religion partly based on their institutions 657

Brauron: one of twelve cities where Cecrops I resettled a number of smaller towns 388

Britain: history written hundreds of years after the death of @Alexander the Great 202; not populated before navigation beyond the Strait of Gibraltar 397; settled by the @Tyrians 285; traded with @Tyrians 298; unknown to the Greeks long after it was discovered by the @Phoenicians 293; visited by @Tyrians before the death of @Melcartus 292

Britomartis: Greeks built a temple to him 359

Bromios: another name for Bacchus 450

Bromios: peak of Mount Parnassus 450

Bronze Age: next generation after the Silver Age in Greece (c. 975 BC) 28; Talus lived at this time 365; Talus lived in this age (933 BC) 75; third age or generation after the gods 364; 371

Bubaste: daughter of @Isis 363; 431; 478; daughter of @Osiris 241; 363; 431; daughter of @Sesostris 246; granddaughter of @Ammon 246; sister of @Orus 478; 67; another name for Selene 463; killed herself after her brother @Orus was drowned (942 BC) 67; king of Egypt before @Amenophis (912 BC) 85

Bubaste: ruled by Tacellotis (788 BC) 109

Buchalion: king of Arcadia 204

Busiris: another name for Belus (Egyptian) given by Eusebius 445; name derived from lament Greeks heard from the Egyptians for Sesostris (951 BC) 66; Sesostris deified under this name by the Greeks 273

Busiris I: king of Egypt according to Diodorus 513; name Diodorus gave to Osiris 514

Busiris II: king of Egypt according to Diodorus 513; name Diodorus gave to Orus 514

Byblia: another name for Calycopis or Venus (930 BC) 78; 458

Byblus: ruled by @Vulcan 458; ruled by a king 457; temple here in Syria to the deified @Calycopis (930 BC) 78

Byires: corruption of the name Moeris 491

Byrene: home of the Naphtuhim 466

Byzantium: visited by the Argonauts 480

Cabiri: name given to the Curetes in Samothrace 336

Cacus: cave used as a burying place 404

Cadis: maybe another name for the island of Ogygia (896 BC) 91

Cadmeis: former name for Boeotia (844 BC) 100

Cadmia: name given to copper ore in Thebes (Greek) and named after Cadmus 337

Cadmus: brother of @Europa 278; 297; 308; 351; brother of Thasus 356; brother-in-law of @Jasius 318; 357; brother-in-law of Ceres 318; father of Alymnus 297; father of Autonoe 359; 395; father of Ino 11; 327; 329; 52; 63; father of Polydorus 314; 315; 316; grandfather of Labdacus 316; 44; grandfather of Pentheus 417; husband of Harmonia 315; husband of Sithonis 282; @Phoenicians surnamed their kings @Jupiter from his time 369; about the same age as his sister @Europa 351; about the time of his going to Europe writing was introduced into Egypt 441; altars may have been erected in Europe before his time to sacrifice to the old gods of the colonies 361; brought many kinds of learning into Greece 336; brought the *Octaeteris* or the *Great Year* into Greece 240; contemporary with Aethlius, Aeolus, Xuthus, Dorus, Tantalus and Danae 328; contemporary with and older than @Erechtheus, Celeus, Eumolpus, Ceres, @Jasius, Harmonia, @Asterius and Dardanus 319; first sailed from Sidon to @Rhodes and then to Samothrace 315; fled from Sidon to Greece 297; found gold in Mount Pangaeus in @Thrace and copper ore at Thebes (Greek) 337; four generations from him to the destruction of Troy 365; Greeks built a temple to him 359; his grandson Pentheus was killed by @Bacchus 417; initiated into the mysteries of Ceres 357; introduced Phoenician letters to Greece 339; introduced the deification of people into Europe 358; introduced writing into Europe 10; led a colony of @Phoenicians and @Syrians fleeing from Sidon and from David (1041 BC) 28; led a colony to Greece 435; 436; led a group of @Phoenicians and @Arabians into Greece 290; led a group of @Sidonians fleeing from Sidon 283; led colonies from Sidon to Crete around 1041 BC 308; left his brother Thasus on the island of Thasos 356; likely arrived in Greece two or three years before the birth of @Minos 278; married Harmonia in Samothrace 315; oldest towns in Europe about two or three generations older than his arrival into Greece 385; 391; two generations younger than the father of Pelasgus 377; various events that happened in his time and that of his posterity 317; with his brothers led colonies of @Sidonians into Cilicia, Asia Minor and Greece 282

Cadmus Milesius: historian who lived at the time of the Persian invasion of Greece 197; introduced writing in prose to Greece 1

Caduceus: hieroglyphic representation of 460

Caea: Aristaeus led a colony here from Thebes (Greek) 395

Caelus: another name for Ammon 274; one of two gods worshipped by the @Arabians 449; worshipped by the @Arabians 273

Caelus: Cretan name for Uranus 470; name means *Heaven* 470

Caelus: father of Doxius 391

Caesar (Germanicus): saw an inscription at @Thebes (Egyptian) about the conquests of @Ramesses and his large army 490

Caesar (Julius): corrected the Egyptian year by adding an extra day every four years 247; in his time the forest called Hercinian in Germany was forty days' journey long and nine days across 403; started the Roman year at the beginning of winter 243

Cairo: built opposite @Memphis 478

Calachene: on the north side of the @Assyrian Empire 539; part of the Babylonian Empire 621

Calais: son of Orithyia 319; an Argonaut 319

Cales: maybe another name for the island of Ogygia (896 BC) 91

Callias: archon of @Athens when @Xerxes I made his expedition against Greece 661

Callimachus: notes the location of @Jupiter in Crete 346; says that the tomb in Crete of @Jupiter is really the tomb of @Minos 347

Calliope: mother of @Orpheus 450; 58; 417; wife of Oeagrus 58; 417; one of the Muses who accompanied @Sesostris on his expedition 450

Calliste: some @Sidonians fled here 283

Callisthenes: sent astronomical observations from Babylon to Greece 194; student of Aristotle 194

Callisto: daughter of Lycaon 333; 351; 34; mother of Arcas 254; 333; 351; 34; contemporary with Rharus 334; she and her son Arcas associated with the constellations of @Ursa Major and Arctophylax (Bootes) 254

Callithea: daughter of @Piranthus 325; first priestess of Juno Argiva 325

Calneh: conquered by @Assyria 530; 533; conquered by @Belus (Assyrian) or @Pul 547; conquered by @Pul 542; founded by Nimrod on the present site of Bagdad 536; had its own king until it was conquered by the @Assyrians 525; located on the south and southeast side of the @Assyrian Empire 536; only kingdom controlled by the @Assyrians in the time of Amos 531

Calno: another name for Calneh 533; 536

Calpe (Mount): mountain near @Carteia in Spain 291

Calyce: daughter of Aeolus 327; mother of Endymion 327; sister of Athamas 327; sister of Cretheus 327; sister of Sisyphus 327; wife of Aethlius 327

Calycopis: daughter of Otreus 457; husband of @Thoas 457; mother of Aeneas according to Homer 457; wife of @Thoas (930 BC) 78; 59; wife of @Vulcan 458; deified by @Vulcan when she died 458; Venus of the ancients was deified by @Thoas (930 BC) 78

Calydonian Boar: killed by Meleager (931 BC) 77

Calypso: daughter of @Atlas 465; 91; found by Ulysses soon after the Trojan War on the island of @Ogygia 465; lived in a cave on the island of @Ogygia along with her maids 397; Ulysses found her on the island of @Ogygia (896 BC) 91

Cambyses: son of Cyrus 651; 667; @Persians omit his reign 696; called Ahasuerus by the Jews 667; carried away many Egyptian records 517; conquered Egypt 485; 509; 510; derided the statue of @Vulcan in its temple at @Memphis for its small size 459; destroyed the city of @Thebes (Egyptian) 505; destroyed the golden circle denoting the days of the year that was in the sepulchre of @Amenophis 246; he and his successor added only seven new provinces to the empire 620; his history was outlined during his reign 677; history of the Jews can be deduced by comparing the books of @Ezra and Nehemiah 673; Jewish history covers his reign 669; listed by Josephus as a king of @Persia 668; plundered the temples of Egypt (523 BC) 94; ruled the Persian Empire (530 BC) 167; second king of the Persian Empire 205; succeeded Cyrus as king of @Persia 651; times of his reign were determined by eclipses recorded in Ptolemy's Canon 660; took Pythagorus captive from Egypt to Babylon 653

Cambyses: father of Cyrus 595; 633; husband of Mandane according to Herodotus and Xenophon 595

Canaan: composed of city states ruled by kings in the time of Joshua 407; invaded by four kings from the land of Nimrod 525; original inhabitants had a common religion until after the time of Melchizedek 411

Canaanites: called @Shepherds by the Egyptains and fled Joshua into Lower Egypt and conquered @Timaeus (1445 BC) 13; confounded with the Israelites by Manetho 373; did not have temples but worshipped at groves and high places 455; Diodorus did not know that Palestine was inhabited by them before the Israelites under Moses came there 435; driven out of Egypt by @Amenophis (926 BC) 81; fled from Joshua and set up pillars in western North Africa 428; lost the city of Gezer to @Ammon (1012 BC) 37; obtained horses from Egypt 375; occupied Egypt and offered their children to the god @Moloch 436; original settlers of western North Africa 430; settled in North Africa after the wars with Joshua 426; supplied troops for the army of @Osarsiphus 476; worshipped Baal, Ashtaroth and @Moloch 362

Canary Islands: settled by the @Tyrians 285

Cancer: constellation contains the star named South Asellus used to define the colure of the solstices 261; constellation is related to the asses of @Bacchus 254; constellation shaped like the crab killed by @Hercules (Idean) 253; middle of the constellation contains a star that passes through the colure of the solstices 252; summer solstice in eighth degree of this constellation in 432 BC 266; summer solstice was in the middle of this constellation at the time of the Argonaut Expedition 256; Zodiac constellation of the summer solstice at the time of the Argonaut Expedition (935 BC) 73; 249; 250

Canethus: father of Canthus 326; descendant of Abas 326

Canis Major: constellation representing one of the dogs of Orion 254

Canis Minor: constellation representing one of the dogs of Orion 254

Canthus: son of Canethus 326

Capaneus: husband of Euadne 324; son of Elector 324; one of the seven captains against Thebes (Greek) 324

Cappadocia: captured by @Cyaxeres and added to the Median Empire 594; conquered by @Sesostris and @Memnon 526; its princes died in the wars with @Cyaxeres 611; part of the @Assyrian Empire at its height 554; ruled by @Ramesses 490; seized by @Cyaxeres from the @Assyrians (607 BC) 144

Capricorn: constellation contains a star used to define the colure of the solstices 261; constellation is related to Pan and @Jupiter's goat with her kids 254; middle of the constellation contains a star that passes through the colure of the solstices 252; winter solstice was in the middle of this constellation at the time of the Argonaut Expedition 256; Zodiac constellation of the winter solstice equinox at the time of the Argonaut Expedition (935 BC) 73; 249; 250

Capsa: built by @Hercules (Tyrian) according to Orosius 295; city founded by the @Tyrians 285

Car: son of Phoroneus (1001 BC) 43; 378; built a temple to Ceres (1001 BC) 43; 378

Car: town built by the children of Phoroneus in @Italy 384

Caranus: brother of Phidon 302; banished from @Argos in the reign of Phidon 301; banished from Phidon along with Perdiccas (594 BC) 148; co-founded the kingdom of Macedon with Perdiccas 302; 148; descended from the family of Temenus 301; incorrectly thought to be older than the Olympiads 302; king in Macedon 301

Carchemish: @Nebuchadnezzar defeated Pharaoh Necho here 576; attacked by Pharaoh Necho 575; conquered by @Assyria 533; conquered by @Pul 542; conquered by Pharaoh Necho and then lost to the Chaldeans 565; on the west and south side of the @Assyrian Empire 535; town of Mesopotamia on the Euphrates River 575

Caria: some @Sidonians fled here 283

Carians: attacked Attica by sea 388; called Legates 283; infested the Greek seas with piracy 394; informed Herodotus about the Egyptian history 510; subject to @Minos 283

Carina: modern constellation derived from the keel of the constellation Argo 253

Carine: name Ptolemy gave to the city of Kir 537

Carmenta: mother of Evander (939 BC) 70; introduced writing into @Italy (939 BC) 70

Carnea: 26th Olymiad games held here, where Terpander was the first man who won the music awards 213; location of the festival dedicated to @Apollo and instituted by the Piseans 304

Carpathus: island first settled by the soldiers of @Minos 395

Carrhae: another name for Haran 525; 535; 550

Carteia: built in Spain by the @Tyrians and @Hercules (Tyrian) 291; city founded by the @Tyrians 285; formerly called Heracleia 291; shortened name of Melcarteia 292

Carthadas: original name for Carthage 224

Carthage: built in North Africa by the @Tyrians 291; city founded by the @Tyrians 285; destroyed by the Romans 224; 225; founded by @Dido 224; 286; 96; sent an annual tithe to @Hercules (Tyrian) in @Tyre 295

Carthaginians: settled on the island of @Erythea 289

Caspian Sea: @Gozan located on 539; some of Galilee transplanted here by the @Assyrians 549

Cassander: first king of Macedon 205

Cassiopia: constellation is related to Perseus 254

Cassiteris: tin imported from here by @Midacritus 292

Castor: brother of Clytemnestra 324; brother of Helen 324; husband of Phoebe 324; son of Leda 253; twin brother of Pollux 253; 324; an Argonaut 253; Greeks built a temple to him 359; returned from the Argonaut Expedition while Theseus was still imprisoned by @Aidoneus 229; young man when he went on the Argonaut Expedition 324

Castor: constellation shaped like the Argonaut by the same name 253

Catacombs: passages under Rome and Naples used as homes by some 404

Catholikim: titles for the treasurers in Solomon's temple 643

Cato: relates the founding of @Carthage 224

Caucasus (Mount): @Bacchus left Prometheus here 422; @Sesostris left Prometheus here 227; 233; 451; 60; Prometheus freed from here by @

Hercules (Idean) (933 BC) 75; Prometheus stayed here for thirty years until he was released by @Hercules (Idean) 232

Caucon: taught the mysteries of Ceres in Messene (1002 BC) 42

Cecropia: built by Cecrops I in Attica (1076 BC) 20; later called Athens (1076 BC) 20; name of the citadel in @Athens built by Cecrops I 384; one of twelve cities where Cecrops I resettled a number of smaller towns 388

Cecrops I: husband of Agraule 382; before his reign Attica was divided into separate towns, each having magistrates and a town hall 388; built @Cecropia in Attica (1076 BC) 20; built the citadel in @Athens called @Cecropia 384; came with a colony into Greece 436; Egyptian from Sais who sailed to Cyprus and then to Attica 382; in his days the wars of the great gods of Egypt against the Greeks occurred 517; in his time women fought along side men in similar clothes and manner as the @Amazons 464; in his times towns began to be consolidated into cities 391; led a colony into Greece (1121 BC) 14; one of the leaders of a colony of @Shepherds fleeing from Egypt to Asia Minor or Greece 376; reigned in Attica 382; 28; succeeded as king of @Athens by Cranaus 330

Cecrops II: brother of Pandion 319; 43; son of @Erechtheus 319; deposed by Pandion his younger brother with help from Metionides 319; reigned in Attica (1002 BC) 42

Celeus: father of Triptolemus 318; 32; son of Rharus 330; alive when Ceres came into Attica 318; contemporary with @Erechtheus 330; contemporary with @Erechtheus, Eumolpus, Ceres, @Jasius, Cadmus, Harmonia, @Asterius and Dardanus 319; contemporary with Arcas, Eumelus, Triptolemus and @Erechtheus 334; contemporary with Saturn 351; Greeks built a temple to him 359; his family served as priests at Eleusis in the temple to Ceres 318; king of Eleusis 330; 32; lived in the Silver Age 366

Centaur: right hand of the constellation contains a star that passes through the colure of the equinoxes 251

Centaurs: name of the people of @Thessaly (956 BC) 64

Cephalus: husband of Procris 328; son of Deioneus 328

Cepheus: brother of Amphidamus 333; brother of Auge 333; brother of Lycurgus 333; father of Andromeda 325; grandson of Belus (Egyptian) 325; son of Aleus 333; appointed king of Joppa by @Ammon (1010 BC) 38; lived in Joppa in the days of Solomon 326

Cepheus: neck of the constellation contains a star that passes through the colure of the solstices 252; 262

Cephissia: one of twelve cities where Cecrops I resettled a number of smaller towns 388

Cephus: constellation is related to Perseus 254

Ceres: mother of Proserpina 319; 320; 32; wife of @Jasius 318; 321; came into Attica from Sicily looking for her daughter Proserpina 319; 320; Car built a temple to her 378; 43; contemporary with Saturn 351; educated Triptolemus and taught him to sow grain 318; her mysteries taught by Caucon in Messene (1002 BC) 42; lived in the Silver Age 366; mysteries instituted to her by Eumolpus at Eleusis 357; 41; Sicilian women who went to Attica to look for her kidnapped daughter Proserpina (1026 BC) 32

Cerethites: another name for the Crethim 341

Cerpheres: another name for Chephron 493

Cetus: constellation is related to Perseus 254; contained stars on the colure for the equinoxes 259; head of the constellation contains a star that passes through the colure of the equinoxes 251

Chabor: country @Salmanasser deported conquered peoples to 550; likely another name for Iberia 554

Chaboras: another name for Habor 538

Chaddon: name of an @Assyrian god 519

Chaitus: translated Phoenician histories into Greek 296

Chalach: another name for Halah 539; country @Salmanasser deported conquered peoples to 550

Chalach: likely another name for Colchis 554

Chalcidians: settled at Leontini in Sicily 299

Chalcis: centre in @Euboea for its copper works 336; place in @Euboea that sent out a colony to Sicily 299

Chaldea: adopted the Egyptian solar year and began the era of Nabonassar (747 BC) 95; 247; astrology spread here from Egypt 625; conquered by @Sesostris and @Memnon 526; exaggerated their history 518; foundation laid on which to build a more exact chronology for it 309;

idolatry began here and spread to @Phoenicia and the neighbouring countries 362; its army under Nabopolassar 563; its astronomers counted the reigns of their kings by the years of Nabonassar 573; likely conquered by @Belus (Assyrian) or @Pul 547; location of Babylon 548; location of the city of Ur 411; on the southern border of @Babylonia 622; one place the @Edomites propagated their skills to 444; part of the @Assyrian Empire at its height 554; part of the kingdom of Nimrod 524; ruled by Noah 409; source of a fiery wind 502; source of idolatry that spread worldwide 411; writing, astronomy, architecture and agriculture introduced here by sailors 442

Chaldean: nationality of @Zoroaster 656; nationality of Berosus 543

Chaldeans: @Nabonnedus was their last king 632; adopted the Egyptian solar year and began the era of Nabonassar (747 BC) 95; Babylon located in their land 547; bragged they were astronomers for over seven hundred and thirty thousand years 194; called @Sesostris by the name of Belus (Egyptian) 273; captured @Jerusalem and destroyed the temple in the eleventh year of Zedekiah 609; claimed to have observed the stars for almost five hundred thousand years 518; descended from Egyptian colonies to @Babylonia 626; destroyed the @Assyrian Empire with the help of the Medes 564; did not conquer @Persia until after the ninth year of @Nebuchadnezzar 606; did not immediately subdue @Persia after the destruction of @Nineveh 603; imparted their skill in astronomy to @Zoroaster 656; Jehoiakim did not revolt from them while their armies were close by 578; made a celestial sphere 625; monuments used by @Abydenus to write a history 544; Persian religion partly based on their institutions 657; priests appointed by Belus (Babylonian) who observed the stars 445; taught @Zoroaster 654; 655; taught astronomy by Helladius according to Hyginus 442; their priesthood established by the Egyptians (951 BC) 66; used a cycle called *Sarus* for calculating time 243; were colonies of the Egyptians who became famous for astrology 498; worshipped the sun, the fire, dead men and images 659

Chalonitis: another name for Calneh 531; name given to the area controlled by @Chalonitis 536; part of the Babylonian Empire by Mount Zagrus 621; part of the kingdom of Nimrod 524

Charilaus: another name for Charillus (708 BC) 122; 216

Charillus: son of Polydectes 216; killed before his son was born 216; king of Sparta (708 BC) 122; Spartan king descended from the family of Procles 204; tutored by Lycurgus (708 BC) 122

Charops: first decennial archon of the Athenians (647 BC) 135

Chazene: part of the Babylonian Empire 621

Chelae: autumnal equinox was in the middle of this constellation at the time of the Argonaut Expedition 256; middle of the constellation contains a star that passes through the colure of the equinoxes 251; modern name is Scorpio (935 BC) 73; 250; Zodiac constellation of the autumnal equinox at the time of the Argonaut Expedition (935 BC) 73; 250

Chelbes: king of @Tyre 589

Chembis: another name for Cheops 493; 514; king of Egypt according to Diodorus 513

Chemmis: another name for Cheops 493

Chemnis: another name for Cheops 493

Chen-El-Adon: example of an @Assyrian name compounded with the name of one of the @Assyrian gods 519

Cheops: built the largest of the three pyramids at @Memphis 493; in the reduced king list of Diodorus 514; king of Egypt (838 BC) 101; king of Egypt according to Herodotus 483; king of Egypt according to Herodotus and Newton 486

Chephron: father of @Mycerinus 493; father of Nitocris 493; built the second large pyramid 493; 103; in the reduced king list of Diodorus 514; king of Egypt according to Diodorus 513; king of Egypt according to Herodotus 483; king of Egypt according to Herodotus and Newton 486; ruled Egypt 103

Cheres: another name for Mycerinus 493

Cherinus: another name for Mycerinus 493; 513

Chersonesus: visited by the Argonauts 480

Chiniladon: example of an @Assyrian name 519

Chios: island populated by Macarius 395; near the city of @Erythra 287; one of the twelve cities in the common council called Panionium 310

Chiron: father of Hippo 253; son of Philyra 345; 367; 28; son of Saturn (Cretan) 28; 345; 367; born in the Golden Age (c. 1020 BC) 73; colures have drifted 36° 29' from his time until 1689 AD 263; had two grandsons in the Argonaut Expedition 345; helped Musaeus make the celestial sphere to assist in navigation by the Argonauts 256; invented the constellations 367; lived in the Silver Age 367; made a celestial sphere for the Greeks 625; wrote the book *The Battle of the Titans* 253

Chiron: constellation is related to Crolus the son of the nurse of Muses 254; constellation shaped like this man who was the teacher of Jason 253

Chisleu: month Zechariah received a vision from God 571

Chloris: daughter of Amphion 317; daughter of Niobe 317; mother of Periclymenus 317

Christians: called @Artaxerxes Longimanus @*Artahascht* 664; religion derived from the primitive religion of Noah 412

Chryses: mother of Idaeus 358; wife of Dardanus 358; learned about the Samothracian mysteries in Arcadia 358

Chthonius: led a colony into Syme 395

Chyniladon: last king of @Assyria 563; 567; likely another name for Nabuchodonosor 561; succeeded Saosduchinus as king of @Assyria (647 BC) 135; succeeded Saosduchinus at Babylon 558

Cicero: documents how the Sicilians and the Greeks made the lunar and solar years agree 236; documents that Digiti in Crete offered sacrifices at the tomb of @Hercules (Idean) 356; documents the existence of three Jupiters 346; stated that @Hercules (Egyptian) was the son of Nile (951 BC) 66; stated that Cyrus lived to the age of seventy years 595; thought the father of the Cretan @Jupiter was @Saturn (Cretan) who fled to @Italy from Crete 348

Cilicia: abandoned the Medes when the @Assyrians attacked the Medes 558; Cadmus with his brothers led colonies of @Sidonians here 282; conquered by @Bacchus and @Minerva 422; conquered by Holofernes 560; part of the @Assyrian Empire at its height 554; part of the Babylonian Empire 621; ruled by @Sardanapalus 557; ruled by King Syennesis 608; Solon visited here after seeing Croesus 307; some @Sidonians fled here 283

Cilix: led a colony of @Phoenicians and @Syrians fleeing from Sidon and from David (1041 BC) 28; 283

Cimmerians: lived as wanderers in Europe (1121 BC) 14

Cinyras: father of @Gingris 459; husband of @Venus 417; 482; husband of Metharme 225; built Paphos according to Apollodorus 225; built temples 454; called Vulcan 482; consecrated a temple of Paphian @Venus 458; deified his son @Gingris under the name of @Adonis 459; lived until the times of the Trojan War 482; made armour for Egyptian kings 482; name given to Thoas for his skill with the harp 457; reigned over Cyprus and part of @Phoenicia for the kings of Egypt 482

Circutium: another name for Carchemish 535; 565; 575

Cirrha: attacked by the armies of the Amphictyonic Council (570 BC) 156; 302

Cirrheans: conquered by the armies of the Amphictyonic Council (570 BC) 156; conquered in year two of the 47th Olympiad according to the Arundelian Marbles 302; 303

Cissia: mother of @Memnon 477; mother of @Menes 68; wife of Zerah 68; 477

Cisus: son of Temenus 301; his son did not reign in @Argos 305; reigned in @Argos after his father Temenus 301

Clazomenae: one of the twelve cities in the common council called Panionium 310

Cleitarchus: states that @Sardanapalus died of old age after he had lost control of Syria 556

Clement: calls the Idean Dactyli barbarians meaning strangers 339

Cleobulus: described the ancient calendar year of the Greeks 238; one of the seven wise men of Greece 238

Cleodius: father of Aristomachus 222; son of Hyllus 222; killed in the third attempt of the Heraclides to return 222

Cleombrotus: created Heraea by consolidating nine towns 389

Cleomenes: Spartan king descended from Eurysthenes 209

Cleonymus: another name for Cleombrotus 389

Cleostratus: modified the *Octaeteris* cycle in the times of the Persian Empire 240

Cleson: brother of Eurotas 381; brother of Myles 381; brother of Polycaon 381; father of Pylas 381; husband of the daughter of Pandion 381; son of Lelex 381

Clisthenes: father of Agarista 156; 302; commanded the forces of the Amphictyons (570 BC) 156; commander of an army against Cirrha 302; contemporary with Phidon 156; king of @Sicyon 302

Clitior: king of Arcadia 333

Clomas: Greek musician 217

Clydon: brother of Pleuron (1006 BC) 39; son of Aetolus (1006 BC) 39; son of Pronoe (1006 BC) 39; built a city in Aetolia (1006 BC) 39

Clymenus: grandson of @Hercules (Idean) 354; erected statues in Olympia to @Europa, @Hercules (Idean) and the rest of the @Curetes 354

Clytemnestra: sister of Castor 324; sister of Helen 324; sister of Pollux 324; very young at the time of the Argonaut Expedition 324

Cnidia: another name for Calycopis or Venus (930 BC) 78; 458

Cocalus: fought with @Minos (961 BC) 61; king of Sicily 61

Cochome: small pyramids built here by @Amenophis (901 BC) 89

Codrus: father of Androcles 310; father of Cyaretus 310; father of Medon 310; father of Neleus 310; early Athenian king 310; his sons led the Ionic migration (794 BC) 107; killed in the war with Sparta (804 BC) 105; king of the Athenians (804 BC) 105

Coele Syria: ruled by @Nebuchadnezzar 580; ruled by Pharaoh Necho 576

Colchis: @Sesostris left Aeetes here around the fourteenth year of Rehoboam 329; @Sesostris left Aeetes here with a part of his army to guard that pass 314; Aeetes left here by @Bacchus 422; Aeetes left here by @Sesostris (962 BC) 60; destination Phrixus fled to from his stepmother Ino (958 BC) 63; part of the @Assyrian Empire at its height 554; Phrixus and Helle fled here to Aeetes 327; Phrixus fled here 253; place @Sesostris left his geographic tables of his conquests (962 BC) 60; place the Scythians were forced to retreat to by @Cyaxeres (607 BC) 144; populated by @Sesostris 451; ruled by Aeetes until the time of the Argonaut Expedition 227; visited by the Argonauts in the ship *Argo* 479; 480

Colophon: destroyed by internal discord 617; one of the twelve cities in the common council called Panionium 310

Comeas: archon of @Athens when Solon returned from his first travels 307

Conon: relates that Crotopus left @Argos and built a new city for himself in Megaris 326

Constantius: moved the obelisk of @Rhampsinitus in Heliopolis to Rome 490

Coptic: @Memphis called @Manphtha in this language 275; language extended over Egypt 482

Coptos: capital of one of several Egyptian kingdoms under a Shepherd king 13; capital of one of the smaller kingdoms in Egypt 431; Egyptian fleet constructed near this place 438; 439; 446; first capital of Egypt after the expulsion of the @Shepherds 482; its Egyptian inhabitants helped expel the @Shepherds from Egypt 363

Coraebus: victor in the first Olympic Games in 776 BC 209; 211; 215

Corcyra: island home of the Pheaces and their King Alcinous 256

Corcyreans: defeated by the Corinthians in the oldest navel battle in recorded history (657 BC) 132; 298

Corinth: Archias led a colony from here into Sicily 299; 118; built by Sisyphus about the latter end of the reign of Solomon or the beginning of the reign of Rehoboam 329; freed from the rule of tyrants after the death of Periander (557 BC) 159; full of fables about the war of the gods and the Titans according to Lucian 467; one of its shipwrights built four ships for the Samians 298; originally called Ephyra by its founder Sisyphus 384; ruled by Cypselus 221; ruled by Prytanes after the expulsion of its kings (658 BC) 131; ruled by Sisyphus (979 BC) 51

Corinthians: built larger ships with three tiers of oars called triremes 298; defeated the Corcyreans in the oldest navel battle in recorded history (657 BC) 132; first to build ships with three banks of oars, called triremes (697 BC) 125

Corinthius: Greek artist 217

Cornwall: another name for the island of Cassiteris 292

Corona Bornealis: constellation is related to Ariadne's crown 254

Corsica: visited by the Argonauts 480

Corvus: constellation shaped like the raven and associated with the constellation of Hydra 253

Corybantes: another name for the Curetes 457; 28; name of the Curetes who settled in @Phrygia 336

Corybantes: name of the *Priests of Cybele* given to them by Corybas 358

Corybas: called the priests of @Cybele @Corybantes 358

Cos: island populated by Macarius 395

Cossaea: country east of @Babylonia 622

Court of Judicature: located on the eastern gate of the @*People's Court* in Solomon's temple 643

Cranaus: father of Pandion 331; father of Rharus 330; between his reign and @Erechtheus, chronologers added @Erichthonius and his son Pandion 331; flood of Deucalion occurred during his reign 332; king of part of Attica at the same time as Amphictyon (1003 BC) 41; Lycaon died before him leaving time for Deucalion's flood between their deaths 334; received his kingdom from Cecrops I 382; reigned in Attica (1041 BC) 28; successor of Cecrops I 28; 330

Crater: constellation shaped like Medea's cup and associated with the constellation of Hydra 253

Creon: first annual archon of the Athenians (607 BC) 144

Cres: Curete after whom Crete was named and raised @Jupiter 401

Cresphontes: brother of Aristodemus 222; brother of Temenus 222; son of Aristomachus 222; king of Messene 204

Cretan Bacchus: name Greeks gave to Bacchus because he buried his wife there 278

Cretans: identified four ages with their deified kings and princes 364; mythology differed from the Egyptians and Libyans in some points 470; say that @Jupiter was born and buried among them and showed his grave 346; say that @Neptune was the first man to outfit a fleet 466; showed the foundations of the house where @Rhea (Cretan) lived 345; their gods @Saturn (Cretan), @Rhea (Cretan) and @Jupiter correspond to @Asterius, @Europa, and @Minos 342; thought the tomb of @Minos was really the tomb of @Jupiter (Cretan) 348

Crete: @Curetes who settled here were called Idean Dactyli 336; @Europa fled here from Sidon before Cadmus left Sidon around 1042 BC 308; @Minos introduced agriculture and laws here 401; @Saturn (Cretan) expelled from here by his son @Jupiter (Cretan) 349; @Vulcan went here to practise metallurgy 458; *Great Year* of Cadmus and @Minos brought here by the @Phoenicians 240; called the land of the @Curetes 341; colonised by Teutamus 354; contains a promontory called Erythraeum 287; contains the grave of @Minos, which was mistaken for the grave of @Jupiter 347; first inhabitants called Eteocretans 400; home of Talus who was killed by the Argonauts 365; location of Mount Ida 353; 30; location of the cave in Mount Ida in which @Minos was raised 404; location of the cave where @Jupiter was raised 345; location of the grave of the Cretan @Jupiter 346; location of the tomb of @Minos 348; near the Cyclades Islands 395; Phoenician letters introduced here by the @Curetes 339; received eight young men and eight young virgins every eight years from @Athens 277; Rhadamanthus led colonies from here to the Greek islands 457; ruled by @Asterius 342; 367; ruled by @Minos 319; 342; 37; Saturn fled from here to @Italy 351; settled by colonies of @Phoenicians and @Syrians fleeing from Sidon and from David (1041 BC) 28; some @Sidonians fled here 283; Theseus made expedition into 278; visited by @Thoas on his way to Lemnos (975 BC) 53; visited by Lycurgus 216

Cretheus: brother of Calyce 327; father of Aeson 327; son of Aeolus 327

Crethim: people among the @Philistines who may have colonised Crete and were there called Curetes 341

Creusa: daughter of @Erechtheus 228; 31; mother of Achaeus 319; mother of Aegeus 228; mother of Ion 319; wife of Xuthus 319; 328; 31

Croesei: name of gold coins minted by Croesus 614

Croesus: king of Sardis 306; chonologers made Solon too old to be alive to meet with him 5; conquered by Cyrus 596; conquered by Cyrus with the help of @Harpagus 630; incredibly wealthy king 613; interviewed Solon 4; 161; minted gold coins called *Croesei* 614; reigned fourteen years 306; sent messengers to the oracle at Delphi 302; 303; some chronologers thought his interview with Solon was fictitious 200; subdued all of Asia Minor as far as the Halys River by the time he was visited by Solon 307; visited by Solon around 550 BC 308

Crolus: related to the constellation of @Chiron 254

Croton: city founded in @Italy by @Hercules (Egyptian) 399

Crotopus: left @Argos and built a new city for himself in Megaris 326

Ctesias: attributed the destruction of the @Assyrian Empire to the Chaldeans and the Medes 564; greatly exaggerated the age of the @Assyrian Empire 8; made gross errors in the history of @Assyria and Media 521; most of the names in his king list for @Assyria are not @Assyrian 520; says that Arbaces a Mede was admitted to see @Sardanapalus in his palace and he saw his voluptuous life among women 556; states that Semiramis was a widow of one of @Pul's sons and built Babylon 543; thought that the @Assyrian Empire was almost as old as Noah's flood 519; thought the @Assyrian Empire ended over two hundred and fifty years before the Median Empire 523

Cupid: her fishes are related to the constellation of Pisces 254

Curetes: @Hercules (Idean), Poeonius, Epimedes, @Jasius and Ida were @Curetes and went to Elis 353; @Phoenicians skilled in the arts and sciences 336; brought their sciences with them from @Phoenicia 457; Clymenus erected statues to them in Olympia 354; danced around @Jupiter (Cretan) in armour, with a great noise so that his father Saturn (Cretan) might not hear him cry 341; from their arrival in Europe to the destruction of Troy were four generations 365; inhabited a country in Achaia into which Aetolus fled (1006 BC) 39; introduced into Greece letters, music, poetry, dancing and arts and attended to the sacrifices 340; introduced Phoenician letters into @Phrygia and Crete and established the trades of metallurgy and carpentry in Greece 339; likely created the fable of the first four ages 367; name of a mysterious religious sect bringing arts and sciences of @Phoenicia with them (1041 BC) 28; raised @Jupiter in a cave in Mount Ida in Crete 345; were Philistines according to Bochart 401

Curtius: ascribes the building of Babylon to @Belus (Assyrian) or @Pul 543

Cuth: its people transplanted by @Esarhaddon to Samaria 534

Cuth: another name for Susa 536

Cuthah: transplanted by @Esarhaddon into the regions of Samaria and @Damascus 504

Cy: prefix meaning *Prince* 594

Cyaretus: brother of Androcles 310; brother of Medon 310; brother of Neleus 310; son of Codrus 310; went to Asia from @Athens 310

Cyaxeres: brother of Amyite 563; 633; brother of Mandane 633; 147; brother-in-law of @Nebuchadnezzar 563; father of @Darius the Mede 598; 151; 146; son of Astyages 562; 563; 596; 597; 598; 147; uncle of Cyrus (599 BC) 147; also called Ahasuerus or Axeres 596; 597; another name for Achsuerus given by Greek writers 594; attacked Alyattes, the king of Lydia (590 BC) 149; attacked and destroyed @Nineveh with help from the Chaldeans 564; conquered many nations 610; corresponds to the name Lohorasp in Persian history 694; ended the Scythian invasion by killing its leaders at a feast 600; first conqueror and founder of the empire of the Medes 599; forced the Scythians to retreat beyond @Colchis and @Iberia, (607 BC) 144; fourth king of Media and started the conquest of all Asia 593; helped @Nebuchadnezzar overthrow @Nineveh (610 BC) 143; Herodotus and Xenophon confounded him with his father Astyages 595; incorrectly is thought to be the last king of Media by Xenophon 631; killed the Scythian leaders at a feast he held 562; made peace with Alyattes and had his son @Darius marry Alyattes' daughter Ariene 608; made war on Lydia when the Scythians fled there 607; recovered the @Assyrian provinces of @Persia and Parthia 566; 588; reigned for forty years 598; reigned over the Medes (600 BC) 146; seized the @Assyrian provinces of @Armenia, Pontus and Cappadocia (607 BC) 144; warred with @Armenia and Cappadocia after @Nineveh was taken 611; what he did between the conquering of @Nineveh and @Persia is unknown 606

Cy-Axeres: another name for Achsuerus 594; another name for Astibares 576

Cybele: daughter of Meones 358; husband of @Jasius 358; mother of Corybas 358; called the *Mother of the Gods* after her own name 358

Cybele: mysteries of @Rhea (Cretan) were instituted here (1003 BC) 41; mysteries of the goddess the *Great Mother* were observed here 340

Cyclades Islands: near Crete and uninhabited before the times of @Minos 395

Cygnus: colure of the solstice passes within 1° of two stars in this constellation 262; constellation shaped like the swan of Leda the mother of Castor and Pollux 253; right wing and neck of the constellation each contain a star that passes through the colure of the solstices 252

Cyndaraxis: another name for Anacyndaraxis 557

Cynortes: son of Amyclas 324

Cyprian: says that @Calycopis was born from the sea and was painted sailing upon a shell 459; states that @Saturn (Cretan) was driven from Crete by his son @Jupiter (Cretan) 348

Cyprus: @Cinyras smelted copper ore here 459; @Thoas appointed king here by @Sesostris (963 BC) 59; @Thoas built a temple to deify @Calycopis here (930 BC) 78; Agapenor built Paphos here after the Trojan War 333; Cecrops I sailed here from Egypt on his way to Attica 382; city of @Erythra located here 287; inhabited after the @Phoenicians discovered it 402; location of early temples 454; ruled by @Cinyras under the Egyptian kings 482; ruled by @Thoas until he died (912 BC) 85; ruled by @Vulcan 458; ruled by Pharnaces 457; settled by Teucer seven years after the Trojan War 293; stopping off place for colonies of @Shepherds fleeing from Egypt to Asia Minor or Greece 376; Teucer built Salamis here (897 BC) 90; Teucer came here seven years after the destruction of Troy and built Salamis 225; Teucer's family ruled there until Evagoras 293; visited by Solon on his travels 307

Cypselus: between the reign of Lycaon and his reign eleven kings ruled Arcadia 335; king of @Corinth 221; king of Arcadia 204; 333; ruled @Corinth after the reign of the annual archons 329

Cyrene: built on the site of the city of Irasa by Battus (633 BC) 139; 467; ruled by Euripylus 480; visited by the Argonauts 480

Cyrus: brother-in-law of @Darius the Mede 595; father of @Cambyses 651; 667; father of @Smerdis 651; grandson of Astyages 596; 597; son of @Cambyses 633; son of Mandane (599 BC) 147; @Assyrians called @Syrians by the Greeks in his time 554; @Darius Hystaspes reigned after him 687; @Ezra and Nehemiah ratified a covenant during his reign 684; @Persia was not free until his reign 606; @Persians omit his reign 696; @Pherecydes of Syria taught men to write in prose in his reign 197; adversaries of @Judah interrupted their building and hired counsellors against the Jews during his reign 674; captured and ruled in @Babylonia in the fourteenth year of the @Tyrian King Hirom 590; captured Babylon (538 BC) 164; captured Babylon eight years before he died 306; captured Babylon ending the reign of @Nabonnedus 584; captured Sardis 596; 597; 163; captured Sardis in 544 BC, Babylon in 538 BC and Ecbatana 537 BC 308; commissioned Zerubbabel to rebuild the temple 648; conquered Asia 1; conquered Croesus and Asia Minor with the help of @Harpagus 630; conquered Croesus and Sardis 303; cut the Gindus River into three hundred and sixty channels 243; defeated @Darius at @Pasargadae 631; defeated @Darius the Mede 633; defeated @Darius the Mede and the empire became Persian (537 BC) 165; died (530 BC) 167; first king of the Persian Empire 205; 667; 685; found much wealth in Asia Minor 613; Herodotus erred in naming his father 599; his army each year was supplied with provisions by conquered countries 623; his history was outlined during his reign 677; history before his time is too long by almost two hundred per cent 210; history of the Jews can be deduced by comparing the books of @Ezra and Nehemiah 673; in the first year of his reign Nehemiah gives a list of the chief priests 676; insert his story in @Ezra to make that book parallel I Esdras 686; invaded @Babylonia and captured Babylon 591; Jewish history covers his reign 669; Jews returned in his first year 670; listed by Josephus as a king of @Persia 668; lived seventy years 595; 633; punished the Medes by conquering them 603; received the kingdom at Ecbatana 618; reigned seven years 598; revolted from @Darius the Mede 630; ruled after @Darius the Mede 619; ruled all Asia 593; ruled Babylon for nine years according to Ptolemy's Canon 595; ruled Egypt and Ethiopia 509; spent the seven winter months yearly at Babylon and the three spring months yearly at @Susa, and the two summer months at Ecbatana 632; succeeded by his son @Cambyses 651; temple was finished according to his command 688; third king who helped establish the Medo-Persian Empire 594; took @Darius prisoner 631

Cythera: @Calycopis sailed from @Phrygia to this island 459

Cytherea: another name for Calycopis or Venus (930 BC) 78; 458

Cytherus: one of twelve cities where Cecrops I resettled a number of smaller towns 388

Cyzicus: king of the Doliones 480; visited by the Argonauts 480

Daedalus: son of Eupalamus 319; 339; uncle of Talus 48; 339; co-inventor of the chip axe, the saw, the auger, the plumb level, the compass, the turning lath, glue and the potter's wheel 339; created the first statues with their feet apart to appear as though they were walking (985 BC) 48; fled to @Minos (983 BC) 50; murdered his nephew Talus 50; originated the carpentry trade in Europe 48; Theseus came to him from @Athens 278

Dagon: located in @Ashdod where the @Philistines brought the ark 455

Damascus: @Benhadad I built temples here 455; @Esarhaddon transplanted countries here 504; @Syrian army from here defeated by David (1042 BC) 27; @Syrians from here defeated by David 456; abandoned the Medes when the @Assyrians attacked the Medes 558; age of kingdom was exaggerated 194; capital city of Syria (852 BC) 99; capital of Syria from David's time 549; captured by Tiglathpileser, the king of @Assyria (740 BC) 115; conquered by @Assyria 533; conquered by Holofernes 560; conquered by Jeroboam II 528; 529; exaggerated their history 699; had its own king until it was conquered by the @Assyrians 525; location of temple built to @Benhadad II (895 BC) 92; on the west and south side of the @Assyrian Empire 535; people of @Kir transplanted here 534; ruled by Rezin 553; started their year on the vernal equinox 243; supplied troops to fight against David 271

Damascus: another name for the @Syrian King Hadad 456

Damophon: son of Pantaleon 304; suspected of treason by the Eleans 304

Dan: Jeroboam I set up the gods of Egypt here 471

Danae: daughter of Acrisius 324; 359; daughter of Eurydice 318; 324; 325; mother of Perseus 324; contemporary with @Erechtheus, @Jasius and Cadmus 328; Greeks built a temple to her 359; her mother dedicated the temple of Juno Argiva to her 325

Danaus: brother of @Aegyptus 445; brother of @Osiris

Danaus: father of Hypermnestra 325; son of Sthenelus 323; king of @Argos 323

Daniel: calls @Belshazzar the last king of Babylon 585; calls the son of @Cyaxeres, @Darius the Mede and @Cyaxeres, @Ahasuerus 596; deported to Babylon by @Nebuchadnezzar 576; his prophecy incorrectly applied to Herod, Judas, Theudas and Bar Kokhab 669; identifies the last king of the Medes as @Darius 631; states that @Darius the Mede was the son of @Achsuerus or @Ahasuerus 594; thought to be contemporary with @Darius Hystaspes by the @Persians 695

Daniel: priest who returned with @Ezra and Nehemiah in the first year of Cyrus 671

Danube River: @Scythia lays beyond this river 202

Darab: another name for Darius Codomannus 696; another name for Darius Hystaspes 660

Darab the Bastard: another name for Darius Nothus 696

Daranelles: Naea lies between here and Lemnos 396

Dardanus: brother of @Jasius 315; 321; 358; brother of Harmonia 315; father of Idaeus 358; husband of Chryses 358; wife of Chryses 358; contemporary with @Erechtheus, Celeus, Eumolpus, Ceres, @Jasius, Cadmus, Harmonia and Achaeus 319; instituted the Samothracian mysteries after his wife Chryses learned about them in Arcadia 358; second king of Troy 321

Darics: coined by @Darius the Mede after the conquest of Sardis 631; coined by @Darius the Mede from the gold and silver coins taken from Lydia 596; 612; 163; name of gold coins minted by @Darius the Mede 614

Darius Codomannus: confounded by Josephus and the Jews for Darius Nothus 668; conquered by @Alexander the Great 696; last king of @Persia (330 BC) 191; last king of the Persian Empire 678; 681; lost his kingdom at the battle of Gaugamela 666; murdered (330 BC) 191; ruled the Persian Empire (336 BC) 189

Darius Hystaspes: father of @Xerxes I 661; 685; son of Hystaspes 655; 656; 168; @Pherecydes Atheniensis wrote around the end of his reign 1; @Pherecydes of @Athens wrote a history of @Athens during his reign 197; adversaries of @Judah interrupted their building and hired counsellors against the Jews until his reign 674; Aeschylus introduces him complaining about his son @Xerxes I 593; began his reign in 521 BC 571; chosen king because his horse neighed first 653; commissioned Zerubbabel to rebuild the temple 648; contemporary with @Ostanes 657; five kings of the family of Eurysthenes, between the end of the first Messenian War, and the beginning of his reign 204; he and his predecessor added only seven new provinces to the empire 620; his history was outlined during his reign 677; his story is interrupted by the account of two other kings in the book of @Ezra 687; history of the Jews can be deduced by comparing the books of @Ezra and Nehemiah 673; insert his story in @Ezra to make that book parallel I Esdras 686; Jewish history covers his reign 669; Joiakim became the high priest in the sixteenth year of his reign 679; king of the Persian

Empire 685; 168; listed by Josephus as a king of @Persia 668; ordered the completion of the second temple (520 BC) 169; ruled from 521 BC to 485 BC 660; seventy years from @Nebuchadnezzar's invasion of @Judah to his second year 573; sometimes called Kischtasp by the @Persians and was contemporary with Daniel, Jeremiah and @Zoroaster 695; temple was rebuilt during his reign 675; 688; thought by the Jews to be Artaxerxes Longimanus 667; times of his reign were determined by eclipses recorded in Ptolemy's Canon 660

Darius Nothus: bastard son of @Artaxerxes Longimanus 665; father of @Artaxerxes Mnemon 666; @Jonathan became the high priest in the eighth year of his reign 679; called Darab by the @Persians 696; confounded by Josephus and the Jews for Darius Codomannus 668; during his reign Sanballat built a temple for his son-in-law Manasseh on Mount Gerizim 681; Nehemiah called him @Darius the Persian 693; reigned for eighteen years 665; ruled the Persian Empire (424 BC) 184; temple not built during his reign since he lived too long after the destruction of the temple 675

Darius the Mede: brother-in-law of Cyrus 595; husband of Ariene 608; 151; son of @Achsuerus 594; son of @Cyaxeres 596; 597; 598; 151; 146; @Persians sometimes call him Bahaman 696; Babylon was captured when he was sixty-two years old 595; captured Babylon with his brother-in-law Cyrus according to Jerome 618; coined Lydian money into @Darics 596; 597; confounded for Darius Hystaspes 695; defeated by Cyrus 631; 632; 633; 165; defeated twice by Cyrus 630; fifth and the last king of Media 593; finished extending the Medo-Persian Empire over all Asia 611; introduced the immutable laws of the Medes and @Persians to Babylon 619; Jews thought he was the successor of @Belshazzar 667; king in the Medo-Persian Empire 594; last king of the Medes 631; learned the art and use of money from the conquered kingdom of the Lydians 613; married Ariene to make an alliance between Lydia and the Medes 608; raised another army after being defeated by Cyrus 630; ratified a peace treaty with Lydia by marrying Ariene (585 BC) 151; recoined the gold Croesei coins into @Darics 614; recoined the gold coins into @Darics 612; 163; reigned (560 BC) 158; reigned for twenty-three years 598; ruled all of Asia 593; ruled over a hundred and twenty provinces 620; sometimes called Kischtasp by the @Persians 695

Darius the Persian: Jewish name for Artaxerxes Longimanus 667; 668; 693

Dathnis: another name for Tahaphenes 272

David: @Chiron was born about the thirty-fifth year of his reign 367; @Damascus was the capital of Syria from his time 549; @Edomites fled from him with their young king @Hadad to Egypt 441; @Europa and Cadmus left Sidon about the middle of his reign around 1041 BC 308; @Minos was born about the middle of his reign 278; @Sesostris was born near the end of his reign 273; @Tyre and Thebes (Greek) founded about the fifteenth or sixteenth year of his reign 283; Abibalus, Cadmus, Alymnus and @Europa fled from Sidon about the sixteenth year of his reign 297; about the same age as Teucer 321; Amphictyonic Council established toward the end of his reign or the beginning of the reign of Solomon 330; ancestor of Josiah 560; 561; appointed king (1055 BC) 24; captured the Red Sea trade route through @Edom 439; colonies led into Greece from Egypt and @Phoenicia in his time 436; committed adultery with Bathsheba 271; conquered @Edom in the twelfth year of his reign 281; conquered and expelled the @Edomites 438; 440; 25; conquered the @Syrians of Zobah and @Damascus (1042 BC) 27; conquered the king of Zobah 525; contemporary with Hellen 320; Cranaus may have received his kingdom about the beginning his reign 382; defeated @Ammon and Syria 272; defeated the @Syrians from Zobah and @Damascus 456; drove out the @Edomites who fled to @Phoenicia in large numbers 290; during his reign, kings ruled at @Thebes (Egyptian) 699; enemy of the @Philistines 287; flood of Deucalion occurred about the fourteenth year of his reign 335; forced the @Edomites to flee from the Red Sea 286; forced the @Edomites to flee to the @Philistines 282; forced the @Phoenicians and @Syrians to flee to other lands (1041 BC) 28; in his time an earlier @Hercules (Tyrian) from @Tyre may have established trade on the Red Sea 295; in his time writing, astronomy, architecture and agriculture came into Chaldea 442; Labdacus was born at the end of his reign 315; likely conscripted fleeing @Shepherds to help build @Jerusalem and the temple 373; lived about the time of @Erechtheus 325; lived when Polydorus was born 314; Lycaon likely died about the middle of his reign 334; Thebans (Egyptian) and the @Ethiopians built a large empire in his days 460; towns and houses in

Europe did not predate his days 415; writing not mentioned before his time except among the posterity of Abraham 444

Dea Cypria: Calycopis or Venus was the goddess of Cyprus (930 BC) 78; 458

Dea Syria: Calycopis or Venus was the goddess of Syria (930 BC) 78; 458

Decelia: one of twelve cities where Cecrops I resettled a number of smaller towns 388

December: tenth month in the Roman calendar 243

Dehavites: transplanted by @Esarhaddon to Samaria 534; 552

Deioneus: father of Cephalus 328; son of Aeolus 328

Dejoces: father of @Phraortes 561; 561; first king of Media 556; 593; may also be the same man as Arphaxad 558; ruled Media for fifty-three years 561

Delos: island formed in the sea by an earthquake 395; 396

Delphi: council was set up here under the leadership of Acrisius (1003 BC) 41; served by the first priestess to @Apollo named Phemonoe 330

Delphi (Oracle of): received messengers from Croesus 302; 303

Delton: another name for the constellation of Antinous 255

Demaratus: Spartan king descended from Procles 209

Demetrius Phalereus: Athenians built three hundred and sixty statues to him 240

Demophon: king of @Corinth before the return of the Heraclides 329

Demophoon: son of Phaedra (903 BC) 88; son of Theseus (903 BC) 88; early Athenian king 310; ruled @Athens (903 BC) 88

Deucalion: father of Amphictyon 330; 41; father of Hellen 327; 330; 41; 29; father of Protogenia 327; grandfather of Aethlius (1031 BC) 30; about two generations older than @Erechtheus 328; died a few years before the reign of @Erechtheus 332; fled with his sons Hellen and Amphictyon from the flood in @Thessaly to Attica 330; lived around 1076 BC 20; Nyctimus ruled Arcadia during his lifetime (1042 BC) 27

Deucalion: incorrectly thought to be the son of Prometheus 370

Deucalion: father of Idomeneus 344; grandson of @Europa 367; son of @Minos 344; youngest son of @Minos 297; 317; an Argonaut 297; 317; 344; ruled at the time of the Argonaut Expedition 367

Deucalion (Flood of): @Japetus lived two generations after it 370; Clymenus came into Crete fifty years after the flood and held the Olympic Games 354; happened about the fourteenth year of David's reign 335; happened between the deaths of Lycaon and Cranaus 334; happened in the reign of Cranaus 382; happened just after Pelasgus died 377; inundated @Thessaly 330; occurred a few years before the reign of @Erechtheus 332; occurred at most two or three generations after the flood of Ogyges 372; occurred before the generation in Greece called the Golden Age (1041 BC) 28; occurred two or three generations after the days of Lelex 391; preceded the first four ages in Greece 371

Dia: another name for the island of Naxos 277; 310

Dicaearchus: incorrectly inserted two fictitious generations into Egyptian history 419

Dido: wife of Hiabias 224; founded @Carthage 224; 96; sailed along North Africa past the Syrtes to found @Carthage 286; Teucer came from the war of Troy to Cyprus in his days 225; way prepared for him by previous explorations of @Hercules (Tyrian) 295

Dieteris: two year cycle used by the Greeks consisting of twenty-five thirty day months 240

Dii magni maiorum gentium: Great Gods of the Greater Nations (959 BC) 62; 363; 464

Dii Paenates: name of household gods 360

Dinaites: transplanted by @Esarhaddon to Samaria 534; 552

Dindymene: mysteries of the goddess the *Great Mother* were observed here 340

Diocles of Peparethius: early Greek historian from whom Quintus Fabius Pictor copied most of his history 201

Diodorus: ascribes the three hundred and sixty-five day year to the Egyptians at Thebes 245; before his time the Egyptian priests had greatly inflated the number of their kings 9; calls @Minerva by the name of @Myrina 422; confounded the flight of Moses with the expulsion of the @Shepherds to Palestine 435; documented early Greek history according to Apollodorus and Eratosthenes 203; documents the exaggerated claims of the Chaldeans 518; from the time of Herodotus to his time the Egyptian priests had greatly increased the number of their kings 483; his history before Cyrus is too long by almost two hundred per cent 210; his king list contains many extraneous kings 514; his king list when compared to Herodotus exposes the fraud of the priests and his list of kings should not be used to correct Herodotus 517; identifies three men called @Hercules 461; places @Uchoreus between @Osymandias and @Myris, that is, between @Amenophis and @Moeris 492; says @Uranus the father of @Hyperion used a three hundred and sixty-five day year 241; says that @Hercules (Egyptian) went over a great part of the world and set up pillars in North Africa (951 BC) 66; says that @Nilus was that king who constructed canals in Egypt to make the river more useful 453; says that after the reign of Saturn (Egyptian) and Rhea (Egyptian), then reigned @Jupiter and Juno, the parents of @Osiris and @Isis and the grandparents of @Orus and @Bubaste 363; says that the @Amazons lived originally in @Libya, and there reigned over the Atlanteans, and invaded their neighbours and conquered as far as Europe 423; says that the Cyclades Islands near Crete were at first desolate and uninhabited 395; says that the Egyptians of Thebes used no intercalary months, nor deducted any days from the month as was done by most of the Greeks 235; says that the seven islands called the Aeolides between @Italy and Sicily, were uninhabited until Lipparus and Aeolus settled there from @Italy 397; states @Ammon is also called @Uranus 405; states @Osiris built two temples in @Thebes (Egyptian) 425; states that @Antaea had its name from @Antaeus 467; states that many Egyptian cities were founded by the gods 454; states that the Chaldeans are Egyptian colonies in @Babylonia 626; states that the Chaldeans in Babylon were colonies of the Egyptians who became famous for astrology 498; states that the Egyptians sent many colonies into other countries 445

Diomedes: king of Bistones in @Thrace 293; thrown to the horses by @Hercules (Idean) 293

Dionysius of Halicarnassus: says @Hercules (Egyptian) was contemporary with Evander 399; says @Pherecydes of @Athens was one of the best historians 197; says that @Oenotrus found in the western part of @Italy a large thinly populated region suitable for pasture and agriculture 352; says that Dardanus instituted the Samothracian mysteries 358; says that in the time of the Trojan War, Latinus was king of the natives in @Italy, and that in the sixteenth generation after that war, Romulus built Rome 226; says that the Nile was called @Siris by the @Ethiopians and @Nilus by the people of Siene 453; states that the first inhabitants of Sicily were a Spanish people who fled from the Ligures in @Italy 398; states that the new kingdom of Rome, as Romulus left it, consisted of thirty courts or councils in thirty towns 393

Dionysius Petavius: computed the longitude of Pleiades 265

Dionysus: another name for Osiris 461; Arabian name for Bacchus 274; name given to Osiris by Eumolpus 419; worshipped by the @Arabians and the name they gave to Sesostris 273

Diospolis: Greek word meaning the *City of Jupiter Ammon* (998 BC) 44; 425

Dira: place @Sesostris set up a pillar to mark his conquests 446; promontory in the straits of the Red Sea next to Ethiopia 446

Dodona: location of oldest Greek oracle similar to @Jupiter @Ammon in @Thebes (Egyptian) 437; location of the oracle of @Jupiter @Ammon (983 BC) 50

Doliones: ruled by Cyzicus 480; visited by the Argonauts 480

Dolomene: part of the Babylonian Empire 621

Dolphinus: constellation is related to @Neptune's dolphin 254

Dorians: sent a colony under the leadership of Teutamus to Crete 400

Doridas: king of @Corinth before the return of the Heraclides 329

Dorotheus: ancient poet from Sidon 545

Dorus: brother of Aeolus 328; brother of Xuthus 328; son of Hellen 328; 29; expelled Procris from @Thessaly 328

Doryagus: father of Agesilaus 218; Spartan king descended from the family of Eurysthenes 204; 218

Dotadas: king of Messene 204

Doxius: son of @Caelus 391; taught people to construct clay brick houses 391

Draco: archon and legislator of the Athenians (572 BC) 154; archon ten years before Solon 307; 308; 310; Greeks had no public tables or inscriptions older than his laws 197

Draco: constellation shaped like the dragon killed by @Hercules (Idean) 253

Duris: says that when Arbaces saw the decadent lifestyle of @Sardanapalus he murdered him 556

Ecbatana: captured by Cyrus in 537 BC 308; city built by @Arphaxad 558; city built by the Medes for their new king @Dejoces 556; city built in Media after the country revolted from the @Assyrians 406; Cyrus received the kingdom here 618; Cyrus spent his summer months here 632

Ecclesiasticus: Simon Justus died some time before this book was written 682

Echemenes: says that @Minos was that @Jupiter who kidnapped Ganymede 343

Echemus: killed Hyllus when he invaded Peloponnesus 333; 83; king of Arcadia 333

Echestratus: Spartan king descended from the family of Eurysthenes 204

Ecnibalus: king of @Tyre 589

Eden: conquered by @Sennacherib 550; had its own king until it was conquered by the @Assyrians 525; its children inhabited @Thelasar 536; part of the @Assyrian Empire at the time of the fall of Israel 532

Eden (Garden of): kingdoms compared to its trees 609

Edom: conquered by @Nebuchadnezzar 577; 602; 604; 610; 611; conquered by David 438; conquered by Holofernes 560; conquered in the twelfth year of David's reign 281; country plundered by four kings from the land of Shinar and @Elam 408; defeated by David 271; 272; had its own king until it was conquered by the @Assyrians 525; name means *red* 290; 443; name of the country of @Esau 443; original home of the @Tyrians 288; revolted from @Judah 376; revolted from king Jehoram and @Judah 285; 286

Edomites: conquered by David and some fled to Egypt, the Persian Gulf and the Mediterranean Sea (1044 BC) 25; defeated by David 271; drove out the @Tyrians who traded on the Red Sea 298; drove the @Phoenicians from the Red Sea around 892 to 889 BC 308; fled from David and strengthened the @Philistines 282; fled from David from the Red Sea to the @Philistines 286; 287; fled from David with their young king @Hadad to Egypt 441; fled into Egypt shortly before the birth of the Titans 440; helped @Ammon build a fleet on the Red Sea 446; helped the @Philistines fortify @Azoth against David 281; introduced navigational skills to Egypt 438; passed their skills onto the Egyptians 439; sailed the Red Sea in the days of @Esau 443; some accompanied Cadmus to Greece 290; some fled to Egypt with their King @Hadad 271

Egypt: @Amenophis returned here from @Susa after building Memnonia there 270; @Cheops prohibited the worship of its gods 493; @Danaus fled from here to Lindus 322; @Edomites and their King @Hadad fled here from David 438; @Edomites fled here from David 271; 441; @Ethiopians expelled @Shepherds into North Africa 426; @Hercules (Egyptian) returned here after his conquests 399; @Inachus led a colony from here to @Argos 378; @Neptune and his son @Atlas made war on the Egyptian gods 466; @Osarsiphus ruled over its lower region (941 BC) 68; @Sabacon voluntarily relinquished it 501; @Sesostris built temples here 455; @Sesostris left on a nine year expedition 229; 232; @Sesostris left to conquer the east 450; @Sesostris returned here after his conquests 227; 327; 451; 477; 95; @Sesostris returned here after his major defeat by the Greeks and Scythians (962 BC) 60; @Sesostris ruled here in the age of the gods 486; @Shepherds expelled from and many fled to @Phoenicia 435; @Shepherds expelled from here 515; @Shepherds fled from here to the @Philistines 436; @Shepherds fled from here to the @Philistines, Sidon and Cyprus 376; @Shepherds were expelled from here in the days of Eli and Samuel 385; @Thebes (Egyptian), @Memphis and Heliopolis were its three principal cities 499; abandoned the Medes when the @Assyrians attacked the Medes 558; Abas left (1066 BC) 21; Abas left here with a colony for @Euboea and Peloponnesus 326; allied with Zedekiah 579; almost invaded by the Scythians who were bought off by Psammitichus 562; Amosis I expelled most of the @Shepherds from here 377; astrology invented here by @Necepsos and Pelosiris (772 BC) 111; astrology invented here by @Nechepsos and Petosiris 625; attacked by the Titans led by @Atlas 467; broke up into several smaller kingdoms after Asychis died (788 BC) 109; Canaanites fled here from Joshua (1445 BC) 13; Canaanites settled in large numbers here during the reign of Tutimaeus 430; composed of many small kingdoms before the time of @Sesostris 484; conquered by @Amenophis 275; conquered by @Cambyses 485; conquered by @

Esarhaddon 553; 559; conquered by @Nebuchadnezzar 577; 602; 611; 155; conquered by the @Assyrians under @Esarhaddon 516; conquered by the @Ethiopians under @Sabacon 516; conquered by the Thebans (Egyptian) and @Ethiopians 460; contains many cities founded by the gods 454; contains the port of Coptos 446; country the Canaanites first fled to from Joshua 429; country where the @Edomites fled from David 440; developed from villages, towns and cities which grew into the kingdom 409; Dicaearchus inserted two fictitious generations into its history 419; Diodorus listed its kings 513; divided into nomes by @Sesostris 452; 462; divided into thirty-six nomes by @Sesostris (961 BC) 61; divided up by @Moeris among his soldiers 491; dominated and was dominated by Ethiopia 473; Egypt, @Thebes (Egyptian), Ethiopia and @Libya had no common king before the expulsion of the @Shepherds 421; embroiled in civil wars after the death of @Sesostris 472; entire country ruled by Amosis I 437; exaggerated their history 518; expelled the @Shepherds who fled to the @Philistines 282; expelled the @Shepherds who migrated to Greece 373; foundation laid on which to build a more exact chronology for it 309; freed from Ethiopian domination in 670 BC 510; had four ages of the great gods 512; harassed by @Assyria before it was freed under the rule of twelve contemporary kings 557; Hebrew copy of Ecclesiasticus was translated to Greek here 682; held Festival of @Isis to honour Ceres for the gift of agriculture 318; Herodotus wrote of its antiquities 483; idolatry began here and spread to @Phoenicia and the neighbouring countries 362; Ino was alive when @Sesostris returned here 314; invaded and conquered by @Assyria 505; invaded by @Amenophis (926 BC) 81; invaded by @Antaeus 468; invaded by @Cambyses 246; invaded by @Esarhaddon 506; 129; invaded by @Ethiopians (942 BC) 67; invaded by @Sennacherib 551; invaded by the @Ethiopians under @Sabacon 498; 113; Isaiah predicted its subjection to @Assyria 507; its antiquity was greatly exaggerated in only four hundred years 465; its archives destroyed by the @Assyrians and the @Ethiopians 517; its civil disorders were the cause of the commissioning of the ship *Argo* by the Greeks (936 BC) 72; its empire stretched from the Atlantic Ocean to India 416; its gods @Jupiter @Ammon and @Osiris correspond to Arabian gods of @Caelus and @Bacchus 449; its gods were set up by Jeroboam I at Dan and Bethel 471; its history was greatly exaggerated 193; its monuments above the Memnonium contained inscriptions on obelisks, expressing the riches of the kings, and their reigning as far as @Scythia, Bactria, India and Ionia 490; its priests created three hundred and thirty kings who reigned for eleven thousand years 9; its priests made the temple of @Vulcan more than a thousand years older than @Amenophis (912 BC) 85; its priests thought @Sethon was the last king of Egypt who reigned before the division of Egypt into twelve contemporary kingdoms 503; its regional capitals had direct canals to the @Nile River 453; its twelve gods brought into Greece by Amphictyon (959 BC) 62; its war was settled by Mercury according to Solon 469; Jacob and his family migrated here 434; kingdom split and ruled by several kings 495; lived a simple lifestyle before @Menes 481; location of the @Lake of @Moeris 587; location of the port of Sais 382; location of the revolt of @Danaus from his brother @Sesostris 422; lost control of @Judah when it was defeated by Asa 475; lost control of @Nineveh and other territories 527; lost control of Ethiopia after the death of @Sesostris 474; lost control of Syria when @Hadad ruled 456; lost her empire and divided into several small kingdoms 494; lost its empire after the time of the Argonaut Expedition 480; lost its empire when countries revolted from it because of the Argonaut Expedition 276; Lower Egypt began to worship their kings before the days of Moses 363; Lower Egypt revolted under @Osarsiphus then @Amenophis retired into Ethiopia resulting in much civil unrest 479; Lower Egypt ruled by Proteus 488; Media revolted after @Sennacherib's defeat here 555; mythology differed from the Cretans in some points 470; one place the @Edomites propagated their skills to 444; oracles came from here into Greece 361; origin of long ships with sails and one tier of oars 298; originally many smaller kingdoms 231; part of the @Assyrian Empire at its height 554; part of the Babylonian Empire 621; Pharaoh Necho led an army from here against @Carchemish 575; Phoenician @Venus was a foreign deity in this country 459; place Joseph entertained his brothers 433; plundered by @Cambyses (523 BC) 94; Pythagorus taken from here to Babylon by @Cambyses 653; revolted from @Assyria 559; revolted from the @Assyrian Empire 508;

130; ruled a large empire from the time of @Sesostris until after @ Ramesses 526; ruled by @Amenophis 489; ruled by @Ammenemes I, @Gesongeses, @Ammenemes II and @Sesostris according to Manetho 424; ruled by @Ammon 425; 31; ruled by @Bacchus or @Osiris 274; ruled by @Cheops (838 BC) 101; ruled by @Chephron (824 BC) 103; ruled by @Memnon and his young son @Ramesses 476; ruled by @ Menes 478; ruled by @Moeris (860 BC) 98; ruled by @Mycerinus (808 BC) 104; ruled by @Nechaoh (617 BC) 142; ruled by @Osiris 241; ruled by @Osiris, @Bacchus and @Sesostris who were all the same person around 971 BC 308; ruled by @Sabacon 495; 496; ruled by @ Sesostris (998 BC) 44; ruled by @Sesostris and @Bacchus at the same time 278; ruled by Belus (Egyptian) 445; ruled by both @Bacchus and @Sesostris 418; ruled by Cyrus 509; ruled by eleven kings who reigned an average of twenty-five years each 205; ruled by one king 420; ruled by Pharaoh Necho 576; ruled by Psammitichus (655 BC) 133; ruled by Psammitichus and Pharaoh Necho 565; ruled by Tirhakah (687 BC) 126; ruled by twelve princes (670 BC) 129; ruled for fifty years by @ Sabacon (701 BC) 123; ruled over by Atlantis according to chronologers 464; ruled over Cyprus, @Phoenicia and western North Africa 482; sacred rites propagated to Babylon 627; slowly united into one kingdom by Misphragmuthosis and his son Amosis I 431; some @Edomites fled here from David 287; 25; source of grain and craftsmen for Myles 381; started their year on the vernal equinox 247; subdued by @Cambyses 651; supplied a large army to @Sesostris for his invasion of the east 273; supplied by horses from @Libya 448; supplied grain, which @ Erechtheus took to @Athens 375; supplied Solomon with horses (1015 BC) 35; supplied the Canaanites with horses 375; Syringes and Troglodytes lived in caves here 404; terminus of the trade route that originated in @Edom 439; thinly populated before the time of Moses 408; torn by civil wars (940 BC) 69; under @Sethon defeated the @ Assyrians under @Sennacherib 502; under viceroy Proteus, when @ Amenophis was in @Susa (909 BC) 86; upper part ruled by Mephres (1121 BC) 14; used a three hundred and sixty-five day year 247; used the same laws as Ethiopia 432; visited by Solon on his travels 307; western boundary of @Phoenicia 290; when @Japetus died, he was deified here under the name of @Typhon (951 BC) 66; when @Sesostris returned here, @Danaus his brother fled to Greece 228; 230

Egyptian: nationality of @Ammon 463; nationality of @Erechtheus 319; nationality of @Hercules (951 BC) 66; nationality of @Isis 419; nationality of @Japetus 370; nationality of Cepheus 325; nationality of Glaucus 277; nationality of Hermapion 490; nationality of merchandise sold by the @Phoenicians 287; nationality of strangers who migrated to Greece (1121 BC) 14; nationality of the colonies that carried astronomy and science to @Babylonia 626; nationality of the god @Isis 6; nationality of the gods introduced into Greece 363; nationality of the gods Jeroboam I set up in Israel (975 BC) 53; nationality of the people who built obelisks 511; nationality of writers who called the invasion of @Memnon and his son @Ramesses the second expulsion of the @Shepherds 476; not the nationality of the women to whom the temple of @Venus Hospita was built 459

Egyptian Mouse: symbol of destruction 501

Egyptian Sea: border of the lands inhabited by the @Arabians and @ Syrians 621

Egyptian Talent: weighed eighty pounds 613

Egyptian Year: five days added to it during the reign of @Amenophis 440; introduced into Babylon (747 BC) 114; three hundred and sixty-five days long and started on the vernal equinox 270

Egyptians: added five extra days to the year to make it solar (1030 BC) 93; applied the skills of the @Edomites 438; ascribed the invention of writing to @Osiris 441; at Thebes discovered the year was three hundred and sixty-five days long 245; ate separately from the Hebrews 433; began to observe the positions of the stars 439; boasted of a very large empire 416; brought into Europe the practice of deifying the dead 362; built a fleet on the Red Sea near Coptos 438; calculated the reigns of kings equal to the generations of men with three generations to a hundred years 204; 207; called @Ammon by the name of @Jupiter 424; called @Japetus by the names of @Typhon, @Python and @Neptune 275; called @ Sesostris by the name of @Hero or @Hercules before he became king 273; 446; called all the farthest parts of the earth and promontories and whatever bordered on the sea and its coastal areas by the name

of @Neptys 466; called the invading Canaanites by the name of @Shepherds (1445 BC) 13; called their @Hercules (Egyptian) by the name of @Nilus 399; carried into captivity by the @Assyrians 505; considered @Menes the first king to reign after their gods 364; considered @Osiris and @Bacchus to be one and the same king of Egypt 419; corrupted their antiquities 278; dedicated oracles to @ Ammon 437; defeated @Antaeus near @Antaea 467; defeated @ Sennacherib 551; 120; deified @Cinyras under the name of @Baal Canaan or @Vulcan 459; despised animal sacrifices 434; determined the length of the solar year 439; 497; did not reckon @Esarhaddon as one of their kings 508; erected a statue to @Sethon holding in his hand a mouse which is the Egyptian symbol of destruction 551; exaggerated their history 699; first fought with clubs 447; fled from @Sabacon 114; fled from the Ethiopian invasion 498; founded the era of Nabonassar in Egyptian years (747 BC) 114; had difficulty understanding Greek pronunciations for the names of the @Nile River 453; had the oldest of the three men named @Hercules 461; imagined the temple of @Vulcan stood for over eleven thousand years 500; initiated the study of astronomy under @Ammon and @ Sesostris 444; introduced the custom of deifying the dead into Asia Minor and Greece 460; introduced their astrology and astronomy to Babylon 114; introduced their solar year to the Chaldeans (747 BC) 95; invaded and conquered many countries before the Argonaut Expedition 480; invaded by the @Assyrians 557; Isaiah predicted civil war among them 507; learned from the @Ethiopians the custom of deifying their kings 432; made their kingdom nine thousand years old by the time of Solon 484; many fled before the invading @ Ethiopians 625; mastered the skills of the @Edomites 439; named the five extra days of the year after Rhea's children 440; named their cities after their gods 363; nationality the Greeks thought the ancestors of Acrisius were 326; noted the heliacal risings and settings of the stars 497; originally subsisted on the fruits of the earth and the produce from the @Nile River 481; populated many cities @Sesostris conquered 451; ruled by @Assyrians for about three years 557; ruled by @Esarhaddon for three years 506; sent many colonies into other countries 445; studied the stars for navigational purposes (1030 BC) 31; taught astronomy and writing by Oes 442; Theban Egyptians used no intercalary months, nor deducted any days from the month as was done by most of the Greeks 235; used a luni-solar year until the days of @Osiris 241; used a luni-solar year until the time of @ Ammon 246; used a solar year 244; when @Japetus died, Egyptians deified him under the name of @Typhon (951 BC) 66; worshipped the great men of the kingdom to whom the nome, the city, and the temple or grave of the god, were dedicated 452; worshipped the sun, the fire, dead men and images 659

Egyptus: brother of @Danaus (961 BC) 61; another name for Sesostris (961 BC) 61

Egyptus: name given to a channel @Sesostris cut from the @Nile River (951 BC) 66

Eilithyia: founded a city in Egypt 454; one of the gods of Egypt 454

Elam: another name for Persia 603; 611; conquered by @Cyaxeres and @Nebuchadnezzar 610; conquered by @Nebuchadnezzar 602; 148; God broke their military strength 605; origin of the army sent into Palestine under four kings 408; small Persian kingdom and warred with the Scythians 566

Elamites: transplanted by @Esarhaddon to Samaria 534; 552

Elean: nationality of Hippias 1

Eleans: conquered Phidon 301; invaded Pisa 304; restored the Olympic Games 220; said that @Jupiter fought here with Saturn for the kingdom while others said that @Hercules (Idean) instituted these games in memory of their victory over the Titans 353; state that Clymenus from Crete celebrated the games again in Olympia 354; suspected Damophon of treason 304

Eleazar: brother of Simon Justus 678; son of Onias 678; younger brother of Simon Justus 682; third high priest of the Jews after the Persian Empire 678

Elector: father of Capaneus 324; son of Anaxagoras 324

Electryo: brother of @Mestor 324; brother of Gorgophone 324; brother of Sthenelus 324; father of Alcmena 54; 324; grandfather of @Hercules (Idean) 324; husband of Lysidice (974 BC) 54; son of Andromeda 324; son of Perseus 54; 324

Elephantis: capital of one of several Egyptian kingdoms under a Shepherd king (1445 BC) 13; 431

Eleusinians: fought against Ion, the commander of the Athenian army 319; led by Eumolpus who rebelled from their King @Erechtheus 388; original kingdom consisted of many small towns (1076 BC) 20; waged war with the Athenians and killed their King @Erechtheus 318

Eleusinus: son of Ogyges (1076 BC) 20; 383; built Eleusis in Attica (1076 BC) 20; 383

Eleusis: built by Eleusinus (1076 BC) 20; city built in Attica either by Ogyges or his son Eleusinus 383; Eumolpus instituted the mysteries to Ceres here (1003 BC) 41; its mysteries were instituted between the tenth and fifteenth year of Solomon 320; mysteries instituted here later than the battle the Eleusinians fought with @Athens 319; mysteries of Ceres were instituted here 357; one of twelve cities where Cecrops I resettled a number of smaller towns 388; ruled by Celeus 330; 32; temple was erected here to Ceres 318

Eli: @Shepherds were expelled from Egypt in his days 373; 375; 376; 385; Canaanites ruled Lower Egypt until his time (c. 1021 BC) 13; colonies led into Greece from Egypt and @Phoenicia in his time 436; Egyptian history before his time is very uncertain 484; in his days @Inachus came to Greece by sea 378; in his days Lelex led a colony from Egypt to Greece 381; in his time Cecrops I came into Attica 382; Pelasgus came to Greece toward the end of his life 377; towns and houses in Europe did not predate his days 415

Eliadah: father of @Rezon 456

Eliashib: father of Joiada 678; son of Joiakim 678; became the high priest in the tenth year of @Xerxes I 679; high priest and may have had grandsons before the seventh year of @Artaxerxes Longimanus 680; in the third generation of the chief priests after the return from the exile 684; 693; lived during the reign of @Artaxerxes Longimanus not @Artaxerxes Mnemon 683; third high priest of the Jews during the Persian Empire 678

Elis: built by Aethlius 384; 30; built by the consolidation of smaller towns into one 389; documented the origin of the Olympic Games 353; home of the historian Hippias who wrote a breviary of the victors of the Olympic Games 197; recovered by Oxylus for the Heraclides 220; ruled by Clymenus and Endymion 354; two men chosen from here to preside over the Olympic Games (580 BC) 153; two men were chosen by lot from the city to preside over the Olympic Games 304

Elissa: another name for Dido 224; 225

Elmacinus: states that @Zoroaster reformed the religion of the @Persians 656

Eloth: port on the Red Sea captured by David 439

Elul: sixth month of the Jewish Year 692

Elymais: country east of @Babylonia 622; on the east side of the @Assyrian Empire 537; part of the @Assyrian Empire at its height 554

Elymeans: part of the Babylonian Empire 621

Empedocles: wrote his history in verse 196

Encaenia: term for the dedication of the city of @Carthage 225

Endymion: father of Aetolus 220; 337; 354; 39; 46; son of Aethlius 220; 327; 30; son of Calyce 327; deposed Clymenus from ruling at Elis 354; Pelops captured the country of Aetolia in his time 327

Enemessar: name Tobit gave to Shalmaneser or Salmanasser 550

Enephes: corruption of the name of Amenophis 482; 489

England: ruled by thirty kings who reigned an average of twenty-one and a half years each 205

Ennius: twenty years younger than Noevius 312

Epacria: one of twelve cities where Cecrops I resettled a number of smaller towns 388

Epaminondas: incorrectly thought Lycurgus lived at the time of the first Olympiad 199

Epaphus: another name for Apis and incorrectly thought to be a different king 10; another name for Epopeus 316; 317; Greek name for Apis according to Herodotus 379

Epaphus: father of @Lisianassa 445; son of @Io 419; became the god Osiris after his death 419; king of Egypt 445

Ephesian Letters: named after the city they were first taught in and also were called *Phoenician Letters* 339

Ephesus: one of the twelve cities in the common council called Panionium 310; source of the Ephesian letters, which were also called Phoenician letters 339

Ephorus: formed a chronological history of Greece, beginning with the return of the Heraclides into Peloponnesus, and ending with the siege of Perinthus 1; 197

Ephyra: original name for Corinth 384

Epimedes: Curete who accompanied @Hercules (Idean) from Crete to Elis 353

Epimenides: organised his history by genealogies 1; 197

Epimetheus: brother of @Atlas 370; brother of Prometheus 370

Epirus: visited by the Argonauts 480

Epopeus: another name for Apis Epaphus and incorrectly thought to be a different king 10; 39; another name for Epaphus 379; 39; kidnapped Antiope causing a war between him and her father Nycteus 316; king of @Aegialea (later called Sicyon) 316; king of @Sicyon 317

Epytus: king of Messene 204

Equestris: name given to Neptune (1015 BC) 35

Eraphius: another name for Apries 509; another name for Hophra 511

Eratosthenes: computed times by the reign of the kings of Sparta 11; followed Thucydides and documented that the return of the Heraclides was eighty years after the Trojan War 203; gave the Greeks a detailed chronology 2; 3; his Egyptian dynasties were filled with the names of many kings not found in Herodotus 515; his history copied by Apollodorus 197; his king lists show @Moeris listed immediately before @Cheops, three times in the dynasties of the kings of Egypt 486; his list of kings should not be used to correct Herodotus 517; mistakenly thought Lycurgus was much older than the first Olympiad 198; 199; says that originally Cyprus was sparsely populated and heavily forested 402; thought that kings who reigned before the Persian Empire reigned an average of thirty-five to forty years each 205

Erech: another name for the city of Areca 536; built by Nimrod 536

Erechtheus: father of Achaeus 328; father of Cecrops II 319; father of Creusa 228; 31; father of Orithyia 319; father of Orneus 319; father of Pandion 228; 319; 331; 381; father of Procris 319; 351; grandfather of @Sicyon 384; great-grandfather of Menestheus (927 BC) 80; after his death Ion commanded the Athenian army 310; Athenian king killed in a war between the Athenians and the Eleusinians 318; came with a colony into Greece 436; contemporary with Aethlius, Aeolus, Xuthus, Dorus, Tantalus and Danae 328; contemporary with Arcas, Eumelus, Triptolemus and Celeus 334; contemporary with Car 378; contemporary with Celeus 330; contemporary with Saturn 351; daughters of @Danaus were three generations younger than him 228; died between the tenth and fifteenth year of Solomon 320; Egyptian who was appointed king of @Athens for bringing grain to them from Egypt 319; Eleusinians rebelled against him under Eumolpus 388; in his days the wars of the great gods of Egypt against the Greeks occurred 517; in his time women fought along side men in similar clothes and manner as the @Amazons 464; king in Attica (1031 BC) 30; lived about the time of King David 325; lived in the Silver Age 366; name given to him by Homer 6; prevented Amphictyon from succeeding his father-in-law Cranaus 330; successor of Cranaus 331; 332; won the chariot race in the first Panathenaea Festival (1030 BC) 31

Erechthonius: name given to the first Erechtheus chronologers created to try to reconcile their errors 6

Erechthonius: one of his charioteers was the constellation of Auriga 254

Eresos: home of Phanias 307

Erichthonius: son of Gaia 331; Homer called him Erechtheus 331; in his days the wars of the great gods of Egypt against the Greeks occurred 517; in his time women fought along side men in similar clothes and manner as the @Amazons 464; raised by @Minerva 331; third king of Troy 321

Eridanus: constellation is related to the river that Orion crossed 254; contained a star on the colure for the equinoxes 259; extreme flexure of the constellation contains a star that passes through the colure of the equinoxes 251

Eridanus: another name for the Nile River 275

Erigone: daughter of Icareus 254; she and her father are related to the constellations of Bootes, @Plaustrum and Virgo 254

Erycina: another name for Calycopis or Venus (930 BC) 78; 458

Erythea: name given to Gades Island 287; settled by Carthaginians 289

Erythia Acra: promontory in @Libya 287

Erythini: city or country in Paphlagonia 287

Erythra: name means the same as Edom 290; name of a city in Ionia, @Libya, Locris, @Boeotia, Cyprus, Aetolia, Asia Minor near Chios 287

Erythra: another name for Gades Island 448; island beyond the Strait of Gibraltar 399

Erythrae: another name for Gades Island 287

Erythraea: one of the twelve cities in the common council called Panionium 310; translated into @*Phoenicia* (1044 BC) 25

Erythraeum: promontory in Crete 287

Erythras: another name for Edom or Esau 443

Erythrean Sea: @Edomites fled here from David 287; named after the @Edomites 287

Erythreans: another name for Edomites 287; 290

Erythros: place near Tybur 287

Esarhaddon: father of Saosduchinus 557; son of @Sennacherib 551; 121; built Tarsus and Anchiale in one day (710 BC) 121; captured @Ashdod 553; carried Manasseh captive to Babylon 553; carried the remainder of the Samaritans into captivity 552; conquered @Babylonia and @Susiana 566; conquered @Phoenicia, Moab, @Ammon and Egypt 559; conquered Egypt 516; conquered the Jews leading Manasseh captive to Babylon (677 BC) 128; died and succeeded by Saosduchinus (668 BC) 130; died of old age after the revolt of Syria from @Assyria 557; Egypt divided into several kingdoms after his conquest 507; invaded Babylon (681 BC) 127; invaded Egypt (670 BC) 129; king of @Assyria 567; king of @Assyria according to the scriptures 521; name of Sarchedon is derived from it 565; ruled Egypt and Ethiopia 506; ruled the @Assyrian Empire at its height 554; sent Tartan with an army to attack @Ashdod 504; succeeded his father @Sennacherib (710 BC) 121; successor of @Sennacherib 551; three years before he died Egypt revolted from the @Assyrian Empire 508; transplanted the inhabitants of Babylon, @Cuth or the @Sepharvaim, the Dinaites, the Apharsachites, the Tarpelites, the Archevites, the Dehavites, the @Elamites, or @Persians into Samaria 534

Esarhaddon-Pul: another name for Esarhaddon (710 BC) 121; 557; name of Sarchedon is derived from it 565

Esau: buried on an island near the Persian Gulf 443; his posterity built vessels to search for new homes in the Red Sea 444; his posterity worshipped false gods 411; name means *red* 443

Esther: Jews thought she lived in the times of @Ahasuerus 667

Eteocles: brother of Polynices 314; son of Oedipus 314; killed about ten years after the Argonaut Expedition in the war at Thebes (Greek) 314

Eteocretans: first inhabitants of Crete 400

Ethiopia: @Amenophis retired here from Egypt 275; @Amenophis returned from here and conquered Egypt 276; @Memnon and his son @Ramesses left here and invaded Egypt 476; conquered by @Sesostris before he became king 273; contributed troops to the army of @Amenophis (926 BC) 81; country conquered by @Nebuchadnezzar 611; dominated and was dominated by Egypt 473; Egypt, @Thebes (Egyptian), Ethiopia and @Libya had no common king before the expulsion of the @Shepherds 421; governed by @Antaeus 467; harassed by @Assyria 557; invaded and conquered by @Assyria 505; its laws propagated into Egypt 432; its rule over Egypt ended by the invasion of @Esarhaddon of Egypt 553; location of temple and oracle @Sesostris dedicated to his father (998 BC) 44; Meroe its capital 449; part of @Ammon's kingdom 274; part of the @Assyrian Empire at its height 554; place @Amenophis retired to after Lower Egypt revolted under @Osarsiphus 479; place of Dira, a promontory by the straits of the Red Sea 446; revolted from Egypt when @Sesostris died 474; ruled by @Amenophis 488; ruled by @Ramesses 490; ruled by Cyrus 509; ruled by Tirhakah 551; 119; ruled by Zerah and @Memnon 477; under Tirhakah they defeated the @Assyrians under @Sennacherib 502; worshipped @Jupiter @Ammon 448

Ethiopian: home country of @Actisanes 514; nationality of @Sabacon 625; 113; nationality of the colony led into Egypt by @Osiris 432

Ethiopians: @Jupiter @Ammon was their only god 448; called the @Nile River @Siris 453; carried into captivity by the @Assyrians 505; commanded by Pan (964 BC) 58; conquered Egypt and many surrounding countries 460; conquered Egypt under @Sabacon 516; contributed troops to the million man army of Zerah 472; defeated @Sennacherib (712 BC) 120; defeated by Asa (941 BC) 68; destroyed much of the Egyptian archives 517; dominated Egypt until 670 BC 510; driven from Lower Egypt by @Osarsiphus (941 BC) 68; drove the @Shepherds from Egypt into western North Africa and Syria and other places 431; drowned @Orus in the @Nile River (942 BC) 67; Egypt divided into several kingdoms after their conquest 507; expelled the @Shepherds from Egypt into North Africa 426; in the army of @Sesostris 58; 231; independent kingdom in the times of @Amenophis 276; invaded and conquered Egypt under @Sabacon 496; invaded Egypt 479; part of the army of @Sesostris 450; retired with @Amenophis from Egypt to Ethiopia 275; retired with @Memnon from Lower Egypt 476; revolted from the kings at @Memphis 494; ruled by @Esarhaddon for three years 506; some fought with clubs and were called Megabars 461; taught the Egyptians the custom of deifying their kings 432; under @Amenophis retreated from Lower Egypt (940 BC) 69; under @Sabacon invaded Egypt causing the Egyptian priests to flee to @Babylonia 498; under Zerah conquered Egypt and @Libya 474

Euadne: daughter of Iphis 324; wife of Capaneus 324

Euboea: Abas led a colony here from Egypt 326; contained the city of Chalcis 299; 336

Euctemon: computed the lunar cycle starting from the summer solstice of 432 BC 266; from his time to Hipparchus, the equinoxes had gone back four degrees 267

Eudamus: descended from the Heraclides 329; king of @Corinth 329

Eudoxus: colures determined from his description of the primitive sphere 260; defined the colure of the equinoxes by ten stars in the constellations 251; documented the stars he used to determine the colure of the solstices 261; documented the stars through which the colures passed 258; his list of stars was used to determine the colure of the equinox at the time of the Argonaut Expedition 259; his sphere had the equinox and solstice colures running through the midpoints of the constellations of the seasons 250; says @Hercules (Egyptian) was killed by @Typhon (951 BC) 66; says that @Hercules (Egyptian) was killed by @Typhon 461; wrote his history in verse 196

Euhadnes: taught the Chaldeans astronomy according to Hyginus 442

Eumelus: first king of Achaia 334; 34; received grain and learned agriculture from Triptolemus (1016 BC) 34

Eumelus: Greek artist 217

Eumolpus: father of Musaeus 253; calls @Osiris by the name of @Dionysus 419; contemporary with @Erechtheus, Celeus, Ceres, @Jasius, Cadmus, Harmonia, @Asterius and Dardanus 319; his family served as priests at Eleusis in the temple to Ceres 318; instituted mysteries to Ceres in Eleusis 357; instituted the mysteries to Ceres in Eleusis (1003 BC) 41; led the rebellion of the Eleusinians against their King @Erechtheus 388

Eunomus: Spartan king descended from the family of Procles 204

Eupalamus: father of Daedalus 319; 339; son of Metion 319; co-inventor of the anchor 339

Euphaes: king of Messene 204

Euphrates River: @Carchemish located on it in Mesopotamia 575; @Nebuchadnezzar captured from here to the river of Egypt from Pharaoh Necho 576; @Sepharvaim on it 535; Belus (Egyptian) established Egyptian colonies near it 445; bordered the city of Tiphsah and its territories 529; eastern boundary of David's kingdom 271; flowed through @Babylonia 536; flowed through the middle of Babylon 624; king of Zobah ruled on both sides of the river 525; location of the battle between Pharaoh Necho and the @Assyrians over @Carchemish 565; melting snow in @Armenia causes the Euphrates River to flood in the beginning of summer 591; patriarchs used boats to cross 443; some @Arabians and @Syrians lived on the far side of it 621; watered the plains of Chaldea, @Chalonitis and @Assyria 524

Eupolemus: states @Astibares assisted @Nebuchadnezzar in the conquest of @Nineveh 594

Euripylus: king of Cyrene 480; visited by the Argonauts 480

Eurolicus: commanded the forces of the Amphictyons (570 BC) 156; commander of an army against Cirrha 302; contemporary with Phidon 156; king of @Thessaly 302

Europa: grandmother of Deucalion 367; great-grandmother of Idomeneus 367; husband of @Asterius 345; mother of @Minos 308; 344; 345; 358; 367; 394; mother of Rhadamanthus 344; mother of Sarpedon 344; sister of Alymmus 342; sister of Cadmus 278; 297; 308; 351; 359; wife of @Asterius 367; wife of @Jupiter (Cretan) 344; @Phoenicians surnamed their kings @Jupiter from her time 369; about the same age as her brother Cadmus 351; accompanied Alymmus into

Crete along with the Idean Dactyli 342; brought the *Octaeteris* or the *Great Year* into Greece 240; came to Crete about one hundred years before the Argonaut Expedition 345; Clymenus built a statue to her in Olympia 354; contemporary with Saturn (Cretan) 345; fled at the time of one of the Phoenician kings 296; fled from Sidon to Crete 297; fled from Sidon to Crete around 1041 BC 308; from her arrival in Europe to the destruction of Troy were four generations 365; Greeks built a temple to her 359; introduced the deification of people into Europe 358; likely came to Europe two or three years before the birth of @Minos 278; same woman as Rhea (Cretan) 342; Sidonian colonies did not flee to find her as some imagine 282; various events happened in her time and in the time of her posterity 317; young woman when she came to Europe 315

Europe: @Europa and Cadmus likely came here two or three years before the birth of @Minos 278; @Sesostris introduced the knowledge of observing the stars here 625; altars erected here before the arrival of Cadmus 361; beginning of trades here 371; Cadmus introduced writing here 10; Cadmus led a colony here 319; composed of city states before the rise of larger kingdoms 407; crossed by @Minerva and her @Amazons 422; Daedalus and his nephew Talus invented the carpentry trade here (985 BC) 48; documented the origin of villages, market towns, cities, common councils, vestal temples, feasts and fairs 387; early inhabitants did not have written records 372; four ages created to commemorate the first four generations of the arrival of the @Curetes here 367; heavily forested in spite of human activity 403; imagined to be smaller than Atlantis (896 BC) 91; its early inhabitants lived in caves 404; its history about as old as @Libya 405; its oldest towns at most two or three generations older than the arrival of Cadmus into Greece 385; its towns and houses later than the time of Eli, Samuel and David 415; manual trades established here by the @Curetes 339; many of its cities populated by @Sesostris 451; metallurgy introduced here by the Idean Dactyli (1031 BC) 30; occupied by wandering tribes of Cimmerians and Scythians (1121 BC) 14; one place the @Edomites propagated their skills to 444; part of it conquered by @Minerva, the queen of the @Amazons 423; part of it ruled over by @Sesostris 424; practice of deifying the dead brought here by the @Phoenicians and Egyptians 362; ruled by Japheth 524; ruled over by Atlantis according to chronologers 464; some think Polydorus was born before Cadmus came here 315; thinly populated 404; writing introduced here by Cadmus 441; writing, the coining of money and the manual arts introduced here by the @Phoenicians 351

European Historians: @Pherecydes of @Athens was one of the first and one of the best 197

Europeans: after they cut down their forests for hundreds of years, Europe was still heavily forested 403; had no chronology before the times of the Persian Empire 196

Europs: second king of @Sicyon 204; 379; 380

Eurotas: brother of Cleson 381; brother of Myles 381; brother of Polycaon 381; father of Sparta 381; 22; son of Lelex 381; 22; built Sparta 381; in his times towns began to be consolidated into cities 391; king in Laconia (1065 BC) 22; some say he was really the son of Myles 381

Euryalus: brother of Hyperbius 391; taught the Greeks to make and build with clay bricks 391

Eurybatus: Spartan who won the wrestling event in the 18th Olympic Games 215

Eurycrates I: Spartan king descended from the family of Eurysthenes 204; 209

Eurycrates II: Spartan king descended from the family of Eurysthenes 204; 209

Eurycratidas: another name for Eurycrates II according to Herodotus 209

Eurydice: daughter of Lacedemon (1043 BC) 26; daughter of Sparta 381; 26; mother of Danae 318; 324; 325; sister of Amyclas 324; wife of Acrisius (1043 BC) 26; built the temple to Juno Argiva 318; 325; lived about the time of King David and @Erechtheus 325

Euryleon: son of Aegeus 208; commanded a Messenian army 208

Eurymedon: son of @Bacchus 227; 277; son of Ariadne 227; 277; an Argonaut 227; 277

Eurypon: Spartan king descended from the family of Procles 204

Eurysthenes: son of Aristodemus 208; 209; 222; twin brother of Procles 208; 209; head of a dynasty of Spartan kings 204; 218; king of Sparta 222; tutored by Theras 208

Eurystheus: brother of Gelanor 322; father of Amyclas 325; son of Nicippe 323; son of Sthenelus 323; 69; born (961 BC) 61; expelled the Heraclides from Peloponnesus (927 BC) 80; killed by Hyllus (927 BC) 80; killed in the first attempt of the Heraclides to return 222; lived in the time of @Hercules (Idean) 222; ruled Mycene (940 BC) 69

Eusebius: calls Belus (Egyptian) by the name of @Busiris 445; copied errors of Mathetho relating to @Ammon 424; dates the founding of Syracuse in 738 BC 299; documents that the Canaanites who fled from Joshua built Tripoli 428; states Crete was named after the Curete called Cres 401

Evagetus: father of Archias (719 BC) 118; descended from @Hercules (Idean) (719 BC) 118

Evagoras: conquered by @Artaxerxes Mnemon ending the rule of the family of Teucer in Cyprus 293

Evander: son of Carmenta (939 BC) 70; contemporary with @Hercules (Egyptian) 399; introduced writing into @Italy (939 BC) 70; led the third Greek colony into @Italy 351

Evarete: daughter of Acrisius 324

Evilmerodach: son of @Nebuchadnezzar 581; died when @Belshazzar was at least thirty-four years old 586; king of Babylon that the Jews knew about 667; murdered by his brother-in-law @Neriglissaros 582; reigned seven years while his father was insane according to Jerome 581; ruled for two years 582

Evil-Merodach: example of an @Assyrian name compounded with the name of one of the @Assyrian gods 519

Ezekiel: his description of the temple differs slightly from that of Solomon's temple 647; knew of and mentioned the @Assyrian Empire 529; lists the main nations conquered by @Cyaxeres and @Nebuchadnezzar 610; measured the court of the temple 648; relates a parable about the @Assyrians 609

Ezion Geber: port on the Red Sea captured by David 439

Ezra: father of Meshullam 676; son of Seraiah 684; book almost parallels I Esdras 686; by comparing his book with Nehemiah's, one can deduce the history of the Jews under Cyrus, @Cambyses and @Darius Hystaspes 673; came to @Jerusalem in the time of @Artaxerxes 667; chief priest in the first year of Cyrus 676; contemporary with @Darius Hystaspes 695; describes history of the Jews rebuilding the temple and the city of @Jerusalem 685; during the reign of @Artaxerxes Longimanus he left Babylon with offerings and vessels for the temple 688; his book is not in chronological order 687; Jews misunderstood his history 669; lived during the reign of @Artaxerxes Longimanus 677; lived during the reign of @Artaxerxes Longimanus not @Artaxerxes Mnemon 683; only Persian kings in this book and Nehemiah are recognised by the Jews 668; partially repaired the walls of @Jerusalem 691; recorded the list of the sons of Levi in the book of Chronicles 680; returned to @Judah (467 BC) 177; returned with Nehemiah in the first year of Cyrus 671; too old to have lived in the reign of @Artaxerxes Mnemon 684

February: era of Nabonassar began on the 26th of this month (747 BC) 95; 247

Fortunate Islands: another name for the Canary Islands 285

France: ruled by sixty-three kings who reigned an average of nineteen and a half years each 205

Gades: built on the @@Gades Islands by the @Tyrians 285; built on the @Gades Islands by the @Tyrians 291

Gades Island: colonised by @Sesostris 448; fell to the lot of @Neptune 464; location of a temple containing the bones of @Hercules (Tyrian) 294; location of the city of Gades built by the @Tyrians 291; location of the grave of @Hercules (Tyrian) 293; off the coast of Spain 288; populated by the @Phoenicians and also called Erythea or Erythrae 287; settled by @Tyrians 288

Gadir: another name for Gades Island 464; island also known as Erythea 289; maybe the island of Ogygia 465

Gaia: father of @Erichthonius 331

Galeed: conquered by @Nebuchadnezzar 576

Galilee: conquered and its people were transplanted by the @Assyrians 534; conquered by @Nebuchadnezzar 576; its tribes transplanted by Tiglathpileser 549

Gallia: visited by the Argonauts 480

Ganges River: eastern border of the conquests of @Sesostris (968 BC) 56; two pillars set up near its mouth by @Sesostris to mark his conquests 446

Ganymede: son of Tros (1015 BC) 35; 254; kidnapped by @Jupiter but some say more accurately that it was by Tantalus 343; kidnapped by Tantalus (1015 BC) 35; 254

Gate of the Causeway: northern gate of the temple was also called *Shallecheth* 638

Gath: conquered by @Assyria 530; conquered by Uzzah 531; on the west and south side of the @Assyrian Empire 535

Gaugamela: location of battle in which @Darius Codomannus lost his kingdom 666

Gaul: @Hercules (Egyptian) crossed from here over the Alps into @Italy 398; @Sesostris returned to Egypt through its southern coasts 448; 40; history written hundreds of years after the death of @Alexander the Great 202

Gauls: called @Hercules (Egyptian) by the name of @Ogmius 399; sacked Rome destroying its historical records 7; 201

Gaulus: island settled by the @Phoenicians 397

Gauzania: metropolis of Calachene 539

Gedaliah: murdered in the seventh month of the Jews 572

Gelanor: brother of Eurystheus 322; son of Nicippe 323; son of Sthenelus 323; defeated by @Danaus for the crown of @Argos 322

Gelon: expelled the inhabitants of Megara Hyblaea 299

Gemini: constellation of the Zodiac 249; constellation shaped like the twins Castor and Pollux 253

Geminus: documents how the Greeks reckoned time 237

Genealogus: title given to Pherecydes of @Athens for the quality of his history 197

Gentiles: outer court of the temple was left open to them 648; to observe laws about not eating blood 413

Genubah: son of @Tahaphenes 272; son of the king of @Edom 272

George Syncellus: thought that five days were added to the calendar by the last Shepherd king 248

Gerar: located near Mareshah 472

Gerastratus: king of @Tyre 589

Gergesites: fled from Joshua into western North Africa 428; 429; inhabited @Phoenicia 429

Gerizim (Mount): location where Sanballat built a temple for his son-in-law Manasseh 681; 182

Germany: contained a huge forest called the Hercinian 403; no written history before the Roman Empire 10; no written language until about 380 AD 202

Geryon: @Sesostris drove his cattle through Gaul and @Italy 448; conquered by @Hercules (Egyptian) 399; conquered by @Osiris in Spain 461; fought against @Hercules (Egyptian) 398; his cattle driven through @Italy by @Hercules (Egyptian) 352

Geshem: opposed Nehemiah when he rebuilt the walls of @Jerusalem 691

Gesongeses: father of Ammenemes II 424; son of Ammenemes I according to Mathetho 424; corrupted name of Sesonchosis 425

Gezer: captured by @Ammon who gave it to his daughter, Solomon's wife (1012 BC) 37; 231

Ghebers: fire worshippers of India 695

Gibraltar (Strait of): @Erythra and the country of Geryon were outside the strait 399; @Hephaestion set up pillars here 461; @Phoenicians sailed here (883 BC) 96; Geryon conquered here by @Sesostris 448; island of Atlantis beyond it 464; island of Madera outside the strait 397; western limit of the conquests of Tirhakah 503

Gindus River: Cyrus cut it into three hundred and sixty channels 243

Gingris: son of @Thoas (935 BC) 73; 459; deified by his father @Thoas under the name of Adonis (935 BC) 73; 459

Ginnetho: chief priest in the first year of Cyrus 676; priest who returned with @Ezra and Nehemiah in the first year of Cyrus 671

Ginnethon: another name for Ginnetho 671

Gisbarim: titles for the junior treasurers in Solomon's temple 643

Glaucus: husband of Ariadne 277; Egyptian naval commander 277

Glaucus: king of Messene 204

Gnephactus: father of Bocchoris 495; cursed @Menes for his luxury and caused the curse to be recorded in the temple of @Jupiter @Ammon at @Thebes (Egyptian) 495; king in @Upper Egypt before Bocchoris (788 BC) 109; reigned at @Memphis (776 BC) 110

Golden Age: first age or generation after the gods 364; 371; first generation in Greece after the flood of Deucalion (c. 1041 BC) 28; men built a temple to Saturn during this age 353; time @Chiron

born in (c. 1020 BC) 73; times of @Asterius or Saturn (Cretan) and Philyra 367

Gomorrah: city plundered by four kings from the land of Shinar and @Elam 408

Gonussa: daughter of @Sicyon 221

Gordyea: on the western border of @Babylonia 622

Gordyean Mountains: northern boundary of the @Assyrian Empire 539

Gordyeans: tribes near them were part of the Babylonian Empire 621

Gorgons: conquered by @Minerva 422

Gorgophone: daughter of Andromeda 324; daughter of Perseus 324; mother of Leucippus 324; sister of @Mestor 324; sister of Electryo 324; sister of Sthenelus 324; wife of Oebalus 324; wife of Perieres 324

Gozan: also called Gauzania 539; conquered by @Sennacherib 550; located on the Caspian Sea 539; on the north side of the @Assyrian Empire 539; part of the @Assyrian Empire at the time of the fall of Israel 532; some of Galilee transplanted here by the @Assyrians 534; some of Samaria transplanted here by the @Assyrians 534

Gozan River: some of Galilee were transplanted here 549

Gozo: modern name for the island of Gaulus 397

Graces: made a purple cloak for @Bacchus 457; three female attendants to @Venus (930 BC) 78

Graecia Magna: name of the Greek colonies in southern @Italy 299

Great Bear: middle of the constellation contains a star that passes through the colure of the solstices 252

Great Court: outer court in Solomon's temple was also called the *People's Court* 636

Greece: @Curetes established the trades of metallurgy and carpentry here 339; @Danaus fled here from Egypt with his fifty daughters 228; 229; 230; 232; 61; @Minos was its greatest king in its early days 343; @Neptune had many children here 465; @Phoenicians from Sidon sailed here (1043 BC) 26; @Phoenicians of Sidon fled here around 1041 BC 308; @Phoenicians traded here 394; @Phoenicians under Cadmus brought many kinds of learning here 336; @Shepherds fled here after being expelled from Egypt 373; @Xerxes I came here after he crossed the Hellespont (480 BC) 175; @Zoroaster came here with @Xerxes I 657; Alymnus, Cadmus and @Europa fled here from Sidon 297; Amphictyon brought the twelve gods from @Thrace to here 363; Amphictyonic Council managed its state affairs 479; benefited from Egyptian navigation expertise 298; Cadmus came here two or three generations after the days of Lelex 391; Cadmus came here with colonies of @Arabians and @Edomites 290; Cadmus was a bachelor when he came here 315; Cadmus with his brothers led colonies of @Sidonians here 282; Callisthenes sent astronomical observations from Babylon to here 194; Ceres introduced agriculture here 318; 351; Cleobulus was one of its seven wise men 238; country of Nycteus 316; custom of deifying the dead introduced here by the Egyptians, @Phoenicians and @Syrians 460; destination of @Danaus sailed to in a long ship (961 BC) 73; destination many @Shepherds fled to 385; destination the @Shepherds and @Philistines fled to when defeated by David 436; developed from villages, towns and cities which grew into the kingdom 409; Ephorus wrote its chronological history, beginning with the return of the Heraclides in Peloponnesus, and ending with the siege of Perinthus 1; 197; exaggerated their history 518; extreme western destination of Sidonian trade 284; first war against Thebes (Greek) happened (928 BC) 79; foundation laid on which to build a more exact chronology for it 309; had four ages of the gods and demigods 365; Idean Dactyli initiated the study of music here 337; invaded by @Bacchus 278; invaded by @Sesostris 369; invaded by @Xerxes I 593; 661; its cities honoured its eminent citizens with temples 359; its first ages were the Golden, Silver, Bronze and Iron Ages 371; its four ages happened after the use of the metals with the same names 372; its history three to four hundred years too old 2; its islands populated by colonies from Crete led by Rhadamanthus 457; its leaders decided to send an embassy to the countries subject to Egypt (936 BC) 72; its oldest oracle located at Dodona 437; its Olympic Games judged by the *Hellenodicae* 304; its rulers commissioned the Argonaut Expedition 256; its seas cleared of pirates by @Minos (1002 BC) 42; its seven wise men preferred to write in verse 196; its war was settled by Mercury according to Solon 469; knew nothing about @Memphis in the times of Homer 482; large numbers of @Shepherds fled here 377; 14; Lycurgus brought the poems of Homer from Asia to here (710 BC) 121; many colonies of @ Shepherds fled here from Egypt 435; oldest city built by Lycaon 390; oracles came here from Egypt 361; Pelasgians spread idolatry here 362; Pelops came here 327; Pelops came here three to four years before Laius fled to him 317; Phoroneus was its oldest king 378; practice of deifying dead men and women unknown here before the coming of Cadmus and @Europa 358; priestess of @Jupiter @Ammon brought to Greece by the Phoenician merchants (983 BC) 50; resisted the invasion of the Atlanteans 464; sent colonies to Crete 400; sent eight young men and eight young virgins every eight years from @Athens to @Minos in Crete 277; sent out colonies led by @Oenotrus into @Italy (1024 BC) 33; settled by colonies of @Phoenicians and @Syrians fleeing from Sidon and from David (1041 BC) 28; several eminent musicians and poets became popular here as a result of the Pythic Games 217; some @Sidonians fled here 283; some of its women including @Io were kidnapped by the @Phoenicians 287; some of the @Shepherds accompanied Sidonian colonies here 376; source of colonists led by @ Oenotrus into @Italy 392; temples started to be built here (1003 BC) 41; twelve gods of Egypt introduced here by Amphictyon (959 BC) 62; used the *Octaeteris* or the *Great Year* introduced there by Cadmus and @Europa 240

Greece (Great): name of the Greek colonies in southern @Italy 299

Greek: @Apis means @Epaphus in this language 379; @Midacritus is a corruption of a Greek name @Melcartus 293; @Poseidon and @ Amphitrite were the names for the Latin gods of @Neptune and @ Neptys 466; *Proteus* in that language means a *prince* or *president* 488; chronology of the @Persians is accurate 667; created variations in the name of @Sesostris 230; its chronologers thought that kings who reigned before the Persian Empire reigned an average of thirty-five to forty years each 205; its early ships did not have sails 339; its history is too long by almost two hundred per cent before Cyrus 210; its islands were inhabited by @Carians who later migrated to @Caria 283; its seas infested by Carian pirates 394; language Ecclesiasticus was translated into 682; language the Phoenician histories translated into by @Chaitus 296; letters used to identify the order of the brightest stars in a constellation 249; nationality of Diocles of Peparethius 201; nationality of the name Polydorus 315; not spoken by the Pelasgians 377; some of its cities were allies of the Piseans 304; its civilised ways were introduced into @Italy by @Saturn (Cretan) 349

Greeks: @Chaitus wrote an address to them 296; @Minos was famous among them for justice 343; adjusted the length of the months to make the lunar and solar years agree 236; ancient calendar year had twelve lunar months with each month having thirty days 238; *Argo* was the first long ship they built 256; attributed the destruction of the @Assyrian Empire to the Medes 564; began to practise agriculture during the Silver Age 366; built a temple to @Bacchus at @Argos 278; built long ships with fifty oars before the Corinthians built triremes (697 BC) 125; built their first long ship the *Argo* patterned after the long ship, which @ Danaus sailed to Greece (935 BC) 73; called @Amenophis by the name of @Memnon 270; 86; called @Sesostris by the names of @Osiris and @Busiris 273; called @Thebes (Egyptian) by the name of @Diospolis 425; called one of the Muses by the name of Calliope 417; called the @ Assyrians by the name of @Syrians in the times of Cyrus 554; called the city of @Ammon @*Diospolis* (998 BC) 44; called the times before the reign of Ogyges, unknown because they had no written history of them 195; captured the Persian Empire from @Darius Codomannus at the battle of Gaugamela 666; colonised southern @Italy 351; commissioned the Argonaut Expedition to persuade countries to revolt from Egypt 276; commissioned the ship *Argo* 479; commissioned the ship *Argo* to sail on the Black and Mediterranean seas (936 BC) 72; considered @Osiris and @Bacchus to be one and the same king of Egypt 419; considered @Osiris and @Bacchus to be sons of @Jupiter 424; created imaginary kings to inflate the history of @Sicyon 379; dated the Argonaut Expedition three hundred years too early 297; defeated @ Sesostris in a major battle (962 BC) 60; derived the constellations from their history 253; derived the words @*Siris*, @*Sirius*, @*Ser-Apis* and @*O-Siris* from the biblical name of @*Sihor* for the @Nile River 453; did not know about the precession of the equinoxes 250; difficult to correct the genealogies and chronology of its fabulous ages 385; early chronology documented 371; Egyptian chronology synchronised with theirs 416; exaggerated the time for the founding of Syracuse 299;

exaggerated their history 700; extreme limit of their known history was termed *Ogygian* 383; feared the Medes after their conquest of Lydia 615; fought @Darius Hystaspes at the battle of Marathon in 490 BC 660; fought with clubs until the times of the Trojan War according to Homer 461; had no public tables or inscriptions older than the laws of Draco 197; halted the advance of the Atlanteans 464; heard the Egyptian's lament saying, @*Oh* @*Siris* and *Bou* @*Siris,* they called @ Sesostris by the names of @Osiris and @Busiris (951 BC) 66; honoured eminent citizens with temples 359; imagined that @Amenophis was the son of Tithonus (962 BC) 95; incorrectly thought @Amenophis came to the Trojan War (904 BC) 87; its islands were colonised by @Minos (1002 BC) 42; its twelve city states excluding Attica were part of the council of Thermopylae 330; learned how to cultivate grain from Ceres (1026 BC) 32; made the Argonaut Expedition too old by three hundred years 267; Myles was the first among them to set up a hand mill to grind grain 381; offered supplications to @Apollo to drive away the Medes 616; oldest extant historian is Herodotus 368; only knew about Britain long after the @Phoenicians did 293; oracle at Dodona was similar to the one of @Jupiter @Ammon in @Thebes (Egyptian) 437; perfected music and poetry 217; placed the flood of Deucalion at the beginning of the reign of Nyctimus (1041 BC) 28; practice of deification of the dead introduced to them by Cadmus and @Europa 358; received a detailed chronology of their history from Eratosthenes 2; received the celestial sphere from @Chiron 625; reckoned times using a luni-solar year 237; repelled the invasion of @Bacchus 422; said that @Cyaxeres was the first person who helped establish the Medo-Persian Empire 594; said that @Japetus was the father of @Atlas 466; sent colonies to Sicily and @Italy around 750 to 700 BC 300; sent the Argonauts as envoys to many countries 480; set up the Amphictyonic Council at Thermopylae (1003 BC) 41; settled Sicily three hundred years after the Sicels 300; sometimes calculated the reigns of kings equal to the generations of men with three generations to a hundred years 204; sometimes equated the reigns of kings to generations and calculated three generations to a hundred and twenty years 207; taught by Euryalus and Hyperbius to make clay bricks and to build with it 391; their ancient history full of poetic fiction 1; their destruction was predicted by a poet 617; their records were used to establish the times of the kings of the Persian Empire 669; their rites were copied by the Romans 393; their war against the gods of Egypt is related in the poem of Solon 517; thought @Memnon was the son of Tithonus 477; thought Semiramis built Babylon 543; thought that Rome was founded long before the Olympiads 311; thought that Romulus built Rome 312; thought the ancestors of Acrisius were Egyptians 326; traded with the @Sidonians 298; uncertain chronology 3; uncertain history concerning the founding of the Olympic Games 198; used a council of elders in every town for its administration and had a place where the elders and people worshipped their god with sacrifices 386; used a luni-solar year and intercalated months to make it agree with the seasons 240; used intercalary months and deducted days from the month 235; used the year of Philip 247; while they wrote in poetry they had no reliable chronology 196

Gudars: another name for Nebuchadnezzar 694

Gymnosophists: name given a sect of naked philosophers in India 656

Habor: mountainous region between @Assyria and Media forming part of the north-east part of @Assyria 538; some of Galilee transplanted here by the @Assyrians 534; 549; some of Samaria transplanted here by the @Assyrians 534

Hachaliah: father of Nehemiah 684

Hadad: husband of Arathes 99; 456; another name for Benhadad II (895 BC) 92; deified after he died (852 BC) 99; freed the country from Egypt 456; king of Syria 456; ruled @Syrians from @Damascus 99

Hadad: Edomite king who fled from David to Egypt 271; 438; 441; 25

Hadadezer: king of Zobah 456

Hadar: king of Syria 699

Hadon: name of an @Assyrian god 519

Haemon: father of Oxylus 220; son of @Thoas 220; son of Pelasgus 384; 19; king in @Thessaly (1081 BC) 19; reigned in @Haemonia and built a town there 384

Haemonia: original name for Thessaly 384

Haggai: encouraged the Jews to complete the temple 674; times of his prophecies were used to determine the month @Darius started to reign 660

Halah: metropolis of Calachene 539; on the north side of the @Assyrian Empire 539; some of Galilee transplanted here by the @Assyrians 534; 549; some of Samaria transplanted here by the @Assyrians 534

Halone: island that rose from the sea 396

Halys River: boundary between Lydia and the @Assyrian Empire 608; eastern border of the kingdom of Croesus 307; western border of the @Assyrian Empire 554

Ham: king of all Africa 524

Hamath: called *the Great* 525; conquered by @Assyria 530; 533; conquered by Jeroboam II 528; 529; 531; had its own king until it was conquered by the @Assyrians 525; on the eastern border of David's kingdom 271; on the west and south side of the @Assyrian Empire 535; part of the @Assyrian Empire at the time of the fall of Israel 532; transplanted by @Esarhaddon into the regions of Samaria and @Damascus 504

Hananiah: son of Jeremiah 676; chief priest in the days of Joiakim 676

Hanes: another name for Anysis (788 BC) 109; 495

Hara: some of Galilee transplanted here by the @Assyrians 534; 549; some of Samaria transplanted here by the @Assyrians 534; 549

Haran: Abraham left here to avoid its idolatry 411; conquered by @Sennacherib 550; had its own king until it was conquered by the @Assyrians 525; part of the @Assyrian Empire at the time of the fall of Israel 532; royal seat of Mesopotamia 535

Harim: priest who returned with @Ezra and Nehemiah in the first year of Cyrus 671

Harmodius: helped Aristagiton murder Hipparchus (513 BC) 171

Harmonia: mother of Polydorus 315; sister of @Jasius 315; 318; 359; sister of Dardanus 315; wife of Cadmus 315; 318; contemporary with @Erechtheus, Celeus, Eumolpus, Ceres, @Jasius, Cadmus, @Asterius and Dardanus 319; married Cadmus in Samothrace 315

Haron: conquered by @Pul 542

Harpagus: instigated a revolt against @Darius the Mede 630

Harpalus: modified the *Octaeteris* cycle in the times of the Persian Empire 240

Harpocration: says that @Darius the Mede recoined the gold coins of Sardis into @Darics 612

Hattush: priest who returned with @Ezra and Nehemiah in the first year of Cyrus 671

Hazael: deified and worshipped by the @Syrians (852 BC) 99; king of Syria 456; 699

Hebrew: language in which Ecclesiasticus was originally written 682

Hebrews: ate separately from the Egyptians 433; called one of the generals of @Lohorasp by the name of @Nebuchadnezzar 694; Egyptian chronology synchronised with theirs 416; led from Egypt under Moses 429

Hebron: David first ruled here as king 271; 320

Hecataeus: says that in the sepulchre of @Amenophis the priests placed a golden circle of three hundred and sixty-five cubits in circumference and divided it into three hundred and sixty-five equal parts 246

Hector: brother of Alexandra 359; son of Priam 359; Greeks built a temple to him 359

Hegestratus: archon of @Athens, when Solon died (549 BC) 162; 307

Helen: sister of Castor 324; sister of Clytemnestra 324; sister of Pollux 324; wife of Menelaus (924 BC) 83; courted by Agapenor 333; freed by her brothers (934 BC) 74; Greeks built a temple to her 359; kidnapped by Paris (924 BC) 83; kidnapped by Paris twenty years before the taking of Troy according to Homer 317; kidnapped by Pirithous 229; kidnapped by Theseus 74; kidnapped by Theseus just before the Argonaut Expedition 228; Solomon reigned before her kidnapping 297; temple of @Venus Hospita was not dedicated to her 459; very young at the time of the Argonaut Expedition 324

Heliopolis: @Ramesses erected an obelisk here 490; @Shepherds fled from here under the leadership of Pelasgians 377; Bocchoris sent in a wild bull on the god @Mnevis which was worshipped here 495; border city of the kingdom of Mephres (1121 BC) 14; capital of the kingdom of @Mitres 511; custom of human sacrifice abolished here by Amosis I 436; its priests gave Herodotus an account of Egyptian history 499; 510; limit of the kingdom of @Mesphres 512; place of the Phoenician custom of sacrificing men (1066 BC) 21

Helius: grandson of @Uranus 405; son of @Basilea 463; son of @Hyperion 405; 463; another name for Orus 241; 246; 463; sun god 246

Helladius: states that Oes taught the Egyptians astronomy and writing 442

Hellanicus: cited by Athenaeus 213; documented the time of the invasion of Sicily by the Sicels 300; organised his history by the generations of the priestesses of Juno Argiva 1; 197

Helle: daughter of Athamas 329; 52; sister of Phrixus 314; 327; 329; 63; step-daughter of Ino 314; 63; drowned in the Hellespont (958 BC) 63; fled with her brother Phrixus from their step-mother Ino to Aeetes 314; 327; 329; 63

Hellen: brother of Amphictyon (1003 BC) 41; brother of Hellen 330; brother of Protogenia 327; father of Aeolus 29; 327; 328; 329; 384; 51; father of Dorus 328; 29; father of Xuthus 29; 319; 328; 31; grandfather of Salmoneus 220; grandfather of Sisyphus 51; son of Deucalion 330; 41; contemporary with the reign of Saul and to David when he was at Hebron 320; fled with his Deucalion father from the flood in @Thessaly to Attica 330; reigned at @Thessaly a few years before the reign of @Erechtheus 332

Hellenodicae: judges for or in the name of Greece in the Olympic Games 304

Hellespont: before @Bacchus crossed it he was caught in bed with @Venus 278; contained numerous monuments to the Argonaut Expedition 480; crossed by @Bacchus and his army 417; 422; 458; crossed by @Sesostris in his invasion of Greece (964 BC) 58; crossed by @Xerxes I (480 BC) 175; crossed by an Egyptian king who almost lost his army in it (958 BC) 63; named after Helle who drown in it (958 BC) 63; took @Xerxes I a month to cross with his army 662

Hena: part of the @Assyrian Empire at the time of the fall of Israel 532

Hephaestia: city in Lemnos (975 BC) 53; ruled by @Thoas (975 BC) 53

Hephaestion: also called Nilus and was Hercules (Egyptian) according to Ptolemy and was Sesostris 461

Heracleia: former name for the city of Carteia 291

Heracleopolis: capital of one of the smaller kingdoms in Egypt 431

Heracles: another name for Hercules 291; Greek name for Hercules 429

Heraclides: Atreus repelled their invasion 354; between their return into Peloponnesus and the end of the first Messenian War, there were ten kings of Sparta 204; chonologers made their return too ancient 11; Ephorus wrote a history of Greece, beginning with their return into Peloponnesus and ending with the siege of Perinthus 1; expelled from Peloponnesus by Eurystheus (927 BC) 80; from their return to the end of the reign of Agesilaus there were six kings in the family of the Spartan kings who descended from Procles 218; from their return to the first Messenian War was less than two hundred years 207; led by Temenus in their return to Peloponnesus 301; made five attempts to return into Peloponnesus before they were successful 222; returned about forty-five years before the beginning of the Olympiads 209; 305; returned into Peloponnesus 221; 333; 335; 102; returned into Peloponnesus around 825 BC 308; returned into Peloponnesus in 1104 BC according to Diodorus 203; returned two generations before the first Olympiad 220; ruled in @Corinth for one hundred and seventy years 329; six generations from their return to the fifth year of the Messenian War 208; their return into Peloponnesus used as the starting point for the history of Ephorus 197

Heraea: town in Arcadia created from nine towns by @Cleombrotus 389

Hercinian: name of a huge forest in Germany 403

Hercules: constellation shaped like this Argonaut man 253

Hercules (Egyptian): son of Nile according to Cicero (951 BC) 66; another name for Sesostris (951 BC) 66; called Nilus 399; called Ogmius 399; conquered most of the world 461; defeated @Antaeus at the town of @Antaea in @Thebes (Egyptian) 467; defeated @Antaeus when he invaded Egypt 468; deified name for Sesostris 486; drove the cattle of Geryon through @Italy and abolished the custom of human sacrifice 352; hieroglyphic representation of 460; killed by @Typhon 461; king of Egypt who established the Egyptian Empire 416; lived fifteen thousand years before @Amasis according to the Egyptian priests 193; made many western conquests in the days of Solomon 399; name given to Sesostris by the Egyptians before he became king 273; 446; one of the gods of Egypt 431; one of three men called @Hercules 461; opposed by Ligures when he tried to cross the Alps from Gaul into @Italy 398

Hercules (Idean): father of Hyllus 222; 333; 80; grandfather of Clymenus 354; grandson of Electryo 324; son of @Jupiter (Cretan) 366; son of Alcmena 324; 366; 461; @Phoenicians built a temple to him on the island of Thasos 356; @Phoenicians called him by the name of Hercules Olympius 356; @Phoenicians surnamed their kings @Jupiter until his time 369; an Argonaut 223; born (961 BC) 61; born the same year as Eurystheus 323; deified (927 BC) 80; Evagetus and his son descended from him (719 BC) 118; fought against the @Amazons 423; freed Theseus (932 BC) 76; Greeks built a temple to him 359; had sexual intercourse with Auge 333; had sexual intercourse with the fifty daughters of Thespis 319; he and Andraemon married two sisters 220; Hippocrates lived eighteen generations after him 223; Idean Dactyli offered sacrifices to him at his tomb in Crete 356; instituted the Olympic Games at Elis in memory of the war between Saturn and @Jupiter 353; killed Augeas 354; killed by Laomedon, the king of Troy (933 BC) 75; one of three men called @Hercules 461; released Prometheus from Mount Caucasus 227; 232

Hercules (Pillars of): @Phoenicians sailed past them after the Trojan War 291; Canaanites settled as far west as here in their flight from Joshua 429; located at the Strait of Gibraltar 464

Hercules (Tyrian): also called Heracles 291; also called Melcartus 293; 308; annual tithe to him was sent to @Tyre from @Carthage 295; his bones were buried in a temple in the @Gades Island 294; led Phoenician colonies from @Tyre to Spain around 892-889 BC 308; lived after the Trojan War 293; one of three men called @Hercules 461; undertook long voyages on the sea 291

Hercules Egyptius: Mathetho's name for Osarsiphus 476

Hercules Olympius: Phoenician name for Hercules (Idean) 356

Herennius: states that Babylon was built by the son of @Belus (Assyrian) 547

Hermapion: Egyptian priest who interpreted an inscription for Emperor Constantius 490

Hermes: founded a city in Egypt 454; one of the gods of Egypt 454

Hermippus: describes the exploits of @Bacchus 417

Hero: name given to Sesostris by the Egyptians before he became king 273; 446

Herod: altered the temple design 649; false messiah the Herodians created to avoid accepting Jesus as fulfilling Daniel's seventy weeks 669

Herodians: thought Herod was the Jewish messiah to avoid accepting Jesus as fulfilling Daniel's seventy weeks 669

Herodotus: Octaeteris or the Great Year introduced by Cadmus and @Europa into Greece was used until his times 240; attributed the actions of @Shishak to @Sesostris 232; called @Nebuchadnezzar by the name of @Labynitus and his son @Belshazzar by the same name 585; calls @Ramesses by the name of @Rhampsinitus 490; calls @Upper Egypt by the name of Thebes 431; confounded Astyages with @Darius the son of @Cyaxeres 596; confounded Astyages with his son @Cyaxeres 595; consulted with the priests of @Thebes (Egyptian), @Memphis and Heliopolis about the Egyptian history 510; custom of building altars were at first built without temples continued in @Persia until after his days 455; describes the city of Babylon 624; describes the expedition of @Sesostris 230; Egyptian king list of Diodorus was similar to his but confused 513; estimated the size of @Babylonia by the produce it supplied 623; from his time to the time of Diodorus the Egyptian priests had greatly increased the number of their kings 483; his king list between the time of the expulsion of the @Shepherds to @Cambyses is reasonably accurate 485; his king list was smaller than that composed by Manetho and Eratosthenes 515; his king list when compared to Diodorus exposes the fraud of the priests 517; his list of kings for two hundred years after @Amenophis seems valid 499; history of Egypt is accurate from the time of the @Assyrian conquest 516; identified @Otanes as the one who exposed the conspiracy of @Smerdis 657; in his days some of the Egyptian temples of @Sesostris were still standing 452; incorrectly thought Astyages was the last king of Media 631; incorrectly thought the @Assyrian Empire lasted five hundred and twenty years 521; lists the kings of Egypt before @Nebuchadnezzar conquered Egypt 509; name Diodorus gave to @Amasis and @Actisanes, he gave to @Anysis and @Sabacon 514; Newton lists his kings in a different order 486; oldest extant Greek historian 368; omitted many kings of Egypt whom the priests had invented 9; relates the same account of the defeat of the Medes as the book of Judith 558; saw the statue of @Sethon holding a mouse in his hand 501; says @Cyaxeres was the first king to introduce martial discipline to the Median armies 694; says Amphictyon came to Greece from Egypt 363; says some of the pillars of @Sesostris were still around in his days 450; says that @Apis in the Greek language is @Epaphus 379; says that @Cyaxeres was much more valiant than his ancestors and was the first who divided the kingdom into provinces and introduced martial disciple into the Median troops 599; says that @Sabacon reigned for fifty years 506; says that Aristodemus was king of the Lacedemonians 218; says that Perdiccas, @Araeus, or @Argaeus, Philippus, Aeropus, Alcetas, Amyntas and Alexander, reigned successively in Macedon 301; says that Phidon removed the Eleans from presiding over the Olympic Games 304; says that Proteus reigned in Lower Egypt when Paris sailed there at the end of the Trojan War 488; says that the @Persians had nothing rich or valuable before they conquered the Lydians 613; says that the @Phoenicians came from the Red Sea to the Mediterranean Sea 287; says that the Medes revolted first from the @Assyrians 556; says that the region around the temple of @Venus Hospita was inhabited by @Tyrian @Phoenicians 459; says the @Phoenicians originally came from the Red Sea (1044 BC) 25; started to write his histories (444 BC) 180; states Semiramis built the walls, gates and temple of @Belus (Assyrian) in Babylon 543; states that @Dejoces reigned for fifty-three years over the Medes 561; states that @Neptune was first worshipped in North Africa 466; states that @Sethon was the last king of Egypt before the division of Egypt into twelve contemporary kingdoms 503; states that Cyrus died at age seventy 633; states that Hesiod and Homer lived about four hundred years before him (870 BC) 97; states that Nitocris was five generations older than Semiramis 8; states that Semiramis was five generations older than the mother of @Labynitus II 520; states that the @Phoenicians under Cadmus brought many kinds of learning into Greece 336; states that the Greeks called the @Assyrians by the name of @Syrians in the times of Cyrus 554; states that the sons of @Europa where contemporary with Aegeus 344; states that three generations of men equates to a hundred years 193; states the Greek islands were first inhabited by @Carians who later migrated to @Caria 283; states the Lydians were the first to mint gold and silver coins 614; told by the Egyptian priests of almost three hundred and thirty imaginary kings 484; twelve years younger than Hellanicus 1; 197

Hesiod: described the four ages of the gods and demigods in Greece 365; did not know about @Memphis hence he must have lived before @Moeris (860 BC) 98; Greeks before his time thought @Memnon was the son of Tithonus 477; in his time the star Arcturus rose sixty days after the winter solstice 268; knew nothing of the @Tyrian voyages on the Mediterranean Sea 293; lived about four hundred years before Herodotus 368; lived one generation after the war of Thebes (Greek) and Troy (870 BC) 97; only knew of one @Minos 344; places the end of the Iron Age at the end of the Trojan War (904 BC) 28; wrote before the Greeks and Egyptians corrupted their antiquities 278; wrote his history in verse 196

Hestiaeus: wrote a history of Egypt 498

Hezekiah: @Elam prospered in his days 566; about his eighteenth year as king, @Dejoces became the king of the Medes 561; in his fourth year the @Assyrians invaded Israel 501; king of @Judah 551; received an embassy from @Merodach Baladan 551; trusted Pharaoh to deliver him from the @Assyrian armies 502

Hezion: another name for Rezon 456

Hiarbas: husband of @Dido 224; king of @Libya 224

Hiera: island formed in the sea by an earthquake 395

Hieronymus: cited by Athenaeus 213

Hilkiah: father of Azariah 684; son of Shallum 684

Hipparchus: son of Pisastratus (513 BC) 171; murdered by Harmodius and Aristagiton (513 BC) 171

Hipparchus: described the sphere of Eudoxus 250; Greek astronomer who wrote in prose 196; noted that the equinoxes were regressing with time 267

Hippias: from Elis who published a breviary or list of the Olympic victors 1; 197

Hippo: daughter of @Chiron 253; good astronomer 253

Hippocrates: lived about five hundred years after the Argonaut Expedition (c. 433 BC) 75; lived eighteen generations on his father's side after the Argonaut Expedition 223

Hippocratides: Spartan king descended from Procles 209

Hippodamia: daughter of Evarete 324; granddaughter of Acrisius (989 BC) 46; mother of Lysidice 324; wife of Pelops 324; 46

Hippolytus: son of Theseus 359; Greeks built a temple to him 359

Hippothous: king of Arcadia 333

Hiram: son of Abibalus 281; 297; built a temple at @Tyre to an earlier @Hercules (Tyrian) 295; built temples 454; 455; furnished Solomon with timber for building the temple 296; king of @Tyre 280; 281; 296; Solomon married his daughter 296; succeeded his father at @Tyre 297; supplied Solomon with carpenters 280; supplied Solomon with men skilled in carpentry and architecture 444

Hirom: in his fourteenth year Cyrus began to rule in @Babylonia 590; king of @Tyre 589

Hittites: supplied with horses from Solomon (1015 BC) 35

Hodaviah: another name for Hodijah 671; Levite who returned with Zerubbabel to @Judah 672

Hodijah: priest who returned with @Ezra and Nehemiah in the first year of Cyrus 671

Holaeas: king of Arcadia 333

Holofernes: conquered Cilicia, Mesopotamia, Syria, @Damascus, part of Arabia, @Ammon, @Edom and Madian 560; killed by Judith 561

Homai: mother of @Darius Nothus 696; @Persians name her as a queen 696

Homer: calls @Erichthonius by the name of @Erectheus 331; calls most of the places which he notes in Peloponnesus not cities but regions 389; calls Proteus the servant of @Neptune 488; calls the first @Erectheus by that same name 6; did not know about @Memphis hence he must have lived before @Moeris (860 BC) 98; does not mention @Memphis 9; his poems were brought from Asia into Greece by Lycurgus (710 BC) 121; his style imitated by Terpander 217; knew nothing about @Memphis but knew about the glories of @Thebes (Egyptian) 482; knew nothing of the @Tyrian voyages on the Mediterranean Sea 293; knows of Sidon but not of @Tyre 284; lived about four hundred years before Herodotus 368; 97; locates Proteus on the sea coasts making him a sea god 488; Lycurgus brought his poems from Asia to Greece 216; mentions @Bacchus and @Memnon as kings of Egypt and @Persia but knows nothing of an @Assyrian Empire 526; only knew of one @Minos 344; says @Thebes (Egyptian) was in Ethiopia 432; says @Vulcan was honoured primarily in Egypt and was a king of @Lemnos 459; says Calypso was the daughter of @Atlas (896 BC) 91; says Paris kidnapped Helen twenty years before the taking of Troy 317; says that the Greeks fought with clubs until the times of the Trojan War 461; says that Ulysses found the island of @Ogygia covered with forests and uninhibited except by Calypso and her maids 397; 465; states that Adrastus reigned first at @Sicyon and was in the first war against Thebes (Greek) 380; wrote before the Greeks and Egyptians corrupted their antiquities 278

Hophra: another name for Apries 509; king of Egypt some time after @Moeris 512; made a large obelisk 511

Horeb (Mount): location of Ishmaelites and Midianites 438

Horus: another name for Orus according to Diodorus 422; in the reduced king list of Diodorus 514; king of Egypt according to Diodorus 513

Hosea: knew of and mentioned the @Assyrian Empire 529; may have alluded to the @Assyrian kings of @Shalmaneser and @Sennacherib 542; says that @Salmanasser captured Beth-Arbela 550

Hoshea: last king of Israel 501; made an alliance with @Sethon 501; rebelled from @Assyria 501

Hunns: no written language until about 530 AD 202

Hyagnis: Phrygian who invented the pipe (1003 BC) 41

Hyanthidas: king of @Corinth before the return of the Heraclides 329

Hyblon: Sicilian king who gave those who were expelled from Thapsus a place to live 299

Hydra: constellation contains a star used to define the colure of the solstices 261; constellation shaped like a dragon 253; neck of the constellation contains a star that passes through the colure of the solstices 252

Hydra: his statues erected on the island of Gades 293

Hyginus: documents that @Minos was the son of @Jupiter and @Europa 344; says that @Epaphus the Sicyonian impregnated Antiope 379; states that @Sesostris is painted with a club in his hand because he fought with a club 447; states that Euhadnes taught the Chaldeans astronomy 442; tells of the war between the gods of Egypt and the Titans led by @Atlas 467

Hyllus: father of Cleodius 222; son of @Hercules (Idean) 222; 333; 80; killed by Echemus 333; killed by Echemus when he invaded Peloponnesus (924 BC) 83; killed Eurystheus (927 BC) 80; killed in the second attempt of the Heraclides to return 222

Hypenus: won the double foot race in the 14th Olympic Games 215

Hyperbius: brother of Euryalus 391; taught the Greeks to make and build with clay bricks 391

Hyperion: father of @Helius 246; 405; 463; father of @Selene 246; 405; 463; husband of @Basilea 463; son of @Uranus 246; 405; another name for Osiris 241; 463; another name for Sesostris 246; his kingdom was divided among his brothers 463; one generation older than @Jupiter (Cretan) 470

Hypermnestra: daughter of @Danaus 325; third priestess of Juno Argiva 325

Hypsipyle: daughter of @Calycopis (963 BC) 59; daughter of @Thoas 457; 59; left at Lemnos by her parents (963 BC) 59

Hysicrates: ancient historian of the @Phoenicians 296

Hystaspes: father of @Darius Hystaspes 653; 656; 168; son of Arsamenes 653; carried on @Zoroaster's work 655; established a new religion in @Persia from the best of the old ones 657; helped @Zoroaster establish the worship of one god in @Persia (521 BC) 168; helped reform of the @Magi 653; high priest or Archimagus of the @Magi 653

I Esdras: book parallels @Ezra 686; gives events in historical order unlike the book of @Ezra 687

Iareb: maybe the last part of the name of @Sennacherib 542

Iberia: part of the @Assyrian Empire at its height 554; Scythians were forced to retreat here by @Cyaxeres (607 BC) 144; source of a colony of Sicaneans that first settled Sicily according to Philistus 398

Iberians: their naval station was located at @Carteia 291

Icareus: father of Erigone 254; he and his daughter Erigone are related to the constellations of Bootes, @Plaustrum and Virgo 254

Ida: Curete who accompanied @Hercules (Idean) from Crete to Elis 353

Ida (Mount): five @Curetes came from here into Elis 353; location of the cave in which @Minos was raised 404; location of the cave that @Jupiter was raised in (1031 BC) 30; 341; location of the grave of @Hercules (Idean) 356

Idaeus: son of Chryses 358; son of Dardanus 358; instituted the mysteries of the @*Mother of the Gods* in @Phrygia 358

Idalia: another name for Calycopis or Venus (930 BC) 78; 458

Idas: grandson of Gorgophone 324; an Argonaut 324

Iddo: priest who returned with @Ezra and Nehemiah in the first year of Cyrus 671; 676

Idean Cave: Cretan @Jupiter was raised here 346

Idean Dactyli: accompanied Alymnus and @Europa into Crete 342; another name for the Curetes 457; 28; danced in armour at sacrifices in a furious manner 358; discovered iron in Mount Ida in Crete (1031 BC) 30; initiated the study of music 338; invented Ephesian letters and musical rhymes 339; name for the Curetes who settled in Crete 336; 337; offered sacrifices at the tomb of @Hercules (Idean) in Crete 356; raised @Jupiter for @Rhea (Cretan) 353; smelted iron into armour and iron tools (1031 BC) 30

Idean Phrygia: mysteries of the goddess the *Great Mother* were observed here 340

Idolarty: prevalent in Ur and @Haran 411

Idomeneus: grandson of @Minos 297; 317; son of Deucalion 344; fought at Troy 317; 344; 367; Greeks built a temple to him 359; in his prime during the war of Troy 297; lived in the Iron Age 367

Idumaea: its inhabitants had determined the constellations and had a written language before the days of Job (c. 1900 BC) 25; some @Shepherds fled here from Misphragmuthosis (1121 BC) 14

Ilaira: wife of Pollux 324

Iluarodamus: another name for Evilmerodach according to Ptolemy's Canon 581

Ilus: fifth king of Troy 321

Imandes: another name for Amenophis 489

Imbrus: one place the @Curetes settled 336

Inachus: father of @Io 6; 287; 394; 419; 26; father of Aegialeus 378; 384; 20; father of Phegeus 378; 384; father of Phoroneus 20; 287; 378; 384; 389; son of @Oceanus 378; came with a colony into Greece 436; his daughter @Io was kidnapped by the @Phoenicians 394; in his time Doxius taught the Greeks to build houses using clay bricks and establish villages 391; king of @Argos 204; 287; led a colony from Egypt to @Argos 378; led a colony into Greece (1121 BC) 14; lived in the time of Ogyges 383; one of the leaders of a colony of @Shepherds fleeing from Egypt to Asia Minor and Greece 376

Inachus River: @Inachus founded a colony here in @Argos 378

India: @Bacchus conquered as far east as here 417; 418; @Bacchus made an expedition here 310; @Sesostris conquered as far east as here 418; conquered by @Bacchus 277; 278; eastern boundary of the Egyptian Empire 416; eastern destination of @Tyrians' and Aradians' voyages 284; eastern limit of the conquests of @Sesostris 450; Egyptian king conquered as far as here 420; first conquered by @Sesostris 421; great empires to the west of 409; invaded by @Sesostris (968 BC) 56; 273; 274; nationality of the Gymnosophists 656; ruled by @Ramesses 490; subdued by @Bacchus 460; two pillars set up near the mouth of the Ganges River by @Sesostris to mark his conquests 446; worshipped @Jupiter @Ammon 448

Indian Ocean: Ganges River empties into it 446

Indians: @Jupiter @Ammon was their only god 448

Ino: daughter of Cadmus 11; 327; 359; 52; mother of Learchus 329; mother of Melicertus 329; step-mother of Helle 314; 63; step-mother of Phrixus 314; 63; wife of Athamas 329; 52; alive when @Sesostris returned into Egypt 314; drowned herself in the sea with her son Melicertus 329; Greeks built a temple to her 359; her step-son Phrixus and step-daughter Helle fled from her 327; lived a generation before the Argonaut Expedition 11

Io: daughter of @Inachus 287; 394; 419; 26; daughter of @Inachus not @Jasius 6; sister of Phoroneus 287; became the Egyptian Isis 419; kidnapped by the @Phoenicians 394; kidnapped by the Phoenician traders 287; 26; kidnapped into Egypt 419

Iolaus: Greeks built a temple to him 359

Ion: son of Creusa 319; son of Xuthus 310; 319; 328; commander of an Athenian army 310; 319; Ionia was named after him 310

Ionia: country where the city of @Erythra was located 287; named after Ion 310; ruled by @Ramesses 490; some of its cities were destroyed by internal discord 617

Ionians: informed Herodotus about the Egyptian history 510; introduced the Ionian philosophy, astronomy and geometry into Egypt (655 BC) 133; people named after Ion 310

Ionic Migration: led by the sons of Codrus (794 BC) 107

Iphis: father of Euadne 324

Iphitus: son of Praxonidas 220; Aristotle incorrectly thought Lycurgus was his companion in restoring the Olympic Games 214; Aristotle incorrectly thought that he and Lycurgus established the Olympic truce 3; did not restore all the events in the first Olympic Games 215; drove Aetolus from Elis 220; established the Olympic truce 198; presided both in the temple of @Jupiter Olympius and in the Olympic Games 304; restored the Olympic Games (776 BC) 110; some chronologers make Lycurgus as old as him 211; thought to be as old as Lycurgus (708 BC) 122

Irasa: capital of the kingdom of @Antaeus 467; port of @Libya used by @Ammon for his Mediterranean Sea fleet (1030 BC) 31; ruled by @Antaeus (633 BC) 139

Ireland: history written hundreds of years after the death of @Alexander the Great 202; not populated before navigation beyond the Strait of Gibraltar 397

Irib: maybe the last part of the name of @Sennacherib 542

Iron Age: fourth age or generation after the gods 364; 371; fourth generation of the @Curetes in Europe 367; next generation after the Bronze Age in Greece ending with the Trojan War (c. 940-904 BC) 28

Isaiah: calls the city of @Tyre, *The @Daughter of Sidon* 280; knew of and mentioned the @Assyrian Empire 529; predicted captivity of Egypt by @Assyria 507; sawed asunder by the command of Manasseh 505; says that the Medes did not regard silver nor delighted in gold 613; states that the @Assyrians built Babylon 547; states that the old palace was built by the @Assyrians between the Euphrates River and the temple of @Jupiter Belus 624; wrote of the boasts of the king of @Assyria 533

Ishmael: son of Abraham 444; his posterity built vessels to search for new homes on the Red Sea islands 444; his posterity worshipped false gods 411

Ishmaelites: grew rich by trading 439; had gold earings in the days of the judges 438; merchants in the days of Jacob 438

Ishtob: supplied troops to fight against David 271

Isidorus: says that musical study began with the Idean Dactyli 338

Isis: daughter of @Ammon (1030 BC) 93; 245; daughter of Belus (Egyptian) 445; mother of @Bubaste 363; 478; 67; mother of @Orus 363; 422; 423; 431; 440; 478; 67; sister of @Danaus 445; sister of @Osiris 445; sister to @Aegyptus 445; wife of @Osiris 61; 440; 513; wife of @Osiris or @Bacchus 6; wife of @Sesostris 452; another name for Basilea 463; deified after her death (961 BC) 61; deified name of Io 419; Egyptians dedicated one of the five extra days of the year to her (1030 BC) 93; 245; goddess with a crown of towers on her head and a drum in her hand 345; in the reduced king list of Diodorus 514; name given to the queen of @Sesostris 61; queen of @Sesostris worshipped under this name 452; queen of Egypt before @Amenophis (912 BC) 85; reigned before @Amenophis 489; went mad when the @Ethiopians drowned her son @Orus (942 BC) 67

Isis (Festival of): held in Egypt in honour of Ceres 318

Ismandes: another name for Amenophis 489

Isocrates: teacher of Ephorus the historian 1; 197

Israel: Amos predicted its captivity beyond @Damascus 529; attacked @Judah and was opposed by Tiglathpileser 549; conquered @Damascus and Hamath under Jeroboam II 528; expelled the Canaanites who fled to western North Africa 428; had its own king until it was conquered by the @Assyrians 525; Hoshea its last king 501; in prosperity followed false gods and in adversity sought the true God 560; invaded by @Assyrian not Median kings 523; its strangers to observe the *The Precepts of the Sons of Noah* 412; Josiah began to seek its God 561; judged by Samuel (1117 BC) 15; not as skilled in carpentry as the @Sidonians 444; oppressed by Syria during the time of Jonah 527; oppressed by the Egyptians until King Asa (951 BC) 66; ordered by Moses to destroy altars, images, high places and groves of the Canaanites 455; pursued by the Egyptians with only six hundred chariots 375; ruled by Jeroboam II 531; 542; ruled by nineteen kings who reigned an average of seventeen years and three months each 205; ruled by Saul 374; ruled by Zacheriah 542; ruled Syria for a time 456; their animal sacrifices held in contempt by the Egyptians 434; threatened by Amos with the same destruction that happened to the surrounding countries 530; transplanted by @Esarhaddon into @Babylonia and @Assyria 504; transplanted by @Salmanasser, the king of @Assyria (721 BC) 117; transplanted into @Chalach and @Chabor by @Salmanasser 550; without the true religion for a long time 471; worshipped Egyptian gods (975 BC) 53

Israelites: confounded with the @Shepherds by Diodorus 435; confounded with the Canaanites by Manetho 373; given to idolatry 411; Pharaoh was afraid of their large numbers in Egypt 408; some helped the @Ethiopians in their invasion of Egypt 479; some lived in caves from fear of attack by the @Philistines 404; their history to the time of Solomon mentioned no conqueror of Palestine 231; to observe the *The Precepts of the Sons of Noah* 412; used the Egyptian luni-solar year 241; 242

Issus (Gulf of): part of the coast of Syria 621

Ister: states that the @Curetes sacrificed children to @Saturn (Cretan) 401

Isthmian Games: instituted at @Corinth by Sisyphus 329

Isthmius: king of Messene 204

Italus: possible father of Romus 311

Italy: @Asterius fled here from Crete (1012 BC) 37; @Oenotrus built towns here 384; @Oenotrus led a colony here from Greece 392; @Oenotrus led a colony into @Italy before the reign of Solomon 334; @Saturn (Cretan) fled here after being expelled from Crete 349; @Saturn (Cretan) settled here 350; @Sesostris returned to Egypt through here 448; 40; colonised by colonies from Greece 351; colony from here led by Lipparus settled the islands of the Aeolides 397; contains the city of Croton 399; destination Phalantus led the Parthenians to (625 BC) 141; Evander and his mother Carmenta introduced writing here (939 BC) 70; first settled by colonies from Greece led by @Oenotrus (1024 BC) 33; Greeks sent colonies here around 750 to 700 BC 308; home of the Ligures who drove out the Sicaneans 398; home of the Sicels before they invaded Sicily 300; its western part contained a large thinly populated region suitable for pasture and agriculture 352; location of the Catacombs which were used as homes by some 404; many Greek colonies in its southern part 299; place @Saturn (Cretan) fled to after his son @Jupiter (Cretan) expelled him from Crete 348;

ruled by Latinus in the time of the Trojan War 226; Sicels invaded Sicily from here 325; visited by the Argonauts 480

Ithaca: Homer lived here for some time with Mentor 368

Ithobalus: king of @Tyre 589

Ivah: part of the @Assyrian Empire at the time of the fall of Israel 532

Ixion: father of Pirithous (934 BC) 74; 229; descended from the Heraclides and was a king of @Corinth 329

Jacob: Ishmaelites and Midianites were merchants in his time 438; migrated with his family to Egypt 434; seas were sailed in his days 444

Jaddua: brother of Manasseh 181; son of @Johanan (467 BC) 177; became the high priest in the nineteenth year of @Artaxerxes Mnemon 679; confounded by the Jews for the high priest Simeon Justus 668; 682; 693; likely high priest when the priests and Levites were numbered and written in the chronicles of the Jews (422 BC) 185; may have been the high priest before the death of Sanballat and Nehemiah 681; sixth high priest of the Jews during the Persian Empire 678

Jamblicus: says Egypt was divided into nomes in the age of the gods 452

Janias: name of a Canaanite king who reigned in Lower Egypt after Joshua expelled the Canaanites (1445 BC) 13; 430

Janis: name given to the Roman god Janus by the Salii 350

Janiscus: some say he reigned after @Polybus and before Adrastus 380

Janus: another name for Oenotria 351; another name for Oenotrus 384; cordially welcomed @Saturn (Cretan) into @Italy 349; 350; descended from the family of Lycaon 352; Latin god for the man Oenotrus (1024 BC) 33; name the Latins gave to Oenotrus 334; since he offered human sacrifices was the same man as Oenotrus 352

Jao-pater: name given to every king by the @Phoenicians 343

Japetus: brother of @Osiris 370; brother of @Sesostris (951 BC) 66; father of @Antaeus (951 BC) 66; father of @Atlas 370; father of @Atlas according to the Greeks 466; father of Epimetheus 370; father of Prometheus 370; murdered @Osiris in the time of Asa and led the Libyans against Egypt 275; murdered his brother @Sesostris (951 BC) 66; one generation older than @Jupiter (Cretan) 470; one of the gods of Egypt 431; when he died, he was deified in North Africa under the name of Neptune (951 BC) 66

Japheth: ancestor of the Scythians 404; king of all Europe and Asia 524

Jareb: Hosea may have alluded to him using the name @Shalman 542

Jasion: another name for Jasius 318

Jasius: brother of Dardanus 315; 321; 358; brother of Harmonia 315; 318; 359; brother-in-law of Cadmus 357; father of Corybas 358; husband of @Cybele 358; husband of Ceres 318; 321; contemporary with @Erechtheus, Celeus, Eumolpus, Ceres, Cadmus, Harmonia, @Asterius and Dardanus 319; contemporary with Aethlius, Aeolus, Xuthus, Dorus, Tantalus and Danae 328; Greeks built a temple to him 359; initiated into the mysteries of Ceres 357

Jasius: chronologers incorrectly thought @Io was the daughter of @Jasius writing the name corruptly for Inachus 6; Curete who accompanied @Hercules (Idean) from Crete to Elis 353

Jason: son of Aeson 327; an Argonaut 327; numerous monuments in @Armenia and Media and neighbouring places erected to his Argonaut Expedition 480; received from @Thoas the purple cloak, which the Graces made for @Bacchus 457; tamed a bull with brazen hoofs and taught by @Chiron 253; undertook long voyages on the sea 291

Jebus: original name of Jerusalem 411

Jebusites: expelled by Joshua 429; inhabited @Phoenicia 429; original inhabitants of @Jebus or @Jerusalem 411

Jeconiah: son of Jehoiakim 578; @Belshazzar was born before his fifth year of captivity 586; captive for more than eleven years when @Tyre was besieged 590; captive for thirty-seven years during the life of @Nebuchadnezzar 580; captured by @Nebuchadnezzar 578; carried captive in 599 BC 573; held captive for thirty-seven years at Babylon 568; in his fifth year of captivity @Belshazzar was next in line after his father @Nebuchadnezzar 581; reigned for three months before he was carried captive by @Nebuchadnezzar 569

Jedaiah: name of two priests in the first year of Cyrus 676

Jehoahaz: father of Jeroboam II 528; Jonah prophesied toward the beginning of his reign 527; king of Israel 527

Jehoahaz: deposed from being king of @Judah by Pharaoh Necho 575; sent in irons to Riblah 575

Jehoiakim: father of Jeconiah 578; son of Josiah 570; @Assyrian Empire was destroyed in his first year 565; @Elam prospered in his days 566;

appointed king of @Judah by Pharaoh Necho 575; began to reign in 610 BC 573; captured in his eleventh year 578; carried captive in the eighth year of @Nebuchadnezzar's reign 569; his fourth year was the first of @Nebuchadnezzar 601; in his fourth year @Nebuchadnezzar defeated Pharaoh Necho at @Carchemish 576

Jehoram: @Edom revolted during his reign 285; @Edomites revolted from him early in his reign 286

Jehu: killed the prophets of Baal 455

Jeremiah: knew of and mentioned the @Assyrian Empire 529

Jeremiah: father of Hananiah 676; chief priest in the first year of Cyrus 676; contemporary with @Darius Hystaspes 695; priest who returned with @Ezra and Nehemiah in the first year of Cyrus 671

Jeroboam I: set up the worship of Egyptian gods in Israel (975 BC) 53; 471

Jeroboam II: father of Zacheriah 542; son of Jehoahaz 528; 529; conquered @Damascus 528; 529; conquered Hamath 528; 529; 531; interregnum happened after he died 542; king of Israel 528; 529

Jerome: states that @Evilmerodach ruled for seven years while his father @Nebuchadnezzar was insane 581

Jerusalem: @Ezra and Nehemiah came here in the days of @Artaxerxes Longimanus 667; @Ezra came here in the seventh year of @Artaxerxes 684; @Shepherds expelled from Egypt about the time the city was built 231; ancient home of Melchizedek 411; attacked by @Nebuchadnezzar in the ninth year of Zedekiah 574; 675; besieged by @Nebuchadnezzar in 590 BC 573; besieged in the fourth year of Jehoiakim 576; book of Ecclesiasticus was written here 682; captured at the end of Jehoiakim's eleventh year 578; captured by @Nebuchadnezzar 609; conquered and burned by @Nebuchadnezzar 579; 694; destroyed about twenty-two years after the destruction of @Nineveh 570; destroyed before the siege of @Tyre 590; Diodorus thought that Moses not David built @Jerusalem 435; enemies complained to @Artaxerxes Longimanus about the Jews rebuilding its walls 689; few people lived in it after it was rebuilt in the days of Nehemiah 693; fortified by Manasseh 553; its chronology is established 574; its temple plundered by @Sesostris (971 BC) 55; its walls were rebuilt by Nehemiah 691; Jews encouraged to attempt to rebuild the city by @Ezra 688; Jews forbidden to rebuild its walls 690; Jews returned here in the first year of Cyrus 673; location of the Christian council that affirmed that Gentiles are not to eat blood 413; made capital of Israel by David 271; Manetho incorrectly thought the @Shepherds built @Jerusalem 373; one in ten Jews selected to live here 674; purged from idolatry by Josiah 561; purged of high places, groves, carved images and the molten images by Josiah 560; second temple was built here (520 BC) 169; some @Shepherds conscripted to help build it 436; taken in the eleventh year of Zedekiah 569; temple gate led to it 638; threatened with destruction by @Sennacherib 533; wall rebuilt in the days of @Artaxerxes Longimanus 687

Jerusalem Gemara: documents the flight of the Canaanites from Joshua into North Africa 428

Jeshua: father of Joiakim 676; 678; 684; father of Jozabad 684; alive when the temple was rebuilt 675; became the high priest in the first year of the Persian Empire 679; first high priest of the Jews during the Persian Empire 678; high priest 675; in the first generation of the chief priests after the return from the exile 684; Levite who returned with Zerubbabel to @Judah 672; priest who returned with @Ezra and Nehemiah in the first year of Cyrus 671; returned with Nehemiah 676; time of his priesthood was of a normal length 683

Jesus: brother of @Johanan 680; murdered by his older brother @Johanan in the temple 680

Jewish Months: @Artaxerxes Longimanus began to reign between the fourth and ninth months 664; temple burned in the fifth month and Gedaliah murdered in the seventh month 572

Jews: @Sennacherib tried to terrify them by listing the conquests of @Assyria 534; 540; added a new court after Solomon built the temple 648; attributed the destruction of the @Assyrian Empire to the Chaldeans 564; began to rebuild the temple in the second year of @Darius Hystaspes 660; built the temple and the city of @Jerusalem in the days of @Ezra 685; called into Egypt by @Osarsiphus to repel the @Ethiopians (941 BC) 68; confessed their sins after the Babylonian captivity 522; confounded @Darius Nothus with @Darius Codomannus 681; confounded @Jaddua with the high priest

@Simeon Justus 682; conquered by @Esarhaddon (677 BC) 128; defeated at @Megiddo by Pharaoh Necho 575; defeated by the @Assyrians 505; driven out of Egypt by @Amenophis (926 BC) 81; encouraged to attempt to rebuild @Jerusalem by @Ezra 688; forbidden to rebuild the walls of @Jerusalem 690; in great affliction before Nehemiah came to them 691; incorrectly understood the history of @Ezra and Nehemiah 669; independent kingdom in the times of @Amenophis 276; kept fasts on the anniversaries of their tragic days 571; only knew of the Babylonian and Medo-Persian Empires from what they found in their scriptures 667; only know of the Persian kings who are mentioned in @Ezra and Nehemiah 668; priests and Levites were numbered and written in their chronicles (422 BC) 185; rebuilt the wall of @Jerusalem in the days of @Artaxerxes Longimanus 687; rebuilt the walls of @Jerusalem during the reign of @Artaxerxes Longimanus 689; reckon that the fourth year of Jehoiakim was the first of @Nebuchadnezzar 573; 601; religion derived from the primitive religion of Noah 412; restored temple worship after their @Assyrian captivity 559; returned from captivity in the first year of Cyrus 670; 673; 166; supplied troops for the army of @Osarsiphus 476; their biblical history ends with @Darius Nothus 693; their history connects with the rest of secular history 574; their history was outlined during the Persian kings 677; their region of Galeed was conquered by @Nebuchadnezzar 576; used a luni-solar year and used Babylonian month names after the Babylonian captivity 243; worshipped the Lord and offered burnt offerings and gifts after defeating the @Assyrians 561

Joash: Jonah prophesied toward the end of his reign 527; king of @Judah 527

Job: @Edomites had a written language before his days (c. 1900 BC) 25; knew a few of the constellations 444; lived in Arabia Petraea 444; mentions writing in his days 441

Johanan: brother of Jesus 680; father of @Jaddua (467 BC) 177; had a room in the temple (467 BC) 177; likely high priest when the priests and Levites were numbered and written in the chronicles of the Jews (422 BC) 185; murdered his younger brother Jesus in the temple 680

John Marsham: states that @Sesostris was the same person as @Shishak 232

Joiada: father of @Jonathan 678; son of Eliashib 678; became the high priest in the nineteenth year of @Artaxerxes Longimanus 679; 693; fourth high priest of the Jews during the Persian Empire 678

Joiakim: father of Eliashib 678; son of Jeshua 676; 678; 684; became the high priest in the sixteenth year of @Darius Hystaspes 679; in the second generation of chief priests after the return from the exile 684; second high priest of the Jews during the Persian Empire 678; time of his priesthood was of a normal length 683

Joiarib: chief priest in the first year of Cyrus 676

Jonah: prophesied when Israel was in affliction under the king of Syria 527

Jonathan: father of @Jaddua 678; son of Joiada 678; another name for Johanan 680; became the high priest in the eighth year of @Darius Nothus 679; contemporary with Joiakim and his father Jeshua 684; 693; fifth high priest of the Jews during the Persian Empire 678

Jonathan: defeated the @Philistines (1094 BC) 18

Joppa: Cepheus appointed its king by @Ammon (1010 BC) 38; Perseus took Andromeda away from here (1001 BC) 43; 326

Jordan River: patriarchs used boats to cross 443

Joseph: entertained his brothers in Egypt 433; while he lived Pharaoh respected the Israelites 434

Josephus: attributed the destruction of the @Assyrian Empire to the Chaldeans and the Medes 564; called the last king of the Babylonians @Naboandelos 585; calls @Naboandelos @Belshazzar for the name @Nabonnedus 632; confounded @Darius Nothus with @Darius Codomannus 681; lists the kings of @Tyre 589; mentions an earlier @Hercules (Tyrian) to whom Hiram built a temple at @Tyre 295; only knows about Cyrus, @Cambyses, @Darius Hystaspes, @Xerxes I, @Artaxerxes, and @Darius as kings of @Persia 668; relates that the *Annals of @Tyre* were extant in his times and Menander of Pergamus had translated them into Greek 296; says that Cadmus Milesius and Acusilaus lived shortly before the Persian invasion of Greece 197; says that Herodotus described the expedition of @Shishak and attributed his actions to @Sesostris 230; 232; says that the @Syrians worshipped

former kings and queens until his time (852 BC) 99; states that @Laboasserdach reigned nine months after the death of his father 583; states that the @Syrians thought that their kingdom was very ancient 456; states the @Syrians were of recent origin 699

Joshua: @Shepherds were originally Canaanites who fled from him 436; expelled Canaanites from Palestine 426; expelled the Canaanites who fled to western North Africa 427; 428; 429; expelled the Canaanites who retreated to Lower Egypt (1445 BC) 13; found Canaan ruled by city states 407

Josiah: father of Jehoiakim 570; son of Amon 560; @Assyrian Empire still was standing during his reign when Zephaniah prophesied 565; @Elam prospered in his days 566; Holofernes invaded the western countries during his reign 560; killed (610 BC) 143; killed when opposing Pharaoh Necho on his way to @Carchemish 575; Medes defeated by the @Assyrians during his reign 558; purged @Judah and @Jerusalem from idolatry 561; ruled @Judah (641 BC) 136

Jozabad: son of Jeshua 684; chief Levite among the Levites in the seventh year of @Artaxerxes 684

Judah: @Edom revolted from 285; 376; @Ezra prayed for its protection 688; @Ezra returned here (467 BC) 177; @Shepherds who remained here were conscripted by David and Solomon in building @Jerusalem and the temple 436; attacked by @Sennacherib after Israel fell 532; attacked by Holofernes when Josiah was still a child 560; conquered by @Nebuchadnezzar 579; 602; 611; 694; conquered by @Sesostris 450; controlled @Ashdod until Tartan captured it 504; defeated by the @Assyrians 505; fortified by Asa 275; free from Egyptian control after the murder of @Sesostris (951 BC) 66; hired Tiglathpileser against Syria and Israel 549; home of nine out of ten Jews who lived outside of @Jerusalem 674; invaded and conquered by @Nebuchadnezzar twice 573; invaded by @Esarhaddon 553; invaded by @Nebuchadnezzar (607 BC) 144; invaded by @Sennacherib 551; invaded by the million man army of Zerah 472; its cities attacked in the ninth year of Zedekiah 675; its cities were attacked in the ninth year of Zedekiah 574; its King Jeconiah was in captivity until the death of @Nebuchadnezzar 581; its kings in conjunction with the @Tyrians traded on the Red Sea until after the Trojan War 284; Jeremiah predicted its invasion by the Medes and the Babylonians 601; Jeroboam I rebelled in 471; Jews returned here in the first year of Cyrus 673; many nations conquered by the @Assyrians before it was conquered 534; Nehemiah returned here (454 BC) 179; not conquered before the reign of Jehoiakim 578; Pharaoh Necho imposed a tribute on it 575; purged from idolatry by Josiah 561; ruled by eighteen kings who reigned an average of twenty-two years each 205; ruled by Hezekiah and invaded by @Sennacherib 502; ruled by Hezekiah, Manasseh, Josiah and Jehoiakim 566; ruled by Josiah (641 BC) 136; ruled by Manasseh (698 BC) 124; ruled by Uzzah 531

Judah: another name for Hodaviah 671; 672

Judas of Galilee: false messiah the Jews created to avoid accepting Jesus as fulfilling Daniel's seventy weeks 669

Judith: documents the defeat of the Medes by the @Assyrians 558; killed Holofernes in battle 561

Julian: emperor of Rome and said that the Egyptians and the Romans used a solar year 244

Julius Firmicus: states that Babylon was built by Belus (Tyrian) 545

Junius Brutus: first consul of Rome about three hundred and ninety-six years after the fall of Troy 226

Juno: mother of @Isis 363; mother of @Osiris 363; wife of @Jupiter @Ammon 514; wife of @Jupiter Ammon 513; @Thebes (Egyptian) contained a temple dedicated to her and her husband @Jupiter @Ammon 425

Juno (Cretan): daughter of Rhea (Cretan) 470; daughter of Saturn (Cretan) 470; husband of @Jupiter (Cretan) 470

Juno Argiva: expedition to Sicily happened in the twenty-sixth year of her priestess Alcyone 300; Hellanicus organised his history by the generations of her priestesses 1; 197; temple built about the time of Solomon 325; temple to her erected by Eurydice 318

Juno Olympia: another name for Europa 354

Jupiter: name given to every king by the @Phoenicians 343

Jupiter (Cretan): father of @Hercules (Idean) 366; father of @Minos according to Homer 344; father of Argus 369; father of Rhadamanthus according to Homer 344; father of Sarpedon according to Homer

344; husband of @Europa according to Homer 344; husband of Juno (Cretan) 470; son of @Europa 367; son of Rhea (Cretan) 341; 470; son of Saturn (Cretan) 346; 348; 349; 367; 470; Alcmena was the last woman he had sexual relations with 366; another name for Minos 342; 343; 347; 367; expelled his father Saturn (Cretan) from Crete 348; 349; fought with @Saturn (Cretan) his father 353; had sexual relations with Niobe 369; his goat with her kids are related to the constellation of Capricorn 254; his grave was in Crete 346; inscription on the tomb of @Minos (961 BC) 61; raised by the @Curetes of whom Cres was one 401; raised in a cave in Crete during the Golden Age 367; raised in a cave in Crete in Mount Ida by the Idean Dactyli (1031 BC) 30; raised in a cave in Mount Ida by the @Curetes 341; 345

Jupiter Ammon: father of @Isis 363; father of @Osiris 363; father of @Sesostris 425; husband of Juno 513; son of Rhea (Egyptian) 363; son of Saturn (Egyptian) 363; another name for Jupiter Uranus 463; another name for Uranus 463; Arabian god called Caelus 449; deified name of @Ammon (998 BC) 44; Egyptian name for @Ammon 424; founded a city in Egypt 454; granted the honour of having one man rule over Asia 593; Greeks thought he was the father of @Osiris and @Bacchus 424; hieroglyphic representation of 460; in the reduced king list of Diodorus 514; its oracle in @Thebes (Egyptian) 437; king of Egypt according to Diodorus 513; name of Ammon 425; one god of Egypt 454; priestess of him brought into Greece by the Phoenician merchants (983 BC) 50; sacred rites propagated to the temple of @Jupiter Belus in Babylon 627; worshipped in @Ammonia (Libya), Ethiopia, Arabia, and east to India 448

Jupiter Ammon (Temple of): @Tnephachthus inscribed a curse on @Menes here 481; curse of @Gnephactus on @Menes recorded in this temple at @Thebes (Egyptian) 495; name of temple @Sesostris built in @Thebes (Egyptian) 425

Jupiter Belus (Temple of): adorned by @Nebuchadnezzar 577; built in Babylon for sacred rites 627; located in the middle of one section of Babylon 624; Nabonassar erected it to his father @Pul 548; shaped like a huge pyramid 627; used as an astronomical observatory 627

Jupiter Enyalius: its sacred vessels were brought into @Babylonia by Egyptian priests fleeing an Ethiopian invasion 498

Jupiter Olympius: son of Rhea (Cretan) 353; @Curetes introduced mysteries to it in Crete 341; @Hercules (Idean) erected an altar to him at Elis 353; his temple presided over by Iphitus 304; Olympic Games were celebrated here 355

Jupiter Uranus: another name for Jupiter Ammon 463; another name for the Arabian god Caelus 274; 449; name of the temple @Sesostris built in @Thebes (Egyptian) 425

Jupiters: three according to Cicero 346

Justin: calls Perdiccas the successor of Caranus 301; says that the @Amazons first had two queens who called themselves the daughters of @Mars 423; states that @Tyre was founded a year before Troy fell 279

Kadmiel: Levite who returned with Zerubbabel to @Judah 672; priest who returned with @Ezra and Nehemiah in the first year of Cyrus 671

Kai: in old Persian language means *giant* or *great king* 694

Kaianides: another name for the Persians 696; dynasty of the kings of @Persia that followed the Pischdadians 694; dynasty of the Medes and @Persians 697; 698

Kai-Axeres: another name for Cyaxeres 694

Kai-Caus: second king of the @Kaianides dynasty 694

Kai-Cobad: first king of the @Kaianides dynasty 694

Kai-Cosroes: third king of the @Kaianides dynasty 694

Keturah: mother of the Abrahamans 657; her posterity worshipped false gods 411

Kilkiah: chief priest in the first year of Cyrus 676

King's Gate: east gate of the @*People's Court* in Solomon's temple 637

Kir: @Syrians were transplanted by Tiglathpileser 529; city and a large region of Media on the east side of the @Assyrian Empire located between Elymais and @Assyria 537; its people transplanted to @Damascus 534; place in Media to which the @Syrians were transplanted by Tiglathpileser 549

Kirene: another name for Kir according to the Chaldee paraphrase and the Latin interpreter 537

Kischtasp: another name for Darius Hystaspes 695

Laban: worshipped idols 362

Labaris: corruption of the name Moeris 491

Labdacus: father of Laius 314; 315; 316; 47; grandson of Cadmus 316; 44; son of Polydorus 314; 316; born at the end of David's reign 315; ward of @Apis @Epaphus and Nycteus 379; ward of Nycteus and later Lycus 316; warred with Pandion (998 BC) 44

Laboasserdach: grandson of @Nebuchadnezzar 583; 586; son of @Neriglissaros 583; 586; reigned nine months at Babylon 583; 586

Labo-Assur-dach: example of an @Assyrian name compounded with the name of one of the @Assyrian gods 519

Labosordachus: another name for Laboasserdach 583

Labotas: Spartan king descended from the family of Eurysthenes 204

Labynitus: son of @Labynitus (Nebuchadnezzar) 585; son of @Nebuchadnezzar 588; son of Nitocris 543; 585; 588; another name for Belshazzar according to Herodotus 585; his mother was five generations younger than Semiramis 520; last king of Babylon 543; 585

Labynitus: father of @Labynitus (Belshazzar) 585; another name for Nebuchadnezzar according to Herodotus 585

Lacedemon: father of Amyclas 324; father of Eurydice 324; 381; 26; husband of Sparta 324; 381; 22; his father surnamed @Jupiter by the @Phoenicians 369; king in Laconia (1065 BC) 22

Lacedemonians: had good laws before any other land 212; ruled by Aristodemus 218; some used their lists of kings to write history 1

Lachares: corruption of the name Moeris 491

Lachish: besieged by @Sennacherib 502

Laconia: contributed to a colony under the leadership of Teutamus that went to Crete 400; destination of the colony Lelex led from Egypt 381; ruled by Eurotas and Lacedemon (1065 BC) 22

Laius: father of Oedipus 314; 315; 65; son of Labdacus 47; 314; 315; 316; born about the twenty-fourth year of Solomon's reign 315; fled to Pelops 317; forced to flee to Thebes (Greek) when Lycus was killed 47; killed by his son Oedipus (954 BC) 65; king of Thebes (Greek) 47; recovered the kingdom of Thebes (Greek) (976 BC) 52

Lamedon: inherited his kingdom from @Epopeus 316; king of @Sicyon 379; returned Antiope to Lycus (1006 BC) 39

Lamis: led a colony from Megara in Achaia to Sicily 299

Lampeto: left by @Sesostris at the Thermodon River in command of the @Amazons (962 BC) 60; queen of the @Amazons after the death of @Minerva 422

Lampis: Spartan who won the pentathlon event in the 18th Olympic Games 215

Lampsacus: home of Anaximenes 196

Laomedon: father of Priam 465; father of Tithonus (962 BC) 60; killed by @Hercules (Idean) (933 BC) 75; king of Troy 465; 480; 75; 60; sixth king of Troy 321; succeeded by Priam (933 BC) 75; visited by the Argonauts 480

Lapithae: warred with the people of @Thessaly (956 BC) 64

Latin: nationality of Cicero 348; their chronology of the @Persians is accurate 667

Latins: @Asterius was their @Saturn (Cretan) (1012 BC) 37; @Oenotrus was their @Janus 351; called @Asterius who fled to them by the name of @Saturn (Cretan) 367; called @Oenotrus by the name of @Janus 334; coined their first money with the head of Saturn on one side and a ship on the other 352; disputed over who founded Rome 311; exaggerated their history 700; name the inhabitants of Latium gave to themselves 348; named their god @Janus after @Oenotrus 384; ruled by fourteen kings 313; ruled by sixteen kings starting with Latinus and ending with Numitor according to Dionysius of Halicarnassus 226; termed an *age* for each Latin king who reigned at Alba Longa 312; their early chronology is very uncertain 7; their god @Janus was @Oenotrus (1024 BC) 33; their records were used to establish the times of the kings of the Persian Empire 669

Latinus: king of the Latins at the time of the Trojan War 226

Latinus: father or grandfather of Romus 311

Latium: name given to the lurking places of @Saturn (Cretan) in @Italy 348; 349

Latus: another name for Chaitus 296

Learchus: brother of Melicertus 329; son of Athamas 329; son of Ino 329; accidentally killed by his father 329

Lebanon: @Assyria compared to its cedar trees 609; source of cedar trees for Solomon's buildings 280

Lebedos: Naea lies between this island and the Daranelles 396

Lebedus: one of the twelve cities in the common council called Panionium 310

Leda: mother of Castor 253; mother of Pollux 253

Leleges: original inhabitants of @Caria 283; some lived in @Boeotia 383

Lelex: father of Cleson 381; father of Eurotas 381; 22; father of Myles 381; father of Polycaon 381; grandfather of Sparta (1065 BC) 22; came with a colony into Greece 436; came with a colony into Laconia 381; led a colony into Greece (1121 BC) 14; led colonies from Sidon into the Greek islands and @Caria 283; lived in the time of Ogyges 383; lived two or three generations before the flood of Deucalion 391; one of the leaders of a colony of @Shepherds fleeing from Egypt to Asia Minor and Greece 376

Lemnos: @Calycopis was left here by her parents (963 BC) 59; given to @Thoas by Rhadamanthus 457; island of Halone lies between here and Teos 396; one place the @Curetes settled where they assisted @Vulcan 336; place in Crete where @Vulcan worked in metals 458; ruled by @Thoas (975 BC) 53; ruled by @Vulcan 459; south of the island of Samothrace 315

Lentulus: consul when @Carthage was destroyed in 146 BC 225

Leo: constellation of the Zodiac 249; constellation shaped like the lion killed by @Hercules (Idean) 253; solstice colure had drifted into this constellation by 1689 AD 261; 262

Leocides: son of Phidon (570 BC) 156; 302; courted Agarista (570 BC) 156; 302

Leon: Spartan king descended from the family of Eurysthenes 204; 209

Leonidas: Spartan king descended from Eurysthenes 209

Leontini: colony of Lamis in Trotilus moved here 299

Leptis: city founded by the @Tyrians 285

Lepus: constellation is related to the hare Orion hunted 254

Lesbos: uninhabited until it was colonised by Xanthus 395

Leucippus: grandfather of @Aesculapius 324; husband of Phlegia 324; son of Perieres 324

Leutychides I: Spartan king descended from Procles 209

Leutychides II: Spartan king descended from Procles and fled from Sparta to Tegea and died there 209

Levi: his sons were recorded in the book of Chronicles by @Ezra 680

Levites: attended to the temple duties 644; Jozabad and Noadiah were chief men among them in the seventh year of @Artaxerxes 684; names entered in the chronicles of the Jews before Nehemiah died (422 BC) 185; Nehemiah appointed portions for them 692; returned with Zerubbabel to @Judah 672; sealed the covenant 670; their genealogies were recorded in I Chronicles 693

Libnah: besieged by @Sennacherib 502

Libra: constellation of the Zodiac 249

Libya: @Ammon was their first king 405; @Hercules (Egyptian) set up pillars here 461; @Neptune was first worshipped here 466; anciently called Ammonia after @Ammon 425; 448; conquered by @Ammon 460; conquered by @Ammon who civilised its inhabitants (1030 BC) 31; conquered by @Nebuchadnezzar 611; conquered by @Sesostris before he became king 273; conquered by Zerah 474; country where the city of @Erythra was located 287; Cyrene located here (633 BC) 139; destination of some @Sidonians fleeing from David 282; 283; destination the @Shepherds and @Philistines fled to when defeated by David 436; Egypt, @Thebes (Egyptian), Ethiopia and @Libya had no common king before the expulsion of the @Shepherds 421; home of the Canaanites who fled from Joshua 429; invaded by @Sesostris 447; invaded by Tirhakah 503; its war was settled by Mercury according to Solon 469; location of temples erected to the deified @Ammon 437; location of the city of @Carthage 224; mythology differed from the Cretans in some points 470; original home of @Minerva and the @Amazons 422; 423; part of the Babylonian Empire 621; ruled by @Antaeus 467; ruled by @Ramesses 490; ruled by Hiarbas 224; ruled over by Atlantis according to chronologers 464; settled by colonies of @Phoenicians and @Syrians fleeing from Sidon and from David (1041 BC) 28; some of the @Shepherds fled here from Misphragmuthosis (1121 BC) 14; source of horses for Egypt and Solomon (1015 BC) 35; western destination of Sidonian trade 284

Libya: mother of Belus (Egyptian) 445; wife of @Neptune 445

Libyan: nationality of the @Amazons (962 BC) 60; nationality of the women in the army of @Bacchus 422; nationality of the women in the army of @Sesostris (964 BC) 58

Libyan World: lost by @Antaeus to @Hercules (Egyptian) 467

Libyanassa: daughter of @Epaphus 445; wife of @Neptune 445; another name for Libya 445

Libyans: contributed troops to the million man army of Zerah 472; fought with @Sesostris 460; independent kingdom in the times of @Amenophis 276; led by @Japetus and @Atlas against Egypt 275; part of the army of @Sesostris 231; 450; received the celestial sphere from @Atlas 625; routed by @Orus after the death of @Sesostris (951 BC) 66

Ligures: opposed @Hercules (Egyptian) when he returned from his expedition against Geryon in Spain and tried to cross the Alps from Gaul into @Italy 398

Lindus: town in @Rhodes 322

Lipparus: helped settle the Aeolides islands 397

Liris River: border of the colony of @Oenotrus in @Italy 392

Lisianassa: variation on the name Libyanassa 445

Livy: says Caranus was the first king of Macedon 301

Locris: country where the city of @Erythra was located 287

Lohorasp: another name for Darius the Mede 695; fourth king of the @Kaianides dynasty and another name for Kai-Axeres or Cyaxeres 694

Loos: lunar month of the Macedonians and occurred in the same season each year 243

Lucan: says a peak in India was dedicated to @Bacchus 450; says that @Sesostris conquered as far east as India 448

Lucian: historian who noted the age of temples 454; saw temples to @Osiris and @Isis (961 BC) 61; says that the Cretans say that @Jupiter (Cretan) was born and buried among them and showed his grave 346; states *The @Mother of the Gods* was the Cretan Rhea or @Europa 358; states that @Corinth is full of fables about the war of the gods and the Titans 467; states that @Europa, the mother of @Minos, was worshipped by the name of Rhea (Cretan) 345

Ludovicus Balbus: king of France 205

Luna: Egyptians imagined that she played dice with Mercury and lost 440

Lycaon: father of @Oenotrus 334; 392; 33; father of Callisto 333; 351; 34; father of Lycaon and twenty-three other sons 384; father of Nyctimus (1042 BC) 27; grandfather of Arcas 334; 34; son of Pelasgus 377; 390; 20; built Lycosura 384; 20; built the oldest city in Greece 390; died about the middle of the reign of David 333; first king of Arcadia 335; in his times towns began to be consolidated into cities 391; king of Arcadia 333; likely died about the middle of the reign of David 334; offered human sacrifices 352; second king of Arcadia 377

Lycia: ruled by @Ramesses 490

Lycosura: built by Lycaon 384; 20; considered the oldest town in Arcadia 384

Lycurgus: brother of Polydectes 216; grandson of Arcas 334; son of Aleus 333; Aristotle incorrectly thought he was the companion of Iphitus in restoring the Olympic Games 214; Aristotle incorrectly thought that he and Iphitus established the Olympic truce 3; brought the poems of Homer from Asia into Greece (710 BC) 121; contemporary with Terpander the musician 213; gave a discus for the pentathlon in the 18th Olympic Games 215; guardian of @Charillus and travelled through Crete and Asia until the child was fully grown 216; his laws written in verse by Terpander 217; incorrectly made one hundred years older than the first Olympiad 4; incorrectly thought to have established the Olympic truce along with Iphitus 198; incorrectly thought to have lived at the time of the first Olympiad 199; instituted his laws about three hundred years before the Peloponnesian War 212; king of Arcadia 333; published his laws during the reign of Agesilaus 218; reigned at Sparta in 708 BC 308; some chronologers make him as old as Iphitus 211; Spartan king descended from the family of Eurysthenes 218; thought to be as old as Iphitus by Aristotle (708 BC) 122

Lycurgus: killed by @Bacchus 417; killed by @Sesostris (964 BC) 58; killed by an Egyptian king 420; king of @Thrace 58; 417; opposed the crossing of @Bacchus over the Hellespont 422

Lycus: brother of Nycteus (1006 BC) 39; Antiope returned to him by Lamedon (1006 BC) 39; murdered by Amphion and Zethus 317; 47; ward of Labdacus 316

Lycus: king of the Mariandyni 480; visited by the Argonauts 480

Lydia: @Darius the Mede finished capturing its kingdom 594; conquered by @Darius the Mede during the reign of Croesus 596; conquered by the Medes 615; its coins were reminted into @*Darics* 614; ruled by

Alyattes (590 BC) 149; Scythians fled here to Alyattes to escape @Cyaxeres 607; war with the Medes was ended by a total eclipse of the sun 608

Lydian: nationality of Sandanis 613

Lydian Money: recoined into @*Darics* by @Darius (544 BC) 163

Lydians: exceedingly rich 613; first to mint gold and silver coins 614; war with Medes ended by a total eclipse predicted by Thales (585 BC) 151; 585

Lynceus: grandson of Gorgophone 324; son-in-law of @Danaus 323; an Argonaut 324; king of @Argos 323

Lyra: constellation shaped like the harp played by @Orpheus 253

Lysidice: daughter of Pelops 54; 324; mother of Alcmena (974 BC) 54; wife of @Mestor 324; wife of Electryo 54

Maacah: supplied troops to fight against David 271

Maadiah: priest who returned with @Ezra and Nehemiah in the first year of Cyrus 671; 676

Maaseiah: father of Azariah 684; son of Ananiah 684

Maaziah: another name for Maadiah 671

Macarius: populated Samos 395

Macedon: founded by Caranus and Perdiccas (594 BC) 148; kingdom founded by Perdiccas and Caranus 302; ruled by eight kings before Archelaus 301; ruled by eight kings who reigned an average of seventeen years and three months each 205

Macedonian Empire: walls of Babylon lasted until its time 544

Macedonians: their lunar month Loos occurred in the same season each year 243

Machaon: father of @Aesculapius 359; father of Polemocrates 359; Greeks built a temple to him 359

Macrobius: says that @Sesostris travelled as far west as the island of Gades beyond Spain 448; says that after Saturn disappeared, @Janus erected an altar to him with sacred rites as to a god and instituted the Saturnalia and that human sacrifices were offered to him 352

Madera: island settled by the @Phoenicians 397

Madian: conquered by Holofernes 560

Madyes: led the Scythian invasion of Asia 562; 600

Magdolus: another name for Megiddo 575

Magi: @Ostanes was one of their eminent men 657; @Zoroaster was their legislator 625; claimed to have fire that came from heaven 656; killed when @Darius became king (521 BC) 168; killed when @Smerdis was exposed and killed 652; taught Pythagoras 653; used a three hundred and sixty-five day year 654; word means *Priests* 659

Magia: word means *Religion of the Persians* 659

Magna Mater: means the *Great Mother* and its mysteries dedicated to @Rhea (Cretan) 340

Magnesia: destroyed by internal discord 617

Malchijah: another name for Malluch 671

Malluch: priest who returned with @Ezra and Nehemiah in the first year of Cyrus 671; 676

Malta: island settled by the @Phoenicians 397

Manasseh: father of Amon 560; @Elam prospered in his days 566; about his forty-third year as king, @Phraortes became king of Media 561; captured and carried into captivity by the @Assyrians 505; carried captive to Babylon by @Esarhaddon 559; held captive in Babylon for a short time by @Esarhaddon 553; Holofernes invaded the western countries after his reign 560; king of @Judah (698 BC) 124; led captive by @Esarhaddon to Babylon returning the same year (677 BC) 128; sixty-five year captivity of Israel ended in the twentieth year of his reign 504

Manasseh: brother of @Jaddua (438 BC) 181; husband of Nicaso (438 BC) 181; son-in-law of Sanballat (432 BC) 182; expelled by Nehemiah (438 BC) 181; expelled by Nehemiah from the priesthood for marrying Nicaso, the daughter of Sanballat 681; first high priest in the temple Sanballat built (432 BC) 182

Mandane: brother of @Cyaxeres (599 BC) 147; daughter of Astyages 596; 597; 147; mother of Cyrus 633; 147; sister of @Cyaxeres 633; sister of Amyite 633; wife of @Cambyses according to Herodotus and Xenophon 595; incorrectly is thought to be the daughter of the last king of Media by Herodotus 631

Manetho: affirms the @Shepherds were driven out of Egypt shortly before the reign of Solomon 434; called @Osarsiphus by the name of @Hercules Egyptius 476; calls the @Shepherds Phoenician strangers 436; cited by Josephus 230; confounded the exodus of Moses with the expulsion of the @Shepherds to Palestine 435; confounded the expulsion of the @Shepherds with the exodus of Israel 373; documents a two year Egyptian interregnum when the country was invaded by the @Assyrians 557; his Egyptian dynasties were filled with the names of many kings not found in Herodotus 515; his king lists show @Moeris listed only once 486; his list of kings should not be used to correct Herodotus 517; incorrectly lists @Ammenemes I, @Gesongeses, @Ammenemes II and @Sesostris as kings of Egypt 424; says the @Shepherds were expelled from Egypt about the time @Jerusalem was built 231; says the Canaanites came from the east and settled in great numbers in Lower Egypt during the reign of Tutimaeus 430; states @Sesostris ruled Egypt for forty-eight years 472; states that @Sevechus was the successor and the son of @Sabacon 501

Manphtha: Coptic name for Memphis 275

Mantinaea: town in Arcadia created from five towns by the Argives 389

Maraphus: king of @Persia for a few days after @Smerdis was killed 652

Marathon: battle fought here (490 BC) 173; location of the battle between the Greeks and @Persians in 490 BC 660

March: possible month @Darius Hystaspes started to reign 660

Mardocempad: another name for Merodach Baladan 551; example of an @Assyrian name 519

Mardus: another name for Smerdis the Magus 651

Mareshah: Asa defeated a million man army led by Zerah here 472

Mariandyni: ruled by Lycus 480; visited by the Argonauts 480

Maris: another name for Moeris 491

Marmorica: home of the Naphtuhim 466

Marres: another name for Moeris 491

Marrus: another name for Mendes 513; variation on the names of Uchoreus, Mendes and Myris 514

Mars: name given to the queens of the @Amazons 423; name the Phrygians and Thracians gave to Sesostris, which means *Valiant* 273; name the Phrygians gave to Sesostris (951 BC) 66

Marthesia: mother of Antiope 423; mother of Orithya 423; leader of the @Amazons 423; left by @Sesostris at the Thermodon River in command of the @Amazons (962 BC) 60; queen of the @Amazons after the death of @Minerva 422

Masoretes: confounded the name @Achsuerus and @Ahasuerus 594

Ma-sors: name the Phrygians and Thracians gave to Sesostris, which means *Valiant* 273; name the Phrygians gave to Sesostris (951 BC) 66

Mastor: another name for Mestor 324

Mavors: name the Phrygians and Thracians gave to Sesostris, which means *Valiant* 273; name the Phrygians gave to Sesostris (951 BC) 66

Mede: nationality of @Cyaxeres 562; nationality of @Darius 594; 667; nationality of Arbaces 556; nationality of Nitocris according to Philostratus 587; nationality of the wife of @Nebuchadnezzar 588; one nationality attributed to @Zoroaster since he lived here for a while 656

Medea: constellation Crater is shaped like her cup 253

Medes: @Cyaxeres was their greatest warrior 599; @Darius their last king was not @Cyaxeres or Astyages 631; @Darius was of their royal blood 594; abandoned by its allies when attacked by the @Assyrians 558; Babylonian Empire was about the same size as the @Assyrian Empire after the Medes revolted 621; became powerful after the @Assyrian Empire fell 567; built the city of Ecbatana for their new king @Dejoces 556; conquered @Persia 611; conquered before Israel was conquered 549; conquered Lydia 615; conquered the @Persians 605; conquered the cities of Magnesia, Colophon and Smyrna 617; conquered the kingdoms of the east 609; defeated by the Scythians 562; destroyed @Nineveh 521; destroyed the @Assyrian Empire with the help of the Chaldeans 564; did not conquer @Persia until after the ninth year of @Nebuchadnezzar 606; did not regard silver nor delighted in gold 613; foremost in the empire of the Medes and @Persians at its beginning 619; helped @Nebuchadnezzar in his conquests 575; 576; invaded by the Scythians (634 BC) 138; Israel transplanted to their cities 550; its army was feared by the Greeks 616; its war with the Lydians ended with a solar eclipse predicted by Thales 585; Jeremiah predicted their attack on @Judah 601; lost the empire with the defeat of @Darius the Mede 632; may have conquered @Elam 566; Nitocris fortified Babylon against them 588; one of their children was cooked by the Scythians and served to @Cyaxeres 607; Paraetacene was their province 554; punished when they were conquered by Cyrus 603; revolted from @Assyria about the time of @Sennacherib's defeat by the Egyptians 551; revolted from the @Assyrian Empire (712 BC) 120; revolted from the @Assyrians in the latter end of the reign of @Sennacherib 555; ruled by @Cyaxeres (600 BC) 146; ruled by @Darius the Mede 618; 620; ruled by @Dejoces, @Phraortes and Astyages 561; ruled by @Dejoces, @Phraortes, Astyages, @Cyaxeres and @Darius 593; ruled by Astyages (635 BC) 137; ruled by the dynasty of the @Kaianides 697; 698; ruled successively by Astyages, @Cyaxeres and @Darius 595; ruled the @Persians until the end of the reign of @Darius the Mede 630; some of its cities were on the east side of the @Assyrian Empire 537; supplied soldiers for the army of Holofernes 560; their punishment after seventy years was predicted by Jeremiah 602; their year had three hundred and sixty days 243; visited by the Argonauts 480; war with Lydia ended by a total eclipse of the sun 608; 151; warred frequently with the Armenians and the Babylonians 622

Media: age of its kingdom was exaggerated 194; civil unrest in @Assyria made it unsafe for Tobit to travel here 551; conquered by @Sesostris and @Memnon 526; conquered fifty-four years after the Cirrheans were conquered 303; contained numerous monuments to the Argonaut Expedition 480; contained the city of @Kir 537; contains the region of @Kir to which the @Syrians were transplanted by Tiglathpileser 549; developed from villages, towns and cities which grew into the kingdom 409; foundation laid on which to build a more exact chronology for it 309; grew strong after the conquest of @Nineveh 587; invaded by the Scythians 562; invaded by the Scythians in the beginning of the reign of Astyages 600; land adjacent to @Habor 538; on the northern boundary of @Babylonia as far as Mount Zagrus 622; only ruled by two kings, Astyages and @Cyaxeres along with @Persia according to Aeschylus 596; part of the @Assyrian Empire at its height 554; received the kingdom of @Nebuchadnezzar 696; revolted from the @Assyrians 406; 556; ruled by @Phraortes (657 BC) 132; ruled by @Ramesses 490; some of Galilee and Samaria were transplanted here by the @Assyrians 534; some Scythians resided here after making peace with @Cyaxeres 607; territory is more mountainous than @Babylonia 588; Tobit was unable to go here after @Sennacherib's defeat in Egypt 555; when @Darius returned here Cyrus revolted from him 630

Median Empire: Ctesias incorrectly thought it lasted three hundred years 521; Ctesias thought it existed two hundred and fifty years after the @Assyrian Empire 523

Mediterranean Sea: @Amazons journeyed to it as part of the army of @Bacchus 422; @Ammon maintained a fleet on (1030 BC) 31; @Edomites fled here from the Red Sea 281; @Phoenicians explored and traded on it 287; @Phoenicians from @Tyre began to make long voyages on it around 892 to 889 BC 308; @Phoenicians made long voyages here (1043 BC) 26; @Sesostris prepared a fleet and explored its western coasts 448; @Tyrians built ships for trading on it 285; @Tyrians traded on it after being driven from the Red Sea 298; after the @Edomites revolted from Jehoram, the @Tyrians began to make long voyages on it 286; at its entrance @Sesostris set up pillars to his conquests (1004 BC) 40; Atlanteans invaded countries bordering its shores 464; countries around it received Greek envoys to incite them to revolt from Egypt 276; frequented by the @Sidonians 284; Greeks sent out envoys to countries around it 256; navigated by the @Phoenicians using the stars to guide them 394; navigated in the days of Jacob 444; northern border of the lands ruled by @Antaeus and @Atlas 467; sailed on by the @Tyrians after the Trojan War 293; sailed on by the ship *Argo* (936 BC) 72; some @Edomites fled to its coasts from David (1044 BC) 25; surrounding countries contained numerous monuments to the Argonaut Expedition 480; traversed by the ship *Argo* 479

Medon: brother of Androcles 310; brother of Cyaretus 310; brother of Neleus 310; son of Codrus 310; lame 310; ruled at @Athens 310

Medo-Persian: @Darius the Mede was the first king of the empire 612

Medus: another name for Madyes 562

Megabars: name given to the Ethiopians 461

Megacles: son of Alcmaeon (570 BC) 156; 302; courted Agarista (570 BC) 156; 302

Megapenthes: father of Anaxagoras 324; son of Praetus 324

Megara: Car the son of Phoroneus built a temple to Ceres here 378; home of the Greek poet Theognis 615; Lamis led a colony from here in Achaia to Sicily 299

Megara Hyblaea: name of the place Hyblon gave those who were expelled from Thapsus 299

Megaris: Crotopus left @Argos and built a new city here 326

Megiddo: Pharaoh Necho defeated the Jews here killing Josiah 575

Mela: says the bones of @Hercules (Tyrian) are buried in the @Gades Island 294

Melampus: Greeks built a temple to him 359

Melas: son of Antissus 221; descended from Gonussa 221

Melcarteia: original name for Carteia 292

Melcartus: also called Hercules (Tyrian) 293; 308; buried on the island of Gades 293; founded @Melcarteia and named it after himself 292; led Phoenician colonies from @Tyre to Spain around 892-889 BC 308

Melchizedek: followed the same religion as Abraham 411; kept the laws of Noah 410

Meleager: killed the Calydonian boar (931 BC) 77

Melec Kartha: another name for Melcartus 292; means the *king of a city* 292

Melec-cartus: another name for Melcartus 292

Melech: name of an @Assyrian god 519

Melicertus: brother of Learchus 329; son of Athamas 329; son of Ino 329; 359; drowned in the sea with his mother Ino 329; Greeks built a temple to him 359

Melicu: another name for Malluch 671

Melita: visited by the Argonauts 480

Melos: island that lies before Anaphe 396

Membliarius: came with a colony into Greece 436; led a colony of @Phoenicians and @Syrians fleeing from Sidon and from David (1041 BC) 28; 283

Memnon: father of @Ramesses 476; son of Cissia 477; son of Zerah 477; another name for Amenophis 478; 489; conquered many countries 526; contemporary with @Menes 517; deified @Cinyras after his death under the name of @Vulcan and began to build the temple of @Vulcan 482; drove out the Jews and @Phoenicians from Lower Egypt 476; Egyptian astronomical discoveries were made during his reign 497; erected a statue to his mother Cissia 477; Greek name for Amenophis (909 BC) 86; 270; king of Egypt who established the Egyptian Empire 416; ruled at the time of the Trojan War 473

Memnonia: built at @Susa and This 489; city built by @Amenophis in @Susa (909 BC) 86; 270; 276

Memnonium: north of the Egyptian monuments 490

Memphis: @Moeris moved the capital of the empire from @Thebes (Egyptian) 500; @Moeris moved the capital of the empire from @Thebes (Egyptian) to here 483; @Shepherds fled from here under various leaders 377; also called Amenoph 275; built by @Uchoreus according to Diodorus 492; built on the site of the city Mesir 426; capital for the kings of Egypt 494; capital of a small kingdom in Egypt ruled by @Gnephactus, and his son and successor Bocchoris 495; capital of the kingdom of @Gnephactus (776 BC) 110; city built by @Amenophis 275; city built by @Menes 478; fortified by @Amenophis against @Osarsiphus (940 BC) 69; insignificant city in the days of Homer 482; Isaiah predicted that its princes would be deceived 507; its priests gave Herodotus an account of Egyptian history 499; 510; location of the largest pyramid which was built by @Cheops 493; location of the temple of @Vulcan 459; made the capital of Egypt by @Moeris (860 BC) 98; Moph a variation of the name 230; Nitocris ruled here 486; not famous before the days of Homer 9; place @Memnon retired to from Lower Egypt 476; Proteus ruled Egypt from here while @Amenophis was absent 276; ruled by @Amenophis 489; temple built here to @Vulcan by @Amenophis (912 BC) 85

Menahem: bribed @Pul not to invade Israel 542; destroyed Tiphsah and its territories because it did not submit to him 529; king of Israel 529

Menander: from Pergamus 296; says the flight of @Europa was the reason Cadmus came to Greece 297; translated the *Annals of @Tyre* into Greek 296

Mencheres: another name for Mycerinus 493

Mendes: king of Egypt according to Diodorus 513; variation on the names of Uchoreus, Marrus and Myris 514

Menelaus: adopted son of Atreus 317; 83; husband of Helen (924 BC) 83; came into @Phoenicia 296; fought at Troy 317; Greeks built a temple to him 359; his voyage was likely after the destruction of Troy

297; left his wife Helen to look after his father Atreus' inheritance (924 BC) 83; undertook long voyages on the sea 291

Menephes: corruption of the name Amenophis 482

Menes: son of Cissia (941 BC) 68; son of Zerah (941 BC) 68; also called Amenophis who reigned in @Upper Egypt (941 BC) 68; another name for Amenophis 482; 489; 512; 514; 85; began to rule after the defeat of Zerah 499; built @Memphis 478; built the temple of @Vulcan 478; 500; 509; cursed by @Gnephactus 495; first king to reign after the gods of Egypt 364; from his time to @Sethon over eleven thousand years elapsed according to the Egyptian priests 193; introduced luxury and an extravagant lifestyle to Egypt 481; king of Egypt according to Diodorus 513; king of Egypt according to Herodotus and Newton 486; no older than Theseus and @Memnon 517; priests inserted three hundred and thirty kings between him and @Moeris 9; three hundred and thirty kings inserted after his reign by the Egyptian priests 483; visited by the Argonauts 480

Menestheus: great-grandson of @Erechtheus (927 BC) 80; son of Peteos 319; early Athenian king 310; fought against Troy 319; ruled @Athens 80

Menoph: another name for Memphis (912 BC) 85; 478

Mentor: personally acquainted with Ulysses and lived in Ithaca and Homer spent some amount of time with him 368

Menus: another name for Memphis 478; name the @Arabians gave to Memphis (912 BC) 85

Meones: father of @Cybele 358; king of @Phrygia 358

Mephres: reigned over @Upper Egypt from Syene to Heliopolis (1121 BC) 14

Merajah: son of Seraiah 676; chief priest in the days of Joiakim 676

Merbalus: king of @Tyre 589

Mercury: Egyptians imagined that he played dice with Luna and won 440; settled the war between the Titans and the gods 469

Meremoth: priest who returned with @Ezra and Nehemiah in the first year of Cyrus 671; 676

Meres: another name for Moeris 491

Meriones: grandson of @Minos 317; fought at Troy 317; Greeks built a temple to him 359

Merodach: name of an @Assyrian god 519

Merodach Baladan: king of Babylon 551; sent an embassy to Hezekiah 551

Merodach-Empad: example of an @Assyrian name compounded with the name of one of the @Assyrian gods 519

Meroe: capital of Ethiopia 449; city in Ethiopia 437; location of the temple erected to the deified @Ammon 437; only worshipped @Jupiter and @Bacchus 449

Mesheck: conquered by @Cyaxeres and @Nebuchadnezzar 610

Meshezabeel: father of Berechiah 684; son of Azariah 684; returned from exile during the reign of Cyrus 684

Meshullam: son of @Ezra 676; priest in the days of Joiakim 676; priest who returned with @Ezra and Nehemiah in the first year of Cyrus 671

Meshullam: son of Berechiah 684; helped Nehemiah repair the wall of @Jerusalem 684

Mesir: Arabian name for Memphis 478; capital of one of the smaller kingdoms in Egypt 431; city where Memphis was built 426

Mesopotamia: @Persians say it was conquered by @Bahaman 696; conquered by Holofernes 560; country west of @Babylonia 622; its tribes near the Gordyeans were part of the Babylonian Empire 621; location of the town of @Carchemish 575; on the west and south side of the @Assyrian Empire 535; part of the @Assyrian Empire at its height 554; under its own king in the time of the judges 525

Mesphres: extended his kingdom over all @Upper Egypt from Syene to Heliopolis 512; made the first obelisk 511; predecessor of Misphragmuthosis 511

Messana: built by Messenians in Sicily (588 BC) 150

Messene: Caucon taught the mysteries of Ceres (1002 BC) 42; conquered by Polycaon and named after his wife 381; its ten kings reigned an average of thirty-eight years according to chronologers 204; ruled by ten kings from the return of the Heraclides to the end of the first Messenian War 207; 102

Messene: wife of Polycaon 381

Messenian War: began (652 BC) 134; chronologers increased the time from the return of the Heraclides to this war by almost two hundred

years 209; ended (633 BC) 102; first war ended in 632 BC 308; from the return of the Heraclides to this war was less than two hundred years 207; in the time between the return of the Heraclides and it, Sparta had ten kings 204; second war began (607 BC) 144; six generations from the return of the Heraclides to the fifth year of this war 208; started about the end of the rule of the decennial archons at @Athens 310

Messenians: built Messana in Sicily (588 BC) 150; defeated and fled to Sicily 150; led by Euryleon in the Messenian War 208

Mestor: brother of Electryo 324; brother of Gorgophone 324; brother of Sthenelus 324; son of Andromeda 324; son of Perseus 324

Metharme: daughter of Pygmalion 225; husband of @Cinyras 225

Metion: father of Eupalamus 319; son of Pandion 319; younger than Theseus 319

Metionides: helped Pandion depose his older brother Cecrops II 319

Meton: computed the lunar cycle starting from the summer solstice of 432 BC 266; discovered the lunar cycle 240; from his time to Hipparchus the equinoxes had gone back four degrees 267; lived about sixty years before Eudoxus 250; observed the summer solstice in the eighth degree of Cancer (432 BC) 73

Miamin: priest who returned with @Ezra and Nehemiah in the first year of Cyrus 671; 676

Micah: knew of and mentioned the @Assyrian Empire 529

Midacritus: another name for Melcartus 292; corruption of a Greek name Melcartus 293

Midas: incredibly wealthy king 613

Midian: nationality of the daughter of a prince Moses married 441

Midian: son of Abraham 444; his posterity built vessels to search for new homes on the Red Sea islands 444

Midianites: merchants in the days of Jacob 438; rich in gold in the days of Moses 438; taught Moses writing 441

Mijamin: another name for Miamin 671

Miletus: home of Thales and visited by Solon 307; one of the twelve cities in the common council called Panionium 310

Millo: temple gate led to it 638

Mimnermnus: Greek artist 217

Minaeus: another name for Amenophis 489

Minerva: @Danaus erected her statue in Lindus 322; commanded the women in the army of @Bacchus 422; conquered part of Europe and some cities of Asia Minor 423; died in a battle with the Greeks and Scythians (962 BC) 60; led the Libyan women in the army of @Sesostris (964 BC) 58; queen of the @Amazons 60; 422; raised @Erichthonius, the son of Gaia 331; women fought in mens' clothes in her time 464

Mines: another name for Amenophis 489

Mineus: another name for Amenophis 489

Miniamin: another name for Miamin 671

Minies: another name for Amenophis 489

Minois Iovis Sepulchrum: original inscription on the grave of @Minos in Crete 348

Minos: brother of Rhadamanthus 457; father of Androgeus 278; 297; 344; 49; father of Ariadne 227; 277; 344; father of Deucalion 297; 317; father of Phaedra 344; 88; father of Talus 317; 365; 366; 75; grandfather of Idomeneus 317; grandfather of Meriones 317; grandfather of Orion according to some 254; grandson of Teutamus 400; nephew of Cadmus 359; son of @Asterius 342; 345; 351; 37; son of @Europa 308; 342; 344; 345; 358; son of @Jupiter (Cretan) 344; about the same age as Perseus, Perieres and Anaxagoras 324; built a fleet and cleared the Greek seas of pirates 394; 42; built many towns and ships in Crete 401; compelled them to send him eight young men and eight young virgins every eight years 277; contemporary with Aegeus 344; Daedalus fled to him when he murdered his nephew Talus (983 BC) 50; died pursuing Daedalus into Sicily 339; expelled his father from Crete (1012 BC) 37; famous for his maritime supremacy 291; famous for justice and dominion 343; first lawgiver of Crete 401; Greeks built a temple to him 359; his father was surnamed @Jupiter by the @Phoenicians 369; his grave was in Crete 347; his soldiers first settled the island of Carpathus 395; introduced agriculture to Crete 401; iron tools invented in his time 403; killed in a war with Cocalus (961 BC) 61; king of Crete 367; Procris fled from her husband to him 328; raised in a cave on Mount Ida in Crete 404; reigned in the Silver Age 365; 366; 367; ruled the Greek islands 283; same man as

Jupiter (Cretan) 342; 343; 347; 367; second king of Crete 342; sent colonies to the islands of the Greeks (1002 BC) 42; sent out colonies 394; talked with Procris the daughter of @Erechtheus 319; tomb in Crete confused with the tomb of @Jupiter 348; used the *Octaeteris* or the *Great Year* 240; warred with the Athenians for killing his son 277; 49

Minoses: chronologers invented two men with the same name to reconcile their chronology 6; 419; 445

Minotaur: Theseus overcame the beast (965 BC) 57

Misphragmuthosis: father of Amosis I 376; 377; 435; conquered part of Lower Egypt 436; consolidated the smaller Shepherd kingdoms in Egypt into a united Egypt in the days of Eli (1121 BC) 13; drove most of the @Shepherds from Egypt 375; drove out the @Shepherds from Egypt 431; expelled the @Shepherds from Egypt 363; expelled the @Shepherds from most of Egypt and confined the rest in @Abaris 377; made a continual war against the @Shepherds causing many to flee Egypt (1121 BC) 14; reigned in Coptos 482; started to expel the @Shepherds from Egypt 435; succeeded @Mesphres as king of Egypt 511; 512; succeeded by Amosis I (1066 BC) 21

Mitres: another name for Mesphres 511

Mizraim: ancestor of the Naphtuhim 466; means *double straits* or *double people* 426

Mnevis: another name for Amenophis 489; name of a god which was worshipped at Heliopolis 495

Moab: abandoned the Medes when the @Assyrians attacked the Medes 558; conquered by @Esarhaddon 559; conquered by @Nebuchadnezzar 602; 604; 611; country plundered by four kings from the land of Shinar and @Elam 408; defeated by David 271; had its own king until it was conquered by the @Assyrians 525; its inhabitants worshipped false gods 411; revolted from @Assyria 559

Moabites: assisted @Nebuchadnezzar in his conquests 576

Mochus: ancient historian of the @Phoenicians 296

Moeris: son of @Ramesses 491; 527; built large pyramids at @Thebes (Egyptian) 482; built the northern portico of the temple of @Vulcan 478; 491; 500; created the @Lake of @Moeris with two large pyramids of brick in the middle of it 491; did the same deeds as Uchoreus and was likely the same man 492; embellished @Memphis (860 BC) 98; king of Egypt 527; king of Egypt according to Herodotus and Newton 486; location of two brick pyramids 493; made one large obelisk 511; moved the capital of his empire to @Memphis from @Thebes (Egyptian) 483; 500; 98; priests inserted three hundred and thirty kings between him and @Menes 9; successor of @Ramesses 512; 527

Moeris (Lake of): Asychis used its mud to build a large brick pyramid 494; 109; contained two large brick pyramids 491; created by @Moeris 491; 98; location of the labyrinth built by a dozen contemporary kings 508; same lake as the Lake of Uchoreus 492; to fortify Babylon, Nitocris created a similar lake 587

Moloch: god the Canaanites offered their children to 362; 436; name of an @Assyrian god also called Melech 519

Molossians: ruled by @Aidoneus 229; ruled by @Orcus (934 BC) 74

Moors: originally were the Canaanites who fled from Joshua 430

Moph: another name for Memphis 478; 85; 230; contracted Coptic name for Memphis 275

Mopsus: commander of the Thracian forces that helped Perseus repel the invasion of @Bacchus 422

Mordecai: Jews thought he lived in the times of @Ahasuerus 667

Moscheres: another name for Mycerinus 493

Moses: @Shepherds did not rule Egypt during his time 434; before his time the Egyptians wrote using hieroglyphics 460; changed the beginning of the Jewish year to the month of Nisan 573; confounded with @Osarsiphus by the Egyptian writers 476; did not lead the @Shepherds from Egypt as Manetho thought 373; died before the Hebrews entered Palestine 429; Diodorus confounded his exodus from Egypt with the expulsion of the @Shepherds 435; Egypt was thinly populated before his time 408; in his days Egypt only had six hundred chariots 375; in his time the Canaanites sacrificed their children to @Moloch 362; laws concerning not eating blood predated his time 413; learned to write from the @Edomites (c. 1510 BC) 25; Lower Egypt began to worship their kings before his time 363; married the daughter of a Median prince 441; Midianites were rich in gold in his time 438; observed the same religion as Noah 412; ordered Israel to destroy all altars, images,

high places and groves of the Canaanites 455; some chronologers think the first king of Troy was contemporary with him 321

Mother of the Gods: named Cybele after her 358

Mountain of the House: name of the walk that surrounded the sanctuary 636; 638; 639

Mummius: consul when @Carthage was destroyed in 146 BC 225

Munychion: Macedonian month when the battle of Salamis was fought 662

Musaeus: son of Eumolpus 253; along with @Chiron made the celestial sphere to assist in navigation by the Argonauts 256; one of the first Greeks to make a sphere of the constellations 253

Muses: accompanied @Bacchus on his expeditions 417; lived two generations later than the Idean Dactyli 339; name of the singing women of @Sesostris (964 BC) 58; 60; one of their nurses was the mother of Crolus 254; singing women of whom Calliope was one 450

Mycene: @Danaus' capital of the kingdom of @Argos 322; ruled by Eurystheus (940 BC) 69; ruled by Pelops and his son Menestheus (927 BC) 80; ruled by Sthenelus (954 BC) 65

Mycerinus: brother of Nitocris 493; 106; son of @Chephron 493; built the third large pyramid 493; 104; famous for clemency and justice 493; in the reduced king list of Diodorus 514; king of Egypt according to Diodorus 513; king of Egypt according to Herodotus 483; king of Egypt according to Herodotus and Newton 486; ruled Egypt 104; 106

Mygdones: tribe around Nisibis as far as Zeugma and were part of the Babylonian Empire 621

Mygdonia: mysteries of the goddess the *Great Mother* were observed here 340

Myles: brother of Cleson 381; brother of Eurotas 381; brother of Polycaon 381; son of Lelex 381; first Greek to set up a hand mill to grind grain 381; in his times towns began to be consolidated into cities 391

Myrina: another name for Minerva 422; 58

Myris: another name for Moeris 491; Diodorus' name for Moeris 492; king of Egypt according to Diodorus 513; variation on the names of Uchoreus, Mendes and Marrus 514

Mysia: visited by the Argonauts 480

Mytgonus: king of @Tyre 589

Myus: one of the twelve cities in the common council called Panionium 310

Naarmalcha River: new river @Nebuchadnezzar made upstream from Babylon 577

Naboandelos: name Josephus called Nabonnedus 632; name Josephus gave to Belshazzar who was the last king of the Babylonians 585

Nabonadius: son of Nitocris (555 BC) 160; another name for Nabonnedus 584; king of Babylon (555 BC) 160

Nabonassar: husband of Semiramis 548; son of @Pul 548; 549; built the temple of @Jupiter Belus dedicating it to his father @Pul 548; example of an @Assyrian name 519; finished the palace started by his father @Pul in Babylon 624; his first year was the twenty-second year of Bocchoris 498; his reign issues in the era using the Egyptian solar year (747 BC) 95; his years used by the Chaldeans to count the years of the reigns of their kings 573; king of Babylon 205; may be the son of @Belus (Assyrian) or @Pul 547; received Babylon from his father @Pul 549; succeeded @Pul as king at Babylon (747 BC) 114; used the Egyptian year 247

Nabonassar (Era of): based on the Egyptian year 247; began after @Sabacon conquered Egypt 516; began in the twenty-second year of the reign of Bocchoris according to Africanus 496; established by the priests fleeing from Egypt 625; instituted about two hundred years later than Asa's defeat of Zerah 499; started on February 27, 747 BC 247

Nabonnedus: another name for Belshazzar 586; another name for Labynitus 543; another name for the younger Labynitus 585; Babylonian who assisted in the overthrow of @Laboasserdach 583; last king of the Chaldeans 632; reigned for eighteen years until Babylon was captured by Cyrus 584

Nabopolassar: father of @Nebuchadnezzar 563; 570; 145; became the king of Babylon 563; died after reigning twenty-one years 577; died and was succeeded by his son @Nebuchadnezzar (605 BC) 145; in his old age his armies were led by his son @Nebuchadnezzar 564; king of Babylon 567; reigned over Babylon (625 BC) 141; revolted from @Assyria 563; revolted from the @Assyrian Empire 141

Nabuchodonosor: another name for Chyniladon in the book of Judith 558; 561; sent his captain Holofernes with a great army to subdue the western nations that had revolted 560

Naea: island that rose from the sea 396; lies between Lemnos and the Daranelles 396

Nahal: signifies a torrent and from which the word @*Nilus* is derived 453

Nahum: knew of and mentioned the @Assyrian Empire 529; prophesied the destruction of @Nineveh 555; wrote after the last invasion of the @Assyrians 505

Naphtuhim: descended from Mizraim 466; name means *people of the seacoasts* 466; their home was on the coasts of Marmorica and Byrene 466

Naples: its Catacombs were used as homes by some 404

Nauplius: son of Amymone 228; an Argonaut 228

Nausica: daughter of Alcinous 256; invention of the celestial sphere was incorrectly attributed to her 256

Naxos: @Bacchus found Ariadne here 278; first settled in the days of Boreas 395; founded by Thucles with a colony from Chalcis in @Euboea 299; its people distorted history by making @Bacchus two generations older than Theseus 419; its people pretended that there were two Minoses and two Ariadnes 344; 445; Theseus abandoned his wife Ariadne here 277; 310

Nebo: name of an @Assyrian god 519

Nebo-Adon-Assur: example of an @Assyrian name compounded with the name of one of the @Assyrian gods 519

Nebo-Assur-Adon: example of an @Assyrian name compounded with the name of one of the @Assyrian gods 519

Nebo-Chaddon-Assur: example of an @Assyrian name compounded with the name of one of the @Assyrian gods 519

Nebo-Pul-Assur: example of an @Assyrian name compounded with the name of one of the @Assyrian gods 519

Nebo-Shashban: example of an @Assyrian name compounded with the name of one of the @Assyrian gods 519

Nebuchadnezzar: brother-in-law to @Cyaxeres 563; father of @Belshazzar 581; father of @Evilmerodach 581; grandfather of @Laboasserdach 583; 586; husband of Amyite 563; 588; 633; husband of Nitocris 585; son of Nabopolassar 563; 570; 145; assisted in the conquest of @Nineveh 594; attacked @Jerusalem in the ninth year of Zedekiah 675; attacked and destroyed @Nineveh 564; built a new palace in one section of Babylon 624; built a wall around Babylon 544; burned the temple of Solomon (588 BC) 150; called Labynitus by Herodotus 585; captured @Jerusalem and destroyed the temple in the eleventh year of Zedekiah 609; captured @Jerusalem in his nineteenth year 574; captured @Tyre 589; captured Jehoiakim and Jeconiah 578; conquered @Edom, Moab, @Ammon, @Tyre and Sidon 604; conquered @Nineveh 521; conquered @Susiana and @Elam (594 BC) 148; conquered Egypt (571 BC) 155; conquered many countries and enlarged the Babylonian Empire 611; conquered many nations 610; conquered Zedekiah and @Judah 579; defeated Pharaoh Necho at @Carchemish 576; descended from @Pul according to @Abydenus 547; destroyed the city of @Thebes (Egyptian) 505; did not conquer @Persia until after his ninth year 606; died in the end of the winter of 562 BC 581; general of @Lohorasp according to the @Persians 694; helped @Cyaxeres invade and conquer @Assyria 600; helped @Cyaxeres overthrow @Nineveh (610 BC) 143; helped by @Assuerus to destroy @Nineveh 575; his kingdom was given to the Medes 696; in his eighth year he carried Jehoiakim captive 569; invaded @Judah and Syria (607 BC) 144; king of Babylon 567; 608; king of Babylon that the Jews knew about 667; made viceroy with his father about two years before his father died 601; married Amyite a Median for an alliance between Media and the Chaldeans 588; mediated a peace between Alyattes and @Cyaxeres 608; ruled @Phoenicia and Coele Syria 580; ruled the Babylonian Empire at its greatest extent 621; Semiramis lived four generations before him 543; seventy years elapsed from his invasion of @Judah to the second year of @Darius Hystaspes 573; subdued Egypt 509; succeeded his father Nabopolassar (605 BC) 145; warred in the west while @Cyaxeres fought in the east 566; when his father Nabopolassar died he settled his affairs in Egypt and the other countries and returned to Babylon 577

Nebuzaradon: example of an @Assyrian name 519

Necepsos: Egyptian king who invented astrology in Egypt along with Petosiris 625; invented astrology 497; 111; king in Sais 497; 109; ruled from Sais over a small kingdom in Egypt 495

Nechaoh: son of Psammitichus (617 BC) 142; reigned for seventeen years after Psammitichus 509; ruled Egypt (617 BC) 142

Nechepsos: another name for Necepsos 497; 625

Nechus: another name for Nechaoh 509; killed in the Ethiopian invasion under @Sabacon (751 BC) 113; king in Sais (788 BC) 109; king of Egypt 510; king of Egypt according to Herodotus 483; king of Egypt according to Herodotus and Newton 486; omitted in the king list of Diodorus but in the list of Herodotus 514; ruled from Sais over a small kingdom in Egypt 495; 496

Nectabis: made a small obelisk 511

Nectenabis: another name for Nectabis 511

Nehemiah: son of Hachaliah 684; before he died the priests and Levites were numbered and written in the chronicles of the Jews (422 BC) 185; by comparing his book with @Ezra's, one can deduce the history of the Jews under Cyrus, @Cambyses and @Darius Hystaspes 673; came to @Jerusalem in the time of @Artaxerxes Longimanus 667; copied the chronicles of the Jews written before his days 670; expelled Manasseh from the priesthood for marrying Nicaso, the daughter of Sanballat 681; 181; in his thirty-second year @Jerusalem was sparsely populated 693; Jews misunderstood his history 669; lived during the reign of @Artaxerxes Longimanus 677; lived during the reign of @Artaxerxes Longimanus not @Artaxerxes Mnemon 683; only Persian kings in this book and @Ezra are recognised by the Jews 668; opposed by Sanballat, Tobiah and Geshem when he rebuilt the walls of @Jerusalem 691; returned to @Judah (454 BC) 179; returned with @Ezra in the first year of Cyrus 671; too old to have lived in the reign of @Artaxerxes Mnemon 684

Neochabis: another name for Gnephactus 495

Nephthe: daughter of @Ammon (1030 BC) 93; 245; sister of @Typhon (1030 BC) 93; 245; wife of @Typhon (1030 BC) 93; 245; Egyptians dedicated one of the five extra days of the year to her (1030 BC) 93; 245

Nephthys: daughter of Rhea (Egyptian) 440; daughter of Saturn (Egyptian) 440; wife of @Typhon 440

Neptune: brother of @Danaus 228; brother of @Sesostris 228; father of @Antaeus 467; father of @Apollo 465; father of @Atlas 464; 466; 467; father of Belus (Egyptian) 445; 447; father of Nauplius 228; father of Orion 254; husband of @Libya 445; husband of @Neptys 466; another name for Japetus 275; 431; appointed his son @Atlas king of Atlantis 464; called @*Equestris* in the days of Solomon (1015 BC) 35; deified name of Japetus by the Libyans (951 BC) 66; father of sons who were Argonauts 465; first worshipped in @Libya 466; fought with a sword not a club 447; he and his dolphin are related to the constellation of Dolphinus 254; helped by his son @Apollo to fortify the walls of Troy 465; hieroglyphic representation of 460; made war on the gods of Egypt 466; name means *king* 466; one of the gods of Egypt 431; Proteus was his governor 488; received the island of Atlantis 464

Neptys: mother of @Atlas 466; wife of @Neptune 466; name means *queen* 466

Neptys: name given by the Egyptians to all the farthest parts of the earth and promontories and whatever bordered on the sea and its coastal areas 466

Neptys: Greek name for a Roman god called Amphitrite 466

Nergal: name of an @Assyrian god 519

Nergalassaros: murdered his brother-in-law @Evilmerodach 582

Nergal-Assur: example of an @Assyrian name compounded with the name of one of the @Assyrian gods 519

Nergal-Shar-Assur: example of an @Assyrian name compounded with the name of one of the @Assyrian gods 519

Neriglissaros: father of @Laboasserdach 583; another name for Nergalassaros 582; reigned for about four years 583; ward of @Laboasserdach 583

Nicander: Spartan king descended from the family of Procles 204

Nicaso: daughter of Sanballat (438 BC) 181; 681; wife of Manasseh (438 BC) 181; 681

Nicippe: daughter of Pelops 323; mother of Eurystheus 323; mother of Gelanor 323; wife of Sthenelus 323

Nile River: @Ethiopians drowned @Orus here (942 BC) 67; @Menes built a bridge over it (912 BC) 85; @Orus drowned in it by the brothers of @

Hyperion 463; @Orus was drowned in it by the invading @Ethiopians 472; @Sesostris did great works here 273; also called Eridanus 275; birthplace of @Hercules (Egyptian) according to Cicero (951 BC) 66; called Aegyptus, Siris, Nilus, Shihor and Sihor 453; fed canals @Sesostris dug to the capital city of each nome 452; its fish supplied the early Egyptians with food 481; its flood waters were held in the @Lake of @Moeris 492; straddled by @Memphis 426; surrounding land very fertile 362; turned into a new channel by @Memnon 476

Nilus: name for Sesostris given by the people of Siene 453; name for the Nile River given by the people of Siene 453; name given to Hephaestion 461; name the Egyptians gave to Hercules (Egyptian) 399; Sesostris deified under this name 273

Nilus: name given to a channel @Sesostris cut from the @Nile River (951 BC) 66

Nimrod: @Assyrian Empire was unknown after his time 525; built the city called @Erech 536; founded a kingdom at Babylon 524; founded cities without naming them after himself 520; led a rebellion against the government of Noah 409

Nineveh: @Assyrian kings ruled here 563; @Sennacherib returned here after his defeat in @Judah 551; after it fell @Cyaxeres warred with @Armenia and Cappadocia 611; bordered the kingdom of @Calneh 531; capital of the @Assyrian Empire 608; captured by @Cyaxeres and @Nebuchadnezzar (610 BC) 143; conquered by @Cyaxeres and @Nebuchadnezzar 594; 600; 606; Ctesias incorrectly thought it was destroyed three hundred years before @Astibares and @Nebuchadnezzar 521; destroyed about twenty-two years before the destruction of @Jerusalem 570; destroyed by @Assuerus, the king of the Medes, and @Nebuchadnezzar, the king of Babylon 575; destroyed by @Nebuchadnezzar and @Cyaxeres 564; destroyed by the Medes and the Chaldeans 562; destroyed in 610 BC 632; final destruction in the first year of Jehoiakim 565; located near @Sepharvaim 535; Media grew strong after its conquest 587; part of the Babylonian Empire 621; ruled by @Esarhaddon 552; ruled by @Nabuchodonosor 558; threw off its Egyptian yoke and had its own king at the time of Jonah 527; Tiglathpileser succeeded @Pul here 549; 114; Tobit advised his son to leave here for Media 555

Ninus: another name for Nineveh 621; Ctesias claimed the city was founded by the man of the same name 520; incorrectly thought to have a son named @Belus (Assyrian) 519

Niobe: daughter of Phoroneus 369; mother of Argus 369; mother of Chloris 317; sister of Pelops 317; wife of Amphion 317; first to have sexual relations with @Jupiter 369

Nisan: first month of the Jewish New Year 573; 578; regal years for a king determined by the number of these months during his reign 601

Nisibis: location of the tribe of Mygdones 621

Nisus: strove with Cleson about the kingdom of Sparta 381

Nitocris: mother of @Labynitus 543; 585; 588; mother of @Nabonadius (555 BC) 160; wife of @Nebuchadnezzar 585; 588; embellished and fortified Babylon (555 BC) 160; fortified the passes from Media into @Babylonia 587; mother of the last king of Babylon 8

Nitocris: daughter of @Chephron 493; sister of @Mycerinus 106; 493; finished the third large pyramid 493; 106; omitted in the king list of Diodorus but in the list of Herodotus 514; queen of Egypt according to Herodotus and Newton 486; reigned after @Menes 483; successor of @Mycerinus 106; 493

Noadiah: son of @Binnui 684; chief Levite in the seventh year of @Artaxerxes 684

Noah: ancient writers thought the @Assyrian Empire was almost as old as his flood 519; calculated thirty days to a month 235; Canaanites worshipped the true God in his days down to the time of Abraham 411; his laws kept in the eastern nations for some time 410; king of all the world 524; law concerning the killing of animals dates to his time 413; ruled the world from Chaldea 409; Tigris and Euphrates river valleys first settled after his flood 362; used a luni-solar year 439

Noah (Precepts of): primitive religion of both the Jews and the Christians 412

No-Ammon: another name for Thebes (Egyptian) 482; 505; another name for Thebes (Egyptian) meaning the people or city of @Ammon (998 BC) 44; 425; royal city of @Ammon 482

Noevius: thought that Rome was founded about one hundred years before the Olympiads 312

Noph: another name for Memphis 478; 507; 85; contracted Coptic name for Memphis 275

North Africa: @Antaeus ruled over this region to the Atlantic Ocean 467; @Dido sailed along its coast past the Syrtes to found @Carthage 286; @Neptune was first worshipped here 466; @Sesostris introduced the knowledge of observing the stars here 625; @Shepherds driven here by Misphragmuthosis and his son Amosis I 431; @Shepherds fled here from Egypt from invading @Ethiopians 426; @Tyrians built @Carthage here 291; @Tyrians sailed along its northern coasts past Syrtes and founded cities 285; Argonauts crossed over to it in order to confer with Euripylus the king of Cyrene 480; Canaanites who fled from Joshua set up pillars here and built Tripoli 428; Diodorus confounded the exodus of Moses with the expulsion of the @Shepherds to here and @Phoenicia 435; invaded by @Sesostris 40; invaded by Tirhakah 503; its coast explored by @Hercules (Tyrian) 295; navy of @Sesostris explored its coast 448; originally settled by the Canaanites before the @Tyrians 430; Phaurusii lived in caves here 404; traded with @Tyrians 298; when @Japetus died, he was deified here under the name of @Neptune 66

Norway: no written language until much later than 500 AD 202; possible location of Thule 285

November: ninth month in the Roman calendar 243

Numa: conceived and instituted the religion of the Romans 657; created a luni-solar year with intercalary months for the Romans 241; instituted one fire for all the surrounding towns at Rome 393

Numitor: last king of the Latins before Romulus built Rome 226

Nycteis: daughter of Nycteus 316; wife of Polydorus 316

Nycteus: brother of Lycus (1006 BC) 39; father of Antiope 316; guardian of Labdacus 379; killed (1006 BC) 39; killed in the tenth year of the reign of Solomon 379; led a colony of @Phoenicians and @Syrians fleeing from Sidon and from David (1041 BC) 28; made war on @Epopeus for kidnapping his daughter Antiope in which he and @Epopeus died 316

Nyctimus: son of Lycaon (1042 BC) 27; flood of Deucalion occurred in the beginning of his reign (1041 BC) 28; king in Arcadia 333; 27

Nyssean: source of the Ganges River 446

Oannes: led some @Edomites who fled from David to the Persian Gulf (1044 BC) 25; no older than @Esau 443; older than the flood of Xisuthrus according to the Chaldeans 442

Obadiah: another name for Iddo 671

Obdia: another name for Iddo 671

Oceanus: another name for the country of Thrace 290

Oceanus: father of @Inachus 378

Ochus: name of Darius Hystaspes before he became king 653

Octaeteris: eight year cycle used by the Greeks (1041 BC) 28; 240; 277

Octateuchus: name of the book written by @Ostanes about the religion of the @Magi 659

October: eighth month in the Roman calendar 243; month of the battle of Marathon in 490 BC 660; month of the battle of Salamis in 480 BC 662

Odomantes: another name for Edomites 290

Oeagrus: father of @Orpheus 417; husband of Calliope 417; 58; son of Tharops 417; received the kingdom of @Thrace from @Sesostris 58

Oebalus: husband of Gorgophone 324; son of Cynortes 324

Oedipus: father of Eteocles 314; father of Polynices 314; son of Laius 314; 315; 65; born about the seventh year of Rehoboam's reign 315; killed his father Laius (954 BC) 65

Oenotria: old name for Italy before it was called Saturnia 350; 351

Oenotrus: son of Lycaon 33; 334; 351; 384; 392; became the @Janus of the Latins 384; became the Roman god Janus (1024 BC) 33; found in the western part of @Italy a large thinly populated region suitable for pasture and agriculture 352; led a colony into @Italy from Greece 334; 351; 384; 392; led the first colonies into @Italy 33; same man as the Janus of the Latins 334; 351

Oes: taught the Egyptians astronomy and writing according to Helladius 442

Ogmius: name the Gauls gave to Hercules (Egyptian) 399

Ogyges: father of Eleusinus 383; 20; after his time and before the Olympiads, Greek history was composed of fables because their history was much mixed with poetic fiction 195; in his time colonies came to Greece from Egypt (1121 BC) 14; in his time Doxius taught the Greeks to build houses using clay bricks and establish villages 391; king in @Boeotia 383

Ogyges (Flood of): Acusilaus thought it happened one thousand and twenty years before the first Olympiad 196; occurred at most two or three generations before the flood of Deucalion 372

Ogygia: Calypso was found here by Ulysses 465; imagined to be Atlantis, which sank into the sea (896 BC) 91; island covered by forests in the days of Ulysses 397

Ogygian: term Greeks applied to very ancient things 383

Oh Siris: lament Greeks heard from the Egyptians which they thought was the name Osiris (951 BC) 66

Oiolicus: son of Theras 208

Olaeas: king of Arcadia 204

Old Testament: only source of information the Jews used to construct a chronology of the Babylonian and Medo-Persian Empires 667

Olympia: contained a temple built by the men of the Golden Age and dedicated to Saturn 353; contained an Olympic discus with the inscription that records the name of Lycurgus 3; 198; contributed to a colony under the leadership of Teutamus that went to Crete 400; Laius went here to escape his brothers Amphion and Zethus 317; located near the Alpheus River 355

Olympiads: began about forty-five years after the return of the Heraclides 305; began in the reign of Petubastes according to Africanus 496; chronologers incorrectly made Phidon and Caranus older than the first one 302; from the time of Ogyges to this time, Greek history was composed of fables because their history was much mixed with poetic fiction 195; Heraclides returned two generations before they began 220; incorrectly thought to occur one hundred years after Lycurgus 4; occurred about one hundred years after Rome was built according to @Timaeus Siculus 312; restored by Iphitus 211; rule of Athenian kings ended about forty years before they began 310; some used these to organise their history 1; used by @Timaeus Siculus to organise a history 197

Olympiads (Era of): began when Iphitus restored the Olympic Games (776 BC) 110

Olympias: name of the spring near the valley of Bathos 354

Olympus (Mount): home of the Titans 345

Olyntes: early Athenian king 310

Onias: father of @Simeon Justus 678; father of Eleazar 678; son of @Jaddua 678; became the high priest in the third year of @Artaxerxes @Ochus 679; first high priest of the Jews after the Persian Empire 678

Onias: son of @Simeon Justus 682; born when his father was very old 682

Ophir: likely source of David's gold 439

Ophiuchus: constellation created in memory of Phorbas grasping a snake 395; constellation is related to the snake killed by Phorbas 254

Ophiusa: original name for Rhodes 395

Orcus: father of Persephone 74; 229; his dog killed Pirithous, when he attempted to kidnap his daughter (934 BC) 74; killed Pirithous 229; king of the Molossians 74; 229

Orestes: father of Penthilus 222; father of Tisamenus 222; son of Agamemnon 222; young when Troy was captured 222

Orgia: secret rites practised by the priests in worshipping @Calycopis 458

Orion: constellation is related to the man Orion 254

Orion: grandson of @Minos 254; son of @Neptune 254; related to the constellation of Orion 254

Orithya: daughter of Marthesia 423; sister of Antiope 423; leader of the @Amazons 423

Orithyia: daughter of @Erechtheus 319; mother of Calais 319; mother of Zetes 319

Orneus: father of Peteos 319; son of @Erechtheus 319

Ornytion: king of @Corinth before the return of the Heraclides 329

Orosius: says that @Hercules (Tyrian) built Capsa in Spain 209

Orpheus: son of Calliope 417; 450; 58; son of Oeagrus 58; 417; an Argonaut 417; 450; contemporary with Thymoetes 422; 425; deified the son of @Semele by the name of Bacchus (938 BC) 71; Greeks built a temple to him 359; his style imitated by Terpander 217; played a harp and taught Musaeus 253; wrote his history in verse 196

Orpheus: calls @Osiris by the name of Sirius 419

Orus: brother of @Bubaste 478; 67; grandson of @Ammon 246; nephew of @Typhon 478; son of @Isis 363; 419; 422; 423; 431; 440; 478; 67; son of @Osiris 241; 275; 363; 419; 440; 472; son of @Sesostris 246; 450; 66; another name for Apollo 457; 465; 467; another name for

Helius 463; called Sesoosis II and Busiris II by Diodorus 514; deified name for Pheron 487; drowned in the @Nile River after ruling for ten years 472; drowned in the @Nile River by the brothers of @Hyperion 463; drowned in the @Nile River by Zerah 275; drowned in the Nile by the @Ethiopians (942 BC) 67; Egyptian astronomical discoveries were made during his reign 497; hieroglyphic representation of 460; king of Egypt 440; king of Egypt before @Amenophis (912 BC) 85; last god of Egypt along with his mother @Isis, sister @Bubaste, secretary @Thoth and uncle @Typhon 478; made a league with @Minerva 422; part of the army of @Bacchus 423; 431; reigned after @Sesostris and routed @Japetus in @Libya (951 BC) 66; reigned before @Amenophis 489; reigned during the four ages of the great gods of Egypt 512; reigned in @Thebes (Egyptian) 482

Orus Senior: son of @Ammon (1030 BC) 93; 245; son of Rhea (Egyptian) 440; son of Saturn (Egyptian) 440; Egyptians dedicated one of the five extra days of the year to him (1030 BC) 93; 245

Osarsiphus: @Memphis fortified by @Amenophis against him 478; 85; 69; appointed king in Lower Egypt after the defeat of Zerah by Asa (941 BC) 68; conquered by @Amenophis 489; 81; priest who led an army that drove @Memnon from Egypt 476; reigned in Lower Egypt and rebelled against @Amenophis 275; revolted from @Amenophis and forced him to retire into Ethiopia 479

Osimandes: another name for Amenophis 489

Osiris: brother of @Aegyptus 445; brother of @Danaus 445; brother of @Isis 445; brother of @Japetus 370; father of @Bubaste 241; 245; 363; father of @Orus 241; 245; 275; 363; 440; 472; husband of @Isis 61; 440; 513; son of @Ammon (1030 BC) 93; son of @Jupiter (Egyptian) 363; son of Belus (Egyptian) 445; son of Juno 363; @Sesostris worshipped under this name 452; @Thoth his secretary introduced writing to Egypt 441; @Thoth was his secretary 484; another name for Bacchus 6; 422; another name for Hyperion 463; another name for Sesostris 246; 274; 452; 472; as old as the flood of Xisuthrus according to the Egyptians 442; built two temples in @Thebes (Egyptian) according to Diodorus 425; 431; called Sesoosis I and Busiris I by Diodorus 514; conquered Geryon in Spain 461; contemporary with @Bacchus and @Sesostris 423; corresponds to the Arabian god Bacchus 449; deified after his death (961 BC) 61; deified name for Sesostris 486; deified name of Epaphus 419; did similar feats as @Bacchus and @Sesostris 420; Egyptians dedicated one of the five extra days of the year to him (1030 BC) 93; Egyptians used a luni-solar year until his days 241; 245; Greeks thought he was the son of @Jupiter 424; hieroglyphic representation of 460; in his days @Hercules (Egyptian) killed @Antaeus 467; introduced idolatry in Spain 461; king of Egypt 440; king of Egypt according to Diodorus 513; king of Egypt before @Amenophis (912 BC) 85; king of Egypt who established the Egyptian Empire 416; led an Ethiopian colony into Egypt according to the @Ethiopians 432; murdered by his brother @Japetus in the time of Asa 275; name derived from the lament Greeks heard from the Egyptians for Sesostris (951 BC) 66; name given to Sesostris 61; reigned in @Thebes (Egyptian) 482; same man as Bacchus, Sesostris and Shishak 308; Sesostris deified under this name 273

Osiris: name given to a channel @Sesostris cut from the @Nile River (951 BC) 66

O-Siris: another name for the Nile River 453

Osorchon: another name for Osarsiphus 476; ruled from @Tanis over a small kingdom in Egypt 495

Osorchor: another name for Osarsiphus 476

Ostanes: eminent man of the @Magi 657; wrote a book about the religion of the @Magi entitled *Octateuchus* 659

Osymandias: king of Egypt according to Diodorus 513; name Diodorus called Amenophis 246; 492; 514

Osymanthias: another name for Amenophis 489

Otanes: exposed @Smerdis 657; headed the conspiracy against @Smerdis 657; may be another name for Ostanes 657

Otreus: father of @Calycopis 457; king of @Phrygia 457

Ouranus: another name for the Arabian god Caelus 449

Oxus River: @Scythia lay beyond it 566; @Touran located beyond it 557

Oxyares: another name for Achsuerus 594; another name for Xerxes I 661

Oxylus: father of Praxonidas 220; son of Haemon 220; led an army of Aetolians under the Heraclides and recovered Elis 220; led the Heraclides victoriously into Peloponnesus 354

Ozair: another name for Ezra 695

Palestine: @Sesostris was the first Egyptian to conquer it 421; conquered by Joshua forcing the Canaanites fled to western North Africa 429; its seacoast was called @Phoenicia (1044 BC) 25; Manetho incorrectly thought the @Shepherds went through the wilderness into Palestine 373; originally inhabited by the Canaanites 435; place @Curetes came from 341; some of the @Shepherds fled here from Misphragmuthosis (1121 BC) 14

Pallacopas River: new river @Nebuchadnezzar made upstream from Babylon 577

Pamphos: says that @Neptune invented tall ships with sails 466

Pan: son of Penelope 359; founded a city in Egypt 454; from his time to @Amasis over fifteen thousand years elapsed according to the Egyptian priests 193; Greeks built a temple to him 359; hieroglyphic representation of 460; led the @Ethiopians in the army of @Sesostris (964 BC) 58; one of the gods of Egypt 431; 454; related to the constellation of Capricorn 254

Panathenaea Festival: initiated by @Erechtheus (1030 BC) 31

Pandion: adoptive father of Aegeus 228; 319; brother of Cecrops II 319; 43; son of @Erechtheus 228; 319; 331; deposed his older brother Cecrops II 319; Greeks built a temple to him 359; his daughter married Cleson 381; king of @Athens 359; ruled in Attica (1001 BC) 43; warred with Labdacus (998 BC) 44

Pandions: chronologers invented two men with the same name to reconcile their chronology 6

Pangaeus (Mount): gold found here by Cadmus 337

Panionium: common council of cities in Ionia composed of twelve cities 310

Pantaleon: father of Damophon 304

Panyasis: says that @Sesostris travelled as far west as the island of Gades beyond Spain 448

Paphia: another name for Calycopis or Venus (930 BC) 78; 458

Paphlagonia: country containing the city or region of Erythini 287

Paphos: @Vulcan built a temple to his wife @Calycopis here 458; built by @Cinyras according to Apollodorus 225; city in Cyprus built by Agapenor after the Trojan War according to Pausanias 333; location of the temple to the deified @Calycopis (930 BC) 78

Paraetacae: part of the Babylonian Empire 621

Paraetacene: country east of @Babylonia 622; part of the @Assyrian Empire at its height 554

Parbar: temple gate led to it 638

Paris: kidnapped Helen (924 BC) 83; kidnapped Helen twenty years before the capture of Troy 317; sailed to Lower Egypt at the end of the Trojan War 488

Parmenides: wrote his history in verse 196

Parnassus (Mount): one peak dedicated to @Apollo and the other to @Bacchus 450

Parthenians: built Tarentum (625 BC) 141; under Phalantus went to @Italy 141

Parthia: conquered by @Cyaxeres 566; location the Scythians fled to 600

Pasargadae: another name for Persepolis 631; 632

Pashur: priest who returned with @Ezra and Nehemiah in the first year of Cyrus 671

Pasitigris: located east of @Erech 536

Pataeci: name of the gods the @Phoenicians placed as figure heads on their ships 459

Pathros: another name for Upper Egypt 431; capital of one of the smaller kingdoms in Egypt 431

Paulinus: says that @Zoroaster taught the @Magi the mysteries of @Necepsos 625

Pausanias: confounded Astyages with @Darius the son of @Cyaxeres 596; says that @Bacchus was repelled by the Greeks under the leadership of Perseus 422; says that Caranus was the first king of Macedon 301; says that Melas was the son of Antissus of the descendants of Gonussa 221; says that the Eleans called in Phidon and together with him celebrated the 48th Olympiad 304; says that there were three discs kept in the Olympic treasury at Altis 215; states that Phoroneus, the son of @Inachus, was the first who gathered the Argives into one city 389; states that the Babylonian Belus was named after an Egyptian Belus, the son of @Libya 445; states that the grave of Deucalion was near @Athens 330; states that the people of Elis originated the Olympic Games 353

Pegasus: constellation is related to Bellerophon's horse 254

Pekah: Galilee captured by Tiglathpileser in his days 549; invaded @Judah with Rezin 553

Pelasgians: instigators in bringing the worship of the dead into Greece 377; introduced idolatry into Europe 362; original inhabitants of @Caria 283; originally were very numerous in Greece and did not speak Greek 377; sent a colony to Crete by ship from Greece 400

Pelasgus: father of Aegialeus (1076 BC) 20; father of Haemon 384; 19; father of Lycaon 20; 377; 390; came into Greece about two generations earlier than Cadmus 377; first king of Arcadia 333; 377; 390; in his time Doxius taught the Greeks to build houses using clay bricks and establish villages 391; 436; led a colony into Greece (1121 BC) 14; led colonies from Sidon into the Greek islands and @Caria 283; lived in the time of Ogyges 383; one of the leaders of a colony of @Shepherds fleeing from Egypt to Asia Minor and Greece 376

Peleg: world under government of Noah until his time 409

Peloponnesian War: ended (404 BC) 186; ended about three hundred years after Lycurgus instituted his laws 212; ended about three hundred years after Lycurgus instituted the Quinquertium (708 BC) 122; ended in April of 404 BC 665; ended three hundred and thirty-five years after the founding of Syracuse 299; Hippocrates lived about the time of the war (c. 433 BC) 75; in its seventh year, @Artaxerxes Longimanus died 664; occurred about eighteen generations after the Argonaut Expedition 223; occurred five hundred and ninety years after the invasion of Sicily by the Sicels 300; started (431 BC) 183; 266; three hundred years before its end, @Corinth began to build triremes 298

Peloponnesus: @Curetes conquered parts of it 401; @Phoronicum, @Phegea and @Aegialea were its oldest towns 384; Abas led a colony here from Egypt 326; Aletes returned here with the Heraclides 221; contains the territory of Olympia 400; Eurystheus expelled the Heraclides from here (927 BC) 80; Heraclides made five attempts to return here before they were successful 222; Heraclides returned here 11; 204; 207; 218; 333; 335; 102; Heraclides returned here ending the dynasty of kings and descended from Sisyphus 329; Heraclides returned here forty-six years before the first Olympic Games 209; Heraclides returned here in 1104 BC according to Diodorus 203; Heraclides returned here two generations before the first Olympiad 220; Heraclides returned to around 825 BC 308; Heraclides returned under the leadership of Oxylus 354; invaded by Hyllus (924 BC) 83; its division and subdivision of towns create great confusion in its history 385; Lycosura, @Aegialea and @Phoronicum were its oldest towns (1076 BC) 20; most places in the times of Homer were small towns 389; Pelops came here (989 BC) 46; Phidon established weights and measures and coined silver money here 301; return of the Heraclides here was used as the starting point for some histories of Greece 1; time when the Heraclides returned to here, Ephorus started his history 197

Pelops: father of Atreus 317; 80; father of Lysidice 324; 54; father of Nicippe 323; father of Plisthenes 317; father of Thyestes 317; husband of Hippodamia (989 BC) 46; about the same age as Perseus, Perieres and Anaxagoras 324; came to Greece 327; captured Aetolia from Aetolus (989 BC) 46; captured the country of Aetolia in the time of Acrisius and Endymion from Aetolus 327; celebrated the Olympic Games. 354; drove out Aetolus from Aetolia 354; his father was surnamed @Jupiter by the @Phoenicians 369; ruled Mycene (927 BC) 80

Pelosiris: Egyptian priest who helped @Necepsos invent astrology in Egypt (772 BC) 111

Pelusium: @Sethon defeated the @Assyrians here 501; 502; Misphragmuthosis confined the @Shepherds here (1121 BC) 14; seized and fortified by the Canaanites 430

Penelope: mother of Pan 359

Pentecost: time varied depending on the harvest of first fruits 242

Penthesilea: queen of the @Amazons during the time of the Trojan War 423

Pentheus: grandson of Cadmus 417; killed by @Bacchus 417

Penthilus: son of Orestes 222; lived to see the return of the Heraclides 222

People's Court: outer court in Solomon's temple was also called the *Great Court* 636; 637; 638; 639; 640; 642; 643; 645

Perdiccas: banished from @Argos in the reign of Phidon 301; banished from Phidon along with Caranus (594 BC) 148; co-founded the kingdom of Macedon with Caranus 302; 148; descended from the family of Temenus 301; incorrectly thought to be older than the Olympiads 302; king in Macedon 301

Pergamus: home of Menander 296

Periander: after his death @Corinth was freed from the rule of tyrants (557 BC) 159; ruled in @Corinth after Cypselus 329

Periclymenus: son of Chloris 317; an Argonauts 317

Perieres: father of Leucippus 324; husband of Gorgophone 324; son of Cynortes 324; about the same age as @Minos, Pelops, Aegeus and @Sesostris 324

Perinthus: its seige ended in twentieth year of the reign of Philip 197; its siege was the ending point of the history of Ephorus 1

Persephone: daughter of @Aidoneus 229; daughter of @Orcus (934 BC) 74; almost kidnapped by Pirithous (934 BC) 74; Pirithous and Theseus attempted to kidnap her 229

Persepolis: city where Cyrus was buried 632; location of the last battle between Cyrus and @Darius the Mede 631

Perseus: father of @Mestor 324; father of Electryo 324; father of Gorgophone 324; father of Sthenelus 323; 324; 65; grandson of Acrisius 330; husband of Andromeda 324; 325; 54; son of Danae 324; about the same age as @Minos, Pelops, Aegeus and @Sesostris 324; accidentally killed his grandfather Acrisius 330; born (1024 BC) 33; his father was surnamed @Jupiter by the @Phoenicians 369; led the Greeks in repelling @Bacchus 422; left Joppa with Andromeda in the days of Solomon 326; related to the constellations of Perseus, Andromeda, Cephus, Cassiopia and Cetus 254; routed @Bacchus 278; took Andromeda away from Joppa (1001 BC) 43

Perseus: constellation is related to Perseus 254; contained stars on the colure for the equinoxes 259; head of the constellation contains a star that passes through the colure of the equinoxes 251

Persia: @Amenophis led his army here 276; @Zoroaster established his religion here 695; ancient religions were abolished (521 BC) 168; captured by @Cyaxeres and added to the Median Empire 594; conquered by @Alexander the Great 697; conquered by @Cyaxeres 566; conquered by @Phraortes 556; conquered by @Sesostris and @Memnon 526; conquered by the Medes 611; country where @Pasargadae was located 631; country where Cyrus died 632; custom of building altars without temples continued here until after the days of Herodotus 455; Cyrus was likely its satrap 630; developed from villages, towns and cities which grew into the kingdom 409; enjoyed jovial festivals 628; God gave its kings favour toward the Jews 688; invaded by @Sesostris (971 BC) 55; its history is poorly understood by the Jews 669; its king and armies were supplied by conquered territories 623; its last king was @Darius Codomannus (330 BC) 191; list of some of its kings are mentioned in the Bible 685; not immediately subdued by the Medes after the destruction of @Nineveh 603; one of its princes was named @Cambyses who became the father of Cyrus 595; only its kings mentioned in @Ezra and Nehemiah are known to the Jews 668; part of the Babylonian Empire 621; Pischdadians and @Kaianides were the oldest dynasties of its kings 694; raided by the Scythians 557; ruled by @Cambyses 246; ruled by @Darius Hystaspes in 521 BC 571; ruled by @Ramesses 490; ruled by @Xerxes I 301; ruled by ten kings who reigned an average of twenty-one years each 205

Persian: nationality of the @Magi 659; one nationality attributed to @Zoroaster since he lived here for a while 656

Persian Empire: @Darius Codomannus was its last king 678; @Jerusalem temple changed little during its time 649; @Simeon Justus was the high priest when it was conquered 682; Acusilaus wrote at its beginning 196; chronologers increased the time from the first Messenian War to the start of this empire 209; chronology in the Arundelian Marbles before the its founding allowed three kings to reign a hundred years 303; conquered by @Alexander the Great (331 BC) 190; created when @Darius was defeated by Cyrus (537 BC) 165; Cypselus the king of @Corinth reigned before the empire 221; Ephorus wrote around ten years before its fall 1; Eudoxus wrote a history down to within eleven years of its fall 197; Greek chronologers thought its kings who reigned before the empire reigned an average of thirty-five to forty years each 205; in its time the Greeks modified their year 240; its religion was based partly on the institutions of the Chaldeans and partly on the institutions of the ancient Brahmins 657; Jews only knew about it from what they had in their scriptures 667; list of Jewish high priests during the empire 679; overthrown by @Alexander the Great 668; used the Babylonian year of three hundred and sixty-five days 247

Persian Gulf: @Edomites sailed here 444; @Esau buried on an island near it 443; @Sesostris sailed into it 446; city of @Areca located between this place and Apamia 536; contained colonies on the islands of @Aradus and @Tyre founded by the @Tyrians and Aradians (1013 BC) 36; contains islands of @Aradus and @Tyre 284; on the southern border of @Babylonia 622; Red Sea was considered part of it and was red in colour according to Strabo 290; sailors who frequented it brought knowledge to Chaldea 442; some @Edomites fled here from David 271; 25

Persians: @Zoroaster introduced the religion of the @Magi to them 656; also called Elamites 534; called @Artaxerxes Longimanus @*Ardschir Diraz* and @*Bahaman* 664; called a governor a satrap 623; called their priests @Magi 652; conquered by the Medes 605; ended the rule of the descendants of Teucer over Cyprus 293; exaggerated their history 699; fire worshippers 387; first king was Cyrus 633; foremost in the empire of the Medes and @Persians after @Darius the Mede 619; fought and won the battle of Thermopylae (480 BC) 175; fought with Greeks at Marathon 660; had nothing rich or valuable before they conquered the Lydians 613; invaded Greece 661; killed Leonidas at Thermopylae 209; kingdom established by @Cambyses 651; lost the battle of Salamis (480 BC) 175; not conquered until after the ninth year of @Nebuchadnezzar 606; originally their year had three hundred and sixty days 243; originally thought the @Tyrians came from the Red Sea area 286; ruled by @Darius the Mede 620; ruled by a family of kings called the Pischdadians 566; ruled by the dynasty of the @Kaianides 697; 698; ruled by the Medes until the end of the reign of @Darius the Mede 630; said that @Zoroaster lived in the same region as Hystaspes 653; said that the Pischdadians and @Kaianides were the oldest dynasties of their kings 694; supplied soldiers for the army of Holofernes 560; thought the @Phoenicians originally came from the Red Sea (1044 BC) 25; took over the empire from the Medes 631; 632; under the religion of the @Magi 659

Pessinuntia: mysteries of the goddess the *Great Mother* were observed here 340

Peteos: father of Menestheus 319; son of Orneus 319; came with a colony into Greece 436

Petosiris: Egyptian priest who helped @Necepsos invent astrology 497; 625

Petra: on the trade route from the Red Sea to Egypt 439

Petubastes: ruled from @Tanis over a small kingdom in Egypt 495; 496

Phaedra: daughter of @Minos 344; 88; mother of Demophoon (903 BC) 88; sister of Androgeus 344; sister of Ariadne 344; wife of Theseus 297; 88; lived during the reigns of Solomon and Rehoboam 297

Phaestus: some say he reigned after @Polybus and before Adrastus 380

Phaeton: another name of Helius or Orus 463

Phalantus: built Tarentum (625 BC) 141; led the Parthenians into @Italy 141

Phalerus: one of twelve cities where Cecrops I resettled a number of smaller towns 388

Phamenophis: another name for Amenophis 489

Phanias: says that after Solon visited Croesus he went into Cilicia and some other places, and died on his travels 307

Pharamundus: king of France 205

Pharaoh: afraid of the numbers of the Israelites 408; at the time of Joseph was not a Shepherd 433; friendly to King @Hadad 438; his daughter @Tahaphenes married the king of @Edom 272; Isaiah predicted that his councillors would be brutish 507; pursued Israel with only six hundred chariots 375; title given to the king of Egypt who lived after Joseph who was not a Shepherd 434; trusted by Hezekiah to deliver him from the @Assyrian armies 502

Pharaoh Necho: son of Psammitichus 565; attacked the @Assyrians at @Carchemish 575; captured @Carchemish from the @Assyrians 565; defeated by @Nebuchadnezzar at @Carchemish 576; succeeded Psammitichus as king of Egypt 565

Pharnaces: father of @Thoas 457; ruled Cyprus 457

Phaurusii: lived in caves in North Africa 404

Pheaces: lived on the island of Corcyra under their King Alcinous 256

Phegea: built by Phegeus 384; later called Psophis after the daughter of Lycaon 384

Phegeus: son of @Inachus 378; 384; built @Phegea 384; in his times towns began to be consolidated into cities 391

Phemonoe: first priestess to @Apollo at Delphi 330

Pherecydes: says that @Sesostris travelled as far west as the island of Gades beyond Spain 448; taught men to write in prose and wrote a history of the Athenians 197

Pherecydes Atheniensis: first to organise his histories by genealogies and was considered one of the best genealogists 1; says that Pelasgus reigned in Arcadia and was the father of Lycaon and he died just before the flood of Deucalion 377

Pherecydes Scyrius: introduced writing in prose 1

Pheron: son of @Sesostris 487; deified under the name of Orus 487; king of Egypt according to Herodotus 483; king of Egypt according to Herodotus and Newton 486; succeeded by Proteus 488; successor of @Sesostris 487

Phialus: king of Arcadia 204

Phidon: brother of Caranus 302; father of Leocides 302; 156; contemporary with Clisthenes, Alcmaeon and Eurolicus (570 BC) 156; contemporary with Solon (584 BC) 308; Eleans overthrew his kingdom 304; established weights and measures and coined silver money in Peloponnesus 301; in the 49th Olympiad he presided over the Olympic Games (584 BC) 152; 308; introduced weights and measures, and the coining of silver money (594 BC) 148; overthrown from the position of presiding over the Olympic Games (580 BC) 153; regained the right to preside over the Olympic Games 304; tenth generation from Temenus 305

Philip: father of @Alexander the Great 1; 197; siege of Perinthus ended in his reign 197

Philip (Era of): began with the death of @Alexander the Great 247

Philip Valesius: king of France 205

Philippus: king in Macedon 301

Philistia: had its own king until it was conquered by the @Assyrians 525; land of the @Philistines 281

Philistines: @Edomites fled from David to them 281; 286; 287; @Shepherds lived among them after being expelled from Egypt 373; brought the ark of Israel into the house of Dagon in @Ashdod 455; captured Sidon about the fifth to seventh year of David 297; conquered by @Assyria 530; conquered Israel and captured the ark (1117 BC) 15; conquered Sidon and intermixed with them 341; defeated by @Jonathan (1094 BC) 18; enemies of David 271; 287; fear of them caused some Israelites to live in caves 404; greatly strengthened by the @Shepherds (1096 BC) 16; many @Shepherds fled to them 376; oppressed Israel in the days of Saul 374; people conquered by @Nebuchadnezzar 611; strengthened by fleeing @Edomites and @Shepherds 282; strengthened by the influx of @Shepherds from Egypt 375; 436; used a common council composed of its five rulers (1003 BC) 41; were the Curetes 401

Philistus: says that the first inhabitants of Sicily moved into Sicily from the Sicanus River in Spain or @Iberia 398; says that the invasion of the Sicels into Sicily happened eighty years before the Trojan War 300

Philochorus: says that Cecrops I first consolidated one hundred and seventy towns into twelve cities 388

Philostratus: calls Nitocris a Mede who made a tunnel under the river six feet wide in Babylon 587

Philyra: mother of @Chiron 345; 367; mother of Cadmus (1041 BC) 28; wife of @Saturn (Cretan) 28

Phineus: king of the Thracians 480; visited by the Argonauts 480

Phintas: king of Messene 204

Phiops: another name for Cheops 493

Phius: another name for Hophra 511

Phlegia: grandmother of @Aesculapius 324; wife of Leucippus 324

Phlias: son of @Bacchus 227; 277; son of Ariadne 227; 277; an Argonaut 227; 277

Phocis: country where the city Abaea was built 326

Phoebe: wife of Castor 324

Phoebus: another name for Apollo 450

Phoebus: peak of Mount Parnassus 450

Phoenicia: @Amenophis expelled the people which had been called in from here 275; @Curetes came from here bringing their science with them 457; abandoned the Medes when the @Assyrians attacked the Medes 558; arts and sciences highly developed here by the @Curetes 336; benefited from Egyptian navigation expertise 298; conquered by @Esarhaddon 559; contained altars with little houses for eating the sacrifices 455; Diodorus confounded the exodus of Moses with the expulsion of the @Shepherds to here 435; extended from Sidon to Egypt 429; idolatry spread here from Egypt and Chaldea 362; invaded by @Ammon 231; invaded by @Nebuchadnezzar 601; invaded by @Salmanasser 550; invaded by @Sennacherib 551; its people transplanted by Tiglathpileser 549; Menelaus came into it 296; name given to the seacoasts of Palestine (1044 BC) 25; name means the same as Edom in the @Syrian language 290; one place the @Shepherds fled to from Amosis I 436; part of the @Assyrian Empire at its height 554; part of the Babylonian Empire 621; part of this country ruled by @Thoas (912 BC) 85; place Psammitichus met the Scythians and bribed them not to invade Egypt 562; reigned over by @Cinyras for the Egyptian kings 482; revolted from the @Assyrian Empire 559; 130; ruled by @Nebuchadnezzar 580; ruled by Pharaoh Necho 576; temples built here by @Cinyras were as old as the temples in Egypt 454; thinly populated in the time of the patriarchs 407

Phoenicia: another name for Caria 283

Phoenician: likely the nationality of @Thoas 457; nationality of mariners who fled from the Red Sea (1043 BC) 26; nationality of names given to the mysteries of Ceres 357; nationality of the @Shepherds according to Manetho 436; nationality of the goddess Astarte who was similar to the Phrygian goddess 358

Phoenician Language: spoken by the Canaanites 429

Phoenician Letters: inscribed on pillars erected in western North Africa by the Canaanites 427; introduced into Europe by the @Curetes 339

Phoenician Merchants: brought a priestess of @Jupiter @Ammon into Greece (983 BC) 50

Phoenician Venus: foreign god in Egypt 459

Phoenicians: accompanied Cadmus into Greece 290; also called Shepherds 426; ate meat and sacrificed men (1445 BC) 13; brought into Europe the practice of deifying the dead 362; brought many kinds of learning into Greece 336; brought tribute of children from Greece to Crete every eight years 277; built a temple to @Hercules Olympius on the island of Thasos 356; Cadmus led a colony of them to @Rhodes 283; called into Egypt by @Osarsiphus to repel the @Ethiopians (941 BC) 68; called the island off the coast of Spain by the name of Gades 288; came from the Red Sea 376; conquered Lower Egypt 426; discovered Cyprus 402; driven from Egypt by @Memnon 476; driven from the Red Sea by the @Edomites around 892 to 889 BC 308; fled from David into other lands (1041 BC) 28; from @Tyre settled in @Memphis around the temples dedicated to @Vulcan and @Venus Hospita 459; from their arrival in Europe to the destruction of Troy were four generations 365; gave every king the name of @Jupiter 343; introduced the *Octaeteris* or the *Great Year* into Crete and Greece 240; introduced the custom of deifying the dead into Asia Minor and Greece 460; introduced the deification of dead men into Greece 386; introduced the practice of deifying dead men and women among the Greeks and Phrygians 358; introduced writing, the coining of money and the manual arts into Europe 351; kidnapped @Io 394; knew about Britain long before the Greeks did 293; made long voyages past the Pillars of @Hercules after the Trojan War 291; originally came from the Red Sea (1044 BC) 25; originally thought the @Tyrians came from the Red Sea area 286; performed human sacrifices (1066 BC) 21; said that Abibalus, Alymnus, Cadmus and @Europa fled from Sidon 297; sailed the Mediterranean Sea 394; sailed up to the Straits of Gilbraltar (883 BC) 96; sent out colonies to found @Carthage 224; settled the islands of Malta, @Gaulus and Madera 397; surnamed their kings @Jupiter 369; temples similar to theirs were built on the Persian Gulf islands of @Tyre and @Aradus 284; their histories translated into Greek by @Chaitus 296; their theology described by Sanchoniatho (760 BC) 112; traded Egyptian and @Assyrian merchandise to countries bordering the Mediterranean Sea 287; worshipped the sun, the fire, dead men and images 659

Phoenix: came with a colony into Greece 436; led a colony of @Phoenicians and @Syrians fleeing from Sidon and from David (1041 BC) 28

Phorbas: father of Pronoe (1006 BC) 39; father of Triopas 283; 326; came with a colony into Greece 436; fled from @Argos to @Rhodes 326; his snake is related to the constellation of Ophiuchus 254; prince of @Argos 395; purged @Rhodes of snakes 283

192

Phoroneus: brother of @Io 287; brother of Aegialeus 379; father of @Apis 419; father of Car 378; 43; father of Niobe 369; great-grandfather of @Pirasus 325; son of @Inachus 287; 384; 389; 20; began to reign in @Argos about the twentieth year of Saul 380; built @Phoronicum 384; built a city called @Phoronicum (1076 BC) 20; chronologers made him three hundred years younger than his brother Aegialeus 10; consolidated many families into the city of @Phoronicum 389; drove out the @Telchines from @Argos 283; Greeks built a temple to him 359; in his times towns began to be consolidated into cities 391; king of @Argos 204; older than Ogyges according to Acusilaus 383; oldest king in Greece according to Acusilaus, Anticlides and Plato 378; reigned in @Argos 378; thought by Acusilaus to be as old as Ogyges 196

Phoronicum: built by Phoroneus (1076 BC) 20; 384; original name for Argos 20; 384; Phoroneus consolidated many families to create this city 389

Phraortes: father of Astyages 556; 561; 598; son of @Dejoces 561; after his death the Scythians invaded Asia 562; conquered @Persia 556; Herodotus incorrectly thought he was the father of @Cyaxeres 596; killed and succeeded by Astyages (635 BC) 137; killed by the @Assyrians 598; may also be the same man as Arphaxad 558; ruled Media (657 BC) 132; ruled Media for twenty-two years 561; second king of Media 593

Phrixus: brother of Helle 314; 327; 329; 63; son of Athamas 329; 52; step-son of Ino (958 BC) 63; ensign of his ship was a golden ram and was the basis for the fable of the golden fleece 479; fled to @Colchis in the ship Aries 253; fled with her brother Phrixus from their step-mother Ino to Aeetes (958 BC) 63; fled with his sister Helle from their step-mother Ino to Aeetes 314; 327; 329

Phroroneus: father of @Apis @Epaphus (1006 BC) 39

Phrygia: @Bacchus seduced @Venus here 278; @Bacchus was caught in bed here with the wife of @Thoas 458; @Calycopis sailed here 459; @Curetes who settled here were called @Corybantes 336; conquered by @Bacchus and @Minerva 422; location of the city of @Cybele (1003 BC) 41; Phoenician letters were introduced here by the @Curetes 339; practice of the deification of the dead was introduced here by Cadmus and @Europa 358; ruled by Pharnaces 457; ruled by Tantalus (1015 BC) 35; some @Sidonians fled here 283; some of its cities were destroyed by internal discord 617

Phrygia: name of a poem written by Thymoetes about the exploits of @Bacchus 422

Phrygia Minor: invaded and helped destroy Babylon 618

Phrygian: its goddess similar to the Phoenician goddess Astarte 358; nationality of Hyagnis (1003 BC) 41

Phrygians: called @Sesostris by the names of @Ma-sors or @Mavors the @Valiant and shortened his name to @Mars (951 BC) 66; called @Sesostris by the names of @Ma-sors, @Mavors and @Mars 273; exceedingly rich 613; practice of deification of the dead was introduced to them by Cadmus and @Europa 358

Physical Acroasis: book written by Aristotle 243

Pices: constellation of the Zodiac 249; method for determining the position of stars in this constellation on the sphere of @Chiron 264

Pierus: his daughters imitated the Muses and were called by the same name (962 BC) 60

Pindar: Greek artist 217; says that @Antaeus reigned at the town of Irasa 467

Piranthus: son or successor of Argus 325

Pirasus: great-grandson of Phoroneus 325; son or successor of Argus 325; may be another name for Piranthus 325

Pirithous: son of Ixion 229; 74; helped Theseus to try to kidnap Persephone 229; killed by the dog of @Orcus, when he attempted to kidnap his daughter (934 BC) 74

Pisa: invaded by the Eleans when the Eleans suspected Damophon of treason 304; near Olympia 355

Pisastratus: father of Hipparchus (513 BC) 171; tyrant of @Athens (513 BC) 171

Pisces: constellation is related to the fishes of @Venus and Cupid 254

Pisces Austrinus: colure of the solstice passes through the tail of this constellation 262; constellation that represents the parents of @Venus and Cupid 254

Pischdadians: dynasty that ruled the @Assyrians 698; family of kings who ruled @Persia 566; Persian dynasty that came before the @Kaianides 694

Piscis Austrinus: tail of the constellation contains a star that passes through the colure of the solstices 252

Piseans: instituted the festival of Carnea to @Apollo 304; removed by Phidon from presiding over the Olympic Games 301

Pisistratus: Solon died in the second year of his rule 307; tyrant who ruled @Athens (550 BC) 161; 303

Plato: alludes to the story of @Erichthonius from Homer 331; derided Hippias of Elis for his inaccurate history 197; eminent author and philosopher 656; his poem from Solon is used to correct the Egyptian king lists 517; introduces Solon saying that the institutions of Lycurgus were not much more than three hundred years old 212; received a poem written by Solon 464; thought that Phoroneus was the oldest king in Greece 378

Plaustrum: constellation is related to Icareus and his daughter Erigone 254

Pleiades: longitude determined by Dionysius Petavius 265; method for determining the position of stars in this cluster on the sphere of @Chiron 264

Pleuron: brother of Clydon (1006 BC) 39; son of Aetolus (1006 BC) 39; son of Pronoe (1006 BC) 39; built a city in Aetolia (1006 BC) 39

Pliny: documents islands that rose from the sea 396; documents the incredible wealth of Croesus 613; explains the meaning of the name @Erythea 289; places @Ostanes under @Darius Hystaspes 657; says that @Pherecydes of Syria taught men to write in prose in the reign of Cyrus 197; says that Ethiopia dominated and was dominated by Egypt 473; says that the Egyptian obelisks were made from stone dug near Syene in @Thebes (Egyptian) 511; states that tin was first imported by @Midacritus from the island of @Cassiteris 292

Plisthenes: son of Pelops 317

Plutarch: complains of many contradictions in ancient history 12; documents an error concerning the times of Lycurgus as being much older than the first Olympiad 198; documents error in Greek history made by Aristotle 3; 4; documents the uncertainty of early Roman history 201; documents uncertainties in chronology 200; his history before Cyrus is too long by almost two hundred per cent 210; notes that the early Latin chronology is very uncertain 7; relates that the people of @Naxos pretended that there were two Minoses, and two Ariadnes 344; says that Solon died ten years earlier than Newton's calculations 307; says that the philosophers of old delivered their teachings in verse 196; says that the priests of Egypt hated the sea and held @Neptune in contempt 467; says that the syllable O, put before the word @Siris by the Greeks, made it scarcely intelligible to the Egyptians 453

Pluto: name of the mysteries of Ceres on the island of Samothrace 357

Poeonius: Curete who accompanied @Hercules (Idean) from Crete to Elis 353

Polemocrates: son of Machaon 359; Greeks built a temple to him 359

Polemon: says that in Attica, there were one hundred and seventy corporate towns of which Eleusis was one 388

Pollux: brother of Clytemnestra 324; brother of Helen 324; husband of Ilaira 324; son of Leda 253; twin brother of Castor 253; 324; an Argonaut 253; Greeks built a temple to him 359; returned from the Argonaut Expedition while Theseus was still imprisoned by @Aidoneus 229; young man when he went on the Argonaut Expedition 324

Pollux: constellation shaped like this Argonaut man 253

Polybius: started his history where @Timaeus Siculus left off writing 1; 197

Polybus: king of @Sicyon 379; 380

Polybus: another name for Thuor 484

Polycaon: husband of Messene 381; conquered the country of Messene 381; in his times towns began to be consolidated into cities 391

Polydectes: brother of Lycurgus 216; father of @Charillus 216; died before the birth of his son @Charillus 216; died in the beginning of the 18th Olympiad 218; king of Sparta 216; Spartan king descended from the family of Procles 204

Polydorus: father of Labdacus 314; 316; husband of Nycteis 316; son of Cadmus 314; 315; son of Harmonia 315; born a year or so after their arrival into Europe 315; lived in the time of David and Solomon 314; Spartan king descended from the family of Eurysthenes 204; 209

Polymnestor: king of Arcadia 204

Polymnestus: Greek artist 217

Polynices: father of Thersander 314; killed about six years after the Argonaut Expedition in the war at Thebes (Greek) 314

Pomponius: says that the island of Gades was settled after the Trojan War 293

Pompus: king of Arcadia 204

Pontus: part of the @Assyrian Empire at its height 554; seized by @Cyaxeres from the @Assyrians beyond @Colchis and @Iberia (607 BC) 144

Porphyry: says that Pythagoras entered the Idean cave to see @Jupiter's grave 346

Poseidon: Greek name for a Roman god called Neptune 466

Praetus: brother of Acrisius 324; father of Megapenthes 324; son of Abas 326; 21; incorrectly thought to be the son of Abas the king of @Argos 323; lived about the time of King David and @Erechtheus 325

Praxonidas: father of Iphitus 220; son of Oxylus 220

Priam: father of Alexandra 359; father of Hector 359; son of Laomedon 465; younger brother of Tithonus 477; Greeks built a temple to him 359; last king of Troy 321; 465; seventh king of Troy 321; succeeded Laomedon as king of Troy (933 BC) 75; younger brother of Tithonus 270

Priests' Court: altar stood in the middle of it 636; court next to the @*People's Court* in the temple 639; 642; 643; 646; 648; 649

Procles: son of Aristodemus 208; 209; 222; twin brother of Eurysthenes 208; 209; head of a dynasty of Spartan kings 204; 218; king of Sparta 222; tutored by Theras 208

Procopius: describes the extreme poverty of the Moors 430; documents pillars erected in western North Africa by the Canaanites who fled from Joshua 427; Hunns had no written language during his time 202

Procris: daughter of @Erechtheus 319; 351; wife of Cephalus 328; fled from her husband Cephalus to @Minos 328; fled to @Minos 351; talked with @Minos 319

Prometheus: brother of @Atlas 370; brother of Epimetheus 370; father of Amphictyon 363; nephew of @Sesostris 451; son of @Japetus 370; @Bacchus left him at Mount Caucasus to guard the pass 422; defended the passes of Mount Caucasus from the Scythians 451; freed by @Hercules (Idean) on Mount Caucasus 232; 75; left at Mount Caucasus by @Sesostris 233; 60; left by @Sesostris with a body of men at Mount Caucasus to guard that pass 227; stayed on Mount Caucasus thirty years 232

Pronoe: daughter of Phorbas 39; husband of Aetolus 39; mother of Clydon (1006 BC) 39; mother of Pleuron 39

Propodas: king of @Corinth before the return of the Heraclides 329

Propontis: contained numerous monuments to the Argonaut Expedition 480

Proserpina: daughter of Ceres 319; 32; Greeks built a temple to her 359; her mother Ceres came into Attica from Sicily looking for her 319

Proserpina: name of the mysteries of Ceres on the island of Samothrace 357

Protesilaus: Greeks built a temple to him 359

Proteus: in the reduced king list of Diodorus 514; king of Egypt according to Diodorus 513; king of Egypt according to Herodotus 483; king of Egypt according to Herodotus and Newton 486; viceroy for @Amenophis while he absent 276; 488; 86

Protogenia: daughter of Deucalion 327; mother of Aethlius 327; sister of Hellen 327

Prumnis: descended from the Heraclides 329; king of @Corinth 329

Prytanes: ruled @Corinth after the expulsion of its kings (658 BC) 131

Prytanis: Spartan king descended from the family of Procles 204

Psammenitus: king of Egypt 510; king of Egypt according to Herodotus 483; king of Egypt according to Herodotus and Newton 486; reigned for six months after @Amasis 509

Psammis: king of Egypt 510; king of Egypt according to Herodotus 483; king of Egypt according to Herodotus and Newton 486; omitted in the king list of Diodorus but in the list of Herodotus 514; reigned for six years after @Nechus 509; ruled from @Tanis over a small kingdom in Egypt 495

Psammitichus: father of @Nechaoh (617 BC) 142; father of Pharaoh Necho 565; 575; added the southern portico to the temple of @Vulcan 9; 478; bought off the Scythians so they did not invade Egypt 562; built the last portico on the temple of @Vulcan 509; in the reduced king list of Diodorus 514; king of Egypt 510; 565; 575; king of Egypt according to Diodorus 513; king of Egypt according to Herodotus 483; king of Egypt according to Herodotus and Newton 486; reigned

for fifty-four years 509; ruled Egypt (655 BC) 133; temple of @Vulcan not built more than three hundred years before his reign (912 BC) 85

Psophis: city originally called Phegea 384

Psophis: daughter of @Phegea 384; daughter of Lycaon 384

Ptolemy: calls @Gozan by the name of @Gauzania 539; calls @Kir by the name of @Carine 537; calls @Sepharvaim by the name of @Sipphara 535; locates Arrapachitis at the base of the mountains next to @Assyria 538; locates the city of @Thelasar in @Babylonia on the common stream of the Tigris and Euphrates Rivers 536; says that @Hephaestion was also called @Nilus 461

Ptolemy (Canon of): attributed the @Assyrian nationality to all the kings of Babylon 547; called @Esarhaddon by the name of @Assaradin 552; called @Evilmerodach by the name of @Iluarodamus 581; fixes the time of the reign of @Darius Hystaspes by several eclipses 571; its records were used to establish the times of the kings of the Persian Empire 669; listed the kings of Media and @Persia 598; lists the kings of Babylon 567; records eclipses used to date the reigns of @Cambyses and @Darius 660; states Babylon was taken in the year 538 BC 592; states Cyrus captured Babylon eight years before he died 306; states that @Artaxerxes Longimanus reigned for forty-one years 664; states that @Evilmerodach reigned for two years 582; states that @Nabonnedus reigned for eighteen years until Babylon fell 584; states that @Neriglissaros and his son @Laboasserdach reigned for four years 583; states that Cyrus died in 530 BC 632; states that Cyrus lived to seventy and ruled Babylon for nine years 595

Ptolemy Euergetes: follies of Onias were excused to him 682

Ptolemy Lagus: king of Egypt 205

Ptolemy Philadelphus: books of the Jewish law were translated in his reign 682

Pul: father of Nabonassar 548; 549; father of Tiglathpileser 549; @Assyrian god or king of @Assyria 519; @Nebuchadnezzar descended from him according to @Abydenus 547; another name for Belus (Assyrian) 547; conquered Haron, @Carchemish, @Reseph, @Calneh and @Thelasar 542; conquests of Jeroboam II were about ten or twenty years before his reign 528; died (747 BC) 114; founded the @Assyrian Empire 8; 523; 525; 108; Jonah prophesied about sixty years before his reign 527; king of @Assyria according to the scriptures 521; some ascribe the building of Babylon to him 543; started building a palace in Babylon 624; started to fulfil the prophecies of Amos and expand the @Assyrian Empire 529; 541; succeeded at @Nineveh by Tiglathpileser (747 BC) 114; succeeded at Babylon by Nabonassar (747 BC) 114; temple of @Jupiter Belus built by his son Nabonassar 548

Punic War: Noevius fought in it 312

Puppis: modern constellation derived from the poop deck of the constellation Argo 252; 253

Pur: name of a lot used to determine when the Jews would be executed 667

Purim: feast of the Jews 667

Pygmalion: father of Metharme 225; king of @Tyre when @Edom revolted from Jehoram 286; statue of his golden olive in a temple at Gades 293

Pylas: daughter of Cleson 381; mother of Sciron 381

Pythagoras: entered the Idean cave to see @Jupiter's grave 346; saw the tomb of @Minos in Crete (961 BC) 61

Pythagorus: abducted by @Cambyses from Egypt to Babylon 653

Pythic Games: encouraged the development of Greek musicians and poets 217; won four times by Terpander 213

Python: another name for Japetus 275; another name for Neptune 467

Pyxis: modern constellation derived from the compass of the constellation of Argo 253

Quinquertium: five games instituted by Lycurgus in the 18th Olympiad (708 BC) 122; 308

Quintilis: fifth month in the Roman calendar 243

Quintus Fabius Pictor: copied most of his history from Diocles of Peparethius 201; lived about a hundred years after @Alexander the Great 7

Rab-Assur: example of an @Assyrian name compounded with the name of one of the @Assyrian gods 519

Rabbah: capital of the Ammonites and besieged by David 271

Rabbi Yoke ben Halafta: author of the Jewish chronicle called *Seder Olam Rabbah* 668

Rabsaris: example of an @Assyrian name 519

Raham: another name for Nebuchadnezzar 694

Rameses: another name for Ramesses 490

Ramesses: father of @Moeris 491; 527; son of @Amenophis 93; 490; son of @Memnon 476; added the western portico to the temple of @Vulcan 478; 93; built the first portico on the temple of @Vulcan 500; had an army of seven hundred thousand men 490; helped drive out the Jews and @Phoenicians from Lower Egypt 476; Homer was alive when he reigned in Egypt 482; in the reduced king list of Diodorus 514; king of Egypt 490; 527; made two very large obelisks 511; reigned before Nitocris and @Moeris 486; reigned over @Libya, Ethiopia, Media, @Persia, Bactria, @Scythia, @Armenia, Cappadocia, Bithynia and Lycia 490; ruled many countries 526; succeeded @Amenophis as the king of Egypt 512; succeeded his father @Amenophis 93; very rich 491

Ramestes: another name for Ramesses 490

Ramises: another name for Ramesses 490; 511

Ramses: another name for Ramesses 490

Red Sea: @Ammon built a fleet on it 446; @Sesostris set up pillars at its mouth (1006 BC) 39; @Tyre lost access to it when @Edom revolted from Jehoram 285; 286; @Tyre may have established trade here in the days of David and Solomon 295; @Tyrians actively traded on it 284; @Tyrians driven from it by the @Edomites 298; David expelled the @Edomites from around here 281; 282; Egyptians built a fleet to sail this sea 438; first sailed on by small round cargo vessels (1030 BC) 31; location of Solomon's fleet (1013 BC) 36; location of the ports of Eloth and Ezion Geber 439; named after its inhabitants called @Edom 443; Oes appeared from it 442; original home of the @Edomites 290; original home of the @Phoenicians 287; 308; 376; 25; original home of the @Tyrians 288; 289; Phoenician mariners expelled from here (1043 BC) 26; sailed by the @Edomites in search of new homes 444; Troglodytes lived beside it in caves 404; writing used here by Abraham's descendants 441

Rehob: supplied troops to fight against David 271

Rehoboam: @Corinth was built about the beginning of his reign 329; @Danaus fled from Egypt in his reign 322; @Minos died during his reign 339; @Sesostris returned to Egypt in his fourteenth year 451; born in the last year of the reign of David 271; children of @Minos were alive during his reign 297; conquered by @Sesostris (971 BC) 55; Cretheus, Sisyphus and Athamas were in their prime in his days 327; during his reign Alcmena was pregnant with @Hercules (Idean) 366; during his reign, @Sesostris removed the temple vessels 475; during his reign, kings ruled at @Thebes (Egyptian) 699; in his fifth year @Sesostris invaded @Judah 450; in his fourteenth year, Ino was still alive 314; in the fourteenth year of his reign Ariadne died 278; invaded by @Sesostris in 971 BC 308; invaded by @Sesostris in his fifth year 229; 232; king of @Judah (975 BC) 53; Oedipus born in the seventh year of his reign 315; Thebans (Egyptian) and the @Ethiopians built a large empire in his days 460; Trojan War and the Argonaut Expedition occurred after he died 300

Rehum: another name for Harim 671; chief priest in the first year of Cyrus 676

Remphis: another name for Ramesses 490; 514; king of Egypt according to Diodorus 513

Rephaims: country plundered by four kings from the land of Shinar and @Elam 408

Resen: another name for Reseph 550

Reseph: conquered by @Pul 542; conquered by @Sennacherib 550; on the west and south side of the @Assyrian Empire 535; part of the @Assyrian Empire at the time of the fall of Israel 532

Rezin: son of Tobeah 456; defeated by Tiglathpilasser 456; invaded @Judah with Pekah 553; last king of Syria 456

Rezon: son of Eliadah 456; first king of Syria 456

Rhadamanthus: brother of @Minos 457; nephew of Cadmus 359; uncle of @Thoas 457; contemporary with Aegeus 344; Greeks built a temple to him 359; led colonies from Crete to the Greek islands 457

Rhampses: another name for Ramesses 490

Rhampsinitus: added the western portico to the temple of @Vulcan 9; another name for Ramesses (887 BC) 93; 478; contemporary with Proteus 488; Herodotus' name for Ramesses 490; king of Egypt according to Herodotus 483; king of Egypt according to Herodotus and Newton 486

Rharus: father of Celeus 330; son of Cranaus 330; contemporary with Callisto 334

Rhea (Cretan): daughter of @Titaea 470; daughter of @Uranus 470; husband of Saturn (Cretan) 345; mother of @Jupiter (Cretan) 341; 353; 470; mother of @Minos 358; mother of Juno (Cretan) 470; wife of Saturn (Cretan) 470; another name for Europa 345; another name for Europa of Crete 342; had the Idean Dactyli raise her son 353; her mysteries were instituted in the city of @Cybele (1003 BC) 41; hid her son @Jupiter (Cretan) in a cave on Mount Ida in Crete 341; mysteries were dedicated to her in @Phrygia and she was called the *Great Mother* 340; name for Europa 358

Rhea (Egyptian): mother of @Jupiter Ammon 363; wife of @Ammon according to Manetho 431; wife of Saturn (Egyptian) 363; 440; Egyptians imagined that she had secret sexual intercourse with Saturn (Egyptian) 440

Rhianus: Greek artist 217

Rhinocolura: on the trade route from the Red Sea to Egypt 439

Rhodes: @Curetes who settled here were called @Telchines 336; @Danaus fled here 322; @Telchines retired here, when driven from @Argos by Phoroneus 283; Cadmus sailed here from Sidon 315; called Ophiusa Island 395; 396; destination of Abas after he left Egypt (1066 BC) 21; filled with snakes until Phorbas destroyed them 395; 396; formed in the sea by an earthquake 395; 396; Phorbas and his son Triopas fled here from @Argos 326

Riblah: location where Pharaoh Necho may have sent Jehoahaz in irons 575

Roman: nationality of the god @Janus (1024 BC) 33; nationality of the goddess @Neptys the wife of the god @Neptune 466

Roman Empire: Germany had no written history before 10

Romans: calculated the reigns of kings equal to the generations of men with three generations to a hundred years 204; conquered @Carthage and acquired their archives 224; expelled their kings and replaced them with consuls (508 BC) 172; old year started in the spring and the reformed year started in winter 243; Quintus Fabius Pictor was their oldest historian 201; their religion was conceived and established by Numa 657; thought that Rome was founded in 753 BC 312; used a corrected Egyptian year implemented by Julius Caesar 247; used a luni-solar year with intercalary months created by Numa 241

Rome: built by Romulus 226; developed from villages, towns and cities which grew into the kingdom 409; Emperor Constantius moved here the obelisk erected by @Ramesses in Heliopolis 490; founded (627 BC) 140; founded by Romus or Aeneas 311; its Catacombs were used as homes by some 404; not a single city before the days of Numa 393; ruled by seven kings 313; ruled by seven kings who reigned two hundred and forty-four years according to chronologers 204; sacked by the Gauls destroying its early historical records 7; sacked sixty-seven years before the death of @Alexander the Great 201; thought to be founded by Romulus 312

Romulus: son or grandson of Aeneas 312; built Rome and was its first king 226; organised the kingdom of Rome into thirty courts or councils in thirty towns 393; some Latins thought that he founded Rome 312

Romus: son or grandson of Latinus 311; thought to have founded Rome 311

Romus: son of Ulysses or of Ascanius or of Italus 311; thought to have founded Rome 311

Sabacon: father of @Sevechus 501; 123; burned Bocchoris alive, killed @Nechus and forced @Anysis to flee (751 BC) 113; conquered Egypt 516; 625; 114; invaded Egypt 113; king of Egypt according to Diodorus 513; king of Egypt according to Herodotus 483; king of Egypt according to Herodotus and Newton 486; led an Ethiopian invasion of Egypt 496; 498; name Herodotus gave to Actisanes in Diodorus 514; reigned fifty years in Egypt (701 BC) 123; reigned for fifty years according to Herodotus 506; voluntarily relinquished Egypt 501

Sacadas: Greek artist 217

Sacaea: name of a festival the Babylonians celebrated 243

Sagan: assistant to the high priest 643

Sagapeni: country east of @Babylonia 622

Sagitta: constellation shaped like the arrow of @Hercules (Idean) 253; middle of the constellation contains a star that passes through the colure of the solstices 252; 261

Sagittarius: constellation of the Zodiac 249; modern name for the ancient constellation called Chiron 253; 254

Sais: capital of a small kingdom in Egypt ruled by Stephanathis, @ Necepsos and @Nechus 495; its king @Necepsos invented astrology 497; its priests talked with Solon 464; port Cecrops I sailed from on his way to Attica 382; ruled by Stephanathis, @Necepsos and @Nechus (788 BC) 109

Saite: name for a person from Sais 495

Salaminia: another name for Calycopis or Venus (930 BC) 78; 458

Salamis: battle fought here in the month of Munychion 662; built by Teucer in Cyprus (897 BC) 90; built by Teucer seven years after the destruction of Troy 225; 293; Greeks defeated the @Persians in a naval battle here (480 BC) 175; location of the battle between the Greeks and @Persians in 480 BC 660

Salatis: name of a Canaanite king who reigned in Lower Egypt after Joshua expelled the Canaanites (1445 BC) 13; 430

Salii: called the Roman god @Janus by the name of @Janis 350

Sallu: chief priest in the first year of Cyrus 676

Salmanasser: father of @Sennacherib 550; 551; captured the city of Samaria 550; defeated the @Syrians and Israel 456; expanded the @Assyrian Empire 541; invaded all @Phoenicia 550; king of @Assyria 456; 117; succeeded Tiglathpileser as king of @Assyria (728 BC) 116; transplanted Israel into @Chalach and @Chabor, by the @Gozan River in the cities of the Medes 550; transplanted the ten tribes of Israel (721 BC) 117

Salman-Assur: example of an @Assyrian name compounded with the name of one of the @Assyrian gods 519

Salmoneus: grandson of Hellen 220; drove Aetolus out of Elis 220

Samaria: captured by @Salmanasser 550; conquered and its people were transplanted by the @Assyrians 533; conquered by @Assyria 534; conquered by @Nebuchadnezzar 576; governed by Sanballat 681; on the west and south side of the @Assyrian Empire 535; populated by @Esarhaddon with people from other countries of @Assyria 552; ruled by Pekah 553; transplanted by @Esarhaddon into @Babylonia and @Assyria 504

Samaritans: carried into captivity by @Esarhaddon 552; Sanballat built a temple for them 681; used a luni-solar year 243

Samians: had four ships built by a Corinthian shipwright 298

Samos: at first deserted and inhabited only by a great number of fierce wild beasts until Macarius populated it 395; Corinthian shipwright built four ships for the city 298; one of the twelve cities in the common council called Panionium 310

Samothrace: @Curetes who settled here called @Cabiri 336; Cadmus sailed here from @Rhodes 315; mysteries of Ceres instituted here 357; one place the @Sidonians fled to 283

Samothracian: nationality of @Jasius 357

Samothracian Mysteries: instituted by Dardanus after his wife Chryses learned about them in Arcadia 358; marriage ceremony of Cadmus and Harmonica gave rise to these mysteries 315

Samuel: @Shepherds forced to flee from Egypt in his time 376; @Shepherds were expelled from Egypt in his days 373; 385; Canaanites ruled Lower Egypt until his time (1117 BC) 13; colonies led into Greece from Egypt and @Phoenicia in his time 436; died (1060 BC) 23; Egyptian history before his time is very uncertain 484; entertained Saul in a high place 455; in his days @Inachus left his lands to his sons 378; in his days Lelex left his lands to his sons 381; judged Israel (1117 BC) 15; Thebans (Egyptian) and the @Ethiopians built a large empire in his days 460; towns and houses in Europe did not predate his days 415

Sanballat: father of Nicaso 681; 181; father-in-law of Manasseh 182; 681; 181; alive at the time of @Alexander the Great according to the defective history of the Jews 668; appointed his son-in-law Manasseh the first high priest in his new temple (432 BC) 182; built a temple for Manasseh on Mount Gerizim during the reign of @Darius Nothus 681; built a temple in Mount Gerizim 182; opposed Nehemiah when he rebuilt the walls of @Jerusalem 691

Sanchoniatho: wrote his *Theology of the @Phoenicians* (760 BC) 112

Sandanis: advised Croesus that he had nothing to gain by attacking the Medes and everything to loose 613

Sandochus: father of @Thoas according to Apollodorus 457

Sanhedrin: also called the *Supreme Court of Judicature* 643; convened to separate the people from their foreign wives 688

Saophis: another name for Cheops 493

Saosduchinus: son of @Esarhaddon 557; built Tarsus and Anchiale 557; died and was succeeded by @Chyniladon (647 BC) 135; king of @

Assyria 567; reigned over Cilicia 557; succeeded @Esarhaddon as king of @Assyria (668 BC) 130; succeeded by @Chyniladon at Babylon 558

Sappho: Greek artist 217

Sarac: last king of @Assyria 563; 564; name is perhaps a contracted form of *Sarchedon* 565

Sarchedon: name derived from Esarhaddon, Esarhaddon-Pul or Sardanapalus 565; name Tobit gave to Esarhaddon 552

Sardanapalus: son of @Anacyndaraxis 557; another name for Esarhaddon 557; 121; his name likely derived from Esarhaddon-Pul 557; incorrectly thought to be the last king of the @Assyrian Empire by Ctesias 519; 521; lived a voluptuous lifestyle 556; name Sarchedon derived from it 565; only genuine @Assyrian king name mentioned by both Herodotus and Ctesias 520

Sardinia: visited by the Argonauts 480

Sardis: @Darius the Mede reigned before he conquered it 614; capital of the kingdom of Croesus 307; captured by Cyrus (544 BC) 163; 303; captured by Cyrus around 544 BC 308; conquered by @Darius the Mede 611; Medes reigned until after its capture 618; ruled by Croesus for fourteen years 306

Sarpedon: contemporary with Aegeus 344

Sarus: cycle containing two hundred and twenty-two lunar months which are eighteen years, each consisting of twelve lunar months besides six intercalary months 243

Saturn: name of treasury in Latium in @Italy 348

Saturn (Cretan): father of @Chiron 345; 367; father of @Jupiter (Cretan) 341; 346; 348; 349; 470; father of @Minos 367; father of Cadmus (1041 BC) 28; father of Juno (Cretan) 470; husband of @Europa 367; husband of Philyra 28; husband of Rhea (Cretan) 341; 470; son of @Titaea 470; son of @Uranus 470; @Curetes sacrificed children to him 401; @Phoenicians sacrificed men to him 283; according to the Cretans he was expelled from his kingdom and castrated by his son @Jupiter (Cretan) 470; another name for Asterius 342; 345; 37; coins made commemorating his coming to @Italy by sea 352; contemporary with the sons of Lycaon and also with Celeus, @Erechtheus, Ceres and @Asterius 351; defeated by @Hercules (Idean) 354; expelled from Crete by his son 348; 349; gave @Neptune the dominion of the sea 466; men in the Golden Age dedicated a temple to him in Olympia 353; received a cordial welcome from @Janus when he came to @Italy 350; ruled the Titans at Mount Olympus in Crete 345; unaware of the birth of @Jupiter (Cretan) by Rhea (Cretan) 341

Saturn (Egyptian): father of @Jupiter Ammon 363; husband of Rhea (Egyptian) 363; 440; Egyptians imagined that Rhea (Egyptian) had secret sexual intercourse with him 440

Saturnalia: festival to Saturn instituted by @Janus 352

Saturnia: @Italy was originally called Oenotria 351; name of the region of @Italy controlled by @Janus 352; name the Latins called @Italy 348; new name given to the whole of Italy 350

Saturnia: name of the mountain @Saturn (Cretan) lived on 350

Saturnia: @Saturn (Cretan) founded this city in @Italy 349

Saul: @Shepherds forced to flee from Egypt in his time 376; about his twentieth year of reigning Phoroneus began to reign in @Argos 380; appointed king (1095 BC) 17; Arcas born at the end of his reign 334; attacked by a large army of the @Philistines 375; attacked by the @Philistines with thirty thousand chariots, six thousand horsemen, and people as the sand on the seashore for multitude (1094 BC) 18; colonies led into Greece from Egypt and @Phoenicia in his time 436; Cranaus may have received his kingdom about the end his reign 382; delivered Israel from the @Philistines 374; end of his reign was contemporary with Hellen 320; entertained by Samuel in a high place 455; in his days some Israelites lived in caves for fear of the @Philistines 404

Scaliger: cites Sosicrates 306

Scamander: father of Teucer 321

Scenitae: another name for the Arabians living on the west side of Chaldea 622

Scilles: another name for the island of Cassiteris 292

Sciron: son of Pylas 381

Scorpio: constellation of the Zodiac 249; 250; modern name for old constellation Chelae (935 BC) 73; modern name for the constellation Chelae 251; 256; related to the scorpion 254

Scythia: fought with @Elam 566; no written language until about 280 AD 202; ruled by @Ramesses 490

Scythian: nationality of Sipylus 422

Scythians: conquered by @Cyaxeres and @Nebuchadnezzar 610; cooked one of the children of the Medes and served it to @Cyaxeres 607; defeated @Sesostris in a major battle (962 BC) 60; descended from Japheth 404; forced by @Cyaxeres to retreat beyond @Colchis and @Iberia (607 BC) 144; invaded Media and ruled there for about twenty-eight years 600; invaded the Medes and @Assyrians (634 BC) 138; lived along the north coast of the Black Sea 404; lived as wanderers in Europe (1121 BC) 14; Prometheus defended the passes of Mount Caucasus from them 451; raided by @Persia 557; ruled a large part of Asia for twenty-eight years 562; sent forces to Perseus to repel the invasion of @Bacchus 422

Scythopolis: conquered by @Nebuchadnezzar 576

Seder Olam Rabbah: Jewish chronicle of the world history compiled by Rabbi Yoke ben Halafta 668

Selene: daughter of @Basilea 463; daughter of @Hyperion 246; 405; granddaughter of @Uranus 405; another name for Bubaste 241; 246; 463; Egyptian moon goddess 246

Seleucus: king of Syria 205

Semele: daughter of Cadmus 359; mother of @Bacchus 359; deified under the name of Bacchus by his father (938 BC) 71

Semiramis: queen of Nabonassar 548; built Babylon in the time of Tiglathpileser 543; first great queen of Babylon 587; five generations older than Nitocris not fifteen hundred years older 8; five generations older than the mother of @Labynitus 520; her cup still preserved until Darus conquered Croesus 614; her wine bowl weighed fifteen talents 613; in her prime (760 BC) 112

Semiramis: name of a gate in Babylon 548

Sennaar: place in @Babylonia where the Egyptian priests fled 498

Sennacherib: father of @Esarhaddon 557; 121; son of @Salmanasser 550; 551; attacked Syria and @Judah after Israel fell 532; corruption of the name Anacyndaraxis 557; defeated by @Sethon 193; defeated by @Sethon and Tirhakah 551; defeated by @Sethon at @Pelusium 501; 502; defeated by the @Ethiopians and Egyptians (712 BC) 120; during the latter end of his reign Media revolted from @Assyria 555; easily subdued many smaller kingdoms 540; expanded the @Assyrian Empire 541; Hosea may have alluded to him by using the name of @Jareb 542; invaded @Judah and Egypt 551; king of @Assyria (719 BC) 118; king of @Assyria according to the scriptures 521; Medes defected from him near the end of his reign 697; murdered by his two sons 551; 121; ruled the @Assyrian Empire at its height 554

Separate Place: court in Solomon's temple surrounded by buildings without cloisters 645; 649

Sepharvaim: another name for Cush 534; city on the Euphrates River and part of the @Assyrian Empire 535; had its own king until it was conquered by the @Assyrians 525; part of the @Assyrian Empire at the time of the fall of Israel 532; transplanted by @Esarhaddon into the regions of Samaria and @Damascus 504

September: seventh month in the Roman calendar 243

Seraiah: father of Merajah 676; chief priest in the first year of Cyrus 676; priest who returned with @Ezra and Nehemiah in the first year of Cyrus 671

Seraiah: father of @Ezra 684; died during the captivity 684

Serapis: deified name of Apis 419

Ser-Apis: another name for the Nile River 453

Servius: notes that the early Latin chronology was very uncertain 7; 201; related the history surrounding the founding of @Carthage 225

Sesac: another name for Sesostris 230

Sesach: another name for Sesostris 230

Sesoch: another name for Sesostris 230

Sesochis: another name for Sesostris 230; 511

Sesochris: another name for Sesostris 230

Sesonch: another name for Sesostris 230

Sesonchis: another name for Sesostris 230

Sesonchoris: son of Ammenemes I according to Mathetho 424; another name for Gesongeses 424; corrupted name of Sesonchosis 425

Sesonchosis: another name for Sesostris 230; 419; 425; 451

Sesoos: another name for Sesostris 230

Sesoosis: another name for Sesostris 230

Sesoosis I: king of Egypt according to Diodorus 513; name Diodorus gave to Osiris 514

Sesoosis II: king of Egypt according to Diodorus 513; name Diodorus gave to Orus 514

Sesost: another name for Sesostris 230

Sesostris: brother of @Danaus 228; 230; 322; brother of @Japetus (951 BC) 66; brother of @Neptune 228; father of @Bubaste 246; father of @Orus 246; 450; 66; father of @Pheron 487; husband of @Isis 452; husband of Ariadne 227; 278; 60; son of @Ammon 245; 246; 405; 446; 40; 39; son of Ammenemes II according to Mathetho 424; uncle of Prometheus 451; about the same age as Perseus, Perieres and Anaxagoras 324; after he died Ethiopia revolted from Egypt 474; after he returned to Egypt, @Memnon was born 477; also called @Hyperion 405; also called Aegyptus 445; appointed @Thoas king of Cyprus (963 BC) 59; Arabian god called Bacchus 449; before his time Egypt was composed of many small kingdoms 484; built @Thebes (Egyptian) and dedicated it to his father @Ammon 425; built temples about the same time the temples were built in @Phoenicia and Cyprus 454; built temples in Egypt 455; called Dionysus by the @Arabians 274; 275; conquered @Thrace 363; conquered as far east as the Ganges River (968 BC) 56; conquered many countries 526; contemporary with @Bacchus and @Osiris 423; crossed the Hellespont and conquered @Thrace, killing Lycurges their king (964 BC) 58; dedicated Thebes to his father (998 BC) 44; deified by the Egyptians 431; did many exploits during his father's lifetime (1006 BC) 39; did similar feats as @Bacchus and @Osiris 420; divided Egypt into equal square parcels of land for the Egyptians 452; divided Egypt into nomes 462; divided Egypt into thirty-six nomes (961 BC) 61; Egyptian astronomical discoveries were made during his reign 497; Egyptians knew nothing of astronomy before his father's time 444; embellished @Thebes (Egyptian) 44; enlarged Egypt into a great empire 431; first to conquer Syria, India, Asia and @Thrace 421; fought against the Libyans with clubs 460; fought the Africans with clubs 447; Greeks thought @Amenophis was born after @Sesostris returned to Egypt (962 BC) 95; helped @Ammon conquer 437; his captains shared his conquests 464; his expedition was one generation before the Argonaut Expedition 232; his wife Ariadne died just before he returned to Egypt 278; in his time writing, astronomy, architecture and agriculture came into Chaldea 442; introduced knowledge of observing the stars into North Africa, Europe and Asia 625; invaded @Libya 447; invaded @Thrace a generation before the Argonaut expedition 11; invaded North Africa and Spain during his father @Ammon's reign (1004 BC) 40; invaded Rehoboam in his fifth year 229; king of Egypt according to Herodotus 483; king of Egypt according to Herodotus and Newton and deified under the names of Osiris, Hercules and Bacchus 486; king of Egypt who established the Egyptian Empire 416; left Aeetes in @Colchis 329; left by @Sesostris with a body of men at Mount Caucasus to guard that pass 233; left his nephew Prometheus at Mount Caucasus to defend his conquests from the Scythians 451; left Prometheus with a body of men at Mount Caucasus to guard the pass 227; lived before the destruction of Troy 417; lost a major battle with the Scythians and the Greeks (962 BC) 60; made the @Nile River more useful by digging channels from it to all the capital cities of Egypt 453; made two large obelisks 511; murdered by his brother @Japetus (951 BC) 66; murdered in the fifth year of the reign of Asa 273; plundered the temple at @Jerusalem, invaded Syria and @Persia, and set up pillars in many places (971 BC) 55; reigned during the four ages of the great gods of Egypt 512; reigned for forty-eight years according to Manetho 472; reigned in Egypt 44; reigned over all the Libyans, Troglodytes and @Ethiopians 231; removed the temple vessels 475; returned to Egypt 322; returned to Egypt after his expedition 327; returned to Egypt in the fourteenth year of Rehoboam 314; rigorously trained by his father @Ammon 446; same man as Bacchus 418; same man as Bacchus, Shishak and Osiris 308; set up pillars in all his conquests 460; subdued Jeroboam I 471; travelled as far west as Spain and returned to Egypt through Gaul and @Italy 448; two generations younger than @Isis and @Osiris according to Apollonius 419; until he invaded Greece @Phoenicians surnamed their kings @Jupiter 369

Sethon: another name for Sevechus (701 BC) 123; defeated @Sennacherib with a great slaughter 551; defeated the @Assyrians at @Pelusium 501; defeated the @Assyrians under @Sennacherib at @Pelusium 502; from @Menes to him there were over three hundred generations according to the Egyptian priests 193; king of Egypt according to Herodotus 483; king of Egypt according to Herodotus and Newton

486; omitted in the king list of Diodorus but in the list of Herodotus 514; reigned after @Sabacon 501; reigned fourteen years according to Africanus 506; succeeded by Tirhakah 503

Sethon: another name for Sesostris 230

Sethosis: another name for Sesostris 230

Sevechus: son of @Sabacon 123; 501; another name for Sethon 551; priest of @Vulcan (701 BC) 123; ruled in Egypt after his father 123; successor and the son of @Sabacon according to Manetho 501

Sextilis: sixth month in the Roman calendar 243

Shallecheth: name of a temple gate with four porters 638

Shallum: father of Hilkiah 684

Shalman: maybe the first part of the name of @Shalmaneser and may be another name for Jareb 542

Shalmaneser: another name for Salmanasser 550; Hosea may have alluded to him by using the name of @Shalman 542; king of @Assyria according to the scriptures 521

Shamgar-Nebo: example of an @Assyrian name compounded with the name of one of the @Assyrian gods 519

Shar-Assur: example of an @Assyrian name compounded with the name of one of the @Assyrian gods 519

Shebaniah: another name for Shechaniah 671

Shebaniah: another name for Sherebiah 671

Shechaniah: priest who returned with @Ezra and Nehemiah in the first year of Cyrus 671; 676

Shemaiah: father of @Jonathan 684

Shemajah: priest who returned with @Ezra and Nehemiah in the first year of Cyrus 671; 676

Shepherds: also called Phoenicians 426; at the time of Joseph the Egyptians were not @Shepherds 433; before their expulsion, Egypt had no common king 421; Canaanites who fled from Joshua and invaded Egypt and ate meat and sacrificed men like the @Phoenicians (1445 BC) 13; confined by Misphragmuthosis into a part of Lower Egypt called @Abaris or @Pelusium (1121 BC) 14; conquered Lower Egypt 426; driven from @Abaris by @Amosis I (1066 BC) 21; driven into North Africa and Syria by Misphragmuthosis and his son Amosis I 431; driven out of Egypt before Solomon reigned 434; driven out of Egypt by @Amenophis (926 BC) 81; established their own religion abolishing religion of the Egyptians 363; expelled a second time by @Memnon and his son @Ramesses 476; expelled a second time from Egypt by @Amenophis 275; expelled before there were kings over all of Egypt 478; expelled from Egypt 432; 485; 515; expelled from Egypt around the time of the building of @Jerusalem 231; expelled from Egypt by Amosis I 377; expelled from Egypt by Amosis I to Arabia, Troglodytica and @Libya 437; expelled from Egypt by Misphragmuthosis 375; expelled from Egypt by Misphragmuthosis and Amosis I 482; expelled from Egypt by Misphragmuthosis and his son @Amosis I 435; expelled from Egypt in the days of Samuel and Eli 385; fled from Egypt 282; forced to leave Egypt around 1096 BC 376; greatly strengthened the @Philistines (1096 BC) 16; strengthened the @@Philistines against Israel 282; strengthened the @Philistines against Israel (1117 BC) 15; their expulsion from @Thebes (Egyptian) strengthened the @Philistines 436; their expulsion from Egypt was the reason for the first migration of people from Egypt into Greece and the building of houses and villages in Greece 373; their reign over Egypt ended one or two generations before @Ammon 248

Sherebiah: priest who returned with @Ezra and Nehemiah in the first year of Cyrus 671

Sheseb-Assur: example of an @Assyrian name compounded with the name of one of the @Assyrian gods 519

Sheshach: another name for Susiana 603; their punishment after seventy years was predicted by Jeremiah 602

Shihor: biblical name for the Nile River 453

Shinar: all nations once lived here under Noah 413; land from which an army was sent into Palestine under four kings 408

Shishak: another name for Sesostris 229; 230; 231; 232; same man as Bacchus, Sesostris and Osiris 308

Sibotas: king of Messene 204

Sicaneans: first inhabitants of Sicily and were from Spain 398; people @Sesostris brought from Spain and settled in Sicily 448; settled in Sicily by @Hercules (Egyptian) 399

Sicanus River: river in Spain or @Iberia that was the original home of the Sicaneans 398

Sicels: expelled by the colony of @Oenotrus 392; invaded Sicily during the priesthood of Alcyone 300; 325

Sicilians: adjusted the length of the months to make the lunar and solar years agree 236

Sicily: @Minos pursued Daedalus here 339; Archias led a colony here from @Corinth (719 BC) 118; first colonised by Sicaneans 398; 399; 448; Greeks sent colonies here around 750 to 700 BC 308; home of Ceres (1026 BC) 32; invaded by the Sicels during the priesthood of Alcyone 325; left by Ceres when searching for her daughter Proserpina 319; Messenians fled here (588 BC) 150; nationality of @Timaeus 197; on the other side of the islands of Malta and @Gaulus 397; ruled by Cocalus (961 BC) 61; settled by colonies from Greece 299; Sicels invaded the island during the twenty-sixth year of the priesthood of Alcyone 300; visited by the Argonauts 480

Sicyon: father of Gonussa 221; grandson of Erechteus 384; @Sicyon named after him 384; king of @Sicyon 379

Sicyon: chronologers created many imaginary kings for it 383; formerly called Aegialea 316; its king, @Apis @Epaphus was killed by Aetolus 337; kingdom founded by Aegialeus 379; originally called Aegialea (1076 BC) 20; originally called Aegialea but renamed after the grandson of Erechteus called @Sicyon 384; ruled by @Apis @Epaphus 10; ruled by @Epopeus 317; ruled by Adrastus according to Homer 380; ruled by Aegialeus 378; ruled by Clisthenes 302; ruled by twelve kings who reigned an average of forty-four years each according to chronologers 204

Sicyonian: nationality of @Epaphus 316; 379

Sicyonians: their original kingdom consisted of many small towns (1076 BC) 20

Sidon: @Europa carried from here by @Jupiter according to a fable 342; @Phoenicians fled from here during the reign of David around 1041 BC 308; Abibalus, Alymnus, Cadmus and @Europa fled from here to Greece 297; Cadmus and @Europa sailed from here to Greece 358; captured by the @Philistines 282; captured by the Ascalonians 279; conquered by @Nebuchadnezzar 602; 604; 611; conquered by the @Philistines 341; from here to Egypt the country was called @Phoenicia 429; had its own king until it was conquered by the @Assyrians 525; home base for the @Phoenicians on the Mediterranean Sea (1043 BC) 26; home of @Syrians who fled from David into other lands (1041 BC) 28; home of the poet Dorotheus 545; its capture triggered an exodus of its inhabitants to Greece 283; its craftsman founded @Tyre in the reign of David 281; its merchants repopulated the island on which @Tyre was rebuilt 280; known by Homer 284; overrun by @Edomites fleeing from David 290; 25; place Cadmus left with a colony for Greece 385; some think Polydorus was born here 315; stopping off place for colonies of @Shepherds fleeing Egypt to Asia Minor or Greece 376

Sidonian: nationality of Sithonis the wife of Cadmus 282

Sidonians: @Tyrians explored areas not frequented by them 285; called @Phoenicians 290; conquered by @Cyaxeres and @Nebuchadnezzar 610; fled from Sidon to various countries 283; fled from their enemies into Cilicia, Asia Minor, Greece and @Libya 282; founded @Aradus and @Tyre after being displaced by the @Edomites fleeing from David (1044 BC) 25; frequented the Mediterranean Sea 284; intermixed with @Philistines 341; name given to the Tyrians 281; skilled carpenters 280; skilled in carpentry and architecture 444; some fled under Cadmus to find new homes 297; traded with Greece 298

Siene: called the @Nile River the @Nilus River 453

Sihor: name given to a channel @Sesostris cut from the @Nile River (951 BC) 66

Sihor: Sesostris deified under this name 273

Sihor: biblical name for the Nile River 453

Siloceni: country east of @Babylonia 622

Silver Age: @Minos reigned 365; Argus was born near the beginning of it 369; Greeks began to practise agriculture during this age 366; next generation after the Golden Age in Greece (c. 1010 BC) 28; second age or generation after the gods 364; 371; times of Cadmus and @Minos 367

Simeon Justus: brother of Eleazar 678; 682; son of Onias 678; died two years before the death of @Alexander the Great 679; high priest who lived during the times of @Alexander the Great 682; Jews consider him the same man as Jaddua 668; second high priest of the Jews after the Persian Empire 678

Simonides: Greek artist 217

Simplicius: wrote a commentary on Aristotle's *Physical Acroasis* 243

Simus: king of Arcadia 204

Sinope: contained numerous monuments to the Argonaut Expedition 480

Sipparae: conquered by @Belus (Assyrian) or @Pul 547; name Berosus gave for Sepharvaim 535

Sipphara: name Ptolemy gave for Sepharvaim 535

Sipylus: commander of the Scythian forces that helped Perseus repel the invasion of @Bacchus 422

Siris: another name for Sesostris 453

Siris: another name for the Nile River 453; name given to a channel @Sesostris cut from the @Nile River (951 BC) 66

Sirius: formed by the Greeks from the word Sihor 453; name given to Osiris by @Orpheus 419

Sisyphus: brother of Athamas (976 BC) 52; brother of Calyce 327; grandson of Hellen (979 BC) 51; son of Aeolus 327; 384; 51; built @Corinth 329; built @Ephyra, which was later called @Corinth 384; first king of @Corinth 329; instituted the Isthmian Games at @Corinth 329

Sithonis: wife of Cadmus 282; from Sidonian 282

Sittacene: conquered by @Nebuchadnezzar 577; country east of @Babylonia 622

Smaragdine: statue of the golden olive of Pygmalion bearing Smaragdine fruit 293

Smarres: another name for Moeris 491

Smerdis: brother of @Cambyses 651; son of Cyrus 651

Smerdis the Magus: exposed by @Ostanes 657; king of @Persia for eight months before he was exposed as a fraud 652; pretender to the Persian throne 651

Smyrna: destroyed by internal discord 617

So: another name for Sabacon 501

Sochis: another name for Sesostris 511

Socrates: died three years after the end of the Peloponnesian War 212; made the institutions of Lycurgus about three hundred years older than the end of the Peloponnesian War (708 BC) 122

Sodom: city plundered by four kings from the land of Shinar and @Elam 408

Sogdianus: reigned for seven months 665

Soiphis: another name for Cheops 493

Sol: another name for Apollo 467; Egyptians imagined that he prayed that Rhea (Egyptian) would not have a child in any month of the year 440; founded a city in Egypt 454; one of the gods of Egypt 454

Solinus: says that Perdiccas was the successor of Caranus and the first of that line of kings 301

Solomon: @Bacchus returned from India about ten years after his death 310; @Benhadad II invaded Israel seventy-four years after his death 407; @Corinth was built about the end of his reign 329; @Rhodes settled toward the end of his reign 395; @Sesostris became king during his reign 273; @Sesostris started to reign in his eighteenth year 472; @Shepherds driven out of Egypt before his reign 434; about forty-nine years after he died, @Amenophis retook Egypt 489; about his time the temple of Juno Argiva was built by Eurydice 325; about twenty years after his death, @Memnon was born 477; Amphictyonic Council was established toward the beginning of his reign or the end of the reign of David 330; Argonaut Expedition happened about forty-two years after he died 222; 223; 232; 233; 276; Argonaut Expedition occurred about thirty-five years after his death by this astronomical calculation 257; asked Hiram for men skilled in carpentry and architecture 444; before his reign @Oenotrus led a colony into @Italy 334; born about the eighteenth year of the reign of David 271; built a fleet on the Red Sea with the help of the @Tyrians and Aradians (1013 BC) 36; built the temple 636; Cepheus lived in his days 326; children of @Minos lived during his reign 297; conscripted @Shepherds for the building of @Jerusalem and the temple 436; Cretheus, Sisyphus and Athamas were in their prime at the end of his reign 327; died about fifty-three years before the Argonaut Expedition by another astronomical calculation 263; died about forty-two years before the Argonaut Expedition by this astronomical calculation 265; 266; 267; 269; died about one hundred and ten or twenty years before Homer and Hesiod

lived 368; died before many events happened in Greece and Egypt in 975 BC 308; died seventy-one years before Troy was destroyed 225; 226; during his reign @Hercules (Egyptian) sailed to the Strait of Gibraltar 399; during his reign, kings ruled at @Thebes (Egyptian) 699; Egypt supplied him with horses 448; eighty-eight years after his death, the Egyptians started to use a three hundred and sixty-five day year starting on the vernal equinox 247; his kingdom was divided after his death 205; his temple was burned by @Nebuchadnezzar (588 BC) 150; his temple was destroyed in 588 BC by the Babylonians 635; his temple was slightly different than Ezekiel's temple 647; in his days temples began to be built 361; in his tenth to fifteenth year, Ceres and @Erechtheus died and the mysteries at Eleusis were instituted 320; in his tenth year @Apis @Epaphus and Nycteus were killed 379; in his tenth year, Amphion and Zethus captured Thebes (Greek) 317; in his time an earlier @Hercules (Tyrian) may have established trade on the Red Sea 295; in his time writing, astronomy, architecture and agriculture came into Chaldea 442; in the latter part of his reign Daedalus and Talus invented many things 339; laid the foundation for the temple (1012 BC) 37; Laius was born about the twenty-fourth year of his reign 315; likely conscripted fleeing @Shepherds to help build @Jerusalem and the temple 373; lived about ninety-five years before Hesiod 268; married @Ammon's daughter (1015 BC) 35; married Hiram's daughter 296; married the oldest of Pharaoh's daughters 272; no mention of sumptuous temples before his time 455; one hundred fifty-four years after his death the Heraclides returned into Peloponnesus 209; Palestine was not conquered from Abraham's time to his days 231; reign of @Apis @Epaphus ended in his tenth year 380; sought help from Hiram in building the temple 296; Thebans (Egyptian) and the @Ethiopians built a large empire in his days 460; Theseus born about the thirty-third year of his reign 228; traded on the Red Sea in conjunction with the @Tyrians 284; Trojan War and the Argonaut Expedition occurred after he died 300; Troy was destroyed about sixty-nine years after he died 313; used Sidonian carpenters 280

Solon: advised the Amphictyonic Council to declare war on the Cirrheans (570 BC) 156; archon and legislator for @Athens (562 BC) 157; Atlantis could not be found in his days 465; chonologers made him too old to be alive to meet with Croesus 5; contemporary with Phidon, Caranus, Alcmaeon, Clisthenes and Eurolicus 302; did not count the days of the month by adding them to the twentieth, but by subtracting them from the thirtieth, on a descending scale 239; died about 549 BC 303; died, when Hegestratus was the archon of @Athens (549 BC) 162; his poem is used to correct the Egyptian king lists 517; his poem mentions the division of the earth among the gods 463; in his time the Egyptians had magnified the time of their kingdom to over nine thousand years 484; interviewed by Croesus 4; met Croesus (550 BC) 161; one of the annual archons of @Athens 310; some chronologers thought his interview with Croesus was fictitious 200; visited Croesus during the latter part of his reign 307; visited Croesus in 550 BC 308; wrote a poem describing Atlantis 464; wrote in verse 196; wrote of the war in Egypt, @Libya and Greece 469

Soris: corruption of the name Moeris 491

Sosibius: cited by Athenaeus 213

Sosicrates: states that Cyrus captured Sardis a few years before he took Babylon 306

Sous: Spartan king descended from the family of Procles 204

South Asellus: star in the middle of the constellation of Cancer used to define the colure of the solstices 261

Spain: @Sesostris went as far west as here 448; colonised by @Melcartus and the @Phoenicians from @Tyre around 892-889 BC 308; country containing the grave of @Hercules (Tyrian) 293; explored and settled by the @Tyrians 285; explored by @Hercules (Tyrian) 295; history written hundreds of years after the death of @Alexander the Great 202; home of Geryon 461; invaded by @Sesostris (1004 BC) 40; its western parts settled by @Tyrians led by @Melcartus 292; location of @Erythra where @Hercules (Egyptian) had his fleet 399; original home of the Sicaneans 398; place explored and settled by the @Phoenicians 291; traded with @Tyrians 298

Spanish: nationality of the first inhabitants of Sicily 398

Sparta: @Timaeus Siculus used its king lists to help write a history 197; built by Eurotas and named after his daughter 381; city built by Eurotas and Lacedemon (1065 BC) 22; Eratosthenes and Apollodorus computed the times by the reigns of its kings 11; its king lists used by @Timaeus Siculus to write a history 1; its kings used as a basis for chronology 3; its young King @Charillus was tutored by Lycurgus (708 BC) 122; kings of Sparta used to measure historical time 198; 203; Lycurgus published his laws here 218; ruled by Eurystheues and Procles 222; ruled by Lycurgus in 708 BC 308; ruled by nine kings from one family and ten from another from the return of the Heraclides to the end of the first Messenian War 207; 102; ruled by Polydectes, the king of Sparta 216; ruled by ten kings who reigned for an average of thirty-eight years each according to chronologers 204; ruled by two kings at the same time one from the family of Eurysthenes and one from the family of Procles 209

Sparta: daughter of Eurotas 381; 22; mother of Amyclas 324; mother of Eurydice 324; 26; wife of Lacedemon 26; 324; 22

Spartan: nationality of kings descended from Procles 218; nationality of the kings who reigned from the family of Eurysthenes and one from the family of Procles 209

Spartans: allied with the Eleans and helped overthrow the kingdom of Phidon 304; conquered Phidon 301; in the time of Lelex, they lived in individual villages 391; waged war with the Athenians (804 BC) 105

Sphettus: one of twelve cities where Cecrops I resettled a number of smaller towns 388

Stateres Darici: Latin name for *Darics* 612

Stephanathis: king in Sais (788 BC) 109; ruled from Sais over a small kingdom in Egypt 495

Stephanus: prepared a text of the work of Thucydides 212; says that the @Edomites helped the @Philistines fortify @Azoth 281; states that @Libya was anciently called @Ammonia after @Ammon 425

Stesichorus: Greek artist 217

Sthenelus: brother of @Mestor 324; brother of Electryo 324; brother of Gorgophone 324; father of @Danaus 323; father of Eurystheus (940 BC) 69; husband of Nicippe 323; son of Andromeda 324; son of Perseus 323; 324; 65; king of @Argos 323; ruled Mycene (954 BC) 65

Strabo: ascribes the three hundred and sixty-five day year to the Egyptians at Thebes 245; cited Polemon saying that in Attica, there were one hundred and seventy corporate towns of which Eleusis was one 388; describes the extent of the Babylonian Empire 621; documents the exploits of @Hercules (Tyrian) and the @Phoenicians 291; only knew of one @Minos 344; saw the monuments of the kings of Egypt, south of Memnonium with inscriptions on obelisks, expressing the riches of the kings, and their reigning as far as @Scythia, Bactria, India and Ionia 490; says that the @Sidonians helped settle @Thrace 290; says that the Syringes, Troglodytes and the Phaurusii lived in caves 404; states that @Aradus was built by men fleeing from Sidon 280; states that many countries contained numerous monuments to the Argonaut Expedition 480; states that Phidon was the tenth generation from Temenus 305; states that the @Ethiopians who were called @Megabars, fought with clubs 461; states that the Greek islands were first inhabited by @Carians who later migrated to @Caria 283

Strongyle: another name for Naxos 395

Sua: another name for Sabacon 501

Succoth Benoth: another name for the temple of @Venus 629; means the *Temple of Women* 629

Suidas: says Acusilaus was a most ancient historian 197; says that @Darius the Mede recoined the gold coins of Sardis into @*Darics* 612; says that @Ostanes was a follower of @Zoroaster 657; says that @Zoroaster was the author of the name of the @*Magi* 656; says that Caranus was the first king of Macedon 301; says that the *Sarus* of the Chaldeans contains two hundred and twenty-two lunar months, which is eighteen years, each consisting of twelve lunar months besides six intercalary months 243; states that @Thoas was descended from Pharnaces the king of Cyprus 457

Suphis: another name for Cheops 493

Susa: @Amenophis left here for Egypt 247; 270; 276; @Amenophis visited here during the Trojan War (904 BC) 87; @Xerxes I set out from here on an expedition against Greece 661; Cyrus spent his three spring months yearly here 632; emptied of its men by @Xerxes I for his invasion of Greece 593; lay to the east of @Babylonia and the regions of @Susiana and Sitacene lay between Babylon and here 622; location of Memnonia built by @Amenophis 489; 86; metropolis of @Susiana 536

Susanchites: their country located on the south and south-east side of the @Assyrian Empire 536; transplanted by @Esarhaddon to Samaria 552

Susiana: conquered by @Nebuchadnezzar 577; 611; 148; conquered by @Sesostris and @Memnon 526; conquered by the @Assyrians 566; country east of @Babylonia 622; located on the south and south-east side of the @Assyrian Empire 536; not immediately subdued by the Medes after the destruction of @Nineveh 603; part of the @Assyrian Empire at its height 554; part of the Babylonian Empire 621

Sweden: no written language until much later than 500 AD 202

Syene: border city of the kingdom of Mephres (1121 BC) 14; capital of one of the smaller kingdoms in Egypt 431; limit of the kingdom of @Mesphres 512; near @Thebes (Egyptian) 511; source of stone for obelisks 511

Syennesis: king of Cilicia 608; mediated a peace between Alyattes and @Cyaxeres 608

Syme: uninhabited until Triops arrived with a colony under Chthonius 395

Syphaosis: another name for Cheops 493

Syphoas: another name for Cheops 493

Syphuris: another name for Cheops 493

Syracuse: city built by Archias (719 BC) 118; founded by Archias with a colony from @Corinth 299; founded three hundred and ten years before the end of the Peloponnesian War 300

Syria: @Persians say it was conquered by @Bahaman 696; @Sardanapalus died of old age after he had lost control of it 556; @Sesostris returned through here to Egypt (962 BC) 60; @Vulcan built a temple here to his wife @Calycopis 458; abandoned the Medes when the @Assyrians attacked the Medes 558; Amos predicted its captivity in @Kir 529; attacked @Judah and opposed by Tiglathpileser 549; attacked by @Sennacherib after Israel fell 532; conquered by @Bacchus and @Minerva 422; conquered by @Nebuchadnezzar 576; 694; conquered by Holofernes 560; exaggerated their history 518; first conquered by @Sesostris 421; invaded by @Nebuchadnezzar 601; 144; invaded by @Sesostris (971 BC) 55; its towns captured by Pharaoh Necho 575; northern boundary of @Phoenicia 290; on the west and south side of the @Assyrian Empire 535; one place the @Edomites propagated their skills to 444; oppressed Israel during the time of Jonah 527; part of the @Assyrian Empire at its height 554; part of the Babylonian Empire 621; revolted from @Assyria before @Esarhaddon died 557; revolted from the @Assyrian Empire (668 BC) 130; ruled by @Benhadad II 407; 92; ruled by @Rezon, Tabrimon, @Benhadad I, @Benhadad II, Hazael, @Benhadad III and Rezin 456; ruled by sixteen kings who reigned an average of fifteen years and three months each 205; some @Shepherds were driven here by Misphragmuthosis and his son Amosis I 431; some of the @Shepherds fled here from Misphragmuthosis (1121 BC) 14; some of the pillars of @Sesostris were seen here in the days of Herodotus 450; temple here to the deified @Calycopis (930 BC) 78; transplanted by @Esarhaddon into @Babylonia and @Assyria 504; when his father Nabopolassar died @Nebuchadnezzar was in this country 577; while the armies of the Chaldeans were here, Jehoiakim did not rebel 578

Syrian: nationality of @Pherecydes 197; nationality of @Thoas according to Apollodorus 457; used interchangeably with the words Assyrian and Tyrian 546

Syrian Language: @*Erythreans* means @*Phoenicians* in this language 290

Syrians: @Phoenicians and @Syrians fled from Sidon and from David into other lands (1041 BC) 28; assisted @Nebuchadnezzar in his conquests 576; defeated by David 271; 272; 456; 27; deified their kings and queens 456; enslaved by Tiglathpileser, the king of @Assyria (740 BC) 115; exaggerated their history 699; followed the example of the Medes and revolted from the @Assyrians 556; introduced the custom of deifying the dead into Asia Minor and Greece 460; name the Greeks gave to the Assyrians in the times of Cyrus 554; some lived on the far side of the Euphrates River 621; supplied with horses from Solomon (1015 BC) 35; transplanted to @Kir in Media by Tiglathpileser 549; worshipped former kings and queens @Hadad, Arathes and Hazael (852 BC) 99

Syringes: lived in the caves in Egypt 404

Syrtes: @Dido sailed past to it found @Carthage 286; @Tyrians sail past it to settle cities in the western Mediterranean Sea 285

Tabrimon: king of Syria 456; subject to Egypt 456

Tacellotis: king in @Bubaste (788 BC) 109

Tacitus: writes of an inscription seen at @Thebes (Egyptian) by Caesar Germanicus and was interpreted for him by the Egyptian priests 490

Tahaphenes: mother of Genubah 272; married to the king of @Edom who fled from David and gave birth to Genubah 272

Talatha: another name for Thelasar 536

Talus: nephew of Daedalus 339; 48; co-inventor of the chip axe, the saw, the auger, the plumb level, the compass, the turning lath, glue and the potter's wheel 339; murdered by his uncle Daedalus (983 BC) 50; originated the carpentry trade in Europe (985 BC) 48

Talus: son of @Minos (933 BC) 75; 317; 365; Bronze Age man killed by the Argonauts (933 BC) 75; 317; 365

Tanais: visited by the Argonauts 480

Tangieres: another name for Tingis 467

Tanis: capital of a small kingdom in Egypt ruled by Petubastes, @Osorchon and @Psammis 495; Isaiah predicted that its princes would become fools 507

Tantalus: father of Pelops (989 BC) 46; contemporary with @Erechtheus, @Jasius and Cadmus 328; kidnapped Ganymede 343; 35; king of @Phrygia 35

Tarentum: built by Phalantus and the Parthenians (625 BC) 141

Tarpelites: transplanted by @Esarhaddon to Samaria 534; 552

Tarshish: another name for Tartessus 292

Tarsus: city built in a day by @Esarhaddon (710 BC) 121; 557

Tartan: sent by @Esarhaddon with an army to attack @Ashdod 504

Tartars: lived a rambling wild sort of life (1121 BC) 14

Tartarus: place @Jupiter (Cretan) cast @Saturn (Cretan) into 348

Tartessus: city founded by the @Tyrians 285; located in western Spain 292; visited by the @Tyrians under @Melcartus 292

Tatian: relates events from the Phoenician history corresponding to the early Greek and biblical history 296

Taurica: visited by the Argonauts 480

Taurus: colure had moved into this constellation from the time of the Argonaut Expedition 259; constellation of the Zodiac 249

Taurus: colure of the equinox cut through this constellation in 1689 AD 257; 260; constellation shaped like the bull with brazen hoofs tamed by Jason 253

Technatis: another name for Gnephactus 495

Tegea: Leutychides II fled here from Sparta 209; town in Arcadia created from nine towns by the Argives 389

Telamon: father of Teucer 293; banished his son Teucer 293

Telchin: king of @Sicyon 379; third king of @Sicyon 380

Telchines: another name for the Curetes 336; 457; 28; driven from @Argos by Phoroneus and retired to @Rhodes 283

Teleclus: Spartan king descended from the family of Eurysthenes 204

Telestes: descended from the Heraclides 329; king of @Corinth 329

Temenus: brother of Aristodemus 222; brother of Cresphontes 222; father of Cisus 301; 305; son of Aristomachus 222; king of @Argos 301; 305

Tenedos: uninhabited until Tennes sailed there from Troas shortly before the Trojan War 395

Tennes: led a colony to Tenedos from Troas 395

Teos: Halone lies between here and Lebedos 396; one of the twelve cities in the common council called Panionium 310

Terah: left Ur to avoid its idolatry 411

Teredon: city built by @Nebuchadnezzar 577

Terpander: contemporary with Lycurgus the legislator 213; lyrical poet and imitated @Orpheus and Homer 217; won the music awards at Carnea four times 213

Terra: Cretan name for Titaea 470; name means *Earth* 470

Terra Curetum: name given to Crete meaning the *Land of the Curetes* 341; 354

Tertullian: documents the arrival of @Saturn (Cretan) into @Italy 350

Tethmosis: another name for Amosis I 431; 21; 376

Tetraeteris: four year cycle used by the Greeks 240; 277

Tetrapolis: one of twelve cities where Cecrops I resettled a number of smaller towns 388

Teucer: son of Telamon 293; banished by his father Telamon 293; built Salamis in Cyprus 293; 90; came to Cyprus seven years after the destruction of Troy and built Salamis 225

Teucer: son of Scamander 321; about the same age as King David 321; first king of Troy 321

Teutamus: father of @Asterius 354; 400; grandfather of @Minos 400; brought a colony to Crete 354; led a colony of Dorians to Crete from Laconia and Olympia in Peloponnesus 400

Thales: called the last day of the month *triakada, the thirtieth* 239; ended the war between the Lydians and the Medes by predicting a solar eclipse 585; 608; predicted a total eclipse that ended the war between Lydia and the Medes (585 BC) 151; revived astronomy and wrote a book of the solstices and equinoxes and predicted eclipses 265; visited by Solon on his travels 307; wrote his history in verse 196

Thaletas: Greek artist 217

Thammuz: another name for Timaeus (1445 BC) 13

Thamus: another name for Timaeus (1445 BC) 13

Thapsacus: city located near @Reseph by Ptolemy 535

Thapsus: colony of Lamis expelled from here after Lamis died 299

Tharops: father of Oeagrus 417

Thasos: Cadmus left his brother Thasus here 356; some @Sidonians fled here 283

Thasus: brother of Cadmus 356; led a colony of @Phoenicians and @Syrians fleeing from Sidon and from David (1041 BC) 28; 283; left on the island of Thasos by his brother Cadmus 356

Thebans: began to study navigation and astronomy in the reign of @Ammon 246; conquered Egypt and many surrounding countries 460; nationality of the Egyptians who expelled the @Shepherds 432

Thebes (Egyptian): @Moeris moved the capital of the empire from here to @Memphis 483; Amosis I drove the @Shepherds who lived here to the @Philistines 436; another name for Upper Egypt 431; area south of it conquered by @Esarhaddon 553; capital for a king of Egypt who ruled the entire country 420; capital of Egypt before @Moeris moved it to @Memphis 500; capital of one of several Egyptian kingdoms under a Shepherd king (1445 BC) 13; capital of one of the smaller kingdoms in Egypt 431; city destroyed by the many invasions of Egypt 505; contained temples dedicated to @Jupiter @Ammon and @Jupiter @Uranus 425; contains a town called @Antaea 467; contributed troops to the army of @Amenophis (926 BC) 81; curse of @Gnephactus on @Menes recorded in its temple of @Jupiter 495; declined in glory when @Memphis was built 492; Egypt, @Thebes (Egyptian), Ethiopia and @Libya had no common king before the expulsion of the @Shepherds 421; Egyptians here used no intercalary months, nor deducted any days from the month as was done by most of the Greeks 235; Emperor Constantius saw inscriptions here about Egyptian kings 490; former capital of Egypt until @Moeris moved the capital to @Memphis (860 BC) 98; helped expel the @Shepherds from Egypt 363; its priests consulted with Herodotus about the Egyptian history 510; its priests excelled more than others in astronomy and philosophy according to Diodorus 245; its priests gave Herodotus an account of Egyptian history 499; located in Ethiopia according to Homer 432; location of the temple and oracle @Sesostris dedicated to his father (998 BC) 44; location of the temple erected to the deified @Ammon 437; location of the temple of @Jupiter @Ammon 481; 627; near Syene where the stone for the obelisks was quarried 511; royal city for early Egyptian kings 482; ruled by kings during the reign of David, Solomon and Rehoboam 699

Thebes (Greek): Aristaeus led a colony from here to the island of Caea 395; attacked by Adrastus according to Homer 380; attacked by seven captains 324; Cadmus found copper ore here 337; captured by Amphion and Zethus 317; Eteocles and Polynices were killed in a war here 314; founded about the fourteenth year of David's reign 283; its war happened in the Iron Age 365; its wars happened about one generation before Hesiod (870 BC) 97; recovered by Laius (976 BC) 52; ruled by Laius who fortified the city with high walls (986 BC) 47; second war (918 BC) 84; warred against by the seven captains (928 BC) 79

Thebian Columns: set up in India 446

Theias: another name for Thoas 457

Thelasar: city of the children of Eden in @Babylonia on the common stream of the Tigris and Euphrates Rivers 536; conquered by @Belus (Assyrian) or @Pul 547; conquered by @Pul 542; part of the @Assyrian Empire at the time of the fall of Israel 532

Themistius: states that @Erechtheus was the first who harnessed horses to a chariot 331

Theodotus: ancient historian of the @Phoenicians 296

Theognis: Greek artist 217; Greek poet who wrote about the conquest of Lydia by the Medes 615

Theopompus: Spartan king descended from the family of Procles 204; 209

Theras: brother-in-law of Aristodemus 208; father of Oiolicus 208; tutor to the twins Eurysthenes and Procles 208

Thermodon River: @Bacchus left his @Amazons here under their new queens of Marthesia and Lampeto 422; place @Amazons retreated to when defeated by the Greeks 423; place the @Amazons were left by @Sesostris (962 BC) 60; place to which the @Amazons were transplanted from @Thrace by @Sesostris 273

Thermopylae: @Persians defeated the Greeks here (480 BC) 175; Amphictyonic Council met here (1003 BC) 41; battle here happened about one hundred and fifty years after the end of the first Messenian War (633 BC) 102; chonologers made the time from the return of the Heraclides and to this battle much too long 11; location of the Amphictyonic Council, which was established by Amphictyon 330; place @Persians killed Leonidas 209; ruled by Amphictyon 332

Thersander: son of Polynices 314; fought at Troy 314

Theseus: father of Demophoon (903 BC) 88; husband of Antiope 423; husband of Ariadne 6; 277; 297; husband of Phaedra 297; 88; son of Aegeus 228; 278; 310; 319; son of Aethra 229; abandoned his wife Ariadne on the island of @Naxos 277; 310; consolidated twelve cities to create @Athens 388; contemporary with @Menes 517; freed by @Hercules (Idean) (932 BC) 76; gods lived between the times of Cecrops I and his time 464; Greeks built a temple to him 359; helped Pirithous to try to kidnap Helen 229; kidnapped Helen and was captured (934 BC) 74; kidnapped Helen just before the Argonaut Expedition 228; kidnapped the *second* Ariadne whom the people of @Naxos created 344; king of @Athens 359; lived during the reigns of Solomon and Rehoboam 297; made an expedition into Sicily 278; made two generations younger than @Bacchus by the people of @Naxos 419; succeeded his father Aegeus as king of @Athens 310; thrown down from a rock and killed (925 BC) 82; united Attica and ruled there (965 BC) 57

Thespis: grandson of @Erechtheus 319; fathered fifty daughters 319

Thessalus: son of Haemon 384

Thessaly: flooded in the days of Deucalion 330; originally called Haemonia 384; ruled by Eurolicus 302; ruled by Haemon (1081 BC) 19; ruled by Hellen 332; warred with the Lapithae (956 BC) 64; Xuthus expelled from here by his brothers Aeolus and Dorus 328

Thetis: mother of Achilles 359; Greeks built a temple to her 359

Theudas: false messiah the Jews created to avoid accepting Jesus as fulfilling Daniel's seventy weeks 669

This: capital of one of several Egyptian kingdoms under a Shepherd king (1445 BC) 13; 431; location of Memnonia built by @Amenophis 489

Thoantes: another name for Thoas 457

Thoas: father of @Gingris (935 BC) 73; father of Hypsipyle 457; 59; husband of @Calycopis 78; 457; 458; 59; another name for Vulcan 458; captain of Rhadamanthus who gave him the island of Lemnos 457; Cretan metallurgist 457; deified his son @Gingris under the name of @Adonis (935 BC) 73; deified his wife @Calycopis in a temple at Paphos and Amathus (930 BC) 78; deified under the name of Vulcan, when he died (912 BC) 85; king of Cyprus and part of @Phoenicia 85; reigned in Hephaestia (975 BC) 53; sent from Crete to Lemnos (975 BC) 53; went to Cyprus with his wife after @Sesostris appointed him king there (963 BC) 59; worked in copper and iron (975 BC) 53

Thoas: father of Oxylus 220; son of Andraemon 220; fought at Troy 220

Thoas: king of @Corinth before the return of the Heraclides 329

Thomosis: another name for Amosis I 431; 482

Thoricus: one of twelve cities where Cecrops I resettled a number of smaller towns 388

Thoth: advised @Sesostris (961 BC) 61; hieroglyphic representation of 460; introduced writing to Egypt 441; one of the gods of Egypt 431; ruled in Egypt before @Amenophis (912 BC) 85; secretary of @Orus 478; secretary of @Osiris 478; secretary of @Sesostris 460

Thoth (Month of): era of Nabonassar started on this Egyptian month (747 BC) 95; first month of a king's reign 567; first month of the Babylonian New Year 573; first month of the Egyptian year 247

Thrace: @Bacchus and @Sesostris conquered as far as here 418; @Sesostris returned to Egypt from here 314; Cadmus found gold here in Mount Pangaeus 337; conquered by @Bacchus 458; conquered by @Sesostris 363; conquered by @Sesostris and given to Oeagrus (964 BC) 58; Egyptian king halted his conquests here 420; first conquered by @Sesostris 421; invaded by @Bacchus 278; invaded by @Sesostris

about a generation before the Argonaut expedition 11; its king Lycurgus was killed by @Bacchus 417; near the island of Samothrace 315; place from which the @Amazons who called themselves the daughters of @Mars were transplanted from by @Sesostris 273; ruled by Diomedes, the king of the Bistones 293; ruled by Lycurgus 422; settled by the @Edomites who circumcised themselves 290; singing women of @Sesostris called Muses here (962 BC) 60; terminus of the conquests of @Sesostris 450

Thracian: nationality of Mopsus 422; nationality of Pierus (962 BC) 60

Thracians: called @Sesostris by the names of @Ma-sors, @Mavors and @Mars 273; first inhabitants of @Strongyle or @Naxos in the days of Boreas 395; ruled by Phineus 480; sent forces to Perseus to repel the invasion of @Bacchus 422; visited by the Argonauts 480

Thucles: led a colony from Chalcis in @Euboea and founded @Naxos in Sicily 299

Thucydides: documents that the return of the Heraclides was eighty years after the Trojan War 203; only knew of one @Minos 344; relates that the Greeks began to come into Sicily almost three hundred years after the Sicels had invaded that island with an army from @Italy 300; says that the institutions of Lycurgus were about three hundred years older than the end of the Peloponnesian War (708 BC) 122; says that the Lacedemonians had good laws at an earlier time than any other land 212; says that the news of the death of @Artaxerxes came to @Athens in the winter, in the seventh year of the Peloponnesian War 664; says that Troy was captured about eighty years before the Heraclides returned 11; says that Troy was captured seventy-five or eighty years before the return of the Heraclides into Peloponnesus 222; states that the first colony, which the Greeks sent to Sicily, came from Chalcis in @Euboea 299; states that there were eight kings of Macedon before Archelaus 301; states that under Cecrops I and the ancient kings to the time of Theseus, Attica had always been divided into separate towns, each having magistrates and a town hall 388

Thule: settled by the @Tyrians 285

Thuor: husband of Acandra 484; prince in Egypt 484

Thyestes: father of Aegisthus 317; son of Pelops 317

Thymoetes: contemporary with @Orpheus 422; early Athenian king 310; wrote a poem about the exploits of @Bacchus 422; wrote that @Bacchus the son of @Ammon ruled over @Libya and Egypt 425

Tiber River: border of the colony of @Oenotrus in @Italy 392

Tiglathpileser: oldest son of @Pul 549; assisted Ahaz against Israel and Syria 549; Babylon was built by Semiramis during his reign 543; captured @Damascus and enslaved the @Syrians (740 BC) 115; died and succeeded by @Salmanasser (728 BC) 116; expanded the @Assyrian Empire 8; 529; 541; king of @Assyria according to the scriptures 521; ruled @Assyria 115; succeeded @Pul at @Nineveh (747 BC) 114; transplanted some people from Syria and Israel 504

Tiglath-Pul-Assur: example of an @Assyrian name compounded with the name of one of the @Assyrian gods 519

Tigris River: @Calneh located on it 531; flowed a few miles from Babylon 624; flowed through @Babylonia 536; surrounding land was very fertile 362; waters the plains of Chaldea, @Chalonitis and @Assyria 524; western border of @Assyria in the days of @Pul 542

Timaeus: king of Lower Egypt who was conquered by the Canaanites fleeing from Joshua (1445 BC) 13

Timaeus Siculus: calculated about eighty years to a generation 208; his followers have greatly increased the antiquity of historical events 209; thought that Rome was founded about one hundred years before the Olympiads 312; thought the kings who reigned before the Persian Empire reigned an average of thirty-five to forty years each 205; usually equated a king's reign to a generation or about forty years 207; wrote a history based on the Olympiads, comparing the ephori, the kings of Sparta, the archons of @Athens, and the priestesses of Juno Argiva, with the Olympic victors 1; wrote a history down to his time using many sources 197

Timocharis: Greek astronomer who wrote in prose 196

Timosthenes: says that @Carteia in ancient times was called @Heracleia 291

Tin: Pliny states it was first imported by @Midacritus from the island of @Cassiteris 292

Tingis: built by @Antaeus 467

Tiphsah: destroyed by Menahem because the city did not submit to him 529

Tirhakah: conquered west through @Libya and North Africa to the Strait of Gibraltar 503; helped @Sethon defeated @Sennacherib 502; king of Ethiopia 502; 503; 551; 119; reigned eighteen years according to Africanus 506; ruled Egypt (687 BC) 126; succeeded @Sethon as king of Egypt 503

Tirshatha: title given to Nehemiah meaning *governor* 684

Tisamenus: son of Orestes 222; lived to see the return of the Heraclides 222

Titaea: mother of @Basilea 463; mother of @Hyperion 463; mother of Saturn (Cretan) 470; mother of the Titans 440; wife of @Ammon 440; wife of @Uranus 463; 470; another name for *Terra* 470; another name for Rhea (Egyptian) 431; her posterity were the Titans 467; mother of eighteen children 463

Titans: son of @Titaea 440; sons of @Ammon 440; defeated by @Hercules (Idean) 353; descended from @Titaea 467; fought with the gods in the valley of Bathos 354; lived on Mount Olympus and were ruled by @Saturn (Cretan) 345; name given to @Hyperion and his brothers 463; one generation older than @Jupiter (Cretan) 470; warred with the gods of Egypt 275

Titans (The Battle of): written by @Chiron 253

Tithonus: father of @Amenophis according to the Greeks (962 BC) 95; older brother of Priam 477; son of Laomedon (962 BC) 60; carried captive into Ethiopia along with many captives by @Sesostris 477; older brother of Priam and thought to be the father of @Amenophis by the Greeks 270; taken captive by @Sesostris to Egypt (962 BC) 60

Tlesilla: Greek artist 217

Tnephachthus: another name for Gnephactus 495; cursed @Menes for introducing luxury and an extravagant lifestyle to Egypt 481; in the reduced king list of Diodorus 514; king of Egypt according to Diodorus 513

Tobeah: father of Rezin 456

Tobiah: opposed Nehemiah when he rebuilt the walls of @Jerusalem 691

Tobit: advised his son to go into Media 555; attributes the destruction of the @Assyrian Empire to the Chaldeans and the Medes 564; called @Esarhaddon by the name of @Sarchedon 552; called @Salmanasser by the name of @Enemessar 550; names @Assuerus for @Cyaxeres 594; unable to go to Media because of unrest in @Assyria 551

Tosorthrus: physician who invented building with square stones 484; 489

Touran: another name for Scythia 566; country of the Scythians 557

Trieterica Bacchi: triennial festival to celebrate the victories of @Sesostris in the east (968 BC) 56

Triopas: son of Phorbas 283; 326; fled from @Argos to @Rhodes 326; led a colony from @Rhodes to @Caria 283

Triopium: promontory in @Caria 283; settled by Triopas 283

Triops: came with a colony into Syme 395

Tripoli: founded by the Canaanites who fled from Joshua 428

Tripos: three legged stool awarded to the winners of the Olympic Games 304

Triptolemus: son of Celeus 318; 32; contemporary with Arcas, Eumelus, Celeus and @Erechtheus 334; distributed grain about the end of David's reign 320; gave grain to Arcas 351; Greeks built a temple to him 359; in his days an Egyptian king conquered much of the world 420; lived after Myles 381; taught agriculture to Arcas and Eumelus and gave them grain (1016 BC) 34; taught to cultivate grain by Ceres 318; 32

Triton River: near the birthplace of @Minerva in @Libya 422

Troas: Tennes led a colony from here to Tenedos 395

Troglodytes: in the army of @Sesostris 231; lived in the caves between Egypt and the Red Sea 404; part of the army of @Sesostris 450

Troglodytica: conquered by @Sesostris 446; conquered by @Sesostris before he became king 273; location where some of the @Shepherds fled 437

Trojan War: @Amazons present at this war 423; @Amenophis not involved in it 247; 87; @Neptune lived two generations before it 465; @Vulcan lived until this war 482; @Vulcan reigned in Cyprus and Byblus until this war 458; Admeta was priestess of Juno Argiva about this time 325; after it the @Phoenicians began to make long voyages past the Pillars of @Hercules 291; after the war the seas could be safely navigated 402; Agapenor participated in it 333; ended about seventy-one years after the death of Solomon 226; Greeks fought with clubs until its times 461; 270; happened a generation after the Argonaut Expedition 11; happened in 1184 BC according to Diodorus 203; 222; Idomeneus and Meriones fought in it 317; Idomeneus, the grandson of @Minos, was in his prime during the war 297; in its time @Memnon was king 473; interrupted @Tyrian trade on the Red Sea with the kings of @Judah 284; Iron Age generation ended with this war (904 BC) 28; occurred about one generation before Hesiod lived 268; occurred after the time of Solomon and Rehoboam 300; Paris sailed to Lower Egypt after it ended 488; Salamis founded by Teucer seven years after it 293; shortly before it ended the islands of Aeolides were settled by a colony led by Lipparus and Aeolus 397; Tenedos was populated shortly before it 395; two generations later than the time of Aeacus 361

Trojans: ruled by Laomedon 480; visited by the Argonauts 480

Trophonius: Greeks built a temple to him 359

Tros: father of Ganymede (1015 BC) 35; fourth king of Troy 321; king of Troy (1015 BC) 35

Trotilus: Lamis first settled here in Sicily with his colony from Achaia 299

Troy: @Edomites revolted from Jehoram about fifteen years after the city was destroyed 286; @Thoas fought here 220; Callithea was succeeded by Alcyone as priestess of Juno Argiva about three generations before the city was taken 325; captured about eighty years before the return of the Heraclides 11; captured by the Greeks (904 BC) 87; captured by the Greeks around 904 BC 308; captured twenty years after Paris kidnapped Helen 317; city fell about eighty years before the return of the Heraclides 222; destroyed about four generations or about one hundred and forty years later than the flood of Deucalion (904 BC) 28; destroyed about sixty-nine years after the death of Solomon 313; destroyed after @Bacchus and @Sesostris died 417; fell a year after @Tyre was founded 279; founded by Dardanus and others 319; Homer and Hesiod lived about one generation after the city was captured 368; Idomeneus fought against it in the Iron Age 367; Idomeneus fought here 344; its walls fortified by @Neptune and his son @Apollo 465; its war happened in the Iron Age 365; its wars happened about one generation before Hesiod (870 BC) 97; Romulus was in the fifteenth generation after its destruction 312; ruled by Laomedon (962 BC) 60; ruled by Laomedon and Priam (933 BC) 75; ruled by seven kings 321; ruled by Tros (1015 BC) 35; seven years after its destruction, Teucer came to Cyprus and built Salamis 225; Thersander fought here 314

Tubal: conquered by @Cyaxeres and @Nebuchadnezzar 610

Turquestan: another name for Touran 557

Tuthmosis: another name for Touran 431

Tutimaeus: Canaanites settled in large numbers in Egypt during his reign 430

Tybur: near Erythros 287

Typhon: brother of Nephthe (1030 BC) 93; 245; husband of Nephthe (1030 BC) 93; 245; son of @Ammon (1030 BC) 93; 245; son of Rhea (Egyptian) 440; son of Saturn (Egyptian) 440; uncle of @Orus 478; another name for Japetus 275; 431; another name for Neptune 467; deified name of Japetus by the Egyptians (951 BC) 66; Egyptians dedicated one of the five extra days of the year to him (1030 BC) 93; 245; killed @Hercules (Egyptian) 461; killed @Hercules (Egyptian) according to Eudoxus 66; one of the gods of Egypt 431; same man as Neptune 445

Tyre: @Phoenicians fled here after being driven from the Red Sea by the @Edomites around 892-889 BC 308; built by the @Sidonians who were displaced by the @Edomites fleeing from David (1044 BC) 25; called the *Daughter of Sidon* 280; conquered by @Nebuchadnezzar 589; 602; 604; 611; founded a year before the fall of Troy by the inhabitants fleeing from Sidon according to Justin 279; founded about the fourteenth year of David's reign 283; founded by Abibalus 297; founded by fleeing @Sidonians after their city was captured by the @Philistines 282; founded seven years after the destruction of Troy 225; founded the city states of Adrymentum and @Carthage 224; Hiram built temples here 455; its inhabitants called @Sidonians 281; its merchants settled in western North Africa after the Canaanites 430; its siege began in 585 BC 590; received an annual tithe to @Hercules (Tyrian) from @Carthage 295; ruled by @Melcartus 292; ruled by Abibalus 296; ruled by Hiram 296; 444; ruled by Pygmalion 286; some @Sidonians fled here 283; started trading on the Mediterranean Sea after it lost access to the Red Sea 285

Tyre: colony on an island in the Persian Gulf founded by the @Tyrians and Aradians (1013 BC) 36; island in the Persian Gulf containing temples like those of the @Phoenicians 284

Tyre (Annals of): relate conquests of @Salmanasser 550

Tyrian: used interchangeably with the words Assyrian and Syrian 546

Tyrians: assisted Solomon with his Red Sea fleet (1013 BC) 36; began to sail the Mediterranean Sea until after the Trojan War 293; built cities of @Carthage, @Carteia and Gades 291; founded cities around the Mediterranean Sea 285; 286; originally came from the Red Sea 289; sailed into the Persian Gulf and beyond to the coasts of India 284; settled Gades off the coast of Spain 288; settled western Spain 292; traded with North Africa, Spain and Britain 298

Tyris: corruption of the name Moeris 491

Tyrrhene Sea: limit of conquests of the Atlanteans 464

Tyrtaeus: Greek artist 217

Uchoreus: corruption of the name Moeris 491; king of Egypt according to Diodorus 513; king who did the same things @Moeris did and was likely another name for Moeris 492; variation on the names of Mendes, Marrus and Myris 514

Uchoreus (Lake of): same lake as the Lake of Moeris 492

Ulphilas: created the written language for @Scythia 202

Ulysses: possible father of Romus 311; acquainted with Mentor 368; found Calypso on the island of @Ogygia 465; 91; found the island of @Ogygia covered with forests and uninhabited except by Calypso and her maids 397; undertook long voyages on the sea 291

Ur: Terah left to avoid its idolatry 411

Uranus: father of @Hyperion 246; 405; father of @Osiris 241; husband of @Titaea 463; another name for Ammon 245; 246; 431; another name for Ammon according to Diodorus 405; another name for Jupiter Ammon 463

Uranus: father of Rhea (Cretan) 470; father of Saturn (Cretan) 470; husband of @Titaea 470; another name for Caelus 274; 470

Ursa Major: constellation is related to Callisto and her son Arcas 254; Latin name for the Great Bear 252

Usorthon: another name for Osarsiphus 476

Utica: city founded by the @Tyrians 285

Uzzah: conquered Gath 531

Valerius Publicola: first consul of Rome about three hundred and ninety-six years after the fall of Troy 226

Vaphres: another name for Apries 509

Varro: dated the founding of Rome in the spring of 753 BC 312; says that the Egyptian talent weighed eighty pounds 613

Vasaeus: says that @Osiris conquered Geryon in Spain 461

Vela: modern constellation derived from the sail of *Argo* 252; 253

Venephes: corruption of the name Amenophis 482; 489

Venus: mother of Aeneas 278; 417; wife of @Cinyras 417; 482; wife of @Thoas (930 BC) 78; wife of Anchises 417; @Cinyras built a temple to her 458; another name for Calycopis 458; Calycopis 78; her fishes are related to the constellation of Pisces 254; hieroglyphic representation of 460; seduced by @Bacchus 278

Venus (Temple of): women once in their life went here for immoral use by strangers 629

Venus Hospita: temple in @Memphis dedicated to her 459

Vesta: word derived from the word for *fire* 387

Virgil: related the history surrounding the founding of @Carthage 225

Virgo: constellation is related to Icareus and his daughter Erigone 254; constellation of the Zodiac 249; method for determining the position of stars in this constellation on the sphere of @Chiron 264

Vulcan: husband of @Calycopis 458; another name for Thoas 458; assisted by the @Curetes who settled in Lemnos 336; deified his wife when she died 458; deified name of Cinyras 459; 482; name given to Thoas, when he was deified (912 BC) 85

Vulcan (Temple of): @Moeris built its northern portico 491; @Ramesses built its western portico 490; @Sethon was a priest in it 501; @Sevechus was a priest in it (701 BC) 123; about two hundred and eighty years in construction 517; Asychis built its eastern portico 494; built by @Amenophis 489; eastern portico built by Asychis (788 BC) 109; Egyptians imagined it stood for over eleven thousand years 500; had hundreds of generations of priests according to the Egyptian priests 193; its construction was started by @Amenophis 482; its northern portico built by @Moeris (860 BC) 98; porticos added to it by Asychis, Psammitichus and @Rhampsinitus 9; Psammitichus built its last portico about two hundred and sixty years after @Menes started to build it 509; temple built to @Vulcan in @Memphis 478; temple in @Memphis built by @Amenophis 459; western portico built by @Ramesses (887 BC) 93

William Rufus: king of England 205

Women's Court: court in Solomon's temple 649

Xanthus: colonised Lesbos 395

Xenocritus: Greek artist 217

Xenodemus: Greek artist 217

Xenophanes: wrote his history in verse 196

Xenophon: calls @Harpagus by the names of @Artagerses and @Artabazus 630; confounded Astyages with his son @Cyaxeres 595; incorrectly thought that @Cyaxeres was the last king of Media 631; says that Cyrus went to the king of the Medes at Ecbatana and succeeded him in the kingdom 618

Xerxes I: father of @Artaxerxes Longimanus 663; 176; son of @Darius Hystaspes 661; 685; @Persians omit his reign 696; accompanied by @Ostanes into Greece 657; appointed his son @Artaxerxes Longimanus as viceroy (474 BC) 176; contemporary with @Alexander (not the Great) who was the king of Macedon 301; crossed over the Hellespont into Greece (480 BC) 175; Eliashib became the high priest in the tenth year of his reign 679; enemies wrote accusations to him about the Jews 688; his father was not the king who coined the @Darics 612; his history was outlined by Newton 677; his invasion ended the dynasty of the Spartan kings descended from Eurysthenes and Procles 209; invaded Greece 593; known by the Jews as Ahasuerus 685; listed by Josephus as a king of @Persia 668; murdered by Artabanus 663; ruled the Persian Empire (485 BC) 174; spent five years preparing for the Greek expedition 661; succeeded @Darius Hystaspes 687

Xerxes II: son of @Artaxerxes Longimanus 665; reigned for two months 665

Xisuthrus (Flood of): Chaldeans thought Oannes was older than it and the Egyptians thought @Osiris just as old 442

Xuthus: brother of Aeolus 328; brother of Dorus 328; father of Achaeus 319; father of Ion 319; 328; husband of Creusa 319; 328; 31; son of Hellen 31; 319; 328; 29; contemporary with @Erechtheus, @Jasius and Cadmus 328; expelled from his kingdom in @Thessaly by his brothers Aeolus and Dorus 328

Zacheriah: son of Jeroboam II 542; interregnum happened before he started to reign 542

Zagrus (Mount): on the border of @Chalonitis 621; on the northern boundary of @Babylonia in Media 622

Zaradust: another name for Zoroaster 695

Zeboim: city plundered by four kings from the land of Shinar and @Elam 408

Zechariah: encouraged the Jews to complete the temple 674; knew of and mentioned the @Assyrian Empire 529; prophecy came to him from the Lord 571; 573; times of his prophecies were used to determine the month @Darius started to reign 660

Zechariah: son of @Jonathan 684; present when Nehemiah dedicated the wall 684

Zedekiah: @Elam fell during his reign 566; captured in his eleventh year by @Nebuchadnezzar 569; conquered in his eleventh year by @Nebuchadnezzar 579; in his eleventh year @Jerusalem was captured and the temple destroyed by the Chaldeans 609; in his eleventh year, he was captured by @Nebuchadnezzar 574; in his ninth year he was invaded by @Nebuchadnezzar 573; 675; Jeremiah prophesied the conquest of @Edom, Moab, @Ammon, @Tyre and Sidon during his reign 604; Medes conquered the @Persians about the middle of his reign 630; started to reign just after the Jewish New Year 578

Zephaniah: @Assyrian Empire was still standing when he prophesied 565; knew of and mentioned the @Assyrian Empire 529

Zerah: father of @Memnon 477; father of @Menes (941 BC) 68; husband of Cissia 477; 68; conquered Egypt and @Libya 474; defeated by Asa 475; 499; 68; invaded @Judah with a million man army of @Ethiopians and Libyans 472; Lower Egypt revolted from him 476; possible father of @Amenophis 275

Zerubbabel: alive when the temple was rebuilt 675; history of the Jews under him needs corrections 669; leader of the Jews 675; led the return of the Jews back to @Judah 673; received a commission from Cyrus and @Darius Hystaspes to rebuild the temple 648; returned with the Levites to @Judah 672

Zetes: son of Orithyia 319; an Argonaut 319

Zethus: son of Antiope 316; 317; 39; twin brother of Amphion 316; 317; 39; helped Amphion kill Lycus (986 BC) 47

Zeugma: boundary of the tribe of Mygdones 621

Zimri: conquered by @Nebuchadnezzar 602

Zmarres: another name for Moeris 511

Zoan: another name for Tanis 495; 507

Zobah: @Syrian army from here defeated by David (1042 BC) 27; conquered by David 456; its king reigned on both sides of the Euphrates River 525; ruled by Hadadezer 456; supplied troops to fight against David 271

Zoroaster: coined the term @*Magi* 656; description of his god 658; established a new religion in @Persia from the best of the old ones 657; helped Hystaspes establish the worship of one god in @Persia (521 BC) 168; helped reform the @Magi 653; learned astrology from the Egyptians 625; legislator of the Ghebers or fire worshippers 695; skilled in astronomy 654; taught by the Brahmins of India 656; taught many skills by the Chaldeans 655

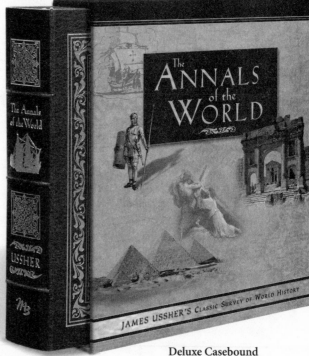